STANDARD
LESSON COMMENTARY
1993-94

International Sunday School Lessons

published by

STANDARD PUBLISHING

Eugene H. Wigginton, *Publisher*

Richard C. McKinley, *Director of Curriculum Development*

James I. Fehl, *Editor*   Hela M. Campbell, *Office Editor*

Forty-first Annual Volume

In This Volume

Autumn Quarter, 1993 (page 1)

Theme: The Story of Beginnings

Writers

Willard W. Winter (1-4),
Stephen M. Hooks (5-8),
Gary Hall (9-13), Lesson Development

Charles R. Boatman, Verbal Illustrations
Jonathan Underwood, Learning by Doing
Kenton K. Smith, Let's Talk It Over

Winter Quarter, 1993-94 (page 113)

Theme: The Story of Jesus

Writers

Edwin V. Hayden (1-9),
Paul W. Patton (10, 11),
Carl Bridges, Jr. (12, 13), Lesson Development

Ward Patterson, Verbal Illustrations
Ronald G. Davis, Learning by Doing
David Morley, Let's Talk It Over

Spring Quarter, 1994 (page 225)

Themes: Good News for God's People
Set Free by God's Grace

Writers

Orrin Root, Lesson Development
Richard W. Baynes, Verbal Illustrations

Mike McCann, Learning by Doing
Kenton K. Smith, Let's Talk It Over

Summer Quarter, 1994 (page 337)

Theme: God Redeems a People

Writers

John W. Wade, Lesson Development
Woodrow Phillips, Verbal Illustrations
Mark A. Taylor, Learning by Doing

Deborah Sue Brunsman (1-4)
R. David Roberts (5-9)
Joe Sutherland (10-13), Let's Talk It Over

Artists

James E. Seward, Title Pages; Ned Ostendorf, Lesson Illustrations;
Robert E. Huffman, Richard Briggs, Maps

Cover design by Schultz Ward

Lessons based on International Sunday School Lessons © 1990 by the Lesson Committee.

II

Index of Printed Texts, 1993-94

The printed texts for 1993-94 are arranged here in the order in which they appear in the Bible. Opposite each reference is the number of the page on which it appears in this volume.

Cumulative Index

A cumulative index for the Scripture passages used in the *Standard Lesson Commentary* for the years September, 1992—August, 1994, is set forth below.

v

The Making of a Leader

by Bob Russell

THE OLD MOVIE, "Viva Zapata," has a dramatic deathbed scene. The elderly Zapata is speaking his last words to his son. "Trouble is coming," he says. "Find a leader. If you cannot find a leader, be a leader." That challenge motivated the son to become one of Mexico's greatest and most colorful military figures.

A leader is simply someone who knows where he is going and is able to persuade others to go along. Not everyone can lead, but I'm convinced that a lot more should lead than do.

Many of you are already leaders. Some of you are administrators, executives, foremen, schoolteachers, or parents. Others of you are leaders in the church. All of you would admit that there is always the need for more insight into your leadership responsibilities. But others of you may be sitting on the sidelines, observing. You need a challenge to leadership.

The apostle Paul will serve as our example. He's the most dynamic Christian leader the world has ever seen. Let's look at what went into making him the great leader he was.

God's Part—Preparation

God had a large part in preparing Saul of Tarsus. Jesus struck Saul down when he was on his way to Damascus to persecute the Christians. A bright light blinded Saul, and he had to admit that he was dead wrong. Saul was humbled by God, and suddenly he had a submissive, teachable spirit.

God further prepared Saul by allowing him to experience failure. Saul began to preach in the synagogue of Damascus with great fervor, but he was overzealous and didn't realize much success. He had to escape from Damascus at night. When he went to Jerusalem he repeated the same mistake. He went into the synagogues and argued with such great fervor with the Jewish people there that they tried to kill him. The believers took Saul down to Caesarea and sent him home to Tarsus. Finally the church enjoyed a time of peace.

For more than a decade Saul lived in obscurity. We are not sure exactly what he did. In Galatians 2:1 Paul wrote, "Fourteen years later I went up again to Jerusalem, this time with Barnabas."* For more than a decade Saul didn't lead anybody. He was being prepared in relative obscurity for his job. You see, before Saul could achieve maximum usefulness, God needed to develop a new spirit in him. Out of the public eye, his fiery spirit had to be tempered. He had to develop a sensitivity for people.

This had to be a frustrating decade for Saul of Tarsus. He knew he had leadership ability. He knew he had been called to lead. Why wasn't he leading? But God, slowly and quietly, was preparing Saul for the task He had in mind.

Often God prepares leaders by putting them either in the crucible of suffering or some place of insignificance. Moses was a shepherd in the wilderness for forty years before God said, "Let's go. Let's lead the children of Israel out of Egypt." Joseph was in a dungeon for two years. Then God tapped him on the shoulder and said, "I want you to be prime minister." After David was anointed to be king, he spent months living in caves, hiding from the jealous King Saul. Jesus lived in obscurity for thirty years before He began His three-year ministry.

Maybe you're a little frustrated with your role right now. You feel that you want to be calling the plays, but you are standing on the sidelines. It may be that God is tempering you, preparing you for the limelight of leadership later. It has been said, "Character is what a man is in the dark." God may be testing you in obscurity to develop the kind of character He needs that can withstand the spotlight. God will more than compensate for those barren years, if you are faithful and wait patiently for Him. "I will repay you for the years the locusts have eaten," He says (Joel 2:25).

The Church's Part—Encouragement

The church's part in preparing Saul was one of encouragement. A special person named Barnabas lived in Antioch. He first appears in the book of Acts when the young church at Jerusalem was undergoing financial stress. A man named Joseph sold his field and gave the money to the church. The apostles called him Barnabas, which means "Son of Encouragement." His generosity encouraged the church.

When Saul of Tarsus was converted, the church kept him at arm's distance because they weren't convinced about him. But Barnabas put his arm around Saul and brought him into the church, introduced him to the people, and said, "Hey, this guy's for real." In Acts 11, Barnabas is at it again. When the Jerusalem church heard that the church at Antioch was growing, they sent Barnabas to help the church and encourage them to remain true to the Lord. Barnabas was a good man, full of the Holy Spirit and faith.

Antioch was the third largest city in the Roman Empire, with about five hundred thousand people. When the Christians in Jerusalem were persecuted, they scattered, and many of them went to Antioch. So the church there started to expand rapidly. Acts 11:21 says, "The Lord's hand was with them, and a great number of people believed and turned to the Lord." When Barnabas saw what was going on in this church—this rapid expansion—he thought, "This church needs more leadership. They need to have an expanded staff. I know just the man, Saul of Tarsus. We haven't heard from him in ten years, but he's the man for the job."

Barnabas didn't ask for volunteers. He selected the right man. Too often in the church we ask for volunteers, when what we need to do is to find the right person and ask that person to serve.

One church had the same minister for about ten years, and they had a successful ministry during that time. But when the minister resigned, the chairman of the board flippantly said, "Well, I need a pulpit committee. Do I have any volunteers?" Some enthusiastic but unperceptive people volunteered, and that church has never recovered from the shallow selection that committee made. Important appointments ought to be the result of prayer and careful selection.

Barnabas wasn't one to say, "It's my job to come up with the ideas. You guys implement them." He put shoe leather into his faith and went to Tarsus and looked for Saul. The Greek word implies that he had to look a long time to find Saul. Saul wasn't in a place of prominence. When Barnabas found him he said, "I want you to come to Antioch, Saul." This had to be an exciting encounter. Barnabas was an encourager. He said, "You're just the man they need, and you can do a good job, Saul." Saul was ready, and the two of them came to Antioch.

Maybe you can't be a leader, but you can be an encourager to leadership as Barnabas was. The church encouraged Saul, too. "For a whole year Barnabas and Saul met with the church and taught great numbers of people" (Acts 11:26). Saul served as an associate minister in this Antioch church for a year. The people responded well to his teaching. Nothing encourages a teacher or a preacher more than responsive people. You can see how God was easing Saul into this role of leadership. He gave Saul a year in a positive situation. (That's why some churches always have interns serving. The interns have a year to serve in a positive situation before they get their feet wet in the real world.)

During this time a prophet named Agabus predicted a severe famine in Jerusalem, and the Christians in Antioch took up an offering to help. Barnabas and Saul were sent to Jerusalem to deliver the gift to the Jerusalem church. Here again God was easing Saul into being a missionary. He had to go to meet strangers on behalf of Christ. Then, "when Barnabas and Saul had finished their mission, they returned from Jerusalem, taking with them John, also called Mark" (Acts 12:25).

The church at Antioch then sent these three men on a special missionary tour. "After they had fasted and prayed, they placed their hands on them and sent them off" (Acts 13:3). In the New Testament, the laying of hands on a man's head was done for one of three purposes. Sometimes it was for healing. Ananias laid his hands on Saul and Saul's sight was restored. Sometimes it was for imparting a special gift of the Holy Spirit. The apostles could lay their hands on people and grant the Holy Spirit. In this case the laying on of hands was for ordination or encouragement.

The church at Antioch had a missionary outlook. When the Jerusalem church was in trouble they took up an offering. When the Holy Spirit said, "I want you to send leaders out," they sent the best they had. The church should be a growing body, but it also needs to reach beyond its own boundaries to the world. Warren Wiersbe tells of a church that had a neon sign that kept flashing "Jesus Only." But the first three letters burned out and it kept flashing "us only, us only, us only." When the church gets introverted, it ceases to have the blessings of God. If we are the church of Jesus Christ there needs to be that constant outreach. Paul was encouraged by the local church to reach out, and they made him a leader.

Saul's Part—Consecration

God had prepared Saul, and the church had encouraged him, but now the rest was up to Saul himself. If he was going to be a leader, he had to have some personal consecration. Saul developed five characteristics in himself. These five characteristics are essential for anyone who wants to be a leader.

The first is *sincerity.* It has been said that the number one ingredient for leadership is sincerity. You can't fake sincerity for very long. Perceptive people begin to see through. They will not follow you if there is an inconsistency in your life, no matter how gifted you are.

Saul was always sincere. Even when he persecuted the church, he was for real. Nobody doubted that he was legitimate—he was not a hypocrite. When he became a Christian, he was one hundred percent a Christian. A sincere leader doesn't just mouth the words. He or she demonstrates the desired goal by living it out.

During World War II, General Patton was leading his troops across Europe. They were tired when they came to a deep, icy cold river, and the men began to grumble. No way were they going to swim across that stiff stream with backpacks. Patton didn't say a word. He waded into the water with his backpack and swam across to the other side. He turned around and looked at the men and swam back. Then he said, "Men, are you ready to go?" They all swam across. People don't need to be told as much as they need to be shown. The Christian leader must be sincere enough to model the Christian life.

The second characteristic of a consecrated leader is *decisiveness*. You cannot be a leader and be wishy-washy. You've got to make up your mind. A lot of people just cannot decide—they keep putting it off. As Charles Swindoll suggests, their favorite color is plaid. But Saul was a decisive person. When Barnabas said, "I want you to come to Antioch," Saul was ready to go. He once said, "But one thing I do: Forgetting what is behind and straining toward what is ahead, I press on toward the goal" (Philippians 3:13, 14).

In the book, *In Search of Excellence*, Peters and Waterman list the number one principle for success as a bias for action—a preference for doing something, anything, rather than sending a question through cycles and cycles of analyses and committee reports. In other words, there comes that time when somebody has to bite the bullet and say, "Let's go; I'll take that responsibility on myself."

The problem is that we want everyone's support, so we delay the decision to avoid criticism. Bill Cosby said, "I don't know what the secret of success is, but I am going to tell you the key to failure. The key to failure is trying to please everybody." If you try to please everybody, you are going to be a weak leader. A successful leader has to be decisive. He or she must have the ability to make decisions and not look back.

The third quality of a consecrated leader is *vision*. A good leader has to be able to dream—to stimulate followers into seeing what can be. Paul always had a vision. He could see beyond Antioch to Asia Minor and Macedonia, to Rome and Spain—into the world for Christ. He had spiritual claustrophobia. A good leader is somewhat of a dreamer. People don't respond to security, they respond to a challenge. They want to stretch and become something more than they are. A good leader is able to inspire people to stretch and believe something can be done and then do it.

The fourth essential characteristic of a leader is *compassion*. A. W. Tozer said, "Nothing can take the place of affection. Those who have it in generous measure have a magic power over men." This is probably the one ingredient Paul needed to develop. He was already sincere, he was already decisive, he was already visionary; but God took ten years to help him develop a spirit of sensitivity for people. I don't think he had that at first. He wouldn't have persecuted people and tortured them if he loved them. But his association with Barnabas and his in-depth training in the school of obscurity taught him to love people.

Paul was not a rigid legalist the way some people portray him. He met with the elders at Ephesus and wept and embraced them. He called Timothy "my dear son"; he loved him like a son and expressed that love. Paul once said that if it were possible, he would go to Hell if his Jewish friends would just believe. He was willing to compromise his personal preference in order to advance the gospel. He learned a sensitivity for people.

It is impossible to be an effective leader if you don't care for people. As Cavitt Roberts said so well, "People don't care how much you know if they don't know how much you care."

The final characteristic of a consecrated leader is *zeal*. Paul never lost his enthusiasm. He was excited all his life. When he came to the end, he said, "I have fought the good fight" (2 Timothy 4:7). His enthusiasm was contagious. He never quit.

Enthusiasm is essential to effective leadership. You don't have to be loud. You don't have to be the "rah-rah" type. But people ought to sense an intensity about your life. Emerson said, "Every great and commanding movement in the annals of history is the triumph of enthusiasm."

The church needs leaders today, perhaps as never before. And if the leaders are the type we have described, they will be worthy of being followed. Leaders who have been prepared by God in the crucible of obscurity. Leaders who have been encouraged by the church to step forward and take charge. Leaders who have developed in themselves a sincerity that's constant, a decisiveness that's wise, a vision that's challenging, a compassion that's obvious, and a zeal that's contagious. That was Paul—Paul, who said, "You follow me as I follow Christ." And maybe that's you, too.

This article is adapted from the book *Making Things Happen* by Bob Russell, © 1987 by the Standard Publishing Company. Used by permission.

*Scripture quotations in this article are taken from the *New International Version*.

Autumn Quarter, 1993

Theme: The Story of Beginnings (Genesis)

Special Features

Lessons

Unit 1: God's Creation of and Relationship With Mankind

Unit 2: The Beginning of a New Relationship

Unit 3: The Promise Is Transmitted

About these lessons

God's loving and total involvement in the beginnings of our universe is seen in this study. The lessons emphasize God's relationship with mankind through Abraham and Sarah, Isaac, Jacob, and Joseph.

Sep 5
Sep 12
Sep 19
Sep 26
Oct 3
Oct 10
Oct 17
Oct 24
Oct 31
Nov 7
Nov 14
Nov 21
Nov 28

The Starting Point

ONE OF THE PRINCIPAL FEATURES of the International Sunday School Lessons is that every major division of the Bible is given appropriate consideration in the six-year cycle of lessons. The lessons for September 1993—August 1994 draw our attention to the books of law, the first major division of the Bible. The first two quarters of last year's studies constituted a survey of the Old and New Testaments. Now, as we begin a more detailed study of individual books and groups of books in the Bible, it is fitting that we begin at the beginning.

The study of Genesis in the Autumn quarter presents the beginnings of our universe and its ongoing history. Emphasis is made on God's relationship with human beings, particularly through His covenant with Abraham, Isaac, and Jacob.

The Summer quarter completes the study of the books of law, picking up where Genesis left off. It traces the early development of the covenant nation that descended from the patriarchs named above.

In between these two studies, the Winter quarter presents the life of Christ as pictured by Luke, and the Spring quarter offers lessons based on Romans and Galatians. Victory over sin and death, and freedom from the bondage of law and works—all of which are ours in Christ—are the themes of the Spring quarter's lessons.

International Sunday School Lesson Cycle
September, 1992—August, 1998

YEAR	AUTUMN QUARTER (Sept., Oct., Nov.)	WINTER QUARTER (Dec., Jan., Feb.)	SPRING QUARTER (Mar., Apr., May)	SUMMER QUARTER (June, July, Aug.)
1992-1993	Old Testament Personalities (Old Testament Survey)	Good News for All (New Testament Survey)	Believing in Christ (John)	Following God's Purpose (Ephesians, Philippians, Colossians, Philemon)
1993-1994	The Story of Beginnings (Genesis)	The Story of Jesus (Luke)	Good News for God's People (Romans) Set Free by God's Grace (Galatians)	God Redeems a People (Exodus, Leviticus, Numbers, Deuteronomy)
1994-1995	From the Conquest to the Kingdom (Joshua, Judges, 1 and 2 Samuel, 1 Kings)	Jesus the Fulfillment (Matthew)	Christians Living in Community (1 and 2 Corinthians)	A Nation Turns From God (1 and 2 Kings, Amos, Hosea, Micah, Isaiah)
1995-1996	The Story of Christian Beginnings (Acts)	God's Promise of Deliverance (Isaiah) God's Love for All People (Jonah, Ruth)	Teachings of Jesus (Matthew, Mark, Luke)	A Practical Religion (James) God Is With Us (Psalms)
1996-1997	God's People Face Judgment (2 Kings, Jeremiah, Lamentations, Ezekiel, Habakkuk)	New Testament Personalities	Hope for the Future (1 and 2 Thessalonians, Revelation)	Guidance for Ministry (1 and 2 Timothy, Titus) A Call to Faithfulness (Hebrews)
1997-1998	God Leads a People Home (Major Prophets, Minor Prophets, Nehemiah)	God's People in a Troubled World (1 and 2 Peter, 1, 2, 3 John, Jude)	The Gospel of Action (Mark)	Wisdom for Living (Job, Proverbs, Ecclesiastes)

Drama in Three Acts

by Willard W. Winter

COULD ANYTHING BE MORE DRAMATIC than the events described in the early chapters of Genesis? There we read of beginnings—of the universe, the earth, mankind, sin, punishment, and redemption. We marvel, we weep, we rejoice over the events that are described. Unit 1 (lessons one through four of this quarter's study) takes us from one dramatic event to another in the first nine chapters of Genesis.

ACT ONE: The Origin of the Universe

The first lesson tells the story of what happened "in the beginning." The Scripture text describes the origin of the universe. The human mind can hardly comprehend the magnificence of the great Creator God, who created heavens and earth *ex nihilo*—out of nothing.

Where in all literature is there a more dramatic statement of action than the very first verse of the Bible: "In the beginning God created the heaven and the earth"? With exciting crescendo the account continues, "And God said, Let there be light: and there was light" (Genesis 1:3). God spoke, and it was done.

The human mind cannot fathom what cataclysmic activity occurred when God said, "Let the waters under the heaven be gathered together unto one place" (Genesis 1:9a). Did great rifts appear in the face of the earth? Did great pressures push mountain peaks high above the surface? Did water drain down the sides of the mountains into pools, lakes, seas, and oceans? What a scene it must have been!

God's steadfast love is equally thrilling. Behind every creative act was His loving-kindness. What else could possibly have moved Him to prepare such a wonderful world as a home for mankind?

ACT TWO: The Origin of Mankind

The second lesson continues the description of God's creative activity reaching a climax as He made human beings in His own image. These verses tell us more about the nature of God, but they also tell us who we are. By them we know our origins, and we also have a better idea of our nature and our destiny.

When we realize that we are created in the image of God, we understand that more is expected of us than of the animal kingdom. This lesson impresses upon us the Biblical teaching that we are stewards of the world God has made. All living things that He placed here were given

for man's benefit and are to be properly cared for by him.

As we read again how God created the first man and woman, a new appreciation of the equality of the two before God bursts on our consciousness. We also gain a better insight of how there can be neither male nor female in Christ (Galatians 3:28).

Adam's dramatic reaction when God presented his helpmate to him guides us in establishing our homes. Part of his statement was, "Therefore shall a man leave his father and his mother, and shall cleave unto his wife: and they shall be one flesh" (Genesis 2:24). Is this not a thrilling and dramatic statement of good counsel for a lasting marriage?

ACT THREE: Mankind's Sin and God's Response

Lessons three and four present the third act of the drama of this first unit of study. Lesson three describes in detail the subtlety of Satan and the origin of sin.

Satan beguiled the woman. She disobeyed God, and Adam joined her in eating of the forbidden fruit. Their sin changed everything. They now knew shame, and they feared God and hid from Him.

God could have destroyed the guilty pair, but His grace prevailed. He penalized them by denying them access to the tree of life. He cursed the serpent and foretold the continuing enmity that would exist between Satan and the human family. God also predicted the final defeat of Satan, stating that the seed of the woman (Jesus Christ), would bruise the head of the serpent, that old dragon, the devil.

The original sin led to increased sin among Adam and Eve's descendants, until the human family was so corrupt that the thoughts of their hearts were continually inclined only toward evil. God responded by sending a flood of waters to destroy all living creatures.

Once again God manifested His grace. He called Noah to prepare an ark to save all who would accept God's salvation. After the flood, God promised that there would never again be such a flood of waters to destroy every living creature. His grace is ageless.

Talk about drama—it is in every line in the early chapters of Genesis. These studies will captivate thoughtful hearts and lead us to a closer walk with God.

"Hope Thou in God"

by Stephen M. Hooks

THE PATHS OF LIFE are strewn with the victims of misplaced hope—people who have been burned by a relationship, betrayed by a friend, disillusioned by a cause gone sour, disappointed by a personal failure. With great expectations, we set out to seize life only to discover that it has a better hold on us than we do on it and that many of our dreams are beyond our ability to turn them into reality. Unfulfilled hope "maketh the heart sick," said the writer of Proverbs (13:12). How well he speaks to our age! We have put our hopes in the wrong things and have come away sick at heart.

There is, at last, only one cure for such a sickness. It is to ground our hopes in that which does not fail. The key to a lasting hope that does not disappoint rests not in *for what* we hope, but *in whom* we hope. In the Bible, hope is not based on the dreams and schemes of men but upon the nature and character of God. Such hope is as firm as God's promises, as dependable as His determination to keep His word and accomplish His will. It is not a hope in the future alone, but in the God who holds the future.

It is this very truth that God sought to teach Abraham. Unit 2 of this quarter's lessons deals with the beginnings of the covenant relationship that God established with "the father of the faithful." Employing texts from Genesis 12—21, these four lessons cover events from the call of Abraham to and including the birth of Isaac.

Lesson five, "God's Commitment to Abram," is based on the printed text of Genesis 15, which records one of the most unusual encounters of God and man in the Bible. God appears in a vision to reassure Abram that he will, indeed, have numerous descendants and that they will inherit the land of Canaan. Abram's response to this promise is to believe in the Lord, to take God at His word. The sovereign Lord of the universe then condescends to His subject's need for further assurance by voluntarily obligating himself to Abram in a manner consistent with the ancient ritual of covenant-making. The Bible asks us, like Abram, to stake our eternal destinies on the promises of God. This lesson demonstrates the degree of God's commitment to the promises He makes to His children. When we put our hope in God, we put our hope in One who is determined to keep His word.

Lesson six, "Sarai Attempts to Manipulate Events," is drawn from Genesis 16 and illustrates the difficulties that can arise when God's children refuse to "wait upon" Him and try to take matters into their own hands. A childless Sarai, desperate for offspring, offers her handmaid Hagar to Abram as a surrogate wife. In the union and child (Ishmael) who comes of it, Sarai and Abram think that they have, by their own initiative, secured the covenant promise. Subsequent events, however, will reveal that, in reality, they have only frustrated the covenant promise by raising up an heir that God never intended, and one who posed a potential threat to plans that God desired to bring about through Isaac. Abram and Sarai will sadly learn that the promises of God are fulfilled in His own time and in His own way.

Lesson seven, "God's Covenant With Abraham," is based on the text of Genesis 17 and discusses God's formal establishing of His covenant with Abram. The promises of numerous offspring and a future homeland are reiterated and made conditional to Abram's full submission to the covenant. This submission is to be symbolized generation after generation through the ritual of circumcision. This formal ratification of the covenant is occasioned by the renaming of Sarai and Abram and the announcement of Isaac's impending birth. From this episode Abraham and Sarah will learn that God's promises are enjoyed by those who meet His conditions.

Lesson eight, "God Keeps His Promise," derives from Genesis 21 and observes the beginning of the fulfillment of the covenant promise in the "out-of-season" birth of Isaac. At a time and in a manner that make it absolutely clear that it is "of God" and not "of men," the Lord acts to fulfill His promise and realize Abraham's highest hopes. That which Abraham and Sarah could not secure for themselves through decades of human relationship and personal initiative is finally secured for them by God—the long-awaited son of promise.

The implications of these events in the life of the ancient patriarch are of great importance for the Christian today. As with Abraham, our personal fulfillment in this life and eternal destiny in the life to come are secured not by what we can propose and achieve, but by what God promises and provides. "Hope thou in God," wrote the psalmist (Psalm 42:5). When we do, we put our hopes in the One who is truly able to save us in every way.

A Life in Conflict

by Gary Hall

THE THIRD UNIT OF LESSONS in this quarter's study covers the life of Jacob, the important ancestor of Israel. His was a life full of conflict and tragedy. Late in his life he could testify that it had been brief and full of trouble (Genesis 47:9). Receiving the continuation of the blessing given to Abraham and Isaac did not exempt Jacob from difficulties and trials, many of which were self-imposed. Focusing on this patriarch offers us the opportunity to reflect on the way God works and the unexpected experiences of those blessed by Him.

Conflict With Esau and Laban

Lesson nine examines the birth and early manhood of the twins, Jacob and Esau. Their birth was marked by conflict between the two in their mother's womb, and by a revelation from God concerning that conflict (Genesis 25:19-34). The word from God prophesied a reversal of status—the older would serve the younger. This lesson will consider the relationship of God's plans regarding Jacob's life and Jacob's manipulations to advance himself. God's selection of Abraham and his descendants impacted on their lives in different ways. Some were more receptive than others. Being part of the favored family obviously did not mean instant perfection. God was working and Jacob was structuring his life at the same time. The word of God in Genesis 25:23 also provides an opportunity for our reflection on the tensions between God's foreknowledge and man's free choice.

The successful effort by Rebekah and Jacob to steal the blessing that Isaac intended for Esau (Genesis 27) forms the basis for lesson ten. Apparently conflict existed in the family because each parent had a favorite of the two sons. This lesson continues the conflict theme as Rebekah and Jacob are pitted against Isaac and Esau over the matter of which son would receive the father's final blessing. This lesson offers the opportunity to reflect on the common human traits of lying and deception and God's attitude toward them. Even though Jacob received the blessing, there was no hint that God approved of his methods. God's blessings should be received in faithfulness and honesty, not deceit.

Lesson eleven subtly hints that divine retribution should not be discounted (Genesis 29). When Jacob met his future father-in-law, he found someone who was in many ways like himself. Laban was not above deceit to promote his own plans. The episode with Laban's two daughters found Jacob deceived and tricked into marrying the older daughter, in addition to the younger daughter, Rachel, whom he dearly loved. Students who reflect on this will not miss the irony. A person reaps what he sows, sometimes in quite unexpected ways.

Jacob's love for Rachel was exemplary, but the tension in the home with his two wives, who were sisters, was strong. A glance at chapter 30 will help the student see the unhappy consequences. Although the children born to Jacob were important for the history of Israel, their births occasioned many hard feelings, even between Jacob and Rachel.

Reconciliation and Blessing

Jacob's reunion with Esau, lesson twelve, was full of anxiety for the younger brother. He made elaborate preparations to soften the wrath that he feared Esau still held for him (Genesis 32). But it seems that the forgiving attitude of Esau made them unnecessary. Esau had forgiven his brother's actions of the past. The reunion of the brothers was a beautiful scene (Genesis 33). This lesson provides an opportunity to reflect on the issues of reconciliation, both with others as well as with God.

Lesson thirteen skips to the end of Jacob's life to help us understand why certain tribes in Israel's later history had such importance (Genesis 48). The background necessary to this lesson is the narrative of Joseph (Genesis 37—47). Jacob's blessing of Joseph's sons completed Joseph's amazing life. But this lesson also brings us back to the second one in this unit, lesson 10. The death bed blessing is at issue again. What was said would stand, whether Esau (earlier) or Joseph (now) liked it or not. There was more to these statements than just the sentiment or wish of a dying patriarch. We are to understand that God's word was behind these events and that Jacob's family was living under great blessing. It was a blessing for the whole world (Genesis 12:1-3).

These lessons should cause every Christian to ponder what it means to live under the blessing of God, who has been at work in human history to draw all people to himself. And they should help us to accept our responsibility to become involved in carrying out His purpose.

Beginning Again

by Mark Mangano

T HE BOOK OF GENESIS is a book of beginnings. The Jews designated the book "in the beginning," the book's opening words. The name *Genesis* is derived from the Greek word meaning "origin, source." Such titles are appropriate for a book concerned with the beginning of all things connected with Biblical faith: the origin of the world, humanity, sin, redemption, and community.

The Beginning of the World and Humanity

In six creative days, God formed and filled this world, as John Calvin says, to be "the theater of His glory." Psalmists and prophets proclaim that from the east to the west God's glory is revealed and praised (Psalms 50:1; 113:3; Isaiah 45:6; 59:19; Malachi 1:11). The glory of God was supremely disclosed in Jesus, by whom, writes the apostle Paul, "were all things created, that are in heaven, and that are in earth, visible and invisible" (Colossians 1:16).

God created mankind, the crescendo of His creative activity, "in his own image" (Genesis 1:26, 27). What does Scripture mean by this expression? Two analogies are here offered.

A photograph or a photocopy resembles the object it pictures. Given that God is spirit (John 4:24; 1 Timothy 1:17; 6:16) and is not conditioned by anything that originates or decays in time (Psalms 90:2, 4; 102:24-27; Isaiah 44:6), whereas man is material and mortal, how can men and women resemble God?

First, Scripture answers this question by focusing on qualities such as holiness (Leviticus 19:2; 1 Peter 1:14-16), humility (John 13:14, 15; Philippians 2:3-8), forgiveness (Colossians 3:13), and love (1 John 4:7-21).

Second, mankind, created in the image of God, represents God. When Adam and Eve were created, God said to them, "Be fruitful, and multiply, and replenish the earth, and subdue it" (Genesis 1:28). Having received this charge, they were to act as representatives of God, extending God's creation as well as His control over all things.

The Beginning of Sin

Created in the image of God, mankind is created with the ability to make moral choices. Adam and Eve exercised this ability and tragically introduced sin into the world. Once sin was introduced, men and women fell prey to the ravaging effects of evil desire (James 1:13-15).

With premeditation Cain killed his brother Abel (Genesis 4:8). With boasting Lamech recounted to his wives that he too had killed another (4:23, 24). With remorse God observed that the "wickedness of [pre-flood] man was great in the earth, and that every imagination of the thoughts of his heart was only evil continually" (6:5). God, therefore, sent the flood as His judgment of mankind. He would have destroyed every last member of the human race, if Noah had not "found grace in the eyes of the Lord" (6:8). God would begin again, as it were, with Noah and his family.

The power and presence of sin did not drown in the flood, however. As earth's population increased following the flood, so did the incidence of sin. We read of the presumption at Babel (11:1-9), the indiscriminate abuse of power (12:10-20; 20:1-18; 26:1-11), quarreling (13:7), war (14:1-16), jealousy and intrigue (16:1-16), sodomy and incest (19:1-38), deception (27:1-40; 29:14-30; 34:1-31), and sexual impropriety (38:1—39:23).

Genesis teaches quite clearly that the wages of sin is ultimately death (2:17; 3:19). "And sin, when it is finished," concurs James, "bringeth forth death" (James 1:15). This connection between death and a sin-filled life is felt most gravely in Genesis 5, where the eulogies of eight men end with the words, "and he died."

The Beginning of Redemption

Sin enslaves the created order to decay and death (Romans 8:18-21). God has promised, therefore, to create "new heavens and a new earth" free from the tyranny of sin (Isaiah 65:17; 66:22; 2 Peter 3:10-13; Revelation 21:1).

Since sin disrupts and defaces those who are created in the image of God, mankind must undergo renewal. That renewal is in Jesus Christ (2 Corinthians 5:17), who is the image of God (2 Corinthians 4:4; Colossians 1:15; Hebrews 1:3).

That re-creation in Jesus was announced for the first time in Genesis 3:15, when God said to the serpent in the garden, "And I will put enmity between thee and the woman, and between thy seed and her seed; it shall bruise thy head, and thou shalt bruise his heel." This first glimmer of the gospel was, of course, God's judgment against the serpent, whom the New Testament unmasks as Satan (Revelation 12:9; 20:2). Jesus, the one born of a woman (Galatians 4:4) and the one identified as the "seed" par excellence (Galatians 3:16), triumphed over the power of Satan, as Paul stated vividly in Colossians 2:15: "And having spoiled principalities and powers, he made a show of them openly, triumphing over them in it [the cross]."

Because of God's love for His creation, He paid the penalty for sin and broke the power of sin by allowing His own Son to die on the cross and then raising Him to life in triumphal procession.

The Beginning of Community

After the flood, God promised that He would never again destroy all flesh in such a manner. When the human race turned again to sin, therefore, God did not eliminate them. Instead, He responded with mercy and grace. He began again, as it were, and called Abram to be the father of a people through whom He would carry out His redemptive purpose.

That purpose is seen in God's promise to Abram: "And I will make of thee a great nation, and I will bless thee, and make thy name great; and thou shalt be a blessing: and I will bless them that bless thee, and curse him that curseth thee: and in thee shall all families of the earth be blessed" (Genesis 12:2, 3).

God promised seed to Abram (Abraham), and that promise to Abraham and his descendants is repeated often in Genesis. From that seed would issue forth the seed of the woman of whom God had spoken in the garden (Genesis 3:15). The promise that the patriarchs Abraham, Isaac, and Jacob were to be a source of blessing to the entire world is also repeated throughout the book (18:18; 22:18; 26:4; 28:14).

Indeed, these two promises find their fulfillment in Jesus. The apostle Paul said it well in Galatians 3:8, 14: "And the Scripture, foreseeing that God would justify the heathen through faith, preached before the gospel unto Abraham, saying, In thee shall all nations be blessed . . . that the blessing of Abraham might come on the Gentiles through Jesus Christ; that we might receive the promise of the Spirit through faith."

God made promises to the patriarchs Abraham, Isaac, and Jacob to establish for himself a people. Genesis is a remarkable record of how God established and preserved His covenant people. In fact, most of the book testifies to the obstacles that God had to overcome to preserve His community.

The barrenness of Sarah, Rebekah, and Rachel stood in the way of God's intention for a people. Old age in Abraham's case was another obstacle (17:17; Hebrews 11:11, 12). On three separate occasions the patriarchs Abraham and Isaac temporarily lost their wives. Famine, war, and the threat of war were other obstacles that God overcame. We read in Exodus 1, that Pharaoh tried to systematically destroy God's people. At the end of Israel's sojourn in Egypt, however, the Israelites numbered about six hundred thousand men, besides women and children (Exodus 12:37).

God intended for man and himself to enjoy fellowship with each other. One of the finest Old Testament expressions of this intimate relationship is found in Exodus 19:5, 6a, where God instructed Moses to speak these words to the nation of Israel: "Now therefore, if ye will obey my voice indeed, and keep my covenant, then ye shall be a peculiar treasure unto me above all people: for all the earth is mine: and ye shall be unto me a kingdom of priests, and a holy nation."

God's desire for community with mankind, which was revealed in His promise to Abraham, Isaac, and Jacob and took form in His relationship with Israel of old, culminates with the new Israel, the church, the elect of God through Jesus Christ.

Through the words of Peter, God uses the same language to describe this intimate relationship of community with the church: "But ye are a chosen generation, a royal priesthood, a holy nation, a peculiar people; that ye should show forth the praises of him who hath called you out of darkness into his marvelous light" (1 Peter 2:9).

As the church shows forth her praises of God, the whole world indeed becomes a "theater of His glory."

Answers to Quarterly Quiz

on page 8

Lesson 1—1. darkness. 2. a firmament. 3. third. **Lesson 2**—1. dominion. 2. that he should be alone. 3. names. **Lesson 3**—1. good and evil. 2. aprons. 3. hid themselves from God. **Lesson 4**—1. cherubim and a flaming sword. 2. destroy all flesh with a flood. **Lesson 5**—1. the stars. 2. four hundred years. **Lesson 6**—1. Hagar. 2. despised her. 3. Ishmael. **Lesson 7**—1. 99. 2. circumcision. **Lesson 8**—1. 100. 2. a great feast. 3. Because she saw Ishmael mocking. **Lesson 9**—1. Jacob's hand took hold of Esau's heel. 2. Esau, Jacob. 3. his birthright. **Lesson 10**—1. hunt for venison and prepare him a meal of it. 2. Esau's clothing and the skins of young goats. 3. he said Isaac's God brought it to him. **Lesson 11**—1. 7. 2. his daughter Leah. 3. 14. **Lesson 12**—1. 400. 2. Rachel and Joseph. 3. false. **Lesson 13**—1. Manasseh and Ephraim. 2. true.

Quarterly Quiz

The questions on this page may be used in several ways: as a pretest at the beginning of the quarter; as a review at the end of the quarter; or as a review after each lesson. The questions are based on the Scripture text of each lesson (King James Version). **The answers are on page 7.**

Lesson 1

1. In the beginning, what was upon the face of the deep of the formless earth? *Genesis 1:2*
2. What did God create to divide the waters from the waters? *Genesis 1:6*
3. On what day of creation did God cause the dry land to appear? *Genesis 1:9, 13*

Lesson 2

1. God created mankind and gave them what over all living things? *Genesis 1:28*
2. What did God say was not good for the man He created? *Genesis 2:18*
3. What did Adam give to all cattle, beasts, and fowls of the air? *Genesis 2:20*

Lesson 3

1. What did the serpent say Eve would know if she ate of the forbidden fruit? *Genesis 3:5*
2. What did Adam and Eve make with fig leaves to hide their nakedness? *Genesis 3:7*
3. What did Adam and Eve do when they heard God's voice in the garden? *Genesis 3:8*

Lesson 4

1. What did God put at the east of the garden of Eden to prevent man's access to the tree of life? *Genesis 3:24*
2. After the flood, what did God say He would never do again? *Genesis 9:15*

Lesson 5

1. God told Abram that his seed would be innumerable, like what? *Genesis 15:5*
2. God said Abram's seed would be strangers in a foreign land, would serve them, and be afflicted by them for how long? *Genesis 15:13*

Lesson 6

1. Sarai bore no children for Abram, so she gave _____ to him as a wife. *Genesis 16:3*
2. After this woman conceived, how did she treat Sarai? *Genesis 16:4*
3. What did Abram name the son this woman bore him? *Genesis 16:15*

Lesson 7

1. How old was Abram when God appeared to him, reaffirmed His covenant with him, and changed his name to Abraham? *Genesis 17:1*

2. What was the token of the covenant between God and Abraham and all of Abraham's seed after him? *Genesis 17:11*

Lesson 8

1. How old was Abraham when Sarah bore Isaac to him? *Genesis 21:5*
2. What did Abraham make for Isaac on the day Isaac was weaned? *Genesis 21:8*
3. Why did Sarah demand that Abraham send away Hagar and Ishmael? *Genesis 21:9, 10*

Lesson 9

1. What action took place between the twins Esau and Jacob at their birth? *Genesis 25:26*
2. Regarding the twins, Isaac loved _____ but Rebekah loved _____ . *Genesis 25:28*
3. What did Esau sell to Jacob for a meal of lentil stew? *Genesis 25:33, 34*

Lesson 10

1. Before Isaac blessed Esau, what did he ask Esau to do? *Genesis 27:7*
2. To make Jacob seem as Esau, what all did Rebekah put on Jacob? *Genesis 27:15, 16*
3. What explanation did the pretender give for finding "venison" so quickly? *Genesis 27:20*

Lesson 11

1. Jacob agreed to serve Laban for (3, 5, 7) years for his daughter Rachel. *Genesis 29:18*
2. On the wedding night, whom did Laban give to Jacob instead of Rachel? *Genesis 29:33*
3. Altogether, Jacob had to serve _____ years for his wives. *Genesis 29:20, 27*

Lesson 12

1. On Jacob's return to Canaan, Esau came with how many men to meet him? *Genesis 33:1*
2. Jacob arranged his caravan so that what two persons were in the rear? *Genesis 33:2*
3. Esau and Jacob's reunion was filled with bitterness and accusation. T/F *Genesis 33:4*

Lesson 13

1. The two sons of Joseph were name _____ and _____ . *Genesis 48:13*
2. Joseph was displeased when his father gave the greater blessing to the younger son. T/F *Genesis 48:17*

The Origin of the Universe

September 5
Lesson 1

DEVOTIONAL READING: Isaiah 40:21, 25, 26, 28-31.

LESSON SCRIPTURE: Genesis 1:1-25.

PRINTED TEXT: Genesis 1:1-15.

Genesis 1:1-15

1 In the beginning God created the heaven and the earth.

2 And the earth was without form, and void; and darkness was upon the face of the deep. And the Spirit of God moved upon the face of the waters.

3 And God said, Let there be light: and there was light.

4 And God saw the light, that it was good: and God divided the light from the darkness.

5 And God called the light Day, and the darkness he called Night. And the evening and the morning were the first day.

6 And God said, Let there be a firmament in the midst of the waters, and let it divide the waters from the waters.

7 And God made the firmament, and divided the waters which were under the firmament from the waters which were above the firmament: and it was so.

8 And God called the firmament Heaven. And the evening and the morning were the second day.

9 And God said, Let the waters under the heaven be gathered together unto one place, and let the dry land appear: and it was so.

10 And God called the dry land Earth; and the gathering together of the waters called he Seas: and God saw that it was good.

11 And God said, Let the earth bring forth grass, the herb yielding seed, and the fruit tree yielding fruit after his kind, whose seed is in itself, upon the earth: and it was so.

12 And the earth brought forth grass, and herb yielding seed after his kind, and the tree yielding fruit, whose seed was in itself, after his kind: and God saw that it was good.

13 And the evening and the morning were the third day.

14 And God said, Let there be lights in the firmament of the heaven to divide the day from the night; and let them be for signs, and for seasons, and for days, and years:

15 And let them be for lights in the firmament of the heaven to give light upon the earth: and it was so.

GOLDEN TEXT: In the beginning God created the heaven and the earth.—Genesis 1:1.

Lesson Aims

After this lesson a student should be able to:
1. Appreciate God's purpose and plan in providing a home for mankind.
2. Have a deeper love for God and serve Him with a grateful heart.

Lesson Outline

INTRODUCTION
   A. "I Made It Myself!"
   B. Lesson Background
 I. THE BEGINNING (Genesis 1:1-5)
   A. God Creates the Universe (vv. 1, 2)
      Simple, But Sufficient
   B. God Speaks Light Into Being (v. 3)
   C. Light Divided From Darkness (vv. 4, 5)
 II. THE FIRMAMENT (Genesis 1:6-8)
   A. The Firmament's Purpose (v. 6)
   B. The Firmament Made (vv. 7, 8)
III. THE EARTH (Genesis 1:9-13)
   A. Dry Land Appears (v. 9)
   B. Earth and Seas Named (v. 10)
   C. Plants Called Forth (vv. 11-13)
      Good for Something, After All!
IV. THE LUMINARIES (Genesis 1:14, 15)
   A. God Gives the Order (v. 14a)
   B. The Purpose of the Lights (vv. 14b, 15)
CONCLUSION
   A. The Light of the World
   B. Let Us Pray
   C. Thought to Remember

Display visual 1 of the visuals packet and let it remain before the class throughout this and next week's lesson. The visual is shown on page 13.

Introduction

A. "I Made It Myself!"

Johnny wanted to give a wedding present to his cousin Marie. She was twelve years older than he, but she had always been his favorite cousin. He didn't have enough money to buy a gift, so he went to the lumberyard and bought a piece of wood; and with his jigsaw, he cut out a doorstop in the shape of a cat. Then he sanded it carefully and painted it with the finest black and white enamel he could buy.

Friends gave Marie a wedding shower. As she unwrapped Johnny's gift, she held it up for all to admire. When she announced who had given it, Johnny spoke out with pride, "I made it myself!"

The first chapter of Genesis contains the Bible's clear and straightforward account of the origin of everything in the physical universe, all things inanimate and all forms of life, including mankind. God himself created them. Mankind was the central feature and crowning glory of God's creation. But first, a place fit for their habitation must be provided.

B. Lesson Background

This lesson is the first in a series of thirteen providing a survey of the book of Genesis. The lessons are divided into three units of four, four, and five sessions respectively. The main theme of the first unit of lessons is the relationship of God the Creator with His universe and the human beings He created. Today's lesson presents God as a loving and benevolent Creator.

The background of this lesson is found in eternity. There, in the indescribable counsels of Father, Son, and Holy Spirit, God's wisdom and love conceived the material universe. And in this almost unbelievably vast universe, one little globe, the earth, was prepared as the home of man, who would be created in the image and likeness of the Creator.

I. The Beginning
(Genesis 1:1-5)

A. God Creates the Universe (vv. 1, 2)

1. In the beginning God created the heaven and the earth.

The first word of the Bible takes us back to the beginning of time, to the beginning of God's creation of the physical universe, to the beginning of His preparations for the creation of human beings. Genesis is a book of beginnings, and the title itself points to the theme of origins.

Notice that God's activity is described in this verse as creating, not making. In some of His later activity, God is described as making parts of the physical universe. In the very beginning, He *created* out of nothing those elements out of which He later fashioned the finished products of the heavens and the earth.

The heaven. The word translated *heaven* is plural, and should be "heavens." Nothing is said in Genesis about the origins of heaven, God's dwelling place. God himself is timeless, and so is the place of His dwelling. This verse refers to the heaven through which the birds fly, and to the vast reaches beyond, in which God set the sun, moon, and stars.

SIMPLE, BUT SUFFICIENT

Isaac Asimov was a very prolific author. He wrote more books on more subjects than anyone else. He had more than four hundred to his credit.

Asimov's claim to fame was not just the sheer number of words he put into print. It was also his ability to restate difficult concepts and technical information in a way that common persons could understand. Most of us need such help as this to illuminate the complex world in which we live.

The first verse of Genesis does an outstanding job of meeting this need of ours. Scientists and theologians alike have spent lifetimes studying in their respective fields and then making solemn pronouncements on the creation—when it occurred, how it was accomplished. But complete agreement on these questions escapes the "experts."

"In the beginning God created" says all we really *need* to know about the origins of life. It is a simple statement, but sufficiently profound to encompass all the truth. This tells us "who" and "what"; it is where faith begins. The "when" and "how" are much less important.   —C. R. B.

2. And the earth was without form, and void; and darkness was upon the face of the deep. And the Spirit of God moved upon the face of the waters.

Verse 1 describes God's creative activity as He called into being the elements of the physical universe. It does not describe God's creation in its final form. The verse may be considered a heading for the entire first chapter, followed by the detailed account of creation.

God called the heavens and the earth into being in an unfinished form, choosing to bring them to their final form in stages. In its primeval state, the earth was *without form, and void.* It was just a great blob of material encircled by a mass of clouds. No light shone upon the earth; darkness was everywhere. *The deep* is a term used often for the ocean, and in this early stage the ocean covered all the face of the earth. But the creative Spirit of God was moving, hovering, brooding over the unfinished earth, and some changes were made. God was in the process of bringing earth to a condition appropriate as a dwelling place for mankind.

B. God Speaks Light Into Being (v. 3)

3. And God said, Let there be light: and there was light.

God spoke, and it was done. Notice how many times this phrase, *God said*, appears in the account of creation.

The first chapters of Genesis are not a textbook on science. We are not told how God made the light that began to shine on earth when He gave the order—whether it was from a heavenly body that was heated until it became luminous, or from some other source. This succinct account of God's creative activity simply states that God said, "Let light be." And light was! Just like that! Presumably the heavy clouds and vapors that enshrouded the earth thinned sufficiently to let in the light.

C. Light Divided From Darkness
(vv. 4, 5)

4. And God saw the light, that it was good: and God divided the light from the darkness.

God saw the light. The meaning is that God examined His newly-finished product and took note that it corresponded with what He had intended it to be. And so He pronounced that *it was good.*

God divided the light from the darkness, thus light did not come to all the world at once. Presumably the light came from one direction, as it does now, so that one side of the earth was in the light and the other side was in the dark. And presumably the earth was turning, as it does now, so that day followed night and night followed day.

5. And God called the light Day, and the darkness he called Night. And the evening and the morning were the first day.

Having divided the light from the darkness, God himself gave names to them. He gave to light the name *Day* and to darkness the name *Night.* So the coming of light was the dawn of earth's first day.

The period of darkness that prevailed until God called light into being formed the *evening.* God's calling forth of light is called *morning.* For that reason man developed the custom of counting the beginning of a day with the coming of darkness, as is still the custom among Jewish people.

The days of creation have occasioned much discussion, and it centers around the question, How long were the days that are mentioned in the first chapter of Genesis? The question cannot be decided by referring to the root meaning of the Hebrew word for *day*.

Some have considered the days of creation to be, not days of twenty-four hours each, but six consecutive geological eras. Attention is called to the fact that the word *day* is sometimes used to indicate an indefinite period of time, as when we refer to the day of George Washington. In this connection, the words of Peter come to mind: "One day is with the Lord as a thousand years, and a thousand years as one day" (2 Peter 3:8). However, in Genesis the reference to day and night, to evening and morning, seems to indicate ordinary days as we know them, especially in 1:16.

Does this mean that God created the universe in six such days as we know? It may indeed be so. He who could speak light into existence in a moment could surely bring worlds into being as easily.

II. The Firmament
(Genesis 1:6-8)

A. The Firmament's Purpose (v. 6)

6. And God said, Let there be a firmament in the midst of the waters, and let it divide the waters from the waters.

God was preparing the earth so that it would be able to sustain all forms of life that He planned to create. He began by calling light into existence, for life as we know it would not be possible without light. It would provide for the growth of grasses, plants, and trees, on which the animals and man would depend for food.

Air for breathing was another requirement, so God created a band of atmosphere to encircle the surface of the earth. This atmosphere was the *firmament* that God called into being.

The word *firmament* may be misleading. God did not call into being something firm, like a glass bowl turned upside down over the earth. The Hebrew word for *firmament* comes from a verb that means "to spread out." As a noun, the word describes an expanse, something spread out. The firmament, therefore, is the space spread out above us, the space into which we look from the earth. At first that space was not very high. It reached out only to the cloud cover that still surrounded the whole earth. Thus, with the creation of the firmament a division was made in the waters that enshrouded the globe.

B. The Firmament Made (vv. 7, 8)

7. And God made the firmament, and divided the waters which were under the firmament from the waters which were above the firmament: and it was so.

Notice that God's activity is here described by the word *made*, and not *created*. In forming the firmament, God used elements that He had already brought into being.

God's purpose in making the firmament was expressed in verse 6. Verse 7 tells us that the firmament fulfilled God's purpose. It divided *the waters which were above the firmament* (the clouds) from *the waters which were under the firmament* (all the waters on the surface of the earth). And with this division God put into operation the processes by which the waters above would condense and fall to earth as rain. The cycle would be completed as the waters in the ponds, lakes, rivers, and oceans evaporated into the atmosphere and were carried to the heights, there to begin the process again.

8. And God called the firmament Heaven. And the evening and the morning were the second day.

Heaven. Sometimes the dwelling place of God is called Heaven (see 1 Kings 8:30; Psalm 11:4; Matthew 6:9). But we see in this verse that God gave the name *Heaven* to the firmament described in verses 6 and 7, that is, the band of atmosphere that surrounds the surface of the earth. By it the clouds are borne up, and in it the birds fly (v. 20). Verses 14-17 reveal that the word *firmament* is extended to include the vast expanse of space beyond earth's atmosphere, that in which the sun, moon, and stars appear. Thus we may speak of the birds of heaven, the clouds of heaven, or the stars of heaven.

We notice that there is no repetition of the statement, "it was good," concerning the making of the firmament. This does not imply that there was anything wrong with God's work; for at the end of the six days of creative activity, "God saw everything that he had made, and, behold, it was very good" (Genesis 1:31).

Once again, the time was counted beginning with the period of darkness and concluding with the period of light. Thus God's activities of the second day were completed.

III. The Earth
(Genesis 1:9-13)

A. Dry Land Appears (v. 9)

9. And God said, Let the waters under the heaven be gathered together unto one place, and let the dry land appear: and it was so.

Once again God spoke, *and it was so.* His creative activity of the third day consisted in the rearrangement of the surface of the earth. Dry land was made to appear, and pools of water were formed. The gathering of water formed earth's lakes, rivers, seas, and oceans.

THE EARTH IS THE LORD'S, AND THE FULNESS THEREOF.

Again, we are not told what method God used to gather the waters together so dry land would appear. Perhaps that part of the globe that would become dry land was raised above the surface of the waters. At the same time, God may have caused other areas on the earth's surface to be depressed, making reservoirs of water. As we now study the surface of the earth, we see that there are depths in the oceans that are as extensive as some of the peaks of the highest mountains.

Nearly three-fourths of the earth's surface is covered with water. If some should think that such a vast expanse of water is wasted area and useless, let them consider that there is a delicate balance between rainfall and the water needs of the earth. With less ocean surface, the lessened evaporation would result in extensive barren, arid wastelands of the earth. God made the proportion just right to serve the needs of man.

B. Earth and Seas Named (v. 10)

10. And God called the dry land Earth; and the gathering together of the waters called he Seas: and God saw that it was good.

Once again God named the things He made. He *called the dry land Earth.* The word *Earth* may have a meaning akin to "that which is lower." Under the expanse of the firmament (v. 6), we have "the flats," the dry land. The word *earth* is used appropriately here without the article *the,* thus discriminating the dry land from the seas. When it became understood that the solid earth was under the waters, and that this globe was one, continuous mass, the term *earth* was applied to its entire surface.

The word *Seas* comes from a word that means to boil or foam. The restlessness and turbulence of the vast bodies of water on the surface of the earth are thus aptly described.

And God saw that it was good. Even though at this time the dry land was comprised only of bare, rocky peaks, mud flats, and valleys with no coverings of grasses, plants, or trees, still God looked on His work and pronounced it good.

C. Plants Called Forth (vv. 11-13)

11. And God said, Let the earth bring forth grass, the herb yielding seed, and the fruit tree yielding fruit after his kind, whose seed is in itself, upon the earth: and it was so.

God's purpose in separating the dry land from the seas becomes apparent in His next act. He ordered the earth to bring forth all kinds of plant life—grass, herbs, and trees.

Plant life was the first animate phase of creation. Plants have seeds within themselves, causing them to reproduce. Furthermore, God ordained that a plant would reproduce itself *after his kind.* This phrase makes it clear that grass will not grow into herbs or trees. Each reproduces its own kind.

12. And the earth brought forth grass, and herb yielding seed after his kind, and the tree yielding fruit, whose seed was in itself, after his kind: and God saw that it was good.

God said it, and it was done. God ordered the earth to bring forth vegetation, and it did. The phrase *after his kind* is repeated twice in this verse. Note its use in verses 21, 24, and 25 also. There is no indication in any of these recorded instances that any species evolved from some lower form of life. Each species reproduced itself only.

God approved of the processes He had set in motion. For a second time in the account of day three, it is said that God saw that what He had created was good.

13. And the evening and the morning were the third day.

We read for the third time that the counting of time began with evening and proceeded into morning.

GOOD FOR SOMETHING, AFTER ALL!

Have you ever wondered why God created certain things? The tobacco industry insists their product is good, in spite of the health hazards that statistics suggest are associated with its use by human beings. Yet there is some good in it: tobacco is said to make an effective insecticide! Marijuana has made "potheads" of many people, but medically supervised dosages have been used to treat glaucoma.

In the animal kingdom are many examples of creatures some might consider "useless." What good could a spitting, smelly camel be? Desert dwellers know its value: it can go for long periods of time without food or water, and special eyelids enable it to endure sandstorms that stop other beasts of burden.

And what can we say for the strange-looking ostrich? Ostrich meat is white, low in fat and cholesterol, and tastes like beef tenderloin. Ostriches can live in the desert, need little water, and can live on weeds. Some are predicting that ostriches will become a plentiful new meat source in this decade.

Out of an unorganized mass of material, God brought forth a creation that is repeatedly said to be "good." He can also take lives that the world discounts as unattractive and worthless and make of them something beautiful and good.   —C. R. B.

IV. The Luminaries
(Genesis 1:14, 15)

A. God Gives the Order (v. 14a)

14a. And God said, Let there be lights in the firmament of the heaven to divide the day from the night.

Verse 16 describes these lights. The "greater light" certainly is the sun, and the "lesser light" the moon. The stars also are mentioned. We are not told the source of the light mentioned in verse 3, whether the sun and moon or some other. After day four, however, the light bearers mentioned here provided light for the earth and divided day from night.

B. The Purpose of the Lights
(vv. 14b, 15)

14b, 15. And let them be for signs, and for seasons, and for days, and years: and let them be for lights in the firmament of the heaven to give light upon the earth: and it was so.

Several purposes of the celestial light bearers are given. They were to be for *signs*. We note that God used a star as a sign of the birth of Christ. See also Luke 21:25. By these lights we mark *seasons*, those periods that return yearly. By the earth's position in relation to the sun, we measure days and years—the passing of time. And, of course, the sun, moon, and stars *give light upon the earth*—that which is essential to sustain our lives and to enable us to move about freely. Surely God's gracious provision for man may be seen in all of His activities of creation.

Conclusion

A. The Light of the World

When God said, "Let there be light," light broke forth upon the earth. Until that time, darkness held dominion, and the earth could only have been a barren and desolate waste. No animal nor vegetable life was possible, for without light there is no life. Think what the world would soon become if suddenly we were deprived of the light of the sun. There would be a quick freezing of the entire earth, a cold so intense that nothing could survive. The fact that one of the first creative acts of God was to call light into being is significant. Since it is the condition of all life, its creation reflects the good will of the Creator. Thus even before man's creation, the Lord was preparing for his welfare.

What light is to the natural world, Christ is to the moral and spiritual world (John 8:12). Just as the physical life of man is not possible without the sun, so the spiritual life depends upon the Christ. Where that light has not shone, men walk in darkness, and all the terrible effects of darkness are the result. How much of evil, even in the lives of His followers, needs to be exposed to that purifying light! And how that light needs to be shed abroad in our society and in the world! What a challenge that our Lord calls upon us to share His light with those who are in spiritual darkness. Christians are called sons of light. Their lives ought to radiate warmth and brightness. Light is clean and pure and health-giving, bringing blessings to the world. No wonder John admonishes us to walk in the light, even as He is in the light (1 John 1:7). We, too, are to be the light of the world (Matthew 5:14-16).

B. Let Us Pray

Dear God, You have made a wonderful world in which we may live. Accept our gratitude, we pray, for the gracious provision You have made for us. May we remember that this world, beautiful as it is, is not our home. Guide us so that our journey through life may ever be heavenward, through Jesus our Lord. Amen.

C. Thought to Remember

To look upon the beauty of the land, sea, and sky is to see the handiwork of God.

Home Daily Bible Readings

Monday, Aug. 30—In the Beginning God (Genesis 1:1, 2; John 1:1-5)

Tuesday, Aug. 31—Let There Be Light (Genesis 1:3-5; Jeremiah 31:35-37)

Wednesday, Sept. 1—God Made the Firmament (Genesis 1:6-8, 14-19)

Thursday, Sept. 2—God Made the Earth and Sea (Genesis 1:9; Isaiah 40:21-26)

Friday, Sept. 3—Earth Produces Plants (Genesis 1:11,12, 29, 30)

Saturday, Sept. 4—Living Creatures of Seas (Genesis 1:20-22; Psalm 8:3-8)

Sunday, Sept. 5—Living Creatures of Earth (Genesis 1:24, 25; Isaiah 40:9-11)

Learning by Doing

*This page contains an alternate lesson plan emphasizing learning activities. Classes
desiring such student involvement will find these suggestions helpful.*

Learning Goals

This lesson will help your students:

1. Describe the events on each day of creation recorded in Genesis 1.

2. Compare and evaluate the presuppositions of the creationist and the secular scientist.

3. Describe the assurance and motivation that the Biblical account of creation gives us.

Into the Lesson

Display the words *creation* and *science* prominently at the front of the classroom. When all the students have arrived, ask them to consider the two words as they relate to the origin of the universe. Are they consistent with each other or are they contradictory? Why?

After a few minutes, discuss the issue. Point out, if someone in the class does not, that the dispute is between creationists and secular scientists, not the Biblical account of creation and true science. Those scientists who presuppose that there is no God and that the Bible is merely the product of human beings often reach conclusions that are in opposition to the Biblical account.

Add the word *bias* to the display. Then say, "It is the secular scientist's bias that throws him or her into conflict with the Scripture. There are many qualified scientists who are Christians, who believe in the Biblical account. Their bias leads them to see harmony between science and the Bible.

"We all have a bias, a starting point. Science cannot take us back to the beginning and allow us to observe how the universe began. Scientists must make some presuppositions about the relationship between what they can observe happening in nature now and what happened then. Christians as well start with a bias, a bias called faith. We cannot go back to the beginning either, but we accept a Book that bears testimony to the Creator. It is that testimony that we will consider today."

Into the Word

Ask a volunteer to read Genesis 1:1-25 aloud to the class. Then divide the class in half. Have the students in the first half work in groups of three or four. Give each small group a copy of the chart in the next column and ask them to complete it by indicating what God created on each day of creation. (Reproduce the chart in a size large enough for the students to have room to write, or refer them to the student book.)

Day	Creative Activity
1	
2	
3	
4	
5	
6	

Have the students in the second half of the class work in similar small groups also. Give each group the following list of questions and ask them to answer each one.

1. What was the condition of the earth "in the beginning"?

2. Where was the Spirit of God?

3. How were the limits of each day defined?

4. What was the designated purpose of the lights in the firmament of the heaven?

5. How did God evaluate His creation on days one, three, four, five, and six? How did He evaluate it after creating humans (v. 31)?

6. According to what (or "after" what) were the plants and animals to reproduce themselves?

After about ten minutes, ask the groups in each half of the class to report on their findings. Discuss each point and its significance.

Into Life

Ask the class, "What difference does it make whether the Biblical account of the origin of the universe or the secular scientist's view is correct?" Bring the following points into your discussion:

1. The Biblical account gives purpose to our existence; the secular view offers none.

2. The existence of a Creator suggests that His power is available to us, providing for our needs.

3. If there is no God, the Bible's message concerning sin, judgment, punishment, and redemption is false.

Close with prayer that we may all have a stronger faith in and deeper commitment to God our Creator.

Let's Talk It Over

The questions on this page are designed to encourage review of the lesson Scriptures and to promote discussion of the lesson by the class. The answers provided are only discussion starters. Let your class talk it over from there.

1. "How did God do it?" Our inquiring minds raise such a question as we read the creation account. Why must we be careful in raising such a question?

The danger is that we will not believe unless we can understand the processes involved. It is natural, of course, for us to ask how God did what He did, and it is not harmful to speculate as to His methods. When we read that God called light into being (Genesis 1:3), while apparently He had not yet made the sun, moon, and stars (v. 16), we are understandably puzzled by this, and we may want to suggest some explanations. But we must at last say, "I do not understand how God did it, but I believe in God, and I believe He did all that the Bible says He did." This willingness to believe also applies to such a miracle as Jesus' virgin birth. We certainly do not understand all that was involved in the miracle briefly described in Luke 1:35, but if we believe in an all-wise, all-powerful God, we can accept even what we do not fully comprehend.

2. The creation account speaks of evening and then morning comprising a day. How might it be beneficial to us if we thought of sunset as the beginning of a new day?

It would cause us to think differently of rest. At present we may regard our sleep as the conclusion of a wearisome day of labor, while it may instead be viewed as a means of preparing our minds and bodies for the ensuing period of work and activity. Perhaps this would aid us in securing for our bodies the amount of rest they need. Another possible benefit might relate to our devotional life. Instead of situating ourselves in front of the television set or taking off on a variety of errands, it could be spiritually profitable to schedule a period of devotional Bible reading for early evening. In that way we could have God's word working in our minds as we prepare for our night's rest.

3. Geologists observe the mountains, canyons, oceans, and rivers and announce that it must have required millions of years for all of these features to develop. How can this be harmonized with the "days" of creation in Genesis?

The word *day* is used in Scripture to refer to a twenty-four-hour period, but it is also used in describing a longer period of time. Therefore, some Bible teachers suggest that the "days" of creation may have been lengthy periods of time, perhaps even millions of years. Such an explanation is not necessary, however. With His divine power, God easily could have accomplished in twenty-four-hours what some might think would have taken millions of years. Later in the Biblical record we read of His covering the earth with a flood for more than a year, overthrowing the infamous cities of Sodom and Gomorrah, and parting the waters of the Red Sea. These are examples of His awesome power to transform the natural world.

4. God created plants with their seeds in them, so they could reproduce themselves. What are some ways in which this aspect of creation should affect us?

We should be filled with a sense of wonder as we see that the seed planted in the earth not only supplies grain and vegetables for our food, but seed as well for replanting and repeating the same cycle. Farmers or gardeners, who work with this process, surely should experience a grand feeling of cooperation with the Creator. This aspect of creation also should cause us to realize how abundantly God has provided for the needs of His creatures. And that should inspire us to thanksgiving. God's wonderful gift of agriculture is well described in Psalm 65:9-13, which even in an age of industry we would do well to ponder.

5. We take few blessings for granted more than we do the marvel of light. What are some of the ways it benefits us?

God could have made us capable of dwelling in continual darkness, but what a dismal thought that is! How much better it is that we can move about, work, and play in the presence of light. Even at night the moon and stars provide illumination, and of course God gave us the light afforded by fire and electricity. The darkness of night would be much more dreadful and dangerous without these. Light also makes possible our enjoyment of beauty. Because of light we can view the pleasing array of colors and shapes in nature and art and we can look upon the faces of our family members and friends.

The Origin of Mankind

DEVOTIONAL READING: Psalm 8:3-9.

LESSON SCRIPTURE: Genesis 1:26-31; 2:4-9, 15-25.

PRINTED TEXT: Genesis 1:26-28; 2:18-25.

Genesis 1:26-28

26 And God said, Let us make man in our image, after our likeness: and let them have dominion over the fish of the sea, and over the fowl of the air, and over the cattle, and over all the earth, and over every creeping thing that creepeth upon the earth.

27 So God created man in his own image, in the image of God created he him; male and female created he them.

28 And God blessed them, and God said unto them, Be fruitful, and multiply, and replenish the earth, and subdue it: and have dominion over the fish of the sea, and over the fowl of the air, and over every living thing that moveth upon the earth.

Genesis 2:18-25

18 And the LORD God said, It is not good that the man should be alone; I will make him a help meet for him.

19 And out of the ground the LORD God formed every beast of the field, and every fowl of the air; and brought them unto Adam to see what he would call them: and whatsoever Adam called every living creature, that was the name thereof.

20 And Adam gave names to all cattle, and to the fowl of the air, and to every beast of the field; but for Adam there was not found a help meet for him.

21 And the LORD God caused a deep sleep to fall upon Adam, and he slept; and he took one of his ribs, and closed up the flesh instead thereof.

22 And the rib, which the LORD God had taken from man, made he a woman, and brought her unto the man.

23 And Adam said, This is now bone of my bones, and flesh of my flesh: she shall be called Woman, because she was taken out of Man.

24 Therefore shall a man leave his father and his mother, and shall cleave unto his wife: and they shall be one flesh.

25 And they were both naked, the man and his wife, and were not ashamed.

GOLDEN TEXT: God created man in his own image, in the image of God created he him; male and female created he them.—Genesis 1:27.

Lesson Aims

As a result of studying this lesson, the students will:

1. Be reminded that God created human beings in His own image.

2. Understand that God appointed human beings stewards of the earth and everything in it.

3. Know God's plan for marriage.

4. Give thought to the meaning and purpose of life as response to God's love and grace.

Lesson Outline

INTRODUCTION

    A. The Main Event

    B. Lesson Background

I. GOD CREATES MANKIND (Genesis 1:26-28)

    A. God's Plan (v. 26)

    B. The Act of Creation (v. 27)

       In God's Image

    C. God's Blessing on Mankind (v. 28)

II. MAN NAMES THE ANIMALS (Genesis 2:18-20)

    A. God Plans a Help Meet for Man (v. 18)

    B. Names Given to the Animals (v. 19)

    C. Man Without a Mate (v. 20)

III. MAN AND HIS MATE (Genesis 2:21-25)

    A. The Creation of Woman (vv. 21, 22)

    B. Man and Woman Together (v. 23)

    C. The Guiding Principle of Marriage (v. 24)

    D. A Pure Relationship (v. 25)

       A Beautiful Wedding

CONCLUSION

    A. "It Was Very Good"

    B. Let Us Pray

    C. Thought to Remember

Display visual 2 of the visuals packet and let it remain before the class throughout this session. The visual is shown on page 22.

Introduction

A. The Main Event

The freshman basketball team played a good game. Mothers and fathers, classmates, friends, and neighbors had nearly filled the gymnasium. The score was close, and the home team won.

When the game was over, however, only a few persons left. In fact, many arrived at the close of the game. Hardly an empty seat could be found. The reason? The varsity teams were going to play. Their game was the main event.

Last week we studied God's creation of the heavens and the earth. Noting the progression of the Genesis account, we can see that God's creative activity of the first five days was preliminary. Something greater—the main event, as it were—was yet to come. That is the subject of today's lesson.

B. Lesson Background

Having begun His work of creation, God called light into being to penetrate the darkness that enshrouded the earth. After that, He made the firmament, setting in motion the processes that occur in the atmosphere. Next came the dividing of land from sea, followed by the emergence of vegetation on the land. Then the sun, moon, and stars were commissioned as lightbearers.

On the fifth day God created fowls to fly in the open firmament of heaven and marine life to fill the waters of the sea. These creatures were the first to have the breath of life.

God's creative activity on the sixth day was twofold. First, He created living creatures to move upon the face of the earth. Then He came to the crowning act of creation—the creation of human beings.

I. God Creates Mankind (Genesis 1:26-28)

A. God's Plan (v. 26)

26. And God said, Let us make man in our image, after our likeness: and let them have dominion over the fish of the sea, and over the fowl of the air, and over the cattle, and over all the earth, and over every creeping thing that creepeth upon the earth.

Let us make man. To whom did God say this? Some say the angels. However, He who created the angels themselves would have no need to consult with them when He was ready to create man.

It has been suggested that this use of the plural pronouns *us* is the "plural of majesty," after the manner of kings. Such a usage is like the editorial "we" used by authors and speakers. Nothing in the context of this verse, however, calls for such usage.

Others see in this a foreshadowing of the Biblical doctrine of the Trinity. Scripture tells us that Christ, the Word, was with God in the beginning, that all things were made by Him, and that "without Him was not any thing made that was made" (John 1:1-3). The account of creation in Genesis notes that "the Spirit of God moved upon the face of the waters" (Genesis 1:2). The expression, *Let us make,* does not explicitly set forth the doctrine of the Trinity, but it is in keeping with that doctrine. God, the heavenly Father, intended to make man with the imprint of a divine image—the image of God the Father, God the Son, and God the Holy Spirit.

In our image, after our likeness. Genesis 2:7 states that "the Lord God formed man of the dust of the ground." Thus man's material unity with the earth is clearly indicated. But of far greater significance is the fact that man was made in the *image* and *likeness* of God. Physical likeness is not to be understood here, for "God is a Spirit" (John 4:24). And "a spirit hath not flesh and bones" (Luke 24:39). Man is made in the spiritual likeness of God. This means that man is an intelligent being. He is a person, capable of thinking, feeling, willing. And because he has will, the power of choice, he is a moral being. He was created perfect, sharing in the holiness of God. In all these ways he was like his Creator, separate and distinct from the animal world.

One godlike quality is especially noted in our text: he has *dominion* over all other creatures, and even over earth itself. Thus he has a share in God's rule of the world. Since man shares God's rule, man must also share God's concern for earth's resources. God's gracious provision of pure air to breathe, plants and trees for food, and animals for man's benefit in so many ways was not given for any one particular generation. These were intended for man's use for as long as he inhabits the earth. Thus, each generation must fulfill its responsibility of stewardship of God's gifts and see to it that these resources are preserved for succeeding generations.

B. The Act of Creation (v. 27)

27. So God created man in his own image, in the image of God created he him; male and female created he them.

What greater honor could be bestowed upon a being than that he should be created in the image of God! The body of man is wonderfully made, but his intellect and his spirit are akin to God, and to that extent he partakes of the nature of God. Not that man is divine—the Scriptures never teach this. But man possesses characteristics and attributes that indicate a likeness to the divine Lord and Creator.

Notice that here it is said that *God created man in his own image.* This is a commentary on the words "our image" of the preceding verse. It is the *image of God* that is meant, even when the plural pronoun "our" is used.

Further details of the creation of man are given in chapter 2, but here in chapter 1 we see that God made mankind in two sexes, male and female.

Note that the words *make* and *create* are both used in describing the process of God's bringing the first man and the first woman into being (vv. 26, 27). God *made* their bodies from the dust of the earth. By endowing them with His own image and likeness, He *created* a being that was intrinsically different from every other form of life. Their earthly bodies were *made;* but as human beings who possessed the image of God, they were *created.* God had brought into existence an entirely new, separate, and distinct creature, one who was absolutely unique—a human being.

IN GOD'S IMAGE

Religion is the "opium of the people!" So says the gospel according to Karl Marx. He thought that belief in God was an idea the downtrodden, lower classes of humanity clutched to their bosoms in order to survive the daily misery of their lives. Marx thought that his social revolution would elevate the status of common people to the point where they would realize they no longer needed the neurotic concept of God.

Just to make sure that people realized they did not need God, the heirs of the Bolshevik Revolution in 1917 outlawed God; the Communists wrote His obituary. God no longer existed—Soviet law said so!

But most people didn't get the message. Throughout seventy years of Communist rule and suppression of religion, the church survived. And when the Soviet Union collapsed, the church emerged again as a visible, powerful force of life in the lands that once lay behind the "iron curtain."

Christianity survived everything the Communists could do to exterminate it for one simple reason: human beings are created in God's image. We were created to respond to our Maker. The prayer of one of the great saints of the ages puts it this way: "Our hearts are restless until they find their rest in Thee."   —C. R. B.

C. God's Blessing on Mankind (v. 28)

28. And God blessed them, and God said unto them, Be fruitful, and multiply, and replenish the earth, and subdue it: and have dominion over the fish of the sea, and over the fowl of the air, and over every living thing that moveth upon the earth.

This succinct account of God's blessing on mankind reveals God's love for them. One provision of God's blessing was that human beings were to reproduce themselves and fill the earth with their descendants. The word in the original text, which is translated "replenish," conveys not only the idea of filling up that which was emptied but also that which was never full. A better translation of God's command in this verse, therefore, is, "Be fruitful and increase in number; fill the earth and subdue it" (*New International Version*).

The blessing bestowed upon mankind included also their having jurisdiction over everything God had made on earth. They were to learn how to use its resources—its water, air, soil, minerals, plant life, fish, fowl, and animals—to provide all things needful for their lives. When God pronounced that mankind was to subdue the earth and have dominion over everything in it, He likewise blessed them with every faculty and attribute needed to accomplish their divinely appointed purpose on earth. Privilege, however, always brings responsibility. Human beings are accountable to God for the nature of the dominion that they exercise over all that God has put into their hands.

II. Man Names the Animals (Genesis 2:18-20)

The second chapter of Genesis is not another account of creation that has been handed down from a second source, different from the source of the first chapter. Biblical evidence points to Moses as the author of Genesis as well as Exodus through Deuteronomy. The book of Genesis is not the result of an editor's weaving together a single book from a number of divergent sources.

In chapter 2 of Genesis, the author is expanding on the account of creation he has given in chapter 1. The first chapter is an account in chronological order of the different steps God took in creating all things. The second chapter is more an account of man and his environment. In chapter 2, the author says nothing about the creation of light, the firmament, or the heavenly bodies.

The main focus in the second chapter is an elaboration of the creation of mankind, which was briefly noted in chapter 1. Since plants, fowl, and animals are closely associated with man's needs, chapter 2 contains details regarding these life forms. The principal object is to give a clearer picture of God's creation of human beings and their home in Eden.

A. God Plans a Help Meet for Man (v. 18)

18. And the LORD God said, It is not good that the man should be alone; I will make him a help meet for him.

The description of the creation of Adam is given in Genesis 2:7: "And the Lord God formed man of the dust of the ground, and breathed into

his nostrils the breath of life; and man became a living soul." He was then put in the Garden of Eden, and with him were the animals that had previously been formed. However, no creature like Adam existed in all the animal kingdom. He was alone, and God saw that that was not good.

Animals make great pets and frequently provide a measure of companionship for lonely people. They also are helpful as beasts of burden. But not one of them has the spiritual, intellectual, emotional, or moral capacity of a human being. God saw that man needed the companionship of a being like himself, and so He set out to make a mate for the man He had created. The two would stand side by side. They would complement each other, aid each other, and in every way be suitable for each other.

B. Names Given to the Animals (v. 19)

19. And out of the ground the LORD God formed every beast of the field, and every fowl of the air; and brought them unto Adam to see what he would call them: and whatsoever Adam called every living creature, that was the name thereof.

Here is additional detail about the creation of the animals and the birds. The *King James* translation of Genesis 1:20 reads as follows: "And God said, Let the waters bring forth abundantly the moving creature that hath life, and fowl that may fly above the earth in the open firmament of heaven." This translation creates the impression in the minds of some that fowl came from the waters or evolved from fish.

A better translation of 1:20 is found in the *New International Version:* "Let the water teem with living creatures, and let birds fly above the earth across the expanse of the sky." This translation is in accord with the second chapter's

Home Daily Bible Readings

Monday, Sept. 6—Human Beings Created in God's Image (Genesis 1:26-31)

Tuesday, Sept. 7—God Breathed Life Into Man (Genesis 2:1-9)

Wednesday, Sept. 8—Man Not Made to Be Alone (Genesis 2:15-20)

Thursday, Sept. 9—God Created Woman (Genesis 2:21-25)

Friday, Sept. 10—Remember: Extol God's Work (Job 36:22-33)

Saturday, Sept. 11—God Accomplishes All Things (Job 37:1-13)

Sunday, Sept. 12—God: Superior to Every Person (Job 38:1-11)

account of the creation of birds: *And out of the ground the Lord God formed every beast of the field, and every fowl of the air.*

Chapter 2 elaborates further on the creation of the birds and animals: God caused them to pass before Adam to see what he would call them. As the man looked at them, he gave them names suggested by their appearance. Whatever man called them, that was the name of them.

C. Man Without a Mate (v. 20)

20. And Adam gave names to all cattle, and to the fowl of the air, and to every beast of the field; but for Adam there was not found a help meet for him.

No creature like man appeared in the animal kingdom. He was different, because he alone was created in the image of God. He had an intellectual, spiritual, emotional, volitional, and rational nature modeled after the nature of God.

The expression *help meet* is sometimes used interchangeably with "helpmate." Generally speaking, these terms are used to describe a good wife. The phrase *help meet* describes a helper who is appropriate. Horses, donkeys, oxen, and dogs may be a help for man, but none of these or any other member of the animal kingdom can be a *help meet*, a help appropriate for man.

III. Man and His Mate (Genesis 2:21-25)

A. The Creation of Woman (vv. 21, 22)

21. And the LORD God caused a deep sleep to fall upon Adam, and he slept; and he took one of his ribs, and closed up the flesh instead thereof.

What was first mentioned in Genesis 1:27 is now described in detail. The two accounts are not contradictory; the second account merely spells out the details of the first.

God brought a deep sleep upon Adam in preparation for the operation He was about to perform on him. *And he slept.* Rather, while Adam slept, or was unconscious, God removed one of Adam's ribs. Perhaps it would be better for us to understand that both rib and flesh were taken, for later Adam said, "This is now bone of my bones, and flesh of my flesh" (v. 23). The man was not aware of the procedure until after it was finished.

22. And the rib, which the LORD God had taken from man, made he a woman, and brought her unto the man.

We are not told God's reason for choosing a rib from which to make Adam's helpmeet. Some find a symbolical significance in this choice, holding that it is indicative of the place woman is to occupy in relation to man. The bone was not taken from Adam's head to suggest the woman was to rule man. Nor was it taken from his foot to imply that she was to be "walked on" by man. Rather, the woman was to be the man's helper in the truest sense of the word, a companion to walk by his side in all of life's experiences.

And brought her unto the man. God conducted her to Adam and presented her to him. The word implies that she was solemnly given to the man in marriage. Adam recognized God's intention and received his bride with joy.

B. Man and Woman Together (v. 23)

23. And Adam said, This is now bone of my bones, and flesh of my flesh: she shall be called Woman, because she was taken out of Man.

The man recognized the similarity between himself and the "help meet for him." She was flesh and blood, as he was. Her bones were like his bones. Her flesh was like his flesh. The two of them were essentially the same. Furthermore, he understood that she was derived from him—*she was taken out of Man.* He knew that she was the female counterpart of his male being. The words in the original text reflect this clearly. The word translated *Woman* is the feminine form for the word translated as *Man.* We are not told how Adam knew this. Either in his original state he possessed intuitive perception, which was lost through the fall, or he spoke under divine inspiration.

C. The Guiding Principle of Marriage (v. 24)

24. Therefore shall a man leave his father and his mother, and shall cleave unto his wife: and they shall be one flesh.

Some regard these words as being spoken by Adam; others feel that Moses, who wrote this record, was the author. In either case they must be considered as an inspired declaration of the divine plan for marriage in the human family.

Although the expression puts the primary emphasis on the man, it applies equally to the woman. A husband should not give primary allegiance to his mother and father after he is married. Neither should a wife cling to her parents rather than to her husband. The married couple are to *cleave* to each other, that is, to cling to each loyally, without wavering.

The fact that a husband and wife are *one flesh* denotes more than the union of their bodies in the marital relationship. It speaks of a unity of persons, a sharing of aims, hopes, dreams, and plans. They are to be one in mind and spirit as well as in flesh.

D. A Pure Relationship (v. 25)

25. And they were both naked, the man and his wife, and were not ashamed.

The man and his wife. From this point onward the first pair of human beings are recognized as husband and wife. *They were naked* as they stood in each other's presence and in the presence of God, who created them and brought them together, and they *were not ashamed.* How could they be? They were as God had made them. Their souls were pure, and "their bodies were made holy through the spirit which animated them" (Keil). They saw each other without the blinding and perverting influences of sin. The man and the woman were good in every aspect of their being—in their being created in the image of God.

A Beautiful Wedding

The city of Los Angeles owns a beautiful Japanese-style garden with a lake, a waterfall, ferns, willows, cherry trees, azaleas, and thousands of other plants. It is the site of scores of weddings each year.

This is an unusual garden: its lake is filled with reclaimed water, and the garden's official name is the "Donald C. Tillman Water Reclamation Plant." In other words, all these weddings take place at a sewage treatment plant.

The "first marriage" was also in a garden, but one as yet unpolluted by either civilization or sin. The purity of life in Eden was symbolic of what God wanted the institution of marriage to be. But the ideal would not be realized: sin would soon enter the picture, and antagonism would enter the marriage relationship.

Unfortunately, the garden in Los Angeles is symbolic of what many marriages become: lovely on the surface perhaps, but the inner workings of the relationship are less delightful to look at. Almost anyone can have a beautiful wedding. Having a beautiful marriage is much more difficult. But when we strive for God's ideal, we find that the work of making a marriage what God intended brings more satisfying results than we could ever imagine.   —C. R. B.

Conclusion

A. "It Was Very Good"

God looked on everything He had made; and "behold, it was very good" (Genesis 1:31). The light functioned properly. The regular recurrence of a period of light marked the division of time into days.

The firmament divided the waters above it from the waters that were beneath it. Condensed

visual 2

into clouds, the water above the earth brought needed moisture to the face of the ground. The waters beneath the firmament gathered into the oceans, seas, lakes, rivers, and ponds; and the dry land, called Earth, appeared. The Earth produced grass, herbs, and trees, which provided food for both animals and mankind.

Heavenly bodies ruled over day and night. Light was resident in the sun, which "ruled over" the day. The reflection of this light on the moon prevailed in the night. These two greater lights and the stars indicated signs and seasons and marked out months and years by their positions in relation to the earth.

Fish swam in the waters, as did the great sea monsters. Fowl flew above the earth; creeping things, cattle, and beasts moved upon dry land.

Especially good was the first couple. They were created in God's image. Their garden home was ideal, and their responsibilities were fitting. The man and the woman understood their relationships to each other, and there was nothing of which they were ashamed.

God paused in His creative activities and was prepared for unbroken fellowship with the human beings He had created. Only a failure on their part could bring disharmony to all the good things that God had created.

B. Let Us Pray

Our Heavenly Father, You have made us in Your image and have given us the power to choose our way. We thank You, for now our service to You may be an expression of the love that is in our hearts. Accept our love and our service as from the grateful hearts of those whom You have called to labor at Your side. Thank You for preparing a wonderful world for us. Help us to take care of it. In Jesus' name we pray. Amen.

C. Thought to Remember

"I will praise thee; for I am fearfully and wonderfully made" (Psalm 139:14)

Learning by Doing

This page contains an alternate lesson plan emphasizing learning activities. Classes desiring such student involvement will find these suggestions helpful.

Learning Goals

As a result of participating in this lesson, the students will be able to do the following:

1. Recall several of the details of the creation of the first man and woman.

2. Mention two characteristics included in man's being created in the image of God.

3. Choose one way to improve their use of God's creation this week.

Into the Lesson

Before class, display this statement before the class: "Man is the crown of God's creation." As the students arrive, ask them to consider the statement and be prepared to suggest reasons why it is true. Allow a few minutes for fellowship and informal discussion.

When it is time to begin the class, ask the students, "What makes man the crown of God's creation?" As they suggest reasons, write them on the chalkboard.

Naturally, the expression "made in God's image" should be on your list. Refer to that entry and say, "This is the key reason why we are the crown of creation. All other reasons are ultimately related to this one. Mankind, both men and women, are made in the image of God. We will consider that concept today."

Into the Word

Begin by telling the class that you are going to read aloud Scripture passages from Genesis 1 and 2, and you want them to listen for answers to certain questions. Have the following questions written on small index cards, one question on each. Distribute the cards to your students. Make enough sets so that each student will have a question. More than one student can listen for the answer to a question. Read Genesis 1:26-31; 2:7, 8, 15-25.

1. God made "man" in the image of God. What of "woman"? (She also was made in the image of God, 1:27.)

2. What role did God give to humans relative to the rest of creation? (They were to subdue the earth and rule over all living things, 1:28.)

3. From what material did God make man? (The dust of the ground, 2:7.)

4. What was the assignment given to Adam in the Garden of Eden? (To cultivate it and keep it, 2:15.)

5. Again and again God said His creation was "good." What did He say was "not good"? (For man to be alone, 2:18.)

6. What did God say He would make for man? (A help meet for him, that is, a suitable helper, 2:18.)

7. From what material did God make the animals and the fowl? ("The ground," 2:19.)

8. From what did God make the woman? (Man's rib, 2:21, 22.)

9. Why was the woman called "woman"? (She was taken out of man, 2:23.)

10. What principle regarding the marriage relationship is seen in this text? (The unity of husband and wife, 2:24.)

When you have finished reading, go over the questions and the students' answers. Add explanatory material from the commentary section as needed.

Into Life

Because we are made in the image of God, it is clear that God designed man to be in some degree like himself. God is Creator. Ask the class how we are like God in this respect. In the discussion, point out that man has a mind to plan and the ability to build in new ways. Animals also build, but they do it by instinct, building the same way generation after generation. They do not build skyscrapers or space shuttles.

God rules everything, and He has shared dominion of the earth with man. How well is man doing in this regard? Place the following words in two columns on the chalkboard or on a poster: *soil, water, air, forests, oil, waste, domestic animals, wildlife, fish, minerals, food.* Have each student evaluate mankind's management of each by rating it on a scale of 1 to 5, 1 being lowest. Discuss their responses, then lead a discussion using the following questions. How important is it that man be an effective manager of God's creation? What are the consequences if man mismanages God's creation? What do these consequences have to do with man's relationship to God?

Now ask each student to look at the list and evaluate his or her own management of God's creation. These evaluations need not be shared with the class, but ask each person to select a way in which he or she will begin this week to manage God's creation more responsibly.

Let's Talk It Over

The questions on this page are designed to encourage review of the lesson Scriptures and to promote discussion of the lesson by the class. The answers provided are only discussion starters. Let your class talk it over from there.

1. "God created man in his own image" (Genesis 1:27), and this is true of every human being. Why is this an important consideration for our time?

It speaks compellingly to the continuing problem of racial strife. If we could realize more clearly that every human being, whatever the color of skin or the shape of his or her eyes, is created in God's image, we could take a giant step toward harmony among the races. This Biblical truth also applies to our attitude regarding people caught up in poverty and illiteracy. We can also say that in spite of the wickedness in which many human beings indulge, they continue to be people created in God's image. Such a consideration can spur us to stronger efforts in benevolent works and evangelism on behalf of all our fellow human beings.

2. Should Christians be in the forefront of those who advocate the preservation of earth, and if so, why?

Some environmentalists are concerned only with the quality of life on earth. The pollution of soil, water, and air will lower that quality, and so they fight such pollution. Christians share the concern of such persons, but since "this world is not our home," we have a higher motivation. God created the world; He created it so that it was good; and we want to keep it as good as possible. Our viewpoint is based on Genesis 1, 2 and the great declaration of Psalm 24:1. Therefore, our zeal for advocating a wise and constructive use of the earth and its resources should be even warmer than that of the humanistic philosophers and politicians whose efforts receive wide publicity.

3. God said, "It is not good that the man should be alone" (Genesis 2:18). What kinds of human problems result from one's being alone? How can we minister to persons who are alone?

Loneliness probably comes to mind first. To have no one to talk to, no one with whom we can share our joys and burdens, is a truly tragic circumstance. A person who is alone can also become very self-centered. We need human companionship to offset the tendency to become preoccupied with our own little world. Another result of being alone is bitterness. When we have no person to whom we can express our anger or unhappiness, these can spread like poison within us. No Christian should ever have to suffer from acute aloneness. The New Testament places a strong emphasis on ministry to widows (1 Timothy 5:3-16); and widowers, shut-ins, and any others in the church who are alone should be given plenty of opportunities for fellowship and service.

4. It has been said that God formed the woman from a bone from man's side to signify that man and woman are to be true companions, walking side by side in life's experiences. What does this indicate in regard to the attitude men and women should have toward one another?

In the present-day "battle of the sexes," old stereotypes have come under fire. Men who have characterized women as lacking intelligence and being too much swayed by emotion have been forced to revise that viewpoint. Women who have lumped all men under the heading of narrow-minded, insensitive brutes have learned to avoid such generalization. The creation account indicates that a spirit of mutual respect and cooperation should exist between the sexes. It leads us to appreciate the dignity, ability, and potential of both men and women.

5. The account of the origin of marriage in Genesis 2:21-25 emphasizes the commitment of husband and wife to one another. How is this commitment realized in marriage?

From the human standpoint a husband and wife's first allegiance is to each other. They are specifically said to owe a greater allegiance to their spouse than to their parents, but it is clear that marital commitment should take priority over relationships with children, employers, and friends. Many marital conflicts have resulted from a spouse's allowing those other relationships to interfere. Also, the expression "one flesh" speaks vividly of mutual commitment. While it is descriptive of sexual union, it clearly goes beyond that to indicate mutual goals, sharing of responsibilities, cooperation in dealing with problems, etc. Paul seems to expand on this "one flesh" concept in 1 Corinthians 7:4.

The Origin of Sin

DEVOTIONAL READING: **Psalm 51:1-4, 6, 9-17.**

LESSON SCRIPTURE: **Genesis 3:1-13.**

PRINTED TEXT: **Genesis 3:1-13.**

Genesis 3:1-13

1 Now the serpent was more subtile than any beast of the field which the LORD God had made. And he said unto the woman, Yea, hath God said, Ye shall not eat of every tree of the garden?

2 And the woman said unto the serpent, We may eat of the fruit of the trees of the garden:

3 But of the fruit of the tree which is in the midst of the garden, God hath said, Ye shall not eat of it, neither shall ye touch it, lest ye die.

4 And the serpent said unto the woman, Ye shall not surely die:

5 For God doth know that in the day ye eat thereof, then your eyes shall be opened, and ye shall be as gods, knowing good and evil.

6 And when the woman saw that the tree was good for food, and that it was pleasant to the eyes, and a tree to be desired to make one wise, she took of the fruit thereof, and did eat, and gave also unto her husband with her; and he did eat.

7 And the eyes of them both were opened, and they knew that they were naked; and they sewed fig leaves together, and made themselves aprons.

8 And they heard the voice of the LORD God walking in the garden in the cool of the day: and Adam and his wife hid themselves

from the presence of the LORD God amongst the trees of the garden.

9 And the LORD God called unto Adam, and said unto him, Where art thou?

10 And he said, I heard thy voice in the garden, and I was afraid, because I was naked; and I hid myself.

11 And he said, Who told thee that thou wast naked? Hast thou eaten of the tree, whereof I commanded thee that thou shouldest not eat?

12 And the man said, The woman whom thou gavest to be with me, she gave me of the tree, and I did eat.

13 And the LORD God said unto the woman, What is this that thou hast done? And the woman said, The serpent beguiled me, and I did eat.

GOLDEN TEXT: The serpent said . . . God doth know that in the day ye eat thereof, then your eyes shall be opened, and ye shall be as gods, knowing good and evil.
—Genesis 3:4, 5.

The Story of Beginnings
Unit 1: God's Creation of and
Relationship With Mankind
(Lessons 1-4)

Lesson Aims

This lesson will help the student:

1. Understand that he or she makes choices as a free and accountable creature.

2. Be motivated to make choices that are right and good in the sight of God.

Lesson Outline

INTRODUCTION
A. Paradise Lost/Paradise Restored
B. Lesson Background
I. SATAN PLANTS DOUBT (Genesis 3:1-3)
  A. The Subtlety of Satan (v. 1)
  B. The Birth of Resentment (vv. 2, 3)
II. RESULTS OF BELIEVING A LIE (Genesis 3:4-8)
  A. Satan's Lie (vv. 4, 5)
    Immune to Law?
  B. Yielding to Temptation (v. 6)
  C. The Loss of Innocence (v. 7)
    Satisfying the Senses
  D. Separation From God (v. 8)
III. THE SINNERS ARRAIGNED (Genesis 3:9-13)
  A. God's Call (v. 9)
  B. Man's Humiliation (vv. 10-12)
  C. The Woman's Part (v. 13)
CONCLUSION
A. The Way of Temptation
B. Let Us Pray
C. Thought to Remember

Display visual 3 of the visuals packet and refer to it as you discuss the steps of man's fall. The visual is shown on page 29.

Introduction

A. Paradise Lost/Paradise Restored

The Greeks gave the name *paradise* to the Garden of Eden. It appears in the Greek translation of the Hebrew Bible. The word *paradise* brings to our minds all that is good and beautiful.

Paradise, the Garden of Eden, was a perfect home for Adam and Eve. It was well watered and brought forth all kinds of trees that were pleasing to the eye and good for food. It may be that God intended for the first couple to use the garden as a model. Perhaps they were to expand its borders as the human family multiplied, thus making the whole earth a veritable paradise. But that didn't happen! That first paradise was lost because of man's failure to obey God.

God, however, is gracious, and He has made ready an eternal paradise for mankind. The time will come when those who have been redeemed in Christ will enjoy the blessings of God's presence. They will live forever in that place where the tree of life stands by the river that flows from the throne of God. This will be Heaven, paradise restored.

B. Lesson Background

The exact location of the Garden of Eden cannot be determined. Two of the four rivers associated with the river that flowed through Eden were the Hiddekel (or Tigris) and the Euphrates (Genesis 2:14). This leads most Bible students to believe that man's first home was located near Mesopotamia, in the general area of the modern countries of Iraq and Iran.

Among the trees that grew in the Garden of Eden was the tree of the knowledge of good and evil. Adam and Eve were permitted to eat of the fruit of all the trees except that one. God warned them that if they ate of it, they would surely die.

God's prohibition against eating of the tree of the knowledge of good and evil afforded the pair an opportunity to develop character. By refusing to eat of the tree they would demonstrate their submission to the will of God. Likewise, they would show that they trusted God to provide everything that they needed.

I. Satan Plants Doubt (Genesis 3:1-3)

A. The Subtlety of Satan (v. 1)

1. Now the serpent was more subtile than any beast of the field which the LORD God had made. And he said unto the woman, Yea, hath God said, Ye shall not eat of every tree of the garden?

The incident recorded in this lesson text was much more than an encounter between a woman and a snake. Further revelation in the Bible clearly reveals this. The serpent was the agent of temptation in an environment that God had described as "very good." So we conclude that there was a force or power of evil behind the serpent.

Paul speaks of the beguiling of Eve by the serpent (2 Corinthians 11:3) and later states, "For Satan himself is transformed into an angel [or messenger] of light" (v. 14). Eve was beguiled, therefore, by the serpent, who was Satan (see Revelation 12:9). And Satan had taken on the appearance of a messenger of light. He did not present himself as a hideous creature, but as one of God's created beings that was *more subtile*, that is, crafty, cunning, than any other.

He said unto the woman. Satan did not attack God outright. Rather he sought to create doubt in the woman's mind regarding the goodness of God. He impugned the motive of God and His very nature. Satan asked Eve if it was true that God had placed any restriction on the eating of the fruit of the garden. He would suggest that God was withholding something that man ought to have.

B. The Birth of Resentment (vv. 2, 3)

2. And the woman said unto the serpent, We may eat of the fruit of the trees of the garden.

In her reply, Eve acknowledged the provision God had made for her and Adam. He had given them the privilege of eating *of the fruit of the trees of the garden.* But her reply suggests that she had begun to lose sight of the great extent of God's goodness, for she did not say "all trees." It seems that she had forgotten the *all* and was thinking only of the one that was prohibited.

3. But of the fruit of the tree which is in the midst of the garden, God hath said, Ye shall not eat of it, neither shall ye touch it, lest ye die.

The tree to which the woman referred was the tree of the knowledge of good and evil. She recalled God's command and what would result from eating the fruit of the tree. But God's command recorded in 2:17 does not stipulate that they were not to touch the tree. It is possible that God had given the man and woman more detailed instructions than are included in the written record, so He may have prohibited their touching the tree.

On the other hand, could it be that Eve added these words herself, making the command seem even more unreasonable than the serpent's insinuation had suggested? Human beings often exaggerate prohibitions in this way. A child may complain to his parents, "You won't let me do anything." In truth, the parents merely have forbidden one thing that the child wants to do. The parents' prohibition is blown out of proportion, and the activity prohibited becomes the most desirable of all.

II. Results of Believing a Lie (Genesis 3:4-8)

A. Satan's Lie (vv. 4, 5)

4. And the serpent said unto the woman, Ye shall not surely die.

Ye shall not surely die. The Hebrew is very emphatic: "You most certainly will not die!" Thus

---

> **How to Say It**
>
> EUPHRATES. U-*fray*-teez.
> HIDDEKEL. *Hid*-eh-kell.
> TIGRIS. *Ty*-griss.

Satan, who is the father of lies, flatly contradicted the word of God. It was not until the seeds of doubt were planted in Eve's mind and her feelings of resentment toward God had risen that Satan directly denied God's truth. In so doing, Satan would remove Eve's fear of the consequences of disobedience. Then he proceeded to tell her of the advantages that would come from eating of the forbidden fruit.

5. For God doth know that in the day ye eat thereof, then your eyes shall be opened, and ye shall be as gods, knowing good and evil.

Not only did Satan contradict God, he impugned His motives. He suggested that God's prohibition was a means for God to preserve His superiority over the man and woman, and to exclude them from certain rights and privileges that should be theirs. Satan assured Eve that after they ate of the fruit of the tree, they would have insights that they could not otherwise acquire. Their eyes would be opened. No longer blinded by ignorance, they would be fulfilled. As a matter of fact, he said they would be like superhuman beings, *as gods*, or "as God." The plural word used here most commonly stands for the one true God. *Knowing good and evil.* Satan told Eve that in this newly found fulfillment, she and the man would understand all great moral questions. In truth, he knew that they would know evil because of their deliberate disobedience of God's command.

IMMUNE TO LAW?

An Oregon man turned in his driver's license and license plates and put a Kingdom of Heaven plate on his truck. He said he did it because his religion did not allow him to recognize the laws of the state.

A seventy-five dollar ticket for a broken headlight was the first of some five hundred traffic citations that he refused to acknowledge. He spent more than two months in jail, and finally changed his religion and made a plea bargain with the judge. His new church allows him to recognize the state's legitimate claim to his obedience.

People do strange things while claiming loyalty to God. Professing allegiance to God, this man overlooked the Biblical command to render to Caesar what belongs to him.

The serpent tricked Adam and Eve into rein-terpreting what God had said about the tree of the knowledge of good and evil. They thought they were immune to the laws of God, but they discovered that disobeying them brings punish-ment. When we trust our opinions above the clear statements of God, we risk great loss. God's word is true, regardless of what Satan or any of us may think about what He has said. —C. R. B.

B. Yielding to Temptation (v. 6)

6. And when the woman saw that the tree was good for food, and that it was pleasant to the eyes, and a tree to be desired to make one wise, she took of the fruit thereof, and did eat, and gave also unto her husband with her; and he did eat.

The temptation that Eve faced appealed to three facets of human nature. One is physical hunger, she saw that *the tree was good for food.* This aspect of the temptation urged her to put her physical need above spiritual considerations.

Second, the temptation appealed to her sense of aesthetics, the appreciation for beauty. The tree was pleasing *to the eyes.* It was attractive. Eve may well have asked herself, "How could anything that is so attractive be harmful?" Per-haps at this point she began to give more cre-dence to the serpent's suggestion that this fruit was being kept from her simply because of God's jealousy.

The third aspect of human nature that the ser-pent appealed to was the capacity for wisdom. She concentrated on the serpent's promise that eating the forbidden fruit of the tree would make her as wise as God. At this point, all restraint was cast off. Step by step she had moved closer and closer toward sin. A loyal love of God and a steadfast faith in His truth and goodness would have prevented all of this.

When doubt was once entertained by Eve, the journey on the downward path had begun, and the actual disobedience of God was a natural consequence. So she ate of the fruit and *gave also unto her husband with her; and he did eat.* Having eaten of the fruit, Eve then did what sinners often do; she enticed Adam to join her.

C. The Loss of Innocence (v. 7)

7. And the eyes of them both were opened, and they knew that they were naked; and they sewed fig leaves together, and made themselves aprons.

The eyes of them both were opened. Satan had said that their eyes would be opened if they ate the forbidden fruit, and indeed they were. But the results were not what the pair had antici-pated. They had hoped for happiness, wisdom,

and power, which is what Satan had insinuated would be theirs. Thinking to be like God, they discovered that they were less like Him than be-fore; for they had committed sin, something that God could never do. They had fallen from the state of innocence in which they had been cre-ated. An awakened conscience spoke to them of their guilt. Their nakedness (see 2:25) was now a matter of shame because of their consciousness of sin. So they sewed together flimsy leaves of a tree to form garments like aprons.

Disregarding God's will concerning the tree, they had done as they pleased. But now they were far from being pleased with themselves be-cause of what they had done.

SATISFYING THE SENSES

Bobby Unger was the operator of a successful sales business. He wore a shiny Rolex watch and gold chains; he loved to be seen pulling a big roll of bills out of his pocket; his Jaguar's license plates read, YRUPOOR. He was impressed with wealth and wanted others to know he had it.

A regular bettor at the racetrack, Unger hit it big one day in June 1991. After conspicuously celebrating his victory, he insisted on taking his winnings ($72,000) in cash. Apparently one of the people he impressed was a gunman who fol-lowed him to his hotel, killed him with several shots from a handgun, and escaped with most of the cash.

This text reveals that the human race has al-ways been subject to sensual enticements. Eve was impressed with the fruit the serpent pointed out to her so beguilingly. Adam, in turn, shared Eve's delight. In eating the forbidden fruit, they sought in part to satisfy their physical senses.

However, the story does not end there: that very day they began to die. When we disregard God's warnings and seek sensual gratification, trouble is almost sure to come. The experience of Adam and Eve has been verified by every gen-eration since.   —C. R. B.

D. Separation From God (v. 8)

8. And they heard the voice of the LORD God walking in the garden in the cool of the day: and Adam and his wife hid themselves from the presence of the LORD God amongst the trees of the garden.

It seems likely that the first couple had en-joyed a close fellowship with God before they yielded to Satan's temptation. Apparently a part of God's reason for creating humans was His de-sire to have fellowship with them. The relation-ship was ruptured by man's disobedience.

After they sinned, Adam and Eve tried to hide from God. The Hebrew word translated *voice*

visual 3

may also be translated "sound." God may have been talking to some other creature, but it seems more probable that God made known His presence by the sound of His moving in the garden. Adam and Eve knew that He was present, and they were afraid; so they tried to hide from God who loved them.

The trees of the garden offered no sure hiding place for the man and woman. They should have known that they could not hide from God. Their sin was bound to be uncovered. Just as certainly, none of us today can hide from God, no matter how hard we try.

III. The Sinners Arraigned (Genesis 3:9-13)

A. God's Call (v. 9)

9. And the LORD God called unto Adam, and said unto him, Where art thou?

Some view God's call as the roar of an angry tyrant. God had every right to be angry, of course. His beloved creatures had spurned His love. Adam and Eve apparently did not believe that God would bring death upon them if they ate of the forbidden fruit. Instead they had chosen to believe Satan's lie.

God could have destroyed the disobedient couple immediately had He chosen to do so. With an outstretched arm and a mighty hand He could have smitten them as He smote the first-born of Egypt. Like the terrible giant in the story of Jack and the Beanstalk, God could have come storming into the Garden of Eden threatening to tear the first couple limb from limb.

The God of the Old Testament, however, is the same God of whom Jesus spoke. He is a God of love. It is better to hear a catch in His voice as He called out to Adam, "Where are you?" God knew full well where Adam was. This was a call to account, but it was also a call to mercy. The man and woman would be given the opportunity to examine their hearts, to recognize their shameful condition, and to confess their sin.

B. Man's Humiliation (vv. 10-12)

10. And he said, I heard thy voice in the garden, and I was afraid, because I was naked; and I hid myself.

How awful is fear! Love should have brought the man before God with a contrite heart, openly confessing the sin that had been committed. But guilt led him to turn from the presence of God and to hide. Sin, indeed, separates us from God. And one sin leads to another. Adam admitted that he was afraid, but he did not tell the whole truth when he said he feared *because I was naked.* Actually, he feared because he had disobeyed God, but he did not have the courage to say this.

11. And he said, Who told thee that thou wast naked? Hast thou eaten of the tree, whereof I commanded thee that thou shouldest not eat?

In their sinless state, Adam and Eve were naked; but they were not ashamed. When they sinned, many things changed—their view of themselves, their relationship with each other, and their relationship with God. Sin brought guilt and shame.

Who told thee that thou wast naked? This was a rhetorical question. God did not need an answer to it, for He knew that Adam could have become aware of nakedness and shame only by committing sin.

Hast thou eaten of the tree? God, who is omniscient, was fully aware of what Adam had done. But confession of sin was necessary, and God would give him the opportunity to admit his wrongdoing.

12. And the man said, The woman whom thou gavest to be with me, she gave me of the tree, and I did eat.

Adam's response to God's question has been given differing interpretations by Bible students. Some see it simply as a statement of facts relating to what occurred, and nothing more. His reference to the woman whom God had given him is regarded only as the identification of the one who was the physical means by which the forbidden fruit was brought to him. According to this view, Adam's words, *and I did eat,* were a clear and willing confession of his guilt.

Others, however, regard Adam's statement as an effort to excuse himself as much as possible of any responsibility for his action. The construction of his reply, *The woman . . . she gave me of the tree,* is seen as Adam's attempt to incriminate Eve for his own wrongdoing and to place the blame on her. And by adding the clause *whom thou gavest to be with me,* Adam seems even to be putting some of the blame on God. If this view is correct, Adam's confession of sin must be regarded as very mildly stated and only reluctantly offered.

There is no indication in the record in Genesis that the serpent personally confronted Adam. Indeed, Paul's statement, "Adam was not deceived" (1 Timothy 2:14), leads us to understand that the serpent did not make a direct appeal to him. The temptation came to Adam when Eve gave him some of the fruit. In any case, He knew that eating the fruit was forbidden, and he was responsible for his actions.

C. The Woman's Part (v. 13)

13. And the LORD God said unto the woman, What is this that thou hast done? And the woman said, The serpent beguiled me, and I did eat.

Eve did not deny Adam's account of what happened. Her response to God's question was an unspoken admission that what Adam said was true. She had indeed given of the fruit of the tree to her husband. But notice that her reply was fashioned after that of her husband. She made no mention of her part in tempting him, and attempted to shift the blame for her disobedience to the serpent. Because *the serpent beguiled me,* she said, *I did eat.*

Satan is indeed the great deceiver. He pretends to be a friend of human beings, but he is their worst enemy. He seemed to sympathize with Eve over the restriction God had placed on her and her husband, and he assured Eve that they would not die if they ate the fruit. He deceived Eve. He led her astray. Eve put it well when she said, *The serpent beguiled me.*

We may be certain that Satan is always lurking somewhere to beguile us—to entice, to lead us astray. He will use anything and anyone to tempt us to disobey God's commands. Sometimes he works through our peers, as they try to convince us that what the Bible identifies as evil is an accepted practice or life-style today. He may use the pressures of today's complex life to break down our moral integrity. Whatever the appeal of Satan, we are still not excused from personal responsibility to choose right over wrong. Let us heed Peter's warning and admonition: "Your adversary the devil, as a roaring lion, walketh about, seeking whom he may devour: whom resist steadfast in the faith" (1 Peter 5:8, 9a).

Conclusion

A. The Way of Temptation

The New Testament tells us that God tempts no man (James 1:13). Yet God permitted Adam and Eve to be tempted, and He permits temptations to come today. Why did God make a creature capable of sinning and then condemn him

for his sin? The answer is to be found in the fact that God intended for man to be a self-determining being. Animals live by instinct; man lives according to the exercise of his will.

Man was created in the image of God, with a moral nature. But no action of man can be counted as of moral significance unless it is freely done when right and wrong courses of action are possible. For man to do the will of God simply because he could not do otherwise would reflect no glory upon man and very little upon God. There must be the opportunity of choice before man's behavior takes on a moral quality. That is why there is temptation.

But this is not the whole story. Consider how great is the love and the wisdom of God, who never intended to abandon man even after his fall. Instead, He had a plan for man's redemption from the beginning. Man, the creature, can return to God and find acceptance through His Son Jesus Christ. But this is so because man, a moral being, can choose to respond to the love of God. "Whosoever will," let him come is the invitation of God (Revelation 22:17). But there can be no "whosoever will" unless the choice is given to be a "whosoever won't." Let us choose to come to God and walk in His way.

B. Let Us Pray

Dear Lord, forgive us of our foolish ways. We confess that we are stubborn, proud, selfish, and rebellious. Thank You for sending Jesus to save us. In His name, amen.

C. Thought to Remember

Satan lures us with the promise of a better life, but he lies. Death awaits all who follow him. Life is found only in God through Jesus Christ.

Home Daily Bible Readings

Monday, Sept. 13—Temptation in the Garden (Genesis 3:1-6)

Tuesday, Sept. 14—God Seeks the Sinners (Genesis 3:7-11)

Wednesday, Sept. 15—Sinners Blame One Another (Genesis 3:12, 13; Psalm 139:1-12)

Thursday, Sept. 16—Punishment for All (Genesis 3:14-19)

Friday, Sept 17—How to Love God (Deuteronomy 6:4-14a)

Saturday, Sept. 18—Commit Your Way to the Lord (Psalm 37:3-9, 27-31)

Sunday, Sept. 19—Walk in God's Way (Psalm 119:1-8)

Learning by Doing

This page contains an alternate lesson plan emphasizing learning activities. Classes desiring such student involvement will find these suggestions helpful.

Learning Goals

The study of this lesson will enable the student to:

1. Explain how the temptations we face are similar to the temptation of Eve.

2. Describe how sin separates people from God as well as from other people.

3. State a plan to resist temptation.

Into the Lesson

Before class, display the following phrases prominently at the front of the classroom:

"The lust of the flesh"

"The lust of the eyes"

"The boastful pride of life."

(If your students all use one version of the Bible, look up 1 John 2:16 and word the phrases according to it. The phrases above are from the *New American Standard Bible.*)

Ask which of these temptations is most prevalent in the world today, and why they think so. After a brief discussion, observe that each one is prevalent. In fact, it has always been so since the temptation of Eve in the Garden of Eden, which is the event for our study today.

Into the Word

Arrange to have four readers help you read the text, Genesis 3:1-13. Have one read the words of Eve; another, the words of Satan; a third, the words of Adam; and the fourth, the words of God. Act as narrator and read all the nondialogue parts. Ask the rest of the class to listen to the reading and mentally note how Eve's temptation is related to the ones discussed earlier, "the lust of the flesh," "the lust of the eyes," and "the boastful pride of life."

After the reading, write these three headings on the chalkboard or overhead: *Promises, Perceptions,* and *Results.* Ask the class to identify the promises Satan made to Eve. As they do so, list them under the first heading. List under the second heading Eve's evaluation of the fruit. List under the third what resulted when Adam and Eve believed Satan. The completed lists should contain the following items: *Promises:* not die, eyes opened, be like God, know good and evil. *Perceptions:* good for food, pleasant to the eyes, desirable to make one wise. *Results:* eyes opened to their nakedness, shame (they covered themselves), hid from God, fear, blamed another for

their sin. Note that Eve's perception that the fruit was good for food appealed to the lust of the flesh; that it was pleasant to the eyes appealed to the lust of the eyes; and that it was desirable to make one wise appealed to the pride of life.

To contrast the promises and perceptions with the results, ask the class to imagine it is a law firm that has been retained by Eve to sue the serpent for fraud. See how many lies and misrepresentations the students can find in Satan's approach.

Into Life

We have seen that the temptations we face have the same elements as Eve's temptation. Consider briefly the results of sin now as then.

Ask, "What changes occurred in the relationship between Adam and Eve after they sinned?" (Their covering themselves shows they no longer had a completely open and innocent relationship; Adam blamed Eve for his sin.) Ask what are some of the disruptions in relationships caused by sin today. Discuss briefly.

Note that the disobedient pair's relationship to God was broken. Now they feared Him and tried to hide from Him. Discuss. "In what ways do people try to hide from God today?" (See question 5 in "Let's Talk It Over" on page 32.)

Observe that our broken relationship with God is restored in Jesus Christ. Point out, however, that we still face temptation, for Satan continues his deadly work among us (see 1 Peter 5:8).

Divide the class into three groups. Ask the first to consider the lust of the flesh and to suggest specific measures one can take to recognize and resist this temptation. Have the second do the same with the lust of the eyes, and the third with the boastful pride of life. Give the groups about five minutes for discussion; then ask for reports. Put a chart on the chalkboard. Make two vertical columns with the headings *Recognize* and *Resist* at the top. Down the left side label three horizontal columns "Flesh," "Eyes," and "Pride." Fill in the chart with the students' suggestions.

Ask each student to consider which area of temptation is the most troubling to him or her. Ask each to make a commitment to use the measures suggested to resist that temptation during this coming week.

Let's Talk It Over

The questions on this page are designed to encourage review of the lesson Scriptures and to promote discussion of the lesson by the class. The answers provided are only discussion starters. Let your class talk it over from there.

1. Satan is a sower of doubts. What are some doubts he is effectively sowing today?

The authenticity and reliability of the Bible are the focus of many doubts. Certain scholars play into the devil's hands by their claims that the Bible contains myths, legends, and historical inaccuracies. They deny the historical character of Biblical miracles, including Jesus Christ's resurrection. While these claims have been often refuted by believing scholars, they continue to be made, and young, impressionable Christians are thereby led to doubt. Satan also persists in sowing doubts about God's goodness. The psalmist exclaimed, "Thou art good, and doest good: teach me thy statutes" (Psalm 119:68). But Satan calls attention to the war, disease, poverty, and crime that plague the human race, and he whispers in men's hearts that if God were truly good, He would not allow such things to exist. Can we blame God for what men, working in harmony with Satan, have caused?

2. Satan tried to make Eve feel that God had unfairly restricted Adam and her by prohibiting their eating of the fruit of one tree. How does Satan use a similar tactic in our time?

In approaching people about accepting Jesus Christ as Savior, one frequently hears the complaint that the Christian life is too difficult to live. This reflects Satan's tactic that emphasizes the restrictions imposed by Christian discipleship. It is true that a believer is restricted from immoral sexual behavior, but greater fulfillment, not to mention freedom from sexually transmitted disease, is to be found in marital faithfulness. It is true that Christians are to avoid illicit drugs, and anything else that will harm their bodies, but they are likely to enjoy better physical health as a result. It is also true that followers of Jesus are taught to avoid excessive desire for money, but they are thereby saved from the sorrows often associated with love of money (1 Timothy 6:9, 10).

3. Satan is shown by our text to be a liar, a fact that Jesus underscored (see John 8:44). What are some lies he is spreading today?

Secular humanism is serving as the mouthpiece for one of his most outrageous lies: that man has no need for God or the Bible, but can build a sound society on his own. For those inclined to believe in God and to hope for eternal life, Satan sets forth his well-worn falsehood that people can earn salvation by their good works. In the realm of morals he employs an appealing array of lies, such as the claim that an action is not sin if no one is hurt; or, if everybody else is doing it, then it must be all right. If we were to write the Ten Commandments on one side of a sheet of paper, we would easily be able to list on the other side popular lies that correspond to each of them.

4. The fruit on the tree of the knowledge of good and evil was attractive and appealing. How does Satan make sin attractive and appealing in our time?

Sin is glamorized by many modern celebrities. These "beautiful," seemingly sophisticated people live together outside of marriage, abuse alcohol and drugs, take God's name in vain, and dabble in occult practices, among other things. It is tempting to think, "If it is all right for them, why shouldn't it be all right for me?" But we must resist such temptation. Sin is made to appear more attractive and appealing also by its association with pleasure or "fun." Sin may indeed be pleasurable "for a season" (Hebrews 11:25), but the pain and sorrow that follow sinful pleasure is rarely acknowledged.

5. What are some ways in which people try to hide from God?

Some people live as though God does not exist. One gains the impression that they deny God mainly because they realize that if they were to admit His existence, they would need to make painful changes in their lives. In a sense, they are hiding from God. One suspects the same about people whose lives are constantly caught up in a welter of activity. Could it be that some keep themselves so busy that they will not have time to ponder such weighty matters as God, sin, salvation, and eternity? It also seems likely that many individuals who befog their minds with drugs and alcohol do so in an attempt to escape the reality of God. It is well for everyone to come to the realization as David did that escape from God is impossible (see Psalm 139:7-12).

God's Response to Mankind's Sin

DEVOTIONAL READING: Psalms 36:1-9; 62:1, 2.

LESSON SCRIPTURE: Genesis 3:14-24; 6:5-8, 11-22; 9:8-13.

PRINTED TEXT: Genesis 3:22-24; 6:5-8; 9:8-13.

Genesis 3:22-24

22 And the LORD God said, Behold, the man is become as one of us, to know good and evil: and now, lest he put forth his hand, and take also of the tree of life, and eat, and live for ever:

23 Therefore the LORD God sent him forth from the garden of Eden, to till the ground from whence he was taken.

24 So he drove out the man: and he placed at the east of the garden of Eden cherubim, and a flaming sword which turned every way, to keep the way of the tree of life.

Genesis 6:5-8

5 And God saw that the wickedness of man was great in the earth, and that every imagination of the thoughts of his heart was only evil continually.

6 And it repented the LORD that he had made man on the earth, and it grieved him at his heart.

7 And the LORD said, I will destroy man whom I have created from the face of the earth; both man, and beast, and the creeping thing, and the fowls of the air; for it repenteth me that I have made them.

8 But Noah found grace in the eyes of the LORD.

Genesis 9:8-13

8 And God spake unto Noah, and to his sons with him, saying,

9 And I, behold, I establish my covenant with you, and with your seed after you;

10 And with every living creature that is with you, of the fowl, of the cattle, and of every beast of the earth with you; from all that go out of the ark, to every beast of the earth.

11 And I will establish my covenant with you; neither shall all flesh be cut off any more by the waters of a flood; neither shall there any more be a flood to destroy the earth.

12 And God said, This is the token of the covenant which I make between me and you, and every living creature that is with you, for perpetual generations:

13 I do set my bow in the cloud, and it shall be for a token of a covenant between me and the earth.

GOLDEN TEXT: I will establish my covenant with you; neither shall all flesh be cut off any more by the waters of a flood; neither shall there any more be a flood to destroy the earth.—Genesis 9:11.

The Story of Beginnings
Unit 1: God's Creation of and
Relationship With Mankind
(Lessons 1-4)

Lesson Aims

As a result of this lesson, students should:
1. Understand that disobeying God brings punishment.
2. Rejoice that forgiveness of sin is available through Jesus Christ.
3. Commit themselves to a closer walk with God

Lesson Outline

INTRODUCTION
   A. Light at the End of the Tunnel
   B. Lesson Background
I. GOD'S ACTIONS (Genesis 3:22-24)
   A. What to Do? (v. 22)
   B. Expelled (v. 23)
   C. Punishment and Mercy (v. 24)
     Paradise Lost
II. GOD'S PATIENCE TESTED (Genesis 6:5-8)
   A. Man's Unrelenting Evil (v. 5)
   B. God's Grief (v. 6)
   C. Man's Fate Decided (v. 7)
   D. Noah's Outstanding Goodness (v. 8)
III. GOD'S COVENANT WITH NOAH (Genesis 9:8-13)
   A. Beneficiaries of the Covenant (vv. 8-10)
   B. The Nature of the Covenant (v. 11)
   C. The Token of the Covenant (vv. 12, 13)
     A Promise and a Purpose
CONCLUSION
   A. The First Good News
   B. Let Us Pray
   C. Thought to Remember

Visual 4 of the visuals packet highlights elements of God's response to mankind's sin. The visual is shown on page 35.

Introduction

A. Light at the End of the Tunnel

Greg and Bob were spelunkers. They thoroughly enjoyed exploring the dark recesses of underground passageways. On one occasion, however, they found themselves in a life-threatening situation. Turning and twisting through the corridors of a cave, they became confused and wandered for hours trying to find their way back to the entrance of the cave.

The batteries of their flashlights were nearly gone. In addition, they had no food, and their water supply was running very low. Their situation was becoming increasingly alarming. Suddenly their fears were dispelled. There was light at the end of the tunnel. As they moved steadily forward, the light became brighter, until at last they reached the cave's entrance and safety.

The first human pair were in a dark and discouraging situation after they sinned against God. God announced penalties for all who had participated in the temptation and fall—the serpent, Eve, and Adam. Still God did not leave the man and the woman without hope. Veiled as it was, the promise of God that the seed of the woman would prevail over the seed of the serpent (Genesis 3:15) gave assurance that God would provide a way to overcome the effects of sin and eventually restore the harmonious relationship between man and his Creator.

B. Lesson Background

After hearing the confessions of Adam and Eve, God confronted the serpent. A curse was placed upon the serpent so that henceforth it would make its way by slithering across the ground on its belly. God stated that there would be continuing enmity between Satan and the human family, and that finally Satan would suffer a crushing defeat by one who would arise from among the seed of the woman.

A second curse was pronounced upon the ground. God announced that thorns and thistles would proliferate and make man's tilling of the ground a burden. With difficulty Adam and his offspring must gain the necessities of life, and it will be thus until man returns to the ground from which he was taken. The curses having been pronounced, it was time for God's action.

I. God's Actions (Genesis 3:22-24)

A. What to Do? (v. 22)

22. And the LORD God said, Behold, the man is become as one of us, to know good and evil: and now, lest he put forth his hand, and take also of the tree of life, and eat, and live for ever.

Adam and Eve did not become equal with God, as Satan had implied (Genesis 3:1-6), but they did get something from their experience: they gained knowledge of *good and evil*. They should have known before that it was good to obey God and evil to disobey Him, but after their sin they knew by experience. For the first time they knew the feeling of shame and fear. They knew they were sinners.

Satan constantly urges us to know evil by experience. "Don't knock it till you've tried it," he says. Surely it is not necessary for Christians today to experiment with alcohol or illicit drugs, when the harmful effects of such practice is clearly seen in our society. The dangers associated with promiscuous sex are well documented. Must one engage in such activity to understand the evil effects that it produces in one's body, mind, and spirit?

The second half of verse 22 is an incomplete statement. As it stands, the statement expresses God's concern over man's changed condition, but without telling us what God decided to do. This is an anthropomorphic expression, a style of writing that couches the thoughts of God in man's terminology. Such a statement helps us to see the dilemma God was facing.

Since man had disobeyed God, God might have struck him dead on the spot. God could have made the fruit of the tree of life poisonous and death-dealing. What should He do? The next verse tells us what God did.

B. Expelled (v. 23)

23. Therefore the LORD God sent him forth from the garden of Eden, to till the ground from whence he was taken.

God announced His decision. The first step He took was to drive man out of the garden. The lovely surroundings that man had enjoyed at first were no longer to be his home. At the same time his physical labor was to become more difficult. Now he would have to live by the sweat of his brow (Genesis 3:17-19).

C. Punishment and Mercy (v. 24)

24. So he drove out the man: and he placed at the east of the garden of Eden cherubim, and a flaming sword which turned every way, to keep the way of the tree of life.

God created man to live in a blissful state in the Garden of Eden, enjoying fellowship with his Creator. But man sinned. Instead of blessing and fellowship with his Creator, man now would experience punishment and separation from God.

It would not be good for man to live forever in sin, so God took another step after He drove the first pair from Eden. Lest they attempt to return to the garden and eat of the fruit of the tree of life in their fallen state, God set Heavenly creatures, cherubim, as guardians of the garden. With them was a flaming sword that turned every way to threaten any who attempted to gain entrance. Evidently these remained until the location and identity of the Garden of Eden became unknown to the human family.

visual 4

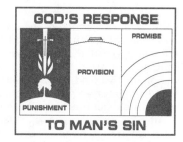

GOD'S RESPONSE
PROMISE
PROVISION
PUNISHMENT
TO MAN'S SIN

Paradise Lost

Imagine being the daughter of one of the world's richest men and spending your youth on the Riviera, on a private island in Greece, and on your father's yacht (longer than a football field), which he named after you. Imagine inheriting more than half a billion dollars before you were thirty years old. Wouldn't that be paradise?

Perhaps not. Christina Onassis was such a person. Her biographer, William Wright, tells us that her parents so ignored her that, at the age of five, she retreated into autism as a plea for love. As an adult, she endured disastrous marriages, and found that most of her "friends" were interested as much in her money as in her. And at age thirty-seven, she died mysteriously.

Adam and Eve literally lived in paradise, where no evil existed until they doubted God's word. When they sinned, the whole dynamic of creation changed. God sent them out of paradise and blocked the path of their return. They had to see the consequences of disbelief, and they could not, as sinners, have access to the tree of life and live forever in their sinful state.

Ever since that time, we have dreamed of the paradise our first parents lost. Too often, our dreams take the form of wishing for the material "blessings" that Christina Onassis found so unsatisfying. But God has something better for us: the spiritual paradise open to all who trust Him and live in tune with the heart of God. —C. R. B.

II. God's Patience Tested (Genesis 6:5-8)

A. Man's Unrelenting Evil (v. 5)

5. And GOD saw that the wickedness of man was great in the earth, and that every imagination of the thoughts of his heart was only evil continually.

As the record in Genesis unfolds, we see that sin continued to plague man. Some time after our first parents were driven from Eden (we are not told how long), two sons, Cain and Abel, were born to them. In time both offered sacrifices to God. Because Abel's sacrifice was acceptable to God and Cain's was not, Cain became filled with envy toward his brother. In spite of God's warning of the danger of sin that was before him, Cain permitted his envy and hatred to control him, and he murdered his brother. As a result, he was condemned to leave the productive land he had tilled and become a wanderer in areas where the earth would not readily yield her fruits for his labor.

After Cain murdered Abel, Adam and Eve had other children, sons and daughters. It must have been one of the latter who became the wife of Cain. The descendants of Cain multiplied. Some were inclined to city life, others to that of nomads. Some developed musical talents, others became skilled workers in bronze and iron. But it seems that the civilization developed by the descendants of Cain became increasingly wicked and depraved.

God blessed Adam and Eve with a son to replace Abel, and they named him Seth. When, in turn, a son was born to him, "then began men to call upon the name of the Lord" (Genesis 4:26). This suggests that the descendants of Seth did worship God. Even so, as mankind began to multiply, ungodliness and wickedness increased upon the earth.

We read in Genesis 6:2 that "the sons of God saw the daughters of men that they were fair; and they took them wives of all which they chose." Most Bible students understand "the sons of God" to be the descendants of Seth, who had maintained the worship of God, and "the daughters of men" to be the godless races around them, of whom the line of Cain may have been the chief representative. When those of Seth's family began to intermarry with the heathen population, the salt of society lost its savor, and the total corruption of mankind ensued. *God saw.* The moral depravity of the age did not go unnoticed. The hearts of men and women are always an open book to God. Man's wickedness was so pervasive that *every imagination of the thoughts of his heart was only evil continually.*

B. God's Grief (v. 6)

6. And it repented the LORD that he had made man on the earth, and it grieved him at his heart.

God was heartbroken over man's all-pervasive sinful condition. In language that man can understand, the author says, *It repented the Lord that he had made man.*

Man's repentance arises from his godly sorrow for his own sin. It generates in him a change of mind that issues in a reformation of character To say that God repented does not imply that He had made a mistake. God does not sin. He has never been, nor can He ever be, guilty of any

evil for which He must repent as is true of men. The shared element in man's repentance and God's repentance is the sorrow. But even here the two are not exactly the same. God grieves because man sins. God's sorrow arises from the failure of mankind and does not at all imply a failure on God's part. Man's sorrow springs from his own failures.

C. Man's Fate Decided (v. 7)

7. And the LORD said, I will destroy man whom I have created from the face of the earth; both man, and beast, and the creeping thing, and the fowls of the air; for it repenteth me that I have made them.

Another element in God's repentance concerning His creation of man is seen in this verse; namely, the approval that God pronounced upon man at creation had to give way to disapproval, because man had turned from God to wickedness. Repentance on the part of God was a change in His *immediate* purpose toward man, a change that had been made necessary because of man's behavior. God's purpose now was to destroy from the face of the earth the creatures that He had made. In view of the depravity to which man had sunk, such destruction was inevitable.

D. Noah's Outstanding Goodness (v. 8)

8. But Noah found grace in the eyes of the LORD.

Among the entire population, one man stood out like an oasis in a parched desert. That man was Noah, one of the descendants in the line of Seth. Noah is described as "just," "perfect in his generations," and one who "walked with God" (Genesis 6:9). This is the type of person that God would have all persons to be. He alone found favor in the eyes of God; so God determined to save him and to use him to start a new population for the earth.

This verse gives us a clue as to how the ultimate purposes of God will be realized, even though mankind possesses freedom of will. Human beings are free to rebel, to turn from God. But God is free to offer mercy and grace, and there are those who will turn to Him. Such a one was Noah.

The verses that follow repeat the depraved condition into which mankind had fallen. His ways were totally corrupt, and violence filled the earth. God then spoke to Noah and revealed that He could no longer tolerate man's wickedness; the time for mankind's destruction had come. He instructed Noah to build an ark and gave him the specifications for it. A flood was coming, and this vessel would be the means of salvation for him, his family, and for every species of living creatures.

In God's appointed time, the flood came. Some hold that the flood was partial, that it covered only that portion of the earth where Noah lived and which was populated at that time. Others, however, contend that the flood was universal, that it covered the entire earth. Both views have been held at certain times by Bible-believing scholars. At any rate, Noah, in obedience to the commandment of God, prepared an ark, into which he took his family and those animals that were to be preserved. The flood destroyed all human beings, and all cattle, fowl, and creeping things that were outside the ark; only those inside were saved from destruction.

Before the flood, God promised to make a covenant with Noah (Genesis 6:18). When the waters finally abated from the earth, Noah came out of the ark and offered sacrifices to the Lord. Now God was ready to establish the covenant He had promised.

III. God's Covenant With Noah (Genesis 9:8-13)

A. Beneficiaries of the Covenant (vv. 8-10)

8, 9. And God spake unto Noah, and to his sons with him, saying, And I, behold, I establish my covenant with you, and with your seed after you.

These words were spoken to Noah and his sons, but the covenant that God was instituting was not with them alone. It was with all mankind. All persons are descended from Noah's family; all are included in his seed after him.

A covenant is an agreement or contract between two or more parties, in which mutual promises are made and obligations stated. This is true of covenants entered into by human beings with one another. God's covenants, however, are better understood as offer and response. God alone states the terms and conditions, and He binds himself to keep the promises that He attaches to the covenant. Man enters the covenant by accepting God's terms and living accordingly. Noah demonstrated his acceptance of the terms of God's covenant with him when he obeyed God and prepared the ark.

10. And with every living creature that is with you, of the fowl, of the cattle, and of every beast of the earth with you; from all that go out of the ark, to every beast of the earth.

God's covenant was not only with mankind, but also with all creatures in which was the breath of life. The animal kingdom shared the penalty that man's sin brought upon the earth. Now the animals would share with man the benefit of God's covenant of mercy announced to Noah and his family.

B. The Nature of the Covenant (v. 11)

11. And I will establish my covenant with you; neither shall all flesh be cut off any more by the waters of a flood; neither shall there any more be a flood to destroy the earth.

Here God stated the nature of the covenant with Noah. In His mercy God promised Noah and his family that there would never again be a flood of water to destroy the earth. Remembering that promise would allay their fears whenever torrential rains began to fall on the earth.

Another feature of the covenant is seen in Genesis 8:22. There we read of this promise of God: "While the earth remaineth, seedtime and harvest, and cold and heat, and summer and winter, and day and night shall not cease." The seasons will continue their perpetual rounds until the end of time. Both man and the animals can, and do, depend on God's faithfulness to keep this promise.

C. The Token of the Covenant (vv. 12, 13)

12. And God said, This is the token of the covenant which I make between me and you, and every living creature that is with you, for perpetual generations.

God appointed a *token*, or sign, to be a continuing reminder of the covenant He was now establishing with all living creatures. That sign would speak to every generation of God's love and concern for His world. The covenant would be *for perpetual generations.* No time limit was placed on this covenant; it would remain in effect for as long as man existed on earth. Whatever covenants God might make with man in the future, this one would not be superseded.

13. I do set my bow in the cloud, and it shall be for a token of a covenant between me and the earth.

The sign God appointed as a reminder of His covenant was the rainbow. The beauty of the rainbow is appropriate. It speaks eloquently of the goodness and mercy of God. Its appearing should stimulate us to give thanks to God for His assurance that floods of water will never again wipe living creatures from the face of the ground. Whether or not the rainbow appeared here for the first time, God declared it to be from that time forward the sign of the covenant that He made with the earth.

A PROMISE AND A PURPOSE

"Water, water, everywhere, nor any drop to drink." The lament of the shipwreck-survivor adrift at sea is just one evidence of the importance of water. Whether we have too little, too much, or the wrong kind, water can be a problem.

Too much spring rain can delay the season so long that farmers cannot plant their crops. Too little rain in a long, hot summer can burn the crops so no grain is produced. Even city dwellers who do not worry about crops can find their lives affected by a drought that extends for years as it does occasionally in the American West. And too much rain too quickly can bring disastrous floods anywhere in the world. History tells us of many such calamities. In 1988, three-fourths of the nation of Bangladesh was covered with water by the heaviest monsoon in a century. More than 1300 people died and 30 million were left homeless.

The wicked who died in the Genesis flood would have said there was too much rain. But the rain that fell was a part of God's plan for saving Noah and purifying the human race. Once that was accomplished, God established a covenant with mankind and all living creatures.

God appointed the rainbow as a sign of His covenant. Whenever we see it, we should remember both God's promise and His purpose: He will never again destroy the world with a flood, but He also intends of us to be pure.

—C. R. B.

Conclusion

A. The First Good News

In the Garden of Eden God confronted the serpent and cursed it. Then God uttered a prophecy that contained elements of both bane and blessing (Genesis 3:15). He said that He would put enmity between the serpent and the woman, and between the serpent's seed and the woman's seed. By this He indicated that the seed of the serpent (mystically Satan and his servants) would continually attack Eve's descendants, the human race. But then the prophecy assumed a personal character as God said, "He will crush your head, and you will strike his heel" (*New International Version*).

This great prediction in the latter part of the verse is the first ray of light relating to the redemption of mankind and the healing of the broken relationship between man and God. Martin Luther said that this first glimmer of good news to the fallen couple included in its fulfillment all the great redemptive acts of God. It set the stage for the conflict of the ages—the war that has raged between good and evil—and envisioned its ultimate outcome.

This one of whom the prophecy spoke was Jesus Christ, the Son of God. Sent from the Father above, He came to earth and took upon himself the form of a man. He was uniquely of the seed of the woman, for no other descendant of Eve had no earthly father. And of Him it is said, "For this purpose the Son of God was manifested, that he might destroy the works of the devil" (1 John 3:8).

Jesus denounced the corrupt religious leaders of His day, saying, "Ye are of your father the devil" (John 8:44). These wicked men were among the seed of the serpent. When they succeeded in crucifying Jesus, Satan did no more than bruise the heel of the seed of the woman. But when Jesus arose from the dead, He crushed the head of the serpent, Satan himself. Satan's power over man was broken.

God's grace, in the garden, which seemed as but a faint ray of light in man's spiritual darkness, in time was "made manifest by the appearing of our Saviour Jesus Christ." In Jesus' victory over Satan, man is rescued from the penalty of death. By the grace of God, Jesus "hath abolished death, and hath brought life and immortality to light through the gospel" (2 Timothy 1:10).

B. Let Us Pray

Our Father, we bow our heads in shame as we think how unfaithful Your creation has been. We are warned by the examples of yesterday, but we know that it is our own sins that stand between us and You. We thank You for Your patience and for Your grace, which You have extended to us through Your Son. Forgive us, O Lord we pledge ourselves anew to live for You. In Jesus' name, amen.

C. Thought to Remember

He who has set the bounds of the seas has set no bounds to His great love.

Learning by Doing

This page contains an alternate lesson plan emphasizing learning activities. Classes desiring such student involvement will find these suggestions helpful.

Learning Goals

As a result of participation in this lesson, each student will be able to do the following:

1. Compare God's response to sin in the Garden of Eden with His response to sin in the days of Noah.

2. Suggest a Christian's appropriate response to sin in the world.

Into the Lesson

As the students arrive, give each one a slip of paper with one of the following questions written on it:

• What is the proper or customary response when someone says, "How are you?"

• What is the proper or customary response when someone sneezes?

• What is the proper or customary response when you spot a police car?

• What is the proper or customary response when the national anthem is played?

• What is the proper or customary response when an athlete or actor gives an impressive performance?

• What is the proper or customary response when someone performs an act of kindness toward you?

Ask the students to think about the answers to the questions as they visit or get ready for the class to begin. Encourage them to share their questions with others and see what questions some of the others have.

When it is time for class to begin, read the first question aloud and ask for response from the students who were given that question. Then let other students give suggestions also. Follow the same procedure with each question.

As you conclude this discussion, point out that the Bible records some of God's responses to man's actions in the past. Ask, "How has God responded to man's sin?" Discuss that briefly. In the discussion, point out that various elements may be seen in God's responses to man's sin. Some of these are punishment, patience, and grace. We see this illustrated in the texts selected for our study in this lesson.

Into the Word

Divide the class into groups of four to six students each. Instruct half of the groups to study Genesis 3:14-24 and the other half to study Gen-

esis 6:5-8, 11-22; 9:8-13. Both sets of groups are to answer the following questions as they pertain to the texts they are studying:

1. What was the punishment God exacted for sin in this case?

2. How did God's response to sin in this case show His patience?

3. How did this event show that sin grieves God?

4. How was God's grace shown in this instance?

Allow the groups about fifteen minutes for their work. Then call the class together. Begin by asking the first set of groups for their answer to the first question. Then ask the second set of groups how they answered the first question. Discuss the difference: why the relatively mild sentence in one case and the harsher one in the other? Treat each question in the same manner, going back and forth between the two sets of groups. Draw from the commentary section for insights to add to the discussion.

Into Life

Ask, "Why do you think it is important to take note of God's response to sin?" List the students' answers on the chalkboard or overhead projector. The following should be included in the list of answers:

• It helps us understand God's holy character.

• It helps us appreciate His grace.

• It motivates us to right behavior.

• It suggests how we ought to respond to sin.

If no one offers this last idea, suggest it yourself. Build on the concept to get the class to explore just how we should respond to sin. Perhaps you could return to the four Bible study questions and apply those concepts:

1. Punishment. When is it proper for Christians to exact punishment for sinful behavior? (In church discipline, when serving in government or the judicial system.)

2. Patience. When should Christians exercise patience in dealing with sinful behavior? What determines the degree of patience to be shown?

3. Grief. Do we truly grieve over sin? Our own or the world's?

4. Grace. How can Christians be channels of God's grace to a world that is lost and dying in sin?

Let's Talk It Over

The questions on this page are designed to encourage review of the lesson Scriptures and to promote discussion of the lesson by the class. The answers provided are only discussion starters. Let your class talk it over from there.

1. Although it seems safe to say that the world is not as wicked as it was in the days of Noah, still humanity shows signs of being headed in that direction. What are some of these signs?

Perhaps the most obvious indications are seen in the realm of entertainment. Assuming that producers of movies and television shows are responding to the public's actual tastes, we find that people have an insatiable appetite for lurid sex, bloody violence, and vulgar language. It is frightening to think about the number of persons who feed their minds with a steady diet of such things. Also, the evil that lurks in human minds too frequently shows up in shocking actions. When we learn of seemingly normal people who have been found guilty of hideous crimes, we gain sobering insights into the depths of wickedness that exist today.

2. How can we imitate Noah's walk with God?

One outstanding characteristic of Noah was his obedience. He built the ark to God's specifications, even though he must have endured much ridicule for doing so and for believing in a God who would direct him to build it. We also are called to obey God, and ridicule is not unknown to one who believes that Jesus was God's Son. We, like Noah, can remain faithful under such circumstances. Another of Noah's characteristics worthy of note was his influence upon his family. It is significant that the only human beings who survived the flood were his family members, who apparently shared his walk with God. Our walk with God also must be the kind that impresses those closest to us with its genuineness, so that they will join us.

3. What comparisons and contrasts can we make between the covenant God made with Noah and the New Covenant under which we live?

Hebrews 8:6 says that the New Covenant "was established upon better promises." The contrast in Hebrews 8 is between the covenant made through Moses and the New Covenant through Jesus Christ, but the "better promises" certainly applies to what we are discussing here. God promised Noah that the earth would never again be destroyed by a flood, but God promises us "a new heaven and a new earth" (Revelation 21:1). The covenant with Noah applies to this life only, but the New Covenant provides eternal benefit and blessing. Both covenants demonstrate the mercy and graciousness of God, but the New Covenant does so much more powerfully.

4. In what ways should a Christian's appreciation of a rainbow differ from that of a non-Christian?

Today we can speak of a rainbow in scientific terms, and describe it merely as bands of color that are formed by the refraction and reflection of the sun's rays through raindrops or mist. But Genesis shows us that the rainbow is a phenomenon that has special significance, and we should be in awe of its beauty. Perhaps the sight of a rainbow makes one think of the proverbial "pot of gold" that some whimsically claim may be found at the rainbow's end. But we recognize something better than gold: a symbol of God's promise first made to Noah and still in effect today, that God will not destroy mankind through another flood. Students of the Bible will find in a rainbow not only these reminders from early in the Bible, but also the fact that the rainbow appears in Heavenly scenes described in Revelation (4:3; 10:1).

5. Why is it significant that a reference to Jesus Christ may be found in Genesis 3:15?

Jesus told the Jews, "Search the Scriptures; . . . they are they which testify of me" (John 5:39). While He walked with the two disciples following His resurrection, Jesus "expounded unto them in all the Scriptures the things concerning himself" (Luke 24:27).

We tend to think first of passages in Psalms and in the prophetical books, which speak more plainly of His suffering, as ones Jesus would have cited on that occasion. But surely He would also have called His hearers' attention to this reference back near the beginning of God's written revelation. Genesis 3 is the chapter that describes sin's entrance into human experience, and it seems quite appropriate that in that same chapter the first mention should be made of Him who would be the conqueror of sin and its attendant woes.

God's Commitment to Abram

DEVOTIONAL READING: Genesis 11:31, 32; 12:1-10; 14:17-20; 15:1-7.

LESSON SCRIPTURE: Genesis 12:1-3; 15:1-18.

PRINTED TEXT: Genesis 15:1-16.

Genesis 15:1-16

1 After these things the word of the LORD came unto Abram in a vision, saying, Fear not, Abram: I am thy shield, and thy exceeding great reward.

2 And Abram said, Lord GOD, what wilt thou give me, seeing I go childless, and the steward of my house is this Eliezer of Damascus?

3 And Abram said, Behold, to me thou hast given no seed: and, lo, one born in my house is mine heir.

4 And, behold, the word of the LORD came unto him, saying, This shall not be thine heir; but he that shall come forth out of thine own bowels shall be thine heir.

5 And he brought him forth abroad, and said, Look now toward heaven, and tell the stars, if thou be able to number them: and he said unto him, So shall thy seed be.

6 And he believed in the LORD; and he counted it to him for righteousness.

7 And he said unto him, I am the LORD that brought thee out of Ur of the Chaldees, to give thee this land to inherit it.

8 And he said, Lord GOD, whereby shall I know that I shall inherit it?

9 And he said unto him, Take me a heifer of three years old, and a she goat of three years old, and a ram of three years old, and a turtledove, and a young pigeon.

10 And he took unto him all these, and divided them in the midst, and laid each piece one against another: but the birds divided he not.

11 And when the fowls came down upon the carcasses, Abram drove them away.

12 And when the sun was going down, a deep sleep fell upon Abram; and, lo, a horror of great darkness fell upon him.

13 And he said unto Abram, Know of a surety that thy seed shall be a stranger in a land that is not theirs, and shall serve them; and they shall afflict them four hundred years;

14 And also that nation, whom they shall serve, will I judge: and afterward shall they come out with great substance.

15 And thou shalt go to thy fathers in peace; thou shalt be buried in a good old age.

16 But in the fourth generation they shall come hither again: for the iniquity of the Amorites is not yet full.

GOLDEN TEXT: I will make of thee a great nation, and I will bless thee, and make thy name great; and thou shalt be a blessing.—Genesis 12:2.

Lesson Aims

This lesson should enable students to:

1. Understand the role that God's promises played in the unfolding of Israel's history.

2. Have confidence in the reliability of God's promises to us today.

Lesson Outline

Visual 5 of the visuals packet highlights features of Abraham's journey of faith as indicated in the Scripture designated for this study. The visual is shown on page 45. The map (visual 14) may be used to locate many of the places referred to in the remaining lessons of this quarter's study.

Introduction

A. "The Word of a Gentleman"

The spiritual giant David Livingston had great confidence in the promises of God. His favorite Biblical verse was one of the compelling promises of Scripture, "Lo, I am with you alway, even unto the end of the world" (Matthew 28:20). His biographers tell us that whenever he was confronted with some special danger or difficulty, he would write the text afresh in his journal along with this affirmation: "It is the word of a Gentleman of the strictest and most sacred honour, and that's an end of it."

"The word of a Gentleman"—such are the promises of God. They are completely reliable, fully credible, because they are grounded in God's character, personally guaranteed by one "of the strictest and most sacred honour." As today's lesson illustrates, personal trust in the promises of God is at the very core of what it means to believe in God. Like Abraham, we live our lives and seek our destinies through faith in the God who always keeps His word.

B. Lesson Background

The first words of chapter 15 ("after these things") suggest a connection with the events of the preceding chapter—a connection that reaches far beyond mere chronological sequence. In fact, a careful reading of the text for this lesson reveals that much of what God said to Abraham was in direct response to and contrast with the events that had just transpired. The battle of the kings (chapter 14) is a classic example of how humans commonly seek to secure their destinies. The dynamics of raw power and unbridled greed, which fueled the conflict recorded there, are unfortunately typical of the forces that drive the human struggle to the "top of the ladder." Abraham, by contrast, had chosen a different way. He would live his life and seek his fulfillment not by force but by faith, not by self-interest but by submission to the will of the sovereign God. Chapter 15 illustrates how God honored this way of life.

I. Promise of an Heir (Genesis 15:1-6)

A. The Appearance of God (v. 1)

1. After these things the word of the LORD came unto Abram in a vision, saying, Fear not, Abram: I am thy shield, and thy exceeding great reward.

There is no way of knowing for certain how much time elapsed between the battle of the kings (chapter 14) and this appearance of God. As noted below, however, several factors in chapter 15 suggest a close connection between the two events. The Lord, who had spoken to Abraham on at least three prior occasions, came *in a vision* to offer words of encouragement.

Fear not, Abram. (Abram's name was later changed to Abraham, Genesis 17:5.) The *fear* of

Abraham that God sought to calm is best understood as a natural fear for his life. He had just returned from an armed conflict during which, for the sake of his nephew Lot, he had put his own life at risk. As the sobering reality of that settled upon him, he was reassured that God would protect him and provide for his needs.

The manner in which God addressed Abraham clearly demonstrates that the blessings He offered His servant were a direct response to the spiritually-minded way in which Abraham behaved during the battle of the kings. It is interesting to note, for example, that the Hebrew word for *shield* (*magen*, v. 1) by which God spoke of himself is an echo of Melchizedek's invocation of "the most high God," who "delivered" (*miggen*, 14:20) Abraham's enemies into his hands. It is as if God was intentionally confirming Melchizedek's blessing, which had attributed Abraham's victory to the power of God. In a similar fashion, God's assurance of *great reward* (v. 1) is clearly to be connected with Abraham's refusal to profit by the spoils of war (14:22-24). In fact, the very word designating the rejected spoils ("goods," 14:21) is employed by God to describe the "great substance" with which God would bless Abraham's descendants (15:14). All of this was designed to show Abraham that any sacrifice he had made out of loyalty to God would be more than recompensed by the even greater blessing of God. This promise likewise sustains God's children today as they sacrifice personal ambition and the desire for material gain to follow the way of the cross.

B. The Apprehension of Abraham (vv. 2, 3)

2, 3. And Abram said, Lord GOD, what wilt thou give me, seeing I go childless, and the steward of my house is this Eliezer of Damascus? And Abram said, Behold, to me thou hast given no seed: and, lo, one born in my house is mine heir.

The prospect of a sudden demise is, in itself, enough to trouble any person, but Abraham's anxiety was deepened by an even greater threat. It was the possibility of dying without a son to inherit his property and carry on his spiritual pilgrimage. In a patriarchal society, people lived their lives as part of an extended family, and all possessions, authority, and family line passed exclusively from father to son. In a very real sense, sons looked to their fathers for their identity and their livelihood, while fathers saw in their sons the means by which they extended themselves into the future. Because he was childless, Abraham had been denied this most important of all family relationships.

How to Say It

CHALDEES. *Kal*-deez.
ELIEZER. El-eye-*ee*-zer or Ee-ley-*ee*-zer.
EUPHRATES. U-*fray*-teez.
MAGEN (Hebrew). mah-gain
MELCHIZEDEK. Mel-*kiz*-eh-dek.
MIGGEN (Hebrew). mig-gen (*g* as in *get*)
TIGRIS. *Ty*-griss.

One born in my house is mine heir. The custom of the day dictated that, should a man die without a son, the oldest houseborn male servant would become heir to the family's estate. Abraham assumed this would be his lot, and that Eliezer of Damascus, who was such a servant in Abraham's house, would inherit all that was his.

C. The Answer of God (v. 4)

4. And, behold, the word of the LORD came unto him, saying, This shall not be thine heir; but he that shall come forth out of thine own bowels shall be thine heir.

God had promised Abraham that He would bring forth a great nation from him (see Genesis 12:2; 13:15, 16). Given the life circumstance of Abraham and Sarah, however, this must have seemed impossible. Their ages (at least seventy-five and sixty-five years old respectively) and Sarah's infertility seemed to doom them to a childless future. But human extremity can often be divine opportunity. In fact, a careful reading of Genesis suggests that God was providentially orchestrating the events of the patriarchs' lives for the purpose of teaching them to be less dependent upon themselves and more dependent upon Him. In each generation of Abraham's family, the covenant promise was moved forward by a son born to a woman who was temporarily barren (Isaac of Sarah, Jacob of Rebekah, and Joseph of Rachel). It is as if God was intentionally interrupting the normal procreation of the patriarchal family in an effort to demonstrate that their destiny lay not in what they could produce but in what God promised.

D. The Assurance of God (v. 5)

5. And he brought him forth abroad, and said, Look now toward heaven, and tell the stars, if thou be able to number them: and he said unto him, So shall thy seed be.

Sensitive to the still developing faith of Abraham, God sought to provide some assurance of His promise. So He took Abraham out into His world and instructed him to look up into the night sky and count the stars, if he could. As the stars seemed countless to Abraham's eye, so also would be the number of his descendants. This same comparison is used in Genesis 22:17; 26:4; and Exodus 32:13. The God whose promises would secure Abraham's future is the same God who "hung the stars in space." His power to fulfill His promises to Abraham and to us is as limitless as His power to create the universe.

E. The Response of Abraham (v. 6)

6. And he believed in the LORD; and he counted it to him for righteousness.

This is the first time "belief" is explicitly referred to in the Bible, and it is one of the most important. The Hebrew word translated *believed* primarily means "to support." The form of the word that is used here signifies "to hold as firm, to rest upon as firm," hence to "accept as true, recognize as valid." It is the word from which the English *amen* ("it shall be so") derives. When Abraham *believed* God, he said "Amen" to God's promise, fully trusting that "it would be so." In other words, he took God at His word. In response to this "faith," God *counted it to him for righteousness.* This means that God took Abraham's faith "into account," "reckoned" him as "just," and considered Abraham to be in "right relationship" with Him.

In Romans 4:3 and Galatians 3:6 the apostle Paul makes reference to this text to demonstrate that we are justified not by works of the law but by faith in Jesus Christ (Galatians 3:5-11). James also cites this text, stating that the faith of Abraham was "made perfect" in his willingness to offer up Isaac (James 2:17-24). In other words, though we are saved by faith apart from works of the law, a saving faith will naturally manifest itself in good works.

II. Promise of a Land (Genesis 15:7, 8)

A. A Promised Land (v. 7)

7. And he said unto him, I am the Lord that brought thee out of Ur of the Chaldees, to give thee this land to inherit it.

God's call of Abraham had set three prospects before him: (1) a land that God would show him; (2) a great nation that would emerge from him; and (3) a blessing that would be extended to all peoples through him and his descendants (Genesis 12:1-3). Abraham began his pilgrimage unsure of its ultimate destination. Having now migrated to Canaan he received assurance that this was the land that God had in mind (see also Genesis 13:14-18).

Ur of the Chaldees. Abraham's ancestors lived in Mesopotamia, a territory somewhere between the Tigris and Euphrates rivers. There is some debate among scholars as to the actual location of Ur of the Chaldees. But the most generally accepted identification of Ur of the Chaldees is with the great city of Ur located on the lower Euphrates River in southern Iraq. Though the exact location of Abraham's homeland remains somewhat of a mystery, the theology of his ancestors does not. It was similar to that of virtually all the peoples of the ancient Near Eastern world: "they served other gods" (Joshua 24:2). Out of a land of idol worshipers, God called Abraham to migrate to Canaan.

B. A Further Need for Reassurance (v. 8)

8. And he said, Lord GOD, whereby shall I know that I shall inherit it?

This was the request of a fledgling faith that had yet to reach full maturity. It was not so much a cry of doubt as it was a cry of weakness. Though God steadfastly resists any human attempt to "test" Him, the Scriptures demonstrate that He has on several occasions condescended to meet the human need for reassurance. He responded to Moses' desire to see his "glory" by showing him His "back" (Exodus 33:18-23). He ministered to Gideon's apprehension by offering him a series of "signs" (Judges 6:16—7:15). The reassurance God would offer to Abraham would come in the form of a formal covenant.

III. Promises Confirmed With a Covenant (Genesis 15:9-16)

A. Ritual Preparations (vv. 9-11)

9-11. And he said unto him, Take me a heifer of three years old, and a she goat of three years old, and a ram of three years old, and a turtledove, and a young pigeon. And he took unto him all these, and divided them in the midst, and laid each piece one against another: but the birds divided he not. And when the fowls came down upon the carcasses, Abram drove them away.

God's instructions to Abraham did not seem nearly as strange to him as they may seem to us. Evidence from Jeremiah 34:18-22 and a text from the ancient city of Mari suggest that the preparations and procedures followed by Abraham were regular features of the ancient custom of covenant-making. In fact, the Hebrew expression translated "make a covenant" (v. 18) literally means "cut a covenant," and may very well owe its origin to the practice of dividing some animal(s) between the two parties entering into the agreement. After placing the halves of the animal(s) in two rows the parties "passed between the parts" as a means of symbolically

visual 5

obligating themselves to the stipulations of the covenant. Apparently those who walked between the two portions of the bisected animal(s) invoked the same fate on themselves if they were unfaithful to the terms of the covenant. What is noteworthy in this account is that the Lord, in the form of a *smoking furnace, and a burning lamp* (v. 17), passed between the pieces, thereby voluntarily obligating himself to Abraham. In similar fashion God would later confirm His promise to Abraham by a sacred oath, swearing "by himself" to make good on His covenant promise (Genesis 22:16). By these condescending acts God demonstrated the level of His commitment to the promises He had made to Abraham.

B. Personal Preparation (v. 12)

12. And when the sun was going down, a deep sleep fell upon Abram; and, lo, a horror of great darkness fell upon him.

This is one of several times that the Old Testament refers to a *deep sleep* that came from God (Genesis 2:21; 1 Samuel 26:12; Job 4:13; 33:15; Isaiah 29:10). This seems to have been a kind of divinely induced trance upon the person rendering him temporarily unconscious. Comparisons with the verses cited above from the book of Job would suggest that what followed came to Abraham in a dream or vision. The nature of the *great darkness* that overwhelmed him is not explained. It may have been related to Abraham's anxiety over the appearance of God or the great difficulties Abraham's posterity would experience in Egypt (see next verse).

C. Historical Implications (vv. 13, 14)

13, 14. And he said unto Abram, Know of a surety that thy seed shall be a stranger in a land that is not theirs, and shall serve them; and they shall afflict them four hundred years; and also that nation, whom they shall serve, will I judge: and afterward shall they come out with great substance.

In this revelation God allowed Abraham to peer several hundred years into the future. The land of Canaan would be occupied by his descendants only after they had experienced a long period of servitude *in a land that is not theirs.* The land of which he spoke was undoubtedly Egypt. The precise length of time Israel is said to have spent in Egypt was 430 years, but here that number is rounded off to four hundred (compare Exodus 12:40; Acts 7:6). That Israel would be freed and come out with great substance was literally fulfilled in the Exodus experience (Exodus 12:34-36). The God who promises is Lord of the future. There is a sense in which history, itself, is the unfolding of His sovereign will.

MIXED BLESSINGS

Robert C. Shannon tells of a visit to Miskolc, Hungary a few years ago. The two hundred Christians with whom he worshiped there met in the former home of Anna Roth, who had begun the congregation in her home before World War II.

Anna Roth was a Christian Jew. When the Nazis began sending Hungarian Jews to concentration camps, they would exempt those who had converted to Christianity. An influential friend offered to provide Anna with exemption papers, but she refused. Thousands of her ethnic family were in those prisons, and they needed to hear about Jesus. She chose to go to prison so she could tell them, and she was never heard from again.

God promised Abraham many descendants, but said also that for four hundred years they would serve another nation and suffer affliction there. This must have left childless Abraham with mixed feelings—joy at the news of a family, but sorrow over the fate awaiting them.

There are few unmixed blessings in life, but the difficulties we encounter serve to help us appreciate the blessings more. As we struggle with trials, our spirits are given opportunity to turn to God. Calamitous circumstances can open the eyes of noble souls to the eternal values that God would have us see.   —C. R. B.

D. Personal Implications (v. 15)

15. And thou shalt go to thy fathers in peace; thou shalt be buried in a good old age.

Though Abraham would not live to witness the fulfillment of the covenant promise, his own life would be filled with God's goodness. Abraham's earthly existence would be characterized by *peace,* which carried with it the connotations of security, personal satisfaction, and fulfillment. The *good old age* that was promised turned out to be 175 years (Genesis 25:7) and was, itself, further evidence of God's blessing.

Abraham might have wished to take possession of Canaan in his own lifetime. But God's time and man's are not always the same. One of the demands of Abraham's faith was the necessity of "waiting upon the Lord," trusting in a promise that would not be totally fulfilled until his earthly life was long past. Similarly, Christians today await a promise of Christ's return that may, or may not, be fulfilled in our day.

E. Theological Implications (v. 16)

16. But in the fourth generation they shall come hither again: for the iniquity of the Amorites is not yet full.

The fourth generation is probably meant to parallel the four hundred years of verse 13. The reason why so much time must pass is explained in the phrase *for the iniquity of the Amorites is not yet full.* This important statement provides us theological insight into the Israelite conquest of Canaan. The campaign under Joshua predicted by verse 16 was not to be purely militaristic or nationalistic but was designed to execute God's judgment upon the inhabitants of Canaan for their sins. As He used the waters of the flood to punish a corrupt world, He would use the army of Israel to punish a corrupt nation. This would not happen for four hundred years, because it would take that long for the iniquity of the Amorites (a general term for the various people groups in Canaan) to reach a level that merited such judgment.

GOD'S SPECIALTY

God seems to specialize in redeeming apparently lost causes and irredeemable situations. Even though he was a very old man, Abraham found comfort in God's gift of a son and in the divine promise that his descendants would be returned to their land even though they would have to endure slavery in Egypt.

This is the story of the Bible. Earlier, when the human race had become so corrupt that God had to purify it by a devastating flood, He established Noah and his family as the channel for the renewal of humanity. More than a thousand years after Abraham's time Israel turned from God to idols. God accomplished His task of renewal by allowing a captivity in Babylon and then returning Israel to her homeland, purged of her idolatrous leanings.

Still later, God accomplished His great work of redemption by sending His Son to save us all. Even in this, God specialized in doing the impossible: He saved the infant Savior by sending Him to Egypt to escape Herod's wrath. When it was safe, God called His Son "out of Egypt" (Matthew 2:15) to return to Nazareth where He would be prepared for His redemptive mission. Through Jesus, God has provided the way for any who wish to return to His presence.

—C. R. B.

Conclusion

A. "Promises, Promises"

A promise is only as good as the person who makes it. For this reason, we have learned to take most promises of men with a grain of salt. Life has taught us that "promises are made to be broken." We have been both victim and victimizer in the underhanded business of the unkept word. This is at least one reason why some people are so skeptical of the promises of God. After all, we have broken so many of our promises to Him, how can we ever expect Him to keep the ones He has made to us?

In the face of this human skepticism comes a clear and powerful affirmation of Scripture: the God who made us and who has offered us eternal life in Jesus Christ is a God who always keeps His word (see Isaiah 45:23; Jeremiah 33:20, 21; Hebrews 6:13-20). God's promises are grounded in His character. He has the absolute ability and uncompromising integrity to fulfill them. We can, therefore, stake our eternal destinies upon them. Like Abraham of old, we can believe in a God who always keeps His word.

B. Let Us Pray

O God of holiness and truth, we bow before You in full confidence that Your will will be done. And to Your promises we say in the name of Christ, "Amen, it shall be so."

C. Thought to Remember

Our lives have meaning and our destinies are secured when we "believe God," when we "take Him at His word."-

Learning by Doing

This page contains an alternate lesson plan emphasizing learning activities. Classes desiring such student involvement will find these suggestions helpful.

Learning Goals

This lesson will help the students:
1. Summarize God's promise to Abram.
2. Explain how the promise was fulfilled.
3. Express their own faith in God.

Into the Lesson

As class members arrive, greet each one by saying, "Thanks for joining us today. Your reward will be very great." Refuse to give any details of the "reward," even if asked.

When it is time to begin, ask the class members what they thought when you told them they would receive a reward. If they were like Abram (better known as Abraham) they wanted to know what the reward would be. When God told him, "Your reward will be very great," Abraham said, "What will You give me?" This lesson will answer Abraham's question, and the students will discover what their reward is.

Into the Word

First, read Genesis 12:1-3 aloud. Then ask the students to summarize God's promise to Abraham. Write the features of the promise on the board as the students call them out. These should be noted:
1. God would show him a land,
2. A great nation would arise from him,
3. All nations would be blessed through him.
Now have Genesis 15:1-18 read aloud. The puzzle shown here is based on this text. Give each student a copy, without answers, and allot ten minutes for them to complete it.

Down

1. God promised that one of Abram's own offspring would be his _____ . (heir)
2. Their iniquity was "not yet full." (Amorites)
3. Abram's seed would be as these. (stars)
4. As the sun went down, this great fear fell on Abram. (horror)
7. Abram's descendants would serve, that is, be _____ to another nation for many years. (enslaved)
8. Abram did this to the animals. (divided)
9. A deep _____ fell upon Abram. (sleep)

Across

3. God promised to be Abram's _____ and great reward. (shield)
5. God said this would be very great. (reward)
6. The Lord called Abram to Canaan so he could inherit, that is, _____ it. (possess)
8. At sunset, a horror of great _____ fell on Abram. (darkness)
10. Because Abram did this, it was credited to him as righteousness. (believed)
11. Abram's descendants would occupy the land from this river to the Euphrates. (Egypt)
12. One of these was part of the covenant sacrifice. (heifer)

Review the answers to the puzzle and use information from the commentary section as needed to clarify the event in today's text.

Into Life

Compare the promises in chapter 15 with those of chapter 12. Point out that each promise was fulfilled. The nation of Israel arose from Abraham. After their bondage in Egypt, they possessed the land of Canaan. Through Israel came Jesus, and in Him all people are blessed. With faith like Abraham's, we too can be credited with righteousness. (This is the reward God has for us. Read aloud Romans 4:3, 20-25.)

Distribute index cards to the class. Have Hebrews 6:13-20 read aloud, and note that God always keeps His promises. Let the students mention some of God's promises. Then ask them to complete the following sentence on their cards:

I believe in God and take Him at His word to—

Let's Talk It Over

The questions on this page are designed to encourage review of the lesson Scriptures and to promote discussion of the lesson by the class. The answers provided are only discussion starters. Let your class talk it over from there.

1. God's exhortation, "Fear not, Abram," is one in which we could appropriately substitute our own names. Why is this so?.

Causes for fear abound in our day. International tensions tend to make us fearful. War has always been an alarming prospect for human beings, but in this nuclear age it is even more so. Economic uncertainty generates fear. We become edgy at the thought of unemployment, rising prices, and tax increases. If we are parents, we probably feel some fear for our children as they face a terrible array of temptations. Will they fall prey to the lure of drugs or alcohol, sexual promiscuity, or vandalism and crime? As Christians we may experience some fearfulness at the growing antiChristian bias in our society. In all of these instances, God is surely trying to tell us, "Fear not. Trust me, for I am able to lead you safely through these hazards."

2. Abram was told to look to the stars for assurance of God's faithfulness regarding Abraham's posterity. What benefit can we gain from gazing at the stars?

Our lives on earth are marked by change. We are born, we live, and we die. But the stars in their heavenly patterns continue as they have throughout history, and they testify to the changelessness of their Creator. In this we take great comfort. It might be beneficial to us to follow God's instruction to Abraham and attempt to count the stars we can see. The exercise can remind us of how the once-childless patriarch has ultimately been blessed with a countless number of descendants (see Galatians 3:27, 29). Our assurance that God will keep those promises that we have embraced through Jesus Christ can thereby be strengthened.

3. Abraham's faith was a matter of accepting God's word as true. Why do we need an emphasis on this kind of faith today?

It is appropriate here to note what John wrote in 1 John 5:9, 10b: "If we receive the witness of men, the witness of God is greater: for this is the witness of God which he hath testified of his Son. . . . He that believeth not God hath made him a liar; because he believeth not the record that God gave of his Son." God has given us His witness or testimony in the Bible concerning His Son Jesus Christ, and we need to accept it as true. Those who deny it or seek to explain it away are guilty of making God out to be a liar. Others, not content with the testimony of Scripture alone, have embraced a faith of their own making. They claim to believe in God and Jesus Christ, but their faith is a mixture of a few Bible concepts, some positive thinking, popular theology, superstition, and the like. This is not a genuine Biblical faith.

4. What value can there be in acknowledging to God the weakness of our faith?

Perhaps we have been able to identify with the father who cried out to Jesus, "Lord, I believe; help thou mine unbelief" (Mark 9:24). Surely God understands those moments when our faith is somewhat shaken; surely He is sympathetic toward our human weakness. By admitting our need for reassurance, we cultivate an open relationship with Him that can lead to our growth in faith and truth. Of course, we should not use this admission as an excuse for spiritual indolence. If our faith is weak, then we should diligently seek through study of the Scriptures to restore it to health and strength. We could speak of a "prescription for a sick faith" in the words of Romans 10:17: "Faith cometh by hearing, and hearing by the word of God."

5. How would it strengthen our faith in God's promises if we were to be more faithful in keeping our promises to Him?

The lesson writer wisely observes that since "we have broken so many of our promises to Him, how can we ever expect Him to keep the ones He has made to us?" Our lack of faithfulness may make us question whether or not He will be faithful to us. Paul assured us in 2 Timothy 2:13 that "if we are faithless, he will remain faithful, for he cannot disown himself" (*New International Version*). It is a relief to know that God does not waver in keeping His promises. But how much better it is for our faith when we follow through with our commitments. If we have committed ourselves to prayer, let us pray. If we have promised to be faithful in worship attendance, let us follow through. If we have stated our intention to rid ourselves of certain unspiritual habits, let us do it.

Sarai Attempts to Manipulate Events

DEVOTIONAL READING: Isaiah 55:8, 9.

LESSON SCRIPTURE: Genesis 16.

PRINTED TEXT: Genesis 16:1-4, 11-16.

Genesis 16:1-4, 11-16

1 Now Sarai, Abram's wife, bare him no children: and she had a handmaid, an Egyptian, whose name was Hagar.

2 And Sarai said unto Abram, Behold now, the LORD hath restrained me from bearing: I pray thee, go in unto my maid; it may be that I may obtain children by her. And Abram hearkened to the voice of Sarai.

3 And Sarai, Abram's wife, took Hagar her maid the Egyptian, after Abram had dwelt ten years in the land of Canaan, and gave her to her husband Abram to be his wife.

4 And he went in unto Hagar, and she conceived: and when she saw that she had conceived, her mistress was despised in her eyes.

11 And the angel of the LORD said unto her, Behold, thou art with child, and shalt bear a son, and shalt call his name Ishmael; because the LORD hath heard thy affliction.

12 And he will be a wild man; his hand will be against every man, and every man's hand against him: and he shall dwell in the presence of all his brethren.

13 And she called the name of the LORD that spake unto her, Thou God seest me: for she said, Have I also here looked after him that seeth me?

14 Wherefore the well was called Beerlahairoi: behold, it is between Kadesh and Bered.

15 And Hagar bare Abram a son: and Abram called his son's name, which Hagar bare, Ishmael.

16 And Abram was fourscore and six years old, when Hagar bare Ishmael to Abram.

GOLDEN TEXT: Sarai said unto Abram, Behold now, the LORD hath restrained me from bearing: I pray thee, go in unto my maid; it may be that I may obtain children by her.—Genesis 16:2.

Lesson Aims

After this lesson, each student should:

1. Understand that humans are not always able to perceive the meaning of the events that God has willed.

2. Recognize the dangers of trying to manipulate events to fulfill one's personal agenda.

3. Learn to "wait upon the Lord" to fulfill His promises in the way that He chooses.

Lesson Outline

INTRODUCTION
  A. "Patience Is a Virtue"
  B. Lesson Background
I. SARAH'S OFFER TO ABRAHAM (Genesis 16:1-4)
  A. Sarah and Her Handmaid (v. 1)
  B. The Barrenness of Sarah (v. 2a)
  C. The Offer of Hagar (vv. 2b, 3)
      Born of Despair
  D. Hagar's Contempt for Sarah (v. 4)
II. THE LORD'S COMPASSION ON HAGAR (Genesis 16:11-16)
  A. Announcement of Ishmael's Birth (v. 11)
  B. Prediction of Ishmael's Future (v. 12)
  C. Hagar's Response to God's Promise (vv. 13, 14)
      The God Who Sees
  D. The Birth of Ishmael (vv. 15, 16)
CONCLUSION
  A. Trust God
  B. Let us Pray
  C. Thought to Remember

Display visual 6 of the visuals packet and refer to it when appropriate. The visual is shown on page 53.

Introduction

A. "Patience Is a Virtue"

If "patience is a virtue" it is one that modern man has lost. In this up-to-the-minute world there are very few things for which we are willing to wait. One might characterize the "now" generation as one that "hatches eggs with a blow torch." It seems that we cannot wait for things to take their natural course. Perhaps the fitting symbol for our time is the instant camera. Push the button, out comes the picture—so typical of our passion for having things "right now." Somewhere in our headlong rush into the future, we have forgotten how to wait.

Sometimes people even grow impatient with God. Because He does not act in a manner or at a time they think appropriate, they begin to wonder if He will act at all. They interpret His "slowness" to act as His inability or unwillingness to act. Delay (by human standards) in the fulfillment of God's promises can lead to doubt over the fulfillment of God's promises. Such would seem to be the case with Sarai (Sarah).

B. Lesson Background

A decade had passed since God had called Abram (Abraham) and had promised to make of him a "great nation" (Genesis 12:2). Though he had been reassured that his "seed" would be as innumerable as the stars (Genesis 15:5) he had yet to father his first son. Sarah's infertility and advanced age (now about seventy-five years) convinced her and Abraham that she would never bear the child of promise. Desperately wanting to see the Lord's promise of a son come true, yet convinced that life's circumstances stood in the way, they acted to take things out of God's hands and help them along. What followed is a classic example of the problems created when God's children "second guess" Him and substitute their own agenda for His.

I. Sarah's Offer to Abraham (Genesis 16:1-4)

A. Sarah and Her Handmaid (v. 1)

1. Now Sarai, Abram's wife, bare him no children: and she had a handmaid, an Egyptian, whose name was Hagar.

This verse is summary in character and fits naturally with the following three verses. In ancient times, women of standing often were assigned their own personal servants (see Genesis 29:24, 29). Such was the Egyptian maiden *Hagar* to Sarah. *Hagar* was probably among the servants given Abraham by Pharoah during the brief time that Abraham and Sarah dwelt in Egypt (12:16). *Hagar* is not an Egyptian name, but Hebrew meaning "flight, fleeing." Some think this name was given her to commemorate Abraham and Sarah's hasty departure from Egypt (12:20). Others think the name was given her after her flight from her angry mistress (16:6).

B. The Barrenness of Sarah (v. 2a)

2a. And Sarai said unto Abram, Behold now, the Lord hath restrained me from bearing.

According to the Bible, God "opens" and "closes" or "shuts" wombs (Genesis 25:21; 29:31;

30:22; 20:18; 1 Samuel 1:5, 6), and children are God's "gifts" to parents (Genesis 33:4, 5; 48:8, 9; Psalm 127:3-5). Thus, when Sarah spoke of her infertility, it was natural for her to say, *the Lord hath restrained me from bearing.* Some interpreters infer from this that all fertility and infertility today are the result of the direct intervention of God. A closer look at the Biblical material, however, reveals an alternative explanation. In each of the above examples of infertility there were extenuating circumstances that might account for the Lord's intervention.

First to be noted is that these incidents involved not just any family or any child. All of the Genesis texts concern the chosen family, and the women in question were the mothers of some key child in the unfolding of the covenant promise (Sarah—Isaac, Rebekah—Jacob and Esau, Rachel—Joseph). It would seem no accident that three successive generations of the line of Abraham were perpetuated through women who were temporarily barren. God was directly intervening in the natural reproduction process for some special agenda. We would suggest that God was intentionally interrupting the normal procreation of this family to show that their future lay not in what they could produce but in what He promised.

Other, more specific, purposes may be found in Genesis 20:17, 18 where God protected Sarah from defilement by Abimelech, or in Genesis 29:30, 31 where He intervened to counteract Jacob's favoritism shown to Rachel over Leah. The latter was also true in the case of Hannah and Peninnah, wives of Elkanah (1 Samuel 1:1-6). The prophet Samuel was born eventually to Hannah. In other words, while each of these cases of barrenness was indeed directly caused by God, there were special circumstances involved that had implications that reached far beyond the barren couple. Something larger was at stake—the unfolding of the very purpose and will of God. The real lesson to be learned from these texts is not that God personally intervenes in every conception, but that He was in control of the destiny of the chosen family. The opening and closing of wombs was simply one of the many ways He demonstrated this. Thus, while all children should be thought of as God's "gifts," the fertility or infertility of a couple today need not be explained necessarily in terms of God's direct intervention.

C. The Offer of Hagar (vv. 2b, 3)

2b, 3. I pray thee, go in unto my maid; it may be that I may obtain children by her. And Abram hearkened to the voice of Sarai. And Sarai, Abram's wife, took Hagar her maid the Egyptian, after Abram had dwelt ten years in the land of Canaan, and gave her to her husband Abram to be his wife.

In the patriarchal culture in which Sarah and Abraham lived, the infertility of a wife was a serious matter. More than a mere personal disappointment to the childless couple, childlessness threatened the very perpetuation of the political and economic structure of their society. Only sons could inherit their father's property. Widows were cared for by the inheritance that their sons received. A marriage that failed to produce a son would ordinarily result in a father with no heir and a mother with no means of financial support.

In order to end a couple's childlessness, a wife could provide a surrogate wife for her husband whereby a son and heir might be raised up to him. Thus when Sarah offered Hagar to Abraham, she was acting according to the custom of her day. Since Hagar belonged to Sarah, Hagar's baby also would belong to Sarah. Rachel would later offer her servant to Jacob for the same purpose (see Genesis 30:3-8).

It should be noted that though the Bible does not overtly condemn the polygamy and surrogate wifedom of the patriarchs, it does expose the potential complications of such relationships. This particular union resulted in tension between Sarah and Hagar, Sarah and Abraham, and Ishmael and Isaac. Of even greater significance for the story of the patriarchs, it had the potential to interfere with the unfolding of the covenant promise itself, by creating a competitor to the true heir (Isaac) that God had in mind.

BORN OF DESPAIR

Despair often leads us to unwise actions and choices. One area in which this is true is the selection of a mate. Recognizing this, a Miami attorney has offered for a number of years a class for women who despair of ever meeting "Mr. Right." The main emphases of the course are: love and marriage are too important to be left to chance; competition is fierce; and women

---

How to Say It

ABIMELECH.   Uh-*bim*-uh-lek.
BEER-LAHAI-ROI (Hebrew).   *Be*-er-luh-*high*-roy (strong accent on *high*).
ELKANAH.   *El*-kuh-nuh or El-*kay*-nuh.
HAGAR.   *Hay*-gar.
ISHMAEL.   *Ish*-may-el.
PENINNAH.   Pe-*nin*-uh.
SARAI.   *Say*-rye.

shouldn't expect magic. In other words, a person's mental attitude is important in finding a mate, and effort is required. A woman who desperately "chases" a man may get one, but not necessarily one who will be good for her. All of this is equally true for men, of course.

Even though God had promised Abraham a son, Sarah was convinced that she could never have a child. In despair, she persuaded her husband to take her servant girl Hagar in the hope that children might come from that union. So intensely was Sarah "chasing" the goal of a child that she lost sight of the real goal she should have had—pleasing God.

May the goal of each of us be to please God and to further His will. Wanting what is right, may we never succumb to the temptation to bring it about in an inappropriate way. —C. R. B.

D. Hagar's Contempt for Sarah (v. 4)

4. And he went in unto Hagar, and she conceived: and when she saw that she had conceived, her mistress was despised in her eyes.

The result of Abraham's union with Hagar was not so satisfying as Sarah had hoped. When Hagar knew that she was pregnant, *her mistress was despised in her eyes.* The idea conveyed by the phrase is that Hagar felt that her conception elevated her to a position above Sarah. She may have even desired to displace Sarah as Abraham's wife (compare Proverbs 30:21-23). We are not told how Hagar showed that she despised her mistress. But it is easy to imagine that she became insolent and neglected her duties.

II. The Lord's Compassion on Hagar (Genesis 16:11-16)

In verses 5-11, we learn of the further complications of this less-than-desirable arrangement. The tension between Sarah and Hagar spilled over into tension between Sarah and Abraham. When Sarah gave Hagar to Abraham as a concubine, she relinquished her authority over her handmaid to her husband. This explains why Sarah held Abraham responsible for the way Hagar was treating her (Genesis 6:5). As a solution to the crisis, Abraham, in turn, returned Hagar to Sarah, reducing her again to the status of a servant. All of this was in accordance with what we know of the legal procedures of the ancient Near Eastern world.

Hagar, again under Sarah's authority, became the victim of abuse. We do not know what form Sarah's harsh treatment of Hagar took; but it was such that Hagar decided to flee, presumably to her native Egypt. On the way she was encountered by the "angel of the Lord" (v. 7) at an oasis

in Shur, a wilderness on the northeastern frontier of Egypt. The angel first ordered her to return to her mistress, then offered her reassurance that the child she was carrying would be but one of many who would descend from her.

This promise is of special significance in view of the circumstances that had produced this particular child. Ancient custom mandated that children who were born to a husband by the wife's handmaid legally belonged to the wife. This is precisely the meaning of the statement that Sarah made when she offered Hagar to Abraham: "it may be that I may obtain children by her" (v. 2). The words of the angel now indicated that that would not be the case, but that the child would be Hagar's descendant ("seed," v. 10), the first of a "multitude." This, it would seem, anticipated the eventual departure of Hagar and Ishmael from Abraham's house to establish a separate nation of their own (Genesis 21:12-21; 25:12-17).

A. Announcement of Ishmael's Birth (v. 11)

11. And the angel of the LORD said unto her, Behold, thou art with child, and shalt bear a son, and shalt call his name Ishmael; because the Lord hath heard thy affliction.

The expression *angel of the Lord* refers to some "messenger" or "agent" who proclaims God's word or does His bidding. In some contexts it refers to some "being," other than God, who appeared in human form to the patriarchs. Such was the case later when "three men" appeared at Abraham's tent, two of whom went on toward Sodom and were later identified as "angels" (Genesis 18:2, 22; 19:1). In Hagar's case, the expression may refer to the Lord himself in some human form, as verse 13 might imply ("the Lord that spake unto her"). Whoever "the angel of the Lord" was here, his purpose was to deliver God's message of hope and encouragement to a troubled Hagar.

Shalt call his name Ishmael. In ancient times names had meaning and significance beyond their function of identifying one person from another. They often owed their origin to some unusual circumstance surrounding the child's birth, some outstanding characteristic that the child displayed, or some great expectation that their parents had for the child. *Ishmael* is just such a name. It means "God shall hear," or "God hears," and owes its origin to God's "hearing" Hagar's cry of distress. This is but one of three places in this brief narrative where a person or place receives a name on the basis of some special event (see also verses 13 and 14).

The Lord hath heard thy affliction. God's compassionate response to what Hagar was suffering is but one of several examples found in the Bible where God intervened to assist a woman who had become a victim of circumstances beyond her control. In the next generation of the covenant family, for example, God showed compassion on Leah, the unwanted and unloved wife of Jacob, by enabling her to bear children while her sister and rival Rachel could not (Genesis 29:31). Though Hagar was not guiltless in the process that led to her desperate situation, there is a sense in which she was but a helpless pawn in a scheme that neither she nor God ever intended to happen. Sensitive to this, God intervened on her behalf.

B. Prediction of Ishmael's Future
(v. 12)

12. And he will be a wild man; his hand will be against every man, and every man's hand against him: and he shall dwell in the presence of all his brethren.

The English translation of this verse needs to be clarified if we are to appreciate the exact intent of this prediction. The Hebrew text literally predicts that Ishmael "will be a wild donkey of a man." The phrase is meant to refer to one who is wild and untamable, not unlike some of the Bedouin tribes who descended from Ishmael. *His hand will be against every man . . . against him* is a common phrase that denotes violence and injury. The phrase translated *in the presence of,* literally means "in front" or "against the face of" and signifies "in defiance/disregard of." In other words, this final phrase simply extends the thought of that which precedes it and describes Ishmael as one who would live in open hostility to his kinsmen. The same is later predicted of his descendants, the Ishmaelites, who "lived in hostility toward all their brothers" (Genesis 25:18, *New International Version*). Some scholars understand Ishmael to be the father of the Arabic peoples and his *brethren* to be the descendants of Isaac (the Israelites), and see in this statement a prediction of struggle between these two people groups.

C. Hagar's Response to God's Promise
(vv. 13, 14)

13, 14. And she called the name of the LORD that spake unto her, Thou God seest me: for she said, Have I also here looked after him that seeth me? Wherefore the well was called Beer-lahai-roi: behold, it is between Kadesh and Bered.

The second person given a name from this episode was God himself. Hagar, convinced that

visual 6

she had actually looked upon the God who had taken note of her, named Him *El-roi,* literally, "the God who sees (me)" or "God who is seen (appears)." *Have I also here looked after him that seeth me?* The intent of the original language is difficult to grasp. Hagar may have been either praising God for having acknowledged her affliction or, as some scholars contend, expressing surprise at having seen God and still surviving to tell of it. The idea that the person who sees God could not survive is quite prevalent in Scripture (Genesis 32:30; Exodus 19:21; 33:20; Judges 6:22, 23; 13:22, 23). The oasis *Beer-lahai-roi* (literally, "well of living seeing" or "well of the Living One who sees") also owes its name to this divine-human encounter. The exact location of this site is unknown.

THE GOD WHO SEES

Amelie Magne, a Frenchwoman, had not received any mail for several months. She assumed that it was because of postal strikes and bad winter weather. In truth, the post office thought she was dead!

Amelie's mail carrier, in training his replacement, had mistakenly pointed to her house and said, "The woman who lived there died recently." The mistake caused all kinds of problems. She has had to present official documents to firms she does business with to prove she is alive. Their computers find it difficult to assimilate contradictory information. Amelie's bank demanded that her husband verify her death with a death certificate, but he has been dead for more than ten years!

When Hagar fled to escape Sarah's harsh treatment of her, she found refuge at a spring in the desert. But it seemed that no one cared whether she was alive. It certainly seemed that Abraham and Sarah, the people who had been her "family," did not care. So it was a great comfort to her when the angel of the Lord pronounced God's blessing upon her. Her delighted response was, "You are a God who sees!"

No matter how desolate our circumstances, or how little recognition other people give to our plight, we can rejoice in the knowledge that we have a God who sees our predicament and will bless us even in the midst of it.   —C. R. B.

D. The Birth of Ishmael (vv. 15, 16)

15, 16. And Hagar bare Abram a son: and Abram called his son's name, which Hagar bare, Ishmael. And Abram was fourscore and six years old, when Hagar bare Ishmael to Abram.

This epilogue emphasizes Abraham's responsibility for Ishmael, which Hagar's return made explicit. Legally speaking, Ishmael was the child of Sarah and Abraham and a potential heir to Abraham's estate. This, of course, was never the intent of God, and it posed a threat to the divine will that a child of Abraham and Sarah (Isaac) be exclusive heir to Abraham's estate and the covenant promise. The undoing of this ill-advised initiative by Sarah would later result in a heart-wrenching separation of Ishmael from the family of Abraham (Genesis 21:8-21).

And Abram called his son's name, which Hagar bare, Ishmael. The angel had told Hagar that she would name the child, but here we learn that Abraham did the actual naming. It was the custom for the father to name the children (Genesis 5:3; 21:3), but this was not always the case (Genesis 30:5-8). It would seem that Abraham was aware of Hagar's encounter with the angel and consented to Hagar's wish to give the child the name revealed by the angel.

Abraham, having lived eleven years in the promised land, was eighty-six years old when Ishmael was born (Genesis 16:3). For the foreseeable future Abraham and Sarah would live under the impression that the action they had taken had indeed provided them the son and heir whom God had promised. Thirteen more years would pass, a full twenty-four years since he had entered Canaan, before Abraham would finally learn how God intended to fulfill His promise to make of Abraham a great nation.

Conclusion

A. Trust God

When God called Abraham to leave his country and go to a land He would show him, God promised to make of Abraham a great nation (Genesis 12:2). The promise of a multitude of descendants was repeated to him on two other occasions before the incident in today's text (13:16; 15:5). At no time did God tell Abraham when the promise would be fulfilled.

Abraham had to wait till he was eighty-six years old to become a father at all, and even then the child (resulting from his union with Hagar) was not the child that God had in mind. It was not until Abraham was one hundred years old, some twenty-five years after entering the promised land, that he saw the first generation of the "great nation" that would come from him (Genesis 12:4; 21:5). We later learn that it was all part of a "test" of faith that would culminate in the command to sacrifice Isaac at Moriah (Genesis 22). Through his faith and patience, Abraham learned that his destiny lay not in what was promised but in the God who made the promise (Genesis 22:14, Hebrews 6:15).

We who are Christians have been given promises by the Lord. Jesus has promised that our Father will provide His children with the physical necessities of life (Matthew 6:25-33); let us, therefore, not be anxious about them to the point that we invest nearly all of our time and energy acquiring material things. Our Lord has promised to be with us as we follow His command to serve Him (Matthew 28:20); let us never doubt it. Preeminently, Jesus has promised His disciples that one day He will return to take them to be with Him (John 14:3). May we labor for Him faithfully while we wait for Him to fulfill His promise. Let us trust God!

B. Let Us Pray

Eternal God, be patient with our impatience. Teach us to measure time and events not by the standard of expediency, but by the standard of eternity. Help us to continue hoping, trusting, and serving You till Jesus comes again. In His name, amen.

C. Thought to Remember

God will fulfill His promises. Trust Him.

Learning by Doing

*This page contains an alternate lesson plan emphasizing learning activities. Classes
desiring such student involvement will find these suggestions helpful.*

Learning Goals

This lesson will help the students:

1. See the need for patience as they await the fulfillment of the Lord's promise to return.

2. Express confidence in God, who sees His peoples' difficulties and gives them aid.

Into the Lesson

Give each student a copy of this coded message. Ask them to work with others to decipher it.

Ω◻↕▼ ●♥ ▼†☆ ✗●→✚

On each copy, give a different clue, such as "Ω=w," "There are two Os and two Ts," and "✗=L." Provide other clues as you choose in order to help the students discover the message: "Wait on the Lord."

After several minutes, ask a volunteer to read the message aloud. Discuss what it means to "wait on the Lord." Perhaps one or two will share experiences when patience was required and the student did or did not exercise patience. Observe that today's lesson tells of a time when Abraham and Sarah failed to exhibit this virtue.

Into the Word

Review last week's lesson and the promise God made Abraham concerning an heir. Point out that ten years had passed since Abraham and Sarah had entered the promised land, and still they had no children. Sarah's barren condition must have seemed an insurmountable obstacle. Indeed, by human ability it was. Yet they waited patiently for a child. This fact is to their credit and must not be overlooked. Even their plan revealed in today's text seems more a matter of their accommodating themselves to the standards of the surrounding culture than it does their disbelieving God's promise.

Read Genesis 16 aloud. Then divide the class into groups of four to six. To half of the groups, distribute copies of the following questions and ask the groups to answer them.

1. What was the name of Sarah's maid? (Hagar)

2. How did Sarah suggest Abraham could have a child? (By her maid Hagar.)

3. What was Hagar's attitude toward Sarah after Hagar conceived? (She despised Sarah.)

4. What did Hagar do when Sarah treated her harshly? (She fled.)

5. When the angel of the Lord spoke to Hagar, what did he tell her? (See verses 11, 12.)

6. What did Hagar call God? (A God who sees.)

7. What was Hagar's son named? (Ishmael)

Give a copy of the following chart to each group in the other half of the class. Omit the words in parentheses and allow room for answers. Ask these groups to compare Abraham and Sarah's situation with our own by completing the chart.

	Abraham and Sarah	Christians
the promise	(a son)	1 Thessalonians 4:16, 17 (the Lord's return)
the present reality	(Sarah barren)	2 Peter 3:9 (the return delayed)
the temptation	(use worldly means)	2 Peter 3:3, 4; Romans 12:1, 2 (abandon faith; be like the world)

Review the answers of the first groups. Use material from the commentary section as needed to clarify the students' understanding of this text. Then lead a discussion based on the charts completed by the other groups. Stress our need to be patient and confident that the Lord will fulfill all His promises to us, including His promise to return.

Into Life

Today's text clearly teaches that God knows what is transpiring in our lives. Hagar said, "You are the God who sees." God was aware of the difficulties she was experiencing, and He gave her encouragement. He was just as aware of Abraham and Sarah's childlessness, and in His own time He would give them the child they desired. We can be sure that God knows and cares about the difficulties we face.

Give each student an index card with the following written on it:

"You are a God who sees. I know You see my own difficulties, and I trust You to help when . . . ." Allow the students a few minutes to complete their cards. Ask them to look at their cards this week to remind themselves of God's care.

Let's Talk It Over

The questions on this page are designed to encourage review of the lesson Scriptures and to promote discussion of the lesson by the class. The answers provided are only discussion starters. Let your class talk it over from there.

1. What are some specific circumstances in which we may become impatient with God?

If we have been praying for the conversion of a family member or a dear friend, we may grow impatient with God over what we perceive as His slowness in awakening our loved one to his or her spiritual need. But we dare not forget that God will not violate a person's free will to choose Him or to reject Him. Another area where impatience develops is in connection with an illness or other physical affliction. We grow restless at the absence of a healing. However, we must recognize the possibility that God desires to work His will through the illness, as He did through Paul's "thorn in the flesh" (2 Corinthians 12:7-10). We may also grow impatient when our prayers for the resolving of a personal problem are unanswered. We may be powerless to change the situation, so we call upon the Lord to bring His divine power to bear upon it. It is difficult to wait on His timing, but we must.

2. Abraham's taking Hagar as a surrogate wife was in harmony with the laws and customs of the time. Did this make it right in God's sight? How does this situation apply to our dealing with the laws and customs of our time?

Although God did not punish Abraham and Sarah for the step they took, He did not use their arrangement as the means by which He provided the promised son. Even though He did not visit direct punishment upon the couple, their household was beset by friction as a result of their choice. Today we recognize that even if a certain practice is permitted by law and accepted by custom, that does not make it right in God's sight. Living together by unmarried couples is but one example. Name others.

3. Our present text is one of those recorded in Genesis that demonstrate the evils of polygamy. What are some of the evils that are demonstrated?

The Genesis record reveals that serious tensions arise in families in which polygamy is practiced. Of course, we also read there of tensions in a monogamous family, such as that of Isaac's. However, the additional conflicts that arise from wives vying for the attention of the same husband, or from sons of different mothers exhibiting jealousy toward one another, are clearly shown. In our own time we are aware of the challenge of living harmoniously within a family consisting of one husband, one wife, and the children born of their union. How much more complex and confusing these relationships would be if other wives and their offspring were to be added in a polygamous arrangement! Surely God has been wise and gracious to us in commanding monogamy.

4. When we consider the circumstances of Ishmael's birth and childhood, we can appreciate how he would become a wild man. How do Ishmael's experiences illustrate the way young people today often go "wild"?

Ishmael must have felt the pain of rejection. He would have felt it first from Sarah, who, as Abraham's wife, must have been a person of great importance to him. Later, he would know the rejection of being sent away from his father and his half-brother Isaac. Today we have many Ishmaels who experience rejection and confusion when their homes are torn by divorce. Others are members of families that remain intact, but the parents' pursuit of money, position, and pleasure rules out the possibility of vital communication between them and their children. Such rejection opens the door to illicit sex, alcohol and drug abuse, and anti-social behavior.

5. Hagar's name for the Lord —"the God who sees me"—is particularly appealing. Why may we want to keep this title in mind?

The promise in Psalm 34:15 comes to mind here: "The eyes of the Lord are upon the righteous, and his ears are open unto their cry." It is comforting to realize that when we are hurting, confused, and fearful, the Lord's eyes are upon us. Hagar was pregnant, poor, alone, and, no doubt, frightened. It must have been very assuring for her to know that she was not alone and on her own after all. We too may feel at times that we are facing severe crises on our own. Other human beings may offer help and encouragement, but we are certain that they cannot fully appreciate how helpless we feel. Then we can remember "the God who sees me" and find assurance that we also are not really on our own.

God's Covenant With Abraham

DEVOTIONAL READING: Galatians 3:6-9.

LESSON SCRIPTURE: Genesis 17.

PRINTED TEXT: Genesis 17:1-14.

Genesis 17:1-14

1 And when Abram was ninety years old and nine, the LORD appeared to Abram, and said unto him, I am the Almighty God; walk before me, and be thou perfect.

2 And I will make my covenant between me and thee, and will multiply thee exceedingly.

3 And Abram fell on his face: and God talked with him, saying,

4 As for me, behold, my covenant is with thee, and thou shalt be a father of many nations.

5 Neither shall thy name any more be called Abram, but thy name shall be Abraham; for a father of many nations have I made thee.

6 And I will make thee exceeding fruitful, and I will make nations of thee, and kings shall come out of thee.

7 And I will establish my covenant between me and thee and thy seed after thee in their generations, for an everlasting covenant, to be a God unto thee and to thy seed after thee.

8 And I will give unto thee, and to thy seed after thee, the land wherein thou art a stranger, all the land of Canaan, for an everlasting possession; and I will be their God.

9 And God said unto Abraham, Thou shalt keep my covenant therefore, thou, and thy seed after thee in their generations.

10 This is my covenant, which ye shall keep, between me and you and thy seed after thee; Every man child among you shall be circumcised.

11 And ye shall circumcise the flesh of your foreskin; and it shall be a token of the covenant betwixt me and you.

12 And he that is eight days old shall be circumcised among you, every man child in your generations, he that is born in the house, or bought with money of any stranger, which is not of thy seed.

13 He that is born in thy house, and he that is bought with thy money, must needs be circumcised: and my covenant shall be in your flesh for an everlasting covenant.

14 And the uncircumcised man child whose flesh of his foreskin is not circumcised, that soul shall be cut off from his people; he hath broken my covenant.

GOLDEN TEXT: I will establish my covenant between me and thee and thy seed after thee in their generations, for an everlasting covenant, to be a God unto thee and to thy seed after thee.—Genesis 17:7.

Lesson Aims

As a result of studying this lesson, each student should:

1. Understand the nature of God's covenant with Abraham.

2. Develop an even greater appreciation for the new covenant God has made with us through Jesus Christ.

Lesson Outline

INTRODUCTION

A. "Signing on the Dotted Line"

B. Lesson Background

I. THE ESTABLISHMENT OF THE COVENANT (Genesis 17:1-8)

A. God Appears to Abram (v. 1)

B. The Declaration of the Covenant (vv. 2-4)

C. Abram's New Name (vv. 5, 6)

What's in a Name?

D. The Extent of the Covenant Promise (vv. 7, 8)

The Blessing of God

II. THE SIGN OF THE COVENANT (Genesis 17:9-14)

A. A Condition of the Covenant (v. 9)

B. The Token of the Covenant (vv. 10, 11)

C. The Practice of Circumcision in Israel (vv. 12-14)

CONCLUSION

A. The "New Covenant" in Christ

B. Let Us Pray

C. Thought to Remember

Display visual 7 of the visuals packet and refer to it in the introduction to this lesson.. The visual is shown on page 61.

Introduction

A. "Signing on the Dotted Line"

Contracts are a way of life in the modern world. The principles of treaty—good faith, mutual privilege and obligation—are fundamental to nearly every relationship. Legal agreements bind husbands to wives, buyers to sellers, and nations to nations. Sooner or later all of us learn what it means to "sign on the dotted line."

Interestingly enough, the Bible uses this same idea of contract to characterize God's relation-

ship with His people. The concept of "covenant" runs as a continuous thread through both the Old and New Testaments. In fact, the word *testament* itself owes its origin to this Biblical idea. Theologically speaking, "covenant" describes the dynamics of the Divine-human relationship that began with Abraham, continued through Israel, and have now been extended to all the nations through Jesus Christ.

B. Lesson Background

The use of covenants to formalize relationships between social, political, and economic partners was widespread in the world of the Biblical patriarchs. Covenants were usually one of two types. *Bilateral* covenants, the most common of these ancient contracts, were negotiated between the two parties with each having input into the requirements and privileges of the arrangement. The terms of *unilateral* covenants, however, were not negotiated but dictated by someone in a high position to someone under his authority.

The covenants that God made with human beings (Noah, Genesis 9:8-17; Abraham, Genesis 17:1-14; Israel, Exodus 24:1-8) were all unilateral. In every case God initiated the covenant, offered promises to His children, and dictated any conditions whereby they might enjoy those promises. It was in this manner that God announced His covenant with Abraham, as we see in our lesson text.

I. The Establishment of the Covenant (Genesis 17:1-8)

A. God Appears to Abram (v. 1)

1. And when Abram was ninety years old and nine, the Lord appeared to Abram, and said unto him, I am the Almighty God; walk before me, and be thou perfect.

Approximately thirteen years passed from the birth of Ishmael to the event recorded in this text (Genesis 16:16). During that time Abram (Abraham) and Sarai (Sarah) may have come to assume that the covenant promise would be carried on through the son born to Hagar (compare Genesis 17:18). God now appeared and revealed to Abram that He had something else in mind. We are not told how God appeared to Abram on this occasion. Earlier God came to him in a vision (Genesis 15:1), and later He would appear in human form (18:1, 2).

I am the Almighty God. Names played an important role in this appearance of God. God (v. 1), Abram (v. 5) and Sarai (v. 15) were all now to be known by a new name. As will be noted more fully below, this was symbolic of the dawning of a new era in the relationship of God and Abram—an era of fulfilled promise and realized hope. The name *Almighty God* translates the Hebrew *El-Shad-dai*. Although scholars disagree over the precise meaning of this name, it especially points to power. It would take a God of power—almighty power—to fulfill the promises that were made to Abram.

Walk before me. This means Abram was to obey God, to trust Him, to walk as though he were always in God's presence. The Hebrew expression translated *be thou perfect* does not imply the impossible requirement of sinlessness. Rather, it means to live "sincerely," "with integrity." This requirement was but one of several made by God of His covenant partner. Others were the command to leave his homeland (Genesis 12:1), the requirement of circumcision (Genesis 17:10, 11), and the near-sacrifice of Isaac (Genesis 22:1, 16-18).

B. The Declaration of the Covenant (vv. 2-4)

2-4. And I will make my covenant between me and thee, and will multiply thee exceedingly. And Abram fell on his face: and God talked with him, saying, As for me, behold, my covenant is with thee, and thou shalt be a father of many nations.

I will make my covenant. At least thirteen years earlier God had appeared to Abram. That appearance was summarized in the statement, "In that same day the Lord made a covenant with Abram" (Genesis 15:18). The verses before us do not speak of an additional covenant. The covenant already concluded was soon to be carried out. We might say that in the first declaration the emphasis was upon God's commitment to the covenant promises, while in the covenant declaration in chapter 17, the emphasis was on the terms or means by which Abram and his descendants would enjoy those blessings.

Will multiply thee exceedingly. The covenant promises that God made to Abram included a great name and blessing (Genesis 12:2), a means of blessing to all peoples (v. 3), and a promised land (Genesis 15:18). But the blessing that is emphasized here (many descendants) was, perhaps, the one that meant the most to Abram. To a man who has fathered but one son in his ninety-nine years of life, no promise could be more inviting than the prospect of fathering *many nations* (see Genesis 15:1-6). To leave behind many children to inherit their property and carry on their name was life's one great ambition for men in ancient patriarchal cultures.

And Abram fell on his face. In Abram's day falling on one's face was a way of showing re-

How to Say It

EL-SHADDAI (Hebrew). El-*Shad*-eye.
EUPHRATES. U-*fray*-teez.
GAZA. *Gay*-zuh.
HAGAR. *Hay*-gar.
ISHMAEL. *Ish*-may-el.
KETURAH. Keh-*too*-ruh.

spect to one's superior and of assuming the role of a servant or subject. According to Genesis, faith (15:6), shown by obedience to God's commands (22:18), is the proper human response to God's call. An attitude of humble submission to the sovereign God produces such a response. Abram's reaction to God's appearance revealed just such an attitude.

And God talked with him. The means of God's communication with Abram is not revealed. God's message breaks down into three sections, each introduced by a similar Hebrew expression. Verses 4-8 begin with "As for me" and discuss God's part in the covenant. Verses 9-14 begin with "As for you" (*New International Version*) and describe how Abram was to "keep" the covenant. Finally, verses 15-22 begin with "As for Sarai" and announce the role she would play as mother to the child of promise.

C. Abram's New Name (v. 5, 6)

5, 6. Neither shall thy name any more be called Abram, but thy name shall be Abraham; for a father of many nations have I made thee. And I will make thee exceeding fruitful, and I will make nations of thee, and kings shall come out of thee.

Among ancient peoples, names did far more than simply distinguish one person from another. They stood for something. It might be an unusual circumstance surrounding the child's birth (see Exodus 2:10; 1 Samuel 1:20) or some personal characteristic of the child (see Genesis 25:25, 30). There was also a custom in Biblical times of giving a person a new name or "nickname" suggestive of some historic milestone in that person's life (see John 1:42; Acts 4:36). Such was the case here. The patriarch's original name *Abram*, "great, or exalted, father," was changed to *Abraham* ("father of a multitude") because of the "many nations" that would come from him (v. 4). With the birth of Isaac the promises of the covenant would start to unfold in a way that would signal the beginning of a new era in the relationship of God and the patriarch. The name *Abraham* commemorates this significant milestone in Biblical history.

I will make nations of thee. Abraham would be the father of Israel and of other nations as well. The *nations* that God had in mind were the descendants of Abraham through Ishmael (Genesis 25:12-16), Keturah (Genesis 25:2-4), and Esau (Edomites, see Genesis 36).

WHAT'S IN A NAME?

Edsel: never will another automobile bear that name. In 1958, Ford Motor Company launched a new car called the Edsel, but it was a merchandising disaster that lasted only three model years. Comedians joked about its styling, and its name came to symbolize poor market planning.

Jezebel: even in Hebrew, it wasn't an attractive name. It meant "unexalted" or "without a husband." But given the behavior of the most famous bearer of the name, the wicked wife of the equally wicked king, Ahab, no modern parent would afflict that name on a beloved daughter.

Names are important. By them we distinguish one person from another; and some names are given in honor of beloved relatives who bore the same name.

To people of Biblical times, names might also be given to commemorate significant events. Such was the case with the event in today's lesson text. The recipient of God's promise had been named Abram—"exalted father." As fine as the name was, God had something even better in mind. He changed the name to Abraham—"father of a multitude"—so that every time Abraham heard his name, he was reminded of the promise of God.

Every time we think of ourselves as Christians, we should be reminded that we are "Christ's ones"—those who belong to Christ, recipients of God's greatest promises.   —C. R. B.

D. The Extent of the Covenant Promise (vv. 7, 8)

7. And I will establish my covenant between me and thee and thy seed after thee in their generations, for an everlasting covenant, to be a God unto thee and to thy seed after thee.

In verses 7 and 8, two promises are extended to Abraham and his descendants. The first concerns a special relationship between the Lord and His people. The Lord said that He would be a God unto Abraham and his descendants. Of all the things that can be said of ancient Israel, this is the most important. Israel is not remembered for its great territory, wealth, political influence, or military might. Israel is remembered for its religion. Ethical monotheism, belief in one God expressed in a distinct way of living, is the great legacy of Biblical Israel to the world. As God later revealed to His people through Moses, Is-

rael was special, not because of their own national standing, but because God "set his love" upon them and chose them to be His people (Deuteronomy 7:6-8).

Abraham was assured that the covenant between himself and God would continue in force for his descendants *in their generations,* or "throughout their generations," *for an everlasting covenant.* The Hebrew word translated "everlasting" may indeed signify "eternal," but sometimes it means "for a long time," or "into the hidden future." For example, reference is made to "the everlasting hills" in Genesis 49:26. The term may even be limited to a lifetime. In Exodus 21:6 provision is made for a servant who wants to remain with his master to "serve him for ever"—obviously only so long as he lives. It is not necessary, therefore, on the basis of this and similar verses, to suppose that the physical seed of Abraham are to continue in the covenant relationship with God on into the millennium. Even in the Old Testament period it was prophesied that God would make a new covenant with the house of Israel (Jeremiah 31:31, 32), "not according to the covenant that I made with their fathers." The *everlasting covenant* with Abraham and his seed, therefore, was to extend throughout their generations until such time that it would be superseded by the new and better covenant. Hebrews 8:1-13 and 9:11-28 show that the redemptive ministry of Jesus Christ established that new covenant between man and God.

8. And I will give unto thee, and to thy seed after thee, the land wherein thou art a stranger, all the land of Canaan, for an everlasting possession; and I will be their God.

The second promise of God's covenant concerned a territory for Abraham and his descendants, *all the land of Canaan.* This repeats the promise God had made earlier to Abram (Genesis 12:7; 15:18). The boundaries of this territory reached all the way from the Euphrates River in the Northeast to the River of Egypt (a stream about fifty miles southwest of Gaza) and would today include all or parts of Syria, Lebanon and Jordan, the land of Israel, and much of the Sinai peninsula. Only during the reigns of David and Solomon did Israel actually control anywhere near the full extent of this territory (1 Kings 4:21, 24; 8:65).

Until this time Abraham did not own one foot of the land in which he was a sojourner. The land had been promised to him and to his seed, but almost twenty-five years had passed since he entered Canaan. Therefore it was fitting that God now renew the promise. The same word, *everlasting,* appears, as in the preceding verse, with a similar meaning—"into the hidden future." It is not necessarily a prediction of eternal tenure of the land by the descendants of Abraham.

I will be their God is not stated as an afterthought. This is the important statement of this verse—indeed, of this entire section of Scripture. This, on God's part, is the significance of the covenant. What greater promise than this could be desired by any people? Elsewhere there is coupled with this statement the words, "They shall be my people" (Jeremiah 24:7). That is the significance of the covenant on their part. The relationship of Abraham's seed to God did not depend alone on God, but also on them. The condition that God placed at this time on His covenant with Abraham and his seed is discussed in the final verses of today's text. Other Biblical texts reveal that Israel's blessing by God, which included their continued presence in the promised land, would be conditioned by their obedience to the terms of the covenant established at Sinai, the law given through Moses (see Deuteronomy 4:40; 5:32, 33; 28:58-68; Leviticus 26:21-33).

THE BLESSING OF GOD

The escapades of Jim and Tammy Bakker became front-page news several years ago. They had built a television "ministry" that brought exorbitant wealth to them. Apparently, they were able to rationalize this as the blessing of God for their service to Him.

Other television "ministries" also proved to be profitable to their principal personnel. At one time in the late eighties, donations to religious programs on more than two hundred stations were estimated to be two billion dollars annually.

The materialism of our culture makes it difficult for us who are Christians to avoid viewing our prosperity as evidence of the blessing of God. We are tempted to think, with the society around us, that wealth is good and great wealth is wonderful.

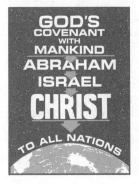

visual 7

God promised that Abraham and his descendants would be given vast expanses of land for their possession. Great as this promise was, the greater blessing that God offered was His lasting promise to be the God of Abraham and his descendants. We who are in Christ are heirs of this promise (Galatians 3:29). This is the eternal blessing of God.   —C. R. B.

II. The Sign of the Covenant (Genesis 17:9-14)

A. A Condition of the Covenant (v. 9)

9. And God said unto Abraham, Thou shalt keep my covenant therefore, thou, and thy seed after thee in their generations.

This was not the first time that God placed a condition upon His promises to Abraham. Years before, when He first called the patriarch, God commanded him, "Get thee out of thy country, and from thy kindred, and from thy father's house, unto a land that I will show thee" (Genesis 12:1). This was no small requirement for a man who lived in a time when people lived their lives and sought their destinies as part of an extended family (clan). Abraham's departure from his kith and kin was a significant act of faith in and obedience to God's call. It was Abraham's obedience that brought him to the promised land and thus put him in a position to begin to enjoy the blessings of the covenant. In this particular repetition of the covenant, God prefaced His promises with a command: "walk before me, and be thou perfect" (Genesis 17:1).

It is obvious from these statements that God's covenant promises to Abraham had a condition attached to them. Abraham and the succeeding generations of his descendants would enjoy the covenant promises if they would *keep* [God's] *covenant.*

B. The Token of the Covenant (vv. 10, 11)

10, 11. This is my covenant, which ye shall keep, between me and you and thy seed after thee; Every man child among you shall be circumcised. And ye shall circumcise the flesh of your foreskin; and it shall be a token of the covenant betwixt me and you.

This turning point in the life of Abraham was to be marked by the act of circumcision, which would become the perpetual symbol of identification with and dedication to the covenant. No explanation is given as to why this act was designated by God to be the *token of the covenant.* One might speculate that it symbolized the very way that the covenant promises were to unfold. God's covenant was with Abraham and his *seed* (descendants). It was to be perpetuated by the procreation of successive generations of Abraham's offspring. Perhaps, too, this act was to serve as a sign that the child promised to Abraham (Isaac) was to be not a child born strictly of a fleshly union, but a child of promise, the gift of God's grace.

C. The Practice of Circumcision in Israel (vv. 12-14)

12-14. And he that is eight days old shall be circumcised among you, every man child in your generations, he that is born in the house, or bought with money of any stranger, which is not of thy seed. He that is born in thy house, and he that is bought with thy money, must needs be circumcised: and my covenant shall be in your flesh for an everlasting covenant. And the uncircumcised man child whose flesh of his foreskin is not circumcised, that soul shall be cut off from his people; he hath broken my covenant.

Circumcision, first performed by Abraham on all the males of his household (Genesis 17:23-27), was to be observed by each successive generation. Every male among his descendants, whether born in their household or bought with money from a foreigner, was to be circumcised on the eighth day. Any male who was uncircumcised would be guilty of breaking God's covenant and was to be *cut off from his people*. Scholars disagree over whether this means execution (as in Exodus 31:14) or excommunication from the covenant community. Apparently, Moses' failure to circumcise his son would later result in God's seeking to "kill him" (Exodus 4:24-26).

The importance of the act of circumcision rested in what it symbolized. It was the God-appointed "sign" of total commitment to the covenant. As has already been noted under verse 8, commitment to God's covenant would manifest itself in obedience to God's commands. As the apostle Paul was later to point out, circumcision apart from obedience is uncircumcision (Romans 2:25-29).

Conclusion

A. The "New Covenant" in Christ

As the New Testament (Covenant) clearly teaches, the Old Covenant that God formed with Israel was but the harbinger of a new and far superior covenant that God offers to all mankind through Jesus Christ. This New Covenant is founded on better promises, mediated by a superior priest, and established through a greater sacrifice (Hebrews 8, 9). There is a sense in which the New Covenant both fulfills and re-

places the Old. It fulfills the Old by providing the means by which "all families of the earth" are blessed through Abraham (Genesis 12:3). As both Peter and Paul testify, this final promise of God's covenant with Abraham was fulfilled in the provision of salvation to all peoples through Jesus Christ (see Acts 3:17-26; Galatians 3:26-29). Once this was accomplished, the Old Covenant became obsolete and was displaced by the New Covenant in Christ (Hebrews 8:6-13). Under this New Covenant all peoples (Jew and Gentile alike) who come to God through Christ are spiritual descendants of Abraham and "heirs according to the promise" (Galatians 3:29).

We live in a world where contracts are "made to be broken." Nations violate treaties, businesses seek loopholes in contracts, and people make commitments they never intend to keep. But not God. He is faithful to His covenant. To accept Jesus Christ as Lord and Savior is to enter into a pact with a God who is trustworthy and reliable. Secured by the blood of Christ, sealed by His resurrection, the Christian is party to a covenant that is steadfast and sure.

B. Let Us Pray

Gracious Heavenly Father, we thank You for making it possible for us to become Your children and heirs to Your eternal promises through Jesus Christ, Your Son. Help us to be faithful in keeping Your covenant. In Jesus' name, amen.

C. Thought to Remember

"All the ways of the Lord are loving and faithful for those who keep the demands of his covenant" (Psalm 25:10, *New International Version*).

Home Daily Bible Readings

Monday, Oct. 11—God Gives Abram a New Name (Genesis 17:1-5)

Tuesday, Oct. 12—God's Covenant Includes: Land, Nations, Descendants (Genesis 17:6-10)

Wednesday, Oct 13—Circumcision: A Sign of the Covenant (Genesis 17:11-14)

Thursday, Oct. 14—Sarah Blessed as Mother of Sons/Kings (Genesis 17:15-19)

Friday, Oct. 15—A Blessing and a Covenant (Genesis 17:21-25)

Saturday, Oct. 16—Keeping Covenant Maintains Faith and Circumcision (Genesis 17:26,27; Hebrews 6:13-20)

Sunday, Oct. 17—Be an Unashamed Worker for Christ (2 Timothy 2:1-15)

Learning by Doing

This page contains an alternate lesson plan emphasizing learning activities. Classes desiring such student involvement will find these suggestions helpful.

Learning Goals

As a result of this lesson, each student will :
1. Be able to list the conditions and promises of the covenant God made with Abraham.
2. Be assured that God keeps His promises.

Into the Lesson

When it is time for class to begin, give each student a slip of paper on which is written a name and Scripture reference from the list below. Make multiple copies of each name and its reference so everyone can have one, but distribute a nearly equal number of each.

Peter ....John 1:42
Barnabas ....Acts 4:36
Jesus ....Matthew 1:21
Samuel ....1 Samuel 1:20
Eve....................................Genesis 3:20
Moses ....Exodus 2:10
Isaac ....Genesis 21:3-6

Have several study Bibles, Bible dictionaries, or Bible encyclopedias on hand. Instruct the students to find the others in the class who have been assigned the same name as they have been given. They are then to work together to discover the meanings of the names. For your convenience, here are the meanings of the names: Peter (a stone or rock), Barnabas (son of consolation, or encouragement), Jesus (Jehovah is salvation), Samuel (asked of God, or God hears), Eve (living), Moses (drawn out [of water]), Isaac (laughter).

When the groups thus formed have had ample opportunity to research and discuss the names assigned to them, ask for reports. Observe that names were very important in Biblical times. They sometimes reflected on unusual circumstance that related to the birth of the child. Names given later in life (as in the case of Barnabas) described one's character. When God was involved in naming a child, the name most often was prophetic of what the child would be or do. As we shall see, names play a prominent role in today's lesson.

Into the Word

Divide the class into groups of four to six students. Give each group a sheet on which you have written the following three assignments. Also give each group a Bible dictionary or Bible encyclopedia. Ask the groups to read Genesis 17:1-19 and then complete the assignments.

Assignment One: List the promises God made to Abraham in connection with the covenant He made with him.

Assignment Two: Identify the conditions God placed on the covenant He made with Abraham and his descendants.

Assignment Three: Explain the significance of the three names cited: God Almighty, Abraham, and Sarah.

After about fifteen minutes, call for reports on each assignment in turn. As the groups share their findings, supplement them as needed with information from the commentary section of this book.

List on the chalkboard these features of God's covenant with Abraham:

Promises: many descendants, nations, kings, land, Jehovah to be his God.
Conditions: moral uprightness, serve God only, circumcision of males.
Recipients: Abraham's descendants through Isaac.
Extent: Perpetual (until fulfilled).

Later, through Moses, God entered into a more detailed covenant with Abraham's descendants. In time, this covenant was fulfilled and replaced by the New Covenant established by Jesus Christ. Have a student read aloud Hebrews 8:6-13. Then ask the class to compare the New Covenant with God's covenant with Abraham. Using the same headings as shown above, list the features of the New Covenant.

Into Life

Note that all of God's promises to Abraham that we have listed were fulfilled. The New Testament reveals more: through Jesus Christ Abraham's descendants have been greatly increased, and God's promise to bless the world in Abraham finds its fulfillment (Genesis 12:3; Galatians 3:7, 8, 26-29).

The message for us in this lesson is, *God keeps His promises.* Distribute index cards to the students and ask them to write the answers to these two questions: Which of God's promises means the most to you, and why? Then close with a prayer of thanks for God's faithfulness.

Let's Talk It Over

The questions on this page are designed to encourage review of the lesson Scriptures and to promote discussion of the lesson by the class. The answers provided are only discussion starters. Let your class talk it over from there.

1. God commanded Abram, "Be thou perfect." This may remind us of Jesus' exhortation in Matthew 5:48: "Be ye therefore perfect, even as your Father which is in heaven is perfect." What did God intend by giving such commands?

Neither Abram nor followers of Jesus Christ were expected to achieve perfection of life. Certainly Abram fell short of perfection—on more than one occasion, for example, he tampered with the truth (Genesis 12:11-20). And yet in comparison with the moral climate of his time, he stands out as a man of righteousness. We need look no further than 1 John 1:7-10 to see that Christians will fall short of perfection. But Jesus' exhortation to us to aim for perfection keeps us from taking lightly our tendencies to sinful attitudes and actions. By pointing toward the goal of perfection, we progress in holiness.

2. Abram fell on his face before God. How can we profit from his example on this occasion?

The Lord may not appear to us as He did to Abram, but we do enter into His presence when we go to Him in prayer. The Bible does not stipulate that one must assume a certain posture while praying. Like Abram, Joshua (Joshua 7:6), Ezekiel (Ezekiel 9:8), and Jesus himself (Matthew 26:39) fell facedown in prayer on occasion. But Solomon at the temple dedication was kneeling (1 Kings 8:54); David offered the prayer recorded in 2 Samuel 7:18-29 while sitting; and Jesus spoke favorably of one's standing while praying (Mark 11:25). We need to consider what posture will best represent our attitude of reverence and submission toward God in a given situation. At mealtimes, simply bowing our heads seems appropriate. When we pray just before retiring, we may kneel by our bedside. But there may be times when we will feel such a tremendous sense of God's majesty and of our needs that we will want to prostrate ourselves before God as Abram did.

3. God's assigning of significant new names to persons, such as He did to Abram, is a practice that the church might do well to consider. How might new titles or nicknames for Christians be beneficial to them?

The best example of this is Jesus' giving Simon the nickname Peter, "the rock." At times that nickname seemed inappropriate for Peter, but it may have helped him through his times of weakness and failure, so that he could become a solid leader in the early church. Perhaps it would seem a bit corny to refer to our fellow Christians as "Steadfast Steve" or "Faithful Phyllis" or "Disciple Dan" or "Ellen the Encourager." However, the use of such nicknames or titles might serve to encourage believers to continue to live up to them and thereby develop into even more effective members of the church.

4. The lesson writer reminds us of the conditional nature of God's promises. What are some of God's promises to us and the conditions related to them?

God's promises of the forgiveness of sin and the gift of eternal life through Jesus Christ are the principal promises of the New Covenant. The conditions of faith, repentance toward sin, confession of our faith, and baptism are clearly stated. The promises related to prayer, which are found throughout the Bible, are also conditional. If we fail to pray in faith (James 1:6-8), if we harbor sinful thoughts in our hearts (Psalm 66:18), if we pray with selfish motives (James 4:3), we will not be fruitful in prayer. Finally, let us note the conditional promise of Revelation 2:10.

5. The New Covenant has fulfilled and replaced the Old Covenant. Why, then, should we study the Old Testament Scriptures?

Many of us have heard the statement, "The Old Testament is the New concealed; the New Testament is the Old revealed." This indicates the unity of the two volumes of Biblical truth. A thorough knowledge of the Old Testament enables us to understand the mission of Jesus Christ and the significance of the New Covenant He put into effect. A study of the Old Testament tells us much about the wisdom, justice, power, and mercy of God. It shows clearly the destructiveness of sin, and its record of countless animal sacrifices makes preparation for the perfect, atoning sacrifice of Jesus Christ. As Hebrews 11 reminds us, the Old Testament provides us with a rich assortment of examples of people who acted on their faith in God.

God Keeps His Promise

DEVOTIONAL READING: Galatians 4:21-31.

LESSON SCRIPTURE: Genesis 21:1-21.

PRINTED TEXT: Genesis 21:1-14.

Genesis 21:1-14

1 And the LORD visited Sarah as he had said, and the LORD did unto Sarah as he had spoken.

2 For Sarah conceived, and bare Abraham a son in his old age, at the set time of which God had spoken to him.

3 And Abraham called the name of his son that was born unto him, whom Sarah bare to him, Isaac.

4 And Abraham circumcised his son Isaac being eight days old, as God had commanded him.

5 And Abraham was a hundred years old, when his son Isaac was born unto him.

6 And Sarah said, God hath made me to laugh, so that all that hear will laugh with me.

7 And she said, Who would have said unto Abraham, that Sarah should have given children suck? for I have borne him a son in his old age.

8 And the child grew, and was weaned: and Abraham made a great feast the same day that Isaac was weaned.

9 And Sarah saw the son of Hagar the Egyptian, which she had borne unto Abraham, mocking.

10 Wherefore she said unto Abraham, Cast out this bondwoman and her son: for the son of this bondwoman shall not be heir with my son, even with Isaac.

11 And the thing was very grievous in Abraham's sight because of his son.

12 And God said unto Abraham, Let it not be grievous in thy sight because of the lad, and because of thy bondwoman; in all that Sarah hath said unto thee, hearken unto her voice; for in Isaac shall thy seed be called.

13 And also of the son of the bondwoman will I make a nation, because he is thy seed.

14 And Abraham rose up early in the morning, and took bread, and a bottle of water, and gave it unto Hagar, putting it on her shoulder, and the child, and sent her away: and she departed, and wandered in the wilderness of Beersheba.

GOLDEN TEXT: Sarah conceived, and bare Abraham a son in his old age, at the set time of which God had spoken to him.—Genesis 21:2.

Lesson Aims

As a result of this lesson, a student should:

1. Understand how God's covenant promises unfolded in the life of Abraham.

2. Develop a greater confidence in the promises God has made to us through Jesus Christ.

Lesson Outline

INTRODUCTION
  A. "And It Came to Pass"
  B. Lesson Background
  I. THE BIRTH OF ISAAC (Genesis 21:1-8)
    A. The Lord's Promise Fulfilled (vv. 1, 2)
    B. Abraham's Reaction to Isaac's Birth (vv. 3-5)
    C. Sarah's Reaction to Isaac's Birth (vv. 6, 7)
       Laughter, the Best Medicine
    D. The Early Childhood of Isaac (v. 8)
  II. CONFLICT IN A HOUSEHOLD (Genesis 21:9-14)
    A. Sarah's Jealousy (vv. 9, 10)
    B. Abraham's Anxiety (v. 11)
    C. God's Reassurance (vv. 12, 13)
    D. Hagar and Ishmael's Departure (v. 14)
       Making the Best of a Bad Situation
CONCLUSION
  A. "Past as Promise"
  B. Let Us Pray
  C. Thought to Remember

Display visual 8 of the visuals packet throughout this session. The visual is shown on page 69.

Introduction

A. "And It Came to Pass"

I once heard an old preacher say that his favorite verse in the Bible was, "And it came to pass." The meaning he took from this expression was that the passing of time takes care of many of life's evils and gives perspective to many of life's events. He would say, "If you're bothered by some problem or bewildered by some puzzle, just be patient; because, sooner or later, it will 'come to pass.' God will either take care of it or He will tell you what it means."

Though this preacher's knowledge of Biblical grammar was woefully inadequate (this expres-

sion actually means nothing of the sort!), his knowledge of Biblical theology was right on the button. The patriarchal narratives of Genesis (chapters 12-50) clearly teach that life's events have meaning and that, in due course of time, God will reveal His eternal purposes and move history toward the end that He has decreed for it. These narratives also emphasize that fulfillment in life is found through trust in God's promises and submission to His will. Abraham saw his faith vindicated as God's promises to him were fulfilled.

B. Lesson Background

Twenty-five years prior to this occasion Abraham's life was transformed by a promise of God: "I will make of thee a great nation" (Genesis 12:2). Abraham, then a seventy-five-year-old husband of a barren wife, first concluded that God would do this through legal custom by elevating his oldest house-born slave, Eliezer of Damascus, to be his heir (Genesis 15:2). God, however, assured him that his own son would be his heir (v. 4). When Abraham was eighty-five years old and still childless, a desperate Sarah gave her maid Hagar to Abraham as a surrogate wife (Genesis 16). It may be that Abraham regarded the child born of this union (Ishmael) as the key to the fulfillment of God's promise. If so, the patriarch again was wrong. What he and Sarah thought impossible, God would bring to pass. A one-hundred-year-old man and his ninety-year-old wife were to be given by God that which all their years of marriage could never produce—a child. In this episode Abraham learned that the God who promises is also the God who provides.

I. The Birth of Isaac (Genesis 21:1-8)

A. The Lord's Promise Fulfilled (vv. 1, 2)

1, 2. And the LORD visited Sarah as he had said, and the LORD did unto Sarah as he had spoken. For Sarah conceived, and bare Abraham a son in his old age, at the set time of which God had spoken to him.

The language of these opening verses is designed to demonstrate that the birth of Isaac was the result of divine intervention in the lives of Abraham and Sarah. The verb *visited* is used regularly in the Old Testament to describe God's supernatural intervention in the lives of His people, either to punish them (Exodus 32:34) or to bless them (Exodus 3:16; Ruth 1:6; Psalm 8:4). In the case of Abraham and Sarah, God blessed their union to produce a child beyond Sarah's normal years of childbearing. The phrase *a son in his old age,* which is repeated in verse 7, draws attention to the extraordinary nature of this out-of-season birth, as does the expression *at the set time.* This later statement recalls the language of God's earlier prediction that the child of promise would be born "at this set time in the next year" (Genesis 17:21; see also Genesis 18:10, 14). This specific prediction and fulfillment demonstrated that the matter was "of God" and not "of men" (compare Exodus 9:5, 6).

However, the phrase *as he had said and as he had spoken,* which is included three times in these two verses, reveals the true significance of Isaac's birth. The author wants us, like Abraham, to realize that when God makes a promise, He keeps it. The Bible asks us to stake our eternal destinies on the promises of God. We do so with great confidence, because of the consistent testimony of Scripture that the God of great promises is a God who always keeps His word.

B. Abraham's Reaction to Isaac's Birth (vv. 3-5)

3-5. And Abraham called the name of his son that was born unto him, whom Sarah bare to him, Isaac. And Abraham circumcised his son Isaac being eight days old, as God had commanded him. And Abraham was a hundred years old, when his son Isaac was born unto him.

There is no way to overstate the joy that the birth of Isaac must have brought to Abraham's life. Even more important than his emotional satisfaction, however, was the affirmation that his faith received at the arrival of his long-awaited son of promise. That Abraham understood Isaac's birth to represent the unfolding of the covenant promise is demonstrated by two specific things he did. First, he named the child *Isaac.* As noted in last week's lesson (see Genesis 17:5, 6) names had special significance for the covenant family. Isaac's name was no exception. It means "laughter" or "he laughs." It remembered the doubt that Sarah showed toward the prospect of the child's birth (Genesis 18:12-15), and which some think Abraham himself expressed (see 17:17), as well as the genuine joy it finally occasioned. Important to remember here is that God had commanded Abraham to so name the child whose birth would begin the unfolding of the covenant (17:19). Abraham's compliance demonstrated his understanding of the spiritual implications of Isaac's birth. So, too, did his circumcising of the boy (v. 4). God had specifically established circumcision as the "token" or symbol of Abraham's submission to the covenant (Genesis 17:9-14). His performance of this on the eight-day-old Isaac was done with

How to Say It	
ABIMELECH.	Uh-*bim*-uh-lek.
BEERSHEBA.	Be-er-*she*-buh.
ELIEZER.	El-eye-*ee*-zer or Ee-ley-*ee*-zer.
HAGAR.	*Hay*-gar.
ISHMAEL.	*Ish*-may-el.
ISHMAELITES.	*Ish*-me-el-ites or *Ish*-may-el-ites.

the full realization that when the conditions of God's covenant are met (see Genesis 17:23-27), the blessings of God's covenant will certainly be realized.

And Abraham was a hundred years old, when his son Isaac was born unto him. It is difficult to explain exactly why God made Abraham wait so long for his "son of promise." The language of this text, however, may supply us a clue (see verses 1, 2, 7). The author seems to be telling us that God delayed the birth of Isaac to demonstrate, without a doubt, that it was of God rather than of man. The impossibility of such a birth occurring naturally only served to prove that it must have occurred supernaturally. The larger lesson, for Abraham and for us, is that personal fulfillment is found not in what we are able to achieve but in what God promises and provides. As the author of the book of Hebrews points out, it was "through faith and patience" that Abraham received the promise. The same is required of God's children today (Hebrews 6:11, 12, 15).

C. Sarah's Reaction to Isaac's Birth (vv. 6, 7)

6, 7. And Sarah said, God hath made me to laugh, so that all that hear will laugh with me. And she said, Who would have said unto Abraham, that Sarah should have given children suck? for I have borne him a son in his old age.

The printed texts in this series of lessons have focused more on Abraham than on Sarah. This is not to imply that she played an insignificant role in the patriarchal narratives. Actually she played a crucial role in the unfolding of the covenant promise. God honored Sarah by announcing that the promised son of Abraham would come through her (Genesis 17:15, 16). She is remembered by Isaiah as the mother of the chosen race (Isaiah 51:2) and by the author of Hebrews as a woman of "faith."

Sarah's initial response to the birth of Isaac, *God hath made me to laugh,* expressed her genuine joy at her great blessing. Her statement contained an allusion to the name *Isaac,* which means "laughter" or "he laughs." Perhaps she was also saying that her laughter now was of a different nature than what it had been when she first heard that she would bear a son (Genesis 18:12-15). Although Sarah bore only one son, she referred to him by the generic word *children*. The plural was appropriate because it anticipated future descendants who would come forth from Isaac.

LAUGHTER, THE BEST MEDICINE

For many years Sarah had carried the onus of being childless—a terrible failing for a wife in the culture in which she lived. Finally, when Sarah was in her old age, God enabled her to give birth to a son.

Sarah's child was named Isaac, a name that comes from the Hebrew root for "laughter." In response to the great blessing she had received, the formerly childless Sarah said, "God has made me to laugh."

Laughter is a gift of God that helps us deal with the demands and the disappointments of life. What is it about laughter that makes it so important to a balanced life? E. B. White said that "humor can be dissected, as a frog can, but the thing dies in the process and the innards are discouraging to any but the pure scientific mind." Most of us don't need an explanation of what makes us laugh; we just need to do it more often. Norman Cousins has written of his bout with cancer and his firm belief that he "laughed himself well."

Someone has said that laughter is the only effective pain-killer available without a doctor's prescription. The older we get, the more important it is that we apply God's gift of laughter to the increasing infirmities of age. It will help us to be better Christians and more enjoyable people to be around.   —C. R. B.

Home Daily Bible Readings

D. The Early Childhood of Isaac (v. 8)

8. And the child grew, and was weaned: and Abraham made a great feast the same day that Isaac was weaned.

In Sarah's culture weaning took place at a later age than it typically does in modern western cultures. Isaac's weaning may have taken place when he was two or three years old. This would mean that Ishmael was now sixteen or seventeen (see Genesis 16:16; 21:5). Evidently it was the normal custom to celebrate the occasion with a family feast.

II. Conflict in a Household (Genesis 21:9-14)

A. Sarah's Jealousy (vv. 9, 10)

9, 10. And Sarah saw the son of Hagar the Egyptian, which she had borne unto Abraham, mocking. Wherefore she said unto Abraham, Cast out this bondwoman and her son: for the son of this bondwoman shall not be heir with my son, even with Isaac.

The events described here may have taken place during the feast mentioned in the previous verse. The exact nature of how Ishmael was behaving toward Isaac is not clear in the text, but it was interpreted by Sarah to typify an attitude of superiority toward the younger boy (Paul, in Galatians 4:29, refers to Ishmael's actions as a "persecution" of Isaac). Such an attitude, coupled with the fact that Ishmael was Abraham's firstborn, caused Sarah to fear that Ishmael might scheme to have Isaac disinherited. Insight gained from extra-biblical, legal literature helps us better understand the meaning of this episode. The Code of Hammurabi suggests that in Abraham's day the sons of a slave-wife shared the inheritance equally with the sons of a free woman, provided that the father made the slave's sons legitimate. Should he refuse to recognize them as sons, the slave and her children were given their freedom. All of this seems to form the legal backdrop to this episode. When Sarah demanded of Abraham, *Cast out this bondwoman and her son,* she was insisting that Hagar and Ishmael be given their freedom, thereby renouncing all claim to a share of the family estate. It would seem that Sarah was acting both out of jealousy and a desire to protect the interests of her son.

B. Abraham's Anxiety (v. 11)

11. And the thing was very grievous in Abraham's sight because of his son.

Sarah's demand for Hagar and Ishmael's expulsion resulted in great anxiety for Abraham.

Ishmael was his son, and it is clear from earlier statements that Abraham regarded him as one of his heirs (Genesis 17:18). He obviously had a deep love for the boy who had grown up before him for more than fifteen years. Further, he must have had some feeling of tenderness for Hagar, who had been to him as a wife (see verse 12). This whole episode dramatically illustrates the complications that can develop when God's children attempt to further His purposes by means that He has neither required nor approved (see Genesis 16:1-3). Had Abraham and Sarah been content to "wait upon the Lord," Ishmael would never have been born and this entire tragedy could have been averted. Paul would later refer to this incident as an illustration of the difference between being children of freedom (in Christ) and children of slavery (to the law, Galatians 4:28-30).

C. God's Reassurance (vv. 12, 13)

12, 13. And God said unto Abraham, Let it not be grievous in thy sight because of the lad, and because of thy bondwoman; in all that Sarah hath said unto thee, hearken unto her voice; for in Isaac shall thy seed be called. And also of the son of the bondwoman will I make a nation, because he is thy seed.

The Lord's response to this difficult situation was in character with other interventions He had made into the lives of Abraham and Sarah. One need only recall the events of the previous chapter (Genesis 20), in which God intervened to set straight another difficult situation created by an ill-advised venture by the patriarch.

God's intervention in the episode recorded in our lesson text demonstrated a similar sensitivity to the persons involved in this situation. Furthermore, it showed His firm commitment to the successful fulfillment of the covenant promise. On the human side, the Lord first addressed the understandable consternation of Abraham. While it is true that this whole domestic mess was the doing of Abraham and Sarah, Genesis 16:1-3, there is no hint of any censure on God's part. Instead, He sought to resolve Abraham's anxiety by reassuring him that the departure of Hagar and Ishmael would turn out for the best, both for Isaac and for Ishmael. Though Ishmael was never part of God's plans for the covenant people, he was, nonetheless, blessed by God out of deference to both Abraham and Hagar (Genesis 21:12, 13, 17). In essence, both Hagar and Ishmael had been innocent pawns of an ill-conceived plot of Sarah and Abraham. Though Ishmael's disinheritance was necessary for the fulfillment of the covenant promise, God acted to see that the boy and his mother were not forced to pay an unfair price.

visual 8

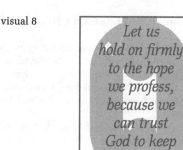

Let us hold on firmly to the hope we profess, because we can trust God to keep his promise.

It was not the human aspects of this episode, however, but their spiritual consequences that prompted God's intervention. All of God's interactions with the patriarchs were motivated by His determination to bring about His will. He had decreed that He would make a "great nation" of Abraham (Genesis 12:2). In this verse God stated that *in Isaac shall thy seed be called.* Whatever the human circumstances of this situation, God simply would not allow them to stand in the way of the unfolding of His covenant promise. This, at last, explains why God told Abraham to *hearken* unto the voice of Sarah. This does not imply that God approved of Sarah's actions or of any of the events that brought them about. Rather, it demonstrates God's uncompromising determination to see the covenant promise come to fruition according to the plan that He, and not circumstance or human initiative, dictates. The overriding truth that emerges from all of this is that God's promises are going to be fulfilled, and His will is going to be accomplished. Sometimes it may be through what people do. Other times it may be in spite of what people do. The patriarchal narratives, indeed all of Scripture, abound with evidence that God can take the very best we do or the very worst we do and turn it to the fulfillment of His eternal purposes. If we doubt this, we need only to look at the cross. From this greatest evil that men ever wrought, God was able to bring the greatest good.

And also of the son of the bondwoman will I make a nation. The *nation* of the Ishmaelites, according to their "princes," is described more fully in Genesis 25:12-18. Ishmael went on to live 137 years, a long life, which, in itself, is evidence of God's blessing (Genesis 25:17). His descendants settled in the desert regions bordering the south and east of Israel (Genesis 25:18). The descendants of Ishmael may be some of those whom God had in mind when he promised that "many nations" would come from Abraham (Genesis 17:4-6).

D. Hagar and Ishmael's Departure (v. 14)

14. And Abraham rose up early in the morning, and took bread, and a bottle of water, and gave it unto Hagar, putting it on her shoulder, and the child, and sent her away: and she departed, and wandered in the wilderness of Beersheba.

This was not the last time that Abraham *rose up early* to perform a difficult task in obedience to God's command. He would do the same when faced with his greatest test, the command to sacrifice Isaac (Genesis 22:3). His obedience in both cases was resolute; he did not hesitate to do what God had commanded. Abraham manifested his love and concern for Hagar and Ishmael by providing them with *bread, and a bottle of water*, which would supply their immediate needs. Having just received God's promise to make a nation of Ishmael, Abraham seemingly believed that God would provide for their further care. The water bottle, probably made of the skin of a goat, was placed on Hagar's shoulder. She was an Egyptian, and records indicate that this was the way Egyptian women normally carried burdens.

And the child. Some scholars take this language to mean that Abraham put Ishmael on Hagar's shoulder. This, of course, would pose a difficulty to our understanding of previous statements in Genesis, which make Ishmael to be around fifteen years old at this time. Though the Hebrew text is admittedly awkward at this point, it is possible to understand it to mean that Abraham provisioned both Hagar and Ishmael, formally "gave" or relinquished his son to her, and then sent them away.

The wilderness of Beersheba. This region would later receive its name in a treaty that Abraham made with Abimelech (Genesis 21:31). It was located in the extreme south of Palestine and served as one of the traditional boundaries to the land of Israel ("from Dan even to Beersheba," 2 Samuel 3:10; 17:11). This geographical note would seem to indicate that Hagar and Ishmael were making their way back to her native country, Egypt.

MAKING THE BEST OF A BAD SITUATION

A San Francisco man was arrested for driving alone in a carpool lane. He explained to the court that he was blind in one eye and only partially-sighted in the other, and his seeing-eye dog was in the front seat with him. The dog, he testified, would bark when they got too close to a vehicle in front of them.

The driver must have figured he was on shaky ground legally, and that perhaps a good story would make the best of a bad situation. What he said as he continued his defense, however, did not help his case. He disputed the arresting officer's claim that he had tried to outrun the highway patrolman in an attempt to escape arrest: he claimed he was just speeding up to cool off his dog! The judge said, "Guilty!"

Sarah's jealousy and anger led her to demand of Abraham that he cast out of his household both the bondwoman, Hagar, and her son, Ishmael. Abraham was torn because of his love for both Sarah and his son Ishmael. Fortunately for all concerned, God stepped into the mess they had created and promised to greatly bless the castaways.

Many of us experience crisis situations for which there is no easy solution. They often arise for the same reason Abraham's crisis did: we lack sufficient faith in God. But in His mercy and grace, He may bless us in spite of our foolishness and show us the means of escape.

—C. R. B.

Conclusion

A. "Past as Promise"

The series of popular motion pictures produced under the title "Back to the Future" based their plots on the premise that the events of the past shape the events of the present and the future. Interestingly enough, a similar concept is affirmed in the pages of Scripture. Biblical scholars have dubbed this theme "Past as Promise." It refers to a Scriptural affirmation that what God has done in the past serves as a promise of what He will do in the future. This is clearly one of the implications that today's lesson has for the modern Christian. Seeing how God, in His own time and in His own way, faithfully acted to fulfill His promises to Abraham, we can rest assured that He will likewise fulfill His promises to us. As the author of Hebrews affirms, "Let us hold unswervingly to the hope we profess, for he who promised is faithful" (Hebrews 10:23 *New International Version*).

B. Let Us Pray

You, Heavenly Father, are the God of the past, present, and future. Unto You we commit our hopes and our eternal destinies. In Jesus' name we pray. Amen.

C. Thought to Remember

Sometimes God's will is accomplished through humans. Other times it is accomplished in spite of humans. But sooner or later, in His own time and in His own way, God's will will be done.

Learning by Doing

*This page contains an alternate lesson plan emphasizing learning activities. Classes
desiring such student involvement will find these suggestions helpful.*

Learning Goals

This lesson will help a student:

1. Cite evidence from the life of Abraham that human failings do not block the fulfillment of God's promises.

2. Express confidence in the fulfillment of God's promises made to us in the New Covenant.

Into the Lesson

Before class, write the word *promise* vertically on the chalkboard or on a poster displayed at the front of the class. Begin the lesson by asking the class to think of words that start with each letter of the word *promise* and that are related to the promises of God. These may indicate promises, describe the promises, or relate in some other way to God's promises. For example, for *p* one may suggest *peace*, a promise in Christ, or *perfect*, a description of His promises, or *patience*, a virtue sometimes needed to receive His promises. Write these three examples on the board (or poster); then ask the class to suggest ideas for the remaining letters. Some ideas are suggested below, but do not be too quick to offer them. Allow the students to express their own ideas, and offer these only if needed.

Patience
Return
Omnipotent
Mysterious
Important
Supernatural
Eternal

Make the transition to the Bible study portion of the lesson by noting that today's lesson reveals the fulfillment of a special promise made to Abraham.

Into the Word

Have someone read Genesis 21:1-14 aloud. Then divide the class into three groups. Assign to each group a different character from the list below. Then ask the students in each group to work together to write three imaginary diary entries for the character assigned to them.

Group 1: Abraham
Group 2: Sarah
Group 3: Hagar

Direct the group to read the text and note the facts that pertain to their assigned character.

Then ask them to imagine that they are that character, with his or her emotions and motives, and to write diary entries for each of the following three days: the day Isaac was born, the day Ishmael mocked Isaac, and the day Hagar and Ishmael were sent away.

Give the groups fifteen or twenty minutes to do their writing. Then have a representative from each group read their first entries, the day of Isaac's birth. Discuss briefly, noting details from the commentary section of this lesson to enhance the discussion. Repeat the process of reading entries and discussion for the other two days. Note the joy of Abraham and Sarah at the birth of Isaac, a joy intensified because it represented the fulfillment of God's promise. Note the potential conflict between Ishmael and Isaac, and the need to dismiss the older son to avoid any problems with the inheritance and to restore family unity.

Into Life

Observe that the birth of Isaac represented the fulfillment of a promise that God made to Abraham many years earlier. Along the way, Abraham had achieved many things, including wealth and power. Discuss how Abraham's being part of God's plan and seeing His promise fulfilled overshadowed all of Abraham's own accomplishments.

After a brief discussion, point out that Abraham made a number of mistakes along the way, too. List the following items for the class to see:

1. God promises to make Abraham a great nation (Genesis 12:1-3).

2. Abraham says Sarah is his sister and nearly loses her in Pharaoh's harem (Genesis 12:10-20).

3. Abraham and Sarah attempt to fulfill God's promise by means of Hagar. (Genesis 16:1-4).

4. Abraham again says Sarah is his sister and allows her to be taken by Abimelech, king of Gerar (Genesis 20:1-7).

5. Isaac, the son of promise, is born (Genesis 21:1-3).

Lead a discussion of how items 2 through 4 represent failings that were potential threats to or complications to Abraham's enjoyment of God's promised blessing. Consider how God dealt with each of those situations. Then ask, What confidence, relative to the promises of the New Covenant, does this inspire?

Let's Talk It Over

The questions on this page are designed to encourage review of the lesson Scriptures and to promote discussion of the lesson by the class. The answers provided are only discussion starters. Let your class talk it over from there.

1. Sometimes we pray for a blessing or victory that seems clearly to be in harmony with the will of God, and yet the answer is delayed. What possible explanation for the delay does this lesson provide?

God's delaying of the birth of Isaac brought greater glory to Him, since the promised birth occurred only after Sarah's normal childbearing years had passed. This is a reminder to us that a major aim in our prayers must be the glorifying of God. It is interesting to note the closing petition in the *King James Version's* recording of the model prayer: "For thine is the kingdom, and the power, and the glory, for ever. Amen" (Matthew 6:13). While that is not found in many early manuscripts of the New Testament, it does fit in well with the spirit of the model prayer in seeking first of all the magnifying of the Heavenly Father and the accomplishing of His will. Perhaps a stronger emphasis on "Thine is the glory" in our prayers will bring the long-delayed answers.

2. We sometimes overlook Abraham's obviously intense love for Ishmael. Why is that remarkable, and how does it apply to parent-child relationships in our time?

It seems clear in the Biblical narrative that if it had been Abraham's decision alone to make, he would have kept Ishmael close to him. And that would have been in spite of Ishmael's mocking of Isaac and in spite of the "wild streak" in Ishmael's character, which had surely already been manifested. We see many "Ishmael's" today, both boys and girls, whose unruly, immoral behavior brings distress to their parents. Even when parents disapprove of their children's behavior, even when they must administer severe discipline, they must hold firmly to their love for those children. Ishmael was blessed by God and became a father of many tribes (Genesis 25:12-18). We still see unruly, rebellious children growing up to be responsible citizens.

3. The lesson writer observes that "God can take the very best we do or the very worst we do and turn it to the fulfillment of His eternal purposes." How is this an encouraging observation?

In our efforts at Christian work in the church and in putting our faith into practice in our daily lives we may see ourselves as stumblers and blunderers. We try to speak an encouraging word to someone who is suffering, and it seems clumsy and ineffective. We teach a Bible lesson or sing a solo or make a call, and we feel keenly our imperfection. It is tremendous to know that just as God worked out His will through the life of a fallible human being such as Abraham, He can also accomplish good things through our sincere but imperfect efforts. Of course, even when we feel that we have performed well, we should humbly offer our service to God and ask Him to use it to further His will.

4. Abraham's faith in God was exemplary, but so too was his obedience. What are some characteristics of his obedience to God.

Abraham's obedience was *prompt*. In sending Hagar and Ishmael away, and in responding later to God's command to sacrifice Isaac, he demonstrated that promptness. When we are made aware of a step of obedience God wants us to take, we should act promptly to do what He wants. Abraham's obedience was *unquestioning*. It is especially remarkable to read the opening verses of Genesis 22 and see that Abraham apparently raised no objections to God's command to sacrifice Isaac. When we clearly understand God's requirements of us as revealed in Scripture, we must learn to halt our questioning of Him and simply do as He commands.

5. If God was faithful in fulfilling His promises to men and women of the Bible, we should be confident that He will do the same for us. How can we strengthen such confidence?

One method is to make a thorough investigation of God's promise-keeping in the Old and New Testaments. As we study and meditate on these Biblical examples, they will become like seed sown within us that will produce the fruit of confidence in God. We can also share with one another examples of promises God has kept to each of us. When we hear our fellow Christians testify to God's comfort in times of sorrow, God's guidance in times of confusion, God's supply when material needs were pressing, we will be stirred to a stronger realization of God's faithfulness.

The Sons of Isaac

DEVOTIONAL READING: Psalm 127.

LESSON SCRIPTURE: Genesis 25:19-34.

PRINTED TEXT: Genesis 25:19-34.

Genesis 25:19-34

19 And these are the generations of Isaac, Abraham's son: Abraham begat Isaac:

20 And Isaac was forty years old when he took Rebekah to wife, the daughter of Bethuel the Syrian of Padanaram, the sister to Laban the Syrian.

21 And Isaac entreated the LORD for his wife, because she was barren: and the LORD was entreated of him, and Rebekah his wife conceived.

22 And the children struggled together within her; and she said, If it be so, why am I thus? And she went to inquire of the LORD.

23 And the LORD said unto her, Two nations are in thy womb, and two manner of people shall be separated from thy bowels; and the one people shall be stronger than the other people; and the elder shall serve the younger.

24 And when her days to be delivered were fulfilled, behold, there were twins in her womb.

25 And the first came out red, all over like a hairy garment; and they called his name Esau.

26 And after that came his brother out, and his hand took hold on Esau's heel; and his name was called Jacob: and Isaac was threescore years old when she bare them.

27 And the boys grew: and Esau was a cunning hunter, a man of the field; and Jacob was a plain man, dwelling in tents.

28 And Isaac loved Esau, because he did eat of his venison: but Rebekah loved Jacob.

29 And Jacob sod pottage: and Esau came from the field, and he was faint:

30 And Esau said to Jacob, Feed me, I pray thee, with that same red pottage; for I am faint: therefore was his name called Edom.

31 And Jacob said, Sell me this day thy birthright.

32 And Esau said, Behold, I am at the point to die: and what profit shall this birthright do to me?

33 And Jacob said, Swear to me this day; and he sware unto him: and he sold his birthright unto Jacob.

34 Then Jacob gave Esau bread and pottage of lentils; and he did eat and drink, and rose up, and went his way. Thus Esau despised his birthright.

GOLDEN TEXT: The LORD said unto her, Two nations are in thy womb, and two manner of people shall be separated from thy bowels; and the one people shall be stronger than the other people; and the elder shall serve the younger.—Genesis 25:23.

Lesson Aims

After studying this lesson the students should:

1. Resolve to allow God to work through them for His glory.

2. Understand that the profane person fails to recognize God's work.

3. Resolve this week to promote brotherly love in the family and in the church.

Lesson Outline

INTRODUCTION
   A. Conflict Resolution
   B. Lesson Background
 I. THE GENERATIONS OF ISAAC (Genesis 25:19, 20)
   A. Isaac Born to Abraham (v. 19)
   B. Isaac Marries Rebekah (v. 20)
 II. SONS ARE BORN TO ISAAC (Genesis 25:21-28)
   A. Isaac Prays for Barren Rebekah (v. 21)
   B. God Foresees Conflict (vv. 22, 23)
   C. The Sons Are Born in Conflict (vv. 24-26)
   D. The Sons Grow in Conflict (vv. 27, 28)
      Playing Favorites
 III. SALE OF THE BIRTHRIGHT (Genesis 25:29-34)
   A. Esau Is Famished (vv. 29, 30)
   B. Jacob Exacts a Price (vv. 31-33)
   C. Esau Despises His Birthright (v. 34)
      Instant Gratification
CONCLUSION
   A. Jacob and Esau
   B. Prayer
   C. Thought to Remember

Display visual 9 of the visuals packet throughout this session. The visual is shown on page 77.

Introduction

A. Conflict Resolution

Mediating conflicts has become a full-time occupation for many people in the modern world. This is partly because it is clearly recognized that the alternative is chaos, and perhaps even worldwide destruction. Though conflict is inevitable in the real world, it can be resolved. Many pastoral care counselors in churches have given themselves to the ministry of resolving conflicts, and many books have been written on the subject. Conflict resolution in the church is not new, however, for many of the New Testament books deal with divisive issues. As the text for this lesson reveals, Jacob and Esau could have benefited from a mediator.

B. Lesson Background

Abraham based his life on God's promises, many of which centered on the patriarch's descendants. Genesis 21 records the birth of Isaac, the child through whom God's promises to Abraham were to be realized. A seeming obstacle to the fulfillment of those promises arose when God himself commanded Abraham to sacrifice this son of promise (Genesis 22). Abraham's obedience stood the test—his faith in God did not falter—and as a result God gave him assurance that the divine promises would be fulfilled (Genesis 22:16-18).

Years passed, and Isaac grew to full manhood. For God's promise to Abraham to be realized, Isaac must have progeny as well. But first he had to find a suitable wife. This issue occupies Genesis 24, which repeatedly stresses God's leading in the matter. The next crucial event in the story of promise was the birth of Isaac and Rebekah's children.

I. The Generations of Isaac (Genesis 25:19, 20)

A. Isaac Born to Abraham (v. 19)

19. And these are the generations of Isaac, Abraham's son: Abraham begat Isaac.

In light of the information we already have in Genesis, this material would seem unnecessary. We already know what it tells us. But it is important here to reemphasize that Isaac was the son of promise and a direct descendant of Abraham. We are to understand that the family of promise will continue to be the subject of the narrative.

B. Isaac Marries Rebekah (v. 20)

20. And Isaac was forty years old when he took Rebekah to wife, the daughter of Bethuel the Syrian of Padan-aram, the sister to Laban the Syrian.

This summary verse takes us back to chapter 24 and the detailed search by Abraham's servant for a wife for Isaac. Rebekah was an ideal woman, and she was discovered through God's guidance. This verse not only looks back, it looks ahead. Twice it emphasizes the Syrian connection of Rebekah. Modern translations prefer Aramean to Syrian, a more accurate ethnic term. These references prepare us for Jacob's long stay with his relatives, specifically with

Laban, in Padan-aram (Northwest Mesopotamia, see map, visual 14 of the visuals packet). The age of Isaac was important also. It underscored the length of time from his marriage to Rebekah to the coming of their sons (twenty years, see verse 26). This note subtly points to a major sub-theme of Genesis—God faithfully keeps His promises, but His timetable does not fit human expectations.

II. Sons Are Born to Isaac (Genesis 25:21-28)

A. Isaac Prays for Barren Rebekah (v. 21)

21. And Isaac entreated the LORD for his wife, because she was barren: and the LORD was entreated of him, and Rebekah his wife conceived.

Rebekah *was barren*. Other women, who also were chosen by God, experienced this same disappointing condition. Sarah was barren, as was Rachel, Hannah (Samuel's mother), and Elisabeth, the mother of John the Baptist. The eventual birth of a son, in each instance, was a statement about the power of God and the dependency of God's chosen on this power. All the details of God's promises were dependent on Him for their fulfillment. There was nothing "natural" about the outcome. The husband and wife may have been specially selected to be participants in the development of God's chosen people, but they must wait for God to open the womb.

So Isaac prayed for his barren wife. The matter was entirely in the hands of God. The expression used here is interesting: *Isaac entreated the Lord. . . and the Lord was entreated*. God responded to the prayer. The verb translated *entreat* here is found also in the narratives of the plagues of Egypt (see Exodus 8:8, 9, 28, 29; 9:28; 10:17, 18).

In Isaac and Rebekah's case, the result of the prayer was conception. One wonders if the boys born to them ever realized that they were special gifts from God, conceived only as a result of prayer?

As Christians, we must realize that we are the children of God only because of His gracious will. Eternal life, which God bestows on us through His Son Jesus Christ, is ours as a gift (John 1:12, 13; Romans 6:23).

B. God Foresees Conflict (vv. 22, 23)

22. And the children struggled together within her; and she said, If it be so, why am I thus? And she went to inquire of the LORD.

As Rebekah's pregnancy advanced, she began to experience difficulties. We learn immediately that she was carrying more than one baby, and that there was conflict between them in her womb. This struggling between the unborn children was indicative of the rivalry that was to exist later between the brothers and between their descendants.

Rebekah, of course, did not know that she would give birth to twins. She was puzzled and disturbed by her experience. Her response, *If it be so, why am I thus?* was cryptic, and its meaning is obscure. She seems to be saying, "If this pregnancy is a result of prayer, then why is such distress coming to me?" She may have thought, "If I am being obedient to God and He is answering my prayers, then shouldn't things go smoothly for me?" Many today seem to share this same theology. But Rebekah found it wasn't so. *She went to inquire of the Lord,* that is to seek an answer from God. We are not told where she went, but there may have been a place where God was worshiped by prayer and sacrifice.

23. And the LORD said unto her, Two nations are in thy womb, and two manner of people shall be separated from thy bowels; and the one people shall be stronger than the other people; and the elder shall serve the younger.

Although we are not told how God spoke to Rebekah, we are told what He said. The divine answer in this verse forms the main point of the text and is the focal point of the whole cycle of narratives centering around Jacob. The words are prophetic, having reference to Esau and Jacob, the two sons in Rebekah's womb. From them would come *two nations,* Edom from Esau and Israel from Jacob. These two *peoples* would be separated, that is divided from and against each other. Thus the conflict between the twins in Rebekah's womb would be continued by those who would descend from them. Furthermore, *the younger* would have the preeminence over *the elder.* Esau himself never served Jacob, but the Old Testament records several instances of the conflict between their descendants and Edom's servitude to Israel (Numbers 20:14-21; 1 Samuel 14:47; 2 Samuel 8:13, 14; 1 Kings 11:14-22; 2 Kings 8:20-22). Some may cite a verse such as this in support of the doctrines of election

---

How to Say It

ARAMEAN. *Ar*-uh-*me*-un (strong accent on *me*).

BETHUEL. Be-*thu*-el.

ISHMAEL. *Ish*-may-el.

LABAN. *Lay*-bun.

PADAN-ARAM. *Pay*-dan-*a*-ram.

and predestination. We need to remember, however, that this text does not speak of individual election for salvation or damnation. It deals with future, concrete, historical developments in two nations in the unfolding of God's purpose for mankind.

In Romans 9:10-12, Paul refers to this passage to support his argument about God's freedom to be God. Paul is concerned to show that God's "purpose" stands. God's purpose is His plan for the salvation of all mankind, and that plan was in existence before the foundation of the world (Ephesians 1:4; 2 Timothy 1:9). That God makes choices relative to His purpose does not determine an individual's future nor eliminate the individual's freedom to exercise his or her will in making moral choices.

Just as Isaac, and not Ishmael, was the son of Abraham through whom God's promise to Abraham was to be carried out, so Jacob, and not Esau, was the son of Isaac who would receive the promise (Genesis 28:13-15). Both Isaac, and Jacob after him, received the promise because it was through their line of descent that God was going to work out His salvation plan.

C. The Sons Are Born in Conflict
(vv. 24-26)

24, 25. And when her days to be delivered were fulfilled, behold, there were twins in her womb. And the first came out red, all over like a hairy garment; and they called his name Esau.

Verse 24 is a brief report of the expected results of the pregnancy. We have already been told that Rebekah would give birth to twins.

The first to be born was reddish, that is, he was of a reddish-brown color. The second feature noted about him was that he seemed as if covered with a kind of fur, a thick down. This latter feature was the basis for his being named *Esau*, which means "hairy." We are not told if Esau's unusual physical appearance at birth bare any relationship to his character in later life.

The hairiness of Esau becomes a factor in a later section of the narrative and seems to fit his being a man of the field (v. 27).

26. And after that came his brother out, and his hand took hold on Esau's heel; and his name was called Jacob: and Isaac was threescore years old when she bare them.

Hosea 12:3 explicitly states that Jacob had grasped the heel of his brother while the twins were still in their mother's womb. (Could this explain, in part, the unusual amount of movement and distress Rebekah had experienced?) After Esau was born, Jacob came out gripping the heel of Esau. This circumstance led to the younger son's being named *Jacob*, for the name literally means "heel-holder." In wrestling one may gain the advantage over his opponent by taking hold of his heel and causing him to fall. Thus this word signifies to "trip up," hence "to supplant." Esau later noted that Jacob had been rightly named (see Genesis 27:36).

Many Bible scholars think there was a positive side to *Jacob's* name also. There is evidence that the word can mean "protect," so it may carry the meaning "may God protect." The events of Jacob's life reveal the appropriateness of this meaning of the name.

D. The Sons Grow in Conflict
(vv. 27, 28)

27. And the boys grew: and Esau was a cunning hunter, a man of the field; and Jacob was a plain man, dwelling in tents.

The boys grew up to become quite different in temperament and occupation. Though we could make too much of this, they chose separate lifestyles that have a long history of conflict—the *hunter* and the settled farmer/herder. There perhaps was another contrast here as well, that of the rough-and-ready uncivilized person and the calm, settled, civilized man. Esau preferred to rove over the country in search of excitement, even danger. Jacob, by contrast, stayed at home with his folks, tending to the family's business. The word to describe Jacob, *plain*, is often translated "even-tempered."

28. And Isaac loved Esau, because he did eat of his venison: but Rebekah loved Jacob.

This statement of parental preference seems innocent enough, but it portended a difficult future for everyone concerned. It was not enough that the sons grew in conflict, even the parents became involved by their favoritism. Isaac was of a quiet and retiring disposition. Perhaps he admired and was drawn to the bold and energetic nature of Esau, which stood in contrast to his own. It is specifically stated that Isaac enjoyed the wild game that Esau provided by his hunting. We are not told why Rebekah favored Jacob. Perhaps it was because he was of a quieter, gentler spirit and was helpful around the home. We must note that Rebekah's love for Jacob may be related to the word she had received from the Lord when she was pregnant with the twins. At that time the Lord had said, "The elder shall serve the younger," and this may have influenced her feelings toward Jacob.

One wonders how later events would have been different if there had not been this parental rivalry. Can any family survive the kind of competition and favoritism we see portrayed in this one? Paul's instructions for the husbands, wives, parents, and children would seem to speak directly to the problems so evident here (Ephesians 5:21—6:4).

PLAYING FAVORITES

Bill Cosby provided television viewers with wholesome, family-oriented entertainment. He began his entertainment career as a stand-up comedian, telling stories of his childhood. He related one outburst of sibling rivalry that resulted in his telling his brother, Russell, "You ain't really my brother. We got you from the police. The police are your mother and father."

The story is a humorous reminder to many people of childhood struggles with others (and within themselves) as to whether they were really loved by their parents, or at least loved as much as their siblings. In some families, that insecurity is well-founded: parents either do not love the children or love one of them more than the others. Sometimes, as in the case of Jacob and Esau, parental love is divided—one parent loving one child, the other loving another.

The result of this parental failure is documented in the bitter rivalry of Jacob and Esau, as well as in the later case of Joseph and his brothers. These were victims of poor parenting, and the lives of all concerned were filled with heartbreak for many years because of it.

Children may differ in their gifts and "likeableness," but wise parents will overcome the temptation to play favorites.   —C. R. B.

III. Sale of the Birthright (Genesis 25:29-34)

A. Esau Is Famished (vv. 29, 30)

29, 30. And Jacob sod pottage: and Esau came from the field, and he was faint: and Esau said to Jacob, Feed me, I pray thee, with that same red pottage; for I am faint: therefore was his name called Edom.

The incident recorded briefly in the remaining verses of our text had far-reaching consequences. It helped to reveal the nature of both Esau and Jacob, and it resulted in Jacob's supplanting Esau as the head of the tribe and assuming the responsibilities and privileges that that honor bestowed.

On this occasion, Jacob was cooking some stew, perhaps of lentils. It may be that he knew from experience Esau would come in from the hunt famished, and that he was preparing this tasty dish to entice Esau. Whether or not this was so, when Esau approached him after a grueling day in the field, Jacob determined to take advantage of the situation.

visual 9

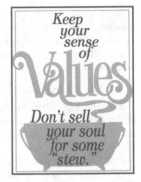

Esau is pictured as a profane man who was driven only by his appetites. He came gasping from the hunt. *Feed me*, he said. The words depict a vehemence of appetite: "Let me devour," or "Let me gulp down." He wanted only food.

That same red pottage, literally, "that red, that red there," referring to the brown-red lentil stew.

Therefore was his name called Edom, that is, red. The combination of his reddish complexion and this episode involving the red pottage, which was a turning point in Esau's life, resulted in his being given this new name. His descendants became known as Edomites.

B. Jacob Exacts a Price (vv. 31-33)

31, 32. And Jacob said, Sell me this day thy birthright. And Esau said, Behold, I am at the point to die: and what profit shall this birthright do to me?

Among the patriarchs, possession of the birthright carried the privilege of leadership of the family. Along with priority of position and control of the inheritance came the responsibility of caring for the family members. In the family of Abraham there were also the unique spiritual privileges bestowed by God first on Abraham and then on his son Isaac. Both Esau and Jacob must have been aware of all this. Jacob desired this birthright.

Was he motivated solely by the desire for priority and status, or did he cherish the thought of having a part in the fulfillment of God's promises to Abraham? It is difficult to tell. Esau's response, however, showed that he had little regard for what the birthright embraced. When his appetite was crying to be satisfied, discussion of a birthright was irrelevant. His focus was on immediate need.

33. And Jacob said, Swear to me this day; and he sware unto him: and he sold his birthright unto Jacob.

By Jacob demanding an oath, Jacob showed that he did not trust his brother. The oath was binding and made the agreement irreversible.

Jacob's conduct in this instance cannot be defended. Even if he desired the birthright for the noblest of reasons, he is to be condemned for securing it by taking advantage of his brother's weakness.

C. Esau Despises His Birthright (v. 34)

34. Then Jacob gave Esau bread and pottage of lentils; and he did eat and drink, and rose up, and went his way. Thus Esau despised his birthright.

Esau's hasty eating is described with four verbs of quick action: he ate, drank, got up, left. His hunger satisfied, he went his way with no thought about the serious transaction he had just completed. His attitude was the crucial problem. Esau despised his position of honor and responsibility in the family—he held it in contempt as totally worthless. Thus the author of Hebrews regarded him as godless (Hebrews 12:16, 17).

INSTANT GRATIFICATION

One of the ongoing themes in Charles Schultz's "Peanuts" comic strip is the unrequited love of Lucy for Schroeder, the virtuoso piano player. As the young musical genius pounds away on his toy piano, extracting from it the music of his idol, Beethoven, Lucy is frequently seen leaning against the piano, looking longingly for some crumb of affection to be thrown her way.

One day's dialogue has Lucy saying, "Do you love me? I need to know right now!" Without looking up from his piano, Schroeder says, "No, I don't love you." Looking away, Lucy sighs, "I could have waited until tomorrow."

Lucy is typical of most of us: we want the good things of life *right now*, but we are willing

to wait forever for the bad. Ironically, in their quest for immediate gratification many often bring about what they do not want. No better example of this exists than the epidemic of AIDS and other sexually transmitted diseases that have resulted from our culture's uninhibited quest for sexual gratification.

The need for immediate gratification is typical of children. When the need persists past adolescence, it becomes a disease of the spirit that may bear wrenching consequences, as in Esau's case. A lifetime of blessings can be lost in pursuit of momentary pleasure.   —C. R. B.

Conclusion

A. Jacob and Esau

The text of our lesson reveals little that is admirable in the character of either of the twin sons of Jacob.

Jacob's covetousness and callousness are made manifest. Esau possessed the birthright, and Jacob wanted it. But the means he employed to obtain the birthright were reprehensible. Catching Esau in a moment of weakness, Jacob saw an opportunity to take advantage of his brother and gain what he himself desired. The result was further distrust and disharmony in the family.

Esau is revealed to be a sensual person, seeking only that which promises pleasure for the moment. His birthright had no value except in the distant future, and even then a *religious* value chiefly. For this reason he was willing to part with it for a bowl of stew.

May we learn from both, Let us seek our place in God's purposes by employing the principles of love and brotherhood that He has revealed. And let us treasure our spiritual inheritance in Christ Jesus above all that this world offers in the way of momentary pleasure.

B. Prayer

Dear Lord, lead us to recognize our place in Your purposes. May we not grasp futilely for power or position, but instead serve others in a spirit of humility. Thank You for Your gift of salvation in Your Son. Help us to share this glorious message with our neighbors and fellow workers. Through Christ we pray. Amen.

C. Thought to Remember

"What will it profit a man if he gains his cause, and silences his adversary, if at the same time he loses that humble, tender frame of spirit in which the Lord delights, and to which the promise of his presence is made."

—John Newton

Home Daily Bible Readings

Monday, Oct. 25—God Tests Abraham's Faith (Genesis 22:1-13)

Tuesday, Oct. 26—God Blesses Abraham's Progeny (Genesis 22:14-19)

Wednesday, Oct. 27—The Search for Isaac's Wife (Genesis 24:7-18, 25-27)

Thursday, Oct. 28—Isaac and Ishmael Bury Abraham (Genesis 25:5-11)

Friday, Oct. 29—Before Birth, Rebekah's Twins Struggled (Genesis 25:19-23)

Saturday, Oct. 30—Isaac Loved Esau; Rebekah Loved Jacob (Genesis 25:24-28)

Sunday, Oct. 31—Esau Sells His Birthright to Jacob (Genesis 25:29-34)

Learning by Doing

This page contains an alternate lesson plan emphasizing learning activities. Classes desiring such student involvement will find these suggestions helpful.

Learning Goals

As a result of participation in this lesson, the students will be able to:

1. Describe the unworthy attitudes displayed by Jacob and Esau in the lesson text.

2. Suggest some means to promote brotherly love in their families and in the family of God.

Into the Lesson

Write the word *brothers* prominently on the chalkboard. As students arrive, ask them to come to the board and write the names of some famous brothers under the heading. If they need some prompting, write one or more of the following: Cain and Abel, Tom and Dick Smothers, Joseph and his eleven brothers, Peter and Andrew, James and John.

When it is time for class to start, ask the class to think about the way brothers often get along. Look at the jealousy and violence between Cain and Abel, or in the relationship of Joseph and his brothers. Tom and Dick Smothers' routine, "Mom always liked you best!" evoked laughter because it had a ring of truth to it. Discuss the rivalry that often develops between brothers.

After a few minutes, make the transition to the Bible study by saying something like the following: "Though not all brothers are or were known for their rivalries, it is not hard to believe that most engage in some. Our lesson today focuses on two brothers who are known for their rivalry. (If the names of Jacob and Esau were written on the board, circle them. If they were not, write them now.) Jacob and Esau were rivals even before they were born, and their rivalry continued through much of their life. Yet even amid the rivalry, we see God's purposes being carried forward."

Into the Word

Ask a volunteer to read Genesis 25:19-28. Divide the class into two groups. Ask the first group to study verses 19-23 and answer the following questions:

1. What problem did Rebekah have, and what did Isaac do about it? (She was barren; Isaac prayed for her.)

2. What problem developed during Rebekah's pregnancy, and what did she do about it? (The children "struggled" within her; she prayed about it.)

3. What prophecy was given about the two children Rebekah would bear? (They would father nations; the older would serve the younger.)

Ask the second group to study verses 24-28 and answer these questions:

1. What event occurred at the birth of Jacob and Esau that pictured their future strife? (Jacob grabbed Esau's heel.)

2. Describe the personalities of the two as they grew. (Esau was an outdoorsman, a hunter; Jacob was a "plain man," an indoors type.)

3. What attitudes by their parents fueled the rivalry between Jacob and Esau? (Isaac showed preference to Esau; Rebekah to Jacob.)

Give the groups about six minutes to complete their assignment; then ask each to report. Observe the importance of prayer in this episode. Note also that the future was known to God and the events that transpired between the brothers advanced God's covenant purposes.

Have another volunteer read verses 29-34 of the text. List the following attitudes on the chalkboard: selfish, opportunistic, uncaring, competitive, godly, worldly. Ask the class which words describe Jacob in this event. Which describe Esau? Which describe both? Which describe neither? Discuss the attitudes displayed by these two brothers and how it affected their lives and choices later. Use the commentary section of this lesson to explain the significance of the events.

(Both Jacob and Esau were selfish and competitive. Esau in particular was uncaring and worldly—despising his birthright. Jacob was opportunistic. Neither displayed godly characteristics in this episode.)

Into Life

Discuss how competitiveness or worldliness prevents us from working together as we should, either in our families or in the body of Christ. Ask the class to suggest three or four things the church could do to enhance cooperation among the members. Then ask them to suggest three or four others that apply to the family. Discuss briefly. To conclude, have the students list privately three or four things they themselves can do (or stop doing) that will promote brotherly love within their own families or within the church. Ask each to select one item from his or her list and put it into practice this week.

Let's Talk It Over

The questions on this page are designed to encourage review of the lesson Scriptures and to promote discussion of the lesson by the class. The answers provided are only discussion starters. Let your class talk it over from there.

1. Isaac prayed for Rebekah because of her barrenness. What are some prayers husbands and wives should offer for each other today?

If the wife is home all day with the children, her husband should ask the Lord to supply her with patience, wisdom, and love. The wife at the same time will want to pray that her husband will be strong in facing the pressures and temptations of the workaday world. Of course, the latter prayer in many families will also be appropriate for the wife. In an era in which sexual temptations abound, each partner will want to intercede for the other for the power to resist and remain faithful. A special danger is the lure of material things. Husbands and wives both need to pray that their mates will not fall prey to the worship of money and what money buys, but value first that which is eternal.

2. What are some prayers parents should offer for their children? What is the benefit for children to know that their parents pray for them?

With children facing a terrible array of temptations regarding sex, drugs, alcohol, the occult, and the like, parents will want to pray that their children will be wise enough and strong enough to resist. As we seek to teach our children to follow Jesus, we will also need to pray that they will stand firm against the efforts of those teachers, friends, and others who might try to disparage God and His Word. If our children know that we are praying for them, surely they will be made stronger by this evidence of our love and concern for them.

3. In Isaac's and Rebekah's preferential treatment of their sons we see the perils of favoritism. How can parents avoid this kind of treatment of their children?

Prospective parents should give serious thought to the expectations they have for their children. Isaac may have anticipated having a son who was an outdoorsman, and so he was inclined to favor Esau. Fathers today desiring a son who will be involved in sports or interested in mechanical things may favor such children over those who take greater pleasure in fine arts. Certainly we must give children freedom to pursue their own areas of interest, so long as these are wholesome and constructive. For Christian parents the most important aim regarding their children should be that they learn to follow Jesus Christ. In this aim parents must give equal effort to teaching those children who are responsive and those who seem slow to respond.

4. Esau demonstrated contempt for his family heritage. What are some present-day examples of contempt for one's heritage?

It is distressing to read of young people desecrating our nation's flag and making disparaging comments about our country. That there are many wrongs done in our nation, many circumstances that need to be changed, is undeniable. But it is troubling that a blanket condemnation of our society ignores the positive heritage of freedom, justice, and opportunity that we possess. In some families of today, children will spurn the moral values of their parents. We feel a sense of outrage when this happens to parents we know. In the church, we see some who abandon the religious heritage passed on to them by faithful men and women of previous generations. They may exhibit a scornful attitude toward their spiritual forebears' belief in the divine inspiration of the Bible, the reality of Biblical miracles, the importance of adhering to New Testament doctrine, and similar views.

5. The unhealthy competitiveness that existed between Esau and Jacob is rampant in our society. How can we avoid an excessive level of competition in the church and the home?

Some want to do away entirely with competition. They feel that team competitions at Christ camp, attendance contests at church, and the like are contrary to the spirit of Christ. Others, however, point out that competition can be a tool in promoting learning and fellowship and that it can be healthy. Certainly it should be understood in Christian competition that winning at any cost, seeking to embarrass or dishearten an opponent, or allowing success to engender a haughty kind of pride are not legitimate features. The key to a Christian approach to any activity is in fulfilling Philippians 2:3: "Let nothing be done through strife or vainglory; but in lowliness of mind let each esteem other better than themselves."

Jacob Steals the Blessing

DEVOTIONAL READING: Hebrews 12:14-17.

LESSON SCRIPTURE: Genesis 27.

PRINTED TEXT: Genesis 27:6-8, 15-27.

Genesis 27:6-8, 15-27

6 And Rebekah spake unto Jacob her son, saying, Behold, I heard thy father speak unto Esau thy brother, saying,

7 Bring me venison, and make me savory meat, that I may eat, and bless thee before the LORD before my death.

8 Now therefore, my son, obey my voice according to that which I command thee.

. . . .

15 And Rebekah took goodly raiment of her eldest son Esau, which were with her in the house, and put them upon Jacob her younger son:

16 And she put the skins of the kids of the goats upon his hands, and upon the smooth of his neck:

17 And she gave the savory meat and the bread, which she had prepared, into the hand of her son Jacob.

18 And he came unto his father, and said, My father: and he said, Here am I; who art thou, my son?

19 And Jacob said unto his father, I am Esau thy firstborn; I have done according as thou badest me: arise, I pray thee, sit and eat of my venison, that thy soul may bless me.

20 And Isaac said unto his son, How is it that thou hast found it so quickly, my son? And he said, Because the LORD thy God brought it to me.

21 And Isaac said unto Jacob, Come near, I pray thee, that I may feel thee, my son, whether thou be my very son Esau or not.

22 And Jacob went near unto Isaac his father; and he felt him, and said, The voice is Jacob's voice, but the hands are the hands of Esau.

23 And he discerned him not, because his hands were hairy, as his brother Esau's hands: so he blessed him.

24 And he said, Art thou my very son Esau? And he said, I am.

25 And he said, Bring it near to me, and I will eat of my son's venison, that my soul may bless thee. And he brought it near to him, and he did eat: and he brought him wine, and he drank.

26 And his father Isaac said unto him, Come near now, and kiss me, my son.

27 And he came near, and kissed him: and he smelled the smell of his raiment, and blessed him.

Nov 7

GOLDEN TEXT: [Isaac] said, Thy brother came with subtilty, and hath taken away thy blessing.—Genesis 27:35.

Lesson Aims

After studying the lesson, the students should be able to:

1. Understand that God cannot be deceived.
2. Resolve to seek God's blessing honestly.
3. Commit themselves to honesty in all relationships.

Lesson Outline

INTRODUCTION
  A. To Tell the Truth
  B. Lesson Background
I. REBEKAH PLANS THE DECEPTION (Genesis 27:6-8)
    Secrets
II. REBEKAH PREPARES FOR THE DECEPTION (Genesis 27:15-17)
    A. Clothes and Coverings Provided (vv. 15, 16)
    B. The Food Prepared (v. 17)
III. JACOB IMPLEMENTS THE DECEPTION (Genesis 27:18-27a)
    A. Jacob Claims to Be Esau (vv. 18, 19)
    B. Isaac Has Doubts (vv. 20-24)
    C. Jacob Receives the Blessing (vv. 25-27a)
CONCLUSION
    A. What Justifies the Means?
    B. God's Purposes
    C. Prayer
    D. Thought to Remember

Visual 10 of the visuals packet highlights events in the lives of Jacob and Esau prior to Jacob's flight from home. The visual is shown on page 86.

Introduction

A. To Tell the Truth

The old television show "To Tell the Truth" was a fascinating program. With only one of three contestants committed to telling the truth, it was very difficult to determine which of them was the person who was described in the affidavit that was read.

The show was entertaining, for it involved no malicious intent. It illustrated, however, the ease with which people may deceive others. And while that resulted in no harm on a TV program, deception and dishonesty, when practiced in life, lead to trouble of all kinds.

We expect our government leaders to be honest. If we discover that they are not, their credibility is damaged and unrest arises among the citizenry. Businesses are expected to operate with integrity. If they do not, public confidence in the products or services they offer is damaged. Certainly the relationships between spouses, siblings, and parents and children must be founded on the principles of truthfulness and honesty. If not, the peace and harmony of the home will be shattered.

The event we are studying in this lesson clearly reveals the damaging effect of deception practiced in the home. The results were lasting alienation, separation, sadness, and fear.

B. Lesson Background

Some thirty, and perhaps as many as fifty, years passed from the time when Esau sold his birthright to Jacob (see last week's lesson) to the event that we are studying in this lesson. Chapter 26 records the little we know of what took place in Isaac's family during this time. A severe famine drove them from the south country to Gerar in the land of the Philistines, where they stayed "a long time" (v. 8). As Abraham before him did, Isaac passed his wife off as his sister so the men of that place would not kill him to take her, and he too was rebuked for his duplicity (vv. 7-11). As time passed God blessed Isaac with abundant harvests and increasing herds. So great was his wealth and numerous his servants that the Philistines envied as well as feared him. Conflict arose over Isaac's wells, and so gradually he withdrew from the Philistines' territory and established himself in Beersheba (vv. 12-33).

Chapter 26 closes with the notation that at the age of forty, Esau married two Canaanite women, and this caused grief of mind to his parents. It is apparent that they wanted their sons to marry women from their extended family rather than choosing wives from among the surrounding peoples (Genesis 27:46—28:2).

The time came when Isaac, old and virtually blind, believed that he soon would die. Although he was mistaken in this, he did proceed with arrangements to pronounce his blessing upon his favorite son, Esau. So he called Esau to him and asked him to go into the field to hunt for venison. When it was found and prepared, Isaac would eat it and then pronounce the blessing. This blessing was more than a benediction. It placed the recipient in close and favored covenant relationship with the Lord. It was prophetic in nature, indicating in a measure the future listing of the one blessed. Once the blessing had been given, it could neither be altered nor revoked.

Rebekah overheard Isaac and immediately set in motion a plan to secure the blessing for Jacob.

I. Rebekah Plans the Deception (Genesis 27:6-8)

Rebekah no doubt had treasured in her heart God's word that her younger son Jacob, whom she loved, would rule over Esau, whose wild life-style and Cannaanite wives were distressing to her (see Genesis 25:23). She probably knew that Jacob had bought Esau's birthright. But in spite of it all, it seemed that Esau would yet receive his father's blessing and regain the preeminence he had given up. To prevent that, she took matters into her own hands.

What would have happened if Rebekah had done nothing? No one knows. Perhaps the blessing would have been interrupted in some way before Isaac bestowed it. One thing is certain, however. God's promise would have stood, regardless of the maneuverings of men.

6, 7. And Rebekah spake unto Jacob her son, saying, Behold, I heard thy father speak unto Esau thy brother, saying, Bring me venison, and make me savory meat, that I may eat, and bless thee before the Lord before my death.

The fragmentation in the family is evident in this episode, as both Isaac and Rebekah made plans for this important event without considering one another. One can raise questions about Isaac's motives. Did he know about God's pronouncement to Rebekah while she was carrying the twins? Surely Rebekah would have shared it with him. If so, had he forgotten God's word that the younger son was to have the preeminence over the elder, or was he trying to bypass it?

How is it that Rebekah overheard Isaac speak to Esau? Did it happen by chance, or did she constantly watch Isaac to guard against just such a move as he planned? If the latter, then the family lived for some time in great tension and competition. The fact that Isaac was blind (v. 1) aided Rebekah in her scheming.

When Rebekah told Jacob about Isaac's request of Esau, she reported that Isaac said he would give his blessing *before the Lord*, that is, "in the presence of the Lord." Although Isaac

---

How to Say It

GERAR.   *Gee*-rar (*G* as in *get*).
PADAN-ARAM.   *Pay*-dan-*a*-ram.

---

didn't include this phrase when speaking to Esau, Rebekah may have understood it to be implied in what her husband had said. This was an indication of the solemnity of the blessing. God's own person would guarantee it. So Rebekah knew that her intrigue would not be hidden from God, yet she went ahead. Did she believe that God was on her side? Most of the time schemers and deceivers operate as if no one, including God, can see them or will know what they do.

SECRETS

"Inside Story" and "Now It Can Be Told" are just two of many TV programs that tantalize viewers with the promise of learning secret information that can now be divulged. TV "soap operas" have long pandered to viewers' desires to observe the secret lives of imaginary people whose twisted morality is presented as true-to-life.

This doesn't differ very much from the old-fashioned practices of gossiping over the backyard fence or sitting in on gab sessions down at the barber shop or gas station. Our interest in discovering someone else's secrets is an age-old human trait.

In a family setting that a modern counselor would call "dysfunctional," Rebekah's eavesdropping on the conversation between Isaac and Esau set the scene for conspiracy. In a healthy family situation, the very normal decision that "now is the time to bestow the blessing on Esau" would have been a matter of open, unashamed discussion. But because of her hidden agenda, Rebekah connived to trick Isaac into bestowing the birthright on Jacob, the younger son. Isaac may also have been playing the game by trying to make the birthright ceremony a private matter.

Regardless, healthy families are able to openly discuss family business and find ways to accommodate each member's need for love and acceptance without hurting the others.   —C. R. B.

8. Now therefore, my son, obey my voice according to that which I command thee.

Jacob was not a young lad at this time. He was a mature man, perhaps as old as seventy-seven. So she was not giving commandment to an unquestioning child. Rather it appears that she knew Jacob shared her craftiness, and that by appealing to their close relationship she would gain his cooperation in her scheme.

The verses that are omitted from the printed text contain the details of Rebekah's scheme. Jacob was to go to the flock and bring her two young goats so that she could prepare some of the "savory meat" that Isaac loved so much. She knew exactly how he liked it, and she had the ability to make goat meat taste like the wild game that Esau was hunting. With this food Jacob could go to his father, feed him, and receive the blessing in Esau's place (vv. 9, 10).

Jacob could see one flaw in the plan—he was quite different from Esau in physical appearance. He had smooth skin, but Esau was hairy (a factor that was noted at the time of birth, 25:25). Isaac might be blind but he would be able to feel the difference between smooth and hairy skin. Jacob knew that if his father touched him, the scheme would be revealed. Jacob was fearful, because that would bring a curse on him. Just as the blessing carried with it a real vitality and a picture of the future, so did a curse. Jacob was not objecting to the overall scheme; he just recognized a potential weakness in it.

Rebekah had already planned for such a contingency (see v. 16), but she didn't share that part of her plan with Jacob just yet. She was willing to bear the curse herself, such was her desire for Jacob to receive the blessing. She again urged him to do as she directed, and Jacob did so (vv. 11-14).

Why did Rebekah scheme to secure the blessing for Jacob, in view of the fact that his future had already been assured by the Lord? Because she could not trust God to do what He said He would do. She felt her efforts could help the promise along and fill in what God might overlook. She displayed a weakness of faith, similar to that of Abraham and Sarah (Genesis 16). Many Christians do likewise. Even with the promises of Scripture (such as Psalm 27:14; Matthew 6:25-33; Hebrews 13:5), some find it difficult to adjust their anxieties to God's timetable. But He is faithful and will do what He has promised (2 Peter 3:9).

II. Rebekah Prepares for the Deception (Genesis 27:15-17)

A. Clothes and Coverings Provided (vv. 15, 16)

15, 16. And Rebekah took goodly raiment of her eldest son Esau, which were with her in the house, and put them upon Jacob her younger son: and she put the skins of the kids of the goats upon his hands, and upon the smooth of his neck.

Goodly raiment. Rebekah took some of Esau's best clothes and gave them to Jacob to wear. These would match the solemnity of the occasion and its festive nature also. The success of the plot depended on making Jacob as much like Esau as possible. The clothing would play an important role in this. The outdoors smell re-

tained by the clothing would provide a crucial identifying mark (see v. 27).

The covering of goatskin was the answer to what Jacob perceived as a weakness in the plot. Only his hands and neck were covered, for they were the only places not covered by the robe.

B. The Food Prepared (v. 17)

17. And she gave the savory meat and the bread, which she had prepared, into the hand of her son Jacob.

Everything was ready for the deception when Rebekah handed Jacob the food. He and his mother were in full agreement as to what needed to be done, and he proceeded without hesitation.

III. Jacob Implements the Deception (Genesis 27:18-27a)

A. Jacob Claims to Be Esau (vv. 18, 19)

18, 19. And he came unto his father, and said, My father: and he said, Here am I; who art thou, my son? And Jacob said unto his father, I am Esau thy firstborn; I have done according as thou badest me: arise, I pray thee, sit and eat of my venison, that thy soul may bless me.

We come now to the actual deception of Isaac. Jacob must have been very tense as he approached his bed-ridden father. Would Jacob be found out by his father despite the disguise? Would Esau return while Jacob was there (see verse 30). The scheme could disintegrate at any moment.

Respectfully Jacob addressed his father, and when Isaac asked who was there, Jacob answered with the first of three lies. Boldly he identified himself as Esau. Then he asserted that he had done what his father had wanted him to do, whereas, in fact, he was implementing the scheme of his mother. Finally he urged, *Eat of my venison* (which was not venison at all). Rarely does one who embarks on a cause of deception stop at one falsehood.

If Jacob attempted to imitate his brother's voice, he did not succeed. Isaac's ensuing remarks reveal his suspicions concerning who was standing before him.

B. Isaac Has Doubts (vv. 20-24)

20. And Isaac said unto his son, How is it that thou hast found it so quickly, my son? And he said, Because the Lord thy God brought it to me.

Adding to Isaac's initial skepticism was the fact that the food had been brought to him so soon. Jacob's quick reply was another lie, this one bordering on blasphemy. He claimed that God helped him find the animal. *The Lord thy God.* Notice that he did not say *my* God, but *your* God. Had Jacob not yet established his own relationship with the Lord God? As solemn as this pronouncement was, it still did not eliminate Isaac's suspicions.

21. And Isaac said unto Jacob, Come near, I pray thee, that I may feel thee, my son, whether thou be my very son Esau or not.

Perhaps Jacob and Rebekah did not think that Isaac would be so careful or hear so well. They no doubt envisioned a quick transaction. The tension built as Isaac proved reluctant to eat and bless. The wily old man was determined to use all of his senses to confirm the recipient of the blessing. The foresight of Rebekah was vindicated.

22, 23. And Jacob went near unto Isaac his father; and he felt him, and said, The voice is Jacob's voice, but the hands are the hands of Esau. And he discerned him not, because his hands were hairy, as his brother Esau's hands: so he blessed him.

What Jacob had feared earlier (v. 12) now came about; Isaac wanted to touch him. We can imagine that Jacob's heart was in his throat, and that his legs trembled with fear. The critical moment had arrived. Everything Jacob had hoped for, everything his mother had cherished for her son and had conspired with him to secure, hung in the balance. Jacob's entire future was at stake. We can almost see the scene in slow motion as Jacob approached his aged father.

Isaac was blind, but not deaf. He had heard the voice of this son, and it sounded to him like Jacob's even though he claimed to be Esau. But when he touched Jacob's hands, Isaac found that the skin was *hairy* like Esau's. The evidence provided by Isaac's sense of touch was such that it overrode any doubts imposed by his sense of hearing.

So he blessed him. Here the outcome of the ruse is stated before the details of the blessing are actually recorded. They are given in the verses that follow.

24. And he said, Art thou my very son Esau? And he said, I am.

Apparently Isaac still needed a final word of reassurance, and so he asked his son's identity one more time. Once again Jacob glibly repeated his lie. Each lie was a little easier, and each one added to the guilt that Jacob already carried. It is true that a deceptive scheme like this one soon takes on a life of its own. Each new turn needs another lie to support the scheme until the web woven has enmeshed the deceiver totally and securely.

C. Jacob Receives the Blessing
(vv. 25-27a)

25. And he said, Bring it near to me, and I will eat of my son's venison, that my soul may bless thee. And he brought it near to him, and he did eat: and he brought him wine, and he drank.

In the ancient Near East the meal was central to the whole concept of hospitality and friendship. Even enemies would eat meals together to solemnize treaties. But here a meal became the center of deceit. Trust and confidence and important social values were violated.

26, 27a. And his father Isaac said unto him, Come near now, and kiss me, my son. And he came near, and kissed him: and he smelled the smell of his raiment, and blessed him.

When Isaac had finished eating the meal, Isaac asked his son to come near and kiss him. This request seems to have been motivated by fatherly affection and not in order for Isaac to remove any lingering doubt. But as Jacob came close and kissed his father, Isaac accidently caught the smell of Esau's garments, and his belief that this person was Esau was confirmed. Of the five senses, three—touch, taste and smell—combined to assure Isaac that he was bestowing his blessing on his favored son, Esau. These were the very senses Rebekah had planned to appeal to with the goatskins, food, clothing, She knew Isaac well.

Isaac then proceeded to give the blessing, and once given, it was irrevocable. Jacob, the deceiver, succeeded in getting what he wanted. Although Jacob seemed the winner, he lost much by his deception. He lost the opportunity to see God at work in his life to bring the blessing. Furthermore, he very soon was separated from his

Home Daily Bible Readings

Monday, Nov. 1—Isaac Seeks the Ways of Peace (Genesis 26:12-22)

Tuesday, Nov. 2—Isaac Joins Philistines in Covenant (Genesis 26:23-29)

Wednesday, Nov. 3—Isaac's Servants Dig Another Well (Genesis 26:30-35)

Thursday, Nov. 4—Isaac Prepares to Bless Esau (Genesis 27:1-4)

Friday, Nov. 5—Rebekah Schemes to Bless Jacob (Genesis 27:5-17)

Saturday, Nov. 6—Isaac Unwittingly Blesses Jacob (Genesis 27:18-29)

Sunday, Nov. 7—Esau Weeps Bitterly: Hates Jacob (Genesis 27:31-46)

family and friends, for he had to flee to a distant land in order to escape Esau's wrath. Rebekah lost much also. She lost the opportunity to see her favorite son marry and to be able to enjoy her grandchildren. As far as we know, she never saw Jacob again after sending him to her brother in Padan-aram.

Conclusion

A. What Justifies the Means?

In our lesson we have seen that Jacob was destined by the Lord to continue the line of Abraham. God's choosing of the younger son was not because he deserved it and certainly not because of mobility of character, for this he did not have. But God knew what Jacob was capable of becoming and would become. If God's mercy were extended only to the deserving, if His call came only to the worthy, there would be no hope for any of us.

By so easily selling his birthright, Esau had shown that he cared little for the rights and responsibilities that fell to the firstborn. It revealed a like unconcern about spiritual matters, in particular the promise that God had made to Abraham.

Jacob, on the other hand, desired the position of family leadership and everything that went with it. However, he set about to attain them in an unethical way. An evil act cannot be cleansed simply by devoting it to "a good cause." It is wrong to steal anything for the church. It is wrong to gamble for the church. It is wrong to lie for the church. What Jacob did was devoted to a good cause. It was, nonetheless, a sin.

It is not wrong to have spiritual aspirations. But if we desire a position of spiritual leadership in the church, we must ask ourselves, Why? Is it because of the prestige involved? Is it to lighten some burden of guilt? Is it to help fulfill a thwarted sense of ambition? Is it to find release from frustrations and failures in other areas of life? Or do we seek positions of responsibility because we desire to serve others and want to build God's kingdom among men?

Not only the motives but the methods of attaining spiritual leadership are important. Jacob was too impatient. He did not allow God time to work things out in His own way. First, Jacob tried hard bargaining. Like a skillful politician he took advantage of his opponent in a weak moment and made a deal with him. Having obtained the birthright by this means, he employed deceit to obtain his father's blessing. But Jacob's means were unworthy of the goal he sought.

Let us never degrade the high spiritual qualities of life by choosing unworthy means. God is not honored by such action. Indeed, Jacob's haste and Jacob's methods betrayed a weakness of faith. The accomplishment of God's purposes does not depend on the cunning strategy of men. He desires rather faithful, loving obedience.

B. God's Purposes

Everywhere we look in this episode we see scheming and deceit. Without informing the rest of the family, Isaac and Esau planned a private ceremony in which the father would bestow his blessing on his firstborn son. Having overheard this, Rebekah developed her own scheme to thwart Isaac's intention, and Jacob adroitly carried out the deception.

Amid all this deceit, God's purposes were worked out. How could that be? We don't know, for God's ways are beyond our understanding (Isaiah 55:8, 9). We may as well attempt to explain how "in all things God works for the good of those who love him, who have been called according to his purpose" (Romans 8:28, *New International Version*). But God is faithful to His promises as all of Scripture illustrates.

What we do know for sure is that as God's people we are not to usurp His prerogatives, nor are we to gain our way by scheming and deceit (2 Corinthians 4:1-6). We are to be honest and faithful (Ephesians 4:25; Colossians 3:9).

C. Prayer

Dear Lord, we are so easily tempted to gain our way by small deceptions and "white" lies. We too often regard situations from our perspective and with our personal goals at the forefront. Remind us daily that You are working out our salvation and that You desire our faithfulness, not our cleverness. Dear Father, we commit our ways into Your hands. In Jesus' name, amen.

D. Thought to Remember

"Do not be deceived: God cannot be mocked. A man reaps what he sows" (Galatians 6:7, *New International Version*).

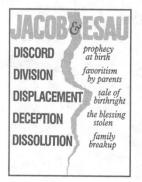

JACOB & ESAU

DISCORD	*prophecy at birth*
DIVISION	*favoritism by parents*
DISPLACEMENT	*sale of birthright*
DECEPTION	*the blessing stolen*
DISSOLUTION	*family breakup*

visual 10

Learning by Doing

This page contains an alternate lesson plan emphasizing learning activities. Classes desiring such student involvement will find these suggestions helpful.

Learning Goals

As a result of participating in this lesson, the students will:

1. Be able to summarize the story of Jacob's deception of his father Isaac in order to receive his blessing.

2. Suggest what Jacob could have done to receive blessing without resorting to deceit.

3. Commit themselves to live in truthfulness and honesty before God.

Into the Lesson

List the following words on the chalkboard before class: *actor, magician, spy.*

When the students arrive, draw their attention to the three words and ask them to try to determine what the three occupations have in common. After some discussion, point out that the success of each depends on deception. The person in each role must appear to be something he or she is not.

A magician's sleight-of-hand tricks, however, are not the same as deceptions perpetrated against us in our everyday lives. Ask the class to mention some situations in which the latter occurs. After some discussion of the resentment we feel about such situations, ask, "What about interpersonal relationships? What happens when deception enters that area—such as between friends, or husband and wife, or parent and child?" Discuss the breakdown caused by deception. Observe that no relationship can be healthy when deception is part of it.

Note that today's lesson involves deception that occurred within a family in Bible times and that it produced extremely unhappy results.

Into the Word

Read Genesis 27:6-8 aloud. Observe that Isaac had spoken to Esau apparently in secret, about giving him the birthright blessing. Discuss the possible reasons for the secrecy. Did Isaac know that Esau had sold his birthright to Jacob but sought to engineer a deception of his own? Note that Rebekah overheard—was she eavesdropping? Discuss the potential for problems to arise in a family when secrecy and suspicion are a way of life.

After a brief discussion, point out that Rebekah was prepared with a plan by which Jacob could deceive his father and receive the bless-ing. The next part of the text describes how the plan was carried out.

Divide the class into groups of four to six students. Give each group the following list of assignments and have them study Genesis 27:15-27 for the answers.

1. List the lies Jacob told to secure the blessing.

2. List as many points of evidence as you can that indicate Isaac was suspicious.

3. List the senses Isaac used to determine which son he was blessing.

Allow fifteen minutes or so for the groups to complete their work. Then go over the questions and have the groups share their findings.

Now have the groups work on one more project. Ask them to suggest some things Jacob could have done in an attempt to receive the blessing without deception. Possible suggestions:

1. Confront Esau before he returned with the venison and ask him to admit to their father that he had sold the birthright.

2. Discuss with his father why it was proper for him (Jacob) to receive the blessing.

3. Trust God to fulfill His promise in His own way. (Recall the prophecy given to Rebekah while the boys were still in the womb.)

Give the groups about five minutes to brainstorm and then have a brief time of reports.

Into Life

Ask the class to recast this Bible event in a modern setting, perhaps that of an employee using deception to get a promotion. Let the whole class work together on this. After the students have developed the fictitious situation, lead them in a discussion of the prevalence of such deception in our society and the harmful, long-term effects it produces.

Consider the modern situation once more and have the class suggest how the person might have achieved the goal without deception. Discuss what attitudes and commitments are required for a person to achieve his or her goals honestly. Note that one of the most important attitudes is one of submission to God's will, trusting Him to provide for our needs.

Close with a prayer of commitment to live in God's way, seeking to be honest and truthful in all our dealings.

Let's Talk It Over

The questions on this page are designed to encourage review of the lesson Scriptures and to promote discussion of the lesson by the class. The answers provided are only discussion starters. Let your class talk it over from there.

1. It seems correct to say that the family of Isaac and Rebekah suffered from a lack of communication. Why is communication an essential element in building a healthy home?

In the culture in which they lived, perhaps Isaac and Rebekah could not have openly expressed to one another their feelings and expectations each harbored regarding their sons. If they had done so, and if they had also brought Esau and Jacob into the circle of communication, they may have been able to avoid the fragmentation of their family. In our society, a husband and wife can and should discuss their mutual expectations from the beginning of their marriage. When the children are old enough to do so, they can join in the family discussion. By airing their desires, hopes, problems, grievances, etc., all the family members can contribute to an atmosphere of understanding and caring. Of course, in a Christian home prayer and attention given to the Bible will be part of this process.

2. In government, in business, and in other areas of modern life, lies and deception have become acceptable tactics. What can Christians do about this?

First of all, we should not let the world's example influence us into using the same tactics. We must remember Paul's admonition to the Colossians: "Lie not one to another, seeing that ye have put off the old man with his deeds" (Colossians 3:9). Then we must let our leaders know that we disapprove of the employment of these tactics. If this trend toward falsehood is to be stopped, young people particularly must be impressed with the importance of truthfulness. Christians especially must give them an example by telling the truth even when it is not convenient or comfortable to do so.

3. Do people who engage in lying and deception actually believe they can hide their tactics and motives from God? Why is this impossible?

"O Lord, thou hast searched me, and known me . . . thou understandest my thought afar off. . . . For there is not a word in my tongue, but, lo, O Lord, thou knowest it altogether" (Psalm 139:1-4). In spite of David's acknowledgment of God's omniscience, he himself behaved as if he could hide from God when he committed adultery with Bathsheba and arranged the death of her husband. This reminds us that we human beings are capable of a kind of self-deception, so that, even though we know better, we are sometimes able to convince ourselves that God does not see our actions or read our motives. Psalm 139 is a passage that we should read frequently as an antidote to such self-deception. Taking everything to God in prayer can also aid us in remembering that He knows all that we think, say, and do.

4. What are some of the negative results that lying and deception produce?

One result is the loss of trust. When a person has told us a damaging lie, it takes a long time to rebuild the relationship of trust that once existed. This tragic result is in evidence in the area of citizens' attitudes toward their governmental leaders. Lies can kindle jealousy and anger also and in turn can trigger violent words and actions. They can contribute to division within the family and in the church. Revelation 21:8 and 22:15 state that the destiny of liars is Hell rather than Heaven. When we consider the bitter fruit lies can produce, we see that lying is not to be taken lightly, but avoided altogether.

5. God worked out His purpose for Jacob in the midst of that man's deceitful activity. What are some other Biblical examples of God's working out His will in the midst of human sin?

David's sins of adultery and murder, mentioned in connection with question 3, afford one example. Even though David's marriage to Bathsheba came about in a way contrary to God's laws, He used that union to continue the Messiah's bloodline through Solomon (see Matthew 1:6). Of course, the greatest example is Jesus' cruel death on the cross, which God used along with the resurrection to bring salvation and eternal life to man. Later, the death of Stephen led to the scattering of the church in Jerusalem, with the positive result that "they that were scattered abroad went every where preaching the word" (Acts 8:4). And still later Paul could say of his imprisonment in Rome: "The things which happened unto me have fallen out rather unto the furtherance of the gospel" (Philippians 1:12).

Jacob's Experiences With Laban

DEVOTIONAL READING: Psalm 130.

LESSON SCRIPTURE: Genesis 29:1-30.

PRINTED TEXT: Genesis 29:15-30.

Genesis 29:15-30

15 And Laban said unto Jacob, Because thou art my brother, shouldest thou therefore serve me for nought? tell me, what shall thy wages be?

16 And Laban had two daughters: the name of the elder was Leah, and the name of the younger was Rachel.

17 Leah was tender eyed; but Rachel was beautiful and well-favored.

18 And Jacob loved Rachel; and said, I will serve thee seven years for Rachel thy younger daughter.

19 And Laban said, It is better that I give her to thee, than that I should give her to another man: abide with me.

20 And Jacob served seven years for Rachel; and they seemed unto him but a few days, for the love he had to her.

21 And Jacob said unto Laban, Give me my wife, for my days are fulfilled, that I may go in unto her.

22 And Laban gathered together all the men of the place, and made a feast.

23 And it came to pass in the evening, that he took Leah his daughter, and brought her to him; and he went in unto her.

24 And Laban gave unto his daughter Leah Zilpah his maid for a handmaid.

25 And it came to pass, that in the morning, behold, it was Leah: and he said to Laban, What is this thou hast done unto me? did not I serve with thee for Rachel? wherefore then hast thou beguiled me?

26 And Laban said, It must not be so done in our country, to give the younger before the firstborn.

27 Fulfil her week, and we will give thee this also for the service which thou shalt serve with me yet seven other years.

28 And Jacob did so, and fulfilled her week: and he gave him Rachel his daughter to wife also.

29 And Laban gave to Rachel his daughter Bilhah his handmaid to be her maid.

30 And he went in also unto Rachel, and he loved also Rachel more than Leah, and served with him yet seven other years.

Nov
14

GOLDEN TEXT: What is this thou hast done unto me? did not I serve with thee for Rachel? wherefore then hast thou beguiled me?—Genesis 29:25.

Lesson Aims

After completing this lesson study, the students should:

1. Understand that God's justice works out in subtle ways.

2. Be willing to reflect on their own strengths and weaknesses.

3. Renew their commitment to honesty and integrity of life.

Lesson Outline

INTRODUCTION
  A. To See Ourselves
  B. Lesson Background
 I. JACOB BELIEVES LABAN (Genesis 29:15-19)
  A. Wages Offered (v. 15)
  B. Laban's Daughters Described (vv. 16, 17)
  C. Agreement Reached (vv. 18, 19)
 II. LABAN DECEIVES JACOB (Genesis 29:20-27)
  A. Service Completed (vv. 20, 21)
   How Fast Time Passes!
  B. Substitution Made (vv. 22-24)
  C. The Trickster Tricked (vv. 25-27)
   "What Goes Around Comes Around"
 III. JACOB RECEIVES RACHEL (Genesis 29:28-30)
  A. Jacob Marries Rachel (vv. 28, 29)
  B. Jacob Serves for Rachel (v. 30)
CONCLUSION
  A. Blessing and Discipline Are Intertwined
  B. Prayer
  C. Thought to Remember

Display visual 11 of the visuals packet throughout this session. The visual is shown on page 93.

Introduction

A. To See Ourselves

The lady, dressed in her Sunday finest, was seated in church. No doubt confident in the neatness and appropriateness of her appearance, she was unaware that a loathsome louse was crawling on her bonnet! This incongruous situation was observed by the Scottish poet Robert Burns, and it prompted him to write the poem, "To a Louse." The thrust of the poem was expressed in the mature wish that God would give us the gift "to see ourselves as others see us."

The Old Testament scholar Victor Hamilton said that God showed Jacob himself, then He showed him Himself. Hamilton was referring to Jacob's encounter with Laban (the text for this lesson) and to the time later when Jacob wrestled with the angel (Genesis 32:22-32). In Laban Jacob found one like himself: clever, manipulative, deceptive. Was Jacob able to see himself in Laban? Did Jacob have the maturity and insight to see himself as others saw him?

If we were to see ourselves as others see us, would we like what we saw? If we didn't like what we saw, what would we do? The mature person would sincerely attempt to change.

B. Lesson Background

When Esau learned that Jacob had stolen his blessing (last week's lesson), he planned to kill Jacob. Rebekah learned of this and warned Jacob of his brother's intention. At the urging of his mother and the blessing of his father, Jacob fled to Padan-aram, the land where his mother's family lived (Genesis 27:41—28:5). While on the way, he came to Bethel and there he lay down to sleep. That night God appeared to Jacob in a dream and extended to him the covenant promise, which he had first given to Abraham and then to Isaac (28:10-14). Furthermore, to the fugitive he made this promise: "I am with you and will watch over you wherever you go, and I will bring you back to this land. I will not leave you until I have done what I have promised you" (v. 15, *New International Version*). It was in the assurance of this promise that Jacob continued his flight to Padan-aram and sojourned in that land.

The account of Jacob's arrival in Padan-aram is recorded in Genesis 29:1-14. Arriving at a well, Jacob met some shepherds who were from Haran. Upon inquiry he discovered that his uncle Laban lived in the vicinity, for these shepherds knew him. Just then Rachel, Laban's daughter, came with her father's sheep to water them at the well. Jacob watered the sheep for her and then told her who he was. As a result of this meeting, Jacob was warmly welcomed by Laban into his home. In this series of events we see God's providence at work. They were all small events, but so far-reaching in their results.

How to Say It

LABAN.   *Lay*-bun.
PADAN-ARAM.   *Pay*-dan-*a*-ram.
ZILPAH.   *Zil*-pa.
BILHAH.   *Bil*-ha.
HARAN.   *Hay*-run.

Perhaps Laban's warmth and friendliness lulled an unsuspecting Jacob into completely trusting his host. The events of our text, however, reveal another side to Laban, one that surprised the extraordinarily shrewd Jacob.

I. Jacob Believes Laban
(Genesis 29:15-19)

A. Wages Offered (v. 15)

15. And Laban said unto Jacob, Because thou art my brother, shouldest thou therefore serve me for nought? tell me, what shall thy wages be?

Jacob remained with Laban for a month, during which time, as this verse implies, Laban observed that he was a good and useful shepherd. At the end of that time, Laban wanted Jacob to stay on and work for him. Appearing not to want to take advantage of Jacob just because he was a relative, Laban offered to pay Jacob for his services. Again, seeming most generous and kind, Laban asked Jacob to name his price.

The word *brother* covers a range of relationships in the Old Testament including, as here, nephew. Earlier, Abraham referred to Lot as his brother, whereas, to be specific, he was Abraham's nephew (Genesis 13:8).

B. Laban's Daughters Described
(vv. 16, 17)

16, 17. And Laban had two daughters: the name of the elder was Leah, and the name of the younger was Rachel. Leah was tender eyed; but Rachel was beautiful and well-favored.

These two women, though sisters, became the focal point of conflict, not only at the time of Jacob's marriage, but also for his family life as seen in the latter part of chapter 29 and in chapter 30. We must not miss the reference to *the elder* and *the younger* here. Jacob himself was the younger of two brothers, and that had a significant bearing on his being in Padan-aram, far from his family. We cannot help but remember that in Jacob's case, "the elder was to serve the younger" (Genesis 25:23). We sense from the descriptions in these verses that *the younger* daughter, who was beautiful, would be favored by Jacob over *the elder*.

Leah was said to be *tender eyed*. This is sometimes translated as "weak" eyed. It is an obscure thought, but it probably refers to the fact that her eyes were pale and did not have a luster. Bright and shining eyes were regarded as a mark of beauty in Eastern women. Rachel, on the other hand, was not only beautiful in form and appearance but also *well-favored*, that is, very graceful.

C. Agreement Reached (vv. 18, 19)

18. And Jacob loved Rachel; and said, I will serve thee seven years for Rachel thy younger daughter.

Jacob loved Rachel. Because of the way this account has unfolded from the beginning, we have been led to expect this declaration. In all likeli hood this was an instance of "love at first sight" for both Jacob and Rachel. Jacob had fled from his father's house with only a staff (Genesis 32:10), so he could give neither the customary dowry nor presents for a bride (see Genesis 24:53). So he offered to work for Laban for seven years, if he would give him Rachel as his wife. Jacob's situation with Esau also required that he stay with Laban for some time.

19. And Laban said, It is better that I give her to thee, than that I should give her to another man: abide with me.

Laban, whose grasping, selfish nature would be seen more clearly later, was only too happy to accept Jacob's proposal. He won everything—labor and a husband for his daughter. Furthermore, Laban preferred that his daughter marry someone in the circle of his kindred rather than someone who was outside it. Given Laban's shrewdness, we cannot help but wonder if he did not also immediately see the potential for a way in which he might gain a husband for his less attractive older daughter.

II. Laban Deceives Jacob
(Genesis 29:20-27)

A. Service Completed (vv. 20, 21)

20. And Jacob served seven years for Rachel; and they seemed unto him but a few days, for the love he had to her.

Jacob wins our approval here for his deep love for Rachel. The seven years that he served Laban seemed to Jacob to be but a few days in comparison with the reward he would receive.

HOW FAST TIME PASSES!

"How fast time passes when you're having fun." There are other times, however, when a person simply becomes so engrossed in an endeavor that he or she does not notice, or at least does not begrudge the passing of time.

Frenchman Gerard d'Aboville wanted to be known as the preeminent solo sailor in the world. In 1980 he rowed a boat, solo, across the Atlantic Ocean, but someone else beat him in conquering the Pacific. Undaunted, d'Aboville decided to become the first person to cross the Pacific from west to east—the most difficult form of the passage. Enduring 133 days at sea and three capsizings, he reached his goal on November 21, 1991. His dream compelled him to persevere.

Jacob loved the beautiful Rachel. To have her as his wife became the most important thing in his life. He agreed to serve her father for seven years in order to marry her. This might seem an amazing display of self-discipline to many people in our time, who seem unable to wait even a few months until marriage to enjoy the fruits of love. However, the years seemed "but a few days" to Jacob, so intent was he on his dream of marrying Rachel. And like the French sailor, d'Aboville, there were two parts to his quest: because of Laban's trickery, Jacob had to agree to another seven years of labor in order to have Rachel as his wife.   —C. R. B.

21. And Jacob said unto Laban, Give me my wife, for my days are fulfilled, that I may go in unto her.

Both Jacob and Laban knew when the seven-year period of service expired, but it seems that Laban was in no hurry to fulfill his part of the agreement. Jacob, therefore, requested that Laban give him his *wife*, that is, the daughter who had been promised to him, so that he might marry her.

B. Substitution Made (vv. 22-24)

22. And Laban gathered together all the men of the place, and made a feast.

In that part of the world in ancient times, weddings were accompanied by a time of feasting. The feast Laban prepared was to last seven days (v. 27), and *all the men of the place* were invited to it. This does not mean the entire population, but the principal inhabitants along with friends and family members. Laban had long ago planned his deceit and the wedding customs aided his scheme.

23. And it came to pass in the evening, that he took Leah his daughter, and brought her to him; and he went in unto her.

Apparently there was no wedding ceremony, such as we know today, during which the bride was presented to the groom. Instead, after the first evening of the feast, the bride was brought heavily veiled to the dwelling of the groom. This custom made the deception possible, for the veil was long and fitted closely so that the bride's face and much of her figure also were concealed. Furthermore, it was dark and the groom would have been less than alert after a day of feasting.

Nothing is said about Leah in this situation. Some, thinking that she was a luckless pawn of her father, feel that our hearts should go out to her. They conclude that Laban not only was not faithful to his contract with Jacob, but also that he was not faithful to his oldest daughter by using her in this manner to further his own interests. Others, however, find it difficult to understand how Leah could agree to participate in a deception to wrong her sister by marrying someone who neither loved nor sought her.

24. And Laban gave unto his daughter Leah Zilpah his maid for a handmaid.

It was the custom for a bride to be given one or more handmaids at the time of marriage (see Genesis 24:61). Some think that the fact that Laban gave Leah only one handmaid is an indication of his lack of generosity. It should be pointed out, however, that Laban already intended to bestow another of his maids on Rachel.

C. The Trickster Tricked (vv. 25-27)

25. And it came to pass, that in the morning, behold, it was Leah: and he said to Laban, What is this thou hast done unto me? did not I serve with thee for Rachel? wherefore then has thou beguiled me?

The outcome of the deception is told with great reserve. *In the morning . . .* Leah! In the light of day Jacob discovered that he had been tricked. What a shock this must have been. We can imagine Jacob's anger when he confronted Laban, but he had no recourse. The wedding had taken place, and there was no going back. The trickster had been tricked. In Laban, clever Jacob had met his match.

Jacob claimed that Laban had *beguiled* him. The irony is that Isaac used the same word to describe Jacob's deceitfulness in stealing Esau's blessing (Genesis 27:35). There the word is translated "subtilty." We recall from an earlier lesson in this series that Eve in the Garden of Eden explained her eating of the forbidden fruit by stating that the serpent beguiled her (Genesis 3:13). Deceitfulness is a mark of sin (Hebrews 3:13), and an inherent characteristic of Satan himself (Revelation 20:7-10).

We must not miss the further irony in Jacob's words. He complained that he had already served Laban for Rachel. Yet the blessing of his father had said that he would be lord over his brothers and that even nations would serve him. Here was one brother, however, who not only did not serve Jacob, he required Jacob to serve him. Certainly we are to understand that God was overseeing the testing and transforming of Jacob in the events that transpired in his dealings with Laban. Jacob was confronted with one like himself, and he must learn that even God's chosen one would reap what he sowed. That he was standing squarely in the middle of God's plan did not exempt him from moral behavior or the consequences of his moral deficiencies.

26. And Laban said, It must not be so done in our country, to give the younger before the firstborn.

Laban appealed to the local marriage customs to explain his action, but what a feeble attempt at self-justification! If it was the custom in Haran for the older daughter to marry before the younger, Laban knew it seven years earlier when he agreed to give his younger daughter to Jacob in exchange for seven years of service. But he made no mention of it to Jacob at the time. Clearly deceit characterized this arrangement from the beginning. Laban's lame excuse could hide neither his greed of gain nor his callousness in using and abusing the affections of his two daughters.

27. Fulfil her week, and we will give thee this also for the service which thou shalt serve with me yet seven other years.

Laban was not opposed to Jacob's having Rachel as his wife; the word *this* in this verse refers to her. But in return for Rachel, Laban required another seven years of work. We don't hear a protest from Jacob. He had been legally wed to Leah, he was caught in the trap of his father-in-law, and if he wanted to marry the girl he loved, he had to comply with Laban's requirements. Laban came out a winner. He was able to marry off both of his daughters, and he would get another seven years of free labor from Jacob.

Fulfil her week. The wedding feast that had been planned was to last a week, and Laban asked Jacob to honor Leah by fulfilling that unsought obligation. Weddings in ancient times were happy occasions, when family and friends got together for food and fellowship and had respite from their hard life of work. Great social harm would have been done to Laban and Jacob if the feast had been cut short.

"WHAT GOES AROUND COMES AROUND"

"What goes around comes around," it is said. For example, think about names. Some cities in eastern Europe have changed their names in recent years. City names had been changed by the Communists to erase the memory of the czarist era (for example, St. Petersburg became Leningrad). With the fall of Communism came a desire to erase the memories of that era, and the historic names were revived.

A name change occurred in a western Missouri town, but for different reasons. Poston's Landing was founded in 1836. Several years later the name was changed to Napoleon. In the 1850s the town became Lisbon. By 1887, the town had developed a rivalry with Wellington to

visual 11

become the commercial center of that part of Missouri. To honor the French emperor who was the rival of the English Duke of Wellington, the residents named the town Napoleon once again. Interestingly, there is a Waterloo about halfway between!

Since Jacob earlier had tricked his father into giving him the blessing intended for Esau, Jacob must have pondered the irony of his being cheated by Laban. Wouldn't it be interesting to know what Jacob was thinking? It *does* seem that what goes around comes around. Regarding sinful behavior, the Bible expresses it this way: "Be sure your sin will find you out" (Numbers 32:23.)
                                                              —C. R. B.

III. Jacob Receives Rachel (Genesis 29:28-30)

A. Jacob Marries Rachel (vv. 28, 29)

28, 29. And Jacob did so, and fulfilled her week: and he gave him Rachel his daughter to wife also. And Laban gave to Rachel his daughter Bilhah his handmaid to be her maid.

Jacob honored Laban's request and spent the week with Leah. It could not have been a happy time for either of them. Jacob's seven years of service had flown by because of his love for Rachel, but these seven days must have dragged slowly and painfully.

At the end of the week's festivities, Rachel was given to Jacob for a wife. What a disappointing situation was created for all of the principals in this episode because of deception and greed. The bridal festivities planned for Rachel and Jacob suddenly became Leah's, but how could they satisfy her knowing that her husband's affections were directed toward her sister? The marriage of Jacob and Rachel, long anticipated by both, now had the unexpected and undesired complication of the presence of a second wife for Jacob. And to make matters more galling still, Jacob had to give his father-in-law free service for another seven years. The first seven years of service seemed but a short time to Jacob because he anticipated the remainder of his life spent with his beloved. The second seven years receive no such evaluation (v. 30). They are just served.

B. Jacob Serves for Rachel (v. 30)

30. And he went in also unto Rachel, and he loved also Rachel more than Leah, and served with him yet seven other years.

At last the marriage Jacob worked for took place. Nothing is said about the wedding night or the feasting. We are probably to assume that custom was followed, though in many ways it would have been anticlimactic.

He loved also Rachel more than Leah. This statement indicates that Leah had some place in Jacob's affections, but that his love for Rachel was much greater. This, of course, would have created ill feelings and jealousy in both women—in Leah, knowing that she was the less preferred wife, and in Rachel, resenting the fact that she was not the sole recipient of her husband's love and attention.

Conclusion

A. Blessing and Discipline
Are Intertwined

The full significance of this episode in Jacob's life cannot be seen until we understand the events that followed those recorded in the printed text. The concluding verse of the text introduced the thought of impending conflict in the relationship of Jacob with his two wives. The very next verse indicates the basis of the conflict that developed: "And when the Lord saw that Leah was hated, he opened her womb: but Rachel was barren" (v. 31). God had not made His presence known up to this point, but now He intervened. We are not surprised by the barrenness of Rachel; the earlier favored wives of the covenant family (Sarah, Rebekah) had been barren also. Once again the chosen must await God's timing and intervention.

The narrative of the birth of Jacob's children follows (Genesis 29:32—30:24). Not only Leah, but both her handmaid and Rachel's handmaid bore children to Jacob before God finally blessed Rachel with a son. From the sons born of these four women came the tribes that would eventually comprise the nation of Israel. Yet their births were not auspicious. They came about in the midst of conflict, resentment, and jealousy. God blessed, and He withheld. There was love and animosity. Leah kept hoping that through the children God blessed her with she would earn Jacob's love. Rachel found that love was not enough.

Jacob discovered an important truth. Although he had received God's covenant promise, he was not to live a life guided by worldly, unethical principles such as had characterized his dealings with his brother and father. The Jacob who tricked Esau and ran for his life was not the Jacob that God desired. Therefore, Jacob had to be shown a better way. He had to change and grow. To serve God's purposes he had to be converted. Just as in the process of growth of any person, discipline was needed. Through his dealings with Laban, who was as crafty as himself, Jacob was eventually made aware of his own unresolved sin. Through the anguish caused by the barrenness of his beloved wife, Rachel, he learned to depend more fully on the grace of God.

Had Jacob sought God as his partner from the beginning, he may very well have been spared those trials that came on him as a result of his attempt to go it alone. As it was, it took him many years to learn through sad experience that one cannot rely on himself and be truly blessed.

B. Prayer

Dear Lord, we praise You because You are the Father of truth, not of lies. Remove from us all malice and deceit. Control us with truth. Mark our lives with honesty and integrity. We ask for the presence of Jesus Christ in our lives, who himself is the way, the truth, and the life. Through His name we pray. Amen.

C. Thought to Remember

How different Jacob's life would have been if he had realized from the beginning that life's worthwhile goals can be attained only through partnership with God and not through trickery or deceit! What a difference this same realization can make in our lives!

Home Daily Bible Readings

Monday, Nov. 8—Isaac Sends Jacob to Laban (Genesis 28:1-5)
Tuesday, Nov. 9—Esau Resentfully Seeks Foreign Wives (Genesis 28:6-9)
Wednesday, Nov. 10—Jacob's Dream and Promise to God (Genesis 28:10-22)
Thursday, Nov. 11—Jacob Meets Shepherds (Genesis 29:1-8)
Friday, Nov. 12—Jacob Meets Rachel, Laban's Daughter (Genesis 29:9-14)
Saturday, Nov. 13—Bright-eyed Rachel vs. Weak-eyed Leah (Genesis 29:15-30)
Sunday, Nov. 14—Wealthy Jacob Plans to Return Home (Genesis 30:25-36, 43)

Learning by Doing

This page contains an alternate lesson plan emphasizing learning activities. Classes desiring such student involvement will find these suggestions helpful.

Learning Goals

As a result of participation in this lesson, each student will be able to:

1. Compare Laban's deception of Jacob with Jacob's deception of Isaac.

2. Explain how Jacob's experiences with Laban brought change in Jacob's life.

3. Suggest ways to discern and respond to God's discipline today.

Into the Lesson

Before class, write the word *discipline* on the chalkboard or a large poster. When the class is assembled, tell the students you want them to think about discipline, which most persons realize is necessary to an orderly society. Tell the students that you are going to suggest several potential purposes of discipline, and they are to decide whether or not each one is valid. As you read aloud the following seven statements, have the students respond to each one by writing their answers on paper.

1. To prevent the recurrence of improper activity.

2. To get even.

3. To restore the offender to a right relationship with others.

4. To lead the offender to see why his or her behavior is unacceptable.

5. To make the one exercising discipline "feel better."

6. To motivate the offender to practice acceptable behavior.

7. To make the offender feel bad.

After reading the list, poll the students' answers and discuss their reasons for answering as they did. Note that statements 1, 3, 4, and 6 express proper reasons for discipline.

Scripture makes it plain that discipline is involved in God's dealings with His people. With this in mind we may add two more purposes of discipline:

1. To lead the offender to repent.

2. To restore the offender to a right relationship with God.

Make the transition to Bible study by stating that today's lesson deals with events in Jacob's life that led to changes in his character and in his relationship with man and God.

Into the Word

Read Genesis 29:15-30 aloud. Then divide the class into groups of three or four. Instruct the groups to compare the events recorded in this text with Jacob's deceiving of Isaac to obtain the birthright blessing (Genesis 27:6-27). Write the following italicized headings on the chalkboard to suggest areas of comparison. The statements in parentheses are suggested answers.

Lies the Deceiver Told

(Jacob claimed to be Esau, and he stated that he prepared the venison; Laban told Jacob he would give him Rachel as a wife if he served him for seven years.)

How the Deceiver Might Have (or Actually) Justified His Action

(Jacob might have appealed to the prophecy at his and Esau's birth that stated that the older would serve the younger, or to the fact that he had bought Esau's birthright; Laban appealed to the custom that the older must marry before the younger.)

How Others Were Used in the Deception

(Jacob used Esau's own clothing to effect the deception; Laban used Leah as a substitute for Rachel.)

Results of the Deception

(Jacob had to run for his life and stay away from his home and family for years because of his fear of Esau; Laban alienated both his daughters—see Genesis 31:14-16.)

Allot fifteen minutes for this. Then let the groups report and discuss their findings.

Into Life

Observe that while Laban was responsible for his actions, God may well have allowed him to act toward Jacob as he did so that Jacob could see his own sin, repent, and change his behavior. In fact, when Jacob returned to Canaan he expressed a different attitude toward Esau.

Have someone read Hebrews 12:4-11. Then discuss these questions: "Is every difficult circumstance in life some form of discipline?" "Does adversity in one's life always suggest one has sinned?" "How should a Christian respond to adversity?" Help the class to see that life's experiences should lead us to self-examination, repentance when necessary, and a stronger confidence in God's care and concern for our eternal welfare.

Let's Talk It Over

The questions on this page are designed to encourage review of the lesson Scriptures and to promote discussion of the lesson by the class. The answers provided are only discussion starters. Let your class talk it over from there.

1. Jacob's experiences with Laban enabled him to see himself as he was. We in turn can use the Biblical descriptions of Jacob and other persons as a mirror to see ourselves as we are. How do we do this?

James 1:22-25 is the passage that compares the Word of God to a mirror. It indicates that we must listen to the Word in the same way we look into a mirror. A casual glance either way accomplishes little. If we are concerned about our physical appearance, we can examine ourselves carefully in a mirror. In similar fashion, we can closely investigate the character of a Biblical person such as Jacob and compare ourselves with him. We may thereby see some attitudes or habits that must be changed. James stresses that neither a look into a mirror nor a period of attention given to the Word is of value unless we make the changes that are called for.

2. The mention of Rachel's physical beauty reminds us of the high value assigned to physical beauty in our society. What can Christians say to those who are obsessed with beauty?

Isaiah prophesied of Jesus, "When we shall see him, there is no beauty that we should desire him" (Isaiah 53:2). The New Testament tells us nothing about Jesus' physical appearance, and yet we are inclined to think of Him as an attractive person. We think this because of what we read about His sinlessness, His compassion, and His merciful deeds. Even so we recognize that true beauty today is more a matter of character and of words and deeds than it is a matter of outward appearance. And so we can say to those who lament their lack of beauty: "Let Jesus Christ dwell within you. Develop a Christlike character. Imitate the deeds of Jesus. Then you will have genuine beauty."

3. Jacob became outraged when he was subjected by Laban to the same kind of deceit he himself had earlier practiced. Can you think of some present-day examples of this kind of reaction?

We sometimes say, "He can dish it out, but he can't take it." That may be said of a person who makes other people victims of his attempts at humor, but who protests vigorously when he is subjected to a practical joke. More serious, however, are those marital situations in which one partner is unfaithful, and then becomes livid with anger upon learning that his or her mate has also succumbed to infidelity. Another common example is the person who relishes passing on gossip about others, but cries foul when he or she becomes the subject of gossip. Paul's uncovering of the Jews' hypocrisy in Romans 2:17-24 speaks to all those who would hold to a double standard.

4. It seems accurate to say that God used Laban's dealings to humble Jacob. How does God humble us, and why is it important that we respond positively to His humbling of us?

Scripture makes it clear that human pride displeases God. In Proverbs 21:4 we read that "a high look, and a proud heart . . . is sin." Proverbs 16:18 describes the peril of pride by reminding us that "pride goeth before destruction, and a haughty spirit before a fall." So if we perceive that God is working to humble us, it is for our own good to respond by yielding up our excessive pride. Perhaps we also have a "Laban," who has confounded us, grieved us, or infuriated us. Perhaps we are experiencing problems regarding our health, our finances, or our family. We do not need to feel that God is actually causing these, but He may allow them as a means of humbling us.

5. How can one develop a disciplined Christian life?

To determine that we will set aside a significant time each day for personal Bible study and prayer is a simple, but vital step. To plan on being present on a consistent basis for the services of the church is also a decision that does not require overwhelming effort. Once we have given priority to these matters, other aspects of Christian discipline can more readily fall in place. We must develop a careful stewardship of our material wealth. We must learn to exercise control over our tongue. We must use discretion in forming our friendships and selecting the kinds of entertainment we will indulge in. And we must master the habit of mental discipline, so that we "take captive every thought to make it obedient to Christ" (2 Corinthians 10:5, *New International Version*).

Jacob Is Reconciled With Esau

November 21
Lesson 12

DEVOTIONAL READING: Matthew 5:23-26.

LESSON SCRIPTURE: Genesis 33.

PRINTED TEXT: Genesis 33:1-14.

Genesis 33:1-14

1 And Jacob lifted up his eyes, and looked, and, behold, Esau came, and with him four hundred men. And he divided the children unto Leah, and unto Rachel, and unto the two handmaids.

2 And he put the handmaids and their children foremost, and Leah and her children after, and Rachel and Joseph hindermost.

3 And he passed over before them, and bowed himself to the ground seven times, until he came near to his brother.

4 And Esau ran to meet him, and embraced him, and fell on his neck, and kissed him: and they wept.

5 And he lifted up his eyes, and saw the women and the children, and said, Who are those with thee? And he said, The children which God hath graciously given thy servant.

6 Then the handmaidens came near, they and their children, and they bowed themselves.

7 And Leah also with her children came near, and bowed themselves: and after came Joseph near and Rachel, and they bowed themselves.

8 And he said, What meanest thou by all this drove which I met? And he said, These are to find grace in the sight of my lord.

9 And Esau said, I have enough, my brother; keep that thou hast unto thyself.

10 And Jacob said, Nay, I pray thee, if now I have found grace in thy sight, then receive my present at my hand: for therefore I have seen thy face, as though I had seen the face of God, and thou wast pleased with me.

11 Take, I pray thee, my blessing that is brought to thee; because God hath dealt graciously with me, and because I have enough. And he urged him, and he took it.

12 And he said, Let us take our journey, and let us go, and I will go before thee.

13 And he said unto him, My lord knoweth that the children are tender, and the flocks and herds with young are with me; and if men should overdrive them one day, all the flock will die.

14 Let my lord, I pray thee, pass over before his servant; and I will lead on softly.

Nov
21

GOLDEN TEXT: If now I have found grace in thy sight, then receive my present at my hand: for therefore I have seen thy face, as though I had seen the face of God, and thou wast pleased with me.—Genesis 33:10.

Lesson Aims

This lesson should help students:

1. Be grateful that God has made it possible for us to be reconciled to Him through Christ.

2. Seek to be reconciled to those persons with whom they presently are in conflict.

3. Resolve to adopt a forgiving attitude.

Lesson Outline

INTRODUCTION
  A. Reconciliation
  B. Lesson Background
 I. THE BROTHERS MEET (Genesis 33:1-11)
  A. Fearful Anticipation (vv. 1-3)
    Risking Rejection
  B. Happy Reunion (vv. 4-7)
    The Wisdom of Forgiveness
  C. Unnecessary Gifts (vv. 8, 9)
  D. Jacob's Insistence (vv. 10, 11)
 II. THE BROTHERS SEPARATE (Genesis 33:12-14)
  A. Esau's Offer (v. 12)
  B. Jacob Declines (vv. 13, 14)
CONCLUSION
  A. Brothers Reconciled
  B. The Ministry of Reconciliation
  C. Prayer
  D. Thought to Remember

Display visual 12 of the visuals packet throughout this session. The visual is shown on page 100.

Introduction

A. Reconciliation

At this moment there are families that are experiencing conflict among some of the family members. If heartache, bitterness, and alienation are to be avoided, reconciliation is essential.

An article in a national magazine some months ago dealt with the subject of broken families and suggested several practical steps that may be taken to heal family strife. The article emphasized the importance of intercession by a third party and pointed out that intercession should be made as quickly as possible after a rift has occurred. If the proper steps are taken and the participants sincerely desire reconciliation, broken relationships can be restored.

The church is sometimes represented as a family. As in many families, conflicts sometimes arise that threaten the church's fellowship and ministry. If, however, reconciliation can take place in a family, it can occur among members of God's family.

This lesson shows us the blessedness that results when brothers who have been estranged are reconciled.

B. Lesson Background

At least thirteen years elapsed from the time of Jacob's marriages to Leah and Rachel (last week's lesson) to the event recorded in the text for this lesson. During that time eleven sons and one daughter were born to Jacob by his wives and their two handmaids (Genesis 29:31—30:24).

The increase in the size of Jacob's family was accompanied by an increase in wealth. This gain in wealth was due partly to natural growth and partly through manipulation by Jacob. This led to more conflict with Laban (30:27-43).

As things turned sour with Laban, God instructed Jacob to return home, assuring him of divine protection. Jacob then called his wives to him in the field and explained Laban's change of feelings toward him. They agreed that Jacob should do as God had directed him, so Jacob gathered his wives, children, and all his property that he had acquired in Padan-aram and fled for Canaan. On the third day afterward, Laban learned of Jacob's flight. Gathering his men, he pursued Jacob's slower moving caravan, and in a week's time overtook them in the mountains of Gilead. God warned Laban in a dream, however, not to harm Jacob. So after some discussion the two men entered into an agreement and set up a heap of stones as a witness to it. Both agreed that they would never go beyond that heap to do the other any harm. The next day Laban said his good-byes to his children and returned to his home.

Jacob then continued on his journey southward and toward home. Hoping to find acceptance by his brother Esau, Jacob sent messengers to him in his home in Edom to tell of his arrival. Jacob greatly feared meeting his brother, and his fear was compounded when he learned that Esau was coming to meet him with four hundred men. Assuming that Esau was bent on vengeance, Jacob moved quickly to protect at least some of the people and livestock in his caravan. He divided them into two groups. He thought if Esau destroyed one group, he might conclude that there were no more, and so the other group would escape. Next, he prayed earnestly that God would deliver them from Esau's wrath. Then, hoping to lessen Esau's wrath, Jacob sent ahead to him a series of gifts consisting of various kinds of livestock (32:1-21).

The most significant spiritual experience of Jacob's life occurred on the night before he met Esau. He sent his wives and sons over the ford of the Jabbok River, and he remained on the northern bank. While there alone, Jacob wrestled with a man, called an angel by Hosea (12:4) and God by Jacob (Genesis 32:22-32). After this, Jacob was a changed man. He came from this mysterious encounter with a new name (Israel), a new blessing, and a limp. The name looked to a new future, the blessing gave him assurance of God's presence as he met his brother, and the limp was a memorial of his struggle with the divine.

With the rising of the sun, Jacob's antagonist departed, and Jacob himself prepared to meet Esau.

I. The Brothers Meet
(Genesis 33:1-11)

A. Fearful Anticipation (vv. 1-3)

1. And Jacob lifted up his eyes, and looked, and, behold, Esau came, and with him four hundred men. And he divided the children unto Leah, and unto Rachel, and unto the two handmaids.

The setting of the meeting was east of the Jordan River just south of the Jabbok River. This area was called Gilead later in the Old Testament. Jacob had crossed Jabbok, rejoining his family and the rest of his flocks and herds, and all began to move slowly southward. Esau came from the land of Seir, which was located in the land of Edom, south and east of the Dead Sea. He would have traveled about a hundred miles to get to where Jacob was.

Jacob's strategy for meeting Esau was to divide his family into little groups, putting the children with their mothers. No mention is made of Jacob's flocks and herds and those who tended them. Perhaps he separated his family from them so that when Esau arrived there would be no sizable group of armed men present who might possibly alarm him.

How to Say It

JABBOK. *Jab*-ok.
LABAN. *Lay*-bun.
PADAN-ARAM. *Pay*-dan-*a*-ram.
PENIEL. Pe-*nye*-el.
PHILIPPI. Fih-*lip*-pie or *Fil*-ih-pie.
SEIR. *See*-ir.
SUCCOTH. *Suck*-oth.

2. And he put the handmaids and their children foremost, and Leah and her children after, and Rachel and Joseph hindermost.

The mothers with their children were arranged in a long procession, with the least favored children and mothers first and the most favored last. It seems that Jacob felt that Rachel and Joseph would be the least exposed to danger by being in the rear.

RISKING REJECTION

Joyce Schultz's three children were taken from her by the court and adopted into other families. For twenty years Joyce lived in hope of a reunion. She even gave up the habits that had caused her to lose her children.

Joyce was working in a convenience store when she discovered that a twenty-one-year-old co-worker, Tammy Harris, was searching for her parents. Tammy showed Joyce her birth certificate, but Joyce withheld belief, fearing it was a mistake. When Tammy gave Joyce a picture of herself as a baby, Joyce knew she had found her daughter. She waited three days to reveal her identity, however, fearing that Tammy might reject her. At last, the truth came out, and relationship was restored.

Fear of rejection is a common emotion when long-separated relatives are reunited, particularly when the sin of one caused the disruption of the relationship. It was certainly so when Jacob approached Esau. Years before, Jacob had tricked their father and stolen Esau's blessing. Intervening years had brought alienation, but now maturity and spiritual renewal had brought Jacob to seek his brother's forgiveness and a restoration of family ties.

Sometimes it takes years of maturing before we outgrow our youthful sins enough to risk making life what it ought to have been. But when we have grown enough, the risk needs to be taken.   —C. R. B.

3. And he passed over before them, and bowed himself to the ground seven times, until he came near to his brother.

Jacob then went out in front of the procession so he would be the first to meet his brother. Esau's anger was toward him personally, and so if there was danger he would be the first to encounter it. When Jacob had sent messengers to tell Esau that he was coming, Jacob made it plain that Esau was the "lord," the master, and that Jacob was his "servant" (Genesis 32:4). Now he confirmed that attitude as he *bowed himself to the ground seven times.* He did not fall on the ground, but rather bent forward from the waist until the upper part of his body was parallel with the ground. After each bow he took a few steps until at last he came to Esau. Thus did he express his reverence and respect for his elder brother. First by his gifts and now by his sincere humility, Jacob hoped to win his brother's favor.

B. Happy Reunion (vv. 4-7)

4. And Esau ran to meet him, and embraced him, and fell on his neck, and kissed him: and they wept.

Without question, Jacob was surprised, and tremendously relieved, by this response of Esau. Jacob had probably thought about and lived through this meeting many times in his imagination. Expecting the worst, he received the best. Esau's actions showed that he had forgiven Jacob for all past wrongs. For whatever reason, the bitterness and anger that Esau had held for Jacob in the past had melted away during the twenty years of their separation. Embracing each other, their emotions overflowed *and they wept.* Their tears expressed the release of tension and the joy of reunion better than any words could.

THE WISDOM OF FORGIVENESS

Terry A. Anderson was playing tennis with a friend in Beirut when the terrorists stole six and one-half years from his life. After his kidnapping, he was kept in darkened rooms or cells—chained to the walls and occasionally to other prisoners. He saw neither sky, sun, nor stars for 2454 days.

Some people are embittered by such circumstances, but a "new" Terry Anderson began to grow in the midst of adversity. When he was finally released in December, 1991, his sister said, "This is not the same Terry, and it's one I like a whole lot better." His friends and family saw a new tenderness in him. His own explanation was, "I'm a Christian . . . and it's required of me that I forgive, no matter how hard that may be. And I'm determined to do that."

Years had passed since Jacob had stolen Esau's blessing, but in that time Esau disciplined himself so that he might prosper in spite of what had happened. When Jacob finally sought his forgiveness, Esau was ready to offer it. He could have focused on his disadvantage, but he chose not to. Instead, he got on with life, forgiving his persecutor. Forgiveness gives freedom and spiritual prosperity at least to the one who offers it, regardless of what happens to the one who needs to receive it.   —C. R. B.

5. And he lifted up his eyes, and saw the women and the children, and said, Who are those with thee? And he said, The children which God hath graciously given thy servant.

This was the first of two questions by Esau that gave Jacob the opportunity to explain how God had cared for him over the years. Esau could not help but be impressed with Jacob's' large family—four women with their twelve children. A fundamental Old Testament truth was stated by Jacob here. Children were regarded as gifts of God. This was true not only in the special cases of barren women, but in every case. Jacob's wives, and their handmaids, who bore his children were very aware of God at work in conception (see chapters 29 and 30).

6, 7. Then the handmaidens came near, they and their children, and they bowed themselves. And Leah also with her children came near, and bowed themselves: and after came Joseph near and Rachel, and they bowed themselves.

Jacob probably beckoned for the women and children to come. They came forward by groups as he had arranged them. First the handmaids and their children, then the wives and their children. Each followed Jacob's example and showed humility and respect for Esau by bowing down before him.

C. Unnecessary Gifts (vv. 8, 9)

8. And he said, What meanest thou by all this drove which I met? And he said, These are to find grace in the sight of my lord.

What meanest thou by all this drove which I met? Esau referred to the gifts that Jacob had sent to him, which were mentioned briefly in the "Lesson Background" section. As Esau was approaching, he kept encountering drove after drove of animals. There were 220 goats, 220 sheep, thirty camels with their colts, fifty cattle, and thirty donkeys. Each group was separated from the other by some distance, and the servants who were in charge of each drove were instructed to say the same thing—that this was a gift from Jacob to Esau. Jacob answered Esau honestly—he had sent them *to find grace,* to win his brother's favor. *My lord.* Jacob continued to acknowledge Esau as the lord, the chief.

HOW GOOD AND PLEASANT IT IS WHEN BROTHERS LIVE TOGETHER IN UNITY!

visual 12

9. And Esau said, I have enough, my brother; keep that thou hast unto thyself.

Esau himself was a wealthy sheik with a large family and many servants. He had no need of any more. The loss of his father's blessing (see chapter 27) had no apparent negative effect on Esau. He had prospered and become powerful in his own right. The gift that meant so much to Jacob meant little to Esau.

My brother. Jacob had greatly feared this meeting with Esau, for he felt, with good reason, that Esau regarded him as perhaps his worst enemy. But instead of coming to him with a sword, Esau greeted him with an embrace. Jacob's attitude and posture of a servant notwithstanding, Esau received him as his brother. Certainly Esau's generous, forgiving, and affectionate spirit commands our admiration.

D. Jacob's Insistence (vv. 10, 11)

10. And Jacob said, Nay, I pray thee, if now I have found grace in thy sight, then receive my present at my hand: for therefore I have seen thy face, as though I had seen the face of God, and thou wast pleased with me.

Jacob could not accept the refusal. He begged his brother to accept the gift he had sent. Esau's acceptance of the gift would be a token, an outward sign, that Jacob had received what he valued more than the gift—the goodwill of his brother.

As though I had seen the face of God. Jacob chose this means to express his profound relief at Esau's response to him. As God had the power to destroy him completely, so Jacob esteemed Esau's capability to do him great harm. Jacob may well have had in mind the event of the night before, when he wrestled with the angel of God. He named the place where that encounter occurred, "Peniel," for he felt that he had seen God face to face, and his life had been preserved (Genesis 32:30). Even so now, his life had been spared again because Esau was gracious to him.

11. Take, I pray thee, my blessing that is brought to thee; because God hath dealt graciously with me, and because I have enough. And he urged him, and he took it.

My blessing. Jacob referred to his gift to Esau. The word signifies a gift by which one seeks to express goodwill (see 1 Samuel 25:27; 30:26). During the twenty years that Jacob had lived in Padan-aram, he had accumulated servants and flocks and herds. He rightly understood that he had all this wealth because God had been gracious to him. He wanted to share it with Esau. He could well afford the gift, he said, because God had given him so much. So Jacob kept on insisting, and finally Esau accepted the gift.

II. The Brothers Separate (Genesis 33:12-14)

A. Esau's Offer (v. 12)

12. And he said, Let us take our journey, and let us go, and I will go before thee.

As a further indication of his friendship, Esau suggested that he and Jacob travel on together. It is not certain whether Esau offered to accompany Jacob to the latter's destination, which was Canaan, and probably in particular, Hebron, where Isaac still lived, or whether Esau invited Jacob to go with him to Mount Seir in the land of Edom. Because Jacob told Esau that he would come to him in Seir (v. 14), some have concluded that Jacob was saying that that was his immediate destination. But that is not necessarily so. He may simply have been saying that at some time in the future he would visit Esau there. At any rate, Esau offered to go on ahead of Jacob and his caravan a short distance and be an escort for them as they traveled through desert regions with which he, Esau, was familiar. Esau's graciousness and generosity throughout this episode reflect favorably upon him. It seems that he had changed much in the twenty years during which he and Jacob had been separated.

B. Jacob Declines (vv. 13, 14)

13. And he said unto him, My lord knoweth that the children are tender, and the flocks and herds with young are with me; and if men should overdrive them one day, all the flock will die.

As generous as Esau's offer was, Jacob desired to travel alone. It was enough for Jacob to have been reunited with his brother, to have been forgiven by him for the misdeeds of the past, and to know that friendship would characterize any dealings between them in the future. Although reconciliation had occurred between them, their differences in personalities and life-styles still existed. Jacob, therefore, declined Esau's offer, and the reasons that he gave were valid ones. A caravan the nature and size of Jacob's could not possibly keep up with Esau and his horsemen without doing harm to the children (Joseph was little over six years old) and to the animals. At this time the sheep and cattle were with young, and to drive them too hard might kill them all.

14. Let my lord, I pray thee, pass over before his servant; and I will lead on softly.

With proper humility and politeness, Jacob requested that Esau *pass over* before Jacob, that is, go on ahead. Jacob himself then would *lead on softly*, would proceed onward at his company's slow pace.

The following verse records that Esau offered to leave some of his men for an escort, but Jacob politely refused that offer as well, stating that it was unnecessary. Esau, therefore, left that day and went on home to Seir.

Jacob then journeyed west to Succoth, which was near the Jordan on the east side of the river. There he built shelters for his herds and a house for himself. After some time he left Succoth and moved to Shechem (v. 18). This marked his arrival in the promised land after his long absence.

At God's direction, Jacob left Shechem and dwelt at Bethel, where God had appeared to him in a dream before Jacob had left for Padan-aram so many years earlier. Once again God appeared to him there and confirmed to him the blessing of His covenant with Abraham. With God's blessing upon him and his conflict with Esau resolved, the wanderer then moved southward and at length came to his father Isaac at Hebron. There, apparently, he resided for many years. The promise of God recorded in Genesis 28:15 had been kept.

Conclusion

A. Brothers Reconciled

The meeting of Jacob and Esau after many years of separation is a touching one, filled with drama and pathos. The men who met were so changed that they little resembled the ones who had separated years before.

How different was the attitude of Jacob. Listen to him pray: "O God . . . I am not worthy of the least of all the mercies, and of all the truth, which thou hast shewed unto thy servant" (Genesis 32:9, 10). He pleaded for deliverance rather than trust in his own strength, "Deliver me" (v. 11). And in conversation with his brother he spoke of "the children which God hath graciously given thy servant" (33:5). Jacob bowed low before Esau seven times, and called him "my lord," offering him a share of his possessions. Esau, however, desired no gift from his brother, but welcomed him and wept with him.

Jacob and Esau both were changed men. This change resulted in changed relationships. Reconciliation was the road to peace and happiness.

B. The Ministry of Reconciliation

Estrangement between God and mankind has existed since the sin of Adam and Eve, and the message of the Bible centers around the divine plan to remove that estrangement. Only God could provide the means for the separating chasm to be bridged, and He has done that through His Son Jesus Christ. "God was in

Home Daily Bible Readings

Monday, Nov. 15—God Orders Jacob's Return (Genesis 31:1-8, 15-18)

Tuesday, Nov. 16—Laban and Jacob Covenant Together (Genesis 31:36, 37, 44-54)

Wednesday, Nov. 17—Jacob Prepares to Meet Esau (Genesis 32:3-8, 13-18)

Thursday, Nov. 18—Jacob, in Fear, Seeks Appeasement (Genesis 32:19-32)

Friday, Nov. 19—Jacob's Family Introduced to Esau (Genesis 33:1-7)

Saturday, Nov. 20—Jacob and Esau Are Reconciled (Genesis 33:8-14)

Sunday, Nov. 21—Jacob Buys Land and Builds (Genesis 33:15-20)

Christ, reconciling the world unto himself," Paul asserts in 2 Corinthians 5:19. To be reconciled to God through Jesus Christ is the message of the gospel, and those who have been reconciled now have peace with God.

Having been reconciled with God, Christians are given the responsibility of the ministry of reconciliation. What sadness there is in the heart of God when this ministry is enfeebled by conflict within the church itself.

One thinks of the conflicts that Paul addressed in the early churches. The church at Corinth was troubled by a divisive spirit. The church at Philippi experienced conflict between two of Paul's trusted co-workers. Paul's exhortations to resolve these conflicts had a very practical concern—to restore the churches to unity and thereby, effective ministry. The goal then was that the gospel might be preached and God glorified. The church's purpose has not changed in the nearly two thousand years since that time. Let us be united with our brothers and sisters in Christ and fulfill the task committed to us.

C. Prayer

Dear Lord, we sometimes find ourselves at odds with each other. We easily put ourselves, not You, at the center of our world. Reconciliation with our brothers and sisters is difficult. Grant us first peace with You so that we can live in peace with each other. Help us to practice reconciliation and be ministers of reconciliation. In Jesus' name, amen.

D. Thought to Remember

"Behold, how good and how pleasant it is for brethren to dwell together in unity!" (Psalm 133:1).

Learning by Doing

This page contains an alternate lesson plan emphasizing learning activities. Classes desiring such student involvement will find these suggestions helpful.

Learning Goals

This lesson will help the students:

1. Compare and contrast forgiveness and reconciliation.

2. Explain the role of forgiveness in the healing of broken relationships.

3. Commit themselves to whatever action is necessary to effect forgiveness and reconciliation in strained church or family relationships.

Into the Lesson

Give each student a copy of one of the following case studies. Ask each student to find two others with the same case study, consider it, and discuss the questions that follow it.

Case One: Frank and Jim were friends and co-workers for several years. Then Frank was promoted to a position that Jim had hoped he would be given. Jim tried to congratulate his friend, but Frank seemed to avoid him. Later, it turned out that Frank had spread the false rumor that Jim was an alcoholic. Believing the rumor, upper management had passed over Jim in considering candidates for the promotion.

What would it take to enable Jim to forgive Frank? Would that also restore the friendship between the two? If not, what would it take?

Case Two: Betty and Carol work together in the same office, but they have never been close friends. They work together well, but it is all business. Betty has long felt that Carol has not been entirely honest; even so, they have been able to work together efficiently. Recently, however, Betty has learned that much of Carol's success has been achieved by dishonest means—with the company's blessing. Betty has applied for a job with another company. She will earn less, but she feels she cannot stay in such an office.

What would it take to enable Betty to forgive Carol? Could there ever be friendship between the two? Explain.

Give the groups about ten minutes for discussion; then ask for reports. After the reports of the first case study, observe that forgiveness by the offended party does not by itself bring reconciliation (restored friendship). Both must also be deliberately sought by the offender. In the second case, developing a friendship seems unlikely since one had not already developed and the two will no longer be working together. Again, deliberate action would be required to effect it.

Into the Word

Read Genesis 33:1-14 aloud to the class. Then have those who discussed case study one form groups of four to six. Have those who discussed case study two do the same. The first groups are to review Genesis 25:29-33; 27:15-29, 41 and then list the parallels between the situation of Jacob and Esau and case study one. The second groups are to study Genesis 31:1-7, 14-16, 22-24, 36-42, 51-53 and list the parallels between the situation of Jacob and Laban and case study two. Allow fifteen minutes for study; then ask for reports.

The first groups' reports should include the following: It seems that in his heart, Esau had forgiven Jacob some time before this reunion. Reconciliation did not occur, however, because Jacob was still in another country and did not know about Esau's change of heart. Jacob had apparently repented and returned to seek forgiveness and reconciliation. Had he not returned, he could not have benefited from Esau's forgiving spirit.

The second groups' reports should include the following: It seems that Jacob and Laban's relationship was an uneasy partnership at best in which trust was lacking. They could forgive one another and put aside ill feelings, but there was little hope for friendship between them.

Into Life

Write the following two statements on the chalkboard:

Forgiveness may be given by the offended, regardless of the attitude or response of the offender.

Forgiveness must be both given and received to effect a change in a relationship.

Ask the students how many agree with the first statement. Then ask how many agree with the second statement. Point out that the two are not contradictory. One can forgive another, whether or not that person receives it. To heal a broken relationship, however, both parties must desire reconciliation.

Jacob and Esau were reunited because each desired reconciliation and took the steps necessary to achieve it. In humility and penitence Jacob sought his brother's forgiveness, and Esau was willing to give it. Urge your students to have the same attitudes if they are in need of reconciliation with another.

Let's Talk It Over

The questions on this page are designed to encourage review of the lesson Scriptures and to promote discussion of the lesson by the class. The answers provided are only discussion starters. Let your class talk it over from there.

1. Jesus said, "Blessed are the peacemakers: for they shall be called the children of God" (Matthew 5:9). One way we can fulfill this is by seeking to reconcile two or more persons at odds with one another. How can we do this?

First, we must examine our motives for doing this. Is it a matter of pride? Do we stand to gain some advantage? Or are we genuinely concerned about those who are separated by misunderstandings or careless words or actions? Then we should speak privately with the parties involved, to see if there is a mutual willingness to work toward a reconciliation. Prayer and patience will be required to make each party face up to his or her role in creating the rift and to be willing to admit that to one another. If we are dealing with Christians, we will surely want to emphasize the importance of "forgiving one another, even as God for Christ's sake hath forgiven you" (Ephesians 4:32).

2. There is a familiar ring to Jacob's efforts to regain Esau's favor by sending him gifts. What are some common examples of this kind of tactic today?

When problems arise in a married couple's relationship, one partner may attempt to "buy back" the love of the other with gifts. If the giving of gifts is the only action taken by the offending partner, such an effort fails to deal with the causes of disharmony. Another example is that of a rift between parents and children. Parents may hold out something such as an item of clothing or jewelry as "bait" to draw an offended son or daughter back into the family circle. That kind of practice sets a dangerous precedent. Perhaps the most tragic example of this tactic is the case of those persons who lavish gifts upon churches or charitable organizations in an attempt to win God's favor.

3. Why should we acknowledge regularly that God has dealt graciously with us in giving us all that we possess?

Jacob had worked hard for Laban and had also done quite a bit of scheming in order to obtain his wealth. He finally recognized, however, that he had that wealth because of God's grace. Perhaps we could describe how we have worked, planned, saved, and sacrificed in order to accumulate our possessions. We may be inclined, therefore, to feel proud of our accomplishments. But we must beware of the kind of attitude that King Nebuchadnezzar exhibited when he exclaimed, "Is not this great Babylon, that I have built for the house of the kingdom by the might of my power, and for the honor of my majesty?" (Daniel 4:30). God humbled Nebuchadnezzar, and He may humble us, too, if we forget that He is the real source of our wealth.

4. Why is the New Testament doctrine of reconciliation difficult for many to accept?

Paul wrote, "And you, that were sometime alienated and enemies in your mind by wicked works, yet now hath he reconciled in the body of his flesh through death" (Colossians 1:21, 22). To admit the need for reconciliation to God is to admit that one is His enemy. Many persons today, however, resist the idea that they are enemies of God. Even though they are not Christians, they may live generally upright lives and show a significant measure of compassion toward the needy. "Why should God regard me as an enemy?" they ask. They fail to recognize the seriousness of sin—the fact that it separates the creature from his Creator. By a variety of popular devices they justify, excuse, or minimize their sins. They must be made to see the dreadful nature of sin and then urged to be reconciled to God (2 Corinthians 5:20).

5. What are some principles we must keep in mind in promoting reconciliation within the church and overcoming conflicts and divisions?

Effective lines of communication must be developed so that persons with misunderstandings and grievances can voice these to their leaders. Conflicts must be dealt with promptly; otherwise, they may spread like a cancer. The principle of "blind justice" must prevail in the church. James 2:1-9 warns against favoritism shown to the wealthy. We must likewise avoid giving preference to a person with greater influence in the church, one who contributes more money, or one who has a more pleasing personality. Above all, we must recognize Jesus Christ as the head of the church indeed and approach every problem in the light of Scripture and with reliance on prayer.

Jacob Blesses Joseph and His Sons

November 28
Lesson 13

DEVOTIONAL READING: Psalm 103:15-18.

LESSON SCRIPTURE: Genesis 48.

PRINTED TEXT: Genesis 48:9-19.

Genesis 48:9-19

9 And Joseph said unto his father, They are my sons, whom God hath given me in this place. And he said, Bring them, I pray thee, unto me, and I will bless them.

10 Now the eyes of Israel were dim for age, so that he could not see. And he brought them near unto him; and he kissed them, and embraced them.

11 And Israel said unto Joseph, I had not thought to see thy face: and, lo, God hath showed me also thy seed.

12 And Joseph brought them out from between his knees, and he bowed himself with his face to the earth.

13 And Joseph took them both, Ephraim in his right hand toward Israel's left hand, and Manasseh in his left hand toward Israel's right hand, and brought them near unto him.

14 And Israel stretched out his right hand, and laid it upon Ephraim's head, who was the younger, and his left hand upon Manasseh's head, guiding his hands wittingly; for Manasseh was the firstborn.

15 And he blessed Joseph, and said, God, before whom my fathers Abraham and Isaac did walk, the God which fed me all my life long unto this day,

16 The angel which redeemed me from all evil, bless the lads; and let my name be named on them, and the name of my fathers Abraham and Isaac; and let them grow into a multitude in the midst of the earth.

17 And when Joseph saw that his father laid his right hand upon the head of Ephraim, it displeased him: and he held up his father's hand, to remove it from Ephraim's head unto Manasseh's head.

18 And Joseph said unto his father, Not so, my father: for this is the firstborn; put thy right hand upon his head.

19 And his father refused, and said, I know it, my son, I know it: he also shall become a people, and he also shall be great: but truly his younger brother shall be greater than he, and his seed shall become a multitude of nations.

GOLDEN TEXT: His younger brother shall be greater than he, and his seed shall become a multitude of nations.—Genesis 48:19.

Lesson Aims

After studying this lesson each student should:

1. Understand afresh the significance of how God's promises shape the future of His people.

2. Be determined to remain faithful to God because He is faithful to His people.

3. Be determined to live each day in hope.

Lesson Outline

INTRODUCTION

    A. Inheritance and Conflict

    B. Lesson Background

I. JOSEPH PRESENTS HIS SONS (Genesis 48:9-13)

    A. Joseph Brings the Sons (vv. 9, 10)

       An Ethical Will

    B. Jacob's Gratitude (v. 11)

    C. Joseph Presents the Sons (vv. 12, 13)

II. JACOB BLESSES THE SONS (Genesis 48:14-19)

    A. Reversal (v. 14)

    B. Jacob Gives the Blessing (vv. 15, 16)

       Living On

    C. Joseph Protests (vv. 17, 18)

    D. Jacob Persists (v. 19)

CONCLUSION

    A. Living Under Blessing

    B. Prayer

    C. Thought to Remember

Display visual 13 of the visuals packet throughout this session. The visual is shown on page 109.

Introduction

A. Inheritance and Conflict

In November 1991 Robert Maxwell, a wealthy tycoon, died and left a large and troubled financial empire. Two sons, with sharply different personalities, were left to carry on the business. Uncertain, however, was whether or not there would be a smooth transition to new leadership and an orderly resolution of the problems facing the empire.

A striking issue was the fact that the younger son was favored over the elder by the father. The question thus was raised, Would the two sons be able to work together with the younger having more power?

This modern story is as old as that of Jacob and Esau, and Joseph and his brothers. In this lesson we see the older/younger reversal with the sons of Joseph.

B. Lesson Background

Many years elapsed from the time of Jacob's return to Canaan (last week's lesson) and the event for our study in this lesson. Jacob apparently took up residence at Hebron, the home of his father Isaac, and continued to dwell there after Isaac's death (Genesis 35:27-29; 37:1, 14).

At this point, the Biblical narrative takes up the story of Joseph. He was Jacob's favorite son and received preferential treatment by his father. As a result, Joseph's brothers hated him. When he dreamed dreams that suggested his ascendancy over his older brothers, they hated him all the more. They conspired to kill him and would have succeeded had it not been for the intervention of Reuben, Jacob's firstborn son. The others succeeded, however, in selling Joseph to a merchant caravan bound for Egypt, and there he was sold into slavery (37:2-36).

After thirteen years, Joseph, by God's providence, was made second in command over Egypt (39:1—41:46a). By divine guidance he made provision for a terrible famine that was to come upon that part of the world. The famine came as predicted, and eventually Joseph's brothers were sent to Egypt by their father so they might buy grain. To do so, they had to appear before Joseph.

Through a series of conversations and tests, Joseph discovered that his brothers were suffering great guilt over their mistreatment of him years earlier. Furthermore, he saw that they were very protective of Benjamin, Joseph's younger brother, and gravely concerned about their father's welfare. Overcome with emotion, Joseph finally revealed himself to them. He then arranged for his entire family, with all of their possessions, to come to Egypt to live (41:46b-45:28).

In the unfolding of all of these events, Joseph saw the hand of God. He realized that God had brought him to Egypt so that he could save his family (45:7, 8; 50:19, 20). In the meantime Joseph had married an Egyptian, and two sons had been born to him (41:50-52).

Jacob lived for seventeen years in Egypt, and then the time of his death drew near (47:9, 28). He would bless all his sons soon, but first he wanted to bless the sons of Joseph. His intention was to adopt into his direct lineage the sons of his favorite child (49:1-5). This would give them comparable status with the other sons and would, in effect, place Joseph in the position of the firstborn as far as the inheritance was concerned (see 1 Chronicles 5:1, 2). Reuben, the actual firstborn, forfeited his position by his sin (Genesis 35:22; 49:4).

Jacob's blessing on the sons was a continuation of the blessing he had received from God (28:13, 14; 35:9-12; 48:3, 4), which in turn was a repetition of the blessing given to Isaac (Genesis 26:3, 4) and to Abraham (Genesis 12:1, 2).

I. Joseph Presents His Sons (Genesis 48:9-13)

A. Joseph Brings the Sons (vv. 9, 10)

9, 10. And Joseph said unto his father, They are my sons, whom God hath given me in this place. And he said, Bring them, I pray thee, unto me, and I will bless them. Now the eyes of Israel were dim for age, so that he could not see. And he brought them near unto him; and he kissed them, and embraced them.

Because of his failing eyesight and his weakened condition, Jacob probably was unaware that anyone else was in the room when he spoke to Joseph about adopting his sons (vv. 1-5). At last, Jacob beheld the forms of the young men and he asked Joseph who they were (v. 8). Joseph then responded, *They are my sons* (of whom you have just spoken).

Whom God hath given me. Just as Jacob had done when he met Esau years earlier, Joseph recognized that his children were a gift from God (see Genesis 33:5). Jacob then asked Joseph to bring his son's near so he could bless them. Joseph did so, and Jacob *kissed them, and embraced them.*

Jacob is called *Israel* in this text. That was the new, covenantal name given to him by God's messenger (Genesis 32:28). It is used here because of the special covenant implications of this blessing.

AN ETHICAL WILL

Israel (Jacob) knew that his days were coming to an end. His strength was failing; his eyes were dimmed; he had some unfinished business. So when his son, Joseph, presented his grandsons, Manasseh and Ephraim to him, Israel said, "Bring them to me that I might bless them."

This blessing relating to God's covenant family was unique. But the idea of spiritual values and insights being conveyed from one who is nearing death to those whose lives are yet before them is worthy of consideration. A recent book encouraging the practice is titled, *So That Your Values Live On: Ethical Wills and How to Prepare Them.*

An ethical will might include a statement of principles by which one's life has been directed and a retrospective judgment regarding them. It could include important lessons one has learned in life. Bible passages that have guided one's life, a listing of great literature or music that has inspired, an expression of thankfulness to those whose influence has blessed—all these things might be appropriately included.

Valuable as such a document may be, more value by far is found in the practice of godly principles and a regular discussion of spiritual values with one's family and friends day by day. We need not wait to the end to make our influence count for God.   —C. R. B.

B. Jacob's Gratitude (v. 11)

11. And Israel said unto Joseph, I had not thought to see thy face: and, lo, God hath showed me also thy seed.

Jacob's emotions, no doubt, were very strong at this moment. At one time Jacob was sure his son Joseph was dead, and his grief had been overwhelming (Genesis 37:31-35). By God's providence, however, Joseph had been protected, and he and his father had been reunited. Not only that, but Jacob had the wonderful blessing of seeing Joseph's children, of seeing the confirmation that his life would go on through his favored son. Jacob recognized the fact that God's providence had been at work to bring this about. This was a significant change in the man who earlier had tried to order everything in his life through his own planning and craftiness.

C. Joseph Presents the Sons (vv. 12, 13)

12. And Joseph brought them out from between his knees, and he bowed himself with his face to the earth.

Joseph brought them out from between his knees. The Hebrew here literally is "from near his knees." When Joseph had brought his sons to his father, Jacob had reached out and drawn them to him in an embrace. Thus the young men were near his knees. Joseph now brought them back from his father. Then, in keeping with the solemnity of the blessing that his father was about to bestow, Joseph *bowed himself* respectfully before him.

Though it may seem as though Joseph's sons were small at this time, they were nearly twenty

---

How to Say It

EPHRAIM. *Ee*-fray-im.
MANASSEH. Muh-*nass*-uh.
SHECHEM. *Shee*-kem or *Shek*-em.

years of age. They were born before the famine (Genesis 41:50-52). Jacob came to Egypt in the second year of the famine, when he was 130 years old (45:6; 47:9); and he gave this blessing near his death at age 147 (47:28).

13. And Joseph took them both, Ephraim in his right hand toward Israel's left hand, and Manasseh in his left hand toward Israel's right hand, and brought them near unto him.

In preparation for the bestowal of the blessing by Jacob (Israel), Joseph brought his sons near to his father once again. He arranged them so that Ephraim was by Jacob's left hand and Manasseh was by Jacob's right hand. Joseph did this so that the nearly blind Jacob could easily place his right hand on Manasseh, the firstborn, and his left hand on Ephraim, the younger of the two.

II. Jacob Blesses the Sons (Genesis 48:14-19)

A. Reversal (v. 14)

14. And Israel stretched out his right hand, and laid it upon Ephraim's head, who was the younger, and his left hand upon Manasseh's head, guiding his hands wittingly; for Manasseh was the firstborn.

Joseph's careful preparation for the blessing went unheeded. Jacob ignored the order of the sons before him. *Guiding his hands wittingly,* fully aware of what he was doing, Jacob crossed his arms to rest his right hand on the head of Ephraim, the younger, and his left hand on the head of Manasseh, who was the firstborn.

This act of the aged patriarch calls to our minds God's announcement to Rebekah, when the twin sons she was carrying struggled in her womb. At that time God stated that the older of her sons would serve the younger (Genesis 25:23). The blessing being bestowed now by Jacob indicated that once again the younger would have preeminence. It seems that the natural order was always being overturned in the covenant family. One would expect that Manasseh, as the older, should receive the blessing, but like Esau he was set aside in favor of the younger. Jacob knew well the implications of his act, but he was the instrument of God here.

This is the first mention in the Bible of the laying on of hands as a symbol of the transference of some supernatural power or gift. It occurs elsewhere in the Old Testament in connection with the offerings of the Mosaic law (Exodus 29:10; Leviticus 1:4; 4:4) and with the dedication to an office (Numbers 28:18, 23; Deuteronomy 34:9). In the New Testament, the laying on of hands was employed in the ordination of Christian office-bearers (Acts 6:6; 1 Timothy 4:14; 2 Timothy 1:6), in the performance of many of the miracles by Christ and the apostles (Mark 5:23; 6:5; Acts 9:17), and in the receiving of the Holy Spirit (Acts 8:17; 19:6).

B. Jacob Gives the Blessing (vv. 15, 16)

15. And he blessed Joseph, and said, God, before whom my fathers Abraham and Isaac did walk, the God which fed me all my life long unto this day.

Joseph himself was blessed by this blessing of his sons. In Jacob's words recorded in this verse and the next, the patriarch refers to God in three different ways.

First, He was the God *before whom my fathers Abraham and Isaac did walk.* That is, He was no strange God, but the same one to whom Jacob's forefathers had given themselves. He was a proven divine power, active in the lives of His chosen family. The patriarchs were aware that they walked, that is, lived in God's presence. They believed He knew their actions and intentions, and they entrusted their lives to Him.

Second, Jacob referred to God as one who had been a shepherd to him. The word *fed* is literally "shepherd." Jacob himself had been a shepherd, so he understood well the significance of the metaphor. A shepherd leads, protects, and provides for the sheep, and that is what God had done for Jacob throughout his life.

Jacob's admission that God was a shepherd to him was significant, for he had not always thought that way. But now, as the time of his death was approaching, he gave expression to the reality that he had always been under the care of God.

We who are Christians are to strive for spiritual maturity in Christ. Those who are spiritually mature recognize the loving care of God in every part of life, and live in faithfulness and loyalty to Him.

16. The angel which redeemed me from all evil, bless the lads; and let my name be named on them, and the name of my fathers Abraham and Isaac; and let them grow into a multitude in the midst of the earth.

In beginning his blessing of Joseph's two sons, Jacob called on the God of his fathers Abraham and Isaac, the God who had been his shepherd (v. 15), and here he continues his series of descriptions by saying *the angel which redeemed me from all evil.* In this triple reference, the term *the angel* is placed on an equality with God; therefore, the reference cannot be to a created angel. Earlier in Genesis we read of "the angel of the Lord" or "the angel of God" appearing and speaking to certain individuals (16:7-13; 21:15-20; 31:11-13). In the contexts of those references

it is clear that the phrase refers to a special manifestation of God, and that the persons involved
were in the presence of God himself. The unusual aspect of Jacob's reference in this verse is
that the word *angel* appears by itself.

Jacob speaks of God as the one who *redeemed*
him. This is the first reference in the Old Testament to this aspect of God's activity. In looking
back on his life, Jacob would have been quite
aware of how often God had protected him. The
Biblical record includes several incidents in
which his safety was threatened, namely by
Esau (Genesis 27:41), Laban (31:29), and the inhabitants near the town of Shechem (34:25-30).
In later Israelite civil law the redeemer was the
relative who could buy a person back who had
been sold into slavery (Leviticus 25:47-49). God
as redeemer had rescued Jacob, not from servitude, but *from evil.*

*Let my name be named on them, and the name of
my fathers.* To call one's name on another was to
consider that person one's own. Jacob was stating that these two sons of Joseph would henceforth be counted as Jacob's sons and the
children of Jacob's ancestors.

The blessing was for the sons to *grow into a
multitude.* The Hebrew term used here is the
word from which the Hebrew word *fish* is derived. Therefore, the blessing was for Ephraim
and Manasseh to multiply rapidly, like the fish
of the sea. Centuries later, as Moses pronounced
a blessing on the tribes of Israel before his death,
he spoke of the myriads of Ephraim and the
thousands of Manasseh, referring to their might.
(Deuteronomy 33:17). This fact is attested to
again in the time of Joshua (Joshua 17:14-18).

LIVING ON

Many are the ways we try to ensure that we
will be remembered after we are gone: mau-
soleums with our names inscribed in stone;
business empires named for us; large sums of
money given so a college hall will bear our
name; pursuit of careers in the public eye. We
even try to live on through our children.

A bizarre attempt at the latter was made last
year. Fourteen convicted killers on Death Row in
San Quentin prison sued the state to allow them
to father children. Insisting that the denial of
their "right to reproduce" amounted to "cruel
and unusual punishment," they demanded the
right to impregnate some willing woman (by artificial insemination) so their names could live
on. The attorney altruistically said he was filing
suit on behalf of the grandparents who would
otherwise have no grandchildren.

Israel's prayer that his name might live on in
his grandsons is a natural longing, not to be dis-

visual 13

paraged. But our yearnings for immortality will
be frustrated if they have their basis only in our
descendants, whether through the carrying on of
our name or the continuation of our genes. Our
only real hope for immortality is to be found in
a saving relationship with Christ. Those who
know Him shall live forever!   —C. R. B.

C. Joseph Protests (vv. 17, 18)

**17, 18. And when Joseph saw that his father
laid his right hand upon the head of Ephraim,
it displeased him: and he held up his father's
hand, to remove it from Ephraim's head unto
Manasseh's head. And Joseph said unto his father, Not so, my father: for this is the firstborn;
put thy right hand upon his head.**

Seeing that Jacob had placed his right hand on
the head of Ephraim, the younger son, Joseph
thought that his blind father had made a mistake. He knew that the oldest should receive the
blessing, and that once again it was irrevocable.
It displeased him to think that the honor that
should rightfully go to Manasseh would mistakenly be given to Ephraim. So Joseph physically
intervened. He took hold of his father's right
hand to move it from Ephraim's head to Manasseh's head and told his father that he was not
blessing the right son.

D. Jacob Persists (v. 19)

**19. And his father refused, and said, I know
it, my son, I know it: he also shall become a
people, and he also shall be great: but truly his
younger brother shall be greater than he, and
his seed shall become a multitude of nations.**

Jacob replied with a quiet confidence. He
knew exactly what he was doing. This was a
blessing of God and initiated by faith. He was
well aware from his own experience that the
firstborn didn't always receive the blessing. The
protest of Joseph did not deter him. The older
received a blessing in his own right, but not of
ascendancy. Manasseh would be great but not
the greater of the two.

In Israelite history Ephraim eventually did gain ascendancy. When the land of Canaan was divided among the tribes of Israel in the days of Joshua, the Joseph tribes (Manasseh and Ephraim) were given the largest territories in the north central hill country and east of Jordan with Manasseh getting the largest portion. Beginning in the time of the Judges, however, Ephraim took the lead of the northern tribes. Ephraim was later called "the strength of mine head" (Psalm 60:7), the great source of warriors for the defense of Israel. Hence, when the nation was split into two kingdoms after Solomon's death, the northern kingdom was often called "Ephraim" (Isaiah 7:17; Hosea 5:3, 5, 9).

The blessing of Jacob was completed in verses 20-22, which immediately follow the printed text. It was a promise that Joseph's descendants would not stay in Egypt indefinitely, but would return to the land that they were to inherit. This promise was first given to Abraham many years before (Genesis 15:13-16), and its fulfillment was a crucial part of God's promise and plan for His chosen nation.

Conclusion

A. Living Under Blessing

Jacob's family had its beginning in the blessing of God (Genesis 12:1-3). Jacob had lived his whole life under that blessing. In his earlier years he did not always trust in that blessing, but often tried to order his own way. Yet in his maturity he realized what it meant to be blessed. Before he died he was determined, under God's direction, to assure the blessing for his descendants. That was true not only of the sons of Joseph, as we have seen in the lesson text, but for all of his sons, as is recorded in Genesis 49.

In conveying this blessing, Jacob wanted his descendants to have a sure hope for the future. They were in Egypt now, but God did not intend for them to stay there permanently. Jacob was confident that they would return to Canaan one day and occupy the land promised to him and his ancestors.

Jacob had known the tragedy of failed hope. Thinking at one time that Joseph was dead, Jacob had been resigned to die in his despair. But the renewal of hope had come with the news that Joseph was alive in Egypt. Reunited with his son, Jacob had even seen Joseph's children. So Jacob wanted his descendants to live in the hope that God would fulfill the promise He had made to their ancestors (48:21).

For anyone else, the words of Jacob would have been incomprehensible. Most people and nations live for the present, not for the future.

Home Daily Bible Readings

Monday, Nov. 22—Joseph Holds No Resentment (Genesis 45:1-9)
Tuesday, Nov. 23—"Thus Says Your Son Joseph" (Genesis 45:10-20)
Wednesday, Nov. 24—Jacob Yearns to See Joseph (Genesis 45:21-28)
Thursday, Nov. 25—Aged Jacob Blesses Pharaoh (Genesis 47:1-12)
Friday, Nov. 26—Joseph Ushers in Land Reform (Genesis 47:13-26)
Saturday, Nov. 27—Jacob Adopts Ephraim and Manasseh (Genesis 48:1-7)
Sunday, Nov. 28—Jacob Blesses Manasseh, Then Ephraim (Genesis 48:8-14, 17-22)

They grasp land and power and control now. Future generations are irrelevant. But Jacob and his family were raised on promises. They could rely on them, because God was the one who promised, and He was the controlling power.

Christians live under blessing, hope, and promise also. In the gospel of Jesus Christ, God fulfilled His promise to Abraham. Through faith in Christ all people can become children of Abraham and recipients of God's promise (Galatians 3:7-14). This ultimate proof of the faithfulness of God is the last in a long line of proofs. Like Jacob, Christians are in a position to trust in God, for He has proved himself completely trustworthy. God's trustworthiness is the basis for Christian hope (Hebrews 7:13-20). The hope we possess provides for us a sure future and gives meaning for the present.

Those outside of Christ have no sure hope governing their future. They have nowhere to turn for meaning in life. The best they can do is invent some mystic vision of the present or search for inward divinity. Both are dead ends.

Christians know the truth that Jacob expressed. The future is in God's hands, and life goes on in the present under His blessing.

B. Prayer

Dear Lord, we often fail You because we allow the hopelessness of our culture to invade our lives. Renew our hope in You, O God, and help us to face tomorrow with fresh faith and energy. Help us to live in complete confidence that You hold the future in Your hands. In Jesus' name, amen.

C. Thought to Remember

"Let us hold fast the profession of our faith without wavering; for he is faithful that promised" (Hebrews 10:23).

Learning by Doing

This page contains an alternate lesson plan emphasizing learning activities. Classes desiring such student involvement will find these suggestions helpful.

Learning Goals

After this lesson, each student will be able to:

1. List several events from the lives of Jacob and his family that demonstrated that God's purpose was being carried out in their lives.

2. Explain how understanding God's eternal purpose provides hope for Christians today.

Into the Lesson

Before class, duplicate the following chart on the chalkboard or with the overhead projector:

Abraham
|
Ishmael   Isaac
|
Esau   Jacob
|
Reuben   Joseph
|
Manasseh   Ephraim

As the students arrive, ask them to study the chart and see if they can determine what unusual circumstance repeated itself in each generation of Abraham's family listed.

In Old Testament times, the firstborn son traditionally received a double portion of the father's estate. This was included in the birthright blessing. Yet in each case noted above, the firstborn son did not receive the greater inheritance. Ishmael was Abraham's firstborn son, but Isaac was the principal heir. We are familiar with Jacob's dealing and deception to obtain the birthright blessing instead of Esau, who was the firstborn. Joseph, who was Jacob's eleventh son, received the double inheritance (through his two sons) instead of Reuben, who was the firstborn (see 1 Chronicles 5:1, 2). In blessing Joseph's two sons, Jacob deliberately gave the blessing of the firstborn to the younger son. God was working in a special way with this family.

Into the Word

Begin by stating that the Biblical record clearly reveals that God has a definite and far-reaching plan that is being carried out in His dealings with mankind. In the past weeks we have seen that God called Abraham out of Ur to go to a land He would show him. Abraham was to be the father of a great people, and through him all peoples would be blessed. Thus was born the Hebrew nation, through whom God's plan of redemption for the world would be carried out. Jacob had his place in this plan. He, like the other patriarchs in the covenant family, received special guidance and protection so that God's plan would go forward.

Read Genesis 48:9-22. Then lecture briefly on the event in this text. Emphasize Jacob's acknowledgement that God had been his shepherd all his life (v. 15). Have different students read the following Scriptures aloud. Discuss how each event demonstrated God's special oversight in the lives of Jacob and his family.

Genesis 25:21-23	Genesis 27:26-30
Genesis 28:10-15	Genesis 31:4-9
Genesis 31:20-24	Genesis 37:23-28
Genesis 41:37-49	Genesis 45:4-8

Write two headings on the chalkboard: "Young Jacob" and "Old Jacob." Observe that, in his youth, Jacob leaned more on his own cunning than on trust in God to bring about the fulfillment of His word (Genesis 25:23). In his later years, however, he demonstrated a mature faith in God and the conviction that His purpose would be accomplished. Have the following three Scriptures read aloud. Under the "Young Jacob" heading on the board write the summary statement that follows the reference here: Genesis 25:29-34 (took advantage of his brother's weakness to obtain the birthright); Genesis 27:18-23 (deceived his father to gain his blessing); Genesis 31:20 (sneaked away from Laban).

Now write the following statements under the "Old Jacob" heading: blessed his grandsons according to God's direction and not according to custom; expressed his faith that God would bring his family back to Canaan.

Into Life

God's plan of redemption, set in motion among mankind through the lives of the patriarchs, was fulfilled in the Messiah, the Lord Jesus Christ. We now have our place in that plan, although we have not been promised the special providential care enjoyed by the patriarchs of old. God's providence, however, still operates, and if we align our will with His will, He will bring us safely into His presence when our journey on earth has ended. Read Romans 8:28. Suggest your students memorize this verse as a reminder of God's concern for His people.

Let's Talk It Over

The questions on this page are designed to encourage review of the lesson Scriptures and to promote discussion of the lesson by the class. The answers provided are only discussion starters. Let your class talk it over from there.

1. The account of Joseph's enslavement in Egypt and his rise to leadership is not part of our lesson text, but it does relate closely to it. What does that account tell us about God's providence?

Joseph's experiences remind us that God's plans sometimes require several years to complete. More than twenty years elapsed from the time when Joseph was sold into slavery until he rescued his family from famine. That offers us hope if we have been waiting a long time for God to give us help or guidance with a difficult situation. When Joseph saw his brothers again after so long a time, he told them that God had worked through their evil deed to send him to Egypt, so that he could preserve life (Genesis 45:5). It is encouraging for us to know that God can exercise His providential guidance of us even in the midst of human evil.

2. Jacob's delight at seeing Joseph's sons is shared by people today who have grandchildren. How can grandchildren be viewed as a special blessing from God?

By the time grandchildren come, we may have achieved many of the goals that distracted us when our children were born. If so, we are likely to be in a more relaxed condition to enjoy our grandchildren. Also, it is satisfying to see our children passing on to their own children some of the values we labored to instill as parents. We are blessed too in the way grandchildren can invigorate us and make us laugh. Their energy, their innocence, and their curiosity can lift us out of a "ho-hum" frame of mind. Finally, we see in grandchildren a reminder of the ongoing nature of life. At a time in our lives, when we have cause to reflect on the brevity of our days on earth, they cause us to contemplate anew God's glorious gift of life.

3. In the *New International Version's* rendering of Genesis 48:15, Jacob speaks of "the God who has been my Shepherd." How does that familiar Biblical figure affect us?

The Twenty-third Psalm with its detailed description of the life of trust in terms of the shepherd's tending his flock, is still a universal favorite. To a certain extent the scenes of this Psalm are foreign to modern life. But the basic idea expressed by Jacob, and by David in the psalm, is one that appeals to all. We often feel a need for the kind of guidance, protection, and provision the shepherd gave his sheep. With our tendency to stray into dangerous situations we can benefit from a "rod" and "staff" to draw us back to safety. "The valley of the shadow of death" was real to Jacob, as it was to David. We too take comfort in knowing that the Lord is with us at that critical time.

4. In ancient Israel, significance was attached to the order of a person's birth in a family. In our time experts point out that our birth order can have a significant effect on our development. Why should we not let this factor inhibit us in achieving a successful life?

While firstborn sons in Bible times enjoyed certain advantages, the Biblical record tells us of many successful second-born persons, such as Isaac and Jacob. Later on, the greatest king in Israel's history, David, was the youngest of eight sons. Today we often hear of jealousy within a family because the firstborn seems to have been blessed with the best mind, the lastborn has come up with the most appealing personality, and similar complaints. Whatever our place in the birth order, however, we possess characteristics and advantages that we can utilize to attain worthwhile life goals.

5. One of our greatest benefits as Christians is that we have a solid hope for the future. How does that differ from the viewpoint many non-Christians have of the future?

Today's society is subjected to an array of pessimistic views of the future. War, and especially nuclear war, remains a chilling possibility. AIDS threatens to ravage mankind. The destruction of our environment, we are told, may ultimately bring an end to life on our planet. Many Christians are concerned about these issues, but our view of the future is not so forbidding, for we know that the almighty God oversees His world. Also, non-Christians often speak of a rather cheerless prospect regarding death. For them it is the end of existence; at its best they see it only as the cessation of toil, pain, and sorrow. Christians, however, see death as the door to a bright, joyous, eternal future.

Winter Quarter, 1993-94

Theme: The Story of Jesus (Luke)

Special Features

Lessons

Unit 1.   Luke: A Savior Is Born

Unit 2.   Luke: Ministry in Galilee

Unit 3.   Luke: The Cross and the Resurrection

About these lessons

The lessons of the Winter Quarter are taken from the Gospel of Luke. A physician and missionary companion of the apostle Paul, Luke has given the world a well-ordered report of the birth, ministry, death, and resurrection of Jesus. It is clear from this Gospel that the message of salvation in Christ is intended for all people.

Dec 5

Dec 12

Dec 19

Dec 26

Jan 2

Jan 9

Jan 16

Jan 23

Jan 30

Feb 6

Feb 13

Feb 20

Feb 27

Quarterly Quiz

The questions on this page may be used in several ways: as a pretest at the beginning of the quarter; as a review at the end of the quarter; or as a review after each lesson. The questions are based on the Scripture text of each lesson (King James Version). **The answers are on page 120.**

Lesson 1

1. What prophet foretold the work of John the Baptist? *Luke 3:4*
2. Whose way did John prepare by his preaching in the country? *Luke 3:4*
3. According to John the Baptist, what should one do who has two coats? *Luke 3:11*

Lesson 2

1. Whom did God send to Nazareth with a message for a girl named Mary? *Luke 1:26, 27*
2. What startling message did God's angel take to Mary in Nazareth? *Luke 1:31*
3. How could Mary have a baby without any help from a man? *Luke 1:35*

Lesson 3

1. Why was a manger used for a newborn baby's bed? *Luke 2:7*
2. How did an angel describe the baby who used a manger for His bed? *Luke 2:11*
3. What did Mary do with the angel's message reported to her by the shepherds? *Luke 2:19*

Lesson 4

1. Who tempted Jesus? *Luke 4:1, 2*
2. What did Jesus use to answer the temptation of the devil? *Luke 4:4, 8, 12*
3. For how long did the devil go away after tempting Jesus? *Luke 4:13*

Lesson 5

1. From what book of the Old Testament did Jesus read in Nazareth? *Luke 4:17*
2. What was Jesus' first comment? *Luke 4:21*
3. How did the hearers feel when Jesus told of God's care for foreign people? *Luke 4:28*

Lesson 6

1. What was it in the teaching of Jesus that amazed the hearers? *Luke 4:32*
2. Jesus set people free from demons. What other miracles did He do? *Luke 4:40*
3. Why did Jesus leave Capernaum when people wanted Him to stay? *Luke 4:43*

Lesson 7

1. What shall we do if people hate us, slander us, and avoid us because we are trying to do as Jesus wants us to do? *Luke 6:22, 23*

2. Jesus says we should love our enemies— and do what else for them? *Luke 6:27, 28*
3. Whose mercy should we imitate? *Luke 6:36*

Lesson 8

1. Jesus sent seventy of His followers to preach in teams of how many? *Luke 10:1*
2. Where were the seventy to go? *Luke 10:1*
3. What were the seventy to say? *Luke 10:9*
4. What were the seventy to do in addition to giving their message? *Luke 10:9*

Lesson 9

1. Give two reasons for the poverty of the boy who had left home. *Luke 15:13, 14*
2. How did the distressed boy plan to escape from his misery? *Luke 15:18, 19*
3. How did the boy's father welcome him when he went home? *Luke 15:20-24*

Lesson 10

1. Did Jesus avoid children or welcome them? *Luke 18:16*
2. What did "a certain ruler" ask Jesus about? *Luke 18:18*
3. Is there any way for a rich man to get into the kingdom of God? *Luke 18:27*

Lesson 11

1. In Jesus' parable, what fate could the wicked husbandmen expect? *Luke 20:16*
2. Who perceived that Jesus had spoken this parable against them? *Luke 20:19*
3. Why didn't the enemies lay hands on Jesus and arrest Him? *Luke 20:19*

Lesson 12

1. In ordaining the Lord's Supper, what purpose did Jesus assign to it? *Luke 22: 19*
2. At their last supper with Jesus, what did the disciples argue about? *Luke 22:24*
3. What should a person do if he wants to be great among Christians? *Luke 22:26*

Lesson 13

1. As Jesus hung on the cross, what surprising thing did He do for His killers? *Luke 23:34*
2. What was over the whole land? *Luke 23:44*
3. What surprised the disciples a few days later? *Luke 24:34*

Be Blessed With Luke

by Edwin V. Hayden

PAUL'S "BELOVED PHYSICIAN," Dr. Luke (Colossians 4:14), invites us during the next three months to share with him in a special blessing promised by the Lord Jesus himself. The blessing is recorded in John 20:29, as addressed to Thomas after that apostle had become fully convinced of the Lord's resurrection from the dead: "Because you have seen me, you have believed; blessed are those who have not seen and yet have believed" (*New International Version*).

Unlike the Gospel writers Matthew and John, who were apostles of Jesus, and probably Mark, whose mother's home became a meeting place for the disciples (Acts 12:12), Luke was not an eyewitness to any of the events he reported in his Gospel. He was nevertheless a firm believer, and he wrote with purpose to confirm the faith of his readers—first, the honorable Theophilus ("friend of God"), to whom the book was addressed, and then whoever might give attention to what he had written (Luke 1:1-4). The readers would not see Jesus in the flesh, but they could still believe and be blessed.

For that purpose, and clearly inspired in the effort, Luke investigated thoroughly, not only in such written accounts as were available during the first generation of the church, but also and especially among persons who had been closest to Jesus during the days of His walk on earth.

The Mother's Story

Luke's personal research becomes dramatically evident in the first two chapters of his Gospel. There the good doctor records, with the utmost tact and simplicity, the experiences of Mary the mother of Jesus relating to His birth and boyhood. To whom more readily than to a Christian physician would Mary unlock her heart's treasures, kept and pondered through the intervening years (Luke 2:19, 51)? It is her story, as told by none but Dr. Luke!

Luke's Favorite Subjects

These same first chapters show several identifying characteristics found throughout Luke's Gospel.

As a careful historian, he links events in the life of Jesus with public happenings in the Roman Empire (1:5; 2:1, 2).

He emphasizes prayer and praise, songs and music (1:10, 13, 14, 46-55, 67-79; 2:10-14). Luke

is the only Gospel writer who mentions Jesus' own praying at the time of His baptism (3:21), and before choosing the twelve apostles (6:12), and before asking the apostles, "Who do you say that I am?" (9:18), and at His transfiguration (9:28, 29), and before teaching the "disciples' prayer" (11:1), and before predicting Peter's denial on the night before His crucifixion (22:31, 32), and in His first and last utterances from the cross (23:34, 46).

Luke especially makes it plain that all mankind—notably the poor, the outcast, and foreigners—are included in God's loving provision for salvation (1:51-53; 2:10). This comes out more clearly in later references to Samaritans (9:51-56; 10:25-37; 17:11-19) and tax collectors (5:27-32; 15:1, 2; 19:1-10).

Luke, more than others, reveals the Lord's appreciation for women and the family (1:5-7, 17; 2:36-38; 8:1-3; 10:38-42). At least one literary critic has called the Gospel according to Luke the most beautiful book ever written.

We Couldn't Cover It All

It is clearly impossible in the scope of thirteen Sunday-school lessons to do justice to anything as extensive and important as "The Story of Jesus (The Gospel of Luke)." Our lesson series does not pretend to do so. Its thirteen printed texts cover only one-sixth of the material in Luke's Gospel. If we include the complete "Background Scripture" assignments, the total is about one-fourth of the whole book. Almost half of Luke's twenty-four chapters are not represented at all in the lesson texts. Many important events in Jesus' life are not mentioned in this series. Among these are His calling of Galilean fishermen to be His disciples (5:1-11); His raising of a widow's son (7:11-17) and a ruler's daughter (8:40-56) from the dead; the conversion of Zaccheus (19:1-10); Jesus' triumphal entry into Jerusalem (19:28-44); and much of His teaching in the temple during the following days (chapter 21). The Lord's resurrection is affirmed in only two verses of the thirteenth lesson text.

Let Students Read for Themselves!

If, therefore, we are to receive the fullest possible blessing from Luke's account, we shall need to go beyond the assignments in reading and studying his book. We urgently recommend that your class engage in a reading campaign covering the entire Gospel of Luke at least once, and preferably more than once during the quarter. That is not a heavy assignment. The whole twenty-four chapters may be read rather easily in a little more than two hours. The assigned texts and topics will become more meaningful for the more complete study of the book.

Meanwhile we have before us thirteen excellent samples from "The Story of Jesus (The Gospel of Luke)." They are presented in three segments, titled "A Savior Is Born" (four Sundays in December), "Ministry in Galilee" (five Sundays in January), and "The Cross and the Resurrection" (four Sundays in February).

A Savior Is Born

The first four lessons deal with preparation for Jesus' public ministry. First we view the work of His forerunner, John the Baptist (Luke 3). Read also Luke 1:5-25 and 57-80, which relate the angel Gabriel's promise of John's birth then the fulfillment of that promise. No other Gospel writer tells of this promise.

Next we consider Gabriel's visit to Mary in Nazareth, saying that she was to become the mother of God's Son. Her acceptance of the responsibility provides the lesson title, "Yielding to God's Will."

Fulfillment of that promise in the birth of Jesus at Bethlehem is the subject of our Christmas lesson. Night-watching shepherds and angels joined in celebration of the event.

The fourth preparatory study picks up with Jesus' commitment to the Messianic ministry announced by John the Baptist. Following Jesus' baptism by John, He was tested through forty days of temptation by Satan in the Judean wilderness. Then He was ready for His public ministry.

Ministry in Galilee

Five lessons for January provide highlights of Jesus' ministry of healing, preaching, and teaching, not only in Galilee, but also in Perea, east of the Jordan, and in the borders of Judea.

First we find Him in Nazareth, where He was brought up, announcing His fulfillment of Isaiah's prophecy that the poor would receive good news, captives would be freed, blind folk would receive their sight, and God's reign would be established. But His neighbors responded with angry rejection.

For January 9 we read of a busy Sabbath Day for Jesus in Capernaum, freeing a demon-possessed man in the synagogue and removing the sicknesses of many, including Simon Peter's mother-in-law. Afterward Jesus left Capernaum to focus on heralding the kingdom of God in other towns and villages.

Central themes of Jesus' preaching provide our study for January 16, as the Lord delivered them to His followers immediately after naming twelve to be His apostles. His "Sermon on the Plain" echoes much that is recorded in Matthew 5—7 from the "Sermon on the Mount."

For January 23 we are provided warnings concerning the seriousness of discipleship, and the account of Jesus' sending seventy disciples as advance agents in cities He intended to visit.

Parables from the Lord's later ministry include three stories demonstrating His insistence that Heaven rejoices when even one lost sinner is found through repentance (January 30). We shall dwell on Jesus' "Welcome Home Story" (recorded only by Luke), celebrating the return of a wayward and wasteful wanderer, to his father's delight and his brother's disdain.

The Cross and the Resurrection

Our first two lessons in February deal with teaching situations in Jerusalem during the tense days leading to Jesus' arrest, His trials, and His crucifixion. For February 6 we find Him among friends discussing the qualifications for entrance into God's kingdom. Jesus welcomed little children, saying that childlike trust is necessary to anyone's salvation. He invited a rich young law-keeper to divest himself of his wealth and become a disciple. Then He said rich people cannot enter the kingdom, but "the things which are impossible with men are possible with God."

For February 13 we consider a parable plainly directed against the religious leaders who rejected and opposed Jesus. It spoke of wicked stewards who refused to yield the return from a vineyard entrusted to their care, and thus came under their lord's most severe judgment. The embittered clergy became increasingly determined to destroy Him.

On February 20 we shall find Jesus spending a final evening with friends at a Passover feast that became His last supper and the basis for the Lord's Supper in the church. Yet even there His disciples contended for positions of honor, and He must point them again in the direction of unselfish service. This is told only by Luke.

Jesus' crucifixion and resurrection is reserved for the final lesson. Luke alone of the Gospel writers tells of the crucified thief who spoke up for Jesus and said to the Lord, "Remember me." Our text declares that Jesus rose again from the grave, but leaves to other studies the responsibility for more adequate treatment.

The blessing of faith is surely available through these studies. It will come in fuller measure from a thorough examination of the entire Gospel of Luke.

Jesus Our Savior

by Jonathan R. Stedman

SIMON PETER was walking on the surface of the Sea of Galilee one night. Exhilarated at first by his unique experience, he did not notice that he was doing it in a gale. When that terrifying thought dawned on him, he spoke a short but fervent prayer: "Lord, save me" (Matthew 14:30). And his walking companion "Immediately . . . caught him" (v. 31), answering his prayer for salvation.

Each one of us who are Christians has, in one way or another, spoken that same prayer to Jesus. And most of us were asked a question that ended with words such as these: "Do you accept Jesus as your Savior?" But did we really understand what a "Savior" is? What has Jesus done for us in His capacity as our "Savior"?

Our purpose here is to see what Jesus has accomplished for us, and what He expects us to do as a result of that salvation.

Saved From Sin

The most obvious application of Jesus' saving work is our salvation from the effects of sin. Even as little children, before we were aware of specific personal sins in our lives, we would echo the prayers of our elders as we asked God to "forgive us from our sins."

Sin is a serious matter, indeed. It produces catastrophic results in our lives, effects that make the most terrifying physical disease pale in comparison. It makes us guilty, unable to stand in the presence of a holy God. It makes us polluted, aware of our spiritual sickness and also aware of our total inability to cure ourselves. It makes us fit for only one appropriate destination: Hell. And yet many people go merrily through their lives thinking that they are reasonably good people, and that God, if He exists, will certainly treat them nicely at the pearly gates.

From this sad situation Jesus our Savior has delivered us Christians. This salvation was accomplished at the cross. It is known by various other words in the New Testament: "redemption" (Romans 3:24), "propitiation" or "sacrifice of atonement" (Romans 3:25, *New International Version*), being "justified" (Romans 3:28). Each of these and other terms has a special meaning, but they all describe the way God has put us in a saved, restored relationship with himself. And it was done at the cross. In the words of P. P. Bliss, "On the cross He sealed my pardon, Paid the debt and made me free."

Saved From Death

In a *Reader's Digest* survey of several years ago, the top ten fears of Americans were listed. Heading the list was the fear of death, the dread that leads people to go to any lengths to postpone their appointment with the "grim reaper." And it *is* an appointment (see Hebrews 9:27). Fear of death is appropriate for one estranged from God, because it is an enemy (1 Corinthians 15:26).

Death is a consequence of sin (see Romans 5:12, 15, 17). And because of its grim inevitability, all the blessings of God's creation and providence would be little more than cruel jokes if we knew that death was the end.

But thanks be to God! It's *not* the end! For the Christian, death is simply another event in his or her life. The sacrifice of Jesus our Savior on the cross defeated the one who uses death as his primary enslaving tool, and it saves us from that awful fear of death with which the devil has held us in bondage (Hebrews 2:14, 15). So in Christ we are saved from death.

But we are faced with a problem: Christ freed us from death, but we still die! Every one of us will pass through that event we call "death," so how do we explain this conundrum? The answer lies in the justice and mercy of God. Death was prescribed as the consequence of sin (Genesis 2:17; 3:19), and this will continue until the

end of the age (Hebrews 9:27). So Jesus took care of the death problem by the resurrection! Oh, yes, we still have to die. But so what! "Death is swallowed up in victory!" (1 Corinthians 15:54).

Saved From Despair

The world around us is filled with despair. While we are not so worried about nuclear annihilation in the post-cold-war years, we still face starvation, environmental disaster, civil wars, and other global concerns. On a personal level, we see people dealing with despair in their families. Marriages are as likely to fail as to succeed, and the ones that "succeed" are often traumatized by concern over economic, ethical, and spiritual pressures.

This problem of despair also is taken care of by Jesus our Savior. He does it by injecting into the mixture an ingredient that lightens the burden. It is called *hope*. Hope is not wishful thinking. It is the assured knowledge that something is yours, but you just don't have it yet. And that blessed assurance comes only as we have been saved by Jesus.

The ultimate object of our hope is, of course, Heaven. We all look forward to it with eager anticipation, and it is this glorious hope that makes us able to live joyfully in a diseased world. Add to this the presence of God's own Spirit living within us, giving strength to our lives and enabling us to do God's will, and there is no good reason for the child of God ever to be discouraged. But even when we are, Jesus our Savior comes and offers to carry the load with us (Matthew 11:28-30). Notice that He doesn't offer to carry the whole load. The yoke in His metaphor is for two animals, not one. But with the Lord carrying His side of the yoke, the burden is lightened considerably.

Saved to Reproduce

To this point we have discussed the blessings given to us by Jesus our Savior: freedom from sin, death, and despair. But wouldn't it seem a bit selfish of us to have the cure for the most disastrous disease of all—sin—and keep it to ourselves?

Jesus used the metaphor of the vine and branches to describe His relationship with His followers (see John 15:1-8). We like to talk about all the benefits we have from being in the vine, and this is fine. But Jesus' point in this passage seems to focus, not on the *benefits* to the branches from being in the vine, but on the *duty* of the branches due to their place in the vine. The branches do the reproducing for the vine (see verses 2, 4, 5, 8). They are to bear fruit.

So we have the greatest news possible: the cure for the disease. And we see the necessity for sharing this with other people: the branches must reproduce. And we have examples of those who have shared their Savior with others, both in the New Testament and in our own experience. Why, then, are so many Christians so reluctant to say anything about Jesus to another person whose eternal destiny is hanging in the balance? "Rescue the perishing," the familiar hymn states; "Duty *demands* it."

Our responsibility to share the news about our Savior can be looked at from another angle. Not only does duty demand it, but it is also our marvelous privilege to be ambassadors on behalf of Christ (2 Corinthians 5:11—6:1). When we appeal to people to decide for Christ, God himself is making the appeal through us!

Isn't it reasonable to assume that if God is speaking through us He will give us the power to present the message courageously? He has! We have His Spirit living in us, enabling us to work His will with His power. In a context of a command to make disciples of all people, Jesus promised: "And surely I will be with you always, to the very end of the age" (Matthew 28:20, *New International Version*).

Conclusion

We use the word *savior* in a number of different contexts. Lucius Quinctius Cincinnatus was the "savior" of Rome in 458 B. C., when he raised an army and defeated the Aequians. Dr. Wilbur A. Sawyer is considered a "savior" for developing the yellow fever vaccine in 1930. Lew Alcindor was the "savior" of the floundering Milwaukee Bucks when he was drafted out of UCLA in 1969. But when we use the word in this way, we understand that, while the individual's accomplishment was noteworthy, someone else could have saved the city or the team or developed the vaccine.

This is not the case with Jesus our Savior. He is the unique Savior because He did something no one else in all earth could do. A human being alone would not be qualified to do what He did, because sin would place him in the position of needing a Savior himself. Nor would a divine being alone be able to do what He did, because it was necessary for a man to undo the effects brought on humanity by Adam (see Romans 5:15, 17, 19). But in Jesus Christ, the perfect God-man, the unique combination necessary and sufficient to save humanity is present.

There is a Savior, what joys expressed!
His eyes are mercy, His word is rest.
For each tomorrow, for yesterday
There is a Savior who lights our way.

Jesus the Servant

by David H. Ray

HOW COULD THEY not understand by now? They had spent the last three years of their lives watching, listening, and learning. But here, on the eve of His death, they once again began to argue. I can just imagine how the spirited exchange might have started.

"Jesus likes me best," one proud disciple prods another. "He let me sit closer to Him than you do."

"Well, He let me say the first prayer," comes the reply. One more joins the fray, then another and another, until the whole room is caught up in an escalating battle of one-upmanship.

Jesus sadly quiets the petty bickering and once more tries to help the disciples understand: "The kings of the Gentiles lord it over them. . . . But you are not to be like that. Instead, the greatest among you should be like the youngest, and the one who rules like the one who serves. For who is greater, the one who is at the table or the one who serves? Is it not the one who is at the table? *But I am among you as one who serves*" (Luke 22:25-27, *New International Version*).

Jesus' words were not new to them. He had met their quarrels with the same instruction many times before. But His thoughts were just too radical for them to accept.

The disciples had tasted of power and were dreaming of a kingdom—an earthly one. They had watched Jesus bring sight to the blind, health to the diseased, and even life to the dead. They had cheered His bold response to those who challenged Him. In the midst of the multitudes who clamored for Jesus' attention, they were the chosen few, the inner circle.

The twelve were little different from most in any day who measure greatness by the standards of prestige and power. They were well-poised on "the ladder." Now it was only a matter of how high they could climb.

We have little trouble identifying with the disciples' attitude. Power tends to intoxicate us as well. The more we get, the greater grows our appetite. We long to be admired, to be served. Along with the whole human parade, we vie to be first in line.

But Jesus jolts the disciples' sense of values with a message that runs counter to the culture of both their day and ours. He offers a head-on challenge to the whole human concept of what it means to be great. Notice how Luke describes Jesus' radical life and message.

A Humble Start

Of all the Gospel writers, Luke offers the most detailed account of Jesus' entrance into the world. He lingers over the first moments with a reverent awe. He notes the amazing response of Mary to the startling announcement that she is to bear God's Son. With simple faith and quiet acceptance, she answers, "I am the Lord's servant" (1:38, *New International Version*).

Then comes Luke's stark picture of the scenes attending Christ's birth. Strips of peasant cloth wrap His tiny new body. A manger doubles for His cradle. And the first visitors to greet Him are lowly shepherds. Strange that glory should find such a starting place—but not if we understand how Christ's coming was intended to help redefine the nature of life's values.

Luke's story reminds us of how it all began for Jesus on earth, not in a throne room but in a cattle stall. It tries to communicate a truth that we still struggle to accept.

Several years ago, I visited ancient Bethlehem's Church of the Nativity. Inside the building are steps that lead down to a hallowed grotto. It was originally a simple cave, but has since been transformed into an ornate place. The once-rough walls are now lined with polished stones. Hanging from the low ceiling are preciously crafted lamps whose flames flicker with a warm glow that bathes the whole area in a soft and beautiful light. And in the marble floor is fixed a silver star. Finely crafted and richly expensive, it marks the place where tradition says the Christ child was born.

Why all the glitter? The keepers of this special site found it hard to let it remain a simple cave. Their sense of values dictated that it be grandly decorated, made into something far different from what it originally was.

Out in a field, though, not far from the grand church and transformed cave, are some rocky outcroppings that could offer simple shelter for a shepherd and his sheep. As our group stood in one of these lowly grottoes and sang the carol, "Silent Night," I somehow found something grander in the simple site than in that of the polished stones and silver star.

Perhaps that is what Luke would have us see as well; perhaps that is why he takes such pains to make sure we know how Jesus made His entrance *humbly* into this world.

A Continuing Lesson

In the midst of Jesus' ministry, Luke describes a teaching moment when the disciples struggled once more to learn about rank and service (9:18-48). Peter makes a magnificent confession of Jesus as "the Christ." The inner trio—Peter, James, and John—accompany Jesus up the mount of transfiguration. There is a dramatic healing of a boy possessed by an evil spirit. But then that old argument resurfaces once again: Who will be the greatest among them?

Perhaps the eleven envied Peter's commendation by Christ (Matthew 16:17-19), or the three grew overconfident after their trip to the mountain, or the whole group was just frustrated because they had failed to heal the demon-possessed boy. Whatever the case, the disciples were at it again. Sensing their struggle, Jesus drew a simple object lesson from the crowd.

Gently picking up a nearby child, Jesus stood the little one in the disciples' midst. Perhaps some of the twelve kneeled to face him on his own level. Maybe Jesus crouched alongside this "kingdom kid" to say, "Whoever welcomes this little child in my name welcomes me; and whoever welcomes me welcomes the one who sent me. For he who is least among you all—he is the greatest" (9:48, *New International Version*).

The small are the great. The humbled are the mighty. The last are the first. An old preacher from the past, Alexander Maclaren, once put it this way: "To sink is the way to rise."

Matthew includes some additional words of Jesus spoken during His response to the disciples' struggle: "I tell you the truth, unless you change and become like little children, you will never enter the kingdom of heaven (Matthew 18:3, *New International Version*). The hard lesson to learn is that life in the kingdom calls for a new way of thinking, a dramatic conversion that allows one to see that the way to up is down.

A Grand Example

Still the disciples went on struggling. They jockeyed for favor, dreamed of power, and wrestled over status down to the end. There may be no greater mark of Christ's humility than His willingness to die for such selfish souls. It is good that Luke lets us know that the disciples' argument over status was a prelude to the cross. It places our sin in stark contrast to the amazing selflessness of Jesus' sacrifice.

I wonder if it wasn't the memory of the cross, etched vividly in the disciples, minds, that finally led them to learn the real truth about greatness. Was it through tears that they finally were able to see and begin to change?

On an afternoon in 1953, reporters and government officials gathered at a Chicago railroad station to await the arrival of the 1952 Nobel Peace Prize winner. As he stepped off the train—a giant of a man, six-feet-four, with bushy hair and a large moustache—cameras flashed and the officials approached him with hands outstretched, telling him how honored they were to meet him. He thanked them, and then asked to be excused for a moment.

Walking through the crowd with quick steps, he reached the side of an elderly woman who was having trouble trying to carry two large suitcases. Picking up the bags in his big hands, he escorted the woman to a bus with a smile. As he helped her aboard, he wished her a safe journey.

The man was Dr. Albert Schweitzer, the famous missionary-doctor who had spent his life helping the poorest of the poor in Africa. Having watched all that had taken place, one of the reporters turned and said to another, "That's the first time I ever saw a sermon walking."

Schweitzer surely learned about the real values in life from the Master. As we study Luke's story of Christ may we do the same.

Answers to Quarterly Quiz

on page 114

Lesson 1—1. Isaiah. 2. The Lord's. 3. Give one away. **Lesson 2**—1. The angel Gabriel. 2. She was going to have a baby. 3. By the power of the Highest. **Lesson 3**—1. There was no room in the inn. 2. "A Saviour, which is Christ the Lord." 3. Pondered it in her heart. **Lesson 4**—1. The devil. 2. The Scriptures. 3. For a season. **Lesson 5**—1. Isaiah. 2. "This day is this Scripture fulfilled." 3. Angry. **Lesson 6**—1. Power. 2. Healed the sick. 3. To preach elsewhere. **Lesson 7**—1. Rejoice. 2. Do good, bless, pray. 3. Our Father's. **Lesson 8**—1. Two. 2. Places where Jesus soon would come. 3. "The kingdom of God is come nigh." 4. Heal the sick. **Lesson 9**—1. He wasted his money, and a famine came. 2. Go back home as a hired servant. 3. Joyfully. **Lesson 10**—1. Welcomed them. 2. Eternal life. 3. Only by God's power. **Lesson 11**—1. Destruction. 2. Chief priests and scribes. 3. They feared the people. **Lesson 12**—1. Remembrance of Him. 2. Which of them should be called the greatest. 3. Serve. **Lesson 13**—1. Asked forgiveness for them. 2. Darkness. 3. Jesus rose.

Preparing the Way

DEVOTIONAL READING: Matthew 1:18-25; 2:1-12.

LESSON SCRIPTURE: Luke 1:5-25; 3:1-18.

PRINTED TEXT: Luke 3:2b-4, 7-17.

Luke 3:2b-4, 7-17

2b The word of God came unto John the son of Zechariah in the wilderness.

3 And he came into all the country about Jordan, preaching the baptism of repentance for the remission of sins;

4 As it is written in the book of the words of Isaiah the prophet, saying, The voice of one crying in the wilderness, Prepare ye the way of the Lord, make his paths straight.

· · · · · · · · · · · · · · ·

7 Then said he to the multitude that came forth to be baptized of him, O generation of vipers, who hath warned you to flee from the wrath to come?

8 Bring forth therefore fruits worthy of repentance, and begin not to say within yourselves, We have Abraham to our father: for I say unto you, That God is able of these stones to raise up children unto Abraham.

9 And now also the axe is laid unto the root of the trees: every tree therefore which bringeth not forth good fruit is hewn down, and cast into the fire.

10 And the people asked him, saying, What shall we do then?

11 He answereth and saith unto them, He that hath two coats, let him impart to him that hath none; and he that hath meat, let him do likewise.

12 Then came also publicans to be baptized, and said unto him, Master, what shall we do?

13 And he said unto them, Exact no more than that which is appointed you.

14 And the soldiers likewise demanded of him, saying, And what shall we do? And he said unto them, Do violence to no man, neither accuse any falsely; and be content with your wages.

15 And as the people were in expectation, and all men mused in their hearts of John, whether he were the Christ, or not;

16 John answered, saying unto them all, I indeed baptize you with water; but one mightier than I cometh, the latchet of whose shoes I am not worthy to unloose: he shall baptize you with the Holy Ghost and with fire:

17 Whose fan is in his hand, and he will thoroughly purge his floor, and will gather the wheat into his garner; but the chaff he will burn with fire unquenchable.

GOLDEN TEXT: The voice of one crying in the wilderness, Prepare ye the way of the Lord, make his paths straight.—Luke 3:4.

The Story of Jesus
Unit 1. Luke: A Savior Is Born
(Lessons 1-4)

Lesson Aims

This lesson should prepare the student to:
1. Briefly tell about John's work.
2. Show clearly at least three ways in which Jesus was greater than John the Baptist.
3. Discover and initiate at least one change the student should make to follow God's will.

Lesson Outline

INTRODUCTION
    A. Who Are You?
    B. Time, Place, and Characters
  I. THE PROMISED PREPARER (Luke 3:2b-4)
    A. Wilderness Preacher (vv. 2b, 3)
    B. Isaiah's Prediction (v. 4)
      Electric Speaking
  II. HARD ON THE HEARERS (Luke 3:7-9)
    A. What a Greeting! (v. 7)
    B. Actions, Not Ancestry (v. 8)
      Improving Our Focus
    C. Good Fruit or Great Fire (v. 9)
  III. ASSIGNMENTS IN ACTION (Luke 3:10-14)
    A. Share With Those in Need (vv. 10, 11)
    B. Stay Within Your Allotment (vv. 12-14)
  IV. MORE TO COME (Luke 3:15-17)
    A. Could This Be the Christ? (v. 15)
    B. The Greater Baptizer to Come (v. 16)
    C. The Judge and His Judgment (v. 17)
      The Threshing Floor
CONCLUSION
    A. Good News!
    B. Let Us Pray
    C. Thought to Remember

Display visual 1 of the visuals packet and let it remain before the class. The visual is shown on page 125.

Introduction

A. Who Are You?

A local politician, eager for advancement, took advantage of his assignment to introduce the governor as the dedication speaker for the new hospital building. The man's "introductory remarks" were long and eloquent. At last one old citizen, weary of waiting for the main event, called out, "We already know the governor and we want to hear him, but who are you, anyway?"

No such self-serving windiness marred the ministry of John the Baptist as he introduced the main event of God's new covenant with men. John's hearers did not know Jesus at all. They expected a heroic ruler in David's line to rescue them from their oppressors, but they did not know when or how he might come. John's spirit and power led some hearers to think he might be that Messiah. Not so! His ministry was not the main event; he was just the introductory speaker, getting them ready for the one to come.

This week's study of John's ministry must be understood in that light. We must see him in his relationship to Jesus, or we shall not see him accurately at all.

B. Time, Place, and Characters

Luke was a careful and thorough historian. He wanted his readers to know when, where, and by whom the most important events were accomplished. To tell how Jesus' ministry was introduced by John's preaching and baptism, he mentioned political and religious rulers on three levels (Luke 3:1, 2). The Roman emperor was Tiberius. Under his authority were four areas associated with Jesus' ministry: (1) Judea was ruled by Pontius Pilate, who would later preside at Jesus' crucifixion. (2) Galilee was under Herod Antipas, who later would order the execution of John the Baptist. This Herod was a son of the Herod who had sought to destroy Jesus as an infant. (3) Iturea, northeast of Palestine, was ruled by Herod Philip, another son of the earlier Herod. (4) Abilene, north of Galilee, was governed by Lysanias. High priesthood was shared by Annas, whom the Romans had deposed, and his son-in-law, Caiaphas, whom the Romans had appointed to replace him. The Jews still recognized Annas, who would later join with Caiaphas in condemning Jesus.

I. The Promised Preparer (Luke 3:2b-4)

A. Wilderness Preacher (vv. 2b, 3)

2b. The word of God came unto John the son of Zechariah in the wilderness.

This is sufficient to identify John as a prophet—one to whom God's word came (compare Isaiah 38:4), with responsibility to deliver the message faithfully. Luke 1:5-25 tells that the angel Gabriel appeared to the aged priest Zechariah as he was busy with priestly duties in the temple at Jerusalem. The angel told Zechariah that his aged wife Elisabeth would bear him a son, to be named John, and this son would be God's messenger "to make ready a people prepared for the Lord" (v. 17). Luke 1:57-80 recounts the birth of John and concludes, "And the child grew, and waxed strong in spirit, and was in the deserts [uninhabited places] till the day of his showing unto Israel."

Concerning John's solitary life in that harsh and forbidding land along the lower Jordan Valley, Matthew 3:4 says his clothing was the rough shepherd's robe of camel's hair, and his food was locusts (a variety of large grasshopper named in Leviticus 11:22 as being edible), along with honey that wild bees had stored in hollows of the rocks. Here John received his orders from God.

3. And he came into all the country about Jordan, preaching the baptism of repentance for the remission of sins.

The fords of the lower Jordan River, where merchant caravans entered Judea from the east, would provide a varied audience of travelers resting in shade near the river. *Repentance*, the rejection of sin in turning to God, was a dominant theme of God's message through the prophets: "If the wicked will turn from all his sins that he hath committed, and keep all my statutes, and do that which is lawful and right, he shall surely live, he shall not die" (Ezekiel 18:21). In His own early appearances "Jesus began to preach, and to say, Repent: for the kingdom of heaven is at hand" (Matthew 4:17).

John's special ministry, however, employed baptism—the immersing of responsive hearers in the waters of Jordan (Mark 1:5)—as the seal of change in the minds and lives of those who came confessing their sins.

Some comparisons and contrasts between John and Jesus become immediately evident. John was the belatedly-born son of Zechariah; Jesus was the virgin-born son of God. God's word came to John; Jesus was the Word who came into the world (John 1:1, 14). People came out of the towns in Judea to hear John; Jesus went into the towns of Galilee to preach, teach, and heal. John's baptism signaled repentance for the forgiveness of sins; Jesus instituted baptism (Matthew 28:19) into himself—His name—for the forgiveness of sins (Galatians 3:27; Acts 2:38).

B. Isaiah's Prediction (v. 4)

4. As it is written in the book of the words of Isaiah the prophet, saying, The voice of one crying in the wilderness, Prepare ye the way of the Lord, make his paths straight.

Luke 3:4-6 quotes Isaiah 40:3-5. That passage speaks God's comfort to Judah when "her warfare is accomplished . . . her iniquity is pardoned" and her people would be returned from their captivity in Babylon. God would then approach His people like a victorious monarch whose way had been prepared by making, grad-

---

> ### How to Say It
>
> ABILENE.   Ab-i-*lee*-neh.
> ANNAS.   *An*-nus.
> ANTIPAS.   *An*-tuh-pas.
> CAESAREA.   Sess-uh-*ree*-uh.
> CAIAPHAS.   *Kay*-uh-fus or *Kye*-uh-fus.
> ITUREA.   *Ih*-tyou-*ree*-uh (strong accent on *ree*).
> LYSANIAS.   Lie-*say*-ne-us.
> PONTIUS PILATE.   *Pon*-shus or *Pon*-ti-us *Pie*-lut.
> TIBERIAS.   Tie-*beer*-ee-us.
> ZECHARIAH.   Zek-uh-*rye*-uh.

---

ing, and straightening roadways over which he would travel. The *voice* is that of the king's messenger summoning the road builders to their task.

This foreshadows the ministry of John the Baptist, who is also prefigured in the words of Malachi 3:1: "I will send my messenger, and he shall prepare the way before me." As a spiritual road builder preparing for the Messiah, John brought down the haughty from their heights, he built up and gave hope to the downcast humble, and he slashed a straight path of truth through the tortuous reasonings of the professionally religious. His thoughtful hearers found him demanding a righteousness beyond their abilities, and so they were prepared to accept the "grace and truth" that came by Jesus Christ (John 1:17).

ELECTRIC SPEAKING

The Japanese combine two characters, one for a cloud and one for lightning, to get their word for electricity. They combine three characters, one for mouth, one for words, and one for tongue, to get their word for speaking. They combine the word for electricity and the word for speaking to make the word for telephone.

There were no telephones in the wilderness, but there was electric speaking. When John spoke, people were electrified by his message: "Prepare ye the way of the Lord."   —W. P.

II. Hard on the Hearers
(Luke 3:7-9)

A. What a Greeting! (v. 7)

7. Then said he to the multitude that came forth to be baptized of him, O generation of vipers, who hath warned you to flee from the wrath to come?

Matthew 3:5-7 describes the *multitude* of hearers as coming from "Jerusalem, and all Judea, and all the region round about Jordan," being "baptized of him in Jordan, confessing their sins." It adds that John's startling reference to the offspring of snakes was addressed to "many of the Pharisees and Sadducees" who had come to his baptism. These were the same kind of legalists and ecclesiastical politicians whom Jesus later addressed in the same terms (Matthew 12:34; 23:33). They are seen here as snakes in grassland fleeing before the flames when the stubble is set on fire. But Luke 7:30 and Matthew 21:25, 32 indicate that most of the professional religionists refused repentance, and departed without John's baptism. Their pride in present position was greater than their fear of God's approaching judgment.

B. Actions, Not Ancestry (v. 8)

8. Bring forth therefore fruits worthy of repentance, and begin not to say within yourselves, We have Abraham to our father: for I say unto you, That God is able of these stones to raise up children unto Abraham.

No mere sorrow for past sins would suffice for the repentance John demanded. He, like Jesus after him, would require a living reality supporting the claim. Paul later sounded the same note, in teaching that men must "repent and turn to God, and do works meet [appropriate] for repentance" (Acts 26:20).

The Jews' appeal to identification with *Abraham* was so natural that John could see it coming. He had spoken of judgment. They saw judgment as being brought by their Messiah, not against the children of Abraham but against the Gentiles. Jesus was to encounter the same argument more clearly spoken, and He answered it much as John did (John 8:33, 39). God, who created mankind from dust of the ground, would find no difficulty in fashioning Jews from rocks in the riverbed.

IMPROVING OUR FOCUS

The Hubble telescope, launched into space in 1990, was expected to send back much new information about the universe. But its huge mirror failed to focus properly, perhaps because a defective measuring device was used years ago in making the telescope. Now scientists hope to correct the fault by installing ten small lenses between the big mirror and the recording instruments.

Many people are living with defective instruments to measure their thinking and conduct. Their lives are out of focus and unsatisfactory. In repentance we acknowledge our faults and install God's Word to correct our focus and bring our living in line with God's will. Such living is "fruits worthy of repentance."   —W. P.

C. Good Fruit or Great Fire (v. 9)

9. And now also the axe is laid unto the root of the trees: every tree therefore which bringeth not forth good fruit is hewn down, and cast into the fire.

This judgment is not limited to *trees* that produce prickers and poisons. It is spoken also of orchard trees that produce nothing at all: "These three years I come seeking fruit on this fig tree, and find none: cut it down; why cumbereth it the ground?" (Luke 13:7).

The order might be conveyed without words by laying a sharp axe at the base of an unfruitful tree. Space is valuable, and firewood is needed. The figure of fire for the fruitless is repeated in the teaching of Jesus (Matthew 7:19).

III. Assignments in Action (Luke 3:10-14)

The idea of repentance found in the bearing of good fruit was still figurative. John's hearers wanted something more concrete and personal.

A. Share With Those in Need (vv. 10, 11)

10, 11. And the people asked him, saying, What shall we do then? He answereth and saith unto them, He that hath two coats, let him impart to him that hath none; and he that hath meat, let him do likewise.

John's answer was as practical and personal as the shirts on their backs. The *coat*, or tunic, was a basic garment, not unlike a long shirt. One tunic at a time was enough; but some people did not have even one. Well, give one of yours to a needy person and stay at home while the one you wear is being laundered! This seems far-fetched to the modern mind, but it says clearly what John meant. We don't need bigger clothes closets; we need bigger hearts. How many of those shirts, skirts, and slacks do we really need, anyway? And how best can we divide with folk who do need them?

The same kind of direct, neighborly sharing of food from the garden, the granary, or the kitchen cupboard will help the hungry and will provide the answer to the troublesome question of 1 John 3:17: If anyone possesses useful material, and sees his brother in need, and turns his back on that need, how can he claim to possess the love of God?

John's prescription is as old as Moses and the prophets, and it is as futuristic as Christ's coming in judgment (Matthew 25:31-46). It is too practical to be popular in the pagan world. But to the extent that it is generally applied, the needs of the poor will be met without the costly complications of public welfare. It will reflect proper glory on the Lord in whose name it is done, and it will build His image in the one who does it.

To the rich young man who asked the way to life eternal, Jesus' instruction was that he sell *all* he had and give to the poor, and then "come, follow me" (Luke 18:18-22). That last is the key to *Christian* charity. Donations made without love don't benefit the donor (1 Corinthians 13:3).

B. Stay Within Your Allotment
(vv. 12-14)

12, 13. Then came also publicans to be baptized, and said unto him, Master, what shall we do? And he said unto them, Exact no more than that which is appointed you.

Different occupations offer different temptations and needs for repentance. John's audience included two groups, apparently of Jews, working for the Roman government and therefore somewhat estranged from their neighbors. They were understandably sensitive to the spiritual need revealed by John's preaching. First were the tax collectors (see Luke 7:29), commonly despised as betrayers of their own people, and constantly tempted to fill their own purses with excessive fees levied on the taxpaying public. These men addressed John respectfully as "Teacher." He perceived their problem and met it squarely. They were steadfastly to resist the occupational enticement; they were to collect what their assignment prescribed, and no more. No one was asked to change jobs; all were to honor God by their performance in the jobs they were doing.

14. And the soldiers likewise demanded of him, saying, And what shall we do? And he said unto them, Do violence to no man, neither accuse any falsely; and be content with your wages.

Soldiers, perhaps assigned to keep order in the crowds that had come to hear and observe John, saw their own need for the baptism of repentance. But how were they to change their behavior? John recognized the soldiers' (and police officers'?) special temptation to "throw their weight around," to bully people and frighten them into offering gifts for protection. False ac-

visual 1

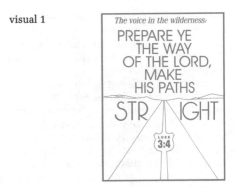

cusations of illegal activity could be used in the same way. John told them to cut it out! They must be satisfied with what they earned, and not to take money on the side. But John didn't advise the soldiers to change their jobs; just to change their behavior.

The repentance demanded of all the inquirers—common people, tax collectors, and soldiers—dealt with money and property in relation to people. God would always have His children use their money and property for the benefit of people, and never the other way around. Christians must always resist the temptation to "double dip"—to seek or demand what they do not earn—or to prize their possessions more than their neighbors. So said Jesus also!

IV. More to Come
(Luke 3:15-17)

A. Could This Be the Christ? (v. 15)

15. And as the people were in expectation, and all men mused in their hearts of John, whether he were the Christ or not.

John's power and persuasiveness convinced people that he was a prophet of God (Matthew 21:25, 26). Was he more than that? Underlying this question was the long expectation of Israel's Messiah (*Christ* is the Greek form of the Hebrew *Messiah*, or anointed one). That one was expected to deliver the nation from submission to Rome and restore the Davidic monarchy in Jerusalem. Could this man from the priestly tribe of Levi do what was expected from the royal line of Judah?

B. The Greater Baptizer to Come (v. 16)

16. John answered, saying unto them all, I indeed baptize you with water; but one mightier than I cometh, the latchet of whose shoes I am not worthy to unloose: he shall baptize you with the Holy Ghost and with fire.

John was not the Messiah, and he said so plainly (John 1:20; 3:28). Even in the most distinctive feature of his ministry—the *water* baptism that sealed his hearers' repentance—he was to be overshadowed by the coming one. In power and in worthiness that one would be infinitely greater than he.

After the church came into being at the great Pentecost (Acts 2), John's baptism of repentance would be superseded by Christian baptism, administered to believers in the name of Christ and by His authority (Matthew 28:19, 20; Acts 2:38-41; 18:25; 19:4, 5). Confession of Jesus as Lord would overshadow confession of sins.

This, however, is not the baptism *with* (or in) *the Holy Ghost*, to be administered by Christ himself. That came to the apostles on the Day of Pentecost (Acts 2:1-4), and in a similar way to the household of Cornelius at Caesarea (Acts 10:44-47).

The baptism *with* (or in) *fire*, also to be administered by Christ himself, is identified most naturally with the "fire unquenchable" cited in the next verse as being visited on the ones found to be worthless in the final judgment.

C. The Judge and His Judgment (v. 17)

17. Whose fan is in his hand, and he will thoroughly purge his floor, and will gather the wheat into his garner; but the chaff he will burn with fire unquenchable.

Messiah's final superiority is seen in His right to judge all the earth (John 5:22; Acts 17:31; Matthew 25:31-46). Here the Judge is compared to a farmer separating his precious harvest from the worthless chaff consigned to the flames. Could there be a more fitting conclusion to a sermon that began, "Repent ye: for the kingdom of heaven is at hand"?

THE THRESHING FLOOR

It is quite a sight, that great golden cloud rising in the air. You can see it from great distances in the Holy Land on a sunny day. The golden cloud shimmers above a threshing floor at the time of harvest. Threshing is still done in the way of the ancients. The cut grain is laid out on a threshing floor, a smooth, flat place. An ox is harnessed to a sled-like instrument. Blindfolded and tethered by a rope to a stake in the center of the threshing floor, the ox walks round and round, pulling the sled behind. Often children happily ride on it. Once the wheat has been pulverized, it is thrown up into the air by means of a wooden pitchfork. The wind catches the light chaff and blows it away. The grain comes down at the thresher's feet. To see this scene is to be reminded of John's words about the Christ. He will come in judgment, separating the righteous from the unrighteous.   —W. P.

Conclusion
A. Good News!

Luke 3:18, following immediately after our printed text, brings a bright surprise to folk accustomed to thinking of repentance as a burdensome duty in response to a harsh demand. The Greek text says John continued to *evangelize*—preach the good news of the gospel—to the people! It is indeed good news that there is a door of repentance from sin's prison, and that people rejoicing in righteousness can rejoice even more in godliness. On the Day of Pentecost, when hearers of the gospel were stabbed with their guilt, they cried for relief. Peter told them to repent and be baptized in the name of Jesus Christ for relief from that guilt (Acts 2:41, 46, 47). Later, when Jewish Christians became convinced that God was offering His grace to Gentiles also, they "glorified God, saying, Then hath God also to the Gentiles granted repentance unto life" (Acts 11:18). Repentance unto life! Good news, preached in prospect and promise by John the preparer, and provided in full by the Prince of Life for whom he prepared the way!

B. Let Us Pray

Thank You, gracious God our Father, for the ministry of John the preparer. May we heed his teaching and make the life changes that will bring us closer to You. May we follow his example in glorifying Jesus our Lord. And may our voices, too, be used to prepare the way of the Lord. In Jesus' name we pray, amen.

C. Thought to Remember

"If anyone is in Christ, he is a new creation; the old has gone, the new has come!" (2 Corinthians 5:17, *New International Version*).

Home Daily Bible Readings

Learning by Doing

This page contains an alternate lesson plan emphasizing learning activities. Classes desiring such student involvement will find these suggestions helpful.

Learning Goals

Following today's study, each learner will be able to:

1. Explain how John filled his role as forerunner of the Messiah.

2. Summarize John's basic message in one word (repent), and give three examples of John's prescribed "fruits worthy of repentance."

3. Give John's probable response to a variety of twentieth-century groups.

Into the Lesson

If members of your class come to the meeting room from the same direction, you can cut large footprints from brightly colored paper and Plasti-Tak them to the floor along the way. When the students have assembled, tell them you are glad they were able to follow the footprints and find the way. Add that God had other methods of preparing the way for Jesus to come to the world and the way for us to come to Jesus.

Write the following references on separate slips of paper and give them to different students to be read to the class. As they are read in order, hold before the class a large Bible with markers in place so you can turn quickly to each passage as it is read, showing the class that we are going through the Old Testament from Genesis to Malachi. Keep emphasizing that God is pointing to His Son all the way.

Genesis 3:15 - God to the serpent
Genesis 22:18 - God to Abraham
Deuteronomy 18:15 - Moses to Israel
2 Samuel 7:16 - God to David
Psalm 45:6, 7 - God to His Son
Isaiah 9:6, 7 - Isaiah to Israel
Micah 5:2 - God to Bethlehem
Malachi 3:1 - God to Israel

Into the Word

Write the following references (without the boldfaced numbers) on slips of paper. Give them to early students so they can become familiar with the passages. To begin the study of the lesson text, read it slowly, asking students to interrupt and read their assigned passages when they hear you read something similar from the lesson text. Boldface numbers below indicate verses of the text at which interruptions should be made. If students do not interrupt, you can prompt them.

3 Mark 1:4	**8** Acts 26:20
4-6 Isaiah 40:3-5	**9** Matthew 7:19
7 Matthew 3:5-7	**11** 1 John 3:17
	17 Matthew 25:31-46

To help the learners remember John's message, prepare the following "sermon notes," each on a separate piece of paper. Present them in scrambled order and let students arrange them in the order in which they appear in the text. (They are printed here in that order.)

generation of vipers	two coats
wrath to come	be content
fruits worthy	one mightier than I
stones . . . children	fan is in his hand
the ax	fire unquenchable

There are various ways of using these:

1. Print the "notes" in big letters on big pieces of paper and post them in random order on the wall. Tell the class, "Here are John's notes for his sermon, but they are all mixed up. Let's put them in order."

2. A small class may stand around a table and work together to put the "notes" in order.

3. If you have access to a copier, you can make enough sets of the "notes" to go around and let students work individually or in pairs.

Into Life

As the lesson writer notes, "The repentance demanded of all the inquirers . . . dealt with money and property in relation to people." Form groups of three or four to discuss and decide what John probably would say to each of these contemporary groups:

Police	Rich entertainers
Merchants	Government workers
Middle-class people	Teachers
Repairmen	Taxi drivers
Office workers	Preachers

Depending on the time available, you may divide these among the discussion groups or give all of them to each group. Remind the discussers to note how John personalized his responses in verses 10-14.

The lesson writer's comments under "Conclusion" are superb. Let a class member read that whole section aloud—about two minutes' worth—before the session is ended with prayer.

Let's Talk It Over

The questions on this page are designed to encourage review of the lesson Scriptures and to promote discussion of the lesson by the class. The answers provided are only discussion starters. Let your class talk it over from there.

1. John prepared the way for Jesus. How may we prepare the way so He will reach others?

John prepared the way for Jesus by preaching and by the witness of his personal austerity and righteousness. We too can speak of Jesus, and our personal integrity is a powerful means of preparing people to listen to the message of the gospel. People who see the beauty of a devout Christian life are more prepared to let Jesus come into their lives.

2. John warned some of his listeners to produce fruit in keeping with repentance. What is this fruit and how do we produce it?

The fruit of repentance is a changed life. We no longer do the evil things we used to do. Changing is not easy, and many who profess repentance and even feel guilty about their sins still do not bear this fruit. Changing may be beyond our power, but the Holy Spirit is promised to those who repent and are baptized in Jesus' name (Acts 2:38). A major task of the Holy Spirit in our lives is to help us bear the fruit of repentance.

3. Some of the Jews trusted in their blood relation to Abraham to save them. John said that would not work. Do we trust in any vain things to save us today? If so, what? How do we become true children of Abraham?

We may trust in the faith of our parents to save us, and never develop a true personal faith of our own. We may trust in our goodness as the Pharisees did, in coming to church, helping in church work, doing right in other ways, and giving some of our money. But we still need the Lord's forgiveness. Jesus is not looking for the blood of Abraham; He is looking for the heart of Abraham. Those who have both the faith and obedience of Abraham are his true children.

4. The trees in John's illustration were fruit trees, but they were fruitless. What is the warning to us today?

Fruit trees are special. We cherish them because they provide nourishment for us. If they do not, we get rid of them. Fruitless trees are fit for nothing but firewood. The Jews should have borne the fruit of faith in the Messiah, and faithful obedience to Him. We who believe in Him are to bear the fruit of righteousness and faithfulness and service. We cannot earn our salvation by the fruit we bear; but if we do not bear any fruit, then it is clear that our tree of faith is dying or dead. Let us bear fruit before the ax is applied.

5. John told the people to share with those who had nothing. How much is enough for us to indulge ourselves? When should we stop buying for ourselves and start giving?

John said two shirts are one too many, because others have none. Perhaps we should not apply this strictly and legalistically today, but the point is clear. We must not pamper and indulge ourselves when we could be helping others. Most of us could be more generous in our giving if we really loved our neighbors as ourselves. If we do not have poor neighbors, then we can give to Christian benevolent organizations.

6. John told the people to resist the temptations that came with their jobs. Suggest some ways in which our jobs tempt us now.

Each job carries its own set of temptations. Police deal with the hardness of life constantly; they may be tempted to become hard and heartless themselves. If we belong to strong unions that make it very difficult for a member to be fired, we may be tempted to do half-hearted work. Those who work with money may be tempted to steal. Employers may be tempted to take advantage of their employees. Each of us must examine his own situation and identify the temptations that confront him. Christians must glorify God through their conduct in their work.

7. How is the Lord separating wheat from chaff now? How do we make sure we are wheat and not chaff?

In John's day farmers separated the chaff from the wheat by tossing both into the air and letting the wind blow the chaff aside. In life God exposes us to the winds of temptation and trial to blow the chaff away. Those who will not stand up to temptations and trials and be faithful to the Lord are not counted worthy of Him. They are blown aside to be burned. We are true wheat if we have sincere faith to withstand these winds. We must strengthen our faith every day so it will not fail us in times of need.

Yielding to God's Will

DEVOTIONAL READING: Luke 1:57-80; Isaiah 11:1-15.

LESSON SCRIPTURE: Luke 1:26-56.

PRINTED TEXT: Luke 1:26-38.

Luke 1:26-38

26 And in the sixth month the angel Gabriel was sent from God unto a city of Galilee, named Nazareth,

27 To a virgin espoused to a man whose name was Joseph, of the house of David; and the virgin's name was Mary.

28 And the angel came in unto her, and said, Hail, thou that art highly favored, the Lord is with thee: blessed art thou among women.

29 And when she saw him, she was troubled at his saying, and cast in her mind what manner of salutation this should be.

30 And the angel said unto her, Fear not, Mary: for thou hast found favor with God.

31 And, behold, thou shalt conceive in thy womb, and bring forth a son, and shalt call his name JESUS.

32 He shall be great, and shall be called the Son of the Highest; and the Lord God shall give unto him the throne of his father David:

33 And he shall reign over the house of Jacob for ever; and of his kingdom there shall be no end.

34 Then said Mary unto the angel, How shall this be, seeing I know not a man?

35 And the angel answered and said unto her, The Holy Ghost shall come upon thee, and the power of the Highest shall overshadow thee: therefore also that holy thing which shall be born of thee shall be called the Son of God.

36 And, behold, thy cousin Elisabeth, she hath also conceived a son in her old age; and this is the sixth month with her, who was called barren.

37 For with God nothing shall be impossible.

38 And Mary said, Behold the handmaid of the Lord; be it unto me according to thy word. And the angel departed from her.

GOLDEN TEXT: Mary said, Behold the handmaid of the Lord; be it unto me according to thy word.—Luke 1:38.

The Story of Jesus

Unit 1. Luke: A Savior Is Born

(Lessons 1-4)

Lesson Aims

This lesson should equip the student to:

1. Tell briefly the story of the angel Gabriel's conversation with Mary.

2. Give Biblical reasons for his or her own feeling and attitude toward Mary.

3. Name ways in which we can follow Mary's example and ways in which we cannot.

Lesson Outline

INTRODUCTION

    A. A Quiet Heir

        Some of the Best

    B. Flashback

  I. MARY RECEIVES GOD'S MESSENGER (Luke 1:26-29)

    A. A Prospective Bride (vv. 26, 27)

    B. A Perplexed Listener (vv. 28, 29)

 II. MARY HEARS GOD'S MESSAGE (Luke 1:30-33)

    A. The Great Favor (v. 30)

        "Fear Not"

    B. The Glorious Promise (vv. 31-33)

III. MARY ACCEPTS GOD'S ASSURANCE (Luke 1:34-38)

    A. Mary's Question (v. 34)

    B. God's Answer (v. 35)

    C. Elisabeth's Example (vv. 36, 37)

    D. Mary's Commitment (v. 38)

        "Behold the Handmaid of the Lord"

CONCLUSION

    A. The Rest of the Story

    B. What's in It for Us?

    C. Let Us Pray

    D. Thought to Remember

Display visual 2 of the visuals packet and let it remain before the class throughout this session. The visual is shown on page 133.

Introduction

A. A Quiet Heir

"Blessed are the meek: for they shall inherit the earth," said Jesus (Matthew 5:5). The truth of His words was demonstrated in His self-giving ministry that won the Father's recognition of Him as the reigning heir, not only of the earth, but of Heaven also (Philippians 2:5-11).

This fact flies in the face of popular opinion and public proclamation in which self-interest and self-assertion, often accompanied by rampant self-indulgence, make the headlines.

The opening chapters of Luke introduce us to just that kind of world. In this setting Luke introduces an aged priest and his wife, both living in humble submission to God, and then their son, John, who grew up in the barren wilderness to become God's prophet and preparer for Christ. Along with these, Luke introduces the devout young woman through whom God chose to send His Son into the world.

Mary seems to have been a descendant of David in the tribe of Judah (Romans 1:3; Luke 1:27), though this is less sure than Jesus' claim to the royal line through Joseph as His legal father. Mary was obviously well taught in the Scriptures and strong in her own faith. Her song of exultation (Luke 1:46-55) demonstrates this. Her identification with "them of low degree" and "the hungry" (vv. 52, 53) would suggest that she had grown up in modest circumstances. So would the fact that she and Joseph made the dove offering of the poor rather than the lamb offering of the affluent when they took the baby Jesus to the temple at the time of her purification (Luke 2:22-24; compare Leviticus 12:6-8).

Mary provides a demonstration that "God chose the weak things of the world to shame the strong. . . . so that no one may boast before him" (1 Corinthians 1:27, 29, *New International Version*).

SOME OF THE BEST

In 1988 a book was published with the title, *One Thousand Nine Hundred and Eleven Best Things Anybody Ever Said.* It contains things like this quote from George Burns: "If you live to the age of a hundred you have it made, because very few people die past the age of a hundred." And there is this line of graffiti: "Bad spellers of the world, untie!" Napoleon Bonaparte observed that "Glory is fleeting, but obscurity is forever."

Some of these sayings are clever, but we might question the assertion that they are the "best things anybody ever said." Our Scripture study today, however, does contain some of the best things ever said. Look at the angel's words to Mary: "The Lord is with you." "Do not be afraid." "You have found favor with God." "You will give birth to a son. . . . He will be great." "Nothing is impossible with God" (*New International Version*).

And there is greatness in Mary's reply to all this: "I am the Lord's servant." Mary's statement contains no play on words, but it expresses an attitude that is great because it acknowledges and pleases God.   —W. P.

B. Flashback

The event we have recorded in today's lesson took place about thirty years before the ministry of John the Baptist (see last week's lesson on "Preparing the Way"). We go back to a time three months before John was born. According to the angel Gabriel's promise to Zechariah at Jerusalem, his wife Elisabeth had conceived and was several months along in her pregnancy. Now we are taken northward from Judea to a town in Galilee.

I. Mary Receives God's Messenger (Luke 1:26-29)

A. A Prospective Bride (vv. 26, 27)

26, 27. And in the sixth month the angel Gabriel was sent from God unto a city of Galilee, named Nazareth, to a virgin espoused to a man whose name was Joseph, of the house of David; and the virgin's name was Mary.

We find that verse 24, concluding the introductory account concerning Zechariah, says, "And after those days his wife Elisabeth conceived, and hid herself five months." At that point God assigned another immense errand to *Gabriel*, who stands "in the presence of God" (Luke 1:19; compare Daniel 8:16; 9:21). Let no one think himself too important to become an "errand boy" for the Almighty!

Galilee was lightly regarded by the Jews in Judea, who thought no prophet could come from there (John 7:41, 52). And *Nazareth*, which is not named either in the Old Testament or in the writings of Josephus, was lightly regarded elsewhere in Galilee (John 1:46).

Gabriel's errand focused, though, not on a place but on a person—*a virgin* named *Mary*. Luke, the physician/historian, emphasizes her virginity, as though knowing it would be questioned at a later time. Jewish girls, customarily betrothed early and married rather young, were expected to be virginal at marriage. But what was commonly taken for granted would come under question at the birth of Jesus. The question must be answered before it was asked. Mary was already Joseph's spouse—*espoused*, betrothed, engaged, under a contract that could be nullified only by divorce, even though the couple had not yet come together.

Joseph was "of the house and lineage of David" (Luke 2:4), and carried a legitimate claim to the royal line for his family. Luke's account of Jesus' genealogy (Luke 3:23-38) suggests that Mary also was descended from Israel's great king.

The Gospel records mention Joseph by name only twice outside the accounts of Jesus' birth and boyhood. Neighbors referred to him as Jesus' father (John 1:45; 6:42). It was a relationship that he accepted with the assurance that God was, in fact, the Father of Jesus (Matthew 1:18-25).

B. A Perplexed Listener (vv. 28, 29)

28. And the angel came in unto her, and said, Hail, thou that art highly favored, the Lord is with thee: blessed art thou among women.

Mary seems to have been in a house when the angel made his sudden appearance. *Hail,* or "hello," is a greeting customary among Luke's Gentile readers. Gentile influence was strong in Galilee. Mary would probably agree that she was *highly favored* in her security as one of God's chosen people, and now as the betrothed of Joseph. Neither would she argue with the assurance that *the Lord is with thee.* Little did she know, however, the reason for the statements and the depth of their meaning.

Blessed art thou among women does not appear at this point in some ancient manuscripts and recent translations. It does appear in Elisabeth's later greeting to Mary (Luke 1:42); and Mary herself was soon to exult, "From henceforth all generations shall call me blessed" (Luke 1:48). The matchless blessing, later to be widely recognized, lay in God's favor, already noted.

29. And when she saw him, she was troubled at his saying, and cast in her mind what manner of salutation this should be.

Gabriel's words set Mary's mind to spinning with questions. She was thoroughly perplexed. What lay behind this strange introduction, with its strong compliments and assurances? Puzzlement set her to debating with herself as to what it all meant. Here was a maiden too thoughtful to ignore the implications of what she heard, and too calm to cry out in fear.

II. Mary Hears God's Message (Luke 1:30-33)

A. The Great Favor (v. 30)

30. And the angel said unto her, Fear not, Mary: for thou hast found favor with God.

Gabriel added another assurance to what he had spoken before. "Don't be afraid!" That was the word of relief often spoken by God's messengers when divine glory broke suddenly into the human consciousness (Luke 1:13; 2:10, etc.). Now Gabriel added comfort in calling *Mary* by name.

His forthcoming announcement would be fraught with all manner of complications, but nothing in it would be impossible with God's help. Phillips' translation paraphrases Gabriel's promise with tender eloquence: "Do not be afraid, Mary; God loves you dearly."

"FEAR NOT"

Eddie Rickenbacker was a war hero during World War II. He led an air attack on Tokyo and survived an ordeal at sea. He said, "Courage is doing what you're afraid to do. There can be no courage unless you are scared."

The sight of the angel, along with his words, must certainly have frightened Mary. His words, however, reassured her. "Do not be afraid, Mary, you have found favor with God." "For nothing is impossible with God," the angel said further.

We will never face the kind of test of faithfulness, obedience, and trust that Mary and Joseph faced, but there will be moments in our lives that will require the courage of faithfulness. With blessing come also responsibility, challenge, and the necessity of conquering fear.
—W. P.

B. The Glorious Promise (vv. 31-33)

31. And, behold, thou shalt conceive in thy womb, and bring forth a son, and shalt call his name Jesus.

How soon, we wonder, did Mary come to realize that Gabriel was not talking about a child who would be born in the normal course of events some time after her marriage to Joseph? Surely, as a responsible Jewish woman, she would expect the blessing of childbirth and family. But how did Gabriel know that the first child would be a son, and why should he specify a name—the name of the great Joshua who succeeded Moses? The name would tell everyone who heard it, "Jehovah is salvation."

Not long after this, when Mary's pregnancy became known, an angel of the Lord would assure a distraught Joseph that Mary's child was of God (Matthew 1:21).

Gabriel's announcement to Mary included three progressive facts, none of which could be naturally known: Mary would be with child; the child would be a son; He would be named Jesus. Was the familiar prophecy of Isaiah 7:14 throbbing by this time in Mary's mind: "Behold, a virgin shall conceive, and bear a son, and shall call his name Immanuel"? If so, it probably came to her in the Greek translation, where the person conceiving is called *parthenos*, definitely indicating virginity, and removing questions that may be raised concerning Isaiah's Hebrew *almah*. (Matthew 1:23 employs *parthenos* in quoting Isaiah 7:14.)

32, 33. He shall be great, and shall be called the Son of the Highest; and the Lord God shall give unto him the throne of his father David: and he shall reign over the house of Jacob for ever; and of his kingdom there shall be no end.

Some women in our time would consider God's favor to Mary as no favor at all! It was wholly contained in the person and ministry of the child she was to bear! She would be blessed in His greatness. He would have a special relationship to God, here called the *Highest* (as He is in six other passages in Luke's Gospel). That divine relationship was shortly to be explained.

The rest of the promise is wholly Messianic. Mary's Son would fulfill the promise given to David: "Thine house and thy kingdom shall be established for ever before thee" (2 Samuel 7:16; compare Isaiah 9:7). Messiah's eternal reign would bless the *house of Jacob*; that is, those persons who would identify themselves as God's people. It would be a spiritual kingdom rather than a political/military one (Luke 17:20, 21; John 18:36). As such it would fulfill Daniel's prophecy of a different kind of kingdom that shall never be destroyed (Daniel 2:44; 7:13, 14).

By this time Mary was fully aware that the angel spoke, not of a child who would be born at some future time to her and Joseph, but of one to come soon according to Gabriel's assurance of favor, his promise of the birth, his direction concerning the child's name, and his prophecy of an eternal reign.

III. Mary Accepts God's Assurance (Luke 1:34-38)

A. Mary's Question (v. 34)

34. Then said Mary unto the angel, How shall this be, seeing I know not a man?

Mary was wholesomely instructed in the facts of life as set forth in Scripture, beginning with Genesis 4:1: "Adam knew Eve his wife; and she conceived." Mary had not entered the marriage relationship; she was a virgin; how could she conceive?

It was a perfectly natural question. Zechariah had expressed doubt when Gabriel promised that he would have a son. "How can I know?" he asked, and was rebuked for his disbelief (Luke 1:18-20). Mary, on the other hand, expressed an interested curiosity, and asked for an explanation: "How can it happen?"

B. God's Answer (v. 35)

35. And the angel answered and said unto her, The Holy Ghost shall come upon thee, and the power of the Highest shall overshadow thee: therefore also that holy thing which shall be born of thee shall be called the Son of God.

Without any rebuke for Mary's question, God's angel supplied the information that she—and the wondering world through all the ages—needed. He did not, of course, supply all the details that curious and skeptical persons might desire or demand. In identifying the *Holy Ghost* as the agent of conception in Mary (compare the angel's assurance to Joseph—Matthew 1:20), Gabriel merely indicated that God can find unusual ways of accomplishing the kind of marvels we take for granted when they happen in the usual manner. This singular divine intervention, however, would identify Mary's baby as *holy*—the one special and unique Son of the Highest.

This divine Father/Son relationship was, in fact, eternal, as set forth in John 1:1-18. It was demonstrated among men, first in Jesus' conception and birth, then in Jesus' life, character, and (ultimately) resurrection from the dead (Romans 1:1-4). It was acknowledged repeatedly by the Father himself (Matthew 3:17; 17:5); it was affirmed by Jesus (John 10:36); it was acknowledged by His apostles (Matthew 16:16); it is to be believed and confessed by all who come to God the Father for life and forgiveness (John 3:16; 20:30, 31).

There are, of course, still doubters and deniers of the facts set forth in our text. They sometimes speak pityingly of folk who are duped into believing such ridiculous stories. And that reminds us of the unlettered gentleman who expressed his pride in not being exposed to books, newspapers, radio, etc. He said that if he had been able to read he, too, might have been fooled into believing such trash as that yarn about men walking on the moon! Some are likewise proud of not being exposed to the incredible stories in the Bible. Do we have news for them!

C. Elisabeth's Example (vv. 36, 37)

36. And, behold, thy cousin Elisabeth, she hath also conceived a son in her old age; and this is the sixth month with her, who was called barren.

Without Mary's asking for it, Gabriel offered evidence to support the promises he had spoken. The news he brought was intensely personal and readily verifiable. Mary's own kinswoman (not necessarily a first cousin), barren through a long lifetime, was now six months pregnant with a son! This angel knew Mary's friend and relative, with intimate details about her, including the sex of her unborn child! He had to be a messenger of God.

Perhaps Mary thought immediately of Abraham and Sarah, to whom God gave Isaac as their son after they were very old (Genesis 17:15-21; 21:1, 2). What God had done once He could do again.

37. For with God nothing shall be impossible.

Here Gabriel said substantially what the Lord had said to Abraham to overcome his and Sarah's doubts about the promise made to them:

visual 2

"Is any thing too hard for the Lord?" (Genesis 18:14). Some things, such as lying, would violate God's very nature and thus would be impossible to Him (Hebrews 6:18; Titus 1:2); but God does not lack the ability to do what He has promised.

To Mary it would be immediately evident that He who could bring life to the wombs of aged Sarah and her own dear Elisabeth could surely bring the child of His promise to her own unfertilized womb. She was convinced.

When, if ever, did Elisabeth learn how much the example of her experience meant to Mary in this crucial hour? Does any one of us know just what the example of his or her experience may mean to a loved one facing some life-changing decision? We don't live to ourselves alone!

D. Mary's Commitment (v. 38)

38. And Mary said, Behold the handmaid of the Lord; be it unto me according to thy word. And the angel departed from her.

Even the young and innocent Mary had to know that the marvelous blessing promised to her would be attended with difficult complications. She was not so naive as to suppose that motherhood itself would be entirely easy; and she had to be aware of severe problems facing motherhood initiated before marriage. What would Joseph think? And her family? And the neighbors? And the leaders in the synagogue at Nazareth?

The way would not be easy; but clearly now it was God's way for her, and she was God's person, owned by Him as though she were a bond-slave. The Phillips translation presents her reply, "I belong to the Lord, body and soul . . . let it happen as you say." Her expression of total commitment foreshadowed Jesus' prayer in Gethsemane: "Not my will, but thine, be done" (Luke 22:42).

This helps to explain why God chose Mary of Nazareth rather than some other virgin in Israel to bear His Son. For her, the joy of perfect obedience overcame any fear of the consequences.

"BEHOLD THE HANDMAID OF THE LORD"

In Nazareth, several places claim to be the "exact" location where the angel of the Lord visited Mary and announced the birth of Christ. One is the Franciscan Church of the Annunciation; another is the Greek Orthodox Church of Saint Gabriel. Other churches are said to mark the "exact" spot of Joseph's carpenter shop and the location of the synagogue that Jesus attended.

It is natural to memorialize events related to the life and ministry of Jesus, but those who follow in the simple faithfulness and obedience of Mary and Joseph do more to memorialize the miracle of the incarnation than any structure ever could.   —W. P.

Conclusion

A. The Rest of the Story

Not many readers of the Bible are satisfied with any brief introduction to Mary of Nazareth. We want to know more, and if we don't find it in the Bible we may accept it from vague tradition or sheer imagination. Yet the one safe source is the Bible, despite the fact that it tells us only a little beyond the accounts of Jesus' birth in Bethlehem and two visits to the temple at Jerusalem (Luke 2). When Jesus was taken there at the age of six weeks, an old saint named Simeon said to Mary, "This child is set . . . for a sign which shall be spoken against; (yea, a sword shall pierce through thy own soul also)" (vv. 34, 35). When Jesus came again with Joseph and Mary twelve years later, Mary became perplexed, first by His unexpected separation from the traveling party, and then by His implied rebuke for her failure to understand His motives (vv. 43-50).

Mary was associated with Jesus' first miracle, performed at a wedding feast in Galilee, when she directed others to do just as He said (John 2:1-5). On two occasions during His public ministry, Jesus said plainly that the spiritual family of believers was more important to Him than His natural family—specifically including His mother (Matthew 12:46-50; Luke 11:27, 28). Yet when He saw Mary nearby as He hung dying on the cross, He committed her to the care of the apostle John (John 19:27).

Mary is named, but without any indication of prominence, among the 120 disciples who prayed together in Jerusalem before the Day of Pentecost (Acts 1:14). And later when Paul wrote that "God sent forth his Son, made of a woman" (Galatians 4:4), he did not name that woman.

We shall do well, therefore, if we regard Jesus' mother as He and His apostles regarded her, a faithful member of God's family, to be appreciated and honored for her commitment to His calling, but not as one toward whom we should direct special devotion or prayers.

B. What's in It for Us?

What practical lessons may we gain, then, from our study of Mary's yielding to God's will? How far can we follow her example?

Most of us will not converse with angels as Mary did. We shall not become related to our Lord in the flesh. And we are not likely to see or participate in miracles as Mary did.

We can give attention to God's messengers as their words come to us in and from the Bible. We can inquire and search for understanding as Mary did. When the evidence is at hand, we can believe and follow it, as Mary did. Most importantly, we can acknowledge God's right to us and our loyalty. When we commit ourselves to His way, we shall probably not know, any better than Mary did, what difficulties may lie ahead; but we can know that difficulties are there, and we can build that expectation into our commitment. Having set our feet on God's course, we can follow it to the end, by His power.

C. Let Us Pray

For the love that gave Your only begotten Son to save us we thank You, our God and Father. For the example of Mary, who committed herself to Your way, we are grateful. May we express that gratitude by accepting and following the way of service available to us. In Jesus' name, amen.

D. Thought to Remember

God can do great things with us, in us, and for us, but only as we willingly yield ourselves to His way.

Home Daily Bible Readings

Monday, Dec. 6—Mary Will Bear a Son (Luke 1:26-31)

Tuesday, Dec. 7—Born Holy (Luke 1:32-37)

Wednesday, Dec. 8—Mary and Elisabeth Rejoice (Luke 1:36-45)

Thursday, Dec. 9—Mary Sings the Magnificat (Luke 1:46-56)

Friday, Dec. 10—His Name Is John (Luke 1:57-66)

Saturday, Dec. 11—Prophet of the Most High (Luke 1:67-80)

Sunday, Dec. 12—The Refiner's Fire Purifies (Malachi 3:1-5; 4:5, 6)

Learning by Doing

*This page contains an alternate lesson plan emphasizing learning activities. Classes
desiring such student involvement will find these suggestions helpful.*

Learning Goals

After today's study, each learner will:

1. Be able to describe the character of Mary.

2. Be able to describe the appropriate response to God's direct revelation.

3. Renew a submissive commitment to the lordship of Christ.

Into the Lesson

Buy a pad of office telephone memos that carry a "message-for-you" heading. Write notes on several—one for each class member, or enough for six to eight sample learners if the class is large. Use such messages as "Ed McMahon stopped by, has $20 million for you"; "Rich uncle died, left you a $1 million home in Coral Gables, FL"; "Macmillan Publishing wants you to write your bio, will give a $500,000 advance"; IRS erred on your recent audit, will return $20,000 plus $5000 interest"; "Boss called, he is making you CEO, beginning tomorrow"; "General Motors likes your ideas for improving the auto line, come to Detroit immediately." Distribute these as class members arrive. As class begins, note the scoffing and laughing you have heard. Ask, "What would it take to make you believe such a message?" After a brief discussion, note how incredible Mary's "memo" from Gabriel must have seemed, yet she believed it completely.

Into the Word

Before the day of meeting, select three readers who will agree to read the text as a short dramatic scene. Have them stand in front of the class as NARRATOR, GABRIEL, and MARY. The narrator reads the text, but stops when he comes to words of Gabriel or Mary. The reader chosen for that part reads those words.

Pass around a box holding small, folded slips of paper, each with one of the following words: *Galilean, Nazarene, virgin, espoused, favored, blessed, troubled, fearful, perplexed, submissive, believing, comforted, holy, overshadowed, privileged, informed, alone.* Add slips with other words describing Mary, but only words that the text clearly shows to be appropriate. Let each member draw a slip. (In a small class, each member may have more than one; in a large class, two or three members may share a slip.) Write on the board, "Mary was . . ." Ask your members to reveal the words they have drawn, one at a time,

and tell where in the text this is revealed about Mary. Add each word to your "Mary was . . ." as it is given. These will help you and the class discuss what kind of a person Mary was.

Have the students use the same small slips to write questions they would like to ask Mary if she were here. Give examples such as these: "Who was the first person you told of the angel's visit?" "Did the angel walk in by the door, or suddenly appear in the room?" After the questions are written, let students imagine how Mary might answer them. As they share speculative comments, remind them of the simplicity of the text. Guided by the Holy Spirit, Luke briefly and beautifully recorded the essential facts.

As an alternate to the preceding activity—or in addition—if you can invite a dramatic young lady of your congregation to "be" Mary, you can interview her before the group. Plan with your actress the questions you will use. Include some questions that can be answered clearly from the text and some that can be answered only from imagination. This will both review the facts of the lesson and allow a thorough discussion of Mary's character and her feelings. Answers given from the imagination can prepare the way for discussion after the interview. Students can judge how reasonable "Mary's" answers are. Some may tell what they think the real Mary would say. Conclude the discussion by a brief review of the facts actually known from the text.

Into Life

Give your class the following "When-Was-the-Last-Time" test. All the students may answer on paper, or volunteers may respond verbally as questions are asked. If time is short read each question and have students answer silently to themselves: (1) "When was the last time you felt that God was speaking directly to you?" (2) "When was the last time you were startled by a revelation from God?" (3) "When was the last time you felt highly favored of God?" (4) "When was the last time you thought, 'With God nothing is impossible'?" (5) "When was the last time you were fearful in God's presence?" (6) "When was the last time you said to God, 'Behold, Your servant; be it to me according to Your word'?" Close by asking how we can become more aware of God's presence with us. How can we learn to shape our thinking so we will want what He wants?

Let's Talk It Over

The questions on this page are designed to encourage review of the lesson Scriptures and to promote discussion of the lesson by the class. The answers provided are only discussion starters. Let your class talk it over from there.

1. What do you think made Mary highly favored with the Lord? What can we do to develop the same qualities?

Mary was humble. God often chooses the meek and humble to serve Him in great ways. We develop humility by reminding ourselves of what we really are: miserable sinners saved only by the grace of God.

Mary was devout: that is, she was truly devoted to the Lord and to His kingdom. She was a pure virgin, and doubtless she was righteous, though not perfect, in all areas of life. God can always use a person who loves Him wholeheartedly, who keeps himself or herself from the corruption of the world. We become devout by spending time with the Lord and growing to love Him by coming to know Him intimately. We become righteous by obeying His will, growing to love the good and hate evil.

Mary was submissive to the point of being self-sacrificing. She must have known she would be scorned and rebuked for becoming pregnant before she was married, yet she did not hesitate. Any person who would follow Jesus and serve Him must be willing to leave family and friends if need be. We learn to be submissive by submitting, by deliberately putting God's will above our own.

Mary was trusting. She started down a road the end of which she could not even imagine. But she trusted the Lord. She was sure He would not call her to a road that she could not walk with His help. God does not always show us the end of a matter; sometimes He only invites us to begin. If we would serve Him, we must trust Him to see us through to the end.

2. Mary's plans changed with the angel's message. Her wedding came sooner than she had expected, and so did motherhood. How do our lives change when we become Christians? How radical a change are we willing to accept?

Of course this varies with the individual. Those who are brought up to love the Lord do not change as much as those who have long gone in godless ways. Yet all of us do change when we become Christians. The more we have participated in evil things, the more radical is our change. Even those who are trained up in the Lord have a new sense of purpose and

commitment when they name Jesus as Lord of their lives. We all must be willing to change in any way necessary to obey and serve the Lord.

3. Mary was an obscure young woman in an obscure village. No one looked for anything special to come from there, but God did cause something very special to happen. How can this bring encouragement to us?

Most of us are ordinary people in ordinary places leading ordinary lives, but are not obscure to God. Much of the work of the kingdom is somewhat ordinary—caring for widows, helping the sick and needy, visiting shut-ins, etc. We may serve God all our lives and not receive much recognition for it, but the Lord is very much aware of every service done for Him. And who knows? God may choose some of us to perform very important tasks for Him.

4. Mary was blessed in an exceptional way, but the blessing cost her something. Do we miss some blessings because we are not willing to pay the cost?

Those who do not go out as missionaries miss the blessing and thrill of taking the gospel to those who have never heard it before. Those who have never given sacrificially, have never known the blessing of having God meet their needs in extraordinary and wonderful ways. Those who never clothe the naked, feed the hungry, or serve the Lord in other ways will never know the blessing of hearing the Lord say, "Well done, good and faithful servant."

5. Elisabeth's example was a great encouragement to Mary. It is the same today. Tell of faithful saints whose examples have been an encouragement to you. If anyone has ever told you that your example was helpful, how did that affect you? What part does the principle of example play in motivating us to faithfulness?

Class members should share personal testimonies. All surely have those who have served as their examples perhaps a faithful preacher, a Sunday-school teacher, an elder, or a saintly widow. When we know that others are looking at us it is a strong motivation to be faithful and true. We must understand that someone else is *always* looking at our example.

Born a Savior

DEVOTIONAL READING: Isaiah 9:2-7.

LESSON SCRIPTURE: Luke 2:1-20.

PRINTED TEXT: Luke 2:4-20.

Luke 2:4-20

4 And Joseph also went up from Galilee, out of the city of Nazareth, into Judea, unto the city of David, which is called Bethlehem, (because he was of the house and lineage of David,)

5 To be taxed with Mary his espoused wife, being great with child.

6 And so it was, that, while they were there, the days were accomplished that she should be delivered.

7 And she brought forth her firstborn son, and wrapped him in swaddling clothes, and laid him in a manger; because there was no room for them in the inn.

8 And there were in the same country shepherds abiding in the field, keeping watch over their flock by night.

9 And, lo, the angel of the Lord came upon them, and the glory of the Lord shone round about them; and they were sore afraid.

10 And the angel said unto them, Fear not: for, behold, I bring you good tidings of great joy, which shall be to all people.

11 For unto you is born this day in the city of David a Saviour, which is Christ the Lord.

12 And this shall be a sign unto you; Ye shall find the babe wrapped in swaddling clothes, lying in a manger.

13 And suddenly there was with the angel a multitude of the heavenly host praising God, and saying,

14 Glory to God in the highest, and on earth peace, good will toward men.

15 And it came to pass, as the angels were gone away from them into heaven, the shepherds said one to another, Let us now go even unto Bethlehem, and see this thing which is come to pass, which the Lord hath made known unto us.

16 And they came with haste, and found Mary and Joseph, and the babe lying in a manger.

17 And when they had seen it, they made known abroad the saying which was told them concerning this child.

18 And all they that heard it wondered at those things which were told them by the shepherds.

19 But Mary kept all these things, and pondered them in her heart.

20 And the shepherds returned, glorifying and praising God for all the things that they had heard and seen, as it was told unto them.

GOLDEN TEXT: Behold, I bring you good tidings of great joy, which shall be to all people. For unto you is born this day in the city of David a Saviour, which is Christ the Lord.
—Luke 2:10, 11.

The Story of Jesus

Unit 1. Luke: A Savior Is Born

(Lessons 1-4)

Lesson Aims

The study of today's lesson should enable the student to:

1. Tell the story of Luke 2:4-20 briefly in his or her own words.

2. Distinguish between fact and fiction in the "Christmas story."

3. Name at least one person to whom he or she will tell the story this week.

Lesson Outline

INTRODUCTION
    A. Hear It as a Child
    B. The Time, Place, and Persons
I. RECEIVING GOD'S GIFT (Luke 2:4-7)
    A. Bethlehem Receives Visitors (vv. 4, 5)
    B. Between Arrival and Departure (v. 6)
    C. Birthplace and Bassinet (v. 7)
       That Baby
II. ANNOUNCING THE GIFT (Luke 2:8-14)
    A. Startling Appearance (vv. 8, 9)
    B. Convincing Message (vv. 10-12)
       Majesty in a Manger
    C. Chorus of Praise (vv. 13, 14)
III. SEEING AND REPORTING IT (Luke 2:15-20)
    A. Seeing for Themselves (vv. 15, 16)
    B. Report and Response (vv. 17-19)
    C. Return and Rejoicing (v. 20)
CONCLUSION
    A. He Dwelt Among Us
    B. Let Us Pray
    C. Thought to Remember

Display visual 3 of the visuals packet and let it remain before the class. The visual is shown on page 141.

Introduction

A. Hear It as a Child

Adults have difficulties with the "Christmas story." Most have heard it for so many years that it tends to lose the luster of the fresh and the new. Most also have heard it so often embellished with traditional and imaginative details that they find it hard to distinguish fact from fiction. We need constantly to "touch base" with Scripture to ask, "Just what does the Bible say about this world-shaking event?"

Fictional elements in Bible stories are not necessarily false, any more than fictional elements in historical novels are necessarily false. But makers of fiction and tradition possess two strong tendencies that must be watched carefully. First, they love to compress events into neat small packages of time and space. It is *possible*, of course, that Jesus was born and the shepherds heard and spread the news, all within a few hours of Mary and Joseph's arrival from Nazareth; but in the light of Luke 2:6 it is not likely. It is *possible* that it was only a few minutes' hike from where the angel found the shepherds with their flocks to the place of Jesus' birth, but a greater distance is suggested by Luke 2:15. It is *not* possible, in the light of Scripture, for the shepherds and the Wise-men of Matthew 2 to have visited the newborn King at the same place on the same day.

Second, merchants of tradition like to identify important events with rocks and caves, which are long lasting, provide convenient bases for shrines, and can be visited throughout the centuries by pilgrims and tourists. It is *possible*, of course, that the manger in which Jesus rested was located in a cave such as the one shown to pilgrims in Bethlehem, but it is highly unlikely.

Can each of us, then, imagine himself or herself as a child hearing for the first time Luke's beautiful account of the birth in Bethlehem? Let us then read the story over and over until, like a child, we resist any changes or omissions. Then perhaps we shall see a new dimension in the wisdom of Jesus, who admonished us adults to repent and become as little children. Bible-story time at Christmas is a wonderful occasion for that repentance.

B. The Time, Place, and Persons

There was nothing fictional about Luke's writing. With bold and careful insistence he connected the works of God with well-known places and persons, making them subject to the most critical investigation. "This thing was not done in a corner" (Acts 26:26).

Public records show that Caesar Augustus authorized an empire-wide enrollment for purposes of taxation and military service several years *before* the birth of Jesus. Naturally it took a few years to make plans and build an organization to complete the enrollment. The process may have been slower in Herod's kingdom than it was elsewhere, for the Jews were allowed to follow their own custom of going to the places of their family origin to enroll.

Public records show Cyrenius (otherwise called Quirinius) as governor of Syria and conductor of a highly unpopular census several years *after* the birth of Jesus; but he appears as *legate* for Augustus, serving in Syria at the earlier date. In his first administration the first enrollment was made.

I. Receiving God's Gift
(Luke 2:4-7)
A. Bethlehem Receives Visitors
(vv. 4, 5)

4. And Joseph also went up from Galilee, out of the city of Nazareth, into Judea, unto the city of David, which is called Bethlehem, (because he was of the house and lineage of David).

Matthew 1:18-25 introduces Joseph of Nazareth as a descendant of David, and himself a man of firm convictions and high principles, devout before God, and considerate of those about him. He, like Mary, was willing to accept and follow the revealed will of God. He seems also to have respected the authority of civil government. Accordingly he made the southward journey of several days, ending in the long climb up to Jerusalem and Bethlehem in the mountains of Judea, to enroll in the required census. Bethlehem was the birthplace and boyhood home of David (1 Samuel 17:12; 20:6).

5. To be taxed with Mary his espoused wife, being great with child.

In obedience to the angel's directive (Matthew 1:20, 24, 25), Joseph had taken Mary as his wife in every way except physical consummation of the marriage. We can only guess by what means they traveled. Consideration for Mary in her advanced pregnancy would naturally cause Joseph to make the journey as early and easily as possible.

How remarkable are the "natural coincidences" by which men—emperor and citizen alike—unknowingly worked together in fulfillment of prophecy that the Messiah, called a Nazarene (Matthew 2:23), would nonetheless be born in Bethlehem of Judea! (Micah 5:2; Matthew 2:4-6).

B. Between Arrival and Departure (v. 6)

6. And so it was, that, while they were there, the days were accomplished that she should be delivered.

Luke says nothing about the couple's arrival in Bethlehem or how many days passed while *they were there* before the time for Mary's delivery. Lodging places in that country are variously described as providing space and shelter, but little privacy. Some offered booths surrounding open spaces, and some no more than space to bed down. These would have served the couple's basic needs before Mary went into labor, but not after.

C. Birthplace and Bassinet (v. 7)

7. And she brought forth her firstborn son, and wrapped him in swaddling clothes, and laid him in a manger; because there was no room for them in the inn.

Room here translates the Greek *topos*, which signifies a place, location, station, position, or even opportunity. Phillips translates the final clause, "There was no place for them inside the inn"; and *Today's English Version* renders it, "There was no room for them to stay in the inn." Clearly, no suitable accommodation for childbirth was available. All we know about the place finally found for Jesus' birth is that it included a *manger*—a feeding trough for animals, sometimes called a crib. Supplied with clean straw, it would serve well the purpose for which Mary used it. Here, then, is where Mary "gave birth to her first child, a son" (Phillips translation).

Mary seems to have brought from Nazareth some cloths in which she now wrapped the newborn infant according to the custom of tender care, before she laid Him in His unusual cradle.

When the Lord came down from His Heavenly glory to live among men, He landed with a thud! But this was only the beginning of a pattern of humble self-giving that He was to follow all the way to Golgotha and the borrowed tomb (Matthew 8:20). For Jesus, and for Mary, it was enough that this was the Father's way, and His lasting approval would more than make up for any temporary discomfort in following it.

THAT BABY

Newsweek carried on its cover a picture of a little baby and the simple option, "That Baby." *Time* described this birth as the most anticipated one in two thousand years.

The eyes of the world were focused on a hospital in Oldham, England. There, in a guarded room of the maternity section, Lesley Brown awaited the birth of her first child. Oldham was in a virtual state of siege. Despite doctors' pleas that all the excitement was endangering both mother and child, journalists swooped like vultures for any morsel of information. A bomb threat was phoned to the hospital.

What made that event so interesting? Researchers Steptoe and Edwards had succeeded in fertilizing a human egg in the laboratory and implanting it into Mrs. Brown's body. That accomplishment drew the attention of the world away from the Middle East, the arms race, and African turmoil.

The theological, philosophical, and scientific communities began a continuing debate about the ethics and ramifications of such procedures.

But Mrs. Brown was quoted as saying, "I realize that this is a scientific miracle, but in a way, science has made us turn to God. We are not religious people. But when we discovered that all was working well and I was pregnant, we just had to pray to God to give our thanks. It seemed right and natural."

That remarkable procedure has been repeated several times since that first time in the late seventies. But today our Bible lesson focuses our attention on a procedure that has never been repeated. The angel told Mary, "The Holy Spirit will come upon you, and the power of the Most High will overshadow you. So the holy one to be born will be called the Son of God. . . . For nothing is impossible with God" (Luke 1:35-37, *New International Version*).   —W. P.

II. Announcing the Gift
(Luke 2:8-14)

A. Startling Appearance (vv. 8, 9)

8. And there were in the same country shepherds abiding in the field, keeping watch over their flock by night.

How appropriate that *shepherds*, whose humbly responsible work is interwoven with divine-human dealings throughout the ages, should be the first to learn about Messiah's birth! When David tended sheep in this same area he wrote, "The Lord is my shepherd" (Psalm 23); and Isaiah said of God, "He shall feed his flock like a shepherd" (Isaiah 40:11). Jeremiah (23:1-4) and Ezekiel (34:1-19) spoke of religious leaders as shepherds responsible for keeping God's flock—His people. Jesus later spoke of himself as the Good Shepherd who would lay down His life for His sheep (John 10:11-18). Addressing Simon Peter, He laid a similar responsibility on His apostles (John 21:15-17). In turn, Peter (1 Peter 5:1-4) and Paul (Acts 20:28-31) directed the same charge to elders in the Lord's church.

It is commonly held that sheep intended for sacrifices in the temple at Jerusalem were grazed in the area about Bethlehem, and that these were kept in the open fields night and day throughout the year. The night watch, which kept the shepherds also living in the fields, would be especially crucial for protecting the flocks from thieves and marauding beasts.

9. And, lo, the angel of the Lord came upon them, and the glory of the Lord shone round about them; and they were sore afraid.

Lo, look, or *behold* prepares the reader for the amazing fact to follow. No name is given to the angel who suddenly *stood by* (literal translation) the shepherds that night. But the bright light of divine presence (compare Matthew 28:3; Acts 12:7; 22:6-9 that suddenly split the quiet darkness terrified the shepherds. It surely got their attention for what followed.

B. Convincing Message (vv. 10-12)

10. And the angel said unto them, Fear not: for, behold, I bring you good tidings of great joy, which shall be to all people.

Observe the effective three-point introduction to the messenger's announcement: *Quit being afraid:* calm down and listen. *My news is good and joyous:* prepare to enjoy it fully. *It is for you and everybody else.* That is its ultimate effect, although the exact message to these Jewish shepherds spoke of "all *the* people" (*American Standard Version*), suggesting the covenant people of God. That would be more fully understood later.

11. For unto you is born this day in the city of David a Saviour, which is Christ the Lord.

Who are the *you* to whom the Savior was born? The shepherds, certainly, and that was very important. The citizens of Judea, surely. The covenant people Israel, according to the promise. But none of us who know the rest of the gospel story will be excluded from that extended *you*.

This day was made eternally significant by the Savior's birth. At what time in *this day* did the birth occur? How long before the angel announced it? *The city of David* was obviously Bethlehem. The angel's reference to David identifies the event with Messianic prophecy.

The Roman world spoke of their emperors and other military heroes as saviors of the people. Perhaps this influenced the Jews' expectations of their Messiah. But the Jews were aware also of their prophets' references to God as their Saviour (Isaiah 43:3; 45:15). They were still to learn that God's Messiah was to be of a special kind, *saving* His people from sin and death (Matthew 1:21; John 4:42; Acts 2:37-40).

Christ is the Greek language equivalent of the Hebrew *Messiah*, both meaning "anointed." By Jewish custom, prophets, priests, and kings were set apart for their God-given calling by the application of oil to their heads. God's Messiah was to be *anointed* with His power and authority.

Lord signified one with authority to command total obedience as owner or ruler. The Jews employed the term in reference to God. It came to be used of Jesus by those who recognized His identity with the Father. In Peter's sermon on the Day of Pentecost he declared that God had made Jesus "both Lord and Christ" (Acts 2:36). But the night-watching shepherds had already heard the full declaration of Jesus' purpose, power, and authority!

12. And this shall be a sign unto you; Ye shall find the babe wrapped in swaddling clothes, lying in a manger.

Did the angel command the shepherds to go and see the newborn Messiah? No, but he told them how they could know the truth of what he had said. The *sign* to Zechariah had been his inability to speak until the promised child was born. The *sign* to Mary had been the pregnancy of her aged kinswoman, Elisabeth. The *sign* to shepherds would involve nothing miraculous, but would be a combination of circumstances so unusual that they could not be known by usual means.

Find a baby; there are many babies. This one is wrapped in the manner customary in caring for newborns; that's not much help. But this cared-for child is lying in an animal's feeding trough; now, there's a solid clue! The shepherds would be right at home in a place like that, even when they found majesty in a manger.

visual 3

MAJESTY IN A MANGER

Our English word *paradox* comes from a Greek word meaning "contrary to expectation." Angels appearing to shepherds. Fear and joy together. A Lord lying in a manger. God becoming man.

The most memorable Christmas of my childhood is, paradoxically, the one that was most difficult. Mom and Dad made a rule that day that we could open only one gift an hour. Talk about time coming to a standstill! An hour seemed interminable. It wasn't so bad when the gift was a toy. My brother and I could play with something like that. But a shirt or a pair of pants? Awful.

Why does that Christmas stand out so vividly in my memory? Is it because I learned a lesson in delayed gratification? Is it because it was so painful to wait that my joy was intensified when the wait was over? Is it that I learned something about patience and anticipation as they relate to satisfaction?

For Mary and Joseph, the birth of her firstborn was filled with paradoxes—joy and pain, anticipation and realization, excitement and peace. Hope held in their arms. The awaited Messiah, now among men.   —W. P.

C. Chorus of Praise (vv. 13, 14)

13, 14. And suddenly there was with the angel a multitude of the heavenly host praising God, and saying, Glory to God in the highest, and on earth peace, good will toward men.

The shepherds had heard joyous good news for all people, and also for the vast armies of angels in Heaven. God, who had thus provided salvation to mankind, must be fervently *praised*!

Did the Heavenly choir *sing* the words recorded in verse 14? What they *said* is so movingly musical that it is a hymn, however the sounds may have been produced. It speaks the grandest good, both in Heaven with God and on earth with men. The dominant theme in the *highest* is recognition and praise of the Almighty. This grows naturally from His grand love gift to men. On earth the dominant theme of Jesus' coming is *peace*—peace restored between God and men; peace within the spirit of each reconciled believer; and the greatest possible peace among men wherever they dwell.

The latter part of verse 14 presents a minor textual difficulty; hence there is some uncertainty between *peace, good will toward men* and a later translation, *peace to men on whom his favor rests*. God's favor gave His Messiah as the Prince of Peace (Isaiah 9:6); and Jesus spoke of peace as the gift He would leave to His followers—"Not as the world giveth, give I unto you" (John 14:27).

III. Seeing and Reporting It (Luke 2:15-20)

A. Seeing for Themselves (vv. 15, 16)

15. And it came to pass, as the angels were gone away from them into heaven, the shepherds said one to another, Let us now go even unto Bethlehem, and see this thing which is come to pass, which the Lord hath made known unto us.

The messengers from Heaven had made known the Savior's birth, and they had convinced the shepherds that the message came from the Lord. Now they returned to His presence, and left the shepherds to accomplish their part in God's program without further help from on high.

"Let's go over to Bethlehem!" they began to say. How far was it? We can only guess. What arrangements did they make for the safety of the sheep in their absence? Luke does not say; but it is evident that Heaven's errand became suddenly more important to them than their regular employment.

16. And they came with haste, and found Mary and Joseph, and the babe lying in a manger.

Excitement gave wings to the shepherds' feet, even where no emergency could be traced. How much more is haste appropriate to our evangelistic labor in fields that are "white already to harvest"! (John 4:35).

How much manger-searching in Bethlehem was necessary before they *found* Mary and Joseph with little Jesus? Scripture provides no hint of divine guidance beyond the angel's instruction, which proved to be adequate and totally accurate.

B. Report and Response (vv. 17-19)

17, 18. And when they had seen it, they made known abroad the saying which was told them concerning this child. And all they that heard it wondered at those things which were told them by the shepherds.

Having found what they came to see, the shepherds explained why they were there. First to Mary and Joseph, "they told what had been said to them about this child" (*Goodspeed*). It is probably safe to assume that the shepherds also told in the manger-place about the joyous worship they had heard from the host of angels. If anyone besides Joseph and Mary was nearby, that one heard it, too. The hearers' amazement at the report could not have been as great as the shepherds' wonderment in their experience.

19. But Mary kept all these things, and pondered them in her heart.

Who would understand, if Mary told of her own experience with an angel in reference to this child? So she gathered more information to establish what she already knew. Gabriel had told her that *Jesus* (Savior) was to be His name, and that He would reign forever on David's throne. But the shepherds spoke of *Christ* and *Lord!* She needed time to weigh and study this.

How long was it before Mary unlocked the treasures of her heart and revealed all these things so they found their way into the Gospel written by Luke, the beloved physician? (Colossians 4:14). Did she not at last reveal them to the gentle doctor himself? (Luke 1:1-4).

C. Return and Rejoicing (v. 20)

20. And the shepherds returned, glorifying and praising God for all the things that they had heard and seen, as it was told unto them.

We can only wonder what the shepherds found when they went back to their flocks in the field. The more important matter is what they found when they took time out and followed the angel's directions to Bethlehem. That finding confirmed exactly what God's messenger had told them. God's Word and God's work do agree! The shepherds responded with glad praise that glorified their lives and status forever. Time out for genuine worship is worth whatever it may cost. The shepherds' enthusiasm surely gave weight to what they said to others about the event.

Conclusion

A. He Dwelt Among Us

When our Lord gave up Heaven's glory to live on earth among men, He came all the way. That becomes the theme of Philippians 2:5-11 and John 1:14: He "dwelt among us." Materially, He identified himself with humble folk and circumstances, in His birth, His manner of life, and His sympathies: "The Son of man hath not where to lay his head" (Matthew 8:20). So "the common people heard him gladly" (Mark 12:37). Yet He was available also to the wealthy and the noble, such as Nicodemus and Joseph of Arimathea, who came to appreciate His wisdom and His worth. No one was, or is, barred from the truth that He lived among men, died for men, and now in glory makes intercession for those who appreciate His presence. His invitation is for "you-all!"

B. Let Us Pray

Thank You, gracious God our Father, for Your only begotten Son, who came to share our humanity and to bear our sins. As we rejoice in His coming, so may we delight in His ways, and talk gladly of His mercy, and look with bright hope to His coming again. In His name, amen.

C. Thought to Remember

God sent His Son! Come and see! Go and tell!

Home Daily Bible Readings

Monday, Dec. 13—The Birth of Jesus (Luke 2:1-7)

Tuesday, Dec. 14—Angels Appear to Lowly Shepherds (Luke 2:8-14)

Wednesday, Dec. 15—Shepherds Find Joseph, Mary, and Jesus (Luke 2:15-20)

Thursday, Dec. 16—Named by the Angel; "Jesus" (Luke 2:21-24)

Friday, Dec. 17—Simeon Blessed God, Mary, and Joseph (Luke 2:25-35)

Saturday, Dec. 18—Joseph and Mary Think Jesus Lost (Luke 2:41-45)

Sunday, Dec. 19—Jesus Amazes His Teachers (Luke 2:46-52)

Learning by Doing

This page contains an alternate lesson plan emphasizing learning activities. Classes
desiring such student involvement will find these suggestions helpful.

Learning Goals

This new look at Luke's record of the birth of Christ will enable the Bible student to:

1. Distinguish between God's revelation and man-made additions to the story.

2. Marvel anew at the simplicity and the profundity of the events.

3. Express a new commitment to make "known abroad the saying which was told them concerning this child," Jesus.

Into the Lesson

As class members arrive, have each one draw a slip of paper from a box you have filled with enough slips for your expected attendance. Each of these designations is written on one-third of the slips: "Jesus and Mary"; "Shepherds"; "Innkeeper and Guests." These groups will be used later in an activity.

If you can borrow a large book of fairy tales with an obvious title on the cover, use that book to hold the following story as you read it. Tell the group you have a fairy tale for them.

Once upon a time, in a land far away, an alien king was ruling while a prince of the true royal family was disguised as a carpenter. The prince took his wife and traveled to a faraway village to register for the census. There the prince's wife gave birth to a baby boy. The innkeeper honored the little family with his best room.

Now three local shepherds were sleepily watching their sheep when the queen of fairies appeared, startling them with the bright light of her wand. "I have good news," she said. "The new king was born today in that village there. You can see him at the inn."

In the blink of an eye all the fairies joined their queen to sing of honor to the king and joy for the people. Then the fairies disappeared with a pop.

The shepherds strolled to town and found the prince and his wife with the new baby. Joyfully they hoped this baby would grow to be a warrior who would overthrow the foreign rulers and set his people free. Then they would live happily ever after.

Close the book and put it aside. Ask the students, "What did you hear in this story that made it sound like a fairy tale?" Expect them to mention the mythical fairies and such phrases as "once upon a time" and "happily ever after."

Be sure they know also that the story is vague about time and place and people—like a fairy tale, but unlike real history or a factual news story.

Into the Word

Have the learners turn to the lesson text in their Bibles. Ask them to read it and then tell how its story differs from the fairy tale they have heard. Be sure the following are noted:

1. The Bible story is clear about the place, Bethlehem. It is a real place.

2. The approximate time also is clear: "in those days" (v. 1), the days when an enrollment was decreed by Caesar Augustus.

3. The main characters are named: Joseph a man of the royal family of David, and his wife Mary. They are real people, not figments of the imagination.

4. The angels come and go miraculously, but with an air of dignity and solemnity that makes them different from the fairies who disappear with a pop.

Now ask students to mention points at which the fairy tale and the Bible story are alike. You may want to read the fairy tale again while the students compare the true story in their Bibles. Several parallels can be noted. There is a country ruled by foreigners. There is a prince of the true royal family, Joseph of the line of David. There is a trip to a village to register. A child is born in that village and visited by shepherds. The child is born to be a king. As similarities are noted, note also how details differ in the two stories.

Into Life

Ask the students to form three groups according to the slips they drew as they arrived. Ask each group to make a list of emotions felt by the people named on their slip. What were the feelings of Joseph and Mary before and after the birth? How did the shepherds feel when they saw the angel and when they saw the baby? Suppose the shepherds talked with some of the guests at the inn. Then how did the guests feel?

As the lists are read, let each student write all of them for himself. Then let students discuss which of these feelings we share at this season of the year. Suggest that each student underline the desirable feelings, then take the list home and use it for a daily attitude check.

Let's Talk It Over

The questions on this page are designed to encourage review of the lesson Scriptures and to promote discussion of the lesson by the class. The answers provided are only discussion starters. Let your class talk it over from there.

1. It must have been a shock to Mary and Joseph to end up in a stable. What a place for God's Son! How can we deal with doubts when the road God gives us is not what we expected?

A missionary couple goes to the field and the husband dies soon after, leaving the widow to labor alone. A conscientious and sincere new deacon begins his work, only to face criticism and opposition. Weren't they, and aren't we, doing God's work? Why are there so many problems? We are involved in a cosmic spiritual battle, and when we begin to work for the Lord Satan begins to work against us. But God's plans and purposes are more far-reaching than we know. He turns apparent defeat into victory. If we stay with the Lord He always leads us in the best path.

2. The angel brought good news for all people. The shepherds were quick to share the news. What were their motives? How can we share it today, and with what motives?

The shepherds wanted to glorify and praise God for sending the promised Christ and inviting them to share in the glory of His birth. They spread the good news by telling it, unable to contain their enthusiasm and excitement.

We share the good news in the same way and with the same motive. When we experience the power and the glory of His presence in our own lives, we tell others about it. If we have lost the joy of telling others about the Christ, then perhaps we have lost sight of the glory of the Lord.

3. One prominent thread in the story of Jesus' birth is the fulfillment of ancient prophecies. How does this strengthen our faith today?

The birth of Jesus Christ fulfilled in exact detail prophecies that were centuries and millennia old. This shows us both God's knowledge of the future and His control over events. If God could so accurately predict what would happen at Jesus' birth, then we can believe and trust Him when He predicts the final victory of the church, the defeat of Satan and death, and the eternal reign of the saints.

4. Most of us have heard the Christmas story so often that it is hard for us to keep up our appreciation for it. How can we feel again the wonder and awe the shepherds felt?

We can turn from the distractions of our current Christmas customs—the shopping, baking, and parties—to focus on the fact that the eternal Word, Creator of the earth and all that is in it, entered into His creation when He was born of Mary. We must remember that upon this one person, Jesus, depends the fate of all the people who ever have lived and ever will live in this world. This includes us. If He had not come we would be doomed to hopeless and eternal death. Because He came to earth and fulfilled His mission, we have the opportunity for eternal life with Him.

5. The angels said that Jesus' birth brought peace. What peace was this? How may we come to experience it?

Jesus brought peace between man and God, reconciling sinful man to his righteous God. We have peace with God when we are personally reconciled to God through the blood of the Savior. Jesus brought peace that dwells in the hearts of redeemed men. When we know God has entered into the world and defeated our worst enemies, sin and death, then we have the peace that comes from knowing that all will be well in the end. This is the peace that martyrs carry with them to their deaths. Jesus brought peace between men. Evil still strives with righteousness, and war still rages, but Jesus teaches us to love our enemies and do good to them. So we live at peace even with those who do not want to live at peace with us.

6. Mary pondered all the wondrous events that accompanied the birth of Jesus. How does similar meditation help us to understand the meaning of Bible events and teaching?

God's words and actions are so marvelous and profound that we can never plumb their full depths. However, we can discover and appreciate more and more about them as we spend time meditating on them and looking at them from every angle. Surely all of us have had the experience of reading a familiar portion of Scripture and seeing something in it that we had never seen before. The more we ponder and learn about God's deeds and words, the more we understand and trust His power and might and wisdom and love.

Testing a Commitment to Service

DEVOTIONAL READING: Matthew 4:1-11.

LESSON SCRIPTURE: Luke 3:21, 22; 4:1-15.

PRINTED TEXT: Luke 4:1-15.

Dec
26

Luke 4:1-15

1 And Jesus being full of the Holy Ghost returned from Jordan, and was led by the Spirit into the wilderness,

2 Being forty days tempted of the devil. And in those days he did eat nothing: and when they were ended, he afterward hungered.

3 And the devil said unto him, If thou be the Son of God, command this stone that it be made bread.

4 And Jesus answered him, saying, It is written, That man shall not live by bread alone, but by every word of God.

5 And the devil, taking him up into a high mountain, showed unto him all the kingdoms of the world in a moment of time.

6 And the devil said unto him, All this power will I give thee, and the glory of them: for that is delivered unto me; and to whomsoever I will, I give it.

7 If thou therefore wilt worship me, all shall be thine.

8 And Jesus answered and said unto him, Get thee behind me, Satan: for it is written, Thou shalt worship the Lord thy God, and him only shalt thou serve.

9 And he brought him to Jerusalem, and set him on a pinnacle of the temple, and said unto him, If thou be the Son of God, cast thyself down from hence:

10 For it is written, He shall give his angels charge over thee, to keep thee:

11 And in their hands they shall bear thee up, lest at any time thou dash thy foot against a stone.

12 And Jesus answering said unto him, It is said, Thou shalt not tempt the Lord thy God.

13 And when the devil had ended all the temptation, he departed from him for a season.

14 And Jesus returned in the power of the Spirit into Galilee: and there went out a fame of him through all the region round about.

15 And he taught in their synagogues, being glorified of all.

GOLDEN TEXT: Thou shalt worship the Lord thy God, and him only shalt thou serve.
—Luke 4:8.

The Story of Jesus

Unit 1. Luke: A Savior Is Born

(Lessons 1-4)

Lesson Aims

After studying this week's lesson the student should be able to:

1. Tell briefly the story of Jesus' wilderness temptation.

2. Tell what special relation the recorded temptations bore to Jesus' life and ministry.

3. Show how the principles found in this lesson apply to the student's life and career.

Lesson Outline

INTRODUCTION
  A. Where Is Commitment?
  B. A Meeting of the Ways
  I. JESUS BECOMES VULNERABLE (Luke 4:1, 2)
 II. SATAN ATTACKS; Jesus Responds (Luke 4:3-13)
  A. How Will He Use God's Gifts? (vv. 3, 4)
    The Destroying Deceiver
  B. What Does He Want Most of All? (vv. 5-8)
  C. Does He Believe God Completely? (vv. 9-12)
  D. When Will the Next Attack Come? (v. 13)
III. JESUS CARRIES OUT HIS COMMITMENT (Luke 4:14, 15)
CONCLUSION
  A. Blessings of Trial
    Struggling for Maturity
  B. Let Us Pray
  C. Thought to Remember

Display visual 4 of the visuals packet and refer to it as you discuss each temptation. The visual is shown on page 148.

Introduction

A. Where Is Commitment?

Where will one find the kind of widespread personal *commitment* that is necessary to a stable society? That question, with all its implications, is being asked by many concerned observers of world affairs today. A minor symptom may be found in frivolity concerning "New Year Resolutions," made by some without any serious intention to perform, and abandoned altogether by many as meaningless.

Widely noted is a "shopper mentality," which always looks for "bargains for me," and for gains

"without cost or obligation." This attitude affects business relationships in employment or in making and paying debts. It affects friendship, marriage, and family. It affects church membership and activity. Where, we are asked, are the persons willing to become involved to the point of sacrifice in service for church or community? Prized indeed are those dependable core persons who will say in word and deed, "With this new relationship I have accepted a new obligation; I am committed; so how do I now go about fulfilling my commitment?"

That kind of commitment must be found first among the followers of Jesus Christ! Committed first to God, to His Word, and to His people, they have set their feet firmly on the course in which He leads. They face recurrent questions as to what is most effective in following that course; but the major issue is settled, and other matters must find their place in related order.

B. A Meeting of the Ways

Our lessons so far in December have worked together in bringing us to this point of commitment. First in the order of events was Mary's acceptance and commitment to mothering God's Son on earth (December 12). Later in Bethlehem she and Joseph accepted the responsibilities attending the Savior's birth (December 19). The lesson for December 5 told of events thirty years later when John the Baptist served in preparation for Jesus' ministry.

Our text for that lesson is followed by an account that leads into the study before us. Luke 3:21, 22 says, "Now when all the people were baptized, it came to pass, that Jesus also being baptized, and praying, the heaven was opened, and the Holy Ghost descended in a bodily shape like a dove upon him, and a voice came from heaven, which said, Thou art my beloved Son; in thee I am well pleased."

At this point, signalling the Lord's emergence into public ministry at the age of thirty, Luke inserts Jesus' genealogy. Then he picks up the narrative where he left it with Jesus' baptism.

Who could have told Luke what happened after this? (Luke 1:1, 2). Only Jesus could have known what happened during those next forty days. Clearly He had His own reasons for telling the apostles, and Luke could hear it from them.

At Jesus' baptism He accepted the awesome responsibilities of Messiah's ministry. How would He conduct that ministry? How would He fulfill His commitment? As if the prospect itself were not enough, Satan, the archenemy of God and slanderer of His saints, invaded the Savior's wild privacy in an all-out effort to warp His course and abort His ministry. Every temptation was directed with devilish cunning to strike Jesus where He was most vulnerable. This the Lord's people needed to know, and so Luke recorded it.

Wherever and whenever God's person enters a new relationship or makes a new resolution, Satan's similar tactics may be expected. Those tactics need to be met with similar weapons of the Word. Jesus' victory thus becomes sharable with all. So today we share it!

I. Jesus Becomes Vulnerable (Luke 4:1, 2)

The highest wave in the sea is commonly followed by the deepest trough. So also in human experience the highest exaltation may be followed by the deepest depression. (Compare the story of Elijah after his victory at Mount Carmel—1 Kings 18, 19.) At His baptism Jesus received the visible presence of the Holy Spirit, and God's own voice acknowledged His pleasure in His one and only Son. Jesus' human nature became an immediate battleground for elation and depression, for high resolve and persistent questions. If ever He would be susceptible to Satan's wiles, now was the time.

1. And Jesus being full of the Holy Ghost returned from Jordan, and was led by the Spirit into the wilderness.

A notable feature in Luke's Gospel is his emphasis on the Holy Spirit as pervasive presence in the life of Jesus. Now, having come upon the Lord at His baptism, the Spirit took possession of Him and "driveth him" (Mark 1:12) to the place of His severe testing. God does not tempt His people, but He permits them—even His Son—to be tested. The same Spirit is available, however, to strengthen the tempted one to stand the test (1 Corinthians 10:13)

So now Jesus, who had come "from Galilee to Jordan unto John, to be baptized of him" (Matthew 3:13), turned away from the river into the *wilderness*. The same word, translated *desert*, is used of the uninhabited region where John the Baptist lived and conducted his ministry (Luke 1:80). Tradition points to the Judean desert west of the Dead Sea as the place of Jesus' temptations. The Arabian Desert east of the Dead Sea is also considered as a possibility. The significant fact is that Jesus was without human support or sustenance, alone "with the wild beasts" (Mark 1:13) in His period of trial.

2. Being forty days tempted of the devil. And in those days he did eat nothing: and when they were ended, he afterward hungered.

It seems that Jesus was so completely absorbed in questions and contemplations of His mission as Messiah and Savior that He was unaware of normal needs and appetites until His hunger became overwhelming. Moses on the "holy mountain" (Exodus 34:28), and Elijah in the same area (1 Kings 19:8) engaged in similar periods of withdrawal. Jesus must have shared the scant water sources with the desert-dwelling animals, but paid no attention to the locusts and wild honey on which John the Baptist fed. All the while His very real accuser and slanderer— the devil—was at hand, probing and searching for any weakness he might exploit to disarm and destroy the Savior. Three specific temptations, coming when hunger and weakness had drained Jesus' physical resources and rendered Him most vulnerable, are described for us. Others during the weeks in the wilderness, plus continual temptations throughout Jesus' ministry, surely justify the summary statement of Hebrews 4:15: "We have not a high priest which cannot be touched with the feeling of our infirmities; but was in all points tempted like as we are, yet without sin."

II. Satan Attacks; Jesus Responds (Luke 4:3-13)

A. How Will He Use God's Gifts? (vv. 3, 4)

3. And the devil said unto him, If thou be the Son of God, command this stone that it be made bread.

There is a brutal reality in the trials described here. The first is based on the physical necessities of the moment. Satan and Jesus both knew that He was in fact the Son of God, able to use His powers in the manner Satan suggested. Jesus didn't need to prove anything. But His forty-day fast had brought Him beyond the point of ordinary hunger. How much longer could His physical body survive? What would happen to that long expected Messianic ministry if it should end in starvation before it began? Didn't Jesus owe it to the world to protect and preserve himself? And that stone lying there probably did look like a flat cake or loaf of bread. What could possibly be wrong with meeting such a practical necessity with the powers so obviously available?

4. And Jesus answered him, saying, It is written, That man shall not live by bread alone, but by every word of God.

Immediately apparent is Jesus' total confidence in Scripture. This Word of God was the final word. Even Satan recognized that it was so.

The book of Deuteronomy provided the Savior with many of His summary statements, including this from Deuteronomy 8:3: "He humbled thee, and suffered thee to hunger, and fed thee with manna . . . that he might make thee know that man doth not live by bread only, but by every word that proceedeth out of the mouth of the Lord doth man live." In this passage Moses spoke of another wilderness, where the people of God were allowed to hunger in order that they might learn to depend on God, who had brought the world into being with His word. With that same word He provided the manna that stayed their hunger and taught them that He, the provider, was more important than any part of His provision.

This is the key to any decision one might make when he or she, like Jesus, embarks on a course or a career. Life's ultimate purpose is to honor, serve, and draw near to God. Any choice that ignores that principle is going to be a wrong choice!

THE DESTROYING DECEIVER

Near Cape Hatteras in North Carolina is a place where hundreds of ships have run aground. In many cases it was accidental, but some were misled by unscrupulous men of Nag's Head, a village where a horse was led back and forth on stormy nights with a lantern tied to its chin. Helmsmen, trying to find their way in a storm, mistook the bobbing lantern for the stern light of a ship making a safe passage. Following it, they ran aground in the shallow water, where their ships became pickings for the thieves who stripped them.

In a book on temptation, Charles Durham compares the work of Satan to the lying lantern of Nag's Head. He is a deceiver who seeks to turn people away from safety within the will of God.   —W. P.

B. What Does He Want Most of All?
(vv. 5-8)

The events recorded here did not necessarily happen in quick succession or in this order. Luke presents two temptations in the wilderness, then one in Jerusalem. Matthew 4:1-11 reverses the order of the second and third. We are helped by knowing that the writers did not get together to contrive any artificial agreement, but each told the truth.

5. And the devil, taking him up into a high mountain, showed unto him all the kingdoms of the world in a moment of time.

Such an instantaneous view of the inhabited earth would be materially impossible from any point in Israel. We must be dealing here with a miraculous vision or a mental perception of the whole world based on the part that was seen. Satan presented the view, and Jesus saw it. That was the basis of a real temptation.

visual 4

6, 7. And the devil said unto him, All this power will I give thee, and the glory of them: for that is delivered unto me; and to whomsoever I will, I give it. If thou therefore wilt worship me, all shall be thine.

Satan was the classic "con artist," judging what his victim wanted most in all the world, and promising instant gratification of the wish.

Jesus did not challenge the boast made by this father of lies and liars. There was enough truth in it to create a real temptation. Jesus later referred to Satan as "the prince of this world" (John 12:31; 14:30). It was a title supported by the lives and accomplishments of Roman emperors and their puppet kings ruling Israel. Using all kinds of wickedness to maintain their power, these men lived in licentious luxury. Yet they accomplished much in building up the empire.

Preachers, politicians, and promoters all are frequently advised to learn early who wields the "real power" in their communities; then to do what is required, including necessary adjustment of principles, to keep those powers friendly and supportive.

So Satan offered Jesus a deal. Instead of having to battle the devil every step of the way in His life and ministry, the Savior Messiah could find the way made easy, just by cooperating sensibly with the ruler of "the real world"—bowing down to him and his way of doing things.

Does it sound familiar? It was, in fact, this temptation to avoid the cross that jabbed Jesus repeatedly, as in Peter's rejection of the Lord's teaching about death (Matthew 16:21-23) and again in Gethsemane (Mark 14:32-42).

8. And Jesus answered and said unto him, Get thee behind me, Satan: for it is written, Thou shalt worship the Lord thy God, and him only shalt thou serve.

Jesus seems to have been stung sharply, perhaps by the massive arrogance of the adversary, and perhaps by the force of the temptation. His reply is again in words from Deuteronomy: "Thou shalt fear the Lord thy God, and serve him" (6:13) and "Thou shalt have none other gods before me" (5:7). The same commandment, repeated with persistent force in many and varied expressions, provides a solid core of Old Testament teaching. To violate that precept would be to nullify any meaningful relationship with the living God. Jesus later responded to Satan's offer in clear and timeless terms: "What is a man profited, if he shall gain the whole world, and lose his own soul?" (Matthew 16:26). God was, and must always be, the ultimate value!

C. Does He Believe God Completely?
(vv. 9-12)

If Jesus could not be persuaded to adopt Satan's program outright, perhaps He could be enticed to another program, a seemingly pious one, to gain instant messiahship. Thus He could be lured away from the hard ministry of teaching and sacrifice prophesied in Isaiah 53. Just how completely did Jesus believe the Father who claimed His sole devotion?

9-11. And he brought him to Jerusalem, and set him on a pinnacle of the temple, and said unto him, If thou be the Son of God, cast thyself down from hence: for it is written, He shall give his angels charge over thee, to keep thee: and in their hands they shall bear thee up, lest at any time thou dash thy foot against a stone.

Matthew 4:5 says Satan "taketh him up into the holy city." That suggests that there were throngs of worshipers gathered where they might see the spectacle Satan suggested. As to the *pinnacle of the temple,* two suggestions are made. One names a lofty platform, from which speakers could address the throngs that were gathered far below in the temple courts. The other suggests a porch at the edge of the temple area, overlooking the Kidron Valley some three hundred feet below. The leap to land unharmed—certainly possible for the Son of God—from either place would be spectacular enough to secure instant Messianic recognition from the crowds. And wasn't that the office Jesus came to fulfill?

Satan changed two significant phrases in quoting Psalm 91:11, 12. The psalm speaks of keeping *thee in all thy ways.* To do what Satan suggested would be to step out of Jesus' proper ways. And the psalm does not say *at any time.* It is highly questionable whether this time and this use of the Scriptural promise made to humble, trusting saints would qualify one to be kept in charge by angels in all one's ways.

Jesus was, in fact, ministered to by angels after the period of temptation (Matthew 4:11; Mark 1:13), but it was not in response to anything like Satan's suggestion.

12. And Jesus answering said unto him, It is said, Thou shalt not tempt the Lord thy God.

With this one brief saying from Scripture Jesus brought to the informed mind—and Satan is not stupid—a complete and sufficient reply. Again from Deuteronomy (6:16) we read, "Ye shall not tempt the Lord your God, as ye tempted him in Massah." That calls up the story from Exodus 17:1-7, telling of God's bringing water from a wilderness rock to quench thirst and quiet the complaining children of Israel. The final verse says, "He called the name of the place Massah [meaning *temptation*] . . . because they tempted the Lord, saying, Is the Lord among us, or not?"

There is the point! The people of Israel did not believe God's assurances, so they tested Him to see whether He meant what He said. So what might seem an act of courageous faith would really be an expression of doubt: "If you are there, God, prove it by doing what I demand!"

Jesus refused to claim a cut-rate messiahship, especially if it meant testing God presumptuously by inviting disaster. "Blessed," He said, "are they that have not seen, and yet have believed" (John 20:29).

D. When Will the Next Attack Come?
(v. 13)

13. And when the devil had ended all the temptation, he departed from him for a season.

Phillips' translation renders this verse, "When the devil had exhausted every kind of temptation, he withdrew until his next opportunity." Jesus was indeed tempted from all directions, as we are, with appeals to the flesh, to pride, and to the avoidance of conflict. But His temptations were peculiarly adapted to Him in His deity and messiahship. Satan tried them all, but was beaten back at every turn by the truth of God's Word. So with Jesus it happened according to the later word of His brother James (4:7): "Resist the devil, and he will flee from you."

But Satan's retreat is always *for a season,* for a time, to wait for another occasion. In the meantime, we need to develop our skills with the sword of the Spirit, the Word of God.

III. Jesus Carries Out His Commitment (Luke 4:14, 15)

By comparing Luke's Gospel with the others—especially John—we learn that several months' time and much activity occurred between Jesus' wilderness temptation and His major ministry in Galilee. In Judea He met several Galileans who later became His apostles (John 1:35-51). At a wedding feast in Galilee, He performed His first miracle (John 2:1-12). At Jerusalem for the Passover, He taught in the temple and drove out the money changers (John 2:13-25). There also He conversed with Nicodemus (John 3:1-21).

Throughout Judea He preached fruitfully among the people (John 3:22-4:2). Turning northward toward Galilee, He taught for several days in Samaria (John 4:3-45).

14. And Jesus returned in the power of the Spirit into Galilee: and there went out a fame of him through all the region round about.

Mark 1:14 says, "Now after that John [the Baptist] was put in prison, Jesus came into Galilee, preaching the gospel of the kingdom of God." *Galilee* was a fertile and well populated area west of the Jordan and the Sea of Galilee. Its cosmopolitan citizenry of both Jews and Gentiles was generally more receptive than were the Judeans. It became the scene of Jesus' most fruitful ministry. John 4:45 says of His arrival that "the Galileans received him, having seen all the things that he did at Jerusalem at the feast [Passover]: for they also went unto the feast." Having been tested and tempered, both by Satan and by critics in Judea and Samaria, Jesus was ready to proceed with His most productive ministry.

15. And he taught in their synagogues, being glorified of all.

Matthew's account of this ministry occupies more than five chapters, beginning and ending with this summary statement: "Jesus went about all Galilee, teaching in their synagogues, and preaching the gospel of the kingdom, and healing all manner of sickness and all manner of disease among the people" (Matthew 4:23; 9:35). His generally enthusiastic popular reception was tempered by some criticism among the Pharisees

---

Home Daily Bible Readings

Monday, Dec. 20—John Baptized for Moral Action (Matthew 3:1-12)
Tuesday, Dec. 21—God's Beloved Son (Matthew 3:13-17)
Wednesday, Dec. 22—Temptations: Bread, Power, and Glory (Luke 4:1-8)
Thursday, Dec. 23—Display Your Power (Luke 4:9-11)
Friday, Dec. 24—Wise-Men Seek Jesus (Matthew 2:1-6)
Saturday, Dec. 25—Wise-Men Worship Jesus (Matthew 2:7-12)
Sunday, Dec. 26—Pleased by the Beloved Son (Isaiah 42:1-9)

---

and by rejection in His hometown synagogue at Nazareth (Luke 4:16-32). But, having won the approval of Heaven, He was content.

Conclusion

A. Blessings of Trial

The final note on Jesus' time of temptation is unqualified rejoicing! Hear it from His brother James: "Consider it pure joy, my brothers, whenever you face trials of many kinds, because you know that the testing of your faith develops perseverance. Perseverance must finish its work so that you may be mature and complete, not lacking anything" (James 1:2-4, *New International Version*).

The victory won by the Lord alone in the desert has been shared with us all, first in His ministry for our salvation, and continually in His example and His Spirit to enable our triumphs over the tempter. Hallelujah!

STRUGGLING FOR MATURITY

Jesus was "tempted in every way, just as we are—yet was without sin" (Hebrews 4:15, *New International Version*). "Because he himself suffered when he was tempted, he is able to help those who are being tempted" (Hebrews 2:18, *New International Version*). All of us face trials and temptations, and Jesus identifies with us in this experience.

In the book mentioned earlier, Charles Durham tells of a man who watched an emperor moth emerge from its cocoon. For a long time the moth tried to struggle through a small opening. Hoping to help, the man took a pair of scissors and enlarged the opening. The moth crawled out with a large body and shriveled wings, and soon died. Apparently the struggle was necessary for developing the wings.

James urges us to consider it joy when we face trials, because the struggle with them develops perseverance and maturity (James 1:2-4). It is part of the process that turns a worm into a butterfly.   —W. P.

B. Let Us Pray

To You, our God and Father, we would bring highest praise for Jesus, who for our sakes endured trials He did not deserve in order that we might participate in the victories we could not win. May our loving commitment to You become daily more like His, single-minded and unswervingly directed by Your Word. Amen.

C. Thought to Remember

Like Jesus, let us trust God completely, worship God only, and believe God without special demonstration.

Learning by Doing

This page contains an alternate lesson plan emphasizing learning activities. Classes desiring such student involvement will find these suggestions helpful.

Learning Goals

After this study each adult will:

1. Identify root causes of temptation that are revealed in the text and related Scriptures.

2. Explain how these specific temptations are representative of all temptation.

3. Explain how Jesus mastered the devil.

4. Adopt Jesus' style of resisting temptation, the "It-is-written" approach.

Into the Lesson

At the door of the room, put the following articles on a table: an open box of chocolates, a "WET PAINT" sign, three one-dollar bills, a TV Guide, and/or other things that represent temptation. Listen to comments of arriving class members. When all are assembled, repeat some of the comments to the whole group.

On each seat have a popular news weekly, a magazine, or a section of newspaper. (You can enlist students in advance to provide some of these.) Ask the learners to look through them to find temptations and/or reports of people who succumbed to temptation. Both will be easy to find, for many advertisements are obviously tempting, and many news stories tell of people who yielded to temptation. As the students "show and tell" their findings, list them on the chalkboard.

Give these references to six students:

James 1:14, 15	Genesis 25:29-34
1 Timothy 6:10	Acts 5:1-5
2 Samuel 11:2-5	John 6:15

As these are read one by one, ask the class to relate each one to something on the chalkboard list. Matches will be obvious.

Into the Word

Enlist two good readers to read Matthew 4:1-11 and Luke 4:1-13. Give both readers the following list of verse numbers to show how they are to read by turns: verse 1 of Matthew followed by verse 1 of Luke, and so on: 1—1; 2—2; 3—3; 4—4; 5—5; 6—6,7; 7—8; 8, 9—9-11; 10—12; 11—13.

Before the reading, tell the listeners to watch for things that are alike in the two records and for things that are different. After the reading, let them tell what likenesses and differences they noticed. If you prefer, you can interrupt the reading to discuss likenesses and differences instead

of waiting till the end. Use the lesson writer's comments as needed to help with the discussion. Point out that there is no contradiction: neither Bible writer denies anything the other says.

Into Life

Give these Scriptures to different students:

Exodus 20:14	Philippians 3:18, 19
Proverbs 20:1	Ephesians 4:25
Malachi 3:8-10	1 Thessalonians 5:16-18
Romans 12:2	Hebrews 10:24, 25

While they are finding the passages, remark that in each temptation the devil said "If" and Jesus answered "It is written." Then read, one by one, the following temptations that misuse Scripture and begin with "if." After reading each one, ask which student has found an appropriate Scripture to respond with "It is written." (Here the appropriate passage is noted after each "if" statement.)

1. If your boss at the office makes sexual advances, God does say, "Servants, be obedient to them that are your masters" (Ephesians 6:5). *Exodus 20:14.*

2. If you are short of money, God does not want an offering from you, for "He careth for you" (1 Peter 5:7). *Malachi 3:8-10*

3. If you are invited to a Sunday-morning picnic, remember "The Sabbath was made for man" (Mark 2:27). Isn't that true of the Lord's Day too? *Hebrews 10:24, 25*

4. If God didn't want you to eat all those rich foods, He wouldn't have provided them. "Every creature of God is good" (1 Timothy 4:4). *Philippians 3:18, 19*

5. If time is limited, cut out prayer. "Your Father knoweth what things ye have need of" (Matthew 6:8). *1 Thessalonians 5:16-18*

6. If the truth hurts, lie a little. God says, "Speak not evil one of another" (James 4:11). *Ephesians 4:25*

7. Don't worry if you go along with the crowd in some minor wrongdoing. Become "all things to all men" (1 Corinthians 9:22). *Romans 12:2*

8. If you like to drink beer or liquor, go ahead. "There is nothing unclean of itself" (Romans 14:14). *Proverbs 20:1*

Suggest that each student keep a diary this week with this daily entry: "Today I was tempted to _____, but it is written _____."

Let's Talk It Over

The questions on this page are designed to encourage review of the lesson Scriptures and to promote discussion of the lesson by the class. The answers provided are only discussion starters. Let your class talk it over from there.

1. We can learn important lessons from Jesus' responses to temptation. First, what can we learn from His response to the temptation to indulge the physical body?

Hunger seems less after a few days of fasting; but after many days, when the body has used up its reserves, hunger becomes very strong. At this time Satan tempted Jesus to use His miraculous power to satisfy the demands of His physical body. Jesus' reply indicated that He trusted God to provide His needs.

Satan tempts us to give high priority to the demands of our physical body, even to ignore God's laws in order to get what we need. We must learn to trust God to provide what we truly need. We must prefer to starve rather than steal.

2. Satan proposed to give Jesus the world without a fight if Jesus would just worship him. What can we learn from Jesus' refusal?

Satan is always trying to lure us into a "short cut" to our goals, even good and worthy goals; but his easy ways demand that we compromise our principles. Jesus shows us that if we allow anything to make us break God's laws, then we have made that thing more important to us than God. We should note that we can never serve God by violating His commands.

3. Satan said Jesus should force God to do a spectacular miracle that would win an instant following. What can we learn from Jesus' refusal?

Christians who are zealous for the Lord's work sometimes grow impatient. Satan whispers that we should launch some impossible program and depend on God to make it succeed. Jesus shows that we should follow the Lord rather than trying to make Him follow us. Christians with sincere trust in the Lord have been empowered to do mighty things, but never by trying to force Him to do the spectacular. Instead, we must make ourselves available for God to use when and how He desires.

4. The devil finally left Jesus until an opportune time arose for further temptation. What is an opportune time for temptation?

An opportune time for Satan is when he can either lure us or pressure us to disobey God. We create opportune times for him when we put ourselves in tempting situations. We are wise to avoid the things that we know tempt us. Sometimes, however, our very desire to obey presents an opportunity for Satan. He tries to pressure us by making it hard and costly to serve the Lord. We can count on him to take advantage of every opportunity, so we must be ready for his attacks.

5. What is the role of temptation and testing? Why does God allow it? How can we withstand it and even profit by it?

Obedience is an empty idea so long as it is easy and brings only rewards. We do not really learn the meaning of obedience until we do what God tells us even though we do not want to do it. It is hard to do it, and it costs us to do it. Jesus learned obedience by going to the cross even when He dreaded it. Temptation and testing give us the opportunity to learn the real meaning of obedience and thereby prove and refine our love and devotion to the Lord.

6. Jesus used the Scripture to refute each of Satan's temptations. In practical terms, how can we use the Scripture to resist Satan?

Jesus did not have to unroll a scroll and look up the references He needed; He had hidden God's Word in His heart so that it was there when He needed it. Moreover, He understood the principles the Word taught, and He could apply them properly. There is no easy way for us to gain such mastery of Scripture. We must study till we understand the meaning of the Word and remember it. When we do this, Satan will not be able to fool us with his lies.

7. Apparently Satan appeared to Jesus in person, in a form easily recognized. It might be easier for us if he would do the same today. Then we would be on guard. How does he tempt us? How can we recognize him?

Satan tempts through things we see and read and hear, through TV, books, and conversations. He tempts through friends, as when Peter rebuked Jesus for talking about His death (Matthew 16:21-23). He tempts through enemies who dare us to do wrong. We can recognize Satan's presence whenever we are impelled to disobey God, even in some very small way.

Jesus States His Mission

DEVOTIONAL READING: Isaiah 61:1, 2; 58:6.

LESSON SCRIPTURE: Luke 4:16-28.

PRINTED TEXT: Luke 4:16-28.

Luke 4:16-28

16 And he came to Nazareth, where he had been brought up: and, as his custom was, he went into the synagogue on the sabbath day, and stood up for to read.

17 And there was delivered unto him the book of the prophet Isaiah. And when he had opened the book, he found the place where it was written,

18 The Spirit of the Lord is upon me, because he hath anointed me to preach the gospel to the poor; he hath sent me to heal the brokenhearted, to preach deliverance to the captives, and recovering of sight to the blind, to set at liberty them that are bruised,

19 To preach the acceptable year of the Lord.

20 And he closed the book, and he gave it again to the minister, and sat down. And the eyes of all them that were in the synagogue were fastened on him.

21 And he began to say unto them, This day is this Scripture fulfilled in your ears.

22 And all bare him witness, and wondered at the gracious words which proceeded out of his mouth. And they said, Is not this Joseph's son?

23 And he said unto them, Ye will surely say unto me this proverb, Physician, heal thyself: whatsoever we have heard done in Capernaum, do also here in thy country.

24 And he said, Verily I say unto you, No prophet is accepted in his own country.

25 But I tell you of a truth, many widows were in Israel in the days of Elijah, when the heaven was shut up three years and six months, when great famine was throughout all the land;

26 But unto none of them was Elijah sent, save unto Zarephath, a city of Sidon, unto a woman that was a widow.

27 And many lepers were in Israel in the time of Elisha the prophet; and none of them was cleansed, saving Naaman the Syrian.

28 And all they in the synagogue, when they heard these things, were filled with wrath.

GOLDEN TEXT: The Spirit of the Lord is upon me, because he hath anointed me to preach the gospel to the poor; he hath sent me to heal the brokenhearted, to preach deliverance to the captives, and recovering of sight to the blind, to set at liberty them that are bruised, to preach the acceptable year of the Lord.—Luke 4:18, 19.

The Story of Jesus

Unit 2. Luke: Ministry in Galilee

(Lessons 5-9)

Lesson Aims

This study should equip the class member to:

1. Tell briefly in his or her own words about Jesus' visit to the synagogue at Nazareth.

2. Show several ways in which Jesus fulfilled the prophecy of Isaiah 61:1, 2.

3. Cite one or more ways in which he or she will participate in the ministry rendered by Jesus.

Lesson Outline

INTRODUCTION
  A. Mission Statement
  B. When Did It Happen?
I. MESSIAH'S ASSIGNMENT (Luke 4:16-19)
  A. The Reader (vv. 16, 17)
    His Custom
  B. The Reading (vv. 18, 19)
    Good News for the Poor
II. MESSIAH'S ACCEPTANCE (Luke 4:20-23)
  A. Jesus Accepts the Assignment (vv. 20, 21)
  B. Jesus Is Accepted Partially (vv. 22, 23)
III. MESSIAH'S AVAILABILITY (Luke 4:24-27)
  A. Hometown Prejudice Hinders It (v. 24)
  B. Elijah Reached Out to Sidon (vv. 25, 26)
  C. Elisha Reached Out to Syria (v. 27)
IV. NAZARETH'S ANGRY REJECTION (Luke 4:28)
CONCLUSION
  A. What Did You Expect?
  B. Prayer for the Home Folks
  C. Thought to Remember

Display visual 5 of the visuals packet and refer to it as you discuss the Messiah's mission as foretold by Isaiah. The visual is shown on page 157.

Introduction

A. Mission Statement

"Let's look again at your mission statement. It's time to give it your periodic review."

The visiting examiner was not talking about how many evangelists our Bible college supported in Cambodia. He wanted to know whether we were maintaining our ability to accomplish our purposes as a Christian college, and—more to the point—whether we were actually doing it. To know that, we had to keep that all-important mission statement in view.

The statement had been drawn up and adopted with a sense of genuine commitment. If other colleges and the prospective employers of our graduates were to respect our credits and degrees, they needed assurance that we had done for our students what we promised to do. The promise was contained in that mission statement, and we must keep it!

In today's lesson we look at a mission statement for Jesus' messiahship. The prophet Isaiah had written it some seven centuries earlier, and here Jesus accepted it as His own. This Promised One was also to be the Savior, Jesus Christ the Lord (Matthew 1:21; Luke 2:11).

Jesus had already come into conflict with Satan on the basis of that statement (last week's lesson). Satan recognized Jesus as the Messiah, but tried to change the nature of His ministry. Today we shall see that the people of Nazareth approved the nature of Messiah's ministry, but refused to consider Jesus' claim to be that Messiah! Jesus himself never lost sight of His Scripturally stated mission. We need to see it, too—His mission as He fulfilled it, and our related mission as He enables it.

B. When Did It Happen?

The final verses of last week's lesson text (Luke 4:14, 15; compare Matthew 4:23) said that Jesus came from Judea into Galilee, where He "taught in their synagogues, being glorified of all." He seems to have taught in synagogues throughout Galilee, and to have performed miracles at the seaside city of Capernaum (Luke 4:23), before He "came to Nazareth," some twenty-five miles away among the hills.

Matthew 13:53-58 and Mark 6:1-6 tell of Jesus' teaching in the synagogue in "his own country" and being rejected in much the same way as Luke 4:16-28 tells it. Some students think that is the same visit that Luke records, and that it took place much later than Luke indicates. It seems more likely that Matthew and Mark tell of another visit at a later time.

I. Messiah's Assignment (Luke 4:16-19)

A. The Reader (vv. 16, 17)

16. And he came to Nazareth, where he had been brought up: and, as his custom was, he went into the synagogue on the sabbath day, and stood up for to read.

Nazareth, the hometown of Joseph and of Mary (Luke 1:26, 27), became their home again after their sojourn in Egypt to escape the murderous jealousy of Herod against the newly-born "King of the Jews" (Matthew 2:13-15, 19-22).

At Nazareth Jesus was *brought up,* much as the sons of godly families have always been brought up. He knew and shared the rugged work habits of Joseph as a carpenter (Matthew 13:55; Mark 6:3). He was instructed in the Scriptures so that by the time He was twelve years old the scholars at the temple in Jerusalem were amazed at His "understanding and his answers," even as Mary and Joseph were amazed at His independence. Yet as a teenager he continued under the discipline of His earthly parents (Luke 2:41-52). Attendance with His family at the Sabbath meetings in the synagogue was habitual in His upbringing. With it all, He developed steadily in mind, in body, and in social graces. The neighbors in Nazareth couldn't think of anything to distinguish Him greatly from any of the other boys brought up in their town.

The *custom* Jesus followed in regard to the synagogue service seems to have been twofold. In His youth He was accustomed to *be there,* with other members of the congregation. Now He was accustomed to *teaching* in the synagogues wherever He went.

The synagogue services lent themselves readily to that kind of participation. A *ruler* was responsible for the service and decided who was to speak and who was to read the Scriptures, whether by invitation or by permission. A reading from the Pentateuch—the law of Moses—customarily came first, then a reading from the Prophets, and then the sermon. An *attendant* took care of the property, and especially the scrolls of sacred Scripture.

He who read from the Law or the Prophets was expected to do so standing, without support. And by custom he who taught would probably sit, cross-legged as did the other men of the congregation, on the floor. A raised area elevated the speaker to be seen, however. So Jesus, by invitation or permission of the synagogue ruler, became the reader of the Prophet, and speaker for the occasion.

17. And there was delivered unto him the book of the prophet Isaiah. And when he had opened the book, he found the place where it was written.

Events were following a customary order. The *book*—or scroll—*of the prophet Isaiah* would be substantial. The Isaiah Scroll found among the famous Dead Sea Scrolls stretches to a length of twenty-five feet unrolled. The columns of text, hand-lettered with meticulous care, are at right angles to the length of the roll. Any passage would have to be found, without the help of chapter or verse numbers, by rolling the parchment from one spindle to the other until the sought-for material appeared in its familiar con-

---

> ### How to Say It
>
> SAREPTA. Sa-*rep*-ta.
> ZAREPHATH. *Zar*-e-fath.

text. Any reader in the synagogue had to know his Scripture!

A reader might insert brief interpretive comments as he read the passage, or in some circumstances he might translate into the commonly spoken Aramaic language what he was reading from the classical Hebrew. Hence we find some differences between Isaiah 61:1, 2 as it appears in our Bibles and as Luke records Jesus' reading of it. We cannot say whether the passage was assigned as reading for the day or Jesus chose it for himself. In either case, the choice is providentially appropriate.

HIS CUSTOM

Jesus was accustomed to be in the synagogue on the Sabbath Day. What are your customs, the habits of your life? If you were to list the things you do most, what would be on the list? Watching the evening news? Reading the Sunday paper? Reading the Bible to your children? Playing golf? Fishing? Baking? Would your list reflect a Christian mind-set? Would it show a yearning for the things of God, as did the priorities of Jesus?

Jesus knew God and the Scriptures well. Probably some things said and done in the synagogue did not please Him, but He was there. He did not disassociate himself from the people dedicated to the worship of God, even though they blundered. We need that same kind of consistency and faithfulness in our worship. —W. P.

B. The Reading (vv. 18, 19)

18. The Spirit of the Lord is upon me, because he hath anointed me to preach the gospel to the poor; he hath sent me to heal the brokenhearted, to preach deliverance to the captives, and recovering of sight to the blind, to set at liberty them that are bruised.

This is one of several passages in which Isaiah described his assignment as a prophet or spokesman for God. Another is at Isaiah 42:1-4, where we read, "I have put my Spirit upon him."

Anointing—the application of oil—was used in conveying the authority and responsibilities of office to a king, a priest, or a prophet. *Messiah* or *Christ* means "anointed." This gesture was linked to God's bestowal of such measure of His Spirit as would enable the appointed one to do the work assigned to him.

Isaiah 61:1 appears in a prophecy of the Israelites' return to Judea at the end of their captivity in Babylon. It is remarkable especially in that Isaiah's words were written almost a hundred years before the Babylonian captivity began!

The *gospel*—good news—of God's special care for *the poor* (*meek* in Isaiah 61:1), appears throughout the Old Testament Scriptures. Included in God's care are the *brokenhearted* sufferers of bereavement and disappointment. (This clause does not appear in some texts and translations of Luke, but it does appear in the Isaiah passage).

Deliverance to the captives is the central message concerning those who were to be released by Cyrus, king of Persia, in Daniel's latter days. *Recovering of sight to the blind* does not appear in Isaiah 61:1, but applies especially to Jesus' fulfillment in delivering and releasing those who were captives to blindness, both physical and spiritual. *To set at liberty them that are bruised* may be translated literally "To send away them that are shattered." It is to heal the wounded ones and restore them to useful activity. This is God's ministry to be announced by His messenger.

19. To preach the acceptable year of the Lord.

Isaiah's hearers might think immediately of the year of Jubilee described in Leviticus 25:8-17, when slaves would go free, when land that had been sold for debt would be returned to its original owners, and the workmen and their fields would enjoy rest. This was to take place every fiftieth year under the law. The *year*, or time of Israel's release from captivity, would be announced as a similar evidence of God's favor.

Yet Isaiah's prophecy sounds a depth not to be found in Israel's release from captivity in Babylon. The prophecy became a part of the Jews' hope for a greater anointed One—their Messiah.

GOOD NEWS FOR THE POOR

Jesus read a passage that focused on the Messiah's concern for the poor, the prisoners, the disabled, and the oppressed. Such people are in our midst today. Current discussions often center on homelessness and poverty, overcrowded jails and burgeoning crime, handicapped people and their needs, and civil rights. Jesus was concerned about such matters. Are we?

Recent statistics tell us that during the last thirty years the gap between the richest and poorest nations has doubled. In 1960 a person in the wealthiest countries made thirty times as much as a person in the poorest. In 1990 that person made sixty times as much as a person in the poorest of the countries. How would Jesus want us to relate to the poor of the world?

However we answer that question, we must remember that many of the poor have problems worse then hunger and homelessness. Jesus did feed the hungry and heal the sick, but His greater aim was "to seek and to save that which was lost" (Luke 19:10). That is our purpose too.

—W. P.

II. Messiah's Acceptance
(Luke 4:20-23)

A. Jesus Accepts the Assignment
(vv. 20, 21)

20. And he closed the book, and he gave it again to the minister, and sat down. And the eyes of all of them that were in the synagogue were fastened on him.

In the usual fashion Jesus rolled up the scroll and delivered it to the synagogue attendant to be replaced in its cabinet. Then He sat down in the area provided for the speaker.

His mother, His brothers, and His sisters may well have been among those whose various emotions riveted their attention on Him. His reputation as a miracle worker and an eloquent speaker had preceded Him. He had just read to them a moving passage of Messianic prophecy. What would this young neighbor say about it?

21. And he began to say unto them, This day is this Scripture fulfilled in your ears.

How is that for openers? This Messianic prophecy was fulfilled while you heard it read! And He went on from there. Obviously we do not have the entire message before us, but this is enough. The man before them was claiming that Isaiah's writing applied to himself more accurately than it applied to Isaiah. He was the Messiah foretold in prophecy, and this was the pattern of His ministry, to the body for time and to the spirit for eternity.

The anointing "Spirit of the Lord" had come upon Him at His baptism. His fullness of the Spirit became a theme of Luke's Gospel.

"Blessed be ye *poor*" (Luke 6:20), Jesus would say in proclaiming the good news of salvation to them as much as to kings and millionaires, and much easier for them to accept.

Healing of the "brokenhearted" marked His ministry, but never more powerfully than in restoring certain of the dead to their loved ones (Luke 7:11-15; 8:49-56; John 11:1-44). Even this is overshadowed, however, by His assurance to all mankind: "I am the resurrection, and the life: he that believeth in me, though he were dead, yet shall he live: and whosoever liveth and believeth in me shall never die" (John 11:25, 26).

We do not read of Jesus' "delivering captives" from material slavery or prison during His earthly ministry (see Matthew 11:2-6), but He released a multitude from bondage to demons, and

His eternal ministry is geared to delivering mankind from slavery to sin and its guilt.

The Gospels tell of several occasions when Jesus gave "sight to the blind" (Matthew 9:27-31; Mark 8:22-26; John 9). He made it clear that spiritual blindness—the failure to see God and His gifts—was the more serious affliction He came to remove (John 9:35-41).

The "acceptable year of the Lord" had arrived! "When the fulness of the time was come, God sent forth his Son . . . to redeem them that were under the law, that we might receive the adoption of sons" (Galatians 4:4, 5). This was the grand Jubilee to which all the years of temporary relief had pointed.

B. Jesus Is Accepted Partially
(vv. 22, 23)

It took a while for Jesus' words to sink in. The hearers first liked what they heard; then they began to perceive how thoroughly this conflicted with their established opinions.

22. And all bare him witness, and wondered at the gracious words which proceeded out of his mouth. And they said, Is not this Joseph's son?

The first responses were all complimentary. Jesus had justified the reports they had heard about the tender eloquence and the evidence of authority in His speech. It began in His boyhood, when at Jerusalem "all that heard him were astonished at his understanding and answers" (Luke 2:47). It continued as thousands hearing Him were astonished, "for he taught them as one having authority" (Matthew 7:28, 29). It impressed officers who were sent to arrest Him and came back empty-handed, declaring, "Never man spake like this man" (John 7:45, 46).

A change is noted, though, in the *and* (we would say *but*) that introduces the people's comment about Jesus' family. They did not know that He was *not* Joseph's son, and they were unprepared to accept the evidences that distinguished Him from His brothers and His neighbors. They had no need to say aloud what they were thinking. Jesus knew!

23. And he said unto them, Ye will surely say unto me this proverb, Physician, heal thyself: whatsoever we have heard done in Capernaum, do also here in thy country.

Jesus perceived that they were curious—and perhaps jealous—to see Him perform miracles such as those they had heard that He performed at Capernaum. That city was witness to many of His "mighty works," but seems to have profited little from the experience (Matthew 11:23). Nazareth would not see miracles because of their unbelief (Matthew 13:57, 58).

III. Messiah's Availability
(Luke 4:24-27)

A. Hometown Prejudice Hinders It
(v. 24)

24. And he said, Verily I say unto you, No prophet is accepted in his own country.

An expanded version of this statement appears in Mark 6:4: "A prophet is not without honor, but in his own country, and among his own kin, and in his own house." Members of Jesus' own family at one time doubted His sanity and sought to remove Him from the public scene (Mark 3:21, 32-35).

The Greek biographer Plutarch said, "You will find that few of the most prudent and wisest of mankind have been appreciated in their own country." Military heroes, athletes, and actors may be given grand receptions at home; but philosophers, prophets, and preachers, dealing with matters in which every man loves the voice of his own opinion, are not highly respected among their childhood playmates. Jesus was not.

The prophet who cannot serve his own people because of their unbelief may find a hearing and render help among foreigners. Jesus cited two Old Testament examples. These suggested something that was to become evident later: His gospel was for all the world, Gentile as well as Jewish.

B. Elijah Reached Out to Sidon
(vv. 25, 26)

25, 26. But I tell you of a truth, many widows were in Israel in the days of Elijah, when the heaven was shut up three years and six months, when great famine was throughout all the land; but unto none of them was Elijah sent, save unto Zarephath, a city of Sidon, unto a woman that was a widow.

First Kings 17:1-16 recounts this aspect of Elijah's conflict with wicked King Ahab of Israel. Ahab was punished by the long drought and famine that was over his kingdom and its

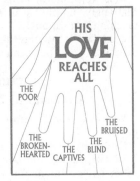

THE POOR

HIS
LOVE
REACHES
ALL

THE BRUISED

THE BROKEN-HEARTED   THE CAPTIVES   THE BLIND

visual 5

neighbors. Elijah found refuge outside of Israel, near the city of Sidon in Phoenicia, in a village called Zarephath, or Sarepta. The widow who shared with him the last of her food supply was rewarded by the miraculous continuance of that supply until food became available again. God's miracle thus came to a foreigner, rather than to a widow in Elijah's home country.

C. Elisha Reached Out to Syria (v. 27)

27. And many lepers were in Israel in the time of Elisha the prophet; and none of them was cleansed, saving Naaman the Syrian.

Second Kings 5:1-14 tells the story of Naaman, captain of the Syrian army in its campaigns against Israel. This enemy's leprosy was healed after he came to "the man of God" in Israel and obeyed (reluctantly) Elisha's instruction to dip himself seven times in the Jordan River. The healing miracle came to an enemy of Israel rather than to any of the lepers in Elisha's homeland.

IV. Nazareth's Angry Rejection (Luke 4:28)

28. And all they in the synagogue, when they heard these things, were filled with wrath.

Jesus' hearers that day were probably stung by His assumption of being superior to the prophet Isaiah—hence to themselves. His claim to fulfilling Messianic prophecy was more than they could understand or tolerate. His rebuke for their lack of faith in Him was even worse. But the crowning insult came with His implication that Gentiles were candidates for God's favor as much as they, His chosen people! (Compare Acts 22:21, 22.)

The measure of the Nazarenes' rage is seen in the verses immediately following our text. They hustled Jesus out of their town to a precipice from which they would have thrown Him to His death, but He escaped from their grasp. He made His way to Capernaum, which became the center for continuous teaching in other synagogues.

Most rejecters of Jesus' claims don't become that angry, simply because they do not take His teaching that seriously. Some Nazarenes, including the Lord's own brothers, finally became His disciples. How about you and your friends?

Conclusion

A. What Did You Expect?

Was ever a story more full of expected surprises?

Wait, now! If something is expected, how can it be surprising? Yet consider this account of Jesus' homecoming. You would certainly expect Jesus to visit Nazareth, and to attend the synagogue service, and to teach if the opportunity afforded, and to read from Isaiah the passage that described Messiah's ministry, and probably to announce His own purposes in relation to it. But why should He wait until His reputation was established and reached Nazareth ahead of Him? And who would expect Him to anticipate His neighbors' doubts concerning Him, and to confront them so bluntly with those doubts, and to add insult to injury by referring as He did to the prophets' help for Gentiles?

Parts of the account seem as natural to us as a summer shower, and parts of it shock us as a bolt of lightning. But the shocking parts are linked in truth with the natural, just as the lightning is linked with the rain.

What kind of servant/Messiah do we see? Just the kind who would later announce, "I am the way, the truth, and the life: no man cometh unto the Father, but by me" (John 14:6). Just the kind whose ministry would bring timely deeds of healing to the hurting ones, while making it abundantly clear that the ultimate purpose of that ministry was eternal, to save His people from their sins. He is Christ the Lord.

B. Prayer for the Home Folks

Our Father God, we thank You for sending Your Son to make His home for a while among us. Please help us to understand Him, as sharing our humanity, and being yet our eternal Lord. Help us to share His compassion for all those folk around us, for whom also He came and lived and died. In His name we pray. Amen.

C. Thought to Remember

Messiah's ministry is for those who recognize their need and accept His provision.

Home Daily Bible Readings

Monday, Dec. 27—Good News for Those in Need (Luke 4:16-19)
Tuesday, Dec. 28—No Prophet Is Acceptable at Home (Luke 4:20-24)
Wednesday, Dec. 29—Jesus Condemned Arrogance and Pride (Luke 4:25-32)
Thursday, Dec. 30—He Feeds His Flock (Isaiah 40:1-11)
Friday, Dec. 31—God's Laws Written in Our Hearts (Jeremiah 31:29-34)
Saturday, Jan. 1—Good Tidings for the Afflicted (Isaiah 61:1-6)
Sunday, Jan. 2—Righteousness and Praise Spring Forth (Isaiah 61:7-11)

Learning by Doing

This page contains an alternate lesson plan emphasizing learning activities. Classes desiring such student involvement will find these suggestions helpful.

Learning Goals

From today's study each adult will:

1. Describe and explain Jesus' reception in His hometown, Nazareth.

2. State Jesus' mission as it is revealed by Isaiah 61:1, 2 and in His ministry.

3. Understand and commit to a personal mission with the gospel.

Into the Lesson

As class members arrive, have the following unfinished statements on the chalkboard:

1. The place where I grew up was _____.
2. Our next-door neighbors were _____.
3. As a child I got in trouble by _____.
4. When I went back after a long absence, my hometown looked _____.

Get students to finish some of the statements, but don't let the talk go on more than six to eight minutes. Then remind the class that Jesus grew up in a small community where He knew almost every resident. When He was about thirty years old He went away for nearly a year, and then returned with a reputation for doing wonderful things He had never done in His hometown.

Into the Word

Select two of your best readers; ask them in advance to be ready to read Matthew 13:53-58 and Mark 6:1-6.

Tell the class the two will read two records of one time when Jesus preached in His hometown. Some people think our lesson text is another record of the same event, but it may be telling about an earlier time when Jesus went back home to Nazareth. Ask class members to watch Luke 4:16-28 in their own Bibles, and notice how it is different from the records in Matthew and Mark.

After the readings from Matthew and Mark, let hearers tell differences they noted. Record them briefly in three columns headed MATTHEW, MARK, and LUKE.

A number of differences may be noted. Matthew and Mark include Mary's name and mention Jesus' half-brothers and sisters. Mark notes the people called Jesus "the carpenter"; Matthew notes why Jesus did not do many mighty works in Nazareth; Mark notes Jesus' marveling at their unbelief. Others may be noted, but the most notable difference is that

Luke says Jesus read a prophecy of the Messiah and said it was being fulfilled in Him. Luke also tells more about the angry response and the reasons for it. These special features of the Luke record may be discussed fully, and the lesson writer's comments will help with the discussion.

Distribute paper and ask each student to write the numbers from 1 to 10 in a vertical column for a "Surprise—No Surprise" quiz. (A similar activity is included in the student book for this series.) Read the following statements one by one, asking each student to put S by its number if the act was a surprise, or N if it was no surprise. Let students explain their answers.

1. Jesus came to His hometown as He was preaching in the towns of Galilee.

2. Jesus attended the synagogue service when He was in Nazareth.

3. Jesus read from the Scripture and spoke in the synagogue service.

4. Jesus easily found the text He was going to read and explain.

5. Jesus turned to the book of Isaiah and read a prophecy of the Messiah.

6. Jesus said He was fulfilling Isaiah's prophecy of the Messiah.

7. Without being told, Jesus knew what His hearers were thinking.

8. Jesus used Old Testament incidents to illustrate His sermon.

9. Jesus indicated that God cared for foreign people as well as people of Israel.

10. Jesus' declarations made the people of Nazareth very angry.

Into Life

Get someone who letters well to use shelf paper and prepare a long banner reading, "1994 IS THE ACCEPTABLE YEAR OF THE LORD." To conclude the class session, read verse 19 of the text and put the following poster under the banner. Ask each student to think silently about his or her own answer to each question.

IN 1994

1. How can I preach the gospel to the poor?
2. How can I heal the brokenhearted?
3. How can I preach deliverance to someone?
4. How can I give sight to someone?
5. How can I help anyone who is bruised?

Close with a prayer for help in making 1994 the acceptable year of the Lord.

Let's Talk It Over

The questions on this page are designed to encourage review of the lesson Scriptures and to promote discussion of the lesson by the class. The answers provided are only discussion starters. Let your class talk it over from there.

1. Jesus said He had come to release the prisoners, give sight to the blind, and relieve the oppressed. How does Jesus free us today? How does He give us sight and relieve our oppression? How can we receive this deliverance?

Jesus frees us from being prisoners of sin and death. He gives us power to overcome sin. He gives us the light of spiritual truth and thus heals us of spiritual blindness. He relieves us of the oppression of guilt. To receive these blessings we must believe His words, submit to His authority, and obey His will. The citizens of Nazareth missed out on Jesus' blessings because they rejected Him. What have you done with Jesus?

2. The people of Jesus' hometown didn't believe that someone they knew so well (or thought they knew) could be the great Messiah. Today people who have grown up in the church sometimes fail to appreciate Jesus' greatness and power. What can we do to appreciate Him as we ought?

Many people would benefit form an in-depth study of what the Bible tells us about the Lord. This would include His preexistence as the Word, His life while on earth, and His return as the Lord of lords. People sometimes fail to appreciate the Lord simply because they don't know much about Him. In addition, it is important to have a healthy prayer life. We cannot know the Father or Son very well if we never talk with them. And we may not be aware of the Lord's involvement in our lives if we do not pray to Him and see the answers He gives.

3. Jesus read a description of His mission from Isaiah. What things are included in the mission of our church?

Our mission is much more than holding services every Sunday, calling on those in the hospital, marrying the young people, and burying the old. We must be active in spreading the gospel, starting with our own community and reaching out to the whole world. Also, we must be sure to bring believers to spiritual maturity. We do this through education, encouragement, and helping them work. Jesus tells us to be a light to the world. We do this by demonstrating integrity, compassion, and generosity in all our dealings with each other and with the world.

4. Each individual, too, should have a clear idea of his or her personal mission for the Lord. How can we develop a personal mission?

We begin by discovering our talents and spiritual gifts. Friends who know us well can give valuable insights into the gifts they see in us, but we need also to be honest in assessing our own abilities. Once our gifts have been identified, we can find opportunities for service in which those gifts will be effective. We ask the Lord's guidance as we look at the service opportunities. Then we commit ourselves to some ministry. We may change areas of service from time to time; but keep in mind that problems that arise do not mean we have chosen the wrong service. Satan always tries to stop a good work.

5. Jesus spoke out even though He knew His words would cause an uproar. Talk may cause an uproar in the church today. How can we know when to speak out, and when it is better to keep quiet?

One important question is whether a matter of principle is involved, or only a matter of opinion. Be very careful about this. Many congregational controversies are disputes about opinions and preferences rather than matters of doctrine or morals, but opinions and prejudices are often dressed up in the garb of principles. The Lord prayed for unity in His church, and that should be a high priority with us, too. As a rule, it is unwise to stir up heated controversy unless the mission of the church is being seriously hindered.

6. Sometimes our convictions force us to speak out on controversial issues. Friends may reject both our message and us personally because of our stand. How should we react to this?

It is very painful to lose a friend because of standing up for what we see to be right. Christian brothers should be able to trust each other's motives even when they disagree. If brothers or sisters withdraw from us, or even attack us as they attacked Jesus, we must be careful not to retaliate. It is important not to let anger or bitterness fill our hearts. Perhaps the best course of action is to stand firm but seek to minimize conflict. Always maintain self-control and display an attitude of love.

Jesus Heals the Sick

DEVOTIONAL READING: Mark 6:1-6a; 9:1-8.

LESSON SCRIPTURE: Luke 4:31-43.

PRINTED TEXT: Luke 4:31-43.

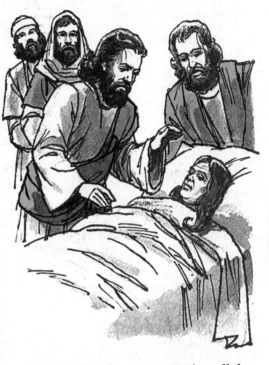

Luke 4:31-43

31 And [Jesus] came down to Capernaum, a city of Galilee, and taught them on the sabbath days.

32 And they were astonished at his doctrine: for his word was with power.

33 And in the synagogue there was a man, which had a spirit of an unclean devil, and cried out with a loud voice,

34 Saying, Let us alone; what have we to do with thee, thou Jesus of Nazareth? art thou come to destroy us? I know thee who thou art; the Holy One of God.

35 And Jesus rebuked him, saying, Hold thy peace, and come out of him. And when the devil had thrown him in the midst, he came out of him, and hurt him not.

36 And they were all amazed, and spake among themselves, saying, What a word is this! for with authority and power he commandeth the unclean spirits, and they come out.

37 And the fame of him went out into every place of the country round about.

38 And he arose out of the synagogue, and entered into Simon's house. And Simon's wife's mother was taken with a great fever; and they besought him for her.

39 And he stood over her, and rebuked the fever; and it left her: and immediately she arose and ministered unto them.

Jan 9

40 Now when the sun was setting, all they that had any sick with divers diseases brought them unto him; and he laid his hands on every one of them, and healed them.

41 And devils also came out of many, crying out, and saying, Thou art Christ the Son of God. And he rebuking them suffered them not to speak: for they knew that he was Christ.

42 And when it was day, he departed and went into a desert place: and the people sought him, and came unto him, and stayed him, that he should not depart from them.

43 And he said unto them, I must preach the kingdom of God to other cities also: for therefore am I sent.

GOLDEN TEXT: All they that had any sick with divers diseases brought them unto him; and he laid his hands on every one of them, and healed them.—Luke 4:40.

The Story of Jesus

Unit 2. Luke: Ministry in Galilee

(Lessons 5-9)

Lesson Aims

This lesson should enable the student to:

1. Relate at least two instances of Jesus' healing the sick and casting out demons.

2. Show the relationship between Jesus' healing ministry and His preaching ministry.

3. Adopt for himself or herself some activity related to Jesus' compassionate ministry.

Lesson Outline

INTRODUCTION

   A. Who Is the Healer?

   B. From Nazareth to Capernaum

I. IMPRESSIVE INSTRUCTION (Luke 4:31, 32)

   A. Continuing Work in a New Place (v. 31)

   B. New Power in Eternal Truth (v. 32)

II. CLEANSING COMMAND (Luke 4:33-37)

   A. Defeating a Demon (vv. 33-35)

      Be Quiet

   B. Amazing the Observers (vv. 36, 37)

      Wonderful Things

III. HEALING HANDS (Luke 4:38-41)

   A. Cooling a Fever (vv. 38, 39)

   B. Dispersing Diseases (v. 40)

   C. Silencing the Spirits (v. 41)

IV. PREVAILING PRIORITY (Luke 4:42, 43)

   A. Popular Request (v. 42)

   B. Purposeful Refusal (v. 43)

CONCLUSION

   A. Partners in Healing

   B. Prayer of a Participant

   C. Thought to Remember

Display visual 6 of the visuals packet throughout this session. The visual is shown on page 164.

Introduction

Included in the Messianic assignment Jesus accepted as the pattern for His ministry was this: "He hath sent me to heal the brokenhearted" (Luke 4:18). This says nothing directly about physical illness, but by implication it points to a practice that was to become prominent in His ministry. Symbolically, He accepted *physician* as applying to himself (Luke 4:23; 5:31). This we noted in last week's lesson. Today we see the Great Physician at work, literally.

A. Who Is the Healer?

I asked our family doctor, "How would you describe the relationship of your medical practice to the ultimate process of healing in your patients?"

He was greatly interested in the question, which reminded him of another: Why do you want to be a doctor? That had been asked of him early in his medical training, and he had answered, "I want to help people to heal." He considered himself an "expediter," making it possible for the patient's own healing forces to work most effectively. Assisted by the physician's setting a broken bone, the body knits the break. Assisted by the cleansing and suturing of a wound, the body rebuilds torn tissues. Assisted by antibiotics' conquest of infections, the body repairs the damage they have done.

How, though, did living creatures come to have this ability to restore themselves? Is not the answer in this: "The Lord God made . . ."? And is not this the basis for the psalmist's reference to God as He "who healeth all thy diseases"? (Psalm 103:3). If God does not in some manner—usual or unusual—heal the affliction, there is no healing. There is only temporary patchwork.

No one should be surprised, then, at the healing ministry wrought by Jesus, God's Son on earth. The marvel is in the speed with which Jesus accomplished the healings that normally require time—hours to months—for restoring disease-damaged tissues. Jesus was more than expediter of healing; He was the healer!

B. From Nazareth to Capernaum

Jesus announced in the synagogue at Nazareth that He had come as the fulfillment of Isaiah's prophecy to bring healing, sight, and liberty to the oppressed. That was too much for His neighbors in the hometown. They rejected Him, violently, and He left their city. It was more than a temporary escape. "Leaving Nazareth, he came and dwelt in Capernaum" (Matthew 4:13). It seems that Jesus and His family had moved their residence there some months earlier (John 2:12). One can only ponder the many kinds of loss suffered by Nazareth in the departure of the citizens who have become its one claim to worldwide notice.

I. Impressive Instruction (Luke 4:31, 32)

Jesus did not allow rejection in any one place to hinder the fulfilling of the ministry given to Him by His Heavenly Father. He exemplified the principle He was later to urge upon His disciples as they went out to announce His coming: "When they persecute you in this city, flee ye into another" (Matthew 10:23). The work of the kingdom goes on!

A. Continuing Work in a New Place (v. 31)

31. And [Jesus] came down to Capernaum, a city of Galilee, and taught them on the sabbath days.

From Nazareth to Capernaum is approximately twenty miles "as the crow flies." Capernaum is on the shore of the Sea of Galilee some 650 feet below the level of the Mediterranean Sea. It was a city of considerable population and radiating influence. Two caravan routes passed through it; hence it was the site of a Roman garrison and a center for the collection of taxes. There Jesus taught on several *sabbath days*; we are not told how many. It becomes immediately evident that He was busy on other days as well.

B. New Power in Eternal Truth (v. 32)

32. And they were astonished at his doctrine: for his word was with power.

The hearers' amazement was as continual as the Lord's teaching. Mark 1:22 expands this comment, saying, "He taught them as one that had authority, and not as the scribes" (compare Matthew 7:28, 29). Jesus' authority rested in His very being, and it was seen in the self-evident truth of what He taught. He had no need to do as the scribes, who bolstered their interpretations of Scripture by quoting extensively from earlier commentators. When Jesus made quotations, even from the Old Testament, it was often to add His own authoritative amendments: "Ye have heard . . . but I say unto you . . ." (see Matthew 5:21, 22, 27, 28, 31-34, 38, 39, 43, 44). In anyone else, this would have seemed insufferably arrogant; but Jesus gave convincing evidence that He had the right to speak as He did. Moreover, what He said was related clearly and forcefully to life as the people knew it.

II. Cleansing Command (Luke 4:33-37)

On one Sabbath at Capernaum, Jesus' teaching procedure was suddenly changed by a noisy interruption. Yet this in itself provided an occasion for still more impressive teaching.

A. Defeating a Demon (vv. 33-35)

33, 34. And in the synagogue there was a man, which had a spirit of an unclean devil, and cried out with a loud voice, saying, Let us alone; what have we to do with thee, thou Jesus *of Nazareth? art thou come to destroy us? I* **know thee who thou art; the Holy One of God.**

Scripture deals with demon possession quite separately from illness, though the same person might be afflicted with both. Demons (not *the* devil, Satan) seem to have inhabited and taken possession of persons in a very irregular fashion—partially or totally, sometimes or continually. The man introduced here may have attended the synagogue services many times as a normal worshiper, but this time the demonic spirit or spirits within him recognized in Jesus a moral enemy and *cried aloud* in fear and frustration. The words were those of the demon or demons; the voice was that of the tormented man.

Us and *we* may indicate the presence of more than one demon, or may indicate that one spoke of himself and the afflicted man. In any case, the evil spirit recognized Jesus and wanted no dealings with Him. "The devils also believe, and tremble" (James 2:19). This demon recognized the man called Jesus—identified precisely by naming His hometown—as the promised Messiah, whose principal mission was to "destroy the works of the devil" (1 John 3:8). The demon said in effect, "I know You and what You are here for." Demons are given to all sorts of evil and falsehood, but when they come face to face with the Son of God they are compelled to speak truth (compare Acts 16:16-18). So will it be in the judgment when every knee shall bow, whether in Heaven, or on earth, or under the earth, and every tongue shall confess Jesus Christ as Lord (Philippians 2:9-11). Believing and trembling do not save, however, without repentance and a changed life.

35. And Jesus rebuked him, saying, Hold thy peace, and come out of him. And when the devil had thrown him in the midst, he came out of him, and hurt him not.

Scripture reveals Jesus as *rebuking*, or calling to account and putting in their place, not only persons and demons, but also an illness and the winds and seas. He is Lord, and all creation must obey Him.

"Quiet!" One word was enough to express Jesus' rejection of demonic testimony that would confuse the hearers and complicate the Lord's teaching ministry. The time for public proclamation of His messiahship would come later.

Come out of him! No mystical or destructive process was required, only the command of Him who had already been acknowledged as the Holy One of God. The defeated demon convulsed the man one final time, throwing him to the floor before them all, but without harming him. Mark 1:26 says the demon "tore" the man in departing, but this simply describes the convulsion that threw him down. Luke, the physician, reflects an interest in the absence of physical injury.

BE QUIET

It is amazing how low-key Jesus was as He began His Galilean ministry. With a modern campaign manager, there would be advance men to be sure everyone in the community knew when Jesus would be arriving. The media would be alerted, and care would be given to timing things just right for the evening news. Jesus would arrive with great fanfare, meeting the dignitaries of the synagogue and town. There would be some photo-ops. Jesus' message would be carefully scripted by speech writers who had studied the issues that would appeal most to that area.

There would be a psychological build-up to the "healing servcie." The camera would pan the crowd, picking out those who seemed most interested. Then the camera would focus on the contorted face of the person possessed by a demon. The murmur going through the crowd would be caught by special long-distance mikes. Then would come the dramatic moment when the demon shouted at Jesus, "Ha! What do you want of us, Jesus of Nazareth? Have you come to destroy us? I know who you are—the Holy One of God!" (Luke 4:34, *New International Version*). The camera would zoom in on the man as he writhed on the ground. "What fantastic footage," the cameraman would think.

Then an offering for the kingdom ministry would be taken, and Jesus would wave "Shalom" to the adoring crowd as He headed toward the next stop on His "Miracle Tour."

Yes, we would know how to "package" Jesus for maximum impact. Jesus, however, did things differently. He came virtually unannounced into the synagogues. He spoke "gracious words" (Luke 4:22). He commanded the demons, "Be quiet!" He forbade the very thing that might have been most useful for drawing a crowd, the shout of the demons coming out of those He healed (Luke 4:41).   —W. P

B. Amazing the Observers (vv. 36, 37)

36. And they were all amazed, and spake among themselves, saying, What a word is this! for with authority and power he commandeth the unclean spirits, and they come out.

Wonderment covered the crowd in the synagogue. The synagogue service, already interrupted, may have been broken up entirely by the buzz of conversation and discussion that followed the miracle.

Mark 1:27 quotes some as saying, "What thing is this? what new doctrine is this?" All seemed to recognize that a teaching, a *word*, was central in the accomplishment. They were yet to learn that it was the eternal Word who was with God from the beginning and had come to dwell among men for their salvation (John 1:1, 14). They did recognize in Jesus the *authority*—the innate right to speak and be heard—and the *power*—the effective force—to accomplish what He determined to do. The cleansing power was in His spoken word. The unclean spirits received the Lord's notice, and they departed!

On this occasion no one seems to have criticized Jesus for casting out a demon on the Sabbath Day! Only later did the critics seek occasion against Him.

37. And the fame of him went out into every place of the country round about.

Capernaum was a place from which news and influence radiated to surrounding communities as tradesmen and fishermen made their contacts and carried their wares. Jesus became news throughout Galilee and beyond.

How unfortunate that the explosive quality of news should depend so much on what is novel and startling, rather than on what is eternal and important! We know more about Jesus than these people did, but all too often we allow the flame of His fame to die down.

WONDERFUL THINGS

Two times in today's lesson we are told that Jesus amazed people. First, they were amazed at His teaching, for it was with power (Luke 4:32). Second, they were amazed at the authority He exercised over evil spirits. He spoke and they obeyed (v. 36).

One of the great moments in the history of archaeology occurred on November 26, 1922, when Howard Carter took an iron rod and poked a small hole in a subterranean door. Dumb with amazement, he peered through the hole till a companion inquired, "Can you see anything?"

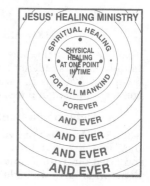

visual 6

"Yes," gasped Carter, "wonderful things."

Indeed they were wonderful things—golden furniture, a golden chariot, and gold mummy cases—the treasures of King Tut's tomb. But there has never been on the face of the earth anything as wonderful and amazing as the deeds and teaching of Jesus. Demons departed, fevers faded, people received a message of hope. These were not dusty objects in a forgotten tomb, but living demonstrations of the power of God at work in life.   —W. P.

III. Healing Hands
(Luke 4:38-41)

After a brief reference to Jesus' spreading fame in the days that followed (v. 37), we come back to Capernaum after the synagogue meeting on that notable Sabbath.

A. Cooling a Fever (vv. 38, 39)

38, 39. And he arose out of the synagogue, and entered into Simon's house. And Simon's wife's mother was taken with a great fever; and they besought him for her. And he stood over her, and rebuked the fever; and it left her: and immediately she arose and ministered unto them.

It seems that Jesus and others were going home with Simon Peter to the traditional Sabbath dinner. Mark 1:29 says Jesus "entered into the house of Simon and Andrew, with James and John." John 1:44 says Peter and Andrew were from Bethsaida. They may have moved the short distance to Capernaum within a few months of the time Jesus moved from Nazareth, or perhaps this Bethsaida was a section of Capernaum.

There was illness in Peter's house when the party arrived. Malarial *fevers* are not uncommon in the marshy areas around the Sea of Galilee; and Luke notes a dangerously high temperature in the patient, Simon's mother-in-law. (This is one of two Scriptures indicating that Peter was a married man. The other is 1 Corinthians 9:5.) Peter and others requested Jesus' help for the sick lady.

It becomes immediately evident that Jesus was not limited to any one procedure in healing sick folk. Here we read that He *stood over*, or "bent over" (*New International Version*) the patient. Matthew 8:15 says He "touched her hand." Mark 1:31 says He "took her by the hand, and lifted her up." He did all these, but Luke emphasizes the spoken word: He "rebuked the fever," and that was the end of it. Healing was immediate and complete. The patient was restored at once to her customary usefulness in waiting on the family.

B. Dispersing Diseases (v. 40)

After that morning in the synagogue, and the noonday healing in the home of a prominent citizen, Capernaum surely buzzed with news of Jesus on that Sabbath afternoon. Would He not heal many others if they were brought to Him? It would violate Sabbath law, though, to carry a sick friend to the place of healing before the holy day was over at sundown.

40. Now when the sun was setting, all they that had any sick with divers diseases brought them unto him; and he laid his hands on every one of them, and healed them.

How wonderful it is to have caring friends! Family members and friends believed in Jesus' healing power, so they provided whatever transportation was necessary to bring the sick to the Great Physician.

In this scene of mass healings we find something of a pattern. Jesus laid His hands on *every one of them.* One at a time, "He was healing them" (*New American Standard Bible*). May we not assume that He had a personally appropriate word for each one also? How acutely He must have been aware that any physical benefit He could render would be temporary! "Heaven and earth shall pass away, but my words shall not pass away" (Matthew 24:35).

C. Silencing the Spirits (v. 41)

41. And devils also came out of many, crying out, and saying, Thou art Christ the Son of God. And he rebuking them suffered them not to speak: for they knew that he was Christ.

In the synagogue that morning Jesus had relieved a man of demon possession, and then at Simon's house He had relieved a patient of high fever. Naturally, then, He would be sought to relieve folk who were suffering either kind—or both kinds—of affliction.

Here again (compare vv. 34, 35), the demons recognized Him and identified Him with God. And again Jesus silenced them, rejecting their testimony. It was essential that people come to recognize Him for who He is, but they must be convinced by His own words and works; they must not receive instruction from demons!

IV. Prevailing Priority
(Luke 4:42, 43)

Jesus' self-chosen program at Capernaum was to teach, beginning in the synagogue. Pressing need and popular demand, however, had brought on a different program to claim His time. Would His ministry continue now in the direction He chose, or in one chosen for him?

A. Popular Request (v. 42)

42. And when it was day, he departed and went into a desert place: and the people sought him, and came unto him, and stayed him, that he should not depart from them.

The Lord had been busy on this Sabbath and past its conclusion into the evening. The next morning, "rising up a great while before day, he went out, and departed into a solitary place, and there prayed" (Mark 1:35). So Jesus sought rest in God's persence on this first day of the week. But even that was not to last long. Peter knew where to look for Him, and others followed Peter to the place (Mark 1:36, 37). So a sizable committee of citizens urged Jesus to make himself continually available in Capernaum as resident physician. Think of it! Not only would the health of their citizens be assured, but they would prosper from the influx of tourist-patients from a distance.

B. Purposeful Refusal (v. 43)

43. And he said unto them, I must preach the kingdom of God to other cities also: for therefore am I sent.

Jesus was polite in declining their invitation. He knew God's purpose for sending Him into the world, and that would not be fulfilled by continuing a healing ministry indefinitely in one place. The *kingdom*—or reign—*of God* was larger than this in several dimensions. It must be eternal, beginning now and continuing forever. It must be spiritual, including but not limited to care for physical needs. It must be for all persons, beginning with us where we are but reaching out to the ends of the earth. To limit the ministry of Christ in any of these particulars would be to frustrate the purposes of God. If any further clarification is needed, it may be found in verse 44, immediately following our lesson text: "And he preached in the synagogues of Galilee."

Conclusion

A. Partners in Healing

Proclaimers of God's reign, beginning with Jesus himself, have always needed to maintain a delicate balance between two aspects of their healing ministry—compassionate service in matters material and zealous evangelism in matters spiritually eternal. Jesus preached, taught, and healed. By His direction, the apostles pursued the same course. Christians have preached the gospel and they have established hospitals—whose ministries are not always as Christ-centered as their names. Missionaries have employed modern medical skills, more or less purposefully related to evangelism. Ministers of the gospel have given themselves variously to encouraging the sick, the sorrowing, the distraught, and the bewildered in their communities. All of these people are, at least potentially, partners with their Lord in the compassionate healing of bodies for time, and mending broken spirits for eternity.

Individual Christians have not always seen their own twofold Christian ministry quite so clearly. They are not inclined to practice medicine without a license, and they are reluctant to accept responsibility for spiritual counseling. The service they can render, though, is doubly helpful because they are amateurs, motivated by genuine compassion, untainted by professional pride or ambition. The convincing force of a kindly word, whether of encouragement or concern, is as effective for good as negative "peer pressure" is for evil. Someone is hurting; let's help him! Someone is wondering; let's give him assurance! Someone is wandering; let's lead him in the way of life! It's an entrance into a healing partnership with the King in His kingdom.

B. Prayer of a Participant

Help us to reflect the character of Jesus, who felt and healed the hurts of strangers about Him and still saw our need for redemption. In His name, may we, to the extent of our ability, heal the hurts of others and include Your saving gospel in our daily conversation. Amen.

C. Thought to Remember

The compassion of Christ worked physical healings to many for a time, but spiritual healing to mankind forever.

Home Daily Bible Readings

Monday, Jan. 3—Jesus Acts With Authority (Luke 4:30-37)
Tuesday, Jan. 4—Jesus Laid Hands on Every One (Luke 4:38-41)
Wednesday, Jan. 5—Jesus Comes to Preach Good News (Luke 4:42—5:3)
Thursday, Jan. 6—Fishers Catching People (Luke 5:4-11)
Friday, Jan. 7—Jesus Healed One With Leprosy (Luke 5:12-16)
Saturday, Jan. 8—Power to Heal (Luke 5:17-26)
Sunday, Jan. 9—Jesus Heals Sinners (Luke 5:27-39)

Learning by Doing

*This page contains an alternate lesson plan emphasizing learning activities. Classes
desiring such student involvement will find these suggestions helpful.*

Learning Goals

Following this study of Jesus' multifaceted ministry as described by Luke the physician, each student will:

1. Recall the main purpose of Jesus' ministry as revealed in verse 43 of the text.

2. Explain how physical healing helped in accomplishing that purpose.

3. Show how various kinds of Christian service help in the main purpose of the church and Christians.

Into the Lesson

Print these letters on separate cards: E, O, P, P, R, S, U. Make them big enough to be seen by the whole class and post them at the front of the room. (Light cards can be taped to the chalkboard or fastened to the wall with Plasti-Tak.) Ask the students to tell what word can be spelled with those letters. If they are slow to get it, help by saying the first letter is P.

When the word *purpose* is discovered, rearrange the letters to spell it. Then let a good reader read this poem to the class:

> Ever get that round-rut feeling,
>   Going round in circles without end,
> Working day by day, or playing,
>   Getting little for the strength you spend?
>
> What you need in life is purpose:
>   Noble goal to which you set your face.
> Meaning, meaning, that's what's missing;
>   All of life is just an endless race.

If you can, put the poem on an overhead transparency and project it for all to see as they discuss it. Ask such questions as these: Do you ever feel this way? Is much of mankind going around in circles and getting nowhere? Mention some activities that have no worthwhile results. After a little discussion, tell students to look at the end of our lesson text and find the purpose for which Jesus was sent. (To preach the kingdom of God v. 43.)

Into the Word

Give each class member a sheet of paper. Ask them to divide it into two columns with the headings "Jesus' Words" and "Jesus' Deeds." Let students read the text, individually or in pairs, and list records of Jesus' sayings in one column and records of His deeds in the other. Get them started by pointing out that in verse 31 "came down to Capernaum" goes under "Deeds" and "taught them" goes under "Words."

Allow time for the lists to be completed, then let some or all of them be read and compared. Do not expect them to be just alike, but note that they can be different without being wrong. Point out that in some cases Jesus' words were also His deeds. For example, He "rebuked the fever" with words (v. 39), but the rebuke was also the act of healing. God's words produced creation in the beginning (Genesis 1:3), and Jesus words repaired damaged creatures.

To consider what the text says about demons, divide your class down the middle. Assign verses 33-36 to one part, and verse 41 to the other. Ask each group to answer this: "What do demons know about Jesus?" Allow two or three minutes for them to jot down ideas, then record their responses on the chalkboard. Probably these items will be noted:

1. Demons know Jesus as the Son of God.

2. Demons know they must submit to Him.

3. Demons know Jesus' purpose is to destroy their power and influence.

Students may want to ask questions and talk more about demons. You can help the discussion with thoughts from the lesson writer's remarks on the subject.

Into Life

Have the following statements written on slips of paper. Distribute them to class members who volunteer to read them:

1. Nothing is more important than making the gospel known, but I must not be insensitive to the physical needs of people.

2. There are powerful forces of evil in the world, but nothing is stronger than the words of God.

3. Many things demand time and attention, but I must not let anything stop me from spreading the good news that Jesus is the Christ.

As the statements are read, ask students if they agree or disagree. Ask what is seen in the text to support each statement. Discuss what class members and the local congregation have done in the past year for the physical needs of people. What have they done for the preaching of the gospel? What can they do this week, this month, or this year?

Let's Talk It Over

The questions on this page are designed to encourage review of the lesson Scriptures and to promote discussion of the lesson by the class. The answers provided are only discussion starters. Let your class talk it over from there.

1. We don't have Jesus' miraculous healing power, but we can have His love. What are some concrete ways in which we can help the sick among us or help those who are caring for sick family members?

While we cannot supply healing, we can supply love, comfort, encouragement, and resources. Chronically ill people need encouragement through phone calls, visits, cards, and prayers. Those incapacitated by disease or injury may need help with activities, chores, or errands. The terminally ill need to be filled with hope. They may need to be told about Jesus, or they may need their faith strengthened. People who minister to sick family members for extended lengths of time need periodic relief, even if only for a few hours. Financial help is sometimes needed.

2. When Jesus was rejected in one place He went to another. Even where He was accepted He stayed only for a while and then went somewhere else to preach. How should we apply this principle to our work for the Lord today?

Some people have hardened hearts and will not accept Jesus. Much as we long to reach such people, we should follow Jesus' example of seeking out and working with those who are responsive. We should help these to grow to the point that they become givers instead of receivers, so workers can be freed to reach out to new people.

3. The people of Capernaum wanted Jesus to settle down in their city so He would be available whenever they needed Him, like the ultimate emergency room. He refused because He needed to visit other cities, too. How are we sometimes like the people of Capernaum? How do you think Jesus reacts when we try to keep Him to ourselves?

It is easy to sit contentedly in our churches and enjoy our fellowship with the Lord and with each other. If we reach out to others, it may be only to those close to us and those like us. But Jesus refuses to be confined to any one group. He constantly went to new cities. If we do not carry Him to others, near and far, similar and dissimilar, is it possible He will withdraw from us as He withdrew from Capernaum?

4. How can we tell whether our church is being selfish with Jesus? What aspects of our programs reveal our priorities and show whether we are serving ourselves or the Lord?

Make a list of the church programs and budget categories. Divide these into one list of things that are directed primarily toward church members and another list of things that are directed primarily outside the congregation. A comparison of these two lists will give a good picture of how selfish or generous our church is with Jesus.

5. People suffer in many ways besides physical disease. Anguish over marriage, children, shattered dreams, guilt, loneliness, or hopelessness plagues many people. How can we as Christians share the healing love of Jesus in ways that relieve the suffering of the heart?

Suffering of the heart is often more excruciating than physical suffering, and Jesus' love is the only true help.

Christians share His love by loving others. True love will find appropriate actions. His love becomes concrete as it is expressed by His people. In this way we introduce people to our loving Lord so that they may come to know Him and welcome Him into their hearts. No one can find true peace until He knows Jesus.

6. Jesus emphasized preaching and teaching more than healing, but He did heal. How should we imitate His priorities as we plan and implement the programs and ministries of our congregation?

This is a hard priority to set, especially for those who work among the poor. Some churches emphasize social programs but do little to proclaim the gospel. Others preach tirelessly but do little to relieve physical burdens. It seems that Jesus would have us do both, but in balance. We cannot use all our resources for relief, because the demand is endless while the resources are limited. However, we should use some in this way. How can we truly love people, or demonstrate the love of Jesus, without trying to ease their suffering? On the other hand, what good is it to relieve earthly pain but leave persons to suffer through eternity because we did not teach them the gospel?

Jesus Teaches His Followers

DEVOTIONAL READING: Matthew 5:3-12, 38-48; 7:12, 24-27; 8:1-4.

LESSON SCRIPTURE: Luke 6:17-36.

PRINTED TEXT: Luke 6:20b-36.

Luke 6:20b-36

20b Blessed be ye poor: for yours is the kingdom of God.

21 Blessed are ye that hunger now: for ye shall be filled. Blessed are ye that weep now: for ye shall laugh.

22 Blessed are ye, when men shall hate you, and when they shall separate you from their company, and shall reproach you, and cast out your name as evil, for the Son of man's sake.

23 Rejoice ye in that day, and leap for joy: for, behold, your reward is great in heaven: for in the like manner did their fathers unto the prophets.

24 But woe unto you that are rich! for ye have received your consolation.

25 Woe unto you that are full! for ye shall hunger. Woe unto you that laugh now! for ye shall mourn and weep.

26 Woe unto you, when all men shall speak well of you! for so did their fathers to the false prophets.

27 But I say unto you which hear, Love your enemies, do good to them which hate you,

28 Bless them that curse you, and pray for them which despitefully use you.

29 And unto him that smiteth thee on the one cheek offer also the other; and him that taketh away thy cloak forbid not to take thy coat also.

30 Give to every man that asketh of thee; and of him that taketh away thy goods ask them not again.

31 And as ye would that men should do to you, do ye also to them likewise.

32 For if ye love them which love you, what thank have ye? for sinners also love those that love them.

33 And if ye do good to them which do good to you, what thank have ye? for sinners also do even the same.

34 And if ye lend to them of whom ye hope to receive, what thank have ye? for sinners also lend to sinners, to receive as much again.

35 But love ye your enemies, and do good, and lend, hoping for nothing again; and your reward shall be great, and ye shall be the children of the Highest: for he is kind unto the unthankful and to the evil.

36 Be ye therefore merciful, as your Father also is merciful.

GOLDEN TEXT: Be ye therefore merciful, as your Father also is merciful.—Luke 6:36.

Lesson Aims

This study should enable the student to:

1. Show how the teachings of Jesus found in Luke 6:20b-36 apply to His followers rather than to unbelievers, and apply most directly to the apostles.

2. Tell specific ways in which Christian love acts, even where no friendship is involved.

3. Name at least one way in which he or she will act this week in reflection of God's love.

Lesson Outline

Display visual 7 of the visuals packet and refer to it as you consider the lesson text. The visual is shown on page 173.

Introduction

One superlative teaching session marks the early and popular ministry of Jesus. Reported in Matthew 5—7, it is called His Sermon on the Mount. Important parts of the same message appear in Luke 6:20-49, sometimes called His Sermon on the Plain (Luke 6:17). Most commentators think that Matthew and Luke both report the same event occurring on an upland plateau near Capernaum, but some think Luke is telling of a similar sermon at another time and place. The whole discourse was surely longer than either report, and Jesus probably repeated the same teachings many times.

A. Sermon Preparation

Jesus prepared with months of living for every minute of His speaking in the teaching session before us. All of His life and ministry finds expression in this sermon.

Moreover, His primary audience had been prepared for it. In it He was to address His disciples—followers whom He had drawn to himself, and some whose commitment He had secured. Four fishermen had left their business and their families to accompany Him (Luke 5:1-11). A tax collector had "left all" to follow Him (Luke 5:27-32). It was for these, and for others who would join them throughout the ages, that the sermon was designed.

Jesus' final preparation for the event occupied a sleepless night and a busy forenoon. In the evening He went out to the mountain alone to pray, "and continued all night in prayer to God" (Luke 6:12). Did He not spend the time in consultation with the Father about His forthcoming choice and instruction of the twelve apostles? That is what happened the next morning. Jesus called together the whole company of His followers and chose from among them the twelve whose names appear in Luke 6:13-16.

With them all Jesus returned to the plateau where a great throng waited for the ministry they had come to expect from Jesus. The message they were to hear was preeminently an ordination sermon, instructing the twelve and the larger "squad" of committed ones from which this "team" had been chosen—and also whoever might be pursuaded to join their ranks. It was not a recruiting sermon; it was a training session. But what would Jesus do with all those other people?

B. Difficult Audience

They were there from near and far, not only from Galilee, but from as far as "all Judea" southward and from Sidon in Phoenicia northward. They came not only to hear Jesus, but especially to obtain healing for such sick or demon-possessed folk as could be brought into the range of His touch.

What a diverse throng, and how difficult to address! Included were curious listeners to be challenged—Jews and Gentiles—idle observers to be amused, and critics to be confronted.

Here was the first lesson of the day for the Lord's disciples. In following their Master, they would not be turning away from folk in need. Freely they had been receiving of Him; freely they were to give in His name (Matthew 10:8). Now, before their verbal instruction began, they would observe Him again radiating compassionate power in healing and cleansing the troubled ones. That being done, the disciples took their places near Jesus as He proceeded to speak.

I. Pursued by Happiness
(Luke 6:20b-23)

The American *Declaration of Independence* presents the "self-evident" truth that all men are endowed by their Creator with an unalienable right to the *pursuit of happiness,* but experience and revelation agree that the chase leads more often to misery instead. God's Son would direct to a different pursuit, with an infinitely better prospect of finding happiness. That better pursuit is what the disciples before Jesus that day had chosen. In committing themselves to Him they had entered the realm of God. That in itself is the ultimate blessing, the highest state of well being. Happiness had found them!

A. Above Wealth and Health
(vv. 20b, 21)

20b. Blessed be ye poor: for yours is the kingdom of God.

In the immediate presence of Jesus were Peter, Andrew, James, John, and Matthew, who only recently had left their substantial businesses to join Him who had "nowhere to lay His head" (Matthew 8:19, 20, *New American Standard Bible*). Others surely had made the same sort of sacrificial commitments. Jesus was later to say, "there is no man that hath left house, or parents, or brethren, or wife, or children, for the kingdom of God's sake, who shall not receive manifold more in this present time, and in the world to come life everlasting" (Luke 18:29, 30). These men had not chosen poverty; they had chosen Christ, and for His sake had accepted poverty. Having become poor for the sake of the spirit (compare Matthew 5:3), they found themselves possessing that most precious treasure, the kingdom of Heaven (Matthew 13:45, 46).

21a. Blessed are ye that hunger now: for ye shall be filled.

The apostles would soon be sent without provisions to "preach the kingdom of God" in communities otherwise unreached, and to depend entirely on the hospitality that was first offered (Luke 9:1-6). They would appreciate whatever was available.

The promise of fulfillment, though, has a spiritual turn, as seen in Matthew 5:6: "Blessed are they which do hunger and thirst after righteousness: for they shall be filled." How wonderful to have a good appetite for God's truth! The listeners to Jesus' sermon were in for a feast!

21b. Blessed are ye that weep now: for ye shall laugh.

The apostles may have shed tears that day over some who had come to Jesus for healing, and may have laughed with delight at the patients' recovery. They had grieved as they saw the ravages of sin among their people, so they were prepared to rejoice in God's gift of salvation from that sin. Concerning their own sin they were acquainted with the godly sorrow that works repentance (2 Corinthians 7:10). They knew that "weeping may endure for a night, but joy cometh in the morning" (Psalm 30:5). Both the weeping and the laughter need to be related to Christ and His kingdom. Self-pity and self-congratulation don't qualify!

B. Above Praise and Popularity
(vv. 22, 23)

22. Blessed are ye, when men shall hate you, and when they shall separate you from their company, and shall reproach you, and cast out your name as evil, for the Son of man's sake.

The key to this affirmation is in the phrase, *for the Son of man's sake.* The disciples would be rejected as their Lord was rejected, because they were committed to Him (John 15:18-21). Punishment for misdeeds would honor no one, but persecution for Christ's sake brought rejoicing to the apostles (Acts 5:41, 42; 1 Peter 4:14-16).

23. Rejoice ye in that day, and leap for joy: for, behold, your reward is great in heaven: for in the like manner did their fathers unto the prophets.

The fellowship of Christ includes celebrations, with dancing for joy, and that under the most amazing circumstances. The Heavenly jubilation here described will bring together such worthies as Elijah, Amos, Isaiah, Jeremiah, and Daniel, concerning whom Stephen charged the Jewish leaders, "Which of the prophets have not your fathers persecuted?" (Acts 7:52, and compare Matthew 23:2-32). The wounded prophets, honored extensively for their faith in the face of rejection (Hebrews 11:32-38), constitute a wonderfully worthy fellowship!

II. Overtaken by Misery
(Luke 6:24-26)

The Lord's attention shifted suddenly from the blessings enjoyed by His loyal followers to the ultimate miseries awaiting those who had chosen an opposite course. Perhaps He was looking at some Galileans who had seen His miracles and attended His teachings but had rejected His claims and resisted His invitation. Having placed their trust in things material and temporary, they faced certain defeat and hopeless frustration in their ultimate failure.

A. From Property and Pleasure (vv. 24, 25)

24. But woe unto you that are rich! for ye have received your consolation.

It is almost as though Jesus had already met the rich young ruler of Luke 18:18-30, and had seen him depart, being "very sorrowful: for he was very rich." That man's wealth would yield him nothing henceforth but bitter disappointment.

Suitable to Jesus' present woe is His epitaph on the "successful" farmer who expected to satisfy his soul with bumper crops filling new barns, but was suddenly deprived of his life with the chilling question, "Then whose shall those things be?" The final word echoes down through time: "So is he that layeth up treasure for himself, and is not rich toward God" (Luke 12:15-21).

25a. Woe unto you that are full! for ye shall hunger.

Misery-producing fullness can come in more than one way. Those who are satisfied with things material—(Philippians 3:19) will never enjoy the hunger and thirst for righteousness that leads to spiritual filling.

Suggested also is a condition described in Amos 8, when the self-satisfied leaders of Israel were "full up to here" with their national religion and didn't want to hear anything more from the prophet. Amos 8:11 predicts a Heaven-sent famine "of hearing the words of the Lord." There would be a great longing, Amos said, for a comforting message from God, but it would not come. Do we not find the same rejection among self-satisfied folk who are "full up to here" with "religion" and desire no more? Where will they turn when they find their present resources inadequate for life's difficult times, and their cry for new resources is met with silence?

25b. Woe unto you that laugh now! for ye shall mourn and weep.

Jesus was fully aware of persons "serving divers lusts and pleasures" (Titus 3:3), being "lovers of pleasure more than lovers of God" (2 Timothy 3:4).

To catch the force of the warning we may look at our word *amusement*. To muse is to reflect, to meditate, to consider thoughtfully. To be *amused* is to be removed from musing, to escape from serious thought. How shall the person who has given major attention to that kind of escapism avoid bitter tears of vain regret when forced at last to face the issues he has spent a lifetime evading? It's not funny!

B. From Popular Applause (v. 26)

26. Woe unto you, when all men shall speak well of you! for so did their fathers to the false prophets.

Jeremiah 5:31; 6:14; 8:11; and Ezekiel 13:10 tell of false prophets who became popular by tickling the ears of their listeners with unfounded pleasantries (compare 2 Timothy 4:3, 4). These folk were such as drew the judgment of Jesus, "All their works they do for to be seen of men" (Matthew 23:5). Having been seen, heard, and admired parading their virtues, "they have their reward" (Matthew 6:2, 5, 16). They will receive no approval from God.

III. Led by Love (Luke 6:27-31)

"Why go to all that trouble? People won't think any more highly of you for it." Fred had stayed after hours to correct an unexpected problem in the office, and that didn't make sense to Bill. The important question to Fred, though, was not other people's attitude toward him; it was his attitude toward them.

With that thought we move from what Jesus said about popularity to what He said about love. The Lord recognized more than one kind of love, and New Testament language distinguishes among them—friendship, affection, approval, sexual attraction—and then that divine love (John 3:16) that has been defined as "looking out for the other person's interests and enjoying doing it." It is mostly action that can be commanded and controlled.

Jesus had been doing a thorough job of turning the world upside down—or right side up—beginning with its sense of values. Now He showed how to put the values to work.

A. Don't React to Abuse (vv. 27-29)

27, 28. But I say unto you which hear, Love your enemies, do good to them which hate you, bless them that curse you, and pray for them which despitefully use you.

The Lord's teaching was given to anyone who would listen. He knew that a lot of worldly-wise folk would be turned off by His "impractical" advice, but He also knew that no other program would meet the need.

First, we must refuse to let another person's attitude or action determine ours. "Be not overcome of evil, but overcome evil with good"

(Romans 12:21). By praising and praying for folk who vilify us we can at least get their attention, and we can do it honestly. There is at least one thing worthy of praise about anyone, and there is no one for whom we cannot pray.

29. And unto him that smiteth thee on the one cheek offer also the other; and him that taketh away thy cloak forbid not to take thy coat also.

The specifics of this verse are subject for much discussion, but its principle is surely found in this: "Do not take revenge . . . but leave room for God's wrath, for it is written: 'It is mine to avenge; I will repay,' says the Lord" (Romans 12:19, *New International Version*). The example of Jesus is much to the point. He never resisted face-slapping personal insults; but until the time came for His ultimate sacrifice, He did move away from physical danger (Luke 4:29, 30; Matthew 12:14, 15), and He directed His disciples to do the same (Matthew 10:23).

Matthew 5:40 presents the taking of one's coat not as personal thievery but as the result of legal action: "If any man will sue thee at the law . . ." The principle goes on, however. Give more than is required. Allow the removal of one's cloak also. Don't be eager in the defense of your rights and property!

PRAY FOR THOSE WHO MISTREAT YOU

Driving toward the university, some students picked up a hitchhiker. He had no money, so they put him up in their lodging, supplied his food, and used their cars to take him to job interviews.

Then came spring break, and the house was closed for a week. The guest found other lodging; but during the week he broke into the house, stole money, stereos, and other valuables, and hauled them away in a car one of the students had left behind.

When the thief was caught, the boy who had lost most kept on praying for him, visiting him in jail, and telling him of Christ. At the trial he begged the judge to be lenient.

It may seem that all this effort was wasted, for the thief did not reform. But what about the boy who helped him? He grew in compassion and kindness and faith, grew in grace and the knowledge of Christ. Was that worth all he lost? —W. P.

B. Give as You Would Receive (vv. 30, 31)

30. Give to every man that asketh of thee; and of him that taketh away thy goods ask them not again.

Perhaps the Lord made His point here with words a bit stronger than the expected result.

visual 7

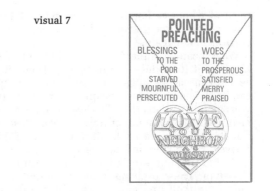

The apostle Paul seemed to think so. He did not recommend limitless handouts to folk unwilling to work (2 Thessalonians 3:10), nor to the members of families who could readily provide their support (1 Timothy 5:3-8). John warned against giving aid to false teachers and false teaching (2 John 9-11). To refuse or ignore the plea of genuine need, however, would betray a lack of the love that the Lord commanded (1 John 3:17, 18).

The main question in Jesus' sermon, though, was not the need of the recipient, but the attitude of the disciple who would either share or miss the spirit and the glory of his Lord.

31. And as ye would that men should do to you, do ye also to them likewise.

Here is the summary guide to loving behavior. "Love thy neighbor as thyself," becomes more than a crowning commandment rescued from its hiding place in Leviticus 19:18. It is the key to the application of Jesus' teaching about the kingdom of Heaven. Loving another as oneself becomes acting toward that other as one would have the other act toward him. A wise person would not desire to have others cater to his every passing fancy or momentary whim. So also he will exercise judgment in his dealing with others.

IV. Like Father, Like Child (Luke 6:32-36)

These are hard sayings; who can heed them? We borrow an answer from another of Jesus' conversations: "The things which are impossible with men are possible with God" (Luke 18:27). The Father's example and support are available to His children.

A. Be Different! (vv. 32-34)

32-34. For if ye love them which love you, what thank have ye? for sinners also love those that love them. And if ye do good to them which do good to you, what thank have ye? for sinners also do even the same. And if ye lend to

them of whom ye hope to receive, what thank have ye? for sinners also lend to sinners, to receive as much again.

What meaning is there to citizenship in God's kingdom if it produces no difference from citizenship in earth's kingdoms? And what credit can be claimed by Jesus' disciples for doing only what non-Christians do? The level exchange of favors will keep you out of trouble with the law, but it will provide no basis for rejoicing in Heaven. Being kind and supportive where those gestures bring a return in kind is not peculiarly Christian. These exchanges may be found also among murderous gangsters and bands of thieves. The way of Christ is very different.

B. Be Godly! (vv. 35, 36)

35. But love ye your enemies, and do good, and lend, hoping for nothing again; and your reward shall be great, and ye shall be the children of the Highest: for he is kind unto the unthankful and to the evil.

The idea of persisting in deeds of love and mercy in spite of rejection may seem unreasonable, but it asks only that God's children shall be like their Heavenly Father. He sends His sunshine and rain on all mankind regardless of their deserving (Matthew 5:45). To be like Him in our distributions of kindness brings its own reward. It establishes and reflects our status as members of His family. And the family resemblance becomes greater as the child becomes more mature. "Be ye therefore perfect, even as your Father which is in heaven is perfect" (Matthew 5:48).

36. Be ye therefore merciful, as your Father also is merciful.

Mercy like God's mercy goes beyond what is deserved to provide what is needed. It does not wait for an emergency to go into action. It moves with opportunity. We are to act in love and mercy because we are God's children; and that is what God did for us before we came into His family.

LOVE YOUR ENEMIES

In a time when it seems that everybody is angrily blaming someone else, it is refreshing to read the words of Terry Anderson, who spent seven years as a hostage in Lebanon.

He recalled being wrapped like a mummy and tied under a truck. He recalled nearly losing his mind when his captors took away some sign-language partners he had learned to communicate with.

More significantly he said the faith that brought him through the years of captivity also kept him from hating his captors. "Hating them

wouldn't hurt them an ounce," he said. "It would only hurt me."

Jesus gave us a profound principle of life: "Love your enemies."   —W. P.

Conclusion

A. The Living Word and His Words

It has been said that Jesus did not practice what He preached; He preached what He practiced. In fact, His life as the embodied Word of God, and the spoken words with which He interpreted that life to His hearers, agreed so completely that it would be hard to distinguish the one from the other. The principles of His ministry were established in what He *did* before they took form in what He said. And even where the words were most startling, we find them fully demonstrated in the continuing ministry of our Lord. He did not take the responsibilities of speech lightly. Hear His warning: "Every idle word that men shall speak, they shall give account thereof in the day of judgment. For by thy words thou shalt be justified, and by thy words thou shalt be condemned" (Matthew 12:36, 37). Thus judged, the living Word of God can still say, "I am . . . the truth" (John 14:6).

B. A Learner's Prayer

Thank You, almighty God, for Your Word, written and spoken, but especially as lived in Jesus our Lord. May we learn from Him in all His ways of instruction, especially when it is most difficult. We pray in His name. Amen.

C. Thought to Remember

"Seek ye first the kingdom of God, and his righteousness; and all these things shall be added unto you" (Matthew 6:33).

Home Daily Bible Readings

Monday, Jan. 10—Jesus Is Lord of the Sabbath (Luke 6:1-5)
Tuesday, Jan. 11—Jesus Heals on the Sabbath (Luke 6:6-11)
Wednesday, Jan. 12—Jesus Chooses Twelve (Luke 6:12-16)
Thursday, Jan. 13—Healings and Blessings (Luke 6:17-26)
Friday, Jan. 14—Love and Prayer for Enemies (Luke 6:27-31)
Saturday, Jan. 15—Ways to Show Our Love (Luke 6:32-38)
Sunday, Jan. 16—Be Like Your Teacher (Luke 6:39-49)

Learning by Doing

This page contains an alternate lesson plan emphasizing learning activities. Classes desiring such student involvement will find these suggestions helpful.

Learning Goals

After our study of Luke 6:20-36, my fellow students and I will:

1. Identify at least seven ways the man or woman of God is or acts opposite to a person of the world.

2. Have a renewed commitment to the true joy and the proper behavior that should characterize a child of God.

3. Demonstrate that joy in acts of kindness and mercy this week.

Into the Lesson

This week's study emphasizes opposites: the opposite ways of godly people and worldly people. You may call attention to this by having your classroom furniture turned in the opposite direction for the study session. (Don't do it if it will complicate procedures, either for your class or for another near by.)

Use the following pairs of opposite words for this activity to begin the class session: poor-rich, hungry-filled, griefstricken-joyous, hated-loved, separated-united, reproached-praised, kind-cruel, merciful-vindictive, blessed-cursed, generous-selfish. Print these on index cards, one word (not a pair) on each card. You may leave out some of these if you expect to have fewer than twenty in the class. If you expect more than twenty, you can add other pairs of opposites, such as feast-famine, weep-laugh, paid-unpaid, misery-delight, serious-silly, friend-enemy, and others that you can relate to the text. You hope to have a card for each person in the class.

Distribute the cards as class members arrive. Let the people mingle till each one finds his or her opposite. If your meeting place has no room for such mingling, simply let each word be read aloud so each person can identify his or her opposite.

Into the Word

Have all the verses of the text written on slips of paper and stacked in reverse order, verse 36 to verse 20. Read a verse aloud and let it be claimed by a person who holds a word to match it. For example, verse 36 will be claimed by one holding the word *merciful.* Give that person the verse, and go on to verse 35 and the rest. If two students claim the same verse, you must make a quick decision and give it to one of them. Possibly some will end up with more than one verse, or with none.

When the verses have been distributed, ask each pair of opposites to meet briefly to answer these questions: Which of our opposite words is approved by the verse we claimed? Which seems to be more popular in the world around us? Does this verse make any suggestion for our Christian thinking or action? (The questions may be displayed on a poster or the chalkboard.) If some students are left without a verse, each of them can join a nearby pair for this discussion. After four or five minutes, let some or all of the pairs express their conclusions.

Now go through the verses of the text in their proper order. Ask those holding a verse to read it aloud and then frame a statement opposite to it. For example, the opposite of verse 20b, may be, "Sad are you poor, for you are shut out of God's Kingdom." Or it may be "Blessed are you rich." However the opposite is expressed, ask the class, "Is that the way many people of the world really think?" Probably you will not have time to do this with all the verses, but a sampling will show that Jesus' prescribed life-style is drastically different from what many people call "really living."

Into Life

If you can collect enough photographic negatives, give one to each person present. If not, bring just one to show to the class. Ask how the negative is different from the real thing. Students will say it is exactly opposite: what is really light is dark in the negative, and what is really dark appears as light. How many people of the world are like that! They call evil good, and call good evil (Isaiah 5:20). Ask students to give some examples that have not yet been mentioned. Advertisements often give a negative picture. Smokers are shown as being healthy and strong. In reality, many are stricken with lung cancer or heart disease. In popular fiction, people in desperate need risk their last dollar in some gambling game and win; in reality, they lose. TV programs abound in promiscuous sex; you have to look elsewhere for the reality of AIDS. Urge your students not to be content with the world's negative pictures, but to demand the reality of God's Word.

Let's Talk It Over

The questions on this page are designed to encourage review of the lesson Scriptures and to promote discussion of the lesson by the class. The answers provided are only discussion starters. Let your class talk it over from there.

1. The four pairs of blessings and woes in today's text call us to choose what manner of life we will live. Jesus said to do the opposite of what the world does. In the first pair, how are we to be poor instead of rich? What blessings come to the poor?

Jesus does bring good news to the financially poor: Even the poorest is welcomed into full citizenship in the kingdom of God. However, all people, rich or poor, must be poor in spirit to enter the kingdom. This means we must be humble, contrite, and repentant. If we recognize our spiritual poverty and come to the Lord and ask from Him, we will receive and be blessed. If we are rich in the sense of being satisfied with possessions, of being proud, self-sufficient, and self-righteous, then we receive nothing from the Lord. Indeed, we will not even understand that we need anything from Him.

2. Jesus blessed those who are hungry, but He pronounced woe on those who are well fed. What kind of hunger and filling was He talking about? How do we develop this hunger? How are we filled?

On at least two occasions Jesus did feed the physically hungry, but His words point to a spiritual hunger. This is the hunger for righteousness, the desire to be right and to do right, the passion for fellowship with God. We develop this hunger when we come to hate sin and its effects in our lives and the lives of our loved ones, when we come to dread eternal death, and when we come to love God in response to His love, which was expressed most forcibly in the sacrifice of His son. We are filled when we surrender to Him, have our sins washed away, and receive the Spirit of holiness into our hearts. He works with us to help us live holy lives.

3. Jesus said He would turn tears into laughter and laughter into mourning. What tears has He dried in our lives? What laughter has He stopped?

Jesus has the power to heal all of life's wounds. Have we cried over our mistakes and sins and guilt? Jesus forgives. Have we cried in our loneliness? Jesus is a faithful friend. Have we wept as we put a loved one in the ground? Jesus is the resurrection and the life. Jesus has a

way of helping us bear life's deepest hurts and then healing us so that we may laugh again. And how long will we laugh with joy when we finally enter Heaven's gate? On the other hand, Jesus stops some kinds of laughter. When He comes into a person's life He stops the laughter of drunken partying or scoffing or filthy jokes or cruelty or callousness. When He returns He will stop all the laughter of His enemies.

4. Most of us have a strong desire to be popular, or at least to be accepted. Jesus warns us that this desire could be our undoing. Those who are welcomed and praised by the world may well be rejected by the Father. How must we live our lives so as to be persecuted by the world but rewarded by God?

While we do not seek persecution, it often comes to those who faithfully serve the Lord. Jesus expects several things of us that will bring the enmity of Satan and the world. First, He demands that we confess Him before men so that none doubt our allegiance. He commands us to do right, even if all about us are corrupt. The prophets were persecuted because they spoke out against sin. We too must not be silent about the rampant sins of our society, such as abortion, homosexuality, divorce, dishonesty, and greed. We must be light and salt and heralds to the world.

5. Jesus' admonition to turn the other cheek and to give to everyone who asks or takes sounds like a sure road to ruin. In practical terms, how must we live out these teachings?

People in our society are obsessed with demanding their rights and getting everything that is coming to them (or even more). Where this attitude prevails it sets every man against his neighbor. This is the reason for many of the fights and lawsuits that plague our society. Jesus set our example of conduct, and it is exactly the opposite of this. He gave up everything to serve our needs, and so He tells us to be less concerned about our own rights and more concerned for peace and righteousness. He asks us to be less concerned with getting and more concerned with giving. The Lord sees and notes our actions, and He will right any injustices and repay any losses.

Jesus Calls and Commissions Disciples

DEVOTIONAL READING: Matthew 8:18-22; 9:38; 10:1-15.

LESSON SCRIPTURE: Luke 9:51—10:12.

PRINTED TEXT: Luke 9:57—10:12.

Luke 9:57-62

57 And it came to pass, that, as they went in the way, a certain man said unto him, Lord, I will follow thee whithersoever thou goest.

58 And Jesus said unto him, Foxes have holes, and birds of the air have nests; but the Son of man hath not where to lay his head.

59 And he said unto another, Follow me. But he said, Lord, suffer me first to go and bury my father.

60 Jesus said unto him, Let the dead bury their dead: but go thou and preach the kingdom of God.

61 And another also said, Lord, I will follow thee; but let me first go bid them farewell, which are at home at my house.

62 And Jesus said unto him, No man, having put his hand to the plow, and looking back, is fit for the kingdom of God.

Luke 10:1-12

1 After these things the Lord appointed other seventy also, and sent them two and two before his face into every city and place, whither he himself would come.

2 Therefore said he unto them, The harvest truly is great, but the laborers are few: pray ye therefore the Lord of the harvest, that he would send forth laborers into his harvest.

3 Go your ways: behold, I send you forth as lambs among wolves.

4 Carry neither purse, nor scrip, nor shoes: and salute no man by the way.

5 And into whatsoever house ye enter, first say, Peace be to this house.

6 And if the son of peace be there, your peace shall rest upon it: if not, it shall turn to you again.

7 And in the same house remain, eating and drinking such things as they give: for the laborer is worthy of his hire. Go not from house to house.

8 And into whatsoever city ye enter, and they receive you, eat such things as are set before you:

9 And heal the sick that are therein, and say unto them, The kingdom of God is come nigh unto you.

10 But into whatsoever city ye enter, and they receive you not, go your ways out into the streets of the same, and say,

11 Even the very dust of your city, which cleaveth on us, we do wipe off against you: notwithstanding, be ye sure of this, that the kingdom of God is come nigh unto you.

12 But I say unto you, that it shall be more tolerable in that day for Sodom, than for that city.

GOLDEN TEXT: No man, having put his hand to the plow, and looking back, is fit for the kingdom of God.—Luke 9:62.

Lesson Aims

This lesson should equip the students to:

1. State the main idea involved in Jesus' response to those who would be His disciples.

2. Summarize the directions Jesus gave to the seventy messengers He sent out.

3. Name a point at which this lesson will make a difference in their own discipleship.

Lesson Outline

INTRODUCTION
   A. Single-Issue Campaign
   B. Following Where?
 I. WOULD-BE DISCIPLES (Luke 9:57-62)
   A. Do Your Homework (vv. 57, 58)
   B. Discipleship Comes First (vv. 59, 60)
     What Is First?
   C. Don't Be Looking Back! (vv. 61, 62)
II. WORKING DISCIPLES (Luke 10:1-12)
   A. Sent to Announce the Kingdom (vv. 1, 2)
     Workers Needed
   B. Security Is in the Sender (vv. 3, 4)
   C. Stay in One Place (vv. 5-7)
     Depending on Others
   D. Serve the City (vv. 8, 9)
   E. Speak God's Judgments (vv. 10-12)
CONCLUSION
   A. Reasons for the Call
   B. The Rest of the Story
   C. Prayer for Growth
   D. Thought to Remember

Visual 8 of the visuals packet relates to the thoughts found in Luke 9:57-62. Display it during the class session. The visual is shown on page 180.

Introduction

Jesus' ministry in Galilee had attracted and convinced many. There He reached the height of His popularity. His immediate disciples concluded and confessed that He was the promised Messiah, the Son of God. But others, less sympathetic and more politically powerful, concluded that He must not be allowed to continue.

Some were firmly determined to destroy Him, and He knew that the time of His sacrificial death was approaching. By various means He began, and continued, to tell His disciples that He must die, but that He would rise again from the grave. Generally they didn't accept what He said about His death, and so they were deaf to what He said about the resurrection.

He knew, however, that His time on earth was limited, and that He could not personally reach all the cities and villages in the land of the Jews with His gospel of God's kingdom. The ones He could reach would be served much better if they were prepared for His coming. It was time to engage His followers in the work He was doing. He needed help, and the disciples needed the preparation for the time when He would no longer be with them.

A. Single-Issue Campaign

Most of us have observed the development of single-issue campaigns in public life around us. When any number of persons become excited enough about any one cause or interest—be it moral, social, or economic—they tend to make all their decisions and direct all their influence on the basis of that one issue, often ignoring any number of equally important reasons to support some other claimant to their attention. So good folk often support bad candidates and destroy good ones simply because of their agreements or disagreements on those single issues.

What, if anything, is worth all that loyalty? There is nothing wrong with choosing a single issue, if you choose the right one! And Jesus Christ is the right issue. That was a point He found it constantly necessary to make with His disciples. Take, for example, the recent incident in Samaria on Jesus' way toward Jerusalem (Luke 9:51-56). Some Samaritans based their hospitality on a single issue—Samaritans versus Jews—and James and John were inclined to respond on the same basis. Jesus had to remind them of the greater issue—the purpose of His ministry.

B. Following Where?

The grand single issue of Christ and His mission becomes the continuing focus of discipleship—learning from Jesus and following Him. It means following where He goes. At the time described in our lesson He was on His way toward Jerusalem, where He had said He was going to die. His disciples did not want to to go there, but they were willing to go with Him, and that was the key to their faithfulness.

They proved to be faithful also in following Jesus' instructions as to what they should do and how they should do it during their journeying. Their example at that point is to be commended to all succeeding generations.

Not every would-be disciple was yet ready for that total commitment. At this point in the narrative Luke introduces the accounts of three who raised questions. Matthew 8:18-22 introduces two of these in an earlier setting. They may have come at various times. We may guess that Luke places the account here because it fits to the present teaching of discipleship rather than because of when it happened. The incidents illustrate the single issue of Christ and willingness to follow where He is going.

I. Would-Be Disciples (Luke 9:57-62)

Jesus' conversations with the three candidates for discipleship do not sound much like speeches for promotion or recruitment. It becomes apparent that He was seeking commitment rather than enrollment. His half brother James later reflected some of the same idea in writing, "Not many of you should presume to be teachers, my brothers, because you know that we who teach will be judged more strictly" (James 3:1, *New International Version*).

A. Do Your Homework (vv. 57, 58)

57. And it came to pass, that, as they went in the way, a certain man said unto him, Lord, I will follow thee whithersoever thou goest.

Jesus frequently taught as He walked from place to place with the twelve and others following. One listener seems to have been deeply stirred. Matthew 8:19 refers to him as "a certain scribe," which is remarkable since the scribes generally opposed Jesus. No fault can be found with the man's voluntary statement. Was he really willing and able to go with the Lord wherever He went? It seems almost too good to be true. Maybe it was. Did he have any idea of the directions and distances involved in Jesus' going?

58. And Jesus said unto him, Foxes have holes, and birds of the air have nests; but the Son of man hath not where to lay his head.

Jesus knew the man's mind, as we do not. He may have seen some hidden motive in the offer. Perhaps the volunteer was hoping for a position of advantage in some expected political kingdom. Perhaps he simply did not know the standard of living accepted by Jesus and His followers. Jesus was to say more later (Luke 14:25-33) about the cost of discipleship, and the need to consider it before making a commitment. For the present the Lord said that the nature of His ministry deprived Him of the simplest securities enjoyed by the wild creatures—a place to go home at night.

B. Discipleship Comes First (vv. 59, 60)

59. And he said unto another, Follow me. But he said, Lord, suffer me first to go and bury my father.

Jesus picked this man to be a disciple, and approached him with the same invitation He gave to each of the apostles. Here was evidently a worthy, thoughtful, and spiritually substantial person. His request for delay to arrange and attend his father's funeral seems entirely reasonable, especially in the light of the high priority given among the Jews to respect for the dead. But we do not know all the circumstances. Jesus did; and as usual He responded to inner thoughts and needs, rather than to words alone.

60. Jesus said unto him, Let the dead bury their dead: but go thou and preach the kingdom of God.

Perhaps the father was not dead, but aged and infirm. In that case an indefinite delay would be involved in the son's "burying" him. Or perhaps the funeral—customarily not later than the day after death—would be followed by delays in settling the estate. In any case, the spiritually dead could bury the physically dead. Other members of the family, not identified with the kingdom of Heaven, could do for the deceased all that could be done. Meanwhile this living disciple should give his attention to bringing spiritual life to persons still physically alive and potentially responsive.

More simply, Jesus was dealing with priorities. Important as respect to the dead may be, discipleship to Jesus and God's kingdom are vastly more important.

WHAT IS FIRST?

If there is anyone who has an excuse for not being an evangelist, it is Mack Wilson. Mack has been horribly crippled by rheumatoid arthritis. The disease and the medicine have taken his eyesight. His legs have been amputated. He has spent much of his life in a nursing home. He has known extreme physical and emotional pain. He has known isolation and loss beyond measure, but his courage and determination are a challenge to all who come to know him.

He recently graduated from college with a degree in gerontology. But much more impressive is the fact that Mack has used his time to grow close to God. He witnesses of his faith to those who come near. He listens to Scripture tapes and has taken Bible correspondence courses. Nurses and others whose lives have crossed his have come to accept Christ as Savior. How feeble my excuses for haphazard faith and evangelism seem when I sit beside Mack!   —W. P.

C. Don't Be Looking Back!

(vv. 61, 62)

61. And another also said, Lord, I will follow thee; but let me first go bid them farewell, which are at home at my house.

This man's request seems reasonable, since he spoke as the head of *my house*. He could cite precedents. When the prophet Elijah called Elisha to accompany him, Elisha made a sacrifice and farewell feast for those in his house (1 Kings 19:19-21). After Matthew "left all" to follow Jesus he made a great feast in his house with friends, including Jesus (Luke 5:27-32). But that was as much introduction as farewell.

We don't know this man's mind. Jesus did.

62. And Jesus said unto him, No man, having put his hand to the plow, and looking back, is fit for the kingdom of God.

Today's English Version puts it this way: "Anyone who starts to plow and then keeps looking back is of no use for the Kingdom of God." Jesus' references to the daily labor of farmers were probably more meaningful to His hearers than they are to us. I once held the handles of a light plow behind a horse, and I can appreciate the need for the first-time plowman behind oxen to give his whole attention to the work, lest he become entangled with harness, hooves, and damaged crops. To keep looking over his shoulder, as the language suggests, would mark the rookie as being totally unsuited to the task.

Jesus may have recognized that the recruit's farewell visit home could easily become an occasion for extended counsel with loved ones who had no interest in God's kingdom, and could dissuade him entirely from it. At the very least, to make that visit the *first* order of business would be to reverse the necessary priorities. "Remember Lot's wife," Jesus once warned (Luke 17:32; Genesis 19:26), and the apostle Paul accepted the warning to focus his attention forward (Philippians 3:13, 14).

II. Working Disciples

(Luke 10:1-12)

Perhaps purposefully, the Bible does not tell us what any of the three would-be disciples did about accepting Jesus' challenge. What would *you* have done? The Gospel writers allowed these candidates to stand as representing many others, some of whom rose to the opportunity and became faithful followers of Jesus, and some of whom went back to a less demanding—and infinitely less fruitful—life-style. The following verses tell of a rather remarkable number whose faith had proved equal to the challenge.

visual 8

A. Sent to Announce the Kingdom

(vv. 1, 2)

1. After these things the Lord appointed other seventy also, and sent them two and two before his face into every city and place, whither he himself would come.

As Jesus had appointed the twelve apostles and had sent them out preaching and healing (Luke 6:12-16; 9:1-6), so now He selected and commissioned *seventy* others of His followers (the number is given as seventy-two in some early manuscripts and some translations). Again as with the twelve (Mark 6:7), He sent them in pairs for mutual support, help, and encouragement. The same pattern was followed after Pentecost by Peter and John, Paul and Barnabas, Paul and Silas, etc.

Jesus had left Galilee (Luke 9:51-53). He now faced a large and populous area in Judea and in Perea east of the Jordan. The disciples would serve as advance agents preparing for His ministry in every place He would reach. This time their mission was not limited to the Jews (see Matthew 10:5).

2. Therefore said he unto them, The harvest truly is great, but the laborers are few: pray ye therefore the Lord of the harvest, that he would send forth laborers into his harvest.

The seventy were like reapers in a huge field of grain. Their urgent cry would be, "Help, Lord! The field is too big for our crew. Please enlist and rush more workers into the field before it is too late!" That is a feeling and a cry shared by Christian workers almost everywhere today.

WORKERS NEEDED

One of the great sights in the western part of our country is the wheat harvest. Throughout the great plains the wheat fields turn golden. Great waves sweep through huge fields of grain. Beginning in Oklahoma and moving north all the way to Canada, the custom cutters move from farm to farm. Driving five or six huge combines, they work day and night to harvest the crop at just the right time. Blue sky above, white clouds towering, the whir of gigantic machinery, golden grain being cut and threshed—the sight of this annual ritual of harvest burns itself indelibly into the memory.

Jesus saw the world as a field ready for harvest. He urged his followers to pray for workers to enter that field. Have we been praying that prayer?   —W. P.

B. Security Is in the Sender (vv. 3, 4)

Grain fields may cause dismay by their size, but they will not rise up and bite the laborer. Jesus' disciples faced danger as well as difficulty.

3. Go your ways: behold, I send you forth as lambs among wolves.

The angry opposers who had determined to destroy Jesus would not deal delicately with disciples announcing His coming. But those disciples must be as He was—refusing to meet force with force. Physically they were to be as defenseless as sheep—nay, rather as lambs—among wolves. More is found in Jesus' words to the twelve on their earlier mission: "Be ye therefore wise as serpents, and harmless as doves. But beware of men: for they will deliver you up to the councils, and they will scourge you in their synagogues" (Matthew 10:16, 17). The wolves would show the clean teeth of piety! But the messengers would not be dependent only on their wits for their safety. It was Jesus who sent them out! And that was enough.

4. Carry neither purse, nor scrip, nor shoes: and salute no man by the way.

Without money or baggage—not even a "beggar's bag" (or knapsack) or extra sandals—they would present no temptation to thieves nor threat to those among whom they labored. No one would be tempted to accept them or their message for the sake of material advantage. Their attention was to be obviously on matters other than their own comfort and convenience (Matthew 6:25-34; Luke 12:22-31). In seeking first God's kingdom and His righteousness, they would find their necessities supplied.

They were to move as men pursuing a purpose, not taking time for long formal greetings nor trivial conversation. They were here on business for their King!

C. Stay in One Place (vv. 5-7)

5, 6. And into whatsoever house ye enter, first say, Peace be to this house. And if the son of peace be there, your peace shall rest upon it: if not, it shall turn to you again.

The disciples' announcement of the kingdom was probably made both in public areas and in homes. In a home the greatest respect and courtesy would be exercised in pronouncing a blessing on that house. It was no mere routine greeting, but an objective spiritual gift, which could be accepted or declined. If the head of the family was receptive and responsive to the blessing, the Lord's messenger would become his guest for the duration of his stay in that community. If not, the spiritual gift would be withdrawn, and the messenger would move on. The decision would rest with the host.

7. And in the same house remain, eating and drinking such things as they give: for the laborer is worthy of his hire. Go not from house to house.

No time was to be spent in shopping around for lodgings. Neither was the guest to be particular about what he would eat, either for ceremonial reasons or for personal preference. God's kingdom was to be announced alike to all. No embarrassment should attach to accepting hospitality, even from the poor. The messenger was not freeloading. He was clearly busy at the Lord's work and earning his keep (1 Corinthians 9:14; 1 Timothy 5:18). The host became a participant in his ministry.

DEPENDING ON OTHERS

A world traveler, commenting on his seven-year journey by motorcycle from Australia and Southeast Asia to Europe, said that when he set out he did not know how to change a tire on his bike. When he had his first flat in Australia he had to flag down a passing motorist to get help to get the tire off. It was embarrassing, he said, because he had painted "Around the World" in large letters on the sidecar in which he had packed all his gear. He said, "I had to learn somewhere, and I found that when I swallowed my pride and depended on others, I made all kinds of friends."   —W. P.

D. Serve the City (vv. 8, 9)

8, 9. And into whatsoever city ye enter, and they receive you, eat such things as are set before you: and heal the sick that are therein, and say unto them, The kingdom of God is come nigh unto you.

The messengers were to make themselves at home and serve each city. They were to leave gifts of healing (compare Acts 3:6) as expressions of gratitude, as a part of Jesus' compassionate ministry, and as substantial evidence of divine authority behind their message. But they must never forget the main purpose of their mission, to announce that God's kingdom was at hand. Jesus the Messiah was in the area and would soon be among them. He himself would soon be saying, "The kingdom of God is within [or among] you" (Luke 17:21). His gospel ministry would soon be accomplished and His kingdom on earth established.

E. Speak God's Judgments (vv. 10-12)

Just as there would be a variety of responses among persons invited to discipleship with Jesus, and a variety of responses among households approached by the commissioned disciples, so the cities they entered would not all respond in the same way, and each would be responsible for its response.

10, 11a. But into whatsoever city ye enter, and they receive you not, go your ways out into the streets of the same, and say, Even the very dust of your city, which cleaveth on us, we do wipe off against you.

The Lord takes seriously the treatment accorded His messengers. He said to them, "He that heareth you heareth me; and he that despiseth you despiseth me; and he that despiseth me despiseth him that sent me" (Luke 10:16). That responsibility must be made plain to the persons involved; privately to individuals, publicly in the open gathering places to the communities. The gesture of dusting off could mean (1) your city that has rejected us we now totally reject—even to the dust of its streets; or (2) the dust of your streets has been more receptive than have you, its citizens. So let the dust remain to testify against you.

11b. Notwithstanding, be ye sure of this, that the kingdom of God is come nigh unto you.

One way or another, the sure message of the kingdom would be delivered. It was still true, whether or not it was believed. To those who accepted it, the nearness of God's reign would bring comfort. To resisters and rejecters it would bring the terrors of judgment and forfeited opportunity. To those who repented of their present rejection and received it, the kingdom would still be available. But perhaps because of the shortness of time Jesus would bypass some of the rejecting cities entirely.

12. But I say unto you, that it shall be more tolerable in that day for Sodom, than for that city.

Genesis 19 tells of God's condemnation and destruction of Sodom for its overwhelming sexual perversions—especially homosexuality (sodomy)—and the name of the city has become a permanent symbol of all that is abhorrent to the Almighty. Nevertheless, Jesus said that in the final judgment a still heavier condemnation would fall on the cities that had received a greater revelation of God's nature and kingdom and had rejected that (Luke 12:48).

Conclusion

A. Reasons for the Call

If we are tempted to think that Jesus' warnings and demands to prospective disciples (Luke 9:57-62) are unrealistic or unreasonable, the thought should disappear when we consider the task to which His disciples were called (Luke 10:1-13). It was no occupation for a person faint in his faith or wavering in his commitment. It is still true that Christian service without faltering is possible only to those who follow Christ without reservation.

B. The Rest of the Story

Did Jesus' seventy disciples follow His instructions? Were they glad for what they did? Was their mission successful? The answer to all these questions is *yes*, found in Luke 10:17-20. We don't know how much later they reported back to the Lord, but it was a joyous report: even the demons were subject to them in His name. Jesus promised them increased measures of power, but reminded them that the greater reason for rejoicing lay in the single fact that their names were written in Heaven. And that is a blessing still available. Have you ever known a devoted Christian who wished he had given *less* to his Lord?

C. Prayer for Growth

Thank You, God, for the grace and mercy of Your firm directives and warnings. Help us to follow them in trust and obedience, as joyous citizens of Your kingdom. In Jesus' name, amen.

D. Thought to Remember

The Lord's faithful followers become His advance agents, preparing others to follow Him.

Home Daily Bible Readings

Monday, Jan. 17—A Centurion Shows Great Faith (Luke 7:1-10)

Tuesday, Jan. 18—Women Who Were With Jesus (Luke 8:1-3; 23:55-56)

Wednesday, Jan. 19—Twelve Receive Power and Authority (Luke 9:1-6)

Thursday, Jan. 20—Jesus Turns Toward Jerusalem (Luke 9:51-56)

Friday, Jan. 21—Priorities of Discipleship (Luke 9:57-62)

Saturday, Jan. 22—"Peace Be to This House" (Luke 10:1-7)

Sunday, Jan. 23—The Kingdom Comes Near (Luke 10:8-12)

Learning by Doing

*This page contains an alternate lesson plan emphasizing learning activities. Classes
desiring such student involvement will find these suggestions helpful.*

Learning Goals

Each disciple, having studied today's text for
what it says, for what it means, and for the "so-
whats" in his or her own life, will:

1. Be able to explain why Jesus appears harsh
and demanding in this text.

2. Compare Jesus' expectations shown in
these verses with His expectations of His disciples in general.

3. Compare his or her own commitment and
behavior with those of the three and of the seventy.

Into the Lesson

Recruit four to six class members in advance
for a short drama; one to be the personnel director and the others to be applicants 1, 2, 3, 4, and
5. (or two of the first three can also play the
parts of 4 and 5).

Set up a "Personnel Office" in the front of the
room: small desk or table with sign reading,
"Personnel Director"; one chair on director's
side, two on applicants' side, three in waiting
area. Give each player a copy of this script:

Director and Applicant 1 sit at table.

DIR: Good morning, Mr. _____. So you'd like
to work with us?

AP. 1: Yes, I want to get a better home nearby
as soon as I land this job.

DIR: Well, Mr. _____, we'll let you know.
Thanks for coming.

Applicant 1 leaves; Applicant 2 enters and sits.

DIR: Well, Mr._____, we're eager to have you
working with us. When can you start?

AP. 2: I want to get my parents settled in a retirement home first. Maybe two or three months.

DIR: We need someone now, so why don't you
come back when you're available?

Applicant 2 leaves; Applicant 3 enters and sits.

DIR: Well, Mr. _____, we're eager for some additional workers. When can you start?

AP. 3: My family's having a big reunion next
week and I have to be there, but I can start in
two weeks.

DIR: Thank you. Don't call us; we'll call you.

Applicant 3 leaves.

DIR: (to intercom): Secretary, send in those
workers who are committed to the job.

Applicants 4 and 5 enter and sit.

DIR: Friends, your assignment is ready. This
will be dangerous, so listen to the rules. One,

take nothing with you; you'll be living with others and depending on them. Two, if a town
doesn't welcome you, just move on—but pronounce a curse on it. Will you take the job?

APS. 4 and 5: Absolutely, Boss! We're ready to
go.

Into the Word

Direct attention to the text and ask students to
tell details in it that are like those in the drama.
Record on the chalkboard those that are mentioned. They may include these and others;

1. Prospective workers are interviewed.

2. Excuses for delay are not accepted.

3. The job is dangerous.

4. Material benefits are few.

5. Workers may sometimes be unwelcome.

Next, ask students to tell how the text is different from the drama. For example:

1. Jesus spoke more sternly to those who
made excuses for delay.

2. Jesus told His workers to pray for more
workers in the same field.

3. Jesus' instructions are more detailed. Let
students mention details not seen in the drama.

Were the seventy successful on the job? Put
that question to the class. If no one answers
promptly and correctly, let an excellent reader
read Luke 10:17-20 aloud. Give special attention
to the main reason for rejoicing.

Into Life

Ask students to pray together silently as you
suggest thoughts for their prayers. Suggest these
and/or others appropriate to the lesson:

1. Thank God for the good news of His kingdom, made so plain that ordinary people like us
can understand.

2. Thank God for the seventy and others in
ancient times who carried the news.

3. Thank Him for Luke and others who
recorded the good news for us.

4. Thank God for people who have helped
you personally to know the good news. Name
specific people.

5. Thank God for recording such people's
names in Heaven.

6. Name someone with whom you can share
what you know about Christ and His kingdom.
Ask for help in finding a time and a way to
share.

Let's Talk It Over

The questions on this page are designed to encourage review of the lesson Scriptures and to promote discussion of the lesson by the class. The answers provided are only discussion starters. Let your class talk it over from there.

1. Excuses, excuses! Apparently the men in our text thought they had good reasons for delay in following Jesus, but Jesus thought otherwise. What are some excuses that modern people offer to evade the duties of discipleship?

We are just as inventive as those men of old. Our excuses seem convincing to us, but do they convince the Lord?

" My contribution has to be small because I'm buying a house." But don't you give higher priority to the Lord's tenth than to anything you buy for yourself?

"When the children are grown, I'll have more time for the church." But your faithful Christian service now has an important part in the up-bringing of your children.

"When I retire I'll have lots of time for the Lord." But if you don't start working for Him now, you won't know how to do it later.

"I don't have any talent." Look again, friend. If you did not have any ability you wouldn't be earning a living or bringing up a family or making friends.

2. What if those three had followed Jesus as Peter, James, and John did? They might have accomplished as much as those apostles did, but they missed their opportunity. What happens when we turn away from a challenge to serve Jesus?

Our faith gets weaker instead of stronger. Our talents stagnate when they could be growing. We drift away from the Lord instead of drawing closer. We become more self-sufficient instead of learning to trust the Lord. In all these ways and more we become poorer when we fail to answer Jesus' call to follow Him.

3. Workers are always scarce in the Lord's kingdom. What can we do to increase their number?

Every Christian should be a worker, but the church needs a continuing force of full-time preachers, teachers, missionaries, benevolent workers, and the like. We can pray earnestly for laborers in the harvest. We can encourage young people who show an interest in Christian careers. We can care less about lucrative careers

for our children and care more about their service to the Lord. We can esteem and praise and support Christian leaders. Young people who hear workers criticized and belittled will not be eager to join their ranks. We can prepare and send workers, helping them with their Bible-college training and supporting them on mission fields. And some of us can go into full-time service ourselves.

4. Jesus said a worker deserves his wages, yet intolerably low wages compel some ministers to leave the ministry. What standards should we have in the way we support God's workers?

All sincere ministers and missionaries are willing to sacrifice for the sake of the kingdom, but they should not do all the sacrificing. A Christian worker's real income should at least equal the average income of the church members, including all perks and benefits. The church should pay his business expenses just as a secular employer would. An adequately paid worker is able to devote his full energy and enthusiasm to his service. Churches that treat the Lord's workers with respect and generosity also honor the Lord who sent them.

5. Jesus said a person who puts his hand to the plow and looks back is not fit for service in the kingdom. He does not want His followers to look back to the old life they used to live. How might we look back? How can we avoid it?

A plowman who keeps stopping and looking back does a slow and poor job of plowing. Just so the worker in the kingdom who keeps turning back and paying attention to the cares of the world will not get much accomplished for the Lord. Once we commit ourselves to serve the Lord we must do it with our whole heart and strength. Vacations in Florida, weekends at the lake, bigger houses, perfect yards, TV, books, career, praise, and security are no longer our main concerns. We can avoid looking back if we keep our eyes and hearts fixed on the job before us and the goal at the end. We see this exemplified in men and women who have given a whole life in service and continue to serve as long as strength allows.

Jesus Tells Parables About the Lost

DEVOTIONAL READING: Isaiah 40:9-11; Ezekiel 34:1-6, 11, 12, 15, 16.

LESSON SCRIPTURE: Luke 15.

PRINTED TEXT: Luke 15:11-24.

Luke 15:11-24

11 And he said, A certain man had two sons:

12 And the younger of them said to his father, Father, give me the portion of goods that falleth to me. And he divided unto them his living.

13 And not many days after the younger son gathered all together, and took his journey into a far country, and there wasted his substance with riotous living.

14 And when he had spent all, there arose a mighty famine in that land; and he began to be in want.

15 And he went and joined himself to a citizen of that country; and he sent him into his fields to feed swine.

16 And he would fain have filled his belly with the husks that the swine did eat: and no man gave unto him.

17 And when he came to himself, he said, How many hired servants of my father's have bread enough and to spare, and I perish with hunger!

18 I will arise and go to my father, and will say unto him, Father, I have sinned against heaven, and before thee,

19 And am no more worthy to be called thy son: make me as one of thy hired servants.

20 And he arose, and came to his father. But when he was yet a great way off, his father saw him, and had compassion, and ran, and fell on his neck, and kissed him.

21 And the son said unto him, Father, I have sinned against heaven, and in thy sight, and am no more worthy to be called thy son.

22 But the father said to his servants, Bring forth the best robe, and put it on him; and put a ring on his hand, and shoes on his feet:

23 And bring hither the fatted calf, and kill it; and let us eat, and be merry:

24 For this my son was dead, and is alive again; he was lost, and is found. And they began to be merry.

Jan 30

GOLDEN TEXT: This my son was dead, and is alive again; he was lost, and is found.
—Luke 15:24.

Lesson Aims

This study should enable the student to:

1. Identify the three lost-and-found parables recorded in Luke 15 and outline the story of the lost-and-found son.

2. Distinguish between the foolish prodigality of the young man and the godlike prodigality of the father in dealing with his two sons.

Lesson Outline

Visual 9 of the visuals packet illustrates a truth contained in the parable for our study. The visual is shown on page 189.

Introduction

A. What and Who Is Prodigal?

If you encounter *prodigal* only in a title given to Jesus' parable in Luke 15:11-32, you may think of it only as describing a sinner—wayward, wasteful, and wicked. But if your attention has been called to the *prodigality* of God's creation—consider the number of seeds produced every year by that tree nearby—you will recognize in the word a different meaning, and not all bad. Your dictionary will define *prodigality* in terms of profusion and extravagance, frequently reckless and wasteful, but perhaps only excessively generous. It is, in fact, a quality manifest in God's giving His one and only Son to save wayward and wicked humanity, as well as God's giving His sunshine and rain to all, without regard to their deserving. In Jesus' parable of the father and his two sons, the younger one was *prodigal* in squandering his inheritance; the father was fully as *prodigal* in giving and forgiving, in welcoming the wanderer at his return, and in dealing patiently with the older brother.

Jesus reflected God's lavish generosity in relating to people who clearly did not deserve it—tax collectors, irreligious folk, and prostitutes. His critics thought that He wasted His spiritual substance with riotous *livers* (Luke 15:1, 2). Jesus did not deny their charge. He acknowledged and defended His actions as being most appropriate with the program of Heaven itself: "Joy shall be in heaven over one sinner that repenteth, more than over ninety and nine just persons, which need no repentance" (Luke 15:7). Now, isn't that an extravagant statement?

B. Lost and Found

Jesus developed the theme of God's extravagant grace by citing three examples finding and restoring treasured items that had been lost. First He assumed that the owner of a hundred sheep would leave his whole flock in order to search out and bring back one stray, and would then publicly celebrate his success (vv. 3-7). To folk who have not owned and cared for animals, that seems almost prodigal, but sheep are living and dependent, though stupid and prone to wander. The owner becomes involved with them, somewhat as God does with His people.

Jesus then spoke of a woman's sweeping and searching the dim corners of her house to find a single coin she had lost, and then rejoicing with her friends when she found it (vv. 8-10). That, too, seems unreasonable, unless the coin possessed great sentimental value. But which of us has not spent ten dollars' worth of time hunting for a misplaced item not worth a dollar, especially if it was a familiar possession?

C. Homecoming Story

Jesus' third lost-and-found parable was entirely different. It dealt with persons. The lostness was not accidental. Unlike the sheep that wandered off or the coin that was misplaced, the young wanderer wanted to get lost. He didn't want to be discovered by anyone he knew.

Hence any effort to restrain him from going or to trace him after he had gone would be a confinement against his will—a violation of his personhood. To be found, he would have to return to his father by the same free choice he exercised in leaving.

What, though, would happen when he repented of his rebellion and surrendered? Would there be celebration, as followed the finding of the lost sheep and the lost coin? That question links the three parables into one, and ties them with the rejoicing in Heaven over a sinner's repenting.

This, then, is a homecoming story. All before the homecoming is background, introducing the characters and telling briefly how they became separated and what led to the young man's return. As in the story's first line, so also in its homecoming conclusion three persons were involved—the welcoming father, the welcomed penitent, and the unwelcoming older brother.

I. Father Gives In and Gives Out (Luke 15:11, 12)

From its earliest words, Jesus' matchless story moves with swift simplicity, couched in terms that touch the experience of people in all times and all places.

11, 12. And he said, A certain man had two sons: and the younger of them said to his father, Father, give me the portion of goods that falleth to me. And he divided unto them his living.

The characters stand out vividly because every one of us is either a parent or a child. More often than not, the older child accepts responsibility: the younger inclines to rebellion. That quality appears immediately in the demand: "I want my share of your estate now!" The demand was stated without *please* or *thanks*. Deuteronomy 21:17 indicates that the firstborn son should receive a "double portion" of the parent's estate: hence the younger son might receive a third of his father's total assets.

How could a worthy father yield to such an unreasonable demand? Would he not know that it would mean providing the tools for his son's self-destruction? Would not fatherly love forbid such a reckless abandonment of responsibility?

But this father, like God, loved and respected this young person before him too much to make a prisoner or a puppet of him. The time had come for the youth to choose, and for the father—prodigal as it might be—to respect that choice. So when humankind, knowing God, rejected God and chose their own self-destructive

course, "God gave them up" to their own wicked ways and to "receiving in themselves that recompense of their error which was meet" (Romans 1:20-32).

So this prodigally recklessly loving father yielded to the son's demand and divided his material assets between the two brothers. Afterward he would say to the older one, "All that I have is thine" (Luke 15:31).

II. The Son Wastes and Wants (Luke 15:13-16)

How did the older son respond to his newly acquired wealth and responsibilities? We can only guess, but from his later comments he seems not to have appreciated nor availed himself of the benefits available at home. His father's continuing presence seems not to have meant much to him (vv. 29-31).

A. Getting Away and Giving Away (v. 13)

13. And not many days after the younger son gathered all together, and took his journey into a far country, and there wasted his substance with riotous living.

The young man acted promptly on his determination to "get lost" from his father and home. First he had to convert his assets into things he could take with him. Then he put as much distance as possible between himself and the disciplines in which he had been reared.

We see a frightening comparison between this and a currently popular American mood in education, communication, entertainment, and social customs. There seems to be a frantic haste to get away from God and the Bible, with whatever influence they might exert on human behavior. The results are not encouraging.

In His parable Jesus said all that is necessary to say about the rebel's life in the fast lane and its effect on his resources—financial, physical, emotional, and moral. The Biblical word for *wasted* suggests something like tossing his money to the wind. There are hundreds of ways—foolish, sinful, or both—in which a rebel spirit and unearned wealth can combine to ruin a young person. The youth can get away from home, but not from the facts of life. There were more difficulties in store.

B. Hard Times and Harder Work (vv. 14, 15)

14, 15. And when he had spent all, there arose a mighty famine in that land; and he began to be in want. And he went and joined himself to a citizen of that country; and he sent him into his fields to feed swine.

The young man was no sooner reduced to living hand-to-mouth for vital necessities than a severe drought removed the normal food supplies. Independence was no longer possible. Desperation drove him to a final embarrassment—attaching himself as a dependent to a man whose habits were as far from those of his father as *that country* was from his home. That citizen saw no reason to deal gently with the young foreigner; hence he laid on him a task as loathsome as possible to a Jew. He made him a swineherd, attending to animals unclean in every way. His work would be to protect his charges from wandering and from attack, and to find food for them.

C. Hunger and No Relief (v. 16)

16. And he would fain have filled his belly with the husks that the swine did eat: and no man gave unto him.

Our young friend was in no position to negotiate a favorable employment contract! His food allowance was the privilege of competing with a herd of hungry hogs for their fodder—stuff that only the poorest of men would eat under the direst of circumstances.

If this seems unrealistic, consider the plight of homeless runaways on the streets of major cities throughout the world. And consider the spiritual starvation of millions who suffer the "famine . . . of hearing the words of the Lord" described in Amos 8:11, 12. Fed on the husks of humanism, a generation starves unnecessarily in the *far country* where they have fled to escape from their Heavenly Father.

III. The Son Faces the Facts
(Luke 15:17-20a)

"When you are flat on your back," they say, "there is no way to look but upward."

A. Realization (v. 17)

17. And when he came to himself, he said, How many hired servants of my father's have bread enough and to spare, and I perish with hunger!

The passage says literally that he *came into himself.* He had been acting like a man "beside himself," denying who he was and whose he was. Now the hammering of hardship had jolted him back to reality. Whereas he had insisted on "being me" he knew now that it was much better to be his father's son and follow in *his* way. At least the son—or even the hired men—would not be hungry at home. How expensively he had learned in the school of experience what he could have learned by listening at home!

B. Repentance and Resolve (vv. 18, 19)

18, 19. I will arise and go to my father, and will say unto him, Father, I have sinned against heaven, and before thee, and am no more worthy to be called thy son: make me as one of thy hired servants.

The choice, determination, and effort that had taken him away from home must now be matched in going the opposite direction. He had left his father and would return to his father. Everything else about home was incidental. Confession and appeal would be addressed directly to him.

The full and frank confession here framed must stand as a model of true repentance. *I have sinned.* No one else is blamed or implicated. No excuse or softening circumstance is suggested. The man's misdeeds are called by their proper name—sin.

Against heaven. Any unholy action is an offense to our holy God. David said this in his penitential Psalm 51:4: "Against thee, thee only, have I sinned, and done this evil in thy sight." Yet sins against God hurt other people, too, as the young penitent recognized in acknowledging his sin, *Father . . . before thee.* He was through with the old self-deception that says, "I am not hurting anyone but myself."

No more worthy to be called thy son. He still *was* a son, however, and as such he hoped to be hired by his father rather than by any of the neighbors. He still depended on the family relationship.

C. Return (v. 20a)

20a. And he arose, and came to his father.

The young man's resolve was translated promptly into action. He got up from where he was sitting. He got up from the depths of helpless despair and self-pity. He retraced the long road between the far country and the family home. But his purposeful approach was not to a place. It was to a person, his father—the same father he had abandoned on his downward course. So at this point the focus of the story shifts to that extravagantly loving father.

THE SCENT OF LOVE

Scott Harrison tells of a sad day in the field when he somehow got separated from Sam, his bird dog. Whistling and calling did no good. Scott had to leave for an important appointment, but he took off his shirt and left it on the ground. When he came back the next morning, Sam was curled up on the shirt. Like that intelligent dog, the prodigal son knew the scent of love.

—W. P.

IV. Father Rejoices in Welcome
(Luke 15:20b-24)

A. He Goes Out to Greet (vv. 20b, 21)

20b. But when he was yet a great way off, his father saw him, and had compassion, and ran, and fell on his neck, and kissed him.

Here is the answer to any question about the father's love for his rebellious son. He respected the young man's demand for his inheritance and allowed him to leave, because he loved him as a person. He refrained from following, searching, or rescuing him in the far country, for the same reason. But he obviously spent much time scanning the horizon on the route of his departure, hoping, longing, and praying for his return. So the returning son was seen and recognized at a distance, despite the changes that must have come in his clothing and in his bearing. A rush of pity for the young man's hardship added force to fatherly love in covering the distance between the two. Words would have added little to the tearful embrace and kiss of welcome. Now wasn't that all a bit much—like the reckless outpouring of God in giving His Son for our salvation? After all, the returning wanderer hadn't said a word yet! He could have been coming back to ask for more money. But he was coming back!

21. And the son said unto him, Father, I have sinned against heaven, and in thy sight, and am no more worthy to be called thy son.

No conditions had been required for his acceptance, but the young man made his confession anyway. Perhaps deliberately he stopped short of asking for a job. He had been given a son's welcome. Perhaps he would not even suggest that he doubted its sincerity. Perhaps in all of the excitement his planned speech was interrupted by the onrush of his father's next command.

CONFIDENCE

Remember "Wrong-way Reigels," the football player? In the Rose Bowl he was rushing the quarterback when he was hit so hard he was dazed for a moment. In that moment the pass

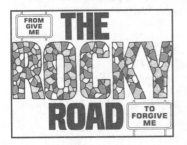

visual 9

was deflected right into his hands, and he had sense enough to grasp it and run. He ran more than half the length of the field—in the wrong direction! Only a tackle by a teammate kept him from scoring for the other team.

You may remember that story, but do you remember that Reigels came back in the second half and played the greatest game of his life? How could he recover so quickly from the shame of his mammoth blunder? He said the coach looked him in the eye at half-time and said, "I believe in you! I expect a great game from you!"

We don't know the rest of our Bible story, but we like to think the father's confidence made a good man out of that prodigal boy.   —W. P.

B. He Commands a Celebration
(vv. 22, 23)

In his reckless love, the father not only failed to require conditions for the son's reinstatement. He didn't even listen to the conditions the offender was prepared to offer!

22. But the father said to his servants, Bring forth the best robe, and put it on him; and put a ring on his hand, and shoes on his feet.

Even the slaves, who seem to have followed their master's rush to meet his son, must have wondered at the impractical nature of the old gentleman's directives. What about a general cleaning up first? Something to get rid of the soil and smell of the pig pasture clinging to his person and his apparel? At least a washing of the feet to make him more comfortable?

Oh, yes, those, too; but the business of first importance is to say in ways that cannot be mistaken, "Welcome home, SON!" Lay on his shoulders—perhaps even over his rags, the royal *robe* of honor; put on his hand the signet *ring* of authority; put on his feet the sandals of a family member to distinguish him from the barefooted servants. This is no strange visitor, nor even an honored guest. This is my son!

23. And bring hither the fatted calf, and kill it; and let us eat, and be merry.

"Let's have a feast and celebrate!" Here is the theme of all three parables in Luke 15—joyous, shared celebration over the finding of that which was lost.

Genesis 18:1-8, with its detailed directions for a dinner quickly prepared for guests, will help us to understand the procedure. Stall-fed veal is ready at hand to provide deliciously marbled, tender steaks on short notice. The cooks will prepare bread, beverages, and other foods quickly from available materials. When the returning son sits at this feast, he will muse, "Until I came home to Father I was starving in a pig pasture!" The joy of finding the lost is not limited to the finders.

C. He Speaks of Resurrection (v. 24)

24. For this my son was dead, and is alive again; he was lost, and is found. And they began to be merry.

My son! the theme of a paternal love is sounded again. God also loves His children.

Was dead, and is alive. For a time he was removed as far as possible from the father. His return was like a resurrection. The theme is echoed in Christian conversion: "When you were dead in your sins . . . God made you alive with Christ" (Colossians 2:13, *New International Version*).

He was lost, and is found. Here is the celebration theme of the chapter—rejoicing at the finding of that which was lost. The lost son had to be found by the operation of his own will. Those who have not known the father must be sought, and taught, and brought. But unless we recognize the lostness of the lost, we are ill prepared to rejoice in the finding.

TURNAROUND

The whale was a lady, but the newsmen didn't know that. They named her Humphrey because she was a humpback whale. Somehow she took a wrong turn and swam up a river. She would surely run aground and die unless she could be turned around.

How do you turn a reluctant forty-five-ton whale? Concerned workers tried tapping pipes under the water. Somehow Humphrey got the message, turned, swam down the river, and back into the Pacific Ocean to the cheers of a nation watching on TV.

The turnaround of an endangered whale was big news to the world, but it was insignificant in comparison with the turnaround of a doomed sinner. There's a turnaround that brings joy in Heaven (Luke 15:10).   —W. P.

Conclusion

A. The Unwelcoming Committee

The opening verses of Luke 15 introduce three kinds of people—Jesus, the commoners who crowded around Him, and the elite who objected to His welcoming the commoners. The opening words of our text introduce three persons—the father and his two sons. The conclusion depicts a celebration centering around two of them, but opposed by the older son. He objected, just as the Jewish elite objected to Jesus' welcoming the commoners (Luke 15:25-32).

Yet even to the objector, the father was extravagantly patient, addressing his very rebuke in terms of tender affection (v. 31). But until the elder could feel the loss of his absent brother, he could not share the jubilation at his rescue and return. The homecoming story is not complete without this sobering reminder.

B. Our Place in the Story

The story before us is unforgettable and powerful because each of us finds himself or herself somewhere in it. But where? Most of us have been at some time to some boundary of the far country with the young rebel and know something of his pain and remorse. In Christ, most of us have come home to our Heavenly Father's welcome. We parents know some part of the father's experience with wayward youth. And we have perhaps shared more than a touch of the older brother's jealous resentment at attention showered on "undeserving" others. And that opens the way to the most profitable identification of all—the place of the elder brother, rebuked, taught, and convinced by a loving Father to be more like Him in caring for the lost, laboring and praying for their salvation, and rejoicing when it is accomplished. That brings us closer to Heaven!

C. Prayer for Godlike Prodigality

Thank you, dear Father in Heaven, for the patient love, the tender mercy, and the forgiving grace that You have lavished without limit on us. May we learn to be more like You in sharing your spirit and your generosity with Your other children. For Jesus' sake, amen.

D. Thought to Remember

"Joy shall be in heaven over one sinner that repenteth, more than over ninety and nine just persons, which need no repentance" (Luke 15:7).

Home Daily Bible Readings

Monday, Jan. 24—How to Inherit Eternal Life (Luke 10:25-37)

Tuesday, Jan. 25—Mary Chooses the Better Part (Luke 10:38-42)

Wednesday, Jan. 26—Proper Place for Treasures (Luke 12:13-21, 32-34)

Thursday, Jan. 27—Rejoice When Lost Are Found (Luke 15:1-7)

Friday, Jan. 28—Finding Lost Coins and Sons (Luke 15:8-24)

Saturday, Jan. 29—Envy Destroys Love (Luke 15:25-32)

Sunday, Jan. 30—Last Will Be First (Luke 13:22-30)

Learning by Doing

This page contains an alternate lesson plan emphasizing learning activities. Classes desiring such student involvement will find these suggestions helpful.

Learning Goals

With this review of Jesus' parable of a prodigal son and father, the learners will:

1. Understand it as a beautiful picture of God's love for sinners and His acceptance of those who repent.

2. Draw at least five parallels between the story and their own relationship with God.

3. Use the story in their evangelistic work.

Into the Lesson

Have the following list on display:

Adam-Cain. Genesis 4:9-14
Abraham-Ishmael. Genesis 21:9-14
Jacob-Joseph. Genesis 37:23-28
David-Absalom. 2 Samuel 13:28, 29, 37

Direct attention to the list and ask, "What do all these pairs of people have in common?" Expect a quick "father-and-son" answer, but persist with, "Yes, but what else do all these pairs have in common?" If no one quickly gives the answer you want, let the accompanying Scripture passages be read. Even then you may have to tell the class the answer: Each pair suffered a painful separation. This week's text tells of another father and son who were separated painfully. Let the students now turn to the text in their own Bibles.

Into the Word

There are four phrases shown below in bold type. Have them printed on separate cards or strips of paper in letters that are large enough to be seen by the entire class. (Or, if available, use an overhead projector to show them.) Display only one of them at a time. Tell the students that each phrase relates to one of the pairs already mentioned; ask students to tell which one. Then ask them to tell how it relates also to the story in our text. You may want to show what you mean by explaining the relations of the first phrase yourself. Students then should be able to see how the others relate. Suggestions are given here with the phrases.

Exile and Isolation. This relates to Adam and Cain, for Cain was exiled and isolated from his family. The son in the text exiled himself, but he also became isolated and desolated.

Distress Before Blessing. This phrase relates to Abraham and Ishmael. Both of them were distressed by their separation, but God promised that Ishmael would prosper and become the head of a nation. In our text the father was distressed when the son left, and the son was distressed when his money was gone; but both were blessed when the son came home.

Anger of the Older. This relates to Jacob and Joseph. Joseph's angry older brothers sold him as a slave and made their father think he was dead. Our text records that the older brother was angry because the younger one was welcomed back home.

How Low Can One Go? This relates to David and Absalom. Absalom sank low enough to murder his half brother and run away to a foreign land. In Jesus' parable the prodigal son sank low enough to be a swineherd. This was the depth of degradation to a Jew, for the law made swine unfit for human use.

If members of the class see other such relationships, accept them and use them to emphasize the pain of broken relationships and the joy of relationships restored.

Into Life

Thinking of God as our Father, ask the learners to make a list of ways in which our experience is like that of the son in the parable. If there is time, let each one make his or her own list first, then read and compare. You may want to suggest a few similarities to get the group started. The following ideas may be among those given.

1. Separation is due to the child.
2. The child may long for more freedom.
3. The child may be looking for profit.
4. The child finds his resources inadequate.
5. The child sinks into sin and degradation.
6. The child sees his mistake and sin.
7. There is the opportunity to go back.
8. The father leaves the choice to the child.
9. The father welcomes one who comes back.
10. Blessings await one who returns.
11. Restoration is like moving from death to life.
12. There is joy in reunion.

Let's Talk It Over

The questions on this page are designed to encourage review of the lesson Scriptures and to promote discussion of the lesson by the class. The answers provided are only discussion starters. Let your class talk it over from there.

1. All are sinners: all of us have gone at least a little away from our Heavenly Father and squandered some of His blessings. According to this parable, what must happen before we return home to be accepted by God?

The boy went through several stages. At first he enjoyed his sinful life, but when he became impoverished he realized his need. He didn't need just money; he needed his home: a place of security, peace, and love. The boy's heart changed. Pride, rebellion, and selfishness were replaced by humility and love for his father. Only then was he ready to return home. When we have gone away from God we must realize our need for Him before we will have any desire to return. Moreover, we must change our hearts from rebellion to submission, from resentment to love. Then we are ready to come to the Heavenly Father and be assured of His acceptance.

2. This parable points to the spiritual poverty that results when a person leaves the presence of the Heavenly Father to follow the ways of the world. What are the signs of such spiritual poverty? How does it drive us back to God? How can Christians show impoverished people the way to the Father?

Just as physical poverty results in an empty stomach, spiritual poverty results in an empty heart. Some of the effects of such poverty are having no purpose in life, receiving no satisfaction from life, hopelessness, despair, depression, loneliness, fearfulness, and alienation. When life apart from God has emptied a person's heart, there is a deep longing to be filled. As Christians we can share the love, strength, hope, and purpose that we receive from our Father, and in this way be able to show others the road to the Father's home.

3. A preacher attended a cocktail party because he wanted to reach out to his lost neighbors. He didn't drink, but he did converse. Eight people from that party eventually accepted Christ, but the preacher lost his job because he went to the party. Would you have gone to the party? How would your church react if your preacher did this?

Many Christians have so little love for lost souls that they don't miss them or have any desire to look for them. However, Jesus did go among the lost (Luke 15:1, 2). We are more like Him if we do the same.

4. Today many people are estranged from other family members. Apply the lessons of the parable to the reconciliation of families. What must each person do to bring it about?

We must begin by admitting our faults. The Father was not at fault in the story, but we are not perfect as He is. We cannot proceed until we recognize our part in the problem. Next we must be genuinely sorry. The boy admitted he had sinned against his father and he was sorry for it. If we can do this, then we can take the next step and reach out to the other person, just as the son went home. Finally, we must be willing to forgive each other.

5. The son wasted jewels and gold, but these are not the kind of inheritance we receive from our Heavenly Father. What is our inheritance? How do we waste it when we sin? What have you wasted? How can it be restored?

Our inheritance from our Heavenly Father includes His image within us, freedom of will, innocence, intelligence, conscience, social nature, and emotions. We waste our free will when we come under the bondage of sin, our innocence when we participate in worldly corruption, our intelligence when we believe the lies of the world, etc. When we return to Him, God restores our inheritance by giving us His Holy Spirit to renew us in the inner person.

6. One of the great tragedies of our society is the large number of young people who leave home to try to make it on their own, only to be used, abused, and destroyed. What concrete steps can our church take to alleviate this problem?

We cannot help all, but we can help some. A church in a community large enough to have runaways may offer emergency shelter or even long-term low-cost or no-cost shelter. Christian business people may hire these young people so they will not turn to prostitution or crime. We can provide a place and leadership for peer support groups. We may hire a staff person for just this ministry.

Jesus Commends Childlike Faith

DEVOTIONAL READING: Matthew 9:13-30.

LESSON SCRIPTURE: Luke 18:15-30.

PRINTED TEXT: Luke 18:15-30.

Luke 18:15-30

15 And they brought unto him also infants, that he would touch them: but when his disciples saw it, they rebuked them.

16 But Jesus called them unto him, and said, Suffer little children to come unto me, and forbid them not: for of such is the kingdom of God.

17 Verily I say unto you, Whosoever shall not receive the kingdom of God as a little child shall in no wise enter therein.

18 And a certain ruler asked him, saying, Good Master, what shall I do to inherit eternal life?

19 And Jesus said unto him, Why callest thou me good? none is good, save one, that is, God.

20 Thou knowest the commandments, Do not commit adultery, Do not kill, Do not steal, Do not bear false witness, Honor thy father and thy mother.

21 And he said, All these have I kept from my youth up.

22 Now when Jesus heard these things, he said unto him, Yet lackest thou one thing: sell all that thou hast, and distribute unto the poor, and thou shalt have treasure in heaven: and come, follow me.

23 And when he heard this, he was very sorrowful: for he was very rich.

24 And when Jesus saw that he was very sorrowful, he said, How hardly shall they that have riches enter into the kingdom of God!

25 For it is easier for a camel to go through a needle's eye, than for a rich man to enter into the kingdom of God.

26 And they that heard it said, Who then can be saved?

27 And he said, The things which are impossible with men are possible with God.

28 Then Peter said, Lo, we have left all, and followed thee.

29 And he said unto them, Verily I say unto you, There is no man that hath left house, or parents, or brethren, or wife, or children, for the kingdom of God's sake,

30 Who shall not receive manifold more in this present time, and in the world to come life everlasting.

Feb
6

GOLDEN TEXT: Whosoever shall not receive the kingdom of God as a little child shall in no wise enter therein.—Luke 18:17.

The Story of Jesus

Unit 3. Luke: The Cross and

the Resurrection (Lessons 10-13)

Lesson Aims

After this lesson a student should be able to:

1. Have a deeper appreciation of the Savior and the salvation He provides.

2. Describe the attitudes that are essential for one to enter the kingdom of God.

3. Cultivate those attitudes in himself or herself.

Lesson Outline

Display visual 10 of the visuals packet and refer to it as you discuss Jesus' conversation with the rich young ruler. The visual is shown on page 196.

Introduction

A. The Importance of Salvation

The supreme need of mankind today is the need for salvation. Man cannot cleanse his past on his own, nor can he defeat death. He cannot keep his motives or his will pure. He cannot control the forces that confront him. Man alone cannot overcome all the temptations he meets. To survive both in this life and throughout eternity, he must have a Savior. To whom can he turn for salvation?

B. The Wonderful Savior

A wonderful Savior is Jesus my Lord,
He taketh my burden away,
He holdeth me up, and I shall not be moved,
He giveth me strength as my day.

Sing or read the other stanzas of Fanny Crosby's hymn entitled "He Hideth My Soul" or "A Wonderful Savior." Note all it says about what Jesus is and does. Take a few minutes to think of what else He does for you personally. Climax your thinking with Hebrews 7:25: "He is able also to save them to the uttermost that come unto God by him, seeing he ever liveth to make intercession for them."

C. Lesson Background

While our lesson centers on little children and a rich man, we cannot completely overlook the others who pass before us in the eighteenth chapter of Luke. They too teach important lessons.

Widows in that time found it hard to make ends meet, and the widow of Luke 18:1-8 was no exception. She was poor, alone, and without social standing, yet she pleaded her case persistently and successfully. This parable encourages Jesus' disciples to pray persistently.

The Pharisee and publican in verses 9-14 teach a different lesson about prayer. The sad thing about the deluded Pharisee was that he imagined he was right in everything. His stubborn pride made him blissfully ignorant of his own heart. On the other hand, the publican knew the enormity of his sin, and such knowledge is one thing that we all need in order to be forgiven.

In sharp contrast to the proud Pharisee are the little children who were brought to Jesus. The rich young ruler, earnestly seeking the way of life, also contrasts with the self-satisfied Pharisee. In another way he contrasts with the children, for he was a man of wealth and influence.

I. Christ Welcomes the Children (Luke 18:15-17)

A. The Bringing (v. 15a)

15a. And they brought unto him also infants, that he would touch them.

Many assume that mothers brought their children to Jesus, but fathers may have been involved as well. Apparently the children were of various ages. Luke speaks of *infants*, but Matthew

19:13 says "little children." Perhaps one walked by a parent's side, another was led by a father's hand, and another was gently carried in a mother's arms.

The children were brought so *he would touch them*, but more than a touch was wanted. Parents hoped Jesus would pray for God's blessing on the children (Matthew 19:13; Mark 10:16). Jesus loved the little children, but that was nothing new. The Jewish people earnestly desired children and treasured them in a time when other people did not. The *Encyclopedia of Religion and Ethics* says Plato recommended exposing sickly children to get rid of them, and Aristotle recommended abortion to prevent overcrowding. Jesus' example demands love and care for all children.

B. The Hindrance (v. 15b)

15b. But when his disciples saw it, they rebuked them.

We are not told exactly what was in the mind of the objectors. If there were sick people seeking healing, the disciples may have thought that that ministry was more important than blessing children. If the disciples were in a house receiving private instruction (Mark 10:10-12), perhaps they wanted to have Jesus to themselves for a while. Or perhaps He had gone in the house to rest, and they wanted to protect Him from interruption. Or possibly Jesus was engrossed in conversation or healing and did not greet the youngsters as soon as they appeared. In that case the disciples may have thought He did not want to take time for the waiting children. Certainly they gave their rebuke with good intentions, "but when Jesus saw it, he was much displeased" (Mark 10:14).

C. The Rebuke (v. 16)

16. But Jesus called them unto him, and said, Suffer little children to come unto me, and forbid them not: for of such is the kingdom of God.

Overruling the disciples' protest, Jesus *called* the children unto him. "And he took them up in his arms, put his hands upon them, and blessed them" (Mark 10:16). He went on to point out that *the kingdom of God* belongs to the childlike. Citizens of that kingdom are not marked by a proud recital of their own virtues (Luke 18:11, 12), but by wholehearted trust like that of a child.

WELCOME TO THE CHILDREN

According to a story that I repeat without verifying, a mother took her young son to hear a concert by Paderewski, the famous Polish pianist. She got front seats so the small boy could easily see the great man.

Before the concert began, the mother turned to talk with someone in the row behind her. In that moment her son raced up to the piano on the stage and began to play "Chopsticks." The audience was shocked, no one more than the mother.

But Paderewski came out from the wings with a smile. Taking his seat beside the boy, he began to improvise an accompaniment to the child's solo. The audience burst into thunderous applause.

Similar to that was Jesus' touch with children. Others might think of them as intruders, but the great one reached out to them in love.   —W. P.

D. The Lesson (v. 17)

17. Verily I say unto you, Whosoever shall not receive the kingdom of God as a little child shall in no wise enter therein.

Jesus wants us to be childlike in a good way, not childish in a bad way. What qualities of *a little child* did He regard as essential to enter the kingdom?

A child who has not been spoiled exhibits great humility, faith, and dependence. He shows us the way into the kingdom through these. Jesus tells us we need a second childhood, a new innocence beyond man's guilty blundering. There must be a second birth to enter the kingdom (John 3:3-6).

II. Christ Instructs a Seeker (Luke 18:18-23)

A. The Sincere Question (v. 18)

18. And a certain ruler asked him, saying, Good Master, what shall I do to inherit eternal life?

The rich young ruler may have been one of the few who came to Jesus and went away in worse condition than when they came. Yet he had so much in his favor! He was moral and religious, earnest and sincere. He was the kind of person most churches would welcome as a member.

We can see a more complete picture of this man by comparing Luke's account of the incident with Matthew 19:16-30 and Mark 10:17-31. Luke alone tells us the man was a *ruler.* This is a general term, but most students take it to mean he was one of the rulers of the local synagogue, a man highly respected in the Jewish community. Matthew tells us he was young, and all three accounts say he was *rich,* or "had great possessions."

Mark says Jesus loved the young man (10:21). This is important. The man's life was one to be admired. He was morally pure (v. 21). He was independent and brave. Otherwise he would not

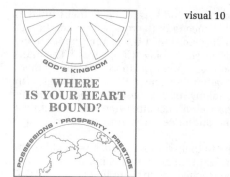

visual 10

had not overtly broken any of the commandments Jesus quoted. But it is not likely that he had any idea of the deeper meaning that Jesus explained in the Sermon on the Mount (Matthew 5:21-48). And what about the rest of God's commandments? For example, did this young man really love his neighbor as himself? It is interesting to note that Jesus did not quote the Tenth Commandment, "Thou shalt not covet" (Exodus 20:17). Instead, He gave a sample test. He asked this seeker to do something that no covetous person would do.

C. The Simple Test (v. 22)

22. Now when Jesus heard these things, he said unto him, Yet lackest thou one thing: sell all that thou hast, and distribute unto the poor, and thou shalt have treasure in heaven: and come, follow me.

The young ruler stood at a turning point. Jesus challenged him to become one of His disciples, and imposed upon him the condition that he *sell* his possessions, *distribute* the proceeds to *the poor*, and thereby gain for himself *treasure in heaven.*

No one is saved by giving to the poor, but no one can be saved who will not repent of his sin, whatever that sin may be. This young man was possessed by the love of money, and he could not escape. He came short of God's requirement. The challenge was one he would not meet. Faced with a choice, he chose his wealth rather than the service of Christ.

Jesus did not make the same demand on all who would follow Him. In this instance He saw that a rich man's love for things of this world was a barrier to wholehearted devotion to the kingdom of God. Before he could serve in that kingdom he must free himself from his loyalty to mammon.

D. The Sad Failure (v. 23)

23. And when he heard this, he was very sorrowful: for he was very rich.

Luke does not actually say that the man refused to do what Jesus asked, but the accounts in Matthew and Mark both say he "went away." It seems plain that Jesus' appeal was in vain. The ruler failed to rise to the challenge. The cost of being a disciple of Jesus was more than he was willing to pay.

A CHALLENGE TO TREASURE HUNTERS

On a small island off the coast of Nova Scotia is a strange pit reputed to be the hiding place of a fabulous treasure. Various search parties have dug there over many years without success. The search is hampered by a series of wooden plat-

have dared to come openly to Jesus and show Him such respect. Most of the Jewish leaders were hostile to that itinerate teacher, and probably would be hostile to a ruler who seemed to favor Him. Eagerly he "came . . . running, and kneeled" before Jesus (Mark 10:17). He addressed Jesus as *Good Master.* In today's English, *Master* is more accurately translated *Teacher.* The ruler thought he could depend on Jesus for the right information. Sincerely he asked an important question: *What shall I do to inherit eternal life?* Apparently he thought eternal life must be earned; but when Jesus told him what to do, he refused to obey. He wanted salvation, but he wanted to make no such sacrifice. This mistake many people make even today.

B. The Willing Answer (vv. 19-21)

19. And Jesus said unto him, Why callest thou me good? none is good, save one, that is, God.

This should not be taken to mean that Jesus was not good. He was and is good, even as God is good. But He was inviting the ruler to think about what he himself was saying and what he believed. Did he mean Jesus was divine, good as only God is good? Or did he mean something less?

20. Thou knowest the commandments, Do not commit adultery, Do not kill, Do not steal, Do not bear false witness, Honor thy father and thy mother.

As a sampling of God's law, Jesus quoted five of the Ten Commandments. In referring another inquirer to the law, Jesus said, "This do, and thou shalt live" (Luke 10:25-28). To the rich young ruler too He implied that eternal life would result from keeping the law. The catch is, of course, that one would have to keep all details of the law fully and perfectly. No one has ever done that.

21. And he said, All these have I kept from my youth up.

There is no reason to doubt that this was substantially true: that is, probably the young man forms, one below another underground to a depth of a hundred feet. Another handicap is the sea water that floods the pit.

No one is really sure that a treasure was ever buried there, or, if it was, that the unknown owner did not later reclaim it. Still, some people have spent all they had in the effort to find a treasure that may be only a myth.

Jesus challenged the rich young ruler to give up all he had for a treasure that is eternal in Heaven, available to those who follow the Master. The rich young ruler would not take up the challenge—and multitudes with less treasure on earth are following his example.   —W. P.

III. Christ Clarifies a Problem (Luke 18:24-30)

A. The Difficulty (vv. 24, 25)

24. And when Jesus saw that he was very sorrowful, he said, How hardly shall they that have riches enter into the kingdom of God!

After the ruler went away, Jesus gave His disciples some explanation of that man's problem. It is hard for a rich man to get into God's kingdom. What hinders him is not so much the possession of wealth as the sense of security that wealth brings. In Mark's account, those who find it hard to enter the kingdom are described as "them that trust in riches" (Mark 10:24).

Very clearly Jesus saw the dangers of material wealth and prosperity. What are those dangers? First, possession of material things tends to attach one's heart to this world. A rich man has so large a stake in this world that it is very hard for him to think beyond it. As Jesus put it at another time, "Where your treasure is, there will your heart be also" (Matthew 6:21)

Second, prosperity tends to make one think in terms of price and not value. The rich young ruler thought of the price he would pay—all he had. He did not know or even estimate the value of eternal life. Anyone with an abundance of the things money can buy is apt to forget that there are things more valuable than money.

Third, if one has a lot of property, the management of it takes a lot of time and attention. The owner may find that he simply has no time for more valuable things.

25. For it is easier for a camel to go through a needle's eye, than for a rich man to enter into the kingdom of God.

The idea of a *camel* going through a *needle's eye* seems so ludicrous that many students have tried to find another meaning here. Some have suggested that the Greek word for camel (*Kamelon*) is an ancient misprint for the word that means cable (Kamilon). But even if this

were true it would not change the meaning. Threading a cable through a needle's eye is just as impossible as driving a camel through it. Other students have suggested that some ancient city wall may have had a small gate called the needle's eye, through which a camel could squeeze if its pack were taken off. But even if such a gate existed, that does not fit Jesus' thought. He was talking about something impossible with men (v. 27), and He emphasized the impossibility with an illustration—a huge camel going through the tiny eye of a needle.

B. The Possibility (vv. 26, 27)

26. And they that heard it said, Who then can be saved?

If the rich with all their advantages cannot be saved, who can? The ruler who had just departed was not only rich, but also good and highly respected. If he could not enter the kingdom, what chance is there for anybody?

27. And he said, The things which are impossible with men are possible with God.

It is not impossible for a rich man to enter the kingdom of God, but it is *impossible with men*. God can do many things that man cannot do.

Zaccheus was one of the richest men in Jericho, but Jesus brought him into the kingdom (Luke 19:2, 9, 10). Joseph of Arimathea was a rich man who donated a costly rock-hewn tomb for the burial of Jesus (Matthew 27:57-60). Nicodemus must have been rich. We deduce this not only because he was a ruler of the Jews (John 3:1), but also because he brought a hundred pounds of costly spices for Jesus' funeral (John 19:39). Joseph timidly kept his allegiance secret while Jesus lived (John 19:38), and it seems that Nicodemus did the same. But when Jesus was dead and other disciples were keeping out of sight, these two boldly came forward as friends of the Master. Without any further information, we like to think they continued openly as disciples and were safely in the kingdom of God.

Salvation is always a gift of God's grace, whether it is received by the rich or the poor. The rich young ruler sounds a warning to people who want a Christian faith that will not upset their values or change their worldly lifestyle. Jesus does not command every seeking sinner to sell everything he has and give away the money, but He does put His finger of conviction on anything in which we are dishonest and that comes between ourselves and Him.

WHAT HAVE YOU SACRIFICED?

We live in an age of conspicuous consumption, not of conspicuous sacrifice. Most of us are more likely to be motivated by what we can get than by what we can give. We like to think of the reward of Christian faith more than of its sacrifices.

Before J. Russel Morse and his wife left for their mission field they had all their teeth pulled—all their good teeth—so they would not be troubled by dental problems in faraway Tibet where dentists are hard to find.

Missionaries well know what it means to give up family relationships, to give up comfort and luxury, even to give up their teeth. What are the rest of us giving up for the kingdom of God.

—W. P.

C. The Reward (vv. 28-30)

28. Then Peter said, Lo, we have left all, and followed thee.

Peter's comment suggests that he had a rather commercial view of discipleship. Matthew 19:27 records his question, "What shall we have therefore?" He and others had done almost what Jesus asked the young ruler to do. They had left homes and jobs and incomes (Matthew 4:18-22; 9:9). What could they expect in return.?

29, 30. And he said unto them, Verily I say unto you, There is no man that hath left house, or parents, or brethren, or wife, or children, for the kingdom of God's sake, who shall not receive manifold more in this present time, and in the world to come life everlasting.

The reward is great for one who gives up things of this life for the sake of the kingdom of God. If his family disowns him because he follows Jesus, he is a member of the much larger and more devoted family of God. If he loses his home, the homes of Christian brethren are open to him. If he loses his income, God's whole great family will see that he has food and clothing (Acts 4:34, 35). And besides all these blessings *in this present time*, there is *life everlasting*. The person of the world gives up his hope of life everlasting, and finds that what he has left with all his riches is a life of disappointment. But the person of the kingdom sacrifices the things of this world and finds complete fulfillment through Jesus Christ.

Conclusion

A. Coming to the Kingdom

Nicodemus came to Jesus by night (John 3:1-21). A nobleman came in the middle of the day (John 4:46-53). A leper disregarded his quarantine to come in the presence of a great crowd (Matthew 8:1-4). A sinful woman invaded a dinner party (Luke 7:37-50). Zaccheus appeared in a tree (Luke 19:2-10). Matthew met Jesus at a toll booth and gave a party for Him at home (Matthew 9:9-13). Many came in search of healing for themselves or others (Matthew 4:23-25). Some came hoping for a free lunch (John 6:26, 27). Some came to find fault (Mark 12:13), but most came with a sense of need. Many came with questions, spoken or unspoken, about how to enter the kingdom and find peace with God and peace within themselves.

Parents brought their children for Jesus' touch and blessing, and a rich young ruler came with his question. Matthew, Mark, and Luke all bring these two incidents together in the record. Probably they were close together in time as well as in teaching.

Other texts deal with such specifics as repentance and baptism, but these two incidents set forth essential attitudes or dispositions one must have in order to enter the kingdom. In one instance the necessary conditions are lowliness, dependence, and trust. In the other instance the necessary condition is an end of trust in worldly wealth. There is no place in the kingdom for those who trust in themselves or in what they own. Salvation comes only to those who place their trust in God.

B. Prayer

Almighty and everlasting God, because of Your tender love for mankind You sent Your Son to take upon himself our flesh and to suffer death upon the cross that all mankind might be saved. Help us to follow the example of His great humility, that through lowliness of mind, renunciation of self, and trust in You, we may become fit subjects for Your kingdom. In Jesus' name, amen.

C. Thought to Remember

Only those can be saved who rely wholly on God, made manifest in His Son.

Home Daily Bible Readings

Monday, Jan. 31—Praising the Steward's Prudence (Luke 16:1-9)

Tuesday, Feb. 1—Be Worthy of True Riches (Luke 16:10-15)

Wednesday, Feb. 2—Rich Man and Lazarus (Luke 16:19-31)

Thursday, Feb. 3—One Healed of Leprosy Thanks Jesus (Luke 17:11-19)

Friday, Feb. 4—Power of Persistent Prayer (Luke 18:1-8)

Saturday, Feb. 5—Humility Better Than False Piety (Luke 18:9-14)

Sunday, Feb. 6—Basic Needs for Eternal Life (Luke 18:15-30)

Learning by Doing

This page contains an alternate lesson plan emphasizing learning activities. Classes desiring such student involvement will find these suggestions helpful.

Learning Goals

After this study the learner will be able to:

1. Tell how the two incidents recorded in the text relate to each other and to the context.

2. Answer the question of Luke 18:26.

3. Give in his or her own words the thought of verse 27 or of verses 29 and 30 in Luke 18.

Into the Lesson

If you can arrange it in advance, let a class of small children come into your meeting place as the session begins. They may even interrupt announcements or opening remarks.

As they make their way to the front of the room, someone asks, "What are these people doing here? This is an *adult* class!"

"We *want* them here," the teacher responds heartily. "They're going to help us with our Sunday-school lesson."

The children sing "Jesus Love the Little Children," then sing it a second time with the adult class joining in. After the singing and the applause, they go back to their own meeting place.

The objection should be made playfully, not realistically. You don't want the children to think anyone really doesn't want them.

As an alternative, one child may stand on a chair (a stable one) with a placard reading KINGDOM STUFF. Ask the class, "Why did Jesus say, 'Of such is the kingdom of God'? In what ways should all of God's people be like little children?" Expect class members to say children are humble, teachable, trusting, obedient, dependent, easily pleased, and so on. If students are slow to respond, perhaps you can get them started by mentioning one or two of these characteristics.

Into the Word

Prepare two copies of the following script and recruit two readers to read it in front of the class. Before the reading starts, ask a third of the class members to be looking at our text, Luke 18:15-30, another third to be watching Matthew 19:13-30, and the third to look at Mark 10:13-31. All of them will be looking for details in the Bible accounts that are not included in the script, or anything in the script that is not found in the Bible.

Ruler: Good Master, what shall I do to inherit eternal life?

Jesus: Why do you call me good? Only God is good. (Pause). You know the commandments: Don't commit adultery; Don't murder; Don't steal; Don't lie; Honor your parents . . .

R (interrupting): From my childhood I have kept all these!

J: Then you lack only one thing: sell everything you have and give the money to the poor. Then you will have treasure in Heaven. And come and follow me.

R: Hey, that's a tough assignment. (Pause). I'll have to have time to think about it. (He departs.)

J (to class): How hard it is to give up material things and value the spiritual! It is easier for a camel to squeeze through a needle's eye than for one who loves riches to get into the kingdom of Heaven!

Take a few minutes for students to tell about any differences they have noted, and to discuss them.

Point out that Matthew, Mark, and Luke all place the coming of the rich young ruler right after the blessing of the children. Divide the class into three groups (perhaps six or nine if it is a big class). Give each group a copy of one of these statements;

These two incidents are placed together to give a positive and a negative answer to the question in Luke 18:26.

These two incidents are placed together to contrast submission and blessing with self-will and disappointment.

Explain that you want each group to see if its statement is supported by the Scripture. Allow five or six minutes, then ask for reports. After the discussion, note that the incidents may be recorded together simply because that is the way they happened, but they also are related in the ways the groups have seen.

Into Life

Display these two statements abbreviated from our text: "Things impossible with men are possible with God." "Anyone who has left anything for the sake of God's kingdom will receive much more." Ask, "Which of these two is more encouraging to you?" Let students answer with a show of hands. Have copies of the statements ready to distribute; give each person his choice. Suggest that each one post it where he will see it every day to think about and memorize.

Let's Talk It Over

The questions on this page are designed to encourage review of the lesson Scriptures and to promote discussion of the lesson by the class. The answers provided are only discussion starters. Let your class talk it over from there.

1. Mention some characteristics seen in young children and explain how we adults can display them.

In a healthy family a child loves his parents wholeheartedly. We must love the Lord above all others. A child trusts his parents—their love, provision, and steadfastness. Christians need this same trust in their Heavenly Father. It may be harder for us because we do not see our Father face to face, but we have His promise to rely on. A well-trained child obeys his parents even if he does not understand the purpose of what they ask. We must be willing to obey the Lord without hesitation or question.

2. Is it possible for us to be active Christians but to have one or more things like this man's riches that have too strong a hold on our lives? If so, how can we detect them and break their hold?

Possessions, position, career, family, and entertainment are a few of the things that may be too important in our lives. List two or three things, other than the Lord and the church, that are important to you. Now ask yourself what challenge would cause you to give them up. What possessions would you sacrifice to meet a special need in the Lord's work? Would you change careers to serve Him better? If you find that nothing would prompt you to give these things up, then perhaps they are too important. If so, begin now to give more importance to your service to the Lord. If you look, you can find some needed work to do.

3. Giving up possessions was only half of Jesus' challenge to the ruler. The Lord also asked the man to follow Him. How do we do this?

If the man had followed Jesus he might have been led into missionary work. He might have been led to suffering. Today, we begin to follow the Lord when we say to Him, without any reservations, that we are willing to do whatever He wants us to do, wherever He wants us to do it. It is appropriate to renew such a promise every day. Then we must pay attention. If we are asked to do something, we do it. If opportunities arise, we take them. If we see a need, we meet it. The Lord will lead those who are truly willing to follow Him.

4. Was Jesus teaching that we are saved by our good works, such as giving to the poor? Does being saved require any more then believing in Jesus?

Jesus expected the man to do more than call Him "Good Master." He demanded drastic action, and so far as we know the man was lost because he would not take that action. His faith was proved false because he would not obey. Faith does us no good unless it is strong enough to move us to obedience. The Bible tells us not only to believe, but also to confess Jesus (Luke 12:8). It tells us to turn from our sins and be baptized (Acts 2:38). It tells us to live righteously (1 John 3:10). If our faith is real, we are eager to do whatever the Lord asks.

5. What should be our relationship to our possessions? Who decides what we keep and what we give up?

We should be willing to sacrifice any possession at any time if our service to the Lord requires it; but for every missionary who gives up everything to go to remote areas, several people stay behind and earn the money to keep him on the field. The Lord does not lead all people to give up everything, but perhaps He would lead more to do so if more were willing to let Him make the decision. Jesus does not take from us against our wills. How much we are willing to give up for Him, is a good indication of the measure of our love.

6. We can't all leave home to become missionaries, nor should we abandon mates or children. Does this mean that those of us who stay at home and serve the Lord must miss out on Jesus' promises in verses 29, 30?

All of us can deny ourselves for the sake of the Lord. Some may choose to remain single so that they can serve without the distractions of family. If we have families, care of them is a part of our service to the Lord (1 Timothy 5:8). Families can choose to work and sacrifice together in their service to the Lord. Parents can encourage their children to enter the full-time work of the kingdom. We may spend less time on our homes and yards so that we have more time for service. Whatever we give up for Jesus, He promises that He will more than repay it "in this present time"—and there is "life everlasting" besides.

God's Patience and Justice

DEVOTIONAL READING: Matthew 21:23-27, 38-46.

LESSON SCRIPTURE: Luke 20:1-19.

PRINTED TEXT: Luke 20:9-19.

Luke 20:9-19

9 Then began he to speak to the people this parable; A certain man planted a vineyard, and let it forth to husbandmen, and went into a far country for a long time.

10 And at the season he sent a servant to the husbandmen, that they should give him of the fruit of the vineyard: but the husbandmen beat him, and sent him away empty.

11 And again he sent another servant: and they beat him also, and entreated him shamefully, and sent him away empty.

12 And again he sent a third: and they wounded him also, and cast him out.

13 Then said the lord of the vineyard, What shall I do? I will send my beloved son: it may be they will reverence him when they see him.

14 But when the husbandmen saw him, they reasoned among themselves, saying, This is the heir: come, let us kill him, that the inheritance may be ours.

15 So they cast him out of the vineyard, and killed him. What therefore shall the lord of the vineyard do unto them?

16 He shall come and destroy these husbandmen, and shall give the vineyard to others. And when they heard it, they said, God forbid.

17 And he beheld them, and said, What is this then that is written, The stone which the builders rejected, the same is become the head of the corner?

18 Whosoever shall fall upon that stone shall be broken; but on whomsoever it shall fall, it will grind him to powder.

19 And the chief priests and the scribes the same hour sought to lay hands on him; and they feared the people: for they perceived that he had spoken this parable against them.

Feb
13

GOLDEN TEXT: The stone which the builders rejected, the same is become the head of the corner.—Luke 20:17.

The Story of Jesus

Unit 3. Luke: The Cross and the Resurrection (Lessons 10-13)

Lesson Aims

After completing this lesson students should be able to:

1. Explain the meaning of the parable of the wicked husbandmen.

2. Better understand God's patience and justice.

3. Find ways to improve their own management of what God has placed under their care and supervision.

Lesson Outline

INTRODUCTION

   A. Teaching Techniques of Jesus

   B. Teaching in the Temple

   C. Lesson Background

  I. THE PARABLE (Luke 20:9-15a)

   A. Preparation of the Vineyard (v. 9)

   B. Mistreatment of the Servants (vv. 10-12)

    He Sent a Third

   C. Mission of the Son (vv. 13-15a)

  II. THE PARABLE DISCUSSED (Luke 20:15b-19)

   A. Question (vv. 15b, 16a)

    Primetime Drama

   B. Opposition (v. 16b)

   C. Explanation (vv. 17, 18)

    The Head of the Corner

   D. Resentment (v. 19)

CONCLUSION

   A. God Is Patient and Just

   B. Application

   C. Prayer

   D. Thought to Remember

Display visual 11 of the visuals packet and cover the right column. Refer to the items in the left column as you discuss verses 9-16a. Then uncover the right column and show the parallels in the remainder of the text. The visual is shown on page 205.

Introduction

A. Teaching Techniques of Jesus

All the Gospel writers give word pictures of Jesus surrounded by large crowds of people and holding their attention by the uniqueness of His teaching. He used several techniques to fascinate His audience. People were impressed by His manner as He spoke with authority (Mark 1:22). He did not quote the rabbis as many teachers did, but sometimes criticized their teaching (Mark 7:8-13). He even dared to place His own statements on a par with the Old Testament teaching (Matthew 5:33, 34, 38, 39). Unlike those religious teachers who loved to engage in the recitation of inconsequential details, Jesus spoke to essential truths. His utterances were marked by great simplicity. He avoided technical terms and chose to use many simple illustrations that are called parables. These have been defined as short earthly stories with Heavenly meaning.

B. Teaching in the Temple

When Jesus was in Jerusalem, His favorite place for teaching was the temple. All male Jews were required to be there three times in the year, at Passover, Pentecost, and Tabernacles (Exodus 23:14-17). This was difficult for Jews scattered all over the Roman world and beyond, but many made the effort at least once during the year. The temple was a customary place for teaching, and Jesus made use of it when He began His ministry of preaching, teaching, and healing.

During the final year of His ministry, He came to the temple to teach in the middle of the autumn feast of Tabernacles (John 7:14). He was there at the winter feast of Dedication (John 10:22, 23). He was also there in the springtime feast of Passover, just before His death on the cross (Luke 19:47).

The synagogues where He often taught were small, but the temple had room for a large crowd. The outer court contained more than twenty acres. A tremendous throng of people could gather here. John 10:23 records that Jesus walked in Solomon's Porch, a roofed and pillared area along the eastern wall of that court. Even the smaller court, reserved for people of Israel, would hold a large crowd. Jesus felt at home in either of the courts, and there He taught the people who were gathered.

C. Lesson Background

There was audacity in Jesus' approach to Jerusalem for the last Passover of His ministry. The hostile authorities had given instructions that anyone who knew where He was should inform them so He could be arrested (John 11:57). But instead of hiding in fear, Jesus came to Jerusalem publicly and triumphantly.

Jesus told two of His disciples to go into a village and get a donkey for Him, a donkey that previously had not been ridden. Unspoiled by previous use, the animal was suitable for sacred purposes (see Numbers 19:2 and 1 Samuel 6:7).

If anyone objected to their taking the ass, the disciples were to say, "The Lord hath need of him." When its owners heard these words they would let the donkey go. Probably Jesus previously had made arrangements to borrow it.

Riding on the borrowed ass, Jesus approached Jerusalem in the midst of a scene of rejoicing. The mount indicated that He was a man of peace. The many people along the way hailed Him as "the King that cometh in the name of the Lord" (Luke 19:38). They saw Him now fulfilling prophecy in showing himself as the Messiah, but they did not stop to reflect that He was also proclaiming himself a man of peace and was giving no support to their nationalistic fervor.

Following Jesus' lament over Jerusalem (Luke 19:41-44), the beloved physician describes His cleansing of the temple. By comparing this account with Mark 11, we learn that Jesus went into the temple at "eventide" and "looked round about upon all things" (Mark 11:11). The next day when He came again to the temple He did not just look. He "began to cast out them that sold therein, and them that bought" (Luke 19:45). Since people came from near and far to worship, it was convenient and proper for them to buy animals in Jerusalem to offer as sacrifices. Also they needed money changers to convert their foreign money into Jewish coins. But Jesus insisted these commercial transactions belonged outside the temple. Further, He charged that the merchants had made God's house "a den of thieves" (v. 46). Apparently they were charging exorbitant prices. Jesus reminded them of the Scripture in which God said, "Mine house shall be called a house of prayer" (Isaiah 56:7).

Matthew tells us that Jesus then proceeded to heal the blind and the lame who came to Him in the temple (21:14), and that children in the temple were crying "Hosanna to the Son of David" (v. 15).

During His time in Jerusalem Jesus taught daily in the temple (Luke 19:47) amidst much opposition by the chief priests, the scribes, and "the chief of the people." The expression, "the chief of the people," is one not seen before. It indicates that Jesus was now finding enemies among the ruling classes generally. His recent actions had greatly disturbed the officials, so "on one of those days" they came to question Him. What authority could justify a man in acting as He did? Jesus countered with a question about the authority of John's baptism. The rulers were silent, so Jesus gave no direct answer to their question about His authority. But in a way He did answer them as He spoke what we call the parable of the wicked husbandmen (Luke 20:9-19).

I. The Parable
(Luke 20:9-15a)

A. Preparation of the Vineyard (v. 9)

9. Then began he to speak to the people this parable; A certain man planted a vineyard, and let it forth to husbandmen, and went into a far country for a long time.

Seven hundred years earlier, the prophet Isaiah spoke about a vineyard when he employed a brief but tender love song to bring God's message to the people of Judah (Isaiah 5:1-7). His lesson of the vineyard was a powerful one! He said the farmer lavished care on his vineyard. He chose a fertile spot, cleared away the many stones covering the ground, fenced the area, planted the finest vines, and constructed a tower where watchmen could guard the vineyard. In anticipation of a good harvest, he also chiseled a stone vat out of the mountain ledge, ready to press the juice from the grapes.

Jesus' parable implies a similar preparation. When it was done, the owner went away, leaving the vineyard under the care and supervision of husbandmen, or sharecroppers.

B. Mistreatment of the Servants
(vv. 10-12)

10. And at the season he sent a servant to the husbandmen, that they should give him of the fruit of the vineyard: but the husbandmen beat him, and sent him away empty.

The rent was to be paid by a share of the produce. The owner had every right to expect this from the vineyard upon which he had lavished so much care. Likewise the Lord has every right to expect that His patient, loving care for His people will produce a bountiful harvest.

In due time the owner sent one of his servants to collect, but instead of paying what they owed, the husbandmen reacted violently, beating the servant and sending him away without any of the produce.

11, 12. And again he sent another servant: and they beat him also, and entreated him shamefully, and sent him away empty. And again he sent a third: and they wounded him also, and cast him out.

The treatment each servant received was shameful. Besides beating some and wounding others, it is said of one that the husbandmen *entreated him shamefully.* Today we would say he *treated* him shamefully. We are left to wonder what shameful treatment was added to the beating. We get the idea as we read of this continual mistreatment that the husbandmen were becoming more arrogant and defiant and the treatment of the servants was becoming worse and worse. And in addition, none collected what was due to the owner.

The husbandmen behaved in a way that was unreasonable and outrageous. We marvel at the patience of the owner! Matthew and Mark indicate that the owner sent even more servants than Luke mentions (Matthew 21:33-41; Mark 12:1-9). It seems that the husbandmen mistook the owner's patience for weakness and concluded they could get away with murder.

In this parable Jesus is picturing an unreasonable and outrageous nation and a patient and compassionate God who, instead of immediately punishing those who rejected the prophets, gave them further opportunities by sending other prophets.

HE SENT A THIRD

How wonderful is the patience of God! Twice the owner sent servants to ask for a proper accounting. Twice his emissaries were humiliated and harmed. Twice the tenants refused to pay what they owed. *Still the owner sent a third servant.* Mark 12:5 indicates that he sent yet more, and the crooked tenants responded by "beating some and killing some." Not till they killed the owner's own son did judgment come to those greedy and malicious tenants.

If God is so patient, why are we so impatient?
—W. P.

C. Mission of the Son (vv. 13-15a)

13. Then said the lord of the vineyard, What shall I do? I will send my beloved son: it may be they will reverence him when they see him.

The lord or the owner *of the vineyard*, having sent servants who were unpaid and mistreated by the husbandmen, gave those husbandmen one more chance, even risking the safety of his own beloved son.

In real life the owner would surely have taken strong action. Having the law on his side, he would have dealt severely with the offenders. But Jesus depicts a God who loves beyond measure and is compassionate when He might be severe. So He speaks of the owner as thinking the matter over and deciding to send his son. No *man* able to command force would risk a son among such ruffians, but *God did!*

14. But when the husbandmen saw him, they reasoned among themselves, saying, This is the heir: come, let us kill him, that the inheritance may be ours.

Upon recognizing the owner's son, the crooked sharecroppers became bolder, plotting to murder the heir and steal the vineyard for themselves. Perhaps they reasoned that the

owner had died and the son had come to take possession. Or the appearance of the son may have given them the idea that the father had transferred ownership to him. In a day when titles were often uncertain and one could claim land after living on it or tending it for a certain period of time, the tenants may have presumed to own it, now that the owner had been away for so long.

15a. So they cast him out of the vineyard, and killed him.

This parable illustrates the insidious nature of sin: the more we sin, the worse it becomes. The husbandmen started off beating some servants and wounding others, but they ended up as murderers!

The tenants underestimated the power of the owner. Since he had not punished them before, they imagined he never would. (See Ecclesiastes 8:11.) The owner's repeated appeals had not softened their hearts, but had caused them to grow harder. If God's repeated appeals do not melt the heart, they harden it. The persistence of His messengers leads to more severe acts of hatred if it does not produce yielding acts of love.

II. The Parable Discussed (Luke 20:15b-19)

A. Question (vv. 15b, 16a)

15b, 16a. What therefore shall the lord of the vineyard do unto them? He shall come and destroy these husbandmen, and shall give the vineyard to others.

To murder the owner's son was intolerable! The greedy and unjust tenants had not imagined how determined the owner would be in dealing with this last crime they had committed. And since the crime was so severe, so should the punishment be. The tenants would be destroyed and the vineyard given to others.

Matthew's longer account indicates that the rulers listening to the parable gave the answer to Jesus' question. It was so obvious they could not avoid it (Matthew 21:41).

PRIMETIME DRAMA

Doesn't it sound like a drama we would see on television?

Act I: The Blackhat cowboys are rustling Rancher's cattle. A Whitehat comes to reclaim them, but he is horsewhipped and sent home with his hands tied behind his back.

Act II: The Blackhats go on rustling till another Whitehat appears. He is lassoed from his horse, dragged through the campfire, and pummeled till he drops—then lashed to his saddle and sent away unconscious.

The music builds as a third Whitehat rides into camp. A shot rings out, and he slumps over the horn of his saddle. The rustling goes on.

Act III: The music becomes more agitated. Into the Blackhat camp rides Rancher's son, the best of the Whitehats. The dastardly Blackhats hang him on a nearby tree. Gleefully they plan to take Rancher's ranch along with his cattle.

Act IV: The Texas Rangers mount up. Rancher rides at their head. The Blackhats suspect no danger till they see the posse on the hilltop. They go for their guns as the Rangers charge into their camp, but the villains are gunned down one by one.

Vividly this parallels Jesus' parable of the crooked tenants. Justice may be slow in coming, but God's justice is sure. Ultimately the Blackhats must perish.   —W. P.

B. Opposition (v. 16b)

16b. And when they heard it, they said, God forbid.

Since the rulers themselves gave the answer to the question as to what should be done to the wicked tenants, it seems that they uttered their protest *God forbid*, after coming to understand that the wicked tenants represented them. They rejected the idea that God would take the leadership away from them.

These men knew the Scriptures and recognized that Jesus was speaking about the "vineyard" of Israel (Isaiah 5:1-7; Psalm 80:8-18). God the Father had planted it, bringing it out of Egypt and establishing it firmly in Canaan. He had blessed the nation abundantly, giving Israel a land that was rich and pleasant. He had put rulers in charge of it, and all He asked was that they obey His statutes and give Him the "spiritual harvest" He deserved. The time came, however, when God was no longer seen in a pillar of cloud or a pillar of fire. It appeared that He had gone to a far country. Instead of being grateful for the blessings God had given them, those managing Israel proceeded to rob God and reject His messengers (Nehemiah 9:26; Jeremiah 7:25, 26; 25:4; Micah 2:2; 3:10, 11). God was patient and sent them one servant after another to ask for the obedience that was due, but they refused to obey (Matthew 23:29-39). The rulers not only refused to obey, but they mistreated God's prophets. In Jesus' time it was agreed that the prophets had been persecuted (Luke 11:47, 48). Finally, He sent His beloved Son (Luke 3:22), and they killed Him.

Would not the owner of the vineyard destroy those murderers and give the vineyard to others? The "others" must be Gentiles. Jesus verified that when He said, "The kingdom of God shall

visual 11

A POINTED PARABLE	
VINEYARD	**ISRAEL**
PLANTED	BROUGHT TO CANAAN
HUSBANDMEN	NATIONAL LEADERS
SERVANTS	PROPHETS
SERVANTS REJECTED	PROPHETS REJECTED
SON MURDERED	CHRIST CRUCIFIED
VINEYARD GIVEN TO OTHERS	KINGDOM OFFERED TO GENTILES

be taken from you, and given to a nation bringing forth the fruits thereof" (Matthew 21:43). But to the leaders it was unthinkable that the privileges of the Jews as God's chosen people could under any circumstances be given to Gentiles. This brought from them the protest *God forbid*. This is the only place this strong expression *God forbid* appears in the New Testament, except in Paul's writing. The words express the revulsion and outrage felt by the guilty rulers.

C. Explanation (vv. 17, 18)

17. And he beheld them, and said, What is this then that is written, The stone which the builders rejected, the same is become the head of the corner?

Jesus pointed them to Scripture. He quoted Psalm 118:22. The rulers knew this was a Messianic psalm, and they had heard it shouted when Jesus rode into the city (compare Luke 19:38 with Psalm 118:26). By applying this verse to himself, Jesus was clearly claiming to be the Messiah.

The head of the corner was an important stone. Some students take *head* to mean the top, and so they translate *capstone*, the stone that completes the building. Others take *head* to mean chief, and translate *chief cornerstone*, the stone with which the building begins. Compare Isaiah 28:16; 1 Peter 2:6; Ephesians 2:20. Even though the Jews rejected Him, Jesus was accepted by God. That is what counts.

18. Whosoever shall fall upon that stone shall be broken; but on whomsoever it shall fall, it will grind him to powder.

To *fall upon that stone* is to attack Jesus, and one who does it will be defeated. To have the stone fall upon one is to be attacked by Jesus, and one who does it will be destroyed. People may reject and oppose Jesus; but it is they, not He, who will suffer. The imagery is similar to that of Isaiah 8:14, 15 and Daniel 2:34, 35. Those who trust Jesus find Him to be the foundation stone and the chief cornerstone (1

Corinthians 3:11; Ephesians 2:20). Unbelievers stumble over Him and are judged by Him who is pictured in Daniel 2 as a stone that crushes all who get in its way.

In this last portion of His address, Jesus threw away the thin veil of parable and spoke the sternest truth in the plainest words possible. He is the cornerstone on which the true kingdom of God is built. The men who stood before Him were incompetent builders who did not know the stone needed for the edifice when they saw it. These are strange words coming from a man who knew that in three days He would be crucified. Yet these words are true. He is the foundation, the pattern of life, the ground of hope for countless individuals. He is the one on whom the church stands, and awful doom awaits those who reject Him.

THE HEAD OF THE CORNER

The temple in which Jesus taught was destroyed by the Romans in A.D. 70, but one vestige of it remains to this day. The famous wailing wall is a retaining wall built to support the platform on which the temple stood.

Early in 1992 a news story called attention to one building block in that wall—a massive stone forty-five feet long, fifteen feet wide, and twelve feet high. Its estimated weight is 570 tons.

Such stones have enabled the wailing wall to stand through centuries, but they are insignificant in comparison with Jesus, "the head of the corner." He is the living stone to whom we come to be built into the structure of His church that will stand forever (1 Peter 2:4, 5).   —W. P.

D. Resentment (v. 19)

19. And the chief priests and the scribes the same hour sought to lay hands on him; and they feared the people: for they perceived that he had spoken this parable against them.

There was no mistaking that Jesus had spoken this parable against the leaders as the "builders" who had rejected the "chief cornerstone." This intensified their anger against Jesus, but they dared not arrest Him because throngs of people favored Him. His arrest could incite a riot, and no one could tell how a riot would end. So Jesus' enemies chose another method: they tried to discredit Him, and that also failed (vv. 20-40).

Conclusion

A. God Is Patient and Just

In this parable there is an emphasis on the patience of God. The apostle Peter wrote that the Lord is patient with us, not wanting anyone to perish (2 Peter 3:9). The owner's patience is evi-

---

Home Daily Bible Readings

Monday, Feb. 7—An Argument About Authority (Luke 20:1-8)
Tuesday, Feb. 8—Parable of the Wicked Husbandmen (Luke 20:9-18)
Wednesday, Feb. 9—Caesar's Tribute and God's (Luke 20:19-26)
Thursday, Feb. 10—God of the Living, Not the Dead (Luke 20:27-40)
Friday, Feb. 11—Beware of False Piety (Luke 20:41-47)
Saturday, Feb. 12—Renewed in Spirit and Mind (Ephesians 4:22-32)
Sunday, Feb. 13—Imitate God by Walking in the Light (Ephesians 5:1-10)

---

denced in the repeated appeals that were made to the husbandmen in the parable. There comes the time, however, when the patient appeals must end and justice be meted out. In the parable, the just thing to do was to "destroy these husbandmen, and . . . give the vineyard to others." God's patience with Israel was turned into justifiable wrath, and even so must He in justice deal with those in every age who continue to reject His patient appeals.

B. Application

The Pharisees said, "If we had been in the days of our fathers, we would not have been partakers with them in the blood of the prophets" (Matthew 23:30). We easily see the faults of the Pharisees, and we say, "If we had been there, we would not have rejected Jesus."

It may be better for us to examine how well we are keeping the vineyard given to us. We all have our own vineyards to keep. That is our work to do for God and our life to live for God. Someday He will call us to account for the way we have kept the vineyard, and for the fruit we have given Him.

C. Prayer

Almighty and most merciful Father, we have so imperfectly kept the vineyard committed to us. We have rejected Your patient appeals and have not been fair and just in our treatment of You and our fellowmen. Forgive our sins and help us to commit ourselves to the patient life and the life that is just, so that we may be more like You. In Jesus name, amen.

D. Thought to Remember

Our actions always carry inevitable consequences.

Learning by Doing

This page contains an alternate lesson plan emphasizing learning activities. Classes desiring such student involvement will find these suggestions helpful.

Learning Goals

Having studied Jesus' parable of the wicked husbandmen, the learner will:

1. Explain the parable as a picture of the Jews' rejection of God's messengers, including Jesus.

2. Relate this parable directly to God's patience and ultimate justice, both for mankind and for the student himself.

Into the Lesson

Have these items on prominent display: grapes, grape juice, raisins, grape jelly. If your setting allows it, you may want to offer arriving students a snack. Raisin cookies and grape juice would be good. Begin the study time by saying, "People who plant grapevines expect to enjoy grapes, but . . ."

By prearrangement, have one of your best readers stand and read Isaiah 5:1-7. At the conclusion of the reading, have today's text read aloud to the class.

Into the Word

Present the following story for your learners to complete. Ask them to make a modern parable similar to the one Jesus told. (This activity is in the student manual for this course, or you can make a copy for each student. If necessary, you can put the story on the chalkboard and let the class work together to complete it.)

Once a man began a _____ and appointed _____ to take care of it. He himself went to _____ and stayed _____. At _____, the owner sent a _____ to the _____ and asked for _____. But the _____ responded by _____ the _____. The owner received _____! He was a patient man, so he sent a _____ to the _____. Again the _____ was _____ and _____. For a third time, the owner sent a _____, but with the same result. Finally the owner thought to himself, "I know what I can do; I'll send my _____. Perhaps, the _____ will _____ him." But the _____ reasoned, "If we _____ this _____, it may be we can _____ the _____." So they did. Now what do you suppose the owner will do? He will _____ and _____!

Allow time for completion, then let several read their parables. Discuss how they match or differ from Jesus' parable.

Present the following headlines and ask learners to match each one with something in a text.

You can do this orally, but it is more effective to print each headline on a separate strip of paper to be stuck to your wall after it is discussed.

1. "Four Strikes and You're Out!"
2. Gone Too Far
3. One Last Hope
4. Empty-Headed and Empty-Handed
5. Stoned to Death
6. Heir Today, Gone Tomorrow,
7. History of Israel
8. Meddle Management
9. Fruitless
10. Taking One Last Trip
11. Going, Going, Gone!
12. Patient Planter Pulverizes.

There will be various answers, but the following samples are given.

1. After three servants and the son were struck, the husbandmen were out.

2. The caretakers thought the owner was so far away they could do anything they wanted.

3. The owner's one last hope was his son.

4. The tenants were not thinking when they sent the servants away without payment.

5. The "Stone" of God will finally crush those who reject Him.

6. The heir to the vineyard is slain, but the killers also are soon destroyed.

7. The parable is a picture of the way Israel often rejected God's messengers.

8. Those who were entrusted to manage wanted to meddle.

9. The owner received no fruit.

10. The "one last trip" is tripping over the stone and being broken.

11. Each step the husbandmen took was a step toward death.

12. God is patient, but He will ultimately obliterate those who reject Him.

Into Life

Hand to each class member a peel-and-stick label with the large letters **W H** printed on it. The text tells of Wicked Husbandmen, but ask the students what they would want the letters to stand for if they were going to wear the label. Such possibilities as Wise Husbandman, Willing Hearer, and Worker for the Head may be given. Suggest that each one wear the label until someone asks, "What does that mean?" Then he can repeat the message of this lesson.

Let's Talk It Over

The questions on this page are designed to encourage review of the lesson Scriptures and to promote discussion of the lesson by the class. The answers provided are only discussion starters. Let your class talk it over from there.

1. The wicked husbandmen grew bolder as they went unpunished, but the day of reckoning did come. What should we learn from their folly?

Many times it seems that our sins aren't producing any negative results. We appear to be getting away with it. Then we are tempted to disobey more. But God is aware of our actions. He sends us warnings and gives us time to repent; but if we are still rebellious when He calls us to stand before Him, we will be condemned just like the wicked husbandmen.

2. Suggest some examples of how unrepented sin leads us into ever bolder disobedience.

A little half-truth, successfully told, tempts us to tell bigger lies. A little cheating, a little pilfering from our employers, a little shoplifting, and we may find ourselves involved in serious white-collar crimes. Lustful fantasies lead us to pornography, and thence to adultery, promiscuity, and perversion. A scrap of gossip over the back fence can lead to a bit of slander told out of spite, and then to vicious character assassination.

3. God gives us spiritual gifts, talents, and resources. Each one of us is like a vineyard that God has prepared and from which He expects fruit. Apply the parable to individual Christians.

If we are vineyards, our individual free wills are the husbandmen. Our Creator and Lord has the right to His due portion of our lives, abilities, and resources. If we lead our lives selfishly, for our own ends and enjoyment, then we are wicked husbandmen. However, if we yield our service to Him we will receive His rewards instead of His wrath.

4. God has also entrusted some vineyard to each congregation. List some of the things that have been entrusted to our church. What is our duty concerning them? Are we guilty of keeping them for ourselves? Do we let them go untended?

For one thing, God gives us the next generation. Our duty is to train up our youth to know the Lord, to be committed to Him, and to be willing workers in His kingdom. We keep them for ourselves if we discourage them from Christian ser-

vice. We neglect them if we do not give full attention to their training.

Another vineyard is our community. It contains people who will respond to the gospel if it is presented to them and demonstrated in the lives of Christians. Our duty is to be out in this vineyard cultivating and harvesting the Lord's fruit. If we do not give Him the fruit of the harvest He may well give it to another congregation who will.

5. God has servants today whose duty it is to call His people to faithfulness and obedience. Who are these servants? Does our congregation heed their call?

On the local level, the elders and ministers have much the same duty as the prophets. They are responsible to instruct, challenge, and rebuke the members of the congregation. Sometimes this calls for them to say things we don't want to hear. They may rebuke us for being stingy or worldly or unwilling to serve. They may challenge us to stretch beyond what is comfortable. When they do any of these things they are likely to meet resistance. Our congregation must be careful to heed their calls. God ordained these leaders to care for His vineyard, the congregation, and so we must submit to them.

6. The owner of the vineyard exhibited great patience toward the husbandmen before He came and destroyed them. Only God has this degree of patience, but we are called to imitate Him. If we put ourselves in the place of the servants who were mistreated, what lessons can we learn about how we should react to mistreatment?

Most of God's faithful servants have been viciously attacked at some time by those they were trying to help. Many preachers have been fired and suffered personal attacks, not for doing a poor job, but for doing their job too faithfully and calling forth the wrath of their hardhearted, worldly flock. Many elders have suffered like fates. In fact, any Christian who dares to stand up for truth and righteousness runs the risk of being attacked. When this happens we must remember the Lord's patience and be patient ourselves. It is our duty to stand up for God. It is His prerogative to punish rebellious people in His own time and in His own way.

One Who Serves

DEVOTIONAL READING: Mark 14:1, 2, 10-25, 42-45.

LESSON SCRIPTURE: Luke 22:1-30.

PRINTED TEXT: Luke 22:14-30.

Luke 22:14-30

14 And when the hour was come, he sat down, and the twelve apostles with him.

15 And he said unto them, With desire I have desired to eat this passover with you before I suffer:

16 For I say unto you, I will not any more eat thereof, until it be fulfilled in the kingdom of God.

17 And he took the cup, and gave thanks, and said, Take this, and divide it among yourselves:

18 For I say unto you, I will not drink of the fruit of the vine, until the kingdom of God shall come.

19 And he took bread, and gave thanks, and brake it, and gave unto them, saying, This is my body which is given for you: this do in remembrance of me.

20 Likewise also the cup after supper, saying, This cup is the new testament in my blood, which is shed for you.

21 But, behold, the hand of him that betrayeth me is with me on the table.

22 And truly the Son of man goeth, as it was determined: but woe unto that man by whom he is betrayed!

23 And they began to inquire among themselves, which of them it was that should do this thing.

24 And there was also a strife among them, which of them should be accounted the greatest.

25 And he said unto them, The kings of the Gentiles exercise lordship over them; and they that exercise authority upon them are called benefactors.

26 But ye shall not be so: but he that is greatest among you, let him be as the younger; and he that is chief, as he that doth serve.

27 For whether is greater, he that sitteth at meat, or he that serveth? is not he that sitteth at meat? but I am among you as he that serveth.

28 Ye are they which have continued with me in my temptations.

29 And I appoint unto you a kingdom, as my Father hath appointed unto me;

30 That ye may eat and drink at my table in my kingdom, and sit on thrones judging the twelve tribes of Israel.

Feb
20

GOLDEN TEXT: He that is greatest among you, let him be as the younger; and he that is chief, as he that doth serve.—Luke 22:26.

The Story of Jesus

Unit 3. Luke: The Cross and the Resurrection (Lessons 10-13)

Lesson Aims

After the lesson a student should be able to:

1. Relate events of the last supper, including what Jesus said about true greatness.

2. Express the difference between greatness as the world understands it and true greatness as Jesus describes it.

3. Discuss the importance of loyalty to Jesus in the Christian life.

Lesson Outline

INTRODUCTION
    A. Who's in Charge?
    B. Lesson Background
  I. THE PASSOVER TRANSFORMED (Luke 22:14-20)
    A. Jesus' Promise (vv. 14-16)
    B. The Bread and Cup (vv. 17-20)
      Sharing the Cup
  II. TREASON PREDICTED (Luke 22:21-23)
    A. The Traitor at the Table (v. 21)
    B. The Traitor's Final Fate (v. 22)
    C. The Disciples' Consternation (v. 23)
  III. TRUE GREATNESS DESCRIBED (Luke 22:24-27)
    A. The Disciples' Dispute (v. 24)
    B. Jesus' Definition (vv. 25, 26)
      Humility
    C. Jesus' Example (v. 27)
      A Helping Hand
  IV. A REWARD PROMISED (Luke 22:28-30)
    A. The Disciples' Faithfulness (v. 28)
    B. The Disciples' Reward (vv. 29, 30)
CONCLUSION
    A. Don't Turn Traitor
    B. Greatness Through Service
    C. "I Appoint Unto You a Kingdom"
    D. Let Us Pray
    E. Thought to Remember

Display visual 12 of the visuals packet and let it remain before the class. The visual is shown on page 213.

Introduction

A. Who's in Charge?

Some people want power more than anything else in the world. More than fifty years ago Adolph Hitler started a world war that caused the death of millions, all because he wanted to exert power over others. Often the newspaper tells us about some dictator who makes his people's lives miserable in his search for power. Some of us even suffer at home or at work from people who can't be happy unless they are controlling others.

There's no place for power-hungry people in God's kingdom. Even Jesus, who had all power in Heaven and in earth (Matthew 28:18), came to serve. In today's Scripture passage we see Jesus' example of humble service in contrast to the power-hungry attitudes of His disciples. From this we can learn to give up our quest for personal power and let God be in charge.

B. Lesson Background

In our study we have followed Jesus through three years of ministry. He planted the seeds of God's kingdom; He won many followers. He healed the sick, raised the dead, and preached good news to hurting people. But by rebuking sin and hypocrisy, He also made powerful enemies. The chief priests and scribes wanted to get Him out of the way (Luke 22:2). His follower Judas Iscariot was ready to betray Him to His enemies (Luke 22:3-6). As He neared the end of His ministry, He did what He could to teach His disciples; but today's passage shows they still had a long way to go.

Jesus had reached the last night of His earthly ministry. Soon He would die and leave His followers to carry on His work. Even after His resurrection from the dead, the disciples would need to be convinced that Jesus was really alive, and they would need the power of the Holy Spirit to enable them to take the gospel to the waiting world. They would need something else too, a clear understanding of "who's in charge" and of where they fit in God's scheme of things. They would need to give up the quest for personal power and follow Jesus' example, learning to become the kind of humble servants that Jesus himself was.

I. The Passover Transformed (Luke 22:14-20)

The verses just before our printed text describe how Peter and John arranged for the Passover meal in an upper room (Luke 22:7-13). Following Jesus' instructions, they went into Jerusalem. There they met a man carrying a pitcher of water. Following him back to his house, they asked the master of the house about the room where Jesus and His disciples were to eat the Passover meal. Once the man showed them the room, Peter and John prepared for the meal. We pick up the story as the meal begins.

A. Jesus' Promise (vv. 14-16)

14. And when the hour was come, he sat down, and the twelve apostles with him.

The Passover lamb had been killed earlier in the day, and the meal took place in the evening (Exodus 12). According to the custom of the time, Jesus and His disciples would have reclined on couches around the table, each man leaning on his left elbow and eating with his right hand.

15. And he said unto them, With desire I have desired to eat this passover with you before I suffer.

With desire I have desired was a Hebrew way of saying, "I have eagerly desired" (*New International Version*). Knowing He would die the next day, Jesus very much wanted to have this quiet evening with His apostles, to give them the teaching recorded in chapters 13—17 of John, and to establish a memorial to be observed through the ages. Passover reminded the Jews of how God had delivered them from Egypt centuries before. Now Jesus was transforming that celebration into a celebration of God's rescuing the whole human race from sin.

16. For I say unto you, I will not any more eat thereof, until it be fulfilled in the kingdom of God.

This statement pointed toward Jesus' death and resurrection, and the founding of the church on the following Pentecost. The Passover would be *fulfilled,* would find its real meaning, when Christ would be sacrificed as our Passover lamb (1 Corinthians 5:7) and God would deliver people from their sins through Him. As God rescued Israel from Egypt at the time of the first Passover, He would rescue them from sin through the cross.

More than that, Jesus' promise foreshadowed "the marriage supper of the Lamb" (Revelation 19:9), the Heavenly feast that will take place when all God's children have come home to Him forever. Each time we eat the Lord's Supper, we are looking forward in a symbolic way to that Heavenly feast; in fact we are preparing ourselves for the final feast when we take part in the weekly feast here on earth.

B. The Bread and Cup (vv. 17-20)

17. And he took the cup, and gave thanks, and said, Take this, and divide it among yourselves.

In the accounts of Matthew and Mark, we see Jesus giving out the bread first, then the cup. Here in Luke's Gospel He gives a cup first, then the bread, and later a cup again. We may think of this first cup as an ordinary part of the Passover meal. The sayings of Jewish rabbis, preserved for fourteen hundred years in the Babylonian Talmud, indicate that a Passover meal included four different cups of wine, taken at different times throughout the evening.

18. For I say unto you, I will not drink of the fruit of the vine, until the kingdom of God shall come.

This repeats the promise of verse 16. *The kingdom of God* would appear in a new way when the church would begin its work on the Day of Pentecost; it will find its culmination in the marriage supper of the Lamb.

19. And he took bread, and gave thanks, and brake it, and gave unto them, saying, This is my body which is given for you: this do in remembrance of me.

At this point Jesus began to institute the Lord's Supper. The *bread* was the unleavened bread of the Passover celebration (Exodus 13:6, 7). It stood as a reminder of how God delivered His people from Egypt in the time of Moses. Jesus gave it new meaning by connecting the bread with His body, *given* on the cross to deliver His people from the power of sin and death.

Jesus died for us, and this leaves us with an obligation to live for Him. We remember Jesus' last Passover, and our debt to Him, when we take the bread *in remembrance* of Him. As Paul said it, Christ "died for all, that they which live should not henceforth live unto themselves, but unto him which died for them, and rose again" (2 Corinthians 5:15).

20. Likewise also the cup after supper, saying, This cup is the new testament in my blood, which is shed for you.

As Jesus' body was *given* for us (v. 19), so His blood was *shed.* The *new testament in my blood* is the New Covenant, the new agreement between God and His people, which came into being through the shedding of Jesus' blood on the cross. As the Old Covenant began with animal sacrifices, so the New Covenant began with the atoning death of God's own Son (Hebrews 9:18-20; Exodus 24:6-8). The writer of Hebrews expressed an important Biblical principle when he said that "without shedding of blood is no remission" of sins (Hebrews 9:22). Jesus paid the price for the wrongs we have done, giving us the right to live with Him forever. His was the pain, ours the gain.

SHARING THE CUP

A group of Christians went to Haiti to help build a hospital. They took their food with them and carefully treated their drinking water so the work would not be hindered by sickness.

Later a campus minister with the group was asked what had been the most difficult part of the trip. He said it was not the primitive living conditions or the hard work in the tropical sun. It was something that happened during a church service.

The group arrived early and saw the elements of the Communion service being prepared under conditions far from sanitary. When Communion time came, the campus minister found himself in a quandary. Sharing in Christ's blood was important to him, and so was fellowship with the Christians about him; but could he risk getting sick and stopping his work? Would anyone notice if he would pretend to drink and put the cup down still full? Was so small a bit of contaminated drink really dangerous? What would Jesus think of his fear and reservation?

Finally love for Christ and His church overcame fear. With a greater sense of trust than he usually felt at Communion time, the man drank from the cup. It was a small crisis, but one he later remembered often at Communion time. Is not trust in God a central part of the Communion?   —W. P.

II. Treason Predicted
(Luke 22:21-23)

A. The Traitor at the Table (v. 21)

21. But, behold, the hand of him that betrayeth me is with me on the table.

Matthew and Mark record what Jesus said about His betrayer before the institution of the Lord's Supper, not after. Luke put the Lord's Supper first, probably because it was the most important thing, then told of something that had already happened during the meal: that is, Jesus' words about Judas the traitor.

These words must have shocked the disciples. One of them would hand the Lord over to His enemies! We need to make sure He can never say the same of us, that one of us who fellowships around His table will never turn traitor. Judas betrayed his Master for thirty pieces of silver (Matthew 26:15), a trivial price for an eternal sin. In our case also, any payoff we might receive for turning away from our Lord is too small (Matthew 16:26). No price is enough to buy our betrayal of our Lord.

B. The Traitor's Final Fate (v. 22)

22. And truly the Son of man goeth, as it was determined: but woe unto that man by whom he is betrayed!

It was determined in God's eternal plan for Jesus to die and redeem His people. But that didn't let Judas escape the responsibility of his betrayal. In the same way, bad things will happen in our time, wrongs will be done; but we need to take care that we are not the ones causing them.

C. The Disciples' Consternation (v. 23)

23. And they began to inquire among themselves, which of them it was that should do this thing.

The disciples not only talked *among themselves*: each of them asked Jesus, "Lord, is it I?" Judas hypocritically asked Him the same thing: "Master, is it I?" (Matthew 26:21-25).

III. True Greatness Described
(Luke 22:24-27)

A. The Disciples' Dispute (v. 24)

24. And there was also a strife among them, which of them should be accounted the greatest.

We wonder what this dispute sounded like. Did the disciples argue over which of them was Jesus' "right hand man"? Did one of them claim to be more spiritual than the others, or a more powerful miracle worker? We don't know; but we do know that whenever God's people stop focusing their attention on Him and start comparing themselves to each other, trouble is not far away. As Paul put it, those caught up in "measuring themselves by themselves, and comparing themselves among themselves, are not wise" (2 Corinthians 10:12). The question is not who *should be accounted the greatest*, but who will serve God by serving His people.

B. Jesus' Definition (vv. 25, 26)

25. And he said unto them, The kings of the Gentiles exercise lordship over them; and they that exercise authority upon them are called benefactors.

Jesus describes the way it is in the world: people who have power use it. The *Gentiles* were pagans, no part of God's chosen people. The way they used power was essentially ungodly. And when they used their power, a strange thing happened: the people under their power praised them for it. How often does a cruel dictator receive praise from his people—at least those whom he is not oppressing at the moment! How often does a religious leader manipulate people until they not only let him take away their freedom of choice but also thank him for taking it! We need to be careful not to be manipulated by frauds who appear godly. More than that, we must be sure we aren't frauds ourselves. "Wherefore let him that thinketh he standeth take heed lest he fall" (1 Corinthians 10:12).

26. But ye shall not be so: but he that is greatest among you, let him be as the younger; and he that is chief, as he that doth serve.

In the world's system, those on the bottom serve those on top. It's the other way around in the kingdom of God. Whoever is *greatest* or *chief,* whoever holds a responsible position in the church, needs to behave as *the younger* or *he that doth serve.* When we meet with the church, we need to leave our worldly notions of prestige and power outside the door and learn to serve. Better yet, we need to carry the kingdom ideal of humble, loving service back to a world that doesn't work that way, trying to transform our office or factory or school into something more like what God prefers.

HUMILITY

Walter Trobisch tells a story about Martin Luther and his barber, Peter Besken. One day the barber asked, "Doctor Luther, how do you pray?"

Luther took the question so seriously that he wrote a letter that later was published in forty printed pages. He said, "A good clever barber must have his thoughts, mind, and eyes concentrated upon the razor and the beard. . . . If he keeps talking or looking around or thinking of something else, he is likely to cut a man's mouth or nose—or even his throat. So anything that is to be done well ought to occupy the whole man with all his faculties and members. . . . How much more must prayer possess the heart completely if it is to be a good prayer."

The letter revealed much about the great man's devotional life, but it also revealed his humility. Luther wrote, "I give you the best I have. I tell you how I pray. May our Lord God grant you and everyone to do it better."   —W. P.

C. Jesus' Example (v. 27)

27. For whether is greater, he that sitteth at meat, or he that serveth? is not he that sitteth at meat? but I am among you as he that serveth.

He that sitteth at meat was the master of the house. *He that serveth* was an employee or slave whose job was to cater to the master. In the world clear lines divide people according to class or occupation or some other measurement. One who serves is considered inferior to one served. But Jesus' example of humble service broke the world's mold. Even though He was God's own Son, He took the place of a servant. Can His people do any less? As Jesus said elsewhere, "The Son of man came not to be ministered unto, but to minister" (Matthew 20:28; Mark 10:45). The more closely we follow Jesus, the more we will resemble Him in the way we serve other people.

A HELPING HAND

A story from the American Revolution has been repeated often and with some variations, but it always carries a message.

A few soldiers were struggling to raise a huge hand-hewn beam to its place in a building that was being built hastily. They were having trouble because of the weight of the beam and because of the slippery mud underfoot, but the corporal in charge offered no sympathy. He just stood by and berated them loudly.

A tall passerby in civilian clothes paused to watch for a minute. Then he inquired, "Why don't you help them?"

The man in charge drew himself up in insulted arrogance. "Sir," he said, "I am a corporal!"

The passerby then took off his coat, waded into the mud, and helped to lift the heavy beam and secure it. Picking up his coat with muddy hands, he said mildly, "Corporal, next time you don't have men enough for a job, send for your commander in chief. I'll be glad to lend a hand." George Washington buttoned his coat and strode away.

The commander in chief must have been learning from the Lord of all.   —W. P.

IV. A Reward Promised
(Luke 22:28-30)

A. The Disciples' Faithfulness (v. 28)

28. Ye are they which have continued with me in my temptations.

Several later translations use the word *trials* instead of *temptations.* Jesus wasn't talking only about the times when the devil tried to get Him to sin, as in the wilderness temptations (Luke 4:1-13). He was speaking more generally, meaning that His disciples had stuck by Him in all His troubles, including the persecution from religious authorities that would lead to His death. As the disciples stayed with Jesus even when

visual 12

things got dangerous, we need to stay faithful to Him, whatever it costs, even being "faithful unto death" (Revelation 2:10).

B. The Disciples' Reward (vv. 29, 30)

29. And I appoint unto you a kingdom, as my Father hath appointed unto me.

Jesus, who has all power, rules over God's kingdom forever. But the kingdom isn't His alone. He will share its joys with His followers.

30. That ye may eat and drink at my table in my kingdom, and sit on thrones judging the twelve tribes of Israel.

As He did in verses 16 and 18, Jesus foretold the Heavenly banquet that is called the "marriage supper of the Lamb" in Revelation 19:9. The disciples, and in fact all believers, will enjoy close fellowship with Jesus in the world to come. And there is more than fellowship to look forward to: God's people will have tasks to perform in the next world. Here Jesus promised His disciples that they would exercise judgment over Israel. We don't know all this involves, but Paul did say that saints will "judge the world" and "judge angels" (1 Corinthians 6:2, 3). Jesus' followers may not have much authority in this world, but He did promise us some sort of authority in the next.

Conclusion

A. Don't Turn Traitor

Eleven of Jesus' disciples were far from perfect men, but they were loyal to Him. The twelfth was a traitor. When the disciples later chose a replacement for Judas, they said it this way: "Judas by transgression fell, that he might go to his own place" (Acts 1:25). It doesn't take much imagination to know what they meant by "his own place," the place where traitors go. Dante, in his famous *Inferno*, reserved the lowest circle of Hell for Judas and all other traitors.

Judas' fate has something to say to us today. The Lord doesn't need brave, brilliant, or beautiful people as much as He needs people He can trust. He can put up with our confusion, He can endure our laziness, He can even forgive our sin, but He can't tolerate our disloyalty. We need to make sure we are true to our Savior in the way we talk, the way we behave, and the way we think. If our loyalty is sound, He can find something in us to work with.

B. Greatness Through Service

In the evening before He died, Jesus showed what greatness is. People who wield power over others are called great in this world; emperors and generals, politicians and judges all have their day. But in God's kingdom, greatness comes through service. Jesus "came not to be ministered unto, but to minister" (Mark 10:45). In the same way, we His people need to think not about what we can get but what we can give.

How does your life measure up? Do you serve, or insist on being served? Do you live your life for what you can get or what you can give? Will the Lord lift you in the end from the humble station you have volunteered for, or will He have to pull you down off the pedestal you have assumed?

C. "I Appoint Unto You a Kingdom"

God's people are called to serve, to give, and even to suffer for Christ; but we won't go unrewarded. Jesus promised His first disciples a kingdom, and the promise is for us as well. If we stay with Jesus through trouble, we will live with Him in glory. As Paul said, "If we suffer, we shall also reign with him" (2 Timothy 2:12).

That's a promise worth holding on to. We shouldn't follow Jesus selfishly because we hope for a reward; but we can take Him seriously when He promises one, and we can trust Him to provide it.

D. Let Us Pray

Father, please forgive us when we seek power for ourselves. Show us the way of the cross, the the way of humble service. Make us truly great by showing us how to serve. Keep our eyes fixed on the eternal kingdom You have prepared for us. Through Christ our Lord, amen.

E. Thought to Remember

"He that is greatest among you, let him be as the younger; and he that is chief, as he that doth serve" (Luke 22:26).

Home Daily Bible Readings

Monday, Feb. 14—The Widow's Gift (Luke 21:1-6)

Tuesday, Feb. 15—Signs of the End (Luke 21:10-24)

Wednesday, Feb. 16—Peter and John Prepare the Passover (Luke 22:1-8)

Thursday, Feb. 17—Finding the Upper Room (Luke 22:9-13)

Friday, Feb. 18—Breaking Bread Together (Luke 22:14-23)

Saturday, Feb. 19—Jesus Serves (Luke 22:24-27)

Sunday, Feb. 20—Jesus Prays for Simon (Luke 22:28-34)

Learning by Doing

This page contains an alternate lesson plan emphasizing learning activities. Classes desiring such student involvement will find these suggestions helpful.

Learning Goals

After this study the adults will be able to:

1. Explain the importance of key words in the text.

2. Contrast the simple facts of the study with its profound truths.

3. Worship more deeply in the Lord's Supper.

Into the Lesson

Have this sign prominently displayed:
THE ABC'S OF SALVATION AND SERVICE

As students come in, hand each one a card with one of the letters of the alphabet. Exclude Q, X, and Z. That leaves twenty-three different letters to be distributed. If there are more than twenty-three people, give some letters on separate cards to two of them; if there are fewer than twenty-three people, hand out leftover letters as you begin the lesson.

Remark that our text has facts that are simple, but truths that are profound. Repeat the alphabet, letting each student hold up his card as you name the letter it bears. Then comment that these few letters can be arranged to present such simple things as *bread* and *cup*, and also such deep ideas as *salvation* and *vicarious*.

Into the Word

```
A B C A B C A K B C A V I N E
B P C U N T I L A B C A E A T
R U O H B N C E T A B W C A B
C C A S G B S A R C T A O B C
A N B D T I B C A E B C A E B
C A O B W L R C S A T B C A B
C M A E E B E T C A B A L C J
A B K C A B A S C A B C E A U
B I C A B M D R I N K H R R D
L C A R E V O S S A P T R B G
C T A N B C A B R C E E A B I
F A T H E R C A A B C V U A N
B E C N A R B M E M E R Q C G
A M B C A B C A L B C E A B C
A B C A B Y O U N G E S T C A
```

After three or four minutes show a big copy of this puzzle on a placard or the chalkboard. (It is also included in the student manual for this course.) Ask each student to find in the puzzle a word beginning with the letter he holds—a word from our lesson text. The word may be spelled from left to right, from right to left, downward,

upward, or diagonally in any direction. As each word is found, mark it on the puzzle. Let the person who holds the letter tell the class what that word is saying in the text, or what is said about it. If some word is hard to find, you can speed up the process by pointing out the first letter of it. To save time you can also post the following words that can be found in the puzzle.

apostles	Israel	Passover
bread	judging	remembrance
cup	Kingdom	serveth
drink	likewise	table
eat	meat	until
Father	New Testament	vine
greater	on	woe
hour	you	

Divide the class down the middle. Ask one half to list simple facts told in the text, and the other half to list profound truths. For example, a simple fact is that Jesus broke the bread and gave it to His disciples. A profound truth is that the bread is His body. After five or six minutes, let the one group read its list of facts. Can anyone in the other group add to it? Then let the other group read its profound truths. Can anyone add to that list?

This will provide an opportunity for the class to discuss the profound truths and any questions that may be raised about them. You can help the discussion with thoughts from the lesson treatment in this book.

Into Life

Divide the class into groups of three or four. Give each group one of these themes. Ask the group to write a Communion meditation using its theme.

1. The Lord's table is no place for feelings of self-importance or conceit (vv. 24-26).

2. The Lord's Supper looks backward in remembrance (v. 19).

3. The Lord's Supper looks forward with expectation of the kingdom (vv. 16, 18).

4. Jesus gave thanks and gave the bread and cup; His body was about to be given (v. 19). What does this suggest about our giving?

5. One may share the Lord's Supper and still deny the Lord. It is appropriate for each of us to ask, "Is it I?" (vv. 21, 22).

Let the completed meditations be read to the class in the closing moments of the session.

Let's Talk It Over

The questions on this page are designed to encourage review of the lesson Scriptures and to promote discussion of the lesson by the class. The answers provided are only discussion starters. Let your class talk it over from there.

1. Describe how Jesus fulfilled the Passover. What part do we have in fulfilling it?

The perfect Passover lamb foretold the sinless perfection of Christ. The lamb was killed in the afternoon; Jesus died in midafternoon. None of the lamb's bones were broken; none of Jesus' bones were broken. Those protected by the blood of the lamb were spared in Egypt; those protected by the blood of Christ will be spared on the Judgment Day. The Passover was eaten with bitter herbs to remind the people of the bitterness of slavery; people who come to Christ experience the bitterness of remorse for sins. As leaven was put out of the house, Christians put sin out of their lives. The Jews ate the flesh of the lamb; Christians eat the Lord's Supper, His flesh and blood.

2. Jesus said to eat the bread and drink the fruit of the vine in remembrance of Him. What do we remember? How does remembrance affect us?

We remember Jesus' suffering and death. We remember that our sins made His suffering necessary. We recall that His love for us drove Him to accept death on the cross. We remind ourselves that we receive eternal life because He died for us. As we remember Jesus' love, we look into our hearts and lives to identify any remaining sinfulness. Confessing our sins and weaknesses, we seek forgiveness and strength to conquer. Thus the purpose of the Lord's Supper is to keep our love for the Lord fresh and strong, and motivates us to lives of righteousness, sacrifice, and service.

3. On the lips of the eleven, the question "Is it I?" revealed real soul-searching and anguish. On the lips of the traitor it was brazen hypocrisy. What does this suggest about our private prayers as we observe the Lord's Supper?

The eleven searched within themselves for any sign of unfaithfulness. Judas, however, knew full well that he had betrayed Christ. We must remember this lesson as we meditate during the Lord's Supper.

Like the eleven, we search our hearts for weakness or unfaithfulness so we can eliminate it. If we come to the Lord's table fully conscious of a sin in our lives, yet do not bring that sin be-fore the Lord to seek His help and forgiveness, then we follow in Judas's steps. Sin that is known and not confessed destroys our communion with the Lord.

4. Give some examples of Jesus' service and tell how we can imitate Him.

Jesus' first miracle served the needs of a host when the wine ran out. He served by teaching about the kingdom of God and by His miracles of healing and feeding. He served by washing the disciples' feet. He served all mankind in His death. We cannot imitate Jesus' miracles, but we can imitate His compassion and helpfulness. We can serve those who need food and clothing. We can minister to the sick and infirm, giving them medicine, comfort, and help. We can minister to one another as each has special need. We minister to the Lord also by supporting the work of proclaiming the gospel.

5. By Jesus' criteria, who are the greatest in our church? Evaluate your own greatness.

The greatest people in a congregation are not necessarily the leaders who are highly visible. The greatest are those who deny self in order to give service to the Lord, to fellow Christians, even to strangers. The greatest among us are those who do this continually and joyfully. Leaders give many hours to meetings and planning. Shepherds spend much time among the flock. Others teach, clean the church building, direct traffic, visit shut-ins. Each congregation has its tasks; the greatest are those who do those tasks. No task is unimportant in the Lord's work. What do you do?

6. The adage says that power corrupts. How can church leaders keep from being corrupted?

Elders and other leaders ought to exercise a certain authority. They must remember that they in turn are under the authority of Christ and they will be called to answer to Him for the way they use their authority. Elders and other leaders can guard against abuse by holding each other accountable. All of us who are leaders will be able to use whatever authority we have in the proper way if we remember that authority is given to us to enable us to be better servants of those we lead.

From Death to Life

DEVOTIONAL READING: Mark 15:33-37.

LESSON SCRIPTURE: Luke 23:32-47; 24:13-35.

PRINTED TEXT: Luke 23:32-46; 24:33, 34.

Luke 23:32-46

32 And there were also two others, malefactors, led with him to be put to death.

33 And when they were come to the place, which is called Calvary, there they crucified him, and the malefactors, one on the right hand, and the other on the left.

34 Then said Jesus, Father, forgive them; for they know not what they do. And they parted his raiment, and cast lots.

35 And the people stood beholding. And the rulers also with them derided him, saying, He saved others; let him save himself, if he be Christ, the chosen of God.

36 And the soldiers also mocked him, coming to him, and offering him vinegar,

37 And saying, If thou be the King of the Jews, save thyself.

38 And a superscription also was written over him in letters of Greek, and Latin, and Hebrew, THIS IS THE KING OF THE JEWS.

39 And one of the malefactors which were hanged railed on him, saying, If thou be Christ, save thyself and us.

40 But the other answering rebuked him, saying, Dost not thou fear God, seeing thou art in the same condemnation?

41 And we indeed justly; for we receive the due reward of our deeds: but this man hath done nothing amiss.

42 And he said unto Jesus, Lord, remember me when thou comest into thy kingdom.

43 And Jesus said unto him, Verily I say unto thee, Today shalt thou be with me in paradise.

44 And it was about the sixth hour, and there was a darkness over all the earth until the ninth hour.

45 And the sun was darkened, and the veil of the temple was rent in the midst.

46 And when Jesus had cried with a loud voice, he said, Father, into thy hands I commend my spirit: and having said thus, he gave up the ghost.

Luke 24:33, 34

33 And they rose up the same hour, and returned to Jerusalem, and found the eleven gathered together, and them that were with them,

34 Saying, The Lord is risen indeed, and hath appeared to Simon.

GOLDEN TEXT: The Lord is risen indeed.—Luke 24:34.

Lesson Aims

After the study of this lesson, a student should be able to:

1. Relate the events of Jesus' death as recorded by Luke.

2. Appreciate the meaning of Jesus' death and resurrection for his or her own salvation.

3. Be committed to a life of personal sacrifice in imitation of Jesus.

Lesson Outline

INTRODUCTION
  A. The Ultimate Service
  B. Lesson Background
  I. JESUS AS VICTIM (Luke 23:32-39)
  A. He Was Crucified (vv. 32, 33)
  B. He Forgave His Murderers (v. 34)
  C. He Endured Abuse (vv. 35-39)
 II. JESUS AS REDEEMER (Luke 23:40-46)
  A. He Comforted a Malefactor (vv. 40-43)
  B. He Caused Mysterious Signs (vv. 44, 45)
  C. He Gave Up His Spirit (v. 46)
III. JESUS AS RISEN LORD (Luke 24:33, 34)
  A. He Caused a Stir (v. 33)
  B. He Appeared to Simon (v. 34)
CONCLUSION
  A. A Death for Us
     Undoing the Dirty Work
  B. A Life for Him
     Carrying a Cross
  C. Let Us Pray
  D. Thought to Remember

Visual 13 of the visuals packet depicts the message of the cross. Display it throughout this session. The visual is shown on page 221.

Introduction

A. The Ultimate Service

In last week's lesson we met Jesus as "one who serves." On the night before His death, we saw Him showing more concern for His disciples than for himself. We saw Him institute the Lord's Supper as a memorial for them to share, and we heard Him warn them that one of them would betray Him. We saw Him settle a dispute among His disciples about which of them was the greatest, and from Him we learned the great principle, "He that is greatest among you, let him be as the younger; and he that is chief, as he that doth serve" (Luke 22:26).

Jesus came to our world as a servant and taught us to serve. He lived out the principle stated in John 15:13, "Greater love hath no man than this, that a man lay down his life for his friends." His life of service climaxed in a death that showed Him servant of the whole human race, and the sacrifice for our sins.

B. Lesson Background

In this quarter we have seen Jesus' words and deeds prove again and again that He is God's own Son. Yet as the common people came to believe in Him more and more, His powerful enemies among the nation's leaders came to hate Him more. Finally they succeeded in their plot to have Him killed.

Judas betrayed Jesus to His enemies, telling them where they could find Him to arrest Him. The spiritual leaders rushed Him through a "religious" trial that resulted in a guilty verdict (Luke 22:66-71). Then they took Him to Pontius Pilate, the Roman governor, hoping to get a sentence of death passed on Him (Luke 23:1-5). Pilate, probably trying to shift responsibility, sent Jesus to Herod Antipas, who questioned and insulted Jesus still more (Luke 23:6-12).

Back in Pilate's hands, Jesus received the death penalty when the Jewish crowd cried out for His crucifixion (Luke 23:13-24). Pilate's attempt to get Jesus released failed, and the governor sent the Savior to His death on a cross.

On Jesus' way to the cross, the Romans made Simon of Cyrene carry the instrument of execution for Him (Luke 23:26). A large crowd followed the procession to the place of execution, including many women who wailed and mourned over Jesus and heard Him pronounce words of doom on Jerusalem (Luke 23:27-31). Now we come to our printed text.

I. Jesus as Victim
(Luke 23:32-39)

A. He Was Crucified (vv. 32, 33)

32. And there were also two others, malefactors, led with him to be put to death.

Jesus was not crucified alone. Along with Him went two men whom Matthew and Mark call "thieves," but the Greek word indicates that they were violent robbers or bandits rather than sneak thieves. They may have been, or may have pretended to be, revolutionaries in rebellion against the Roman government of occupied Palestine. Luke describes these men by the more general term *malefactors*, which means evildoers. Little did those two victims know whom they were meeting in their death; but one of them would realize it before he died.

33. And when they were come to the place, which is called Calvary, there they crucified him, and the malefactors, one on the right hand, and the other on the left.

The place of execution bore a sinister name in keeping with its dark purpose. Matthew, Mark, and John give the Hebrew name *Golgotha* for the place; they also note that *Golgotha* means "place of a skull." The name *Calvary*, which appears here in the *King James Version*, comes from the Latin translation of the Greek word Luke really used, which means "skull." This means that *Calvary* is a modern name for the place the Jews knew as *Golgotha*.

None of the Gospel writers refers to Calvary as a hill or mountain. However, the crucified Jesus could be seen from a distance (Luke 23:49), and the Romans usually crucified their victims in as public a place as possible. This may explain the popular opinion that Calvary was a hill.

Golgotha was a place of horror for those who knew it, but it has become a place of hope for us. The death Jesus died there was not an accident of history or the tragic ending of a human life; it was the redeeming force that gives us hope for eternity.

B. He Forgave His Murderers (v. 34)

34. Then said Jesus, Father, forgive them; for they know not what they do. And they parted his raiment, and cast lots.

Most men in pain will curse or threaten those who torment them; Jesus offered them forgiveness instead. In doing so He showed love for His enemies (see Matthew 5:44) and submission to His Father as He appealed to the Father for the enemies' pardon.

The Roman execution squad had the right to take the victim's clothes; He certainly wouldn't need them anymore! John reports the reason for casting lots: Jesus had a seamless tunic that the soldiers didn't want to tear up, so they cast lots for it (John 19:23, 24), perhaps by throwing dice.

C. He Endured Abuse (vv. 35-39)

35. And the people stood beholding. And the rulers also with them derided him, saying, He saved others; let him save himself, if he be Christ, the chosen of God.

The execution was public in hope of keeping other people from committing similar crimes. The *rulers* who made fun of Jesus were the very religious leaders who had Him arrested and condemned to death. Their response shows how

---

How to Say It

ANTIPAS. *An*-tuh-pas.
ARIMATHEA. Air-uh-muh-*thee*-uh (*th* as in *thin*).
CYRENE. Sye-*ree*-nee.
EMMAUS. Em-*may*-us.

---

deep human evil can go, as they laughed at a man in His death agony.

Let him save himself, if he be Christ was a challenge to Jesus' divine nature. If He really was the Messiah, the anointed Savior God promised, then He ought to be able to rescue himself. The Jewish leaders thought He could not get free, but the truth is that He would not. He was paying the price for our sins, and so He endured what He had to endure.

36, 37. And the soldiers also mocked him, coming to him, and offering him vinegar, and saying, If thou be the King of the Jews, save thyself.

The vinegar the Roman soldiers offered Jesus was a kind of cheap, sour wine favored by people who couldn't afford anything better. Luke's account does not necessarily imply that their offer of a drink was a way of making fun of Jesus. Instead, it may have been an act of rough kindness from these hardened soldiers. But they did make fun of Him, using nearly the same words as Jesus' own people: *let him save himself.*

Once again we see how deep human wickedness can go as these pagan soldiers made fun of a dying, helpless man. But God's sacrificial love cuts deeper than our sin; the Redeemer carried on His work of redemption while being mocked by the very people He came to save.

For these tough Roman soldiers Jesus' death was just another execution. They didn't understand the implications of their actions; they didn't realize they were taking part in a divine drama that would change the world; they didn't know that their actions, evil as they were, would help save the world.

38. And a superscription also was written over him in letters of Greek, and Latin, and Hebrew, This is the King of the Jews.

The Romans often hung a sign over the head of a crucified victim stating his crime; this practice probably acted as a healthy deterrent. In Jesus' case the sign also communicated the Romans' scorn: scorn for the Jews and their hope of an independent kingdom, and scorn for Jesus as a failed claimant to the throne. The sign implied, "This is what happens to people who try to infringe on Rome's right to rule."

When they put up the sign in mockery, the Romans would have been surprised to know how true their words were: that Jesus really was *The King of the Jews*, and that His kingdom would outlast their empire by at least nineteen hundred years of human history and on through eternity.

39. And one of the malefactors which were hanged railed on him, saying, If thou be Christ, save thyself and us.

Note how everyone made fun of Jesus, from the highest to the lowest: not only the Jewish religious leaders, but also the pagan soldiers; not only the pagans, but even a condemned criminal. In great pain as he was, the man wanted to spread his pain to someone else, or maybe to relieve his own agony a bit by pretending he was wiser than the man he was being executed with.

II. Jesus as Redeemer
(Luke 23:40-46)

A. He Comforted a Malefactor
(vv. 40-43)

40. But the other answering rebuked him, saying, Dost not thou fear God, seeing thou art in the same condemnation?

Matthew and Mark record that both of the other victims insulted Jesus; only Luke has any record of the man we call the "good thief." Maybe both men made fun of Jesus at first, but the "good thief" saw Jesus' reaction and had a change of heart.

When the man asked his companion, *Dost not thou fear God?* he may have been referring to the judgment. Many Jews believed that God would raise the dead at the last day and judge their deeds. His point apparently was something like this: "Here you are dying for a crime. Aren't you afraid to go before God for judgment with still another sin on your head, the sin of reviling an innocent man?"

41. And we indeed justly; for we receive the due reward of our deeds: but this man hath done nothing amiss.

The "good thief" knew that he was suffering for what he had done. Even if he was a revolutionary and not a common robber, he could easily see that his violent life had led him to a violent death. In contrast, Jesus was not dying for any wrong He himself had done. Whether the "thief" knew more of Jesus' situation than this we don't know, but what the man said next may lead us to believe he understood something at least of who Jesus was and what His mission was.

42. And he said unto Jesus, Lord, remember me when thou comest into thy kingdom.

The man must have understood that Jesus' kingdom was "not of this world" (John 18:36), because it was plain to all that any hope of earthly glory Jesus might have had was coming to a violent end on the cross. However much or little the man knew about Jesus, at least he knew enough to look to Him for salvation, and that's the most important thing for any sinner to do in that time or this.

43. And Jesus said unto him, Verily I say unto thee, Today shalt thou be with me in paradise.

The man made his request in good faith, and Jesus graciously answered in the same way. To the Jews of that time, *paradise* meant the place where righteous people went when they died. Paul connected paradise with the third heaven (2 Corinthians 12:2-4), the highest heaven, the place where God lives.

Jesus implied that the man would be alive and conscious after his upcoming death, and He gave him the same promise He gave His closest followers: "that where I am, there ye may be also" (John 14:3). This was no less than a commitment to meet the man in God's own presence within a few hours. His promise to us is not so specific as *today* but it is just as firm. We who put our trust in Jesus and follow Him can expect to see Him in eternity.

B. He Caused Mysterious Signs
(vv. 44, 45)

44. And it was about the sixth hour, and there was a darkness over all the earth until the ninth hour.

Since the Jews divided the daylight into twelve hours, from *the sixth hour* to *the ninth hour* was from noon until about three o'clock. The darkness was either *over all the earth*, as the *King James Version* puts it, or "over the whole land" according to the *New International Version*. The word Luke used for *earth* or "land" can be translated either way, meaning either a limited darkness over Palestine or a general darkness over the whole planet.

The unnatural darkness was a sign: nature was protesting the violent death of God's Son. Just as the sign of a light-giving star appeared in the sky when the Savior's life began, the sign of a darkened sun appeared on the day He died.

45. And the sun was darkened, and the veil of the temple was rent in the midst.

The *veil* or curtain *of the temple* separated the outer room, called the Holy Place, from the inner room, called the Holy of Holies or the Most Holy Place, the place where God showed His presence among His people. Matthew and Mark note that the curtain was torn "from the top to the bottom" (Matthew 27:51; Mark 15:38), showing that the tearing was God's action and not a human one.

The inner room of the temple, now revealed to those outside, stood for the presence of God. In Hebrews 10:19-22 we learn that Jesus has made for us a "new and living way" into God's presence, so that we have "boldness to enter into the holiest by the blood of Jesus." More than that, the writer of Hebrews says the veil refers to Jesus' flesh: as His flesh was torn on the cross, and as the curtain in the temple was split in two, God was showing His people that the way to Him was now open. No barrier exists any more; no go-between but Christ is necessary; we who believe in Jesus can go before God with boldness and joy, finding there the forgiveness and help we need.

C. He Gave Up His Spirit (v. 46)

46. And when Jesus had cried with a loud voice, he said, Father, into thy hands I commend my spirit: and having said thus, he gave up the ghost.

Nobody took Jesus' life from Him; He gave it up voluntarily. As He said, "No man taketh it from me, but I lay it down of myself. I have power to lay it down, and I have power to take it again" (John 10:18). Here in Luke's account we read that He addressed God as *Father*, committed His spirit to the Father, and finished the sacrificial death He had come to die.

For some, Jesus' death is the last act in a tragedy, but for Christians it is the centerpiece of God's plan to save the people of His world. For those who accept Jesus, His death means forgiveness of sins and eternal life. For those who reject Him, His death stands as a judgment on them because they have rejected the best God had to offer, His only plan to redeem them.

III. Jesus as Risen Lord
(Luke 24:33, 34)

The verses left out of our printed text tell of what happened after Jesus' death. Luke records the reaction of the centurion, the Roman officer who had supervised the crucifixion, and the reaction both of the crowds and of the women who followed Jesus (vv. 47-49). Next came Joseph of Arimathea to bury Jesus' body in his new tomb carved out of the rock (vv. 50-56). Then on the first day of the week came the marvelous discovery: the tomb was empty; the Lord had risen from the dead! (Luke 24:1-12). Later on that day Jesus appeared to two of His followers on the road between Jerusalem and the town of Emmaus (Luke 24:13-32). They saw Him, but they didn't recognize Him until He blessed the bread they were about to eat and, as Luke says, "their eyes were opened, and they knew him"

visual 13

(Luke 24:31). After Jesus vanished, the men had to tell someone; and that brings us back to our printed text.

A. He Caused a Stir (v. 33)

33. And they rose up the same hour, and returned to Jerusalem, and found the eleven gathered together, and them that were with them.

The two men had just walked at least seven miles from Jerusalem to Emmaus, and the day was nearly over (v. 29). But because of their wonderful news, they turned right around and went back to Jerusalem, finding Jesus' disciples—all but Judas, who probably was dead by now—*gathered together*, along with some other friends of Jesus.

B. He Appeared to Simon (v. 34)

34. Saying, The Lord is risen indeed, and hath appeared to Simon.

The two men from Emmaus were not the only ones who had seen the risen Jesus. He had appeared to Simon Peter also. In other passages we read of appearances to some women (Matthew 28:9, 10; John 20:14-18), to the disciples both with and without Thomas (John 20:19-29), to James the brother of Jesus (1 Corinthians 15:7), to "above five hundred brethren at once" (1 Corinthians 15:6), and to Paul (Acts 9:1-9 and parallels). This large group of witnesses should convince us, as it convinced the first Christians, that "Christ is risen; He is *risen indeed!*"

Conclusion

A. A Death for Us

Although Jesus died as a criminal in the eyes of the law, He died as a sacrifice in the eyes of God. "He himself bore our sins in his body on the tree, so that we might die to sins and live for righteousness; by his wounds you have been healed" (1 Peter 2:24, *New International Version.*)

Here lies the central truth of the Christian faith: God's own Son came into the world, not only to teach and heal and show God's love to people, but primarily to die as a sacrifice for our sins. The whole human race, and each member of it, was alienated from God; but Christ has made us God's friends, those of us who will accept His solution to our problem. As Paul put it, "But now in Christ Jesus you who once were far away have been brought near through the blood of Christ" (Ephesians 2:13, *New International Version*).

UNDOING THE DIRTY WORK

March 6, 1992, was a dreaded day for millions of people who depend on a computer. On that day, Michelangelo's 517th birthday, a computer virus would be activated that could erase or garble irreplaceable files throughout the world. First discovered in the Netherlands in February of 1991, the virus had spread till it was believed that at least 400,000 personal computers were contaminated in the United States, not to mention those in other nations and the large computers of government and business. It is impossible to estimate how much money and effort has been spent to undo the effects of that virus.

The Michelangelo virus reminds us of how simple it is to sow destruction and how difficult it is to undo the results of a malicious act. Satan sowed the seeds of disobedience, destruction, and death centuries ago; and the virus of sin has spread throughout the human race. There came a day, however, when God intervened to nullify that contamination through the suffering and death of His Son.   —W. P.

B. A Life for Him

The fact that Jesus has done so much for us ought to suggest to us what we can do for Him. We owe Him our lives, both now and for eternity. He calls each of us to "take up his cross,

---

Home Daily Bible Readings

Monday, Feb. 21—Praying on the Mount of Olives (Luke 22:39-46)
Tuesday, Feb. 22—Judas Led a Crowd to Jesus (Luke 22:47-53)
Wednesday, Feb. 23—Peter Denies Jesus (Luke 22:54-62)
Thursday, Feb. 24—"He Stirs Up the People" (Luke 23:1-12)
Friday, Feb. 25—Pilate Says Not Guilty! (Luke 23:13-25)
Saturday, Feb. 26—The Crucifixion (Luke 23:32-47)
Sunday, Feb. 27—The Resurrection (Luke 24:1-12)

---

and follow me" (Matthew 16:24), being ready to suffer persecution and even death for Him. But most of us won't be martyrs; we won't find ourselves in a life-or-death situation that will give us the chance to die for Jesus in some dramatic way. God calls most of us to give our lives to Him through Christ in the day-by-day grind of faithful living. If we realize deep within ourselves what we owe Christ, the least we can do is to do our jobs well, raise our families as best we can, live at peace with our neighbors, and honor God through His church. If we commit our lives to Christ in these routine ways, then maybe He will find something for us to do beyond the ordinary! The key is to be ready for whatever the Lord wants us to do for Him.

CARRYING A CROSS

Simon of Cyrene will ever be remembered for his role in the mournful procession to Calvary. Apparently thrust by chance into the role, he will forever be known as the man who carried Christ's cross (Luke 23:26).

Arthur Blessitt, in our time, has devoted his life to carrying a cross around the world. He has borne it across Europe, North and South America, Asia, and Africa. The cross is twelve feet high and has a six-foot crossbeam. A report made several years ago noted that he had carried the cross 23,560 miles through 77 countries. Sometimes suspected of being a gun-runner or spy, he has been arrested at least twenty times. His purpose, however, is to use the curiosity he arouses to share his belief in Christ.

Many look at his efforts as rather silly and pointless. But who knows how many he has led to think seriously of the Savior who died on such a cross? Who knows how many have been reminded of their duty to the Savior? With or without a literal cross of wood, all of us need to remember that Jesus said, "If anyone would come after me, he must deny himself and take up his cross daily and follow me" (Luke 9:23, *New International Version*).   —W. P.

C. Let Us Pray

We thank You, Father, for raising Your Son from the dead and giving us new hope and new life through Him. We thank You for His sacrificial death, which pays the price for our sins. We commit our lives to You through Him. We are ready to do whatever You want us to do, out of gratitude for what You have done. In the name of Jesus we pray. Amen.

D. Thought to Remember

"The Lord is risen indeed" (Luke 24:34). Make sure you live like a follower of His.

Learning by Doing

This page contains an alternate lesson plan emphasizing learning activities. Classes desiring such student involvement will find these suggestions helpful.

Learning Goals

After this lesson, each learner will:

1. Affirm full confidence in the saving power of Jesus' death, and full hope based on the assurance of His resurrection.

2. Complete the statement "Jesus is . . ." in several ways suggested by this lesson.

3. Express daily thanks for Jesus' death that atones for daily sin, and for His resurrection that helps us overcome despondency.

Into the Lesson

L I V E

- - - -

- - - -

- - - -

- - - -

D̄ Ē Ā D

Put this puzzle on chalkboard or poster. Let the class work together to change DEAD to LIVE by changing one letter on each line between the two words. The bold line shows which letter to change. The fill-in words from the bottom upward are LEAD, LOAD, LORD, LORE, LOVE. When all the words are filled in, note that the LORD is at the center of this dramatic and eternally significant change. Emphasize this by circling DEAD, LORD, and LIVE.

Into the Word

Print each of the following heads in bold letters on a three-inch strip cut from shelf paper, or any paper from which you can get strips long enough for these heads:

JESUS IS VICTIM
JESUS IS REDEEMER
JESUS IS RISEN LORD
He is crucified (Luke 23:32, 33)
He forgives His murderers (Luke 23:34)
He endures abuse (Luke 23:35-39)
He comforts a malefactor (Luke 23:40-43)
He causes mysterious signs (Luke 23:44, 45)
He gives up His spirit (Luke 23:46)
He causes a stir (Luke 24:33)
He appears to Simon (Luke 24:34)

Roll each strip separately and hold it with a rubber band. Distribute the strips to class members as your session begins.

Be ready with a bulletin board at least three feet high to which the strips can be fastened with tape or thumb tacks (or they may be fastened to the wall with Plasti-Tak). Have these references already fastened to the board at the right side, and spaced to correspond with the three main headings of the "Lesson Outline": Luke 23:32-39; Luke 23: 40-46; Luke 24:33, 34.

First call for the three class members who have headings printed in capital letters. Let them come forward and decide which heading matches each reference on the board, then attach the headings.

Let someone read the lesson text aloud while those who have the other strips come forward one at a time and attach them to the board as the corresponding verses are read.

Now call attention to the three main headings in the outline on the board. Ask students to look at the text and find other endings that it suggests for a sentence beginning "Jesus is. . . ." For example, they may see these among others; forgiving (v. 34), derided (v. 35), mocked (v. 36), King (v. 38), innocent (v. 41), Lord (v. 42), praying (v. 46), trusting (v. 46).

Into Life

Luke 24:34 is the key verse of our text. Get your learners to affirm its truth in one of these ways:

1. Divide the class into two groups. Lead one group in saying in unison, "The Lord is risen." Let the other group respond, "He is risen indeed." It is said that ancient Christians used to greet each other in that way instead of saying, "Good morning" and "Hello."

2. If the class is seated in a circle, each one may call the next one by name and then make the statement: "(Name), the Lord is risen indeed." This can be done even if the students are seated in rows. As a variation, each one may call the next one by the name of a Bible character such as Simon or Mary instead of the person's real name.

In closing, suggest the following prayers for daily use this week:

When one catches himself doing wrong; "Father, thank You for Jesus' death, which pays for all my sin."

When one is downhearted or discouraged; "Father, thank You for Jesus' resurrection, which always gives me hope."

Use those two thoughts in your closing prayer.

Let's Talk It Over

The questions on this page are designed to encourage review of the lesson Scriptures and to promote discussion of the lesson by the class. The answers provided are only discussion starters. Let your class talk it over from there.

1. Jesus was able to forgive those who killed Him. It is hard for most of us to forgive people for much lesser offenses. How can we learn to forgive as Jesus did?

We must learn to love our enemies, as God loved us when we were His enemies. We must learn to forgive them, hoping they will repent and reform in the future, as God withholds His judgment to give men time to repent. We must remember that we cannot expect forgiveness unless we forgive others.

2. Jesus made the ultimate sacrifice for the redemption of mankind. What sacrifices can we make for the same cause?

During World War II, millions of men and women volunteered because they were committed to the cause of victory. Those at home denied themselves, doing without many things in order to support the war effort. We must have the attitude of people at war. Thousands of us ought to join in the fight as full-time soldiers. The rest of us must be willing to deny ourselves luxuries so we may give to the war effort. The fate of the world is at stake!

3. Jesus died nobly. How can we prepare ourselves now to face death with grace and courage?

Who is not moved by the courage of the martyrs who accepted death rather than deny Christ? Many of us have been inspired by the calm way in which terminally ill Christians look forward to their deliverance. The most important way we can prepare to face death with equal grace is to develop the closest possible relationship with the Father. This is what Jesus had. He knew He was fulfilling God's will. He did not doubt His Father. If we walk with Him daily, putting our trust in Him, then we will glorify Him when we face death.

4. Jesus came into this world and partook of our suffering, and He lifted our lives from hopelessness and misery to victory and joy. On a smaller scale we can enter into the lives of those who are suffering and minister to them. Name some practical ways of doing this.

One way to discover hurting people is to notice those who are on the periphery, lonely and neglected. Befriend such a person and become a part of his or her world. Another good way for people to minister to each other is through small Bible study groups. Such simple things as regularly spending time with shut-ins, prisoners, or those in nursing homes can bring great joy.

5. Sometimes suffering causes even Christians to doubt. How can Jesus' example give us strength and trust in the face of suffering?

First we must understand that suffering is not a sign that God has abandoned us. God does not abandon those who do not abandon Him. Jesus' mission required His suffering, and our missions for Him may require suffering too. If we suffer as Christians, we suffer with the Lord, who suffered before us and more than we do. Christians are at war with the kingdom of Satan, and we can expect injuries and casualties in war. Remember that all loyal soldiers will come to victory, just as Jesus passed from suffering to victory.

6. The repentant thief acknowledged that he was getting what he deserved. Only then did he appeal to Christ for mercy. How can we apply this lesson?

Much of our suffering and trouble comes through no fault of our own, but sometimes our personal sins do cause us suffering. Frequently we try to blame our problems on others, but, like the thief, we will gain no help until we confess our sinfulness to the Lord and appeal for His mercy. God resists the stubborn, but He shows mercy to the contrite.

7. God tore the veil in the temple to show that the way is now open for man to come into His presence through Jesus Christ. We must tear away the veils that separate us from others so that we can reach out to them in Jesus' name. What are some of the veils we must tear apart?

It is right to be repulsed by sin, but we must learn to reach past the sin to the person. We cannot expect one to behave like a Christian until he or she becomes a Christian. People on different social, economic, or educational levels often have difficulty relating to one another. Christians must overcome these barriers. We cannot witness to a person if we do not associate with him or her.

Spring Quarter, 1994

Theme: Good News for God's People (Romans)

Special Features

Lessons

Unit 1.   Righteous Through Faith

Unit 2.   Empowered by the Spirit

Theme: Set Free by God's Grace (Galatians)

About these lessons

The study of Romans explores the gifts that God bestows through Christ, and examines their implications for the believer's life. The lessons from Galatians describe our freedom in Christ and urge us to cherish it and use it properly.

Mar 6
Mar 13
Mar 20
Mar 27
Apr 3
Apr 10
Apr 17
Apr 24
May 1
May 8
May 15
May 22
May 29

Quarterly Quiz

The questions on this page may be used in several ways: as a pretest at the beginning of the quarter; as a review at the end of the quarter; or as a review after each lesson. The questions are based on the Scripture of each lesson (King James Version). ***The answers are on page 228.***

Lesson 1

1. Paul thanked God for the Roman Christians and for the fact that their _____ was spoken of throughout the whole world. *Romans 1:8*
2. To whom was Paul debtor? *Romans 1:14*
3. What did Paul say the gospel is to every one who believes? *Romans 1:16*

Lesson 2

1. If people can become heirs of God by keeping law, what is faith made? *Romans 4:14*
2. Paul describes Abraham as the (ancestor, father, brother) of us all. *Romans 4:16*
3. What was counted as righteousness to Abraham? *Romans 4:20-22*

Lesson 3

1. Being justified by Christ's blood, we shall be saved from what through Him? *Romans 5:9*
2. What entered the world by one man? *Romans 5:12*
3. What passed upon everyone, since all have sinned? *Romans 5:12*

Lesson 4

1. Those who are baptized into Jesus Christ are baptized into His _____. *Romans 6:3*
2. Because Christ was raised from the dead, death has _____ over Him no more. *Romans 6:9*
3. What are we to be dead unto? *Romans 6:11*

Lesson 5

1. What had the women planned to do when they arrived at Jesus' tomb on the morning after the Sabbath? *Mark 16:1*
2. The Spirit of God bears witness with our spirit that we are what? *Romans 8:16*

Lesson 6

1. For a person to be carnally minded is _____; but to be spiritually minded is life and _____. *Romans 8:6*
2. If His Spirit dwells in us, God, who raised up Christ from the dead, will do what to our mortal bodies? *Romans 8:11*

Lesson 7

1. What are Christians to present unto God as a living sacrifice, holy and acceptable unto Him? *Romans 12:1*

2. Rather than being conformed to this world, Christians are to be transformed in what way? *Romans 12:2*

Lesson 8

1. A Christian is to determine not to put a _____ or an occasion to (question, doubt, fall) in his brother's way. *Romans 14:13*
2. Christians are to pursue the things that make for (holiness, peace, joy) and the things by which we may _____ one another. *Romans 14:19*

Lesson 9

1. Whom did Paul correct at Antioch for conduct contrary to the gospel? *Galatians 2:11*
2. What was the improper conduct that drew Paul's criticism? *Galatians 2:12*
3. What other church leader was misled by that improper conduct? *Galatians 2:13*

Lesson 10

1. Paul said, "The law was our _____ to bring us unto Christ." *Galatians 3:24*
2. If we are Christ's, then whose seed are we? *Galatians 3:29*
3. If one is a son of God, then one is an _____ of God through Christ. *Galatians 4:7*

Lesson 11

1. As an indication that the Galatians were turning to the bondage of the Jewish law, what were they observing? *Galatians 4:10*
2. Illustrating the Galatians' regard for him at the first, Paul said they would have plucked out what and given them to him, if it were possible? *Galatians 4:15*

Lesson 12

1. Christians are not to use their liberty for an occasion to the _____. *Galatians 5:13*
2. Those who are Christ's have done what to the flesh with the affections and lusts? *Galatians 5:24*

Lesson 13

1. What are Christians to do in a spirit of meekness to a brother who is overtaken in a fault? *Galatians 6:1*
2. What are Christians not to be weary in? *Galatians 6:9*

Preview

by Orrin Root

NERO IS KNOWN as one of the worst of Roman emperors, and he certainly deserves that reputation. In the early years of his reign, however, he was guided by wise and just advisers. His government then was fair and good. Jews had been banished from Rome by a former emperor (Acts 18:2), but now they were back in large numbers.

No one knows when or how the gospel first came to Rome, but there was a strong church there. Paul heard about it as he was working in lands farther east. As we shall see in our lessons for March, he was eager to visit the Roman Christians, both to strengthen their strong faith and to be strengthened by it.

Paul's visit to Rome was delayed, so about A.D. 57 or 58 he wrote a letter to the Christians there. While the Corinthians still needed elementary teaching (1 Corinthians 3:1, 2), the church at Rome received one of his more profound epistles. From that letter we draw our lessons for March and April, and they are worthy of our best attention.

The lessons for March, April, and May are appropriately divided into three units corresponding to those three months. The first two are from Romans; the third is from Galatians. Here is a short preview of the thirteen lessons.

Unit 1—March
Romans 1—6

The first unit is titled "Righteous Through Faith." In various ways the four lessons will remind us that we are not so good as we ought to be. The only way we can become righteous is by having our sins forgiven, and God forgives us because we have faith—we believe in the Savior, Jesus.

Lesson 1. "The Power of God for Salvation." The gospel, the good news of Jesus, is God's power to bring people to believe in Jesus and find forgiveness and salvation in Him. The Roman Christians had heard that good news, but still Paul was eager to tell it to them again. Are we as eager to carry the good news both to those who have heard it and those who have not?

Lesson 2. "God's Gift of Redemption." In Rome and elsewhere, some of the Jewish Christians were teaching that Gentile Christians must become Jews and keep the Old Testament law in order to be saved. Paul reminded his readers of the great promise made to Abraham and his descendants. Made long before the law was given, the promise did not depend on keeping the law, but on faith in God. The crowning promise was the promise of blessing to all families of the earth, not just to the family of Abraham. Redemption now is offered to all families of the earth, and it is offered as a gift, not as wages. It is given to those who believe in the Redeemer, Jesus.

Lesson 3. "The Gift of Life in Christ." This lesson calls attention to the price of our redemption: the life of Jesus. It calls attention also to the result of redemption: life and joy. But costly as redemption was to Jesus, it is free to us. Our life is the gift of God's grace.

Lesson 4. "Deliverance From Sin." Romans 6 begins with a question. Since our sins are forgiven and life is ours as a gift, why not keep on sinning whenever it seems pleasant or profitable? Paul's answer is sharp: We died to sin, so how can we keep on living in it? When we were baptized into Christ, we were baptized into His death. He was raised from the dead, and we have been raised from baptism to a new way of life. Redemption makes us free from sin. It does not make us free in sin: it does not make us free to keep on sinning. We were slaves of sin, but Christ redeemed us from that bondage. Now we are slaves of God. We obey Him.

Unit II—April
Romans 7—14

Lessons 5-8. form a group that is titled "Empowered by the Spirit." Lesson 4 brought us the vigorous declaration that we are dead to sin. Romans 6 makes that plain. We ought to be separated from sin as completely as death separates us from friends on earth. But Romans 7 adds the sobering thought that sin is not dead to us. Sin is still around, trying to enslave us again. He would succeed if we had to rely on ourselves alone, but God's Spirit is with us.

Lesson 5. "A Glimpse of Glory." The first Sunday in April represents the anniversary of Jesus' resurrection, so a special celebration is in order. Therefore we interrupt our study in Romans to consider Mark's brief record of the empty tomb and the angel's message, "He is risen." From this glimpse of Christ's glory we go back to Romans for a glimpse of our own glory. God raised Jesus from the dead. If His Spirit lives in us, He will raise us too. Therefore we have a debt. We are obligated to live according to the will of the Spirit, not the lusts of the flesh.

Lesson 6. "Life in the Spirit." Lesson 5 chose a bit from the eighth chapter of Romans to be included in our study of the resurrection. Now we drop back to the beginning of Romans 8, to the stirring declaration that "there is therefore now no condemnation to them which are in Christ Jesus." The next breath adds a further description of those who are not condemned: they "walk not after the flesh, but after the Spirit." God's Spirit leads us always to do right. Opposed to Him is "the flesh." Paul uses that term to mean the selfish side of human nature, the greedy side that looks for profit or pleasure or comfort for oneself, regardless of the needs of others. It is up to us to follow the Spirit's leading and choose the right.

Lesson 7. "Using Our Gifts in Serving." If we live as God's Spirit leads us, we shall surely do right. We know that. Now we come to some specifics, some of the attitudes and ways of thinking and acting in which the Spirit leads. Romans 12 provides a good checklist.

Lesson 8. "Living for Others." The thought of this title is included in lessons 6 and 7, of course. But now we see some ways of living for others that may not have occurred to us as we studied the other lessons. We may even see that we ought to give up some rights—a hard lesson for us who have been conditioned to fight for our rights. But even some rights may be sacrificed for the sake of "the things which make for peace, and things wherewith one may edify another."

Unit III—May
Galatians

The Galatian Christians were members of several different congregations in the Roman province of Galatia, but apparently one problem troubled all of them. Some Jewish Christians were saying that Christians could not be saved without becoming Jews and keeping the whole law found in the Old Testament. Vigorously Paul denied that statement. Through centuries the Jews had proved that the law was an intolerable burden. It would be folly for the Gentiles to accept it. The title of this unit is "Set Free by God's Grace." Freedom is to be cherished and preserved—but not abused.

Lesson 9. "Delivered From Bondage." The teaching that troubled the Galatians had been thoroughly investigated and shown to be false. Peter and the other apostles had joined in denouncing it, yet a trace of it still cropped up in Peter's actions. False teaching may have to be opposed again and again.

Lesson 10. "Adopted as God's Children." The law given to the Jews was never meant to be permanent. It was designed to keep them under control, as minor children are controlled by baby-sitters and teachers, and finally to bring them to Christ. Christians, Jewish or Gentile, are like grown-up children of God. They should be able to do His will without minute regulations governing every act.

Lesson 11. "Given the Birthright of Freedom." Lesson 10 pointed out that minor children are like slaves, and that was the condition of Jews under the law. Grown-up children have more freedom, and that is the condition of Christians. Well-adjusted adults accept their freedom and the responsibility that goes with it. They have no wish to be little children again.

Lesson 12. "Bear Fruit of the Spirit." Christian liberty is freedom to do right, not to do wrong. Christians crucify the flesh, the selfish and ungodly side of human nature. Led by the Spirit of God, they are filled with the fruit of the Spirit.

Lesson 13. "Express Christ's Love in All Relationships." Moved by the Spirit of God, Christians love as Christ loves. They help one another when burdens are great; generously they share their blessings. Eagerly they "do good unto all men, especially unto them who are of the household of faith." Sowing the good words and acts the Spirit desires, they wait confidently for the harvest of "life everlasting."

Answers to Quarterly Quiz
on page 226

Lesson 1—1. faith. 2. to the Greeks, the Barbarians, the wise, and the unwise. Lesson 2—1. void. 2. father. 3. his faith. Lesson 3—1. wrath. 2. sin. 3. death. Lesson 4—1. death. 2. dominion. 3. sin. Lesson 5—1. anoint Him with seet spices. 2. the children of God. Lesson 6—1. death, peace. 2. quicken them. Lesson 7—1. their bodies. 2. by the renewing of their mind. Lesson 8—1. stumblingblock, fall. 2. peace, edify. Lesson 9—1. Peter. 2. When certain persons came from Jerusalem, Peter withdrew from the Gentiles and associated only with the Jewish Christians. 3. Barnabas. Lesson 10—1. schoolmaster. 2. Abraham's. 3. heir. Lesson 11—1. days, months, times, and years. 2. their own eyes. Lesson 12—1. flesh. 2. crucified. Lesson 13—1. restore. 2. well doing.

Reconciliation

by Johnny Pressley

THE STORY HAS BECOME COMMONPLACE in twentieth-century America. Labor and management cannot agree on wages and benefits for a new contract, so the union calls for a strike by its members. Sometimes these deadlocks require the mediation of a skilled negotiator. This mediator (the one "in the middle" listens to the arguments of both sides and determines the legitimate claims of each. The mediator then establishes the conditions to be met by both labor and management so relations can return to normal and work can resume.

The idea of two parties in dispute is an age-old situation in the realm of personal relationships. Here, as in the business world, a third party acting as a mediator is sometimes required to help two friends patch up their differences.

The New Testament uses this imagery of mediation to illustrate one aspect of our salvation, namely our reconciliation to God.

The theme of reconciliation is developed in several of Paul's epistles, notably in the epistle to the Romans. Let us consider the following observations regarding the nature of our reconciliation with God.

The Means of Reconciliation

Picture God and mankind in a dispute. The cause lies in mankind's rebellion against God's will. Man has turned his back on his relationship with his Creator, and God has responded with a threat of eternal punishment. The tension between God and man may be felt in Paul's description of mankind as "ungodly," "sinners," and "enemies" of God (Romans 5:6-10).

Enlarge upon your picture of God and mankind in this dispute by imagining the entrance of Christ onto the scene as the mediator. In this role Christ would listen to the claims of both sides, God and mankind, and then issue a ruling. In disputes between human beings, it is common to find legitimate points being made by both sides. Normally, therefore, a settlement will require some give and take by each party. But not so in the dispute between God and mankind. We humans are entirely responsible for the breakdown of friendly relations with God, for we have chosen to violate His law. God, on the other hand, has consistently acted in an honorable and righteous fashion toward us, and thus is entirely in the right to demand a penalty from us for the damage our sin has caused.

To be fair and true, therefore, Christ, as the mediator, must rule in favor of God. The penalty for our sins is obvious and dreadful: sinful mankind is rightfully sentenced to suffer eternally in Hell. God's demand for eternal punishment must be satisfied before the enmity between God and man can be eliminated.

At this point the Biblical doctrine of reconciliation takes a unique turn. In human relations the parties in dispute are responsible for satisfying the terms established by the mediator in order to bring about the reconciliation of the disputants. The mediator's role is simply to establish the terms, not to satisfy them personally. In the case of our dispute with God, however, our Mediator offered to satisfy the terms of the settlement in our behalf and pay the required penalty himself. Christ declared that God was willing to accept the death of His Son on a cross as a substitute for the eternal suffering of mankind in Hell.

Once the terms of the settlement were satisfied at Calvary, friendly relations could be restored between God and man. This is the good news of the gospel! Paul summarizes the means of our reconciliation to God succinctly in this statement: "When we were God's enemies, we were reconciled to him through the death of his Son" (Romans 5:10).*

The Source of Reconciliation

Some may find fault with the use of the foregoing imagery to illustrate our reconciliation to God, because it seems to suggest that God was stuck in His dispute with man until a mediator came along and offered a solution. Although human disputants may come to such an impasse, that was not the case with God.

Once again Biblical reconciliation displays a unique characteristic in that it was God himself who set up Christ as the mediator and devised the solution to the conflict. One of the amazing concepts of Scripture is that Christ's death at Calvary was planned by God even before the creation of the world (1 Peter 1:18-20). As Paul declares in Romans 3:25, God "presented him [Christ] as a sacrifice of atonement [propitiation]." Thus God was not helplessly waiting and looking for someone else to make something happen. From start to finish God has been actively involved in arranging for our reconciliation to Him.

This emphasis on God's initiative should in no way diminish the significance of Christ's participation as part of the Godhead in the planning of the scheme of redemption. Nor should it take away from the glory He deserves for graciously choosing to assume the role of the suffering Savior. But when considering the theme of reconciliation and the source from which it derives, it is good to remember that God "reconciled us to himself through Christ and gave us the ministry of reconciliation" (2 Corinthians 5:18).

The Results of Reconciliation

When we think in general about the salvation that God has made possible for us, a number of blessings come to mind. Those who are saved have been forgiven of their sins, and thus they are exempted from the penalty of Hell. They have received the gift of God's Spirit so that they may draw upon the sanctifying power of God to assist them in their pursuit of godliness. They have been adopted into the family of God and added to the fellowship of the saints of all ages. And they live with the hope that when their lives on earth have ended, they will be given residence in Heaven for eternity.

For the purpose of this discussion, however, let us narrow our focus to the subject of reconciliation. This imagery calls forth one blessing in particular: peace with God. Certainly there was no peace with God during the time of mankind's alienation from Him. We lived in a rebellious state, and as such were subject to His eternal wrath. Calvary, however, made possible a change in our relationship with God. Once the terms of settlement were satisfied by the death of Christ, it was possible for God to put aside His judgments against us and offer us the opportunity to resume peaceful relations with Him. Though we were once "God's enemies," we have now been privileged to become His friends.

Consider how the subject of reconciliation forms a fitting background for the emphasis in Scripture upon Christ's role as peacemaker. The Old Testament prophecies of the coming of the "Prince of Peace" (Isaiah 9:6) incorporated at least two ideas regarding the work of the Messiah. Part of His ministry would be to show us how to break down those walls that we allow to separate us from other persons, walls such as race, social status, and gender (Galatians 3:28), and how to replace these barriers with a spirit of love and peace. But the establishment of peace among people on earth was just a prelude to an even greater dimension of Christ's role as peacemaker. As Paul explains, Christ's "purpose was to create in himself one new man out of the two [Jew and Gentile], thus making peace, and in

this one body to reconcile both of them to God through the cross" (Ephesians 2:15, 16).

It is little wonder, therefore, that Paul begins his discussion of reconciliation in Romans 5 by declaring the great result of it: "Since we have been justified through faith, we have peace with God through our Lord Jesus Christ" (Romans 5:1).

The Responsibility of Reconciliation

In a mediation case among people, peace does not automatically follow the completion of the mediator's work. Harmonious relations are reestablished only if and when the parties choose to act upon the terms of settlement.

God has already done His part in making possible our reconciliation to Him. As we have already stated, He gave His own dear Son to be both the mediator in our estrangement and the means whereby that estrangement could be removed and peaceful relations reestablished. It remains for each person to accept the mediatorial work of Christ on his or her behalf. Until a person does that, he or she remains under God's condemnation.

The responsibilities of reconciliation do not end when we establish an alliance with our Mediator at our conversion. God then expects us to begin living like persons who have been reconciled to Him. For instance, to be restored to fellowship with God is to resume a relationship in which God is Lord and we are His faithful servants. We should be eagerly seeking to follow God's revealed will in every aspect of our lives.

Those who are reconciled with God should be establishing frequent communication with Him. It is the nature of friends to communicate with one another as much as possible. The thought that we have been restored to friendship with God should prompt us to establish a strong pattern of prayer and praise so that we can express our thoughts to Him. Reading and meditating on God's Word every day will enable us to hear what God has to say to us.

Perhaps the most challenging aspect of our reconciliation is the responsibility to tell others that the offer the mediator has made to us is available to them as well. Paul provides an appropriate thought for concluding a study of reconciliation: God "reconciled us to himself through Christ and gave us the ministry of reconciliation. . . . We are therefore Christ's ambassadors, as though God were making his appeal through us. We implore you on Christ's behalf: Be reconciled to God" (2 Corinthians 5:18-20).

---

*Scripture quotations in this article are taken from the *New International Version*.

Called to Freedom

by Jack Cottrell

WE VALUE few things more highly than freedom. Because we are creatures, our freedom, of course, can never be absolute. But because we are human beings made in God's image, certain freedoms are ours by right and are necessary for the full expression of our humanness.

Some of these freedoms are external. Many people live in free countries where they are guaranteed free speech, free assembly, and freedom to choose their religion and their government. As important as these may be, the really significant freedoms are internal. We are not truly free until we are free from such bonds as anxiety, fear, falsehood, frustration, doubt, guilt, hopelessness, and meaninglessness. These are the things that bind our spirits.

Paul's letter to the Galatians is about the latter kind of freedom. "It was for freedom that Christ set us free," he says. "For you were called to freedom, brethren" (5:1, 13).* Exactly what is Paul talking about, and what does this mean for Christians living today?

Freedom in Galatians

The Galatian letter is Paul's response to a specific problem that faced the early church, especially in Galatia. The problem focused on the role of the law of Moses in the Christian life. It was not a question of choosing between Moses and Christ; all agreed that we must become Christians. The question had to do with *how* one becomes a Christian. Exactly what is required for those who want to profess Christ and receive His salvation?

One group of converts from Judaism were unable to make a clean break with the law of Moses. They were called the *Judaizers*. They went around teaching that in addition to faith and baptism (3:26, 27), one must be circumcised in order to be saved (6:12; see Acts 15:1).

The Judaizers were guilty of two specific errors. First, they assumed that the law of Moses (in part, at least) is still binding in the Christian age. Second, they assumed that salvation (specifically justification) comes by means of such law-keeping.

Paul refutes both falsehoods by declaring that the gospel of Christ is a call to *freedom*. It sets us free from the Old Testament law as a way of life, and it sets us free from law as such as a way of salvation.

The law of Moses itself was a source of bondage in two different ways. First, Paul explains how the Jews' existence under the law was more like slavery than sonship, because their place in history excluded them from full possession of the blessings of God's grace. They lived in the childhood stage of God's overall plan of redemption, which in some ways was similar to existing in the bondage of slavery (Galatians 4:1-7).

Second, contrary to God's own intention for the law of Moses, many Jews regarded it as the means of their salvation. They believed they were saved by keeping the law. This seems to have been true of the Judaizers, at least with regard to the command of circumcision. One problem with this, says Paul, is that you cannot stop with circumcision. If you are going to bind this part of the law of Moses upon us, you have to go ahead and require it all (5:3). Thus bondage replaces liberty (2:4), and we become "subject again to a yoke of slavery" (5:1).

Paul affirms, however, that Christians are free from the law of Moses in both senses. First, we do not live in that slave-like childhood age. We live in the age of full sonship, in which we have full possession of the inheritance given through Abraham to his Seed, Jesus Christ, and to those who become one with Him in faith and baptism (3:23-29). The law of Moses was for the former age, not the latter. We are free from the legal requirements of that law, such as circumcision.

Second, we are definitely free from the law of Moses as a way of salvation. In the midst of his discussion of whether we have to "live like Jews" (2:14), Paul sums up the essence of our freedom in Christ: "Nevertheless knowing that a man is not justified by the works of the Law but through faith in Christ Jesus, even we have believed in Christ Jesus, that we may be justified by faith in Christ, and not by the works of the Law; since by the works of the Law shall no flesh be justified" (2:16).

Christian Freedom Today

It is extremely important to see that this last point has a far broader application than just one system of laws. Few Christians today feel any obligation to obey the Mosaic law, and even fewer think of it as a way of salvation. But the truth of Galatians 2:16 applies not just to the law of Moses; that is just one example of the general principle. The fact is that no one can be saved by successful obedience to *any* list of God's rules and commands, including those written on the heart (Romans 2:14, 15) and even those recorded in the New Testament.

This is the very point of Christian freedom; the grace of Jesus Christ sets us free from law—any law—as a means of salvation. We are saved by grace through faith, not by keeping commandments. What follows is a brief discussion of three important aspects of this freedom.

First, as intimated above, we are free from *depending on law-keeping* as a way of salvation. This is indeed a glorious freedom, because there is no more hopeless bondage than thinking our day-to-day obedience is the key to acceptance with God. Such slavery makes us victims either of deception or of despair. On the one hand, if a person really thinks he is good enough to be accepted by God in this way (like the Pharisee), then he is deceiving himself. On the other hand, the person who thinks he has to be "good enough" for Heaven, yet knows he is not, will be filled with anxiety, doubt, fear, and despair. Either way one is in the bondage of law-depending (which is the essence of legalism).

The glory of the gospel of grace is that it frees us from the legalistic mind-set. It frees us from both self-deception and despair. In Christ we are free from law-keeping as a means of being right with God. "For Christ is the end of the law for righteousness to everyone who believes" (Romans 10:4). When we put our trust in Christ, we are confessing that we are *not* able to obey in a way that deserves Heaven, but grace frees us from worrying about it.

A serious error to be avoided here is that somehow the grace of God frees us from our *obligation* to obey God's commandments. Such is not the case; indeed, it is impossible for creatures of God ever to be relieved of their obligation to obey their Creator and Lord. This distinction must be carefully maintained: Christian freedom is not freedom from law-*keeping*, but freedom from law-*depending*.

The reason we are free from law-depending is that Christ's death has set us free from the *condemnation* of the law. This is the second aspect of Christian freedom.

Anyone living under law (in the sense of depending on works for salvation) must be ready to accept the consequences of breaking the law, namely, eternal punishment in Hell. Thus for unsaved sinners, to be under law means to be under its condemnation or curse.

Here is the wonderful truth about Jesus Christ: He has borne this condemnation or curse for us! When we accept Him as Savior and Lord and become united with Him, He sets us free from this curse. "Christ redeemed us from the curse of the Law, having become a curse for us" (Galatians 3:13). "There is therefore now no condemnation for those who are in Christ Jesus" (Romans 8:1).

The third aspect of Christian freedom is that we are set free from *legalistic motives* for obedience to God's commandments. That is, we are free from the law as a taskmaster that forces us to obey—or else! Knowing that we are justified by faith, we can obey the law simply because we *want* to. (It is still true, however, that we *ought* to.)

Motives for Obedience

The Christian life is work. It often takes great effort to live according to God's will. The Bible describes Christian living as taking a yoke, working in a vineyard, reaping a harvest, fighting a battle, bearing a cross, and other such wearisome exercise.

Why does anyone want to work so hard? Why should we persevere in good works? What motivates us?

Living under law, one is driven by the dual motives of fear of punishment and desire for reward. Everything depends on personal obedience. Hence one must obey in order to escape punishment or in order to gain the reward. One may actually hate the things that God's law requires a person to do; but like a sullen slave he or she does them to escape the whip of God's wrath. Such an attitude is true bondage.

The grace of Jesus Christ sets us free from such self-centered motives, and provides the basis for the truly Christian motivation of grateful love. Faith in Christ continues to work, but it works through love (Galatians 5:6). Jesus said, "If you love Me, you will keep My commandments" (John 14:15). Freedom from false motives allows us to cultivate this grateful love, which is the strongest, least selfish, and most Christ-centered of all motives.

The point is that the grace of the gospel of Christ frees us to obey God solely from love. Because of grace we are free from the law's penalty on the basis of what Christ has done. Jesus paid it *all*; nothing we do adds to His payment. Thus if our justification is secure by faith, we are free to work and obey Him out of selfless love. Our daily obedience is not some kind of payment that God extorts or demands in return for His saving favors. It is simply our way of saying "Thank You" to a Savior who has freely given us everything.

---

*Scripture quotations in this article are taken from the *New American Standard Bible*.

The Power of God for Salvation

March 6
Lesson 1

DEVOTIONAL READING: Romans 1:18-25.

LESSON SCRIPTURE: Romans 1:1-17.

PRINTED TEXT: Romans 1:1-17.

Romans 1:1-17

1 Paul, a servant of Jesus Christ, called to be an apostle, separated unto the gospel of God,

2 (Which he had promised afore by his prophets in the holy Scriptures,)

3 Concerning his Son Jesus Christ our Lord, which was made of the seed of David according to the flesh;

4 And declared to be the Son of God with power, according to the Spirit of holiness, by the resurrection from the dead:

5 By whom we have received grace and apostleship, for obedience to the faith among all nations, for his name:

6 Among whom are ye also the called of Jesus Christ:

7 To all that be in Rome, beloved of God, called to be saints: Grace to you, and peace, from God our Father and the Lord Jesus Christ.

8 First, I thank my God through Jesus Christ for you all, that your faith is spoken of throughout the whole world.

9 For God is my witness, whom I serve with my spirit in the gospel of his Son, that without ceasing I make mention of you always in my prayers;

10 Making request, if by any means now at length I might have a prosperous journey by the will of God to come unto you.

11 For I long to see you, that I may impart unto you some spiritual gift, to the end ye may be established;

12 That is, that I may be comforted together with you by the mutual faith both of you and me.

13 Now I would not have you ignorant, brethren, that oftentimes I purposed to come unto you, (but was let hitherto,) that I might have some fruit among you also, even as among other Gentiles.

14 I am debtor both to the Greeks, and to the Barbarians; both to the wise, and to the unwise.

15 So, as much as in me is, I am ready to preach the gospel to you that are at Rome also.

16 For I am not ashamed of the gospel of Christ: for it is the power of God unto salvation to every one that believeth; to the Jew first, and also to the Greek.

17 For therein is the righteousness of God revealed from faith to faith: as it is written, The just shall live by faith.

GOLDEN TEXT: For I am not ashamed of the gospel of Christ: for it is the power of God unto salvation to every one that believeth.—Romans 1:16.

Lesson Aims

After studying this lesson a student should be able to:

1. Explain why Paul was in debt to Greeks and Barbarians, to wise and unwise.

2. Acknowledge his or her own similar debt.

3. Make some payments on his or her debt.

Lesson Outline

Display visual 1 of the visuals packet as you consider the Christian's responsibility for sharing the gospel of Christ. The visual is shown on page 235.

Introduction

A. Power

Paul, an apostle of Christ, was no stranger to worldly power. He was trained in Jerusalem, the center of Jewish power (Acts 22:3). Easily he got the backing of authorities in his campaign to destroy the church. They authorized him to arrest Christians even in foreign cities (Acts 9:1, 2). But on the road to Damascus his earthly power was overpowered by the Lord (Acts 9:3-19). Then in the service of the Lord he often found worldly power arrayed against him (2 Corinthians 11:24, 25). Still his strategy as an evangelist

was to plant the gospel in the centers of power, from which it would spread to the nearby areas. By worldly power Paul was beaten and imprisoned; but he was not intimidated, for he carried a power above all worldly power—"the power of God unto salvation" (Romans 1:16).

It is not surprising, then, that Paul wanted to go to Rome (Romans 1:10, 11). That was the power center of the world. Whatever happened in Rome was soon known everywhere. Already the church there was known throughout the world (Romans 1:8). To strengthen that church would add power to Christian influence everywhere.

B. Lesson Background

Paul's third missionary journey was near its end, and already he was planning a fourth. First he needed to go to Jerusalem with others to take an offering from many churches to the poor Christians there (Romans 15:25, 26). Then he hoped to go to Rome, but not to stay there very long before going on to Spain (Romans 15:24). There was a strong church in Rome already, and Paul's major aim was to take the gospel to places where it was not yet known (Romans 15:20, 21).

No one knows when or how the church began in Rome. But a church was there, a strong church; and Paul was eager to visit it after his trip to Jerusalem. In the meantime he wrote his letter to the Romans from Corinth, about A.D. 57 or 58. We shall be taking our lessons from that letter through the months of March and April.

I. Paul and His Master (Romans 1:1-5)

Paul's letter to the Romans begins by announcing the sender's name. That was the custom of the time. In the opening verses of Romans, however, Paul says little about himself and more about the Master he served.

A. Paul (vv. 1, 2)

1. Paul, a servant of Jesus Christ, called to be an apostle, separated unto the gospel of God.

Like a modern letterhead, the opening line tells Paul's business as well as his name. Most English versions say he was *a servant of Jesus Christ*; but the Greek word indicates a slave, one wholly possessed by Jesus Christ. However, this slave was also *an apostle*, an emissary specially authorized to speak for his Owner. His was a particular task: he was *separated*, dedicated, to *the gospel of God*. His special work was to tell God's good news.

2. (Which he had promised afore by his prophets in the holy Scriptures.)

Paul summarizes God's good news in 1 Corinthians 15:3, 4: "Christ died for our sins according to the Scriptures . . . he was buried . . . he rose again the third day according to the Scriptures." This news was truly new to the world, but God had planned it long before and had promised it *in the holy Scriptures* written by His inspired *prophets.* In telling the good news, Jesus, Paul, and others showed how the Scriptures promised what Jesus did (Luke 24:25-27, 44-47; Acts 2:25-36; 8:32-35; 13:26-41).

B. Paul's Master (vv. 3-5)

3. Concerning his Son Jesus Christ our Lord, which was made of the seed of David according to the flesh.

The *King James Version* puts verse 2 in parentheses, indicating that the first part of verse 3 is to be read with the last part of verse 1: *the gospel of God concerning his Son.* Some students think the first of verse 3 is to be read with the end of verse 2: *the holy Scriptures concerning his Son.* As a matter of fact, *the gospel of God* is *concerning his Son,* and so are *the holy Scriptures* that promise the gospel. Since both these thoughts are true, we need not spend our time trying to decide which one Paul had in mind. Verse 3 tells us that God's Son, Jesus, is a descendant of David *according to the flesh:* that is, in a human and physical way. This is important because *the holy Scriptures* promised that David's descendants would rule forever (1 Chronicles 17:11-14; Psalm 89:3, 4, 35, 36; Acts 2:25-36). The Christ, the king eternal, must be of David's family.

4. And declared to be the Son of God with power, according to the Spirit of holiness, by the resurrection from the dead.

According to the flesh—on the physical and human side—Jesus is the son of David (v. 3). *According to the Spirit of holiness*—on the spiritual and divine side—He is the Son of God. Without any physical contact, the Holy Spirit made a virgin pregnant; and her Son was literally the Son of God, divine as well as human (Luke 1:35). His divine nature was proved again by His *resurrection from the dead.*

Shall we read the phrase *with power* along with what goes just before it: *the Son of God with power?* Or does this phrase belong with *declared: declared with power to be the Son of God?* This is another question that need not trouble us. In fact, Jesus is the Son of God with power; and in fact, that truth is declared with power by His resurrection. Whichever thought was in Paul's mind, it was and is true.

5. By whom we have received grace and apostleship, for obedience to the faith among all nations, for his name.

visual 1

Jesus granted to Paul a special *grace,* a special favor, that made him an apostle, a specially authorized and inspired emissary of the Lord. The purpose of this was to lead people to *faith* in Christ, and to the *obedience* that faith produces. Paul was sent to lead people to faith and obedience *among all nations.* His work was not to gather followers from all nations for himself. He was Jesus' slave (v. 1), and all he did was *for his name*—for Jesus' name, to bring honor and glory to Jesus.

SIAMESE TRUTHS

Every eighty-seventh human birth produces twins. Far more rare is the birth of "Siamese twins"—two babies not totally separated. Often, if joined only superficially, they may be separated surgically. If the two babies share bone structure and/or organs, of course, separation becomes much more complicated and risky, sometimes impossible.

The Scriptural doctrines of *faith* and *obedience* are "Siamese truths"; they cannot be separated. Paul writes of the "obedience that comes from faith" (*New International Version*). Believing in Christ results in obeying Christ. Trusting Jesus produces behavior that conforms to His teaching. As James declares, "I will show you my faith by what I do" (James 2:18, *New International Version*).

As faith matures, obedience is more and more closely joined to it. To faith will be added "goodness . . . self-control . . . godliness . . . brotherly kindness . . . and love" (2 Peter 1:5-7, *New International Version*). Can one's faith be shown without such works?
                                                                —R. W. B.

II. Paul and His Hearers (Romans 1:6-13)

The first five verses have told us a little about Paul the slave and more about Jesus the Master. But verse 5 speaks about bringing people to faith and obedience among all nations, and now the thought turns to some of those people. Specifically we think of the Roman Christians to whom this letter is written.

A. Paul's Hearers (vv. 6, 7)

6. Among whom are ye also the called of Jesus Christ.

Paul is writing to some *among* the people of all nations to whom he has been sent. This letter is not to all those people, but to those who are *called of Jesus Christ.* The next verse tells more about their calling.

7. To all that be in Rome, beloved of God, called to be saints: Grace to you, and peace, from God our Father and the Lord Jesus Christ.

This letter is meant for people who are described in three ways. First, they are *in Rome.* Second, they are *beloved of God.* Third, they are *called to be saints.* In the language of the New Testament, all Christians are *saints.* The name means they are set apart from others in the world, dedicated to Christ. We see, then, that the letter is addressed to the Christians in Rome. God loves everybody in the world, of course; but those who give themselves to Him are beloved in a special way. The difference is illustrated in good Christian parents. A Christian father and mother love everybody, but their own family are beloved as no others are.

For the Christians in Rome Paul wished two things. *Grace* is favor, usually favor that is not earned nor deserved. *Peace* is not necessarily freedom from problems and conflict; it is the kind of calmness that can live in the midst of trouble when one trusts in the Lord.

B. Paul's Prayer (vv. 8-10)

8. First, I thank my God through Jesus Christ for you all, that your faith is spoken of throughout the whole world.

Paul's prayer began with thanks for Christians like those in Rome. Recently he had spent several years in Ephesus, a city busy with traffic from Rome to the East. Then he had traveled in Macedonia and Greece. Everywhere people were talking about the wonderful faith of those Christians in Rome. How did people know the Romans had such faith? By what the Romans did, of course. Their faith was made known by their "obedience to the faith" (v. 5).

9. For God is my witness, whom I serve with my spirit in the gospel of his Son, that without ceasing I make mention of you always in my prayers.

The Romans might suspect Paul was exaggerating his concern for them, so he insisted, "God knows this is true." And the apostle Paul was not one who would take God's name lightly or in vain. He was one whose life was devoted to serving God by telling and retelling *the gospel of his Son.*

10. Making request, if by any means now at length I might have a prosperous journey by the will of God to come unto you.

Paul's prayer began with thanks (v. 8), but it went on to a *request.* For a long time he had been wanting to go to Rome. Now he was praying that at last he would have that privilege.

C. Paul's Purpose (vv. 11-13)

11. For I long to see you, that I may impart unto you some spiritual gift, to the end ye may be established.

Why was Paul so eager to go to Rome? Because he was confident that he could make a substantial contribution, not with money, but with *some spiritual gift.*

Paul mentions a number of spiritual gifts in 1 Corinthians 12. Some are miraculous abilities such as speaking in tongues, prophesying, and healing. Apostles sometimes imparted such gifts to others (Acts 8:14-17; 19:1-6). Possibly there were no such gifts in Rome because no apostle had been there. It would be very helpful to have some inspired prophets to tell the church about God's will.

There were also spiritual gifts that involved nothing miraculous: teaching, helping, governing or leading. With his wide experience in organizing churches, Paul might help in these ways. Whatever *spiritual gift* he had in mind, it was something by which the church would *be established,* strengthened, made firm.

12. That is, that I may be comforted together with you by the mutual faith both of you and me.

The benefit of Paul's visit would not be to the church only. Paul too would gain by his association with Christians of such notable faith (v. 8). *Strengthened* is the basic meaning of *comforted.*

MUTUAL ENCOURAGEMENT

Many Christians are regular attenders of Christian conventions, seminars, and workshops because the fellowship they find there is so stimulating and affirming. The inspiration of singing, sharing, and enthusing with others of "like precious faith" gives participants a spiritual high. Listening to gifted and successful speakers is exhilarating, challenging, comforting.

These gatherings are characterized by the enjoyment of Christian fellowship and motivation for continued service for Christ. Indeed, church folk should develop a keen appetite for such spiritual nourishment.

Basic to the nature of Christian faith is the dynamic of mutual encouragement. When two or more believers share, they give and receive acceptance, support, and understanding. It is more than strength in numbers; it is the unique spirit of community in Christ. It is the joy of togetherness, based upon our mutual convictions.

Such encouragement is available even in small groups: Bible-school classes, Christian coffee clubs, etc. And personal one-to-one encounters are often the most rewarding.

Let your faith encourage others. It will come back to you "a hundredfold."   —R. W. B.

13. Now I would not have you ignorant, brethren, that oftentimes I purposed to come unto you, (but was let hitherto,) that I might have some fruit among you also, even as among other Gentiles.

For a long time Paul had cherished the wish to go to Rome, but always something seemed to keep him from going. In the antique English of our version, *let* means "hindered" or "prevented." Whatever had been hindering him, Paul was longing to go to Rome to produce *some fruit*, some beneficial results, such as he had produced in many places *among other Gentiles.*

III. Paul and His Debt
(Romans 1:14-17)

As Paul saw it, he was under an obligation. He must deliver the good news that had been committed to him. Preaching the gospel cost him his high standing among the Jews (Philippians 3:4-11). It brought persecution and many other hardships (2 Corinthians 11:24-28), but it was something he had to do (1 Corinthians 9:16).

A. In Debt to All (v. 14)

14. I am debtor both to the Greeks, and to the Barbarians; both to the wise, and to the unwise.

The Greeks were intelligent, educated, highly civilized. Sometimes their name was used loosely to mean all the people who had adopted the Greek language and civilization. *The Barbarians* were all the people who had not taken up the Greek language and civilization. Paul was saying he was in debt to all kinds of people. *Both to the wise, and to the unwise* is another way of saying the same thing.

VISUALS FOR THESE LESSONS

The *Adult Visuals/Learning Resources* packet contains classroom-size visuals designed for use with the lessons in the Spring Quarter. The packet is available from your supplier. Order no. 392.

When we are in debt, usually we owe someone from whom we have received something of value. We borrow money from the bank, and we have to pay it back. We buy a car on credit, and we have to make the monthly payments. Paul's case was not quite the same. He had not received anything from the Greeks and Barbarians, but he owed them something. He had received the good news of salvation from the Lord (Galatians 1:11, 12). But it was not given for him alone. It was entrusted to him to be delivered to others, and Paul was in debt till it was delivered. To keep it for himself would not be honest.

This calls for some serious thinking by all of us who have received the good news of salvation. How many of us are in debt to non-Christian neighbors? Are we making any payments? Some of us are gifted with a talent for communication as well as the good news of salvation. We may well be thinking of paying our debt on some mission field. At the very least, all of us had better stop thinking of our missionary offerings as gifts. They are small payments on our debt. The gospel we have received makes the difference between Hell and Heaven. How much is that worth to you? Are you satisfied with the payments you are making?

B. Willing to Pay (v. 15)

15. So, as much as in me is, I am ready to preach the gospel to you that are at Rome also.

As much as in me is, all Paul had and all he was, all his energy and devotion, all his knowledge and skill—everything was expendable in payment of his debt. He was eager to pay in Rome as he had been paying in other places. The Christians in Rome had heard and accepted the good news already, but they could profit by hearing it again. Making disciples is followed by teaching them to observe all that Jesus taught (Matthew 28:19, 20), and Paul was adept at such teaching.

C. Currency to Pay With (vv. 16, 17)

16. For I am not ashamed of the gospel of Christ: for it is the power of God unto salvation to every one that believeth; to the Jew first, and also to the Greek.

"Christ died for our sins" (1 Corinthians 15:3). That is a very important part of the good news. Paul preached "Christ crucified" (1 Corinthians 1:23-25). To the Jews that was a "stumblingblock." They tripped over it and fell flat on their faces: they could not believe that one crucified as a criminal could be their glorious Messiah, the King eternal, the Son of God. And to the Greeks, the preaching of Christ crucified was "foolishness." Their great ones exercised authority over them (Mark 10:42). How could a crucified man do that? The preaching of the resurrection brought only scorn from many of the wise (Acts 17:32). "Scientific" thinkers "knew" that dead persons stay dead. Faced by such opposition from Jews and Greeks, a timid preacher might stop in shame; but not Paul. Boldly he proclaimed the gospel of Christ, for he knew it was *the power of God unto salvation.* This is the message that turns men "from darkness to light, and from the power of Satan unto God, that they may receive forgiveness of sins, and inheritance among them which are sanctified by faith" (Acts 26:18). Foolishness to those who reject it and choose to die (1 Corinthians 1:18), the good news brings salvation *to every one that believeth.* The good news brought salvation because it was given *to the Jew first*; but later it was given also to the Greek, and it brought salvation to Greeks, too.

17. For therein is the righteousness of God revealed from faith to faith: as it is written, The just shall live by faith.

The righteousness of God can be understood in two ways (1) The righteousness of God's own character (Revelation 16:5); (2) the righteousness that God gives to believers when He forgives their sins (Romans 3:21, 22). If we understand the phrase in either of these ways, God's righteousness is revealed in the gospel.

1. Justice demands that wrong be punished. It is not just, not right, for a sinner to escape punishment. Then how can we say God is righteous if He forgives a sinner and lets him escape? The answer is found in the gospel. Christ died for our sins. Our sins have been punished in His death. The demand of justice has been satisfied, so God is still just, still righteous, even while He lets us escape the punishment we have earned.

2. All of us have sinned (Romans 3:23), and the wages of sin is death (Romans 6:23). Only by death can our sins be paid for. If we could live sinless lives from now on, our righteousness still would be marred by past sins. Then how can we possibly be righteous? The gospel reveals that Christ has died for our sins. Because we believe in Him, God takes away our sins and gives us His righteousness (Romans 3:21-26; 2 Corinthians 5:21; Philippians 3:9).

In the gospel all this is *revealed from faith to faith:* that is, people who have faith tell the good news to others and lead them to have faith too. Paul's statement, *The just shall live by faith,* agrees with what is written in Habakkuk 2:4. We live for eternity, not because what we do is good enough to earn that privilege, but because we have faith in Jesus, who died to atone for our sins. Because He atoned for our sins we can be

forgiven. We are forgiven because of our faith, and so by faith we become just and by faith we live. This does not take away any of the importance of doing right. Faith cannot live without "obedience to the faith" (v. 5; James 2:14-26). If we abandon our lives to sin while we say we have faith in Jesus, we show that our statement of faith is a lie.

Conclusion

Power is useless until it is used. No matter how much horsepower is under the hood, your car goes nowhere till the gears are engaged and the wheels start to turn.

The gospel is the power of God unto salvation, and Christians are the machinery through which that power is put to work. The gospel goes nowhere till you and I start to move.

A. Are You Ready?

Paul had in his possession some good news for the whole world. Therefore he was in debt to everybody who did not have that news—and he was ready to pay (Romans 1:14, 15).

Now we have the same good news in our possession. Therefore we are in debt to countless people near and far, for Jesus sent the news to "every creature" (Mark 16:15). It is time to be making payments on our debt. Are you ready?

B. Prayer

What a treasure we have in the gospel! Thank You for entrusting it to us, Father. May we have wisdom and courage to pass it on in a winning way. In Jesus' name, amen.

C. Thought to Remember

"I am debtor."

Home Daily Bible Readings

Monday, Feb. 28—Jesus Christ: Truly Human, Truly God (Romans 1:1-7)

Tuesday, Mar. 1—Thanksgiving for the Romans' Faith (Romans 1:8-12)

Wednesday, Mar. 2—The Power of the Gospel (Romans 1:13-17)

Thursday, Mar. 3—God Loathes Sin (Romans 1:18-23)

Friday, Mar. 4—Sin Dishonors Persons (Romans 1:24-32)

Saturday, Mar. 5—Salvation Comes Only Through Jesus Christ (Acts 4:5-13)

Sunday, Mar. 6—Put on Christ (Romans 13:8-14)

Learning by Doing

*This page contains an alternate lesson plan emphasizing learning activities. Classes
desiring such student involvement will find these suggestions helpful.*

Learning Goals

In this lesson you will lead your students to
accomplish the following:

1. Explain why Paul was eager to share the
gospel.

2. Determine how they can overcome their
fears to share the gospel message with their unsaved friends and acquaintances.

Into the Lesson

Write this statement on your chalkboard: *Most
Christians are ashamed of the gospel message.*

Provide paper and pencils for your class
members and ask them to write whether they
agree or disagree with the statement and to jot
down two reasons for their opinions. Or use the
space provided for this in the student book.
Then have the students pair off and discuss for
ninety seconds whether they agree or disagree
with the statement, and the reason for their
opinions.

After ninety seconds ask, "How many agree?"
Have them raise their hands. Then ask, "How
many disagree?" Again have them raise their
hands. Then let volunteers briefly explain their
opinions. Allow discussion for three or four
minutes.

Lead into today's Bible study by saying,
"Today we begin a study of the book of Romans.
Romans was written by the apostle Paul, and is
the most thorough explanation of the gospel in
Scripture. In today's passage Paul introduces the
power of the gospel and his eagerness to share
it. As we explore the passage, let's look for clues
that tell us how we can gain greater courage to
share our faith with others."

Into the Word

Begin with a brief lecture (two or three minutes) describing the background of this passage.
You will find helpful information in the Introduction of the commentary for this lesson.

Ask a volunteer to read Romans 1:1-17 aloud.
Then follow the steps below:

Step One. Lead the whole class in discussing
the following two questions as a means of ana-
lyzing today's text:

1. What does this passage reveal about the
gospel?

2. What indicates that Paul was eager to share
the gospel?

Allow six to eight minutes for observing the
facts. Be sure to list them on the chalkboard as
insights are suggested.

Step Two. Divide the class into groups of four
to six students each. Give each group this assignment: *You are to create a tract designed for
Christians. The tract is entitled, "How to Develop
Boldness in Witnessing." You may develop it any way
you like, with or without artwork.*

Encourage each group to list from Romans
1:1-17 some insights for becoming bold in witnessing, and then include those principles in
the content for the tract.

Provide each group with enough paper, pencils, and felt-tip pens. Appoint a discussion
leader for each group. Allow the groups twenty-
five minutes to complete the project.

Step Three. Have each group select a reporter
to present the group's tract to the rest of the
class.

Option

Follow the instructions for *Step One* above.
Then divide the class into groups of four to six
students each, and ask each group to develop a
brief sermon outline on the subject of becoming
a bold witness. Appoint a leader for each group
and provide each group with paper and pencils.
After twenty minutes have each group share
their outline with the rest of the class. Here is a
sample outline:

We increase our courage to share our faith as
we—

I. Serve God with our whole heart (v. 9)

II. Participate in mutually encouraging relationships with other Christians (vv. 11,
12)

III. Recognize our obligation to share our faith
(vv. 14, 15)

IV. Focus on the power of the gospel (v. 16)

Into Life

Lead the class in discussing these questions:

1. What makes it difficult for you to share
your faith?

2. How can you overcome these obstacles?

Give each student an index card. Ask each to
write on the card the names of five non-Christians he or she has contact with. Challenge them
to put the card in a place where they will see it,
and pray for these people daily.

Let's Talk It Over

The questions on this page are designed to encourage review of the lesson Scriptures and to promote discussion of the lesson by the class. The answers provided are only discussion starters. Let your class talk it over from there.

1. When we read the New Testament, from beginning to end, the first of the letters we encounter is Romans. Right away in Romans 1:3, 4 we find Paul describing Jesus as both human and divine. Why is this significant?

It informs us immediately that Jesus Christ, who is presented in the Gospels and Acts, is the one of whom Paul wrote in his letter. Some critics have charged that Paul took the simple gospel and expanded it into a theological system that is foreign to the Christ of the Gospels. But we need look no farther than these opening verses of Romans to discover that Paul understood the basic truths of the gospel and to gain assurance that the sublime discussions in Romans are very much in harmony with those basic truths. Paul's mention of the resurrection in verse 4 is especially significant, it is a signal that this mighty event will occupy a place of great prominence throughout this letter.

2. Is it a legitimate aim for a church to desire that their faith be "spoken of throughout the whole world"? Explain.

It is legitimate if by seeking such a reputation a church desires only to glorify Jesus Christ. Congregations can be widely known for many reasons, such as the prominence of their minister, the impressiveness of their building, the support they give to missions, the quality of their teaching programs, and the like. Care must be taken that these factors do not become a matter of congregational pride. Instead, they should be a means of magnifying Christ. This aim can be legitimate also if the church's demonstration of faith can serve as an example for other congregations to follow. An illustration of this is seen in Paul's reference to the Macedonian churches' generosity as a way of encouraging the Corinthians to contribute to the needs of believers in Jerusalem (2 Corinthians 8:1-7).

3. Paul was an inspired apostle, but he desired the spiritual strengthening that would come from fellowship with the Roman Christians. How does this relate to the strengthening of leaders in the church today?

It seems unlikely that the believers in Rome could have imparted to Paul any spiritual truths he did not already know. However, Paul surely would have been encouraged merely by listening to these fellow Christians express their faith in Jesus Christ and declare their certainty regarding the facts of the gospel preached by the apostles and others. In the same way today ministers, evangelists, and missionaries can gain strength from the humblest believer who declares his or her convictions regarding Christ, the power of the gospel, the effectiveness of prayer, and the certainties of Heaven. These messengers receive further encouragement in knowing that their labors, and those of others, have not been in vain. One does not have to possess a college education or a boundless knowledge of the Scriptures in order to strengthen and encourage another in the faith. One simply needs to speak out confidently about what he or she knows and believes.

4. Paul considered himself to be under obligation to take the gospel to the lost. What can we say about how we should pay our debt to the unsaved in regard to sharing the gospel with them?

If we are honest, we strive to pay off our debts completely. In connection with the gospel this suggests that we will not be half-hearted in our attempts to evangelize our friends and neighbors who are lost in sin. Instead, we will do our best to convince them of their need for Christ's salvation. We also try to pay our financial debts promptly. Since life is uncertain and opportunities often seem to drift away, we need to be prompt in communicating the gospel to the persons we know. (See Colossians 4:5, 6.)

5. Why should we be able to say with Paul, "I am not ashamed of the gospel of Christ"?

The gospel's power is still being demonstrated today. People who once were enslaved by drugs or alcohol, caught up in crime and violence, or victimized by physical or sexual abuse have experienced the power of the gospel, and by it have been rescued from the awful realities of their past. Furthermore, the gospel is clearly the only answer to the ravages of sin. Other solutions that people have offered—education, economic programs, other religions and philosophies—have failed to deal with the basic problem of human sinfulness.

God's Gift of Redemption

DEVOTIONAL READING: Romans 2:4b-16.

LESSON SCRIPTURE: Romans 3:21—4:25.

PRINTED TEXT: Romans 4:13-25.

Romans 4:13-25

13 For the promise, that he should be the heir of the world, was not to Abraham, or to his seed, through the law, but through the righteousness of faith.

14 For if they which are of the law be heirs, faith is made void, and the promise made of none effect:

15 Because the law worketh wrath: for where no law is, there is no transgression.

16 Therefore it is of faith, that it might be by grace; to the end the promise might be sure to all the seed; not to that only which is of the law, but to that also which is of the faith of Abraham; who is the father of us all,

17 (As it is written, I have made thee a father of many nations,) before him whom he believed, even God, who quickeneth the dead, and calleth those things which be not as though they were:

18 Who against hope believed in hope, that he might become the father of many nations, according to that which was spoken, So shall thy seed be.

19 And being not weak in faith, he considered not his own body now dead, when he was about a hundred years old, neither yet the deadness of Sarah's womb:

20 He staggered not at the promise of God through unbelief; but was strong in faith, giving glory to God;

21 And being fully persuaded, that what he had promised, he was able also to perform.

22 And therefore it was imputed to him for righteousness.

23 Now it was not written for his sake alone, that it was imputed to him;

24 But for us also, to whom it shall be imputed, if we believe on him that raised up Jesus our Lord from the dead;

25 Who was delivered for our offenses, and was raised again for our justification.

GOLDEN TEXT: The promise, that he should be the heir of the world, was not to Abraham, or to his seed, through the law, but through the righteousness of faith.
—Romans 4:13.

Lesson Aims

After studying this lesson a student should be able to:

1. Describe Abraham's faith and the consequences of it.

2. Describe a Christian's faith and the consequences of it.

Lesson Outline

INTRODUCTION
A. Gifts From God
B. Lesson Background
I. A PROMISED INHERITANCE (Romans 4:13-17)
A. Faith Wins a Promise (vv. 13-15)
B. Grace Gives a Promise (vv. 16, 17)
   Unconditional Promise
II. ABRAHAM'S FAITH (Romans 4:18-22)
A. Faith's Hope (v. 18)
   High Hopes
B. Faith's Strength (vv. 19-21)
C. Faith's Result (v. 22)
III. OUR FAITH (Romans 4:23-25)
A. Result of Our Faith (vv. 23, 24)
B. Items of Our Faith (v. 25)
CONCLUSION
A. Consequences
B. Consider Your Calling
C. The Final Consequence
D. Prayer
E. Thought to Remember

Visual 2 of the visuals packet highlights the thoughts found in the conclusion of the lesson. The visual is shown on page 245.

Introduction

A. Gifts From God

Look out of your window and count the gifts from God. I see a spreading linden tree with frolicsome squirrels, a pair of cardinals, and a turtledove. These are gifts from God. I see sunlight flooding wind-touched leaves and making moving shadows—God's gifts.

On this side of the window I see some bookshelves I made with my own hands; but the material came from a tree, and "only God can make a tree." I see a desk and filing cabinets, products

of mine and steel mill and factory; but God made the iron.

In the mirror I see a human frame, stooped and small and homely, but "fearfully and wonderfully made" (Psalm 139:14). There's no such thing as a self-made man. I may develop a stoop in my shoulders, I may shape my personality within limits, I may polish my intellect a bit; but still Paul asks, "What do you have that you did not receive?" (1 Corinthians 4:7, *New International Version*). It's all a gift from God.

God has still better gifts for us: forgiveness, new birth, eternal life. Praise the Lord!

B. Lesson Background

The gospel is the power of God unto salvation. God's power is enough to save everybody in the world, and those who believe the gospel will be saved (Romans 1:16). Unbelievers throng the wide road to destruction (Matthew 7:13, 14).

Romans 1:18-32 describes the utter depravity of those who do not want to include God in their knowledge. Their actions demand the wrath of God (v. 18).

Chapter 2 of Romans then deals with those who do want to know God, those who have His law to guide them. They too demand the wrath of God, for they do not obey His law (v. 12).

This is made more emphatic in Romans 3:9-20. All the people in the world are sinners, "guilty before God" (v. 19). All of them deserve His wrath. Then is everybody doomed?

No, there is a way out. Sinners can become righteous, not by what they do, but by believing in Jesus Christ. He is the "propitiation," the atoning sacrifice, for the sins of humanity. Those who believe in Him are forgiven and made as pure as if they had never sinned. They cannot boast about their purity, however. It is not their accomplishment; it is God's gift (Romans 3:21-31).

I. A Promised Inheritance
(Romans 4:13-17)

Chapter 4 of Romans takes us back to Abraham, father of the chosen race that had God's law and failed to obey it. Like everyone else, Abraham fell short of perfection in his own life. But Abraham believed in God; and because of his belief, God gave him credit for the righteousness that he did not attain in his way of living (Romans 4:3; Genesis 15:6).

A. Faith Wins a Promise (vv. 13-15)

13. For the promise, that he should be the heir of the world, was not to Abraham, or to his seed, through the law, but through the righteousness of faith.

Repeatedly the Lord promised a certain land to Abraham and *his seed*, his descendants (Genesis 12:7; 13:14, 15; 15:7, 18; 17:8). Primarily this meant the land of Canaan, in which Abraham was a pioneer; but the Hebrew word for land can also mean the whole world. Paul now gave it that wider meaning because he was thinking of Abraham's *seed* in a wider sense, including not only the Jews, his physical descendants, but also Christians who believe as Abraham did (Romans 4:11, 12). Perhaps he was thinking also of the "new earth, wherein dwelleth righteousness" (2 Peter 3:13). Both Abraham and his seed will inherit what God promised, not because they keep the law, but because they believe God, and therefore are credited with *righteousness.*

14. For if they which are of the law be heirs, faith is made void, and the promise made of none effect.

If receiving the promised inheritance depended on keeping the law, then faith would have nothing to do with it—neither the faith of Abraham nor the faith of his Jewish or Christian descendants. Furthermore, if only those who kept the law could have the inheritance, then no one would have it, for no one kept the law. In that case, God's promise would not be kept. The next verse explains this further.

15. Because the law worketh wrath: for where no law is, there is no transgression.

The law prescribed wrath and punishment for lawbreakers. That means everybody, for all have sinned (Romans 3:23). Abraham and others of his time could not transgress a law that did not yet exist, so they would not come under God's wrath for that reason. However, that did not mean they were safe from His wrath if they did wrong. "As many as have sinned without law shall also perish without law" (Romans 2:12). The only way of escape from wrath was Abraham's way. He believed in the Lord, and therefore the Lord credited him with righteousness even though he did not attain righteousness in his living (Genesis 15:6).

B. Grace Gives a Promise (vv. 16, 17)

16. Therefore it is of faith, that it might be by grace; to the end the promise might be sure to all the seed; not to that only which is of the law, but to that also which is of the faith of Abraham; who is the father of us all.

If God gave the inheritance only to those who kept the law, it would be what they earned. No grace would be involved. But that would make His promise void, for none kept the law (v. 14). Therefore He gave the inheritance to those who have faith like that of Abraham. Such faith involves trust and daring obedience (Hebrews

11:8), but still Abraham received the promise because of what he believed rather than what he did. His life was not faultless. In strict justice he could have perished without law (Romans 2:12). Instead, he received the promise *by grace,* by God's favor that Abraham did not deserve.

What is *the end,* the purpose and result, of making the inheritance depend on faith rather than law? It is that *the promise might be sure to all the seed,* all the people of Abraham. They include not only the Jews who are *of the law,* but also the Christians who are *of the faith of Abraham*—who believe and trust and obey God as Abraham did. Jesus said to the Father, "This is life eternal, that they might know thee the only true God, and Jesus Christ, whom thou hast sent" (John 17:3). If we accept that and step out in faith as boldly as Abraham did, it makes no difference whether we are Jew or Gentile, British or American, Russian or Chinese, Hottentot or Eskimo. Abraham *is the father of us all.*

UNCONDITIONAL PROMISE

Most promises are conditional: "If you will . . . then I will. . . ." Whether the conditions are explicit or implied, promises usually have "strings attached." We understand that promised "merit raises" are given to those whose productivity merits an increase. We are accustomed to earning our rewards.

Paul stressed the grace factor in God's promise of redemption. To people who were programmed for receiving what they deserved by obedience to law, it was not an easy concept to grasp. It seemed too good to be true. Many of us also have some difficulty accepting God's unmerited favor. We keep trying to earn our redemption.

The promise of redemption, however, is not entirely without conditions. The one condition we must fulfill for forgiveness and justification is *faith.* We are saved by grace through faith (Ephesians 2:8). And, as Paul makes clear in the text we studied last week (Romans 1), Christian faith is obedient faith and righteous faith. It is a faith like that of Abraham.   —R. W. B.

17. (As it is written, I have made thee a father of many nations,) before him whom he believed, even God, who quickeneth the dead, and calleth those things which be not as though they were.

It is written in Genesis 17:5 that God said to Abraham, "A father of many nations have I made thee." Literally and physically, Abraham was father to the Jews descended from Jacob, the Edomites descended from Esau (Genesis 36), the tribes descended from Ishmael (Genesis 25:12-18), and all of the tribes descended from

Abraham's later sons (Genesis 25:1-6). To these Paul is adding the spiritual descendants, the Christians of many nations who have faith like that of Abraham (v. 16).

Omitting the words in parentheses and connecting what goes before them, with what follows them, we read that Abraham *is the father of us all before him whom he believed, even God.* In other words, in God's sight Abraham is the father of Christians as well as Jews. The Jews are his children by actual physical descent; Christians are his children in a spiritual way because they have inherited his remarkable faith.

Verse 17 closes with two examples of God's unique power. First, He *quickeneth the dead*: that is, He makes them alive. Second, He calls things that do not exist as if they did exist. In response to His call they come into existence. The following verses explain how these examples are suitable to the case of Abraham.

II. Abraham's Faith
(Romans 4:18-22)

Basically, Abraham's faith was belief in God. Two elements of it are seen in the end of verse 17. He believed God could give life to the dead and call into existence things that did not exist. Now we see more about Abraham's faith.

A. Faith's Hope (v. 18)

18. Who against hope believed in hope, that he might become the father of many nations, according to that which was spoken, So shall thy seed be.

Abraham kept on hoping when it seemed that there could be no hope. His wife had been barren all her life (Genesis 11:30). How could he hope to be the father of many nations, as God said he would be? Could it be that God meant for him to take another wife? He tried that, and the second wife produced a son (Genesis 16). But God rejected that son and insisted that the promised progeny would come by the first wife, the barren one (Genesis 17:15-19). So Abraham was ninety-nine years old (Genesis 17:1), and the only son he had was rejected; but still he hoped to be *the father of many nations.* How could he hope? God said it would be so, and Abraham believed God.

HIGH HOPES

Remember that old song about an ant setting about to move a rubber tree plant? The refrain says, "He's got high hopes, he's got high hopes; he's got high apple pie in the sky hopes. " No task too tough for that ant!

"Now faith is being sure of what we hope for" (Hebrews 11:1, *New International Version*). Abra-

ham's faith was so great, he did not give up hope when the fulfillment of God's promise seemed hopeless. Despite the seeming impossibility of his fathering a child by Sarah, Abraham's hope neither weakened nor wavered. And God ultimately honored Abraham's faith, who was "fully persuaded" that God could do what He promised.

High hopes are the essence of faith. Christians thrive on hopes that are generated by God's promises—the hope of forgiveness, a Heavenly home, the crown of life. And all of these center in Jesus Christ.

In times of disappointment, difficulty, and even seeming defeat, remember God's promises and hold on to your high hopes.   —R. W. B.

B. Faith's Strength (vv. 19-21)

19. And being not weak in faith, he considered not his own body now dead, when he was about a hundred years old, neither yet the deadness of Sarah's womb.

Abraham was nearly a hundred years old; his wife was nearly ninety and barren. If he had been weak in faith, surely he would have thought that both of them were as good as dead. Without a powerful faith he would not have hoped for even one child, much less many nations. But Abraham was *not weak in faith.* He believed in the God who gives life to the dead and calls things out of nothing into being (v. 17). If Abraham's reproductive power was now dead, and Sarah's womb had always been dead, God could give life to both of them.

20. He staggered not at the promise of God through unbelief; but was strong in faith, giving glory to God.

In Abraham there was no *unbelief,* no lack of faith, that would allow him to stagger or falter or waver or doubt when the promise of God seemed incredible. He was so *strong in faith* that he gave *glory to God,* honor and praise to Him with whom nothing is impossible.

21. And being fully persuaded, that what he had promised, he was able also to perform.

As Abraham saw it, the promise that seemed incredible was really credible, because God was really able to do whatever He promised.

C. Faith's Result (v. 22)

22. And therefore it was imputed to him for righteousness.

This is the kind of faith that God accepts—a strong faith, a faith that trusts Him completely, an assurance that He can do whatever He wants to do and surely will do whatever He has promised. Abraham had that kind of faith, and that was why God gave him credit for *righteousness* (Genesis 15:6).

III. Our Faith
(Romans 4:23-25)

By the grace of God we have a promise and hope of a homeland better than the one Abraham found in Canaan. Is our faith as strong as Abraham's? Paul leaves us to make the comparison for ourselves, but the final verses of our text point us in that direction.

A. Result of Our Faith (vv. 23, 24)

23. Now it was not written for his sake alone, that it was imputed to him.

God had the story of Abraham *written* in the inspired record so Abraham would be remembered and honored by his descendants both physical and spiritual. To this day he is highly honored by Muslims, Jews, and Christians. But that was not the only reason for preserving this record. Read on.

24. But for us also, to whom it shall be imputed, if we believe on him that raised up Jesus our Lord from the dead.

The record was made and preserved *for us*, for our sake, our benefit. If our faith matches Abraham's faith, righteousness *shall be imputed* to us too. The Greek word for *imputed* is translated *counted* and *reckoned* in this same chapter (vv. 3-10). It is an accountant's word. In God's bookkeeping, Abraham was given credit for more righteousness than he attained. We can get the same extra credit *if we believe on him that raised up Jesus our Lord from the dead.* Abraham believed in "God, who quickeneth the dead" (v. 17). We have a substantial basis for that belief in the fact that He actually did raise Jesus from the dead, a fact proved by a number of capable witnesses (1 Corinthians 15:3-8). When Paul wrote this, most of those five hundred witnesses were still alive. Anyone with interest enough could hear their testimony for himself. Luke must have interviewed dozens of them before he wrote that he had "carefully investigated everything from

the beginning" (Luke 1:3a *New International Version*). We cannot now talk in person with the original witnesses, but we have Luke's report. With it we have the report of Mark, who was even closer to the events he records. We have also the testimony of two eyewitnesses, Matthew and John. We can be sure Jesus rose from the dead. With such a firm basis in fact, our faith ought to be as powerful as Abraham's, and our commitment ought to be as full as his (Hebrews 11:8). For us, as for Abraham, such faith can win extra credit, credit for more righteousness than our lives have earned. Only in this way can the promise be made sure to us who are Abraham's progeny by faith (v. 16).

B. Items of Our Faith (v. 25)

25. Who was delivered for our offenses, and was raised again for our justification.

Here are two items of our faith, two facts we believe about "Jesus our Lord" (v. 24).

First, He *was delivered for our offenses*. We believe not only that "Christ died for our sins according to the Scriptures" (1 Corinthians 15:3), but also that He was delivered to death "by the determinate counsel and foreknowledge of God" (Acts 2:23). We were all sinners (Romans 3:23), and "the wages of sin is death" (Romans 6:23). But because of our faith, Jesus accepted the wages of our sin and gave us credit for His righteousness (Romans 3:21, 22). Therefore we have eternal life as a gift (Romans 6:23). While that gift is free to us who receive it, it was very costly to those who gave it. God gave His Son; Jesus gave His life. He *was delivered for our offenses*.

To that our text adds a second item of our faith: Jesus our Lord *was raised again for our justification.* What is our justification? It is our transformation from sinners to people who are just, people who are righteous. This change takes place when our sins are erased from God's book and we are given credit for righteousness instead.

Then how is our justification related to Christ's resurrection? Sometimes our understanding of reality can be helped by looking at a picture of it. Jesus' atonement for us is pictured in the ceremonies of the Day of Atonement in earlier times. On that day the priest offered sacrifices to atone for his sins and the sins of the people. But atonement was not complete when the victims died. The priest took some of the blood into the inner shrine of the tabernacle or temple, to the holy ark that symbolized God's presence (Leviticus 16:11-16). Only then was atonement completed.

Jesus died to atone for our sins, but atonement was not completed at the moment of His death. Jesus was both sacrifice and priest. As sacrifice

visual 2

He died for our sins; as priest He was raised from the dead to enter not into a holy place made by human hands, but into Heaven itself "to appear in the presence of God for us." When He did that the atonement was complete, and with it our justification was complete (Hebrews 9:6, 7, 11-14, 24).

Conclusion

Redemption is God's gift, as our lesson title indicates. Redemption, justification, salvation—these are not separate and distinct things. They are different aspects of the transformation by which sinners become saints. That transformation is wrought by God. It is His gift.

God's gift is free, but it is not compulsory. No one gets it who does not want it; no one gets it who does not value it; no one gets it who does not believe in the giver. The gift is given freely by God's grace (Romans 3:24), but it is received by man's faith (Ephesians 2:8). How much hangs on our faith!

A. Consequences

Faith cannot live alone. Without consequences it is dead. If it makes no difference in our living, faith itself is not living (James 2:17).

"By faith Abraham, when he was called . . . went out." He didn't know where he was going; but God called, and he went because he believed in God. His going was the natural consequence of his faith (Hebrews 11:8).

Today hundreds of missionaries are toiling in difficult fields as a consequence of their faith. Countless other full-time Christian workers are laboring no less diligently because they believe in God.

Salvation is God's most precious gift, but not His only one. Different people are gifted with different abilities, and butchers and bakers and candlestick makers are using their gifts to glorify the Giver by honest dealing and unselfish living. "Whatsoever ye do, do all to the glory of God" (1 Corinthians 10:31). This is the natural consequence of your faith.

B. Consider Your Calling

Think of what you have done in the past week. Is it a proper response to the call of God in whom you believe? In relation to your spouse, have you responded to the clarion call of God in Ephesians 5:22-33? In relation to parents or children, have you been guided by the call of Ephesians 6:1-4? In the workplace, have you stepped out boldly in response to Ephesians 6:5-9? Has the divine call of Romans 13:1-7 controlled your response to government, even to the IRS? Romans 12 calls us to make good use of our differing gifts. Are you satisfied with your answer to its call?

C. The Final Consequence

Abraham went out without knowing where he was going, but God led him safely to a land that was to belong to him and his children for countless generations. But even in that land that was promised and given, Abraham lived in tents like a nomad, and so did his son and grandson. Wasn't it time to settle down?

No, that promised land was not the end of their journey. It was to be their home for centuries, but they were looking for a place more permanent still—"a city which hath foundations, whose builder and maker is God" (Hebrews 11:8-10).

The last two chapters of the Bible present a picture of that city. There the water of life flows in a river from the throne of God, and the tree of life grows on both its banks. "And the Spirit and the bride say, Come. And let him that heareth say, Come. And let him that is athirst come. And whosoever will, let him take the water of life freely" (Revelation 22:17). That is faith's final consequence.

D. Prayer

Thank You, God, for holding out to us the precious gift of redemption, for calling us to step out and claim it. We have chosen to answer Your call, and now we look to You for wisdom and strength and fortitude to live with the consequences of our choice till we enjoy the final consequence forever. In Jesus' name, amen.

E. Thought to Remember

Faith has consequences.

Learning by Doing

This page contains an alternate lesson plan emphasizing learning activities. Classes desiring such student involvement will find these suggestions helpful.

Learning Goals

As a result of this session, a student will:

1. Demonstrate from Romans 4 that we receive righteousness through faith, not by works.

2. Distinguish between salvation by works and salvation by faith.

Into the Lesson

Say to the class, "I am going to give an illustration to explain salvation by grace, but the illustration I will use has a very serious error. See if you can identify the error." Then tell the following illustration:

A man died and stood at the gate of Heaven. When he was asked by the attendant why he should be allowed to enter, he answered, "Well, I've been a faithful church member all my life."

"Great!" the attendant replied. "That's worth one dollar. But you will need one billion dollars' worth of good works to get into Heaven."

"Well," the man continued, "I've read the Bible and prayed every day."

"Wonderful," the attendant responded. "That's worth another dollar. You need $999,999,998 more."

"Boy, this is tougher than I thought," the man gasped. "Let's see . . . I've been a tither."

"I'm certainly glad you tithed. That's worth another dollar. You need $999,999,997 more to get into Heaven."

"You're kidding. Why, the only way a person could make it into Heaven is by the grace of God," the man exclaimed.

"Ah, the grace of God," the attendant said with a smile. "Now that's worth $999,999,997. By adding that to your three dollars, you have enough to get into Heaven. Come on in."

After telling the illustration say, "Obviously the details of this illustration concerning the judgment are fictitious. But there is a major problem with the main point of the illustration. Let's read Romans 4 and see if it will shed any light on the error in the illustration.

Divide this chapter into several sections and ask several volunteers to read the sections aloud to the class. Then come back to the illustration and ask the students what major error they see in it.

If after two minutes of discussion the error is not detected, point out that according to the illustration a person is admitted to Heaven by a combination of good works (the $3) plus the grace of God (the $999,999,997). But that is contrary to the Scriptures. We are saved by God's grace through faith, and not by our good works (see Ephesians 2:8-10; Titus 3:5). Christ's death paid for one hundred per cent of our salvation; our good works contribute nothing. Good works, of course, are to characterize a Christian's life. But rather than being the means of our salvation, they are the natural expression of our love for Christ.

Into the Word

Have the students form groups of six. Each group is to explore Romans 4 and look for answers to this question: *What arguments are given to prove that we are saved (made righteous) by faith, not works?* Each of the following groups of verses should be considered separately: 1-3; 4-8; 9-12; 13-15; 16, 17; 18-25. Have each group select a person to list the group's ideas on paper.

Allow approximately twenty minutes for study. When time is up, ask the groups to share their observations with the rest of the class.

Into Life

Help your students distinguish between seeking righteousness through works and receiving the righteousness that God gives through faith in Jesus Christ. Copy the chart below onto the chalkboard. Discuss the questions in the left column as they pertain first to the person who seeks righteousness by works. Put the students' responses in the appropriate box. Then do the same for the one who receives righteousness by faith. Conclude by urging the students to share Abraham's faith and give thanks to God for the righteousness He graciously bestows.

	Works	Faith
What is his view of God?		
What is his motivation for doing good works?		
What is his view of the Christian life?		

Let's Talk It Over

The questions on this page are designed to encourage review of the lesson Scriptures and to promote discussion of the lesson by the class. The answers provided are only discussion starters. Let your class talk it over from there.

1. Abraham is "the father of us all," which includes all Christians. How should we respond to this truth?

The spiritual fatherhood of Abraham, to which Paul refers, was established by God (Genesis 17:5). The heritage Abraham has passed on to us is one of bold faith and courageous obedience to the voice of God. Since Abraham's experiences are referred to several times in the New Testament (in addition to Romans 4, note Galatians 3, Hebrews 11, and James 2), it behooves us to become familiar with the record of his life. One way the Bible functions for us is as a mirror (James 1:22-25), and we can use our father Abraham's experiences in this way. How well do we reflect his acceptance of God's promises? His promptness in obeying God's commands? When we see him steadfastly waiting on God, can we find a likeness of this in our lives?

2. We are told that Abraham "against hope believed in hope (Romans 4:18)." Have we also experienced that kind of hope? If so, in what way?

The expression speaks of clinging to hope in the face of a situation that appears hopeless. Most people have gone through crises like that. Perhaps it was an illness or accident suffered by someone dear to us. In spite of the apparent hopelessness of that person's condition, we offered the prayer of hope, and like Abraham we finally enjoyed the realization of our hope. It may have been a relative or friend for whose salvation we were hoping or praying. We continued to hope for that in spite of that individual's resistance to the gospel, and at last he or she yielded to Christ. Or it may be that we clung to hope for a positive change in our job status or financial condition, and only after we endured a period of seeming hopelessness did that change finally come.

3. Unlike Abraham, we may feel that we are weak in faith. What can we do to overcome such weakness?

Abraham was strong in faith because he listened to and heeded God's promises. His faith was not a vague emotion or a mere wishful thinking. It was focused on something real and objective: God's revelation to him. For us also it is still true that "faith comes from hearing the message, and the message is heard through the word of Christ" (Romans 10:17, *New International Version*). We have vastly more of God's faith-producing revelation than Abraham had, but are we hearing it? Are we heeding it? Much of our weakness of faith no doubt reflects the lack of attention we give to the Scriptures. The solution to that weakness, therefore, lies in committing ourselves to regular, consistent study of the Word of God and to the conscientious practice of its principles.

4. *Justification* is a long, formidable term, but it is one that most Christians should be able to appreciate. Why is that? What does the term mean as applied to Christians?

It is a term associated with the courtroom, and most of us are familiar with that. In the courtroom justice is sought. Depending on the jury's verdict, one is declared innocent or guilty of a charge brought against him. Regarding our standing before God, however, there is no question—we are all guilty of sin and deserve punishment (Romans 3:23; 6:23). But Jesus gave himself as an atoning sacrifice for our sin. Admitting our guilt to God and accepting Jesus as our Savior, we are declared not guilty. This transformation from sinners to righteous people, people who are just in the sight of God, is our justification.

5. Why is it important to emphasize the consequences of faith?

It is too easy to think of faith as a kind of mental assent to Biblical truth. We may feel that since a great many people do not believe in God, we have done something praiseworthy in choosing to believe. The New Testament book of James speaks to this issue. While Paul points out that we are saved by God's grace through faith, apart from the works of the law, James makes it clear that genuine faith is active and working. "Yea, a man may say, Thou hast faith, and I have works: show me thy faith without thy works, and I will show thee my faith by my works" (James 2:18). We dare not let church members delude themselves into assuming that a faith in the head and heart is enough. Genuine faith makes a difference in the way one lives.

The Gift of Life in Christ

DEVOTIONAL READING: Colossians 1:9-14, 21-23.

LESSON SCRIPTURE: Romans 5.

PRINTED TEXT: Romans 5:6-17.

Romans 5:6-17

6 For when we were yet without strength, in due time Christ died for the ungodly.

7 For scarcely for a righteous man will one die: yet peradventure for a good man some would even dare to die.

8 But God commendeth his love toward us, in that, while we were yet sinners, Christ died for us.

9 Much more then, being now justified by his blood, we shall be saved from wrath through him.

10 For if, when we were enemies, we were reconciled to God by the death of his Son; much more, being reconciled, we shall be saved by his life.

11 And not only so, but we also joy in God through our Lord Jesus Christ, by whom we have now received the atonement.

12 Wherefore, as by one man sin entered into the world, and death by sin; and so death passed upon all men, for that all have sinned:

13 (For until the law sin was in the world: but sin is not imputed when there is no law.

14 Nevertheless death reigned from Adam to Moses, even over them that had not sinned after the similitude of Adam's transgression, who is the figure of him that was to come.

15 But not as the offense, so also is the free gift: for if through the offense of one many be dead, much more the grace of God, and the gift by grace, which is by one man, Jesus Christ, hath abounded unto many.

16 And not as it was by one that sinned, so is the gift: for the judgment was by one to condemnation, but the free gift is of many offenses unto justification.

17 For if by one man's offense death reigned by one; much more they which receive abundance of grace and of the gift of righteousness shall reign in life by one, Jesus Christ.)

GOLDEN TEXT: God commendeth his love toward us, in that, while we were yet sinners, Christ died for us.—Romans 5:8.

Lesson Aims

After this lesson a student should be able to:

1. Briefly tell how sin and death came through one man, and how redemption and life came through another one Man.

2. Describe the difference between God's free gift and the result of Adam's sin.

3. Accept and appreciate God's gift.

Lesson Outline

INTRODUCTION
  A. Free!
  B. Lesson Background
 I. LOVE STOOPS AND LIFTS (Romans 5:6-11)
  A. Love and Sacrifice (vv. 6-8)
    Supreme Sacrifice
  B. Reconciliation and Salvation (vv. 9, 10)
  C. Joy (v. 11)
    Big Words/Big Ideas
 II. FROM DEATH TO LIFE (Romans 5:12-17)
  A. Sin and Death (vv. 12-14)
  B. Gift of Life (vv. 15-17)
    Guilt (and Grace) by Association
CONCLUSION
  A. Summary
  B. Free Gifts
  C. An Offer I Can't Refuse
  D. Prayer
  E. Thought to Remember

Display visual 3 of the visuals packet and let it remain before the class throughout this session. The visual is shown on page 251.

Introduction

A. Free!

Cheery optimists say, "The best things in life are free," meaning sunshine and rain, the song of birds and the love of friends. But there's something better than all of these, and it's free. Let's think about God's gift of life.

B. Lesson Background

This lesson builds on last week's study of "God's Gift of Redemption." Though free to us, that gift was costly to the giver. God gave His Son to die for us, and Jesus gave His life. Last week's text ended with the statement that we are given credit for righteousness because we believe in God, who raised Jesus from the dead—Jesus who died for our sins and was raised for our justification.

Chapter 5 of Romans then begins with what follows our justification. First, "we have peace with God." Our sins made us His enemies (Colossians 1:21). When our sins were taken away, the enmity was ended. We have this peace "through our Lord Jesus Christ" because He is the one who brings us into God's grace, God's favor in which we stand now that we are redeemed. Being thus in God's favor, we rejoice in the hope of sharing His glory for eternity. This joyous hope lets us rejoice even in our "tribulations": all the troubles and difficulties that try our souls. This is not to say we enjoy tribulations but we delight in them, unpleasant as they are, because they bring good results. If we are true to our faith, all our trials build steadfast endurance in us. That endurance in turn builds strong character, and such character strengthens our hope of glory. That hope will never end in disappointment, "because the love of God is shed abroad in our hearts by the Holy Ghost which is given unto us" (Romans 5:1-5). The text of this week's lesson begins with appreciation of God's love.

I. Love Stoops and Lifts (Romans 5:6-11)

To rescue us from sin and sadness, our Savior came down from glory in Heaven to poverty on earth; and from poverty on earth He stooped to the depths of the grave. What love!

A. Love and Sacrifice (vv. 6-8)

6. For when we were yet without strength, in due time Christ died for the ungodly.

We were yet without strength, helpless and hopeless, utterly unable to get rid of our guilt, and therefore doomed to death. But *Christ died for the ungodly*. Without any guilt of His own, He accepted the death that was due to us; and therefore we can live. He did not do this hastily, but *in due time*, or *at just the right time*, as the *New International Version* has it. First God allowed "all nations to walk in their own ways" for a long time (Acts 14:16). Their own ways turned out to be bad. Then God gave a law to show the right way; and even with the law to guide them, people took wrong ways instead of the right. Through thousands of years the people of earth had every opportunity to choose the right, but the sad verdict had to be, "There is none righteous, no, not one" (Romans 3:10). Then at last,

visual 3

"when the fulness of the time was come, God sent forth his Son" (Galatians 4:4). When ages of history had proved that we were without strength, unable to get rid of wrong, Christ died to redeem us.

7. For scarcely for a righteous man will one die: yet peradventure for a good man some would even dare to die.

Charles Dickens's *Tale of Two Cities* soars to its climax when Sidney Carton cleverly manages to take the place of a man about to have his head lopped off by the guillotine. The one saved from death was an upright and noble man; but even so, the sacrifice of Sidney was unusual enough to become the climax of a famous book. In real life as in fiction, perhaps *for a good man some would even dare to die.* But who would even think of making such a sacrifice for a criminal who deserved to die?

8. But God commendeth his love toward us, in that, while we were yet sinners, Christ died for us.

Christ died for us, not when we were upright and noble people, but *while we were yet sinners.* What a matchless demonstration of God's matchless love! Why should He love us so? He does not love us because of what we are, but because of what He is, "for God is love" (1 John 4:8).

SUPREME SACRIFICE

During my high school years, the brother of one of my buddies drowned in a swimming accident. I learned that my friend's father, who was not a swimmer, nearly lost his own life when he jumped in the water to help his son. It was a futile attempt, made in desperation. But the father clearly would have sacrificed his own life to save his boy.

Parents will risk life and limb, and even die, to protect the lives of their children. These are not uncommon acts of love. We have heard of soldiers in wartime who fell on live grenades to save their buddies. Such selfless sacrifices are

rightly memorialized as acts of valor and courage.

The truly awesome acts of love, though, are those done on behalf of strangers, the undeserving, and even enemies. The ultimate example is Christ's death for sinners. Jesus died to save relatives and friends, but He died also to save strangers, even those who put Him to death. His was the supreme sacrifice.   —R. W. B.

B. Reconciliation and Salvation
(vv. 9, 10)

9. Much more then, being now justified by his blood, we shall be saved from wrath through him.

God loved us when we were sinners, loved us so much that Christ died for us. Now we are *justified by his blood*: our sins are taken away, we are made just. We are upright and noble children of God. Surely God now loves us *much more* than He did when we were sinners. If, while we were sinners, God gave His Son to die for us to rescue us from our sinful state, surely much more will He now save us from the wrath and punishment that unforgiven sin deserves. The next verse repeats this blessed assurance.

10. For if, when we were enemies, we were reconciled to God by the death of his Son; much more, being reconciled, we shall be saved by his life.

We were enemies of God when we were sinners, but even then He was not our enemy. As children of God we are taught to love our enemies and do them good (Luke 6:35). Our Heavenly Father set the example. When we were enemies He loved us and sent His Son to take our punishment. Thus our sins were taken away. We are no longer enemies, for *we were reconciled to God by the death of his Son.* God loved us greatly before; certainly now He does not love us less, but *much more.* Certainly we who were reconciled by Jesus' death *shall be saved by his life.* Jesus died, but He is not dead. He rose to life and ascended to Heaven, "now to appear in the presence of God for us" (Hebrews 9:24). There in the presence of God "he ever liveth to make intercession" for us, and therefore "he is able also to save them to the uttermost that come unto God by him" (Hebrews 7:25).

C. Joy (v. 11)

11. And not only so, but we also joy in God through our Lord Jesus Christ, by whom we have now received the atonement.

Our Lord Jesus Christ is the key to our relationship with God. It is through Him that *we have now received the atonement,* that we have become reconciled to God, that we are His children instead of His enemies, that our sins are erased from the record, that we are free from the threat of death and Hell, that we shall live forever in glory. Therefore it is *through our Lord Jesus Christ* that we find our *joy in God*, and it is "an inexpressible and glorious joy" (1 Peter 1:8, *New International Version*).

Walking with my father one spring day when I was ten, I tried to make adult conversation. I said, "Boy, the flowers sure are fragrant." I mispronounced the word, making the first *a* sound like the *a* in *rat*. Dad replied, "Yes, but don't you mean *fragrant*?" saying the word correctly. My response: "Yeah, I guess so; sometimes I like to try out those big words."

Some of the words Paul used to describe the redemptive works of Christ are big ones: *justification, reconciliation,* and *atonement.* Big ideas often require big words. And the grand plan of God's salvation deserves all the eloquence that human language can afford. A shorter word is used by Paul to summarize the concept: *saved.* Now, there's a word we all can understand—but the bigger words help us to see the depth of meaning in it.   —R. W. B.

II. From Death to Life (Romans 5:12-17)

What's it all about? Atonement, forgiveness, justification, reconciliation, salvation—these are all involved in a magnificent happening in which sinners become righteous by the grace of God. But then what? This magnificent happening brings us to a magnificent outcome—life! We were dead because of our sins. That is, we were under the sentence of death; and there was no way to escape by our own power or wisdom. But God made us alive (Ephesians 2:1-10).

A. Sin and Death (vv. 12-14)

12. Wherefore, as by one man sin entered into the world, and death by sin; and so death passed upon all men, for that all have sinned.

Wherefore means *on account of this.* It refers to what has just been said. Because we are rejoicing that God in His great love has saved us, let's look back and review the beginning of sin and the beginning of redemption.

Sin in the world began with one man, Adam (Genesis 3:1-6). Sin brought death (Genesis 3:22-24) just as God had said it would (Genesis 2:16, 17). Therefore death came to *all men*, not because Adam sinned, but because *all have sinned.*

The *King James Version* indicates that Paul was beginning a comparison, but left it unfinished in order to give the explanation that we see in parentheses in our text. The finished comparison would have been this: "As death came by the sin of one man (Adam), so salvation came by the righteousness of one man (Christ)." That comparison is made clearly in verse 18.

It is possible, however, that the comparison the apostle Paul had in mind in verse 12 is complete in that verse. It may be translated thus: "Wherefore, as by one man sin entered into the world, and death by sin; even so death passed to all men, for that all have sinned." With this translation the parentheses in the following verses are not needed.

With either translation the information of verse 12 is clear: Sin came into the world by way of Adam, death came because of sin, and death passed to all people because they all sinned.

13. (For until the law sin was in the world: but sin is not imputed when there is no law.

Many centuries after the time of Adam, God gave the law to define sin, to tell what people ought not to do. Through all those centuries *sin was in the world,* though there was no law to define it. *But sin is not imputed when there is no law.* What can this mean? As we saw in last week's lesson, *imputed* is an accountant's term. We are reading that sin is not taken into account when there is no law. We can hardly take it to mean that God took no account of sin before the law was given. It seems that He did take account of it. Remember what happened to sinners in the days of Noah? Perhaps the meaning is that the sinners themselves did not take account of sin. They did not understand the deadly nature of it. With no law to tell them, they did not even know what acts were wrong and what were right.

14. Nevertheless death reigned from Adam to Moses, even over them that had not sinned after the similitude of Adam's transgression, who is the figure of him that was to come.

Nevertheless, even though sin was not taken into account, it carried its penalty. *Death reigned* through all those years *from Adam to Moses* before the law was given. The people all died because they all sinned (v. 12), even though they did not sin just as Adam did. Another word now is used for Adam's sin. It was a *transgression,* a going aside, disobedience to an explicit command (Genesis 2:17). The word translated *sin* in these verses means missing the mark. All the sinners from Adam to Moses missed the mark. Their lives were not on target; they did not even know what the target was. Adam had the target plainly set before him, but he aimed in another direction. In spite of his transgression, Adam is *the figure*, the symbol, *of him that was to come;* that is, of Christ. The following verses compare and contrast what happened in and after Adam's time with what happened in and after Jesus' time on earth.

B. Gift of Life (vv. 15-17)

15. But not as the offense, so also is the free gift: for if through the offense of one many be dead, much more the grace of God, and the gift by grace, which is by one man, Jesus Christ, hath abounded unto many.

Now we see yet another word for the sin of Adam. *Transgression* (v. 14) is going aside; *offense* is falling aside. There is no great difference between these two, but both of them are different from missing the mark, especially an unknown mark. *The free gift*, also called *the gift by grace*, is God's gift of redemption, justification, salvation. Here we read that it is *not as the offense*.

It is interesting to note that some students translate the first part of this verse as a question, and so reverse the meaning of it. The *King James* translation means the free gift is not like the offense. Translating as a question, we read, "Is not the free gift like the offense?" Such a question indicates that an affirmative answer is expected: "Yes, they are alike." There must indeed be some similarity, for we have just read that Adam is a figure, a symbol, a picture of Christ.

The rest of the verse shows that the offense and the gift are alike in one way and different in another. They are alike in that each came into the world by one man and affected many. Sin came by Adam (v. 12); the free gift came *by one man, Jesus Christ*. They are different in that *the gift by grace* is *much more*. As Knofel Staton has aptly put it, "God's grace is greater than man's disgrace."

Through the offense of one many be dead. This is an abbreviated way of recalling what is said in verse 12. It is not that *many be dead* in punishment of Adam's sin. But Adam brought sin into the world, sin brought death, and many are dead because they all sinned.

Now we see another difference between the offense and the gift. Adam's sin did not make all his people sinners when they had no sin of their own, but Jesus' sacrifice did make all His people righteous when they did not have complete righteousness of their own. As we saw in last week's lesson, Jesus' people are those who believe in Him and live according to that belief.

This points to yet another difference between the offense and the free gift, and it is a crucial one. The final results are different. The offense brought death; the free gift brings life. That is why this lesson is titled "God's Gift of Life."

The difference between the offense and the free gift is much greater than the similarity between them, so it seems better to take the first part of the verse as a statement: "The free gift is not like the offense." This is verifed in the next two verses. There again we have both similarity and difference, but the difference is greater.

16. And not as it was by one that sinned, so is the gift: for the judgment was by one to condemnation, but the free gift is of many offenses unto justification.

Again the first part of the verse can be either a statement or a question, and to read it as a question is to reverse the meaning. As a statement, the *New International Version* puts it thus: "The gift of God is not like the result of the one man's sin." As a question it would be, "Is not the gift of God like the result of one man's sin?"

The rest of the verse speaks of difference, and again the *New International Version* clarifies it: "The judgment followed one sin and brought condemnation, but the gift followed many trespasses and brought justification." A great difference indeed!

17. For if by one man's offense death reigned by one; much more they which receive abundance of grace and of the gift of righteousness shall reign in life by one, Jesus Christ.)

How is the gift of God like the result of one man's sin? Only in one way: one person led the way to each. Adam led the way to sin and death; Jesus led the way to righteousness and life.

Obviously the difference is what is emphasized here. It is the difference between death and life. Adam started humanity in a way that ended in the reign of death. Jesus is the way that ends with His people living and reigning. Only through Him can we *receive abundance of grace*: "grace that is greater than all our sin," the favor of God by which our sins are forgiven and we receive as a *gift* the *righteousness* that we could never attain by our own efforts.

Only by wonderful grace can we become righteous and escape death, but there is more. Through Jesus we *shall reign in life*. What does that mean? It is not explained in our text. To begin with, we can rule our own lives with God's help. We can overcome our own selfish and sinful desires (1 Corinthians 9:27). We can successfully resist the devil (James 4:7). Thus we can reign over sin, which once reigned over us. But Paul says also that we shall judge the world, and even angels (1 Corinthians 6:2, 3). And in the final chapter of the Bible is the glorious promise that we "shall reign for ever and ever" (Revelation 22:5). The nature and extent of our rule are not described. But we shall serve God, and we shall see His face, and bear His name (Revelation 22:3, 4). Will not our will be so perfectly in tune with His will that the will of all of us will be done? It will be as if we were all kings together.

Guilt (and Grace) by Association

TV's Rob Petrie (played by Dick Van Dyke) bought a motorcycle against the better judgment of his wife, Laura, (played by Mary Tyler Moore). On his first major ride, he stopped at a hamburger stand and was soon joined by a whole gang of motorcycle riders, all wearing black leather jackets similar to Rob's. When he befriended these "hoods" by helping pay for their food, the gang reciprocated by naming Rob their "leader."

The plot really thickens when the police arrive to arrest the gang for riding through some farmer's tomato patch. They, of course, assume that Rob is one of the offenders. He is presumed guilty by association. Only by some fast explaining does Rob narrowly avoid arrest.

As members of Adam's family, we all are sinners (Romans 3:23), and the penalty for sin is death (Romans 6:23). We are guilty by association with Adam in that, like him, each of us has sinned against God. We, however, cannot talk our way out of the punishment we deserve. Since Jesus died in our place, though, we can have our guilt removed and we can be clothed with His righteousness. He provides vicarious virtue, *grace by association*, as it were. Thank God, His grace is greater than our guilt!

—R. W. B.

Conclusion

A. Summary

Verse 18, the one following our text, sums up what we have been reading. There is a similarity and there is a difference between the offense and the free gift: "Therefore, as by the offense of one judgment came upon all men to condemnation; even so by the righteousness of one the free gift came upon all men unto justification of life." The similarity is in the great significance of what one person did. The difference is in the result. The offense brought death; the free gift brought justification and life.

B. Free Gifts

Week after week the mail brings offers of free gifts. I can win a free car, a letter says, or a free trip to Disney World, or a million dollars. Just attach the enclosed sticker to the enclosed card and put it in the mail.

Such a glowing offer lands in the wastebasket. Why? It isn't because I wouldn't like to replace my 1982 car. It's not because I have a prejudice against Disney World. It's not because I wouldn't know what to do with a million dollars. But I think I see two reasons for ignoring the glowing offer.

First, I suspect the offer is phony. If I respond as directed, I will not get the free car. I will get, perhaps, one chance in a million of getting the car; and I may have to buy some merchandise or subscribe to a magazine to get that.

Second, even if I could get the free car I wouldn't want it. It seems to me the human impulse to get something for nothing is not a Christian impulse. "It is more blessed to give than to receive" (Acts 20:35). A Christian likes to give honest value for what he gets—and that seems like a good principle for any self-respecting person.

C. An Offer I Can't Refuse

God offers a free gift, justification and life. That's an offer I can't refuse. Oh, I *could*—many people do. But it wouldn't be reasonable to refuse. It seems to me there are two reasons:

First, the offer is genuine. God can and will deliver.

Second, much as I like to pay for what I get, I *can't* pay for this. I swallow my pride and accept life as a free gift, or I'm dead.

D. Prayer

When we see the limits of our ability, Father, it is good to know that Your ability has no limit. Thank You for the free gift of life that we can have in no other way. Through Jesus, who makes it possible, we pray. Amen.

E. Thought to Remember

Believe in Jesus. Your life depends on it.

Home Daily Bible Readings

Monday, Mar. 14—Justification by Faith (Romans 5:1-5)

Tuesday, Mar. 15—Christ Died for Us (Romans 5:6-10)

Wednesday, Mar. 16—Righteousness Brings Justification (Romans 5:11-16)

Thursday, Mar. 17—As Sin Increased, Grace Abounded More (Romans 5:17-21)

Friday, Mar. 18—God Redeemed My Soul, Offering Light (Job 33:23-28)

Saturday, Mar. 19—God Gives Sinners Life in Christ (Ephesians 2:1-6)

Sunday, Mar. 20—"The Word of God Is Not Bound" (2 Timothy 2:8-15)

Learning by Doing

This page contains an alternate lesson plan emphasizing learning activities. Classes desiring such student involvement will find these suggestions helpful.

Learning Goals

By the end of this session students will:

1. Relate truths from Romans 5 to phrases from Christian hymns.

2. Select concepts from Romans 5 for personal meditation during the Lord's Supper.

Into the Lesson

Before class write these two questions on the chalkboard:

1. What would be different if sin hadn't entered the world?

2. What would be different if Jesus hadn't entered the world?

Begin the session by leading the students in a discussion of the first question, then the second. Allow several minutes for discussion.

Into the Word

For this part of the lesson you will need to have on hand a hymnal for each class member's use. Paper and pens will be needed by the study groups to be formed.

Lead into the Bible study by having volunteers read Romans 5 aloud to the class, following these verse divisions: 1-5, 6-11, 12-14, 15-17, 18-21. Then divide the students into groups of four to six. As they are assembling, write the following three questions on the chalkboard:

According to Romans 5,

1. How do I know that God loves me?

2. Why do I need Jesus?

3. How do I know I have eternal life in Jesus?

Each group is to discuss the questions and be prepared to share their conclusions with the rest of the class. Appoint a leader for each group and encourage the leaders to have one of their group members take notes. Provide paper and pens for this. Allot twelve or fifteen minutes for the groups to discuss. After the time has expired, ask groups to share their insights with the rest of the class. If you have more than two groups, let each group share their answers for only one of the questions.

At this point distribute the hymnals. Encourage students to read some of the hymns to find thoughts that are similar to the truths expressed in Romans 5. Allow five or six minutes for students to browse. Then ask volunteers to share some of the hymns and phrases from the hymns they have found.

Option

After Romans 5 has been read aloud, lead the class in a discussion of the three questions above. Then have your class members read the words to Charles Wesley's hymn, "And Can It Be?" If the hymn is not in your church hymnal, make copies of the stanzas shown below and give each student a copy. If students know the hymn, you might want to have them sing it. After reading or singing the hymn, discuss this question: "What phrases in the hymn contain concepts found in Romans 5?" As students suggest answers, ask them for the specific verse in Romans 5 in which the concepts are found.

And Can It Be?
by Charles Wesley

And can it be that I should gain An interest in the Saviour's blood?

Died He for me, who caused His pain? For me, who Him to death pursued?

Amazing love! how can it be That Thou, my God, should die for me?

He left His Father's throne above, So free, so infinite His grace;

Emptied Himself of all but love, And bled for Adam's helpless race;

'Tis mercy all, immense and free; For, O my God, it found out me.

No condemnation now I dread; Jesus, and all in Him, is mine!

Alive in Him, my living Head, and clothed in righteousness divine,

Bold I approach th'eternal throne, And claim the crown, through Christ my own.

Into Life

Provide each student with a sheet of paper and a pen. Suggest that Romans 5 contains a wealth of information regarding Christ's sacrificial death for us. Ask students to identify three or four truths from the chapter that they would like to reflect upon the next time they partake of the Lord's Supper. They are to write these insights on the paper and add a personal comment about it.

For example, considering Romans 5:9, the student might write, "Because Jesus' death enables me to stand justified before God, I can live without fear of God's judgment."

Let's Talk It Over

The questions on this page are designed to encourage review of the lesson Scriptures and to promote discussion of the lesson by the class. The answers provided are only discussion starters. Let your class talk it over from there.

1. Paul said, "When we were yet without strength, in due time Christ died for the ungodly" (Romans 5:6). What lack of strength did Paul refer to, and why must each of us admit that we have that lack?

Paul was speaking of mankind's moral and spiritual weakness. Each of us has sinned against God, and we are unable to rid ourselves of our sin and guilt. Only the atoning sacrifice of Christ can do that. His sacrifice becomes effective for us when we acknowledge our lack of strength and trust His blood to cleanse us. In our evangelistic efforts we must make people aware that they also are without strength and are totally dependent on God's grace to save them. After we are saved, we must remain continually aware of our need for the strength Christ provides if we are to serve Him effectively. Jesus made this clear when He said, "Without me ye can do nothing" (John 15:5).

2. Many people have sacrificed their lives on behalf of others. How is Jesus Christ's sacrificial death unique.

First, only Jesus could offer a perfect sacrifice, because He is the sinless Son of God. As Paul points out in Romans 5, while other people have given their lives for righteous and good fellow human beings, Jesus died for sinners. Second, in dying for one's fellowmen the most one can do is preserve their physical existence, whereas Jesus died to provide eternal salvation. Furthermore, people who sacrifice their lives for others often do so without thinking. A person who tries to rescue another from a burning building or from drowning may die a heroic death, but his spur-of-the-moment action differs from Jesus' planned, deliberate act of going to the cross for us (see John 10:17, 18; Acts 2:23).

3. How can we help people understand that if they are not Christians, they are enemies of God?

First, of course, we must find out if they believe that God exists and that He created mankind. If they do, then we may point out that God as Creator surely has the right to determine how we should live. Since at times we have chosen to live as we pleased, we have in that way opposed our Creator's will and made ourselves

His enemies. Furthermore, so long as we reject His Son we make ourselves that much more the enemies of God: "He that believeth not the Son shall not see life; but the wrath of God abideth on him" (John 3:36). We must emphasize that the barrier between us and God is of our making, not His. We have violated His laws, but He is ready to break down the barrier by offering us grace, mercy, and peace with Him through His Son Jesus Christ.

4. When we observe in Romans 5 the disastrous results of Adam's sin, we may be inclined to blame him for many of our human woes. What may be said of this reaction?

Like Adam in the Garden of Eden we also have faced situations in which there was a clear choice between right and wrong, and we have chosen the wrong. So we must ask ourselves this question: If we, instead of Adam, had been in the Garden of Eden, would we have done any differently. To be excessively critical of Adam is unwise because it is one form of the convenient device of blaming all our faults on something or someone else. The proper reaction to our sins is to acknowledge our personal responsibility for them. Romans 5 demonstrates the pointlessness of blaming Adam, since Jesus Christ has made atonement for the sins we have personally committed.

5. Since salvation is a free gift, why are many people so reluctant to accept it?

Many do not realize it is free. They view the church and its message as too restrictive and negative. While we must speak out against sin and call for holiness, we must not neglect proclaiming the positive invitation found in Revelation 22:17: "The Spirit and the bride say, Come. And let him that heareth say, Come. And let him that is athirst come. And whosoever will, let him take the water of life freely." People also fail to accept the free gift of salvation because they think they do not need it. They are preoccupied with the goals, duties, and pleasures of this present life and allow themselves no time to think of their eternal needs. Let us pray that they will be awakened to the Holy Spirit's promptings regarding sin, righteousness, and judgment (John 16:8).

Deliverance From Sin

DEVOTIONAL READING: Colossians 3:1-15.

LESSON SCRIPTURE: Romans 6.

PRINTED TEXT: Romans 6:3-14, 20-23.

Romans 6:3-14, 20-23

3 Know ye not, that so many of us as were baptized into Jesus Christ were baptized into his death?

4 Therefore we are buried with him by baptism into death: that like as Christ was raised up from the dead by the glory of the Father, even so we also should walk in newness of life.

5 For if we have been planted together in the likeness of his death, we shall be also in the likeness of his resurrection:

6 Knowing this, that our old man is crucified with him, that the body of sin might be destroyed, that henceforth we should not serve sin.

7 For he that is dead is freed from sin.

8 Now if we be dead with Christ, we believe that we shall also live with him:

9 Knowing that Christ being raised from the dead dieth no more; death hath no more dominion over him.

10 For in that he died, he died unto sin once: but in that he liveth, he liveth unto God.

11 Likewise reckon ye also yourselves to be dead indeed unto sin, but alive unto God through Jesus Christ our Lord.

12 Let not sin therefore reign in your mortal body, that ye should obey it in the lusts thereof.

13 Neither yield ye your members as instruments of unrighteousness unto sin: but yield yourselves unto God, as those that are alive from the dead, and your members as instruments of righteousness unto God.

14 For sin shall not have dominion over you: for ye are not under the law, but under grace.

. . . .

20 For when ye were the servants of sin, ye were free from righteousness.

21 What fruit had ye then in those things whereof ye are now ashamed? for the end of those things is death.

22 But now being made free from sin, and become servants to God, ye have your fruit unto holiness, and the end everlasting life.

23 For the wages of sin is death; but the gift of God is eternal life through Jesus Christ our Lord.

GOLDEN TEXT: For the wages of sin is death; but the gift of God is eternal life through Jesus Christ our Lord.—Romans 6:23.

Good News for God's People
Romans—Unit 1: Righteous Through Faith (Lessons 1-4)

Lesson Aims

After this lesson a student should be able to:
1. Tell in ordinary English what it means to die to sin and rise to walk in newness of life.
2. Specify two or three sins that even Christians sometimes commit.
3. Examine his or her own way of living and make one improvement.

Lesson Outline

INTRODUCTION
  A. Pie in the Sky?
  B. Lesson Background
I. DYING AND LIVING (Romans 6:3-11)
  A. Baptized Into Death (v. 3)
  B. Purpose (v. 4)
    Watery Grave
  C. Explanation (vv. 5-11)
    Greatest Escape
II. A NEW WAY OF LIVING (Romans 6:12-14)
  A. Without Sin (vv. 12, 13a)
  B. With Righteousness (v. 13b)
  C. Explanation (v. 14)
III. RESULTS (Romans 6:20-23)
  A. Sin Brings Death (vv. 20, 21)
  B. Holiness Brings Life (v. 22)
  C. Summary (v. 23)
CONCLUSION
  A. A Look at Ourselves
  B. Prayer
  C. Thought to Remember

Display visual 4 of the visuals packet to picture the Christian's state. The visual is shown on page 261.

Introduction

A. Pie in the Sky?

Skeptics like to ridicule Christianity because, they say, it offers "pie in the sky by and by" rather than pleasure and profit here and now. It is misleading to describe the joy of Heaven by such a trivial term, but it is true that the greatest benefit of Christianity is beyond this life. That has been prominent in several lessons, but this lesson focuses attention on the difference Christianity makes here and now. Christians are "dead indeed unto sin, but alive unto God."

B. Lesson Background

Last week we were thinking about the contrast between the followers of Adam and the followers of Christ. After Adam's sin brought death, everybody died because everybody sinned. But Christ died to atone for the sins of everybody, and since then His people are saved by grace. The closing part of Romans 5 adds that with the coming of the law sin was seen to be even more abundant; but when sin was abundant, saving grace was more abundant still.

That thought might lead someone to ask the question that begins Romans 6. If grace is more abundant when sin is abundant, shall we keep on sinning so God's saving grace will grow more and more? That idea might appeal to one who finds sin pleasant, but Paul rejects it with abhorrence: "God forbid." To explain why continued sin is so abhorrent, Paul begins with a query: "We died to sin; how can we live in it any longer?" (*New International Version*). That introduces our text, which brings more discussion of our death to sin.

I. Dying and Living (Romans 6:3-11)

Most of us have learned that death means separation. One who has died no longer walks beside us. We do not see his face nor hear his voice. He does not greet us with a handshake or a hug. We no longer laugh at his joking or grieve with his distress. We say he lives in memory, and that is true; but beyond that we no longer have anything to do with him. We are cut off completely.

That is what it means to die to sin. We are through with it, finished. We have nothing to do with it anymore.

A. Baptized Into Death (v. 3)

3. Know ye not, that so many of us as were baptized into Jesus Christ were baptized into his death?

We are *baptized into Jesus Christ*, and to be in Him is a very great thing. We put Him on as a garment (Galatians 3:27): we are clothed in His nature and character and likeness, and so we are one with all who are in Him (Galatians 3:28). We are members of His body, the church, through which much of His work is done (Romans 12:4-8). In Christ we have "all spiritual blessings" (Ephesians 1:3). In Christ we triumph (2 Corinthians 2:14). The dead in Christ will rise to meet Him at His coming (1 Thessalonians 4:16).

However, the point of our text is this: In being baptized into Christ we are baptized into His death, for our whole association with Him depends on His death. His death atoned for our sins so we are justified by God's grace "through the redemption that is in Christ Jesus" (Romans 3:24). This makes it possible to be in Christ and have all the blessings mentioned above.

B. Purpose (v. 4)

4. Therefore we are buried with him by baptism into death: that like as Christ was raised up from the dead by the glory of the Father, even so we also should walk in newness of life.

We are baptized into Christ's death (v. 3), and into our own. This is how we become dead to sin (v. 2). We are separated from it completely and permanently. We have nothing to do with it anymore. The purpose of this death is to bring us to a resurrection. *Christ was raised up from the dead by the glory,* the authority and power, *of the Father;* by that same power we are raised up from our death. Dead to sin, we are raised as new creatures to live a new kind of life.

WATERY GRAVE

My young friend at church camp was mentally immature. "Slow," some people called him. David's mind had not developed as rapidly or as fully as his body; his intellectual growth was perhaps two or three years retarded.

But David believed in Jesus, and he wanted to obey Him and be forgiven of his sins. After he made that known to me we talked about what was involved in becoming a Christian.

In our discussion, I explained at length the spiritual symbolism of immersion: the death, burial, and resurrection. David seemed to grasp those concepts, and was eager to fulfill all of the requirements of his commitment. After phoning his mother for her consent, and making the arrangements, I had the privilege that evening of baptizing this young believer.

It was not until a subsequent conversation with David that I understood the strength and courage of his decision. His literal interpretation of my teaching was that he would physically die in the act of baptism, then come back to life. Yet he was eager to be buried with Christ! "Slow" David could teach many of us something about submission and sacrifice!   —R. W. B.

C. Explanation (vv. 5-11)

5. For if we have been planted together in the likeness of his death, we shall be also in the likeness of his resurrection.

Verse 4 presents baptism as death and resurrection; now *planted together* suggests another figure of speech. Baptism is the planting from which a new kind of life grows. Paul may have

had that figure in mind, but it seems more probable that he did not. The Greek word translated *planted together* has a much wider meaning, being used of any close union. Most English versions translate it in other ways. The *American Standard Version,* for example, says, "For if we have become united with him in the likeness of his death." This verse emphasizes the thought of death and resurrection that was begun in verse 4, with special emphasis on the fact that we are united with Christ in both death and resurrection.

We can hardly read these verses without thinking of the glorious assurance that we shall be raised from literal physical death because we are in Christ. That is suggested by the future tense of the verb: *We shall be also in the likeness of his resurrection.* The main thought of our text, however, seems to be that we are raised from our baptismal death to a new kind of life here on earth. Jesus' life after His resurrection was quite different from His life before He died; since we have been baptized into Christ, we are in a life different from our former life. The main difference is that sin no longer rules us. This is clear in the following verses.

6. Knowing this, that our old man is crucified with him, that the body of sin might be destroyed, that henceforth we should not serve sin.

The Christian raised from the water of baptism is a new creature (2 Corinthians 5:17), a different person. The person he was before baptism now is called the *old man,* the man who died and no longer exists. He was *crucified,* he died painfully, but he is gone. That person who died is called also *the body of sin,* the body that belonged to sin. It was sin's slave, doing what sin required. But that sinful body has been *destroyed,* and now we are new people free from bondage to sin.

7. For he that is dead is freed from sin.

A slave who dies is no longer a slave. There is no way for the master to hold him in bondage. When we die to sin (v. 2), we are free from its bondage.

GREATEST ESCAPE

Human nature makes us great escape artists. We watch TV, read books, or go to movies, often to escape the pressures of work, of personal conflicts, or of emotional fatigue. Vacation cruises or weekend getaways are promoted as "great escapes." And such escapes can indeed be therapeutic.

Sometimes escapist behavior is involuntary, such as when an auto accident victim "blacks out" a split second before impact. A mysterious mechanism of the brain transmits an SOS of sorts: "We can't bear the trauma of what is happening, so we will simply take leave of consciousness."

Mankind's greatest need is to escape the clutches of sin. That is not accomplished by temporary distractions or involuntary action. It occurs through death, the voluntary crucifying of our old self with Christ. "For he that is dead is freed from sin." God's grace, Christ's crucifixion, and one's own will combine to execute spiritual deliverance from sin. It is the greatest escape of all. "And how shall we escape, if we neglect so great salvation?" (Hebrews 2:3).   —R. W. B.

8. Now if we be dead with Christ, we believe that we shall also live with him.

The old man is dead (v. 6), but we live on as new creatures. The power of God raised Jesus from the dead, and the same power raises us to live a new life free from sin. That is the assurance we have seen in verses 2-5.

9. Knowing that Christ being raised from the dead dieth no more; death hath no more dominion over him.

Christ was not overpowered by death, but He accepted its *dominion* willingly: He laid down His life (John 10:18). By that sacrifice He redeemed us. But that sacrifice was made once for all (Hebrews 10:10). Since He rose from the dead, death can never claim Him again. This turns our minds again to the thought of resurrection from physical death to eternal life in glory. This will be ours as well as Christ's. But in our joy at that grand thought we should not lose sight of the more immediate matter of a new kind of life here and now.

10. For in that he died, he died unto sin once: but in that he liveth, he liveth unto God.

Having no sin of His own, Jesus died for the sins of others *once*. That once was enough. It paid for all the sins of the world (1 John 2:2). Sin can never again bring Him to death—not even all the sin of the world. *He died unto sin:* He is separated from it forever. Though dead to sin, Jesus *liveth unto God*, and that forever. Never will He be separated from His Father in Heaven.

11. Likewise reckon ye also yourselves to be dead indeed unto sin, but alive unto God through Jesus Christ our Lord.

We must constantly think of ourselves as *dead indeed unto sin*. We must keep ourselves separated from it as completely as Jesus is. We must have nothing to do with it. But in relation to God we are very much *alive*, as Jesus is. We have our new life *through Jesus Christ our Lord*. We owe our life to Him, and so we are obligated to use it for Him. The next part of our text gives instructions for doing this.

II. A New Way of Living
(Romans 6:12-14)

We have died to sin, but we live in a world where sin is all around us and eager to rule the new man as it ruled the old man who died. To avoid its clutches we must use our own effort as well as God's help. By God's help and our own effort, we can maintain a new way of living.

A. Without Sin (vv. 12, 13a)

12. Let not sin therefore reign in your mortal body, that ye should obey it in the lusts thereof.

Back in the morning of human history, sin was pictured as a fierce beast crouching at the door, ready to pounce on the unwary (Genesis 4:7). Cain should have subdued that beast and ruled it, and so should we. Though the new man is forgiven and cleansed and dedicated to the Lord, the *mortal body* still has appetites and desires. It craves food and drink and comfort and sexual satisfaction, and the mortal body itself doesn't care how those things are gotten. The body must be controlled by a godly mind to be sure its desires are satisfied only in proper ways. Otherwise *the lusts* of the body will lead it to obey sin as the old man did. The body continues its craving for the same things, but it is better to do without them than to let sin rule again.

13a. Neither yield ye your members as instruments of unrighteousness unto sin.

Your members—hands and feet and tongues and brains—are *instruments* or tools that can be used in many ways. How they are used depends on who is in control of them. If you turn them over *unto sin*, you can be sure they will be used in *unrighteousness*. Don't let that happen!

B. With Righteousness (v. 13b)

13b. But yield yourselves unto God, as those that are alive from the dead, and your members as instruments of righteousness unto God.

Instead of letting sin take control of you again, turn yourselves over to *God*. He is the proper one to control those who have died to sin and now *are alive from the dead* and walking in newness of life (vv. 1-4). If you put God in control of *your members*, your hands and feet and tongues and brains, you can be sure they will be used as *instruments* or tools *of righteousness*.

C. Explanation (v. 14)

14. For sin shall not have dominion over you: for ye are not under the law, but under grace.

As Christians, we have died to sin and now are living new lives as God's people. But from experience as well as Scripture, we learn that sin is still around and eager to capture and enslave us again. And sometimes, through ignorance or carelessness or the demands of our physical bodies, we do something wrong. As people dead to sin and alive to God (v. 11), we do not want to do any such thing; but sometimes we do. This is discussed in the next chapter of Romans: "What I would, that do I not; but what I hate, that do I." Why? Not because of me, as a person dead to sin; but because of sin that is not dead to me (Romans 7:15-23). Still Paul insists, *Sin shall not have dominion over you.* The law demanded punishment for "every transgression and disobedience" (Hebrews 2:2); but *ye are not under the law, but under grace.* By God's grace, our faith is reckoned for righteousness, as we saw in our lesson two weeks ago. If we really believe in God and not in our wrongdoing, occasional sins can be forgiven (1 John 1:9). So we can still be free from sin's dominion.

III. Results
(Romans 6:20-23)

Verses 15-19 are not included in our text, but we need to note the main thought of them. Paul asks a question similar to the one that begins chapter 6 (vv. 1, 15). Since we are under grace and sin can be forgiven, why should we avoid sin? If we find it profitable or pleasant, why not sin freely and depend on God's grace to rescue us from the consequences? In verse 15 Paul rejects that thought as vigorously as he did in verse 2: "God forbid." In verse 2 he said we have died to sin and therefore we cannot continue to live in it. In verse 16 he takes a practical and pragmatic approach. Regardless of what you say, you actually are servants of the one you obey. If you choose to obey sin, that leads to death. If you choose to obey God, that leads to righteousness and life. The last part of our text says more about the results of our choice.

A. Sin Brings Death (vv. 20, 21)

20. For when ye were the servants of sin, ye were free from righteousness.

Before we became Christians we were willing slaves of sin. We made no effort to obey the right. This was more obvious in ancient Rome than it is in our town today. Our society has been so influenced by Christian principles that many non-Christians abhor lying and stealing and adultery, while they applaud purity and unselfishness and helpfulness. But the pagan Romans had no objection to selfishness and sensuality, deceit and adultery. They imagined that such things were commonly practiced by

visual 4

gods as well as human beings. And we must recognize that some of our pagan neighbors are becoming more like the pagan Romans—slaves of sin and unconcerned about the right.

21. What fruit had ye then in those things whereof ye are now ashamed? for the end of those things is death.

The Romans who died to sin rose to a new and different life, as did we who are Christians now. They had higher moral and ethical standards, as we have. They were ashamed of many things done in the past, as we are. Those things were wrong. They displeased the God we now serve. The memory of them brings us shame and grief.

But Paul's question had to do with results. *What fruit had ye then in those things?* What did you get out of them? Did you get some pleasure, some profit, some admiration from other sinners? Perhaps you did; but Paul bypasses all these and goes straight to the final result: *the end of those things is death.*

B. Holiness Brings Life (v. 22)

22. But now being made free from sin, and become servants to God, ye have your fruit unto holiness, and the end everlasting life.

We Christians have left the way of death. We have died to sin (v. 2), and therefore we are *free* from it (v. 7). We have a new Master: we have *become servants to God.* So now what results can we expect? Paul mentions two. The first is *holiness.* To be holy is to be set apart, dedicated. Since we are dedicated to God's service, to be holy is also to be righteous, good, godly. That leads on to the final result, *the end.* The end is life that has no end.

C. Summary (v. 23)

23. For the wages of sin is death; but the gift of God is eternal life through Jesus Christ our Lord.

Death is *wages.* It is what we earn when we choose to serve sin. Sin is cruel and deceptive. It hides the final payoff under a froth of pleasure and profit and prestige. But in one way it is dependable. It pays off in the end. Wholehearted servants of sin can expect to get their wages—*death!*

Life is *the gift of God.* Nobody earns it. But God does not give it to everybody. Those who choose to serve sin must accept sin's wages, even if they happen to do right sometimes. Those who choose to serve God can expect His gift, even if they happen to do wrong sometimes. How can they escape the wages of their wrong? There is only one way: *through Jesus Christ our Lord.*

Conclusion

"How shall we, that are dead to sin, live any longer therein?" God's Word calls us to "lay aside every weight, and the sin which doth so easily beset us" (Hebrews 12:1). The text of our lesson speaks of sin in general rather than specific sins. Perhaps it will be helpful to think a little about some sins we know; and not sins of the pagan world, but those that "easily beset" Christians.

A. A Look at Ourselves

Though we are not under the law, we recognize the Ten Commandments as a good outline of moral living. Let's look at them first (Exodus 20:3-17). Of course we do not bow down to graven images, but do we *always* put God first in our lives? Do we ever take God's name in vain, either profanely or frivolously? Have we grown-up people become careless about honoring our fathers and mothers? Probably no one among us has ever killed anybody, but we Christians know "whosoever hateth his brother is a murderer" (1 John 3:15). Are we so innocent after

---

Home Daily Bible Readings

Monday, Mar. 21—Walk in the Newness of Life (Romans 6:1-5)

Tuesday, Mar. 22—Freedom From Moral Enslavement (Romans 6:6-11)

Wednesday, Mar. 23—Let Not Sin Reign (Romans 6:12-16)

Thursday, Mar. 24—Set Free From Immorality (Romans 6:17-21)

Friday, Mar. 25—Wages of Sin Versus Eternal Life (Romans 6:22, 23; 7:1-4)

Saturday, Mar. 26—Glorify God With Your Body (1 Corinthians 6:13-20)

Sunday, Mar. 27—Fruit of the Spirit (Galatians 5:16-25)

---

all? Christians do not commit adultery in the gross physical sense, but Jesus extended that Commandment beyond such a sense (Matthew 5:27, 28; Mark 10:11, 12). Are we all as pure as we like to think? Do we steal? Of course not! We wouldn't even go home with a pencil from the office; and if a clerk hands us too much change, we hand back the surplus. Or do we? And false witness? No Christian would stretch the truth to escape a reprimand from the boss, or even to save a little on his income tax. Would he? Then there's the Tenth Commandment: "Thou shalt not covet." Don't bear false witness now: Do you ever feel a twinge of envy because someone else has something you can't afford?

Of course the Ten Commandments don't define all the sins we avoid. Let the self-examination continue.

Hebrews 10:25 says something about "not forsaking the assembling of ourselves together, as the manner of some is." What percentage of our membership is in our assembly this week?

When God made laws for His people, He required a tenth of their income for His service (Leviticus 27:30-32). That was only a start; He required many offerings besides. Can we imagine that we owe less to God because we are not under law, but under grace? How many in our congregation consistently give more than a tenth of their incomes? Will a man rob God? (Malachi 3:8).

"Love your enemies, bless them that curse you, do good to them that hate you" (Matthew 5:44). Have you done good to an enemy lately? Of course you would never think of yourself more highly than you ought to think (Romans 12:3), but don't you know somebody who does think of himself that way?

Check your love by 1 Corinthians 13, your devotion to Christ by Colossians 3:17. Check your death to sin by Colossians 3:5-10. Check your newness of life by Colossians 3:12-15.

Don't stop now. Go on and search every nook and cranny of your way of living. Then pick at least one improvement to be made this week.

B. Prayer

How good it is to be under grace and not under law! In Your great mercy, Father, forgive the sins we have confessed to You. Help us to search out those secret sins we do not see as yet, and help us to die to them as well as to the sins we have found. This we ask in the name of Jesus Christ our Lord.

C. Thought to Remember

"Sin shall not have dominion over you" (Romans 6:14).

Learning by Doing

This page contains an alternate lesson plan emphasizing learning activities. Classes desiring such student involvement will find these suggestions helpful.

Learning Goals

In this lesson you will seek to lead your class members to:

1. Reconstruct Paul's arguments in Romans 6 concerning why we are to have nothing to do with sin and are to live in obedience to God.

2. Create a plan that will help them obey God in their daily lives.

Into the Lesson

Begin class by saying, "Being a Christian means, among other things, that we want to have nothing to do with sin. Sometimes, however, through our carelessness or the demands of our physical bodies, we do wrong. Then we may attempt to justify our sin. Let's brainstorm this question together: *What are some excuses that Christians sometimes make to justify their sin?* Name as many excuses as you can think of."

As students mention excuses, write them on the chalkboard. Allow two or three minutes for this. Then lead into the Bible study by saying, "In Romans 6 the apostle Paul deals with the subjects of sin and obedience to God. Let's see how seriously Paul views them."

Into the Word

Have several volunteers read Romans 6 aloud to the class, using these verse divisions: 1-4, 5-11, 12-14, 15-19, 20-23. Then have the class form groups of six.

Inform the groups that they are to prepare an imaginary interview with the apostle Paul regarding his views on sin and obedience. Give each group a copy of the interviewer's questions below to form the direction of the interview. Students are to use Romans 6 as the basis for what they imagine Paul's response might have been to each question.

Appoint a leader for each group and provide Bibles, paper, and pens for the groups' use. Have each group select two of its members to conduct the interview for the rest of the class, one to read the interviewer's questions and the other to read the group's responses. Allow twenty minutes for the groups to formulate their answers to the questions.

Here are the questions:

Interviewer: Paul, it has been reported that you think a Christian should not take sin lightly. Why is that?

Paul:

Interviewer: So you are convinced that the Christian's only legitimate response to God's grace is to live in obedience to Him. It seems to me that sin is so much a part of life that it is natural for most Christians to continue to sin. How can a Christian make obedience to God a habit?

Paul:

Interviewer: You indicated earlier in Romans that we have forgiveness of sins by God's grace through the redemption that is in Christ Jesus (3:24). Don't you think God's grace gives Christians the freedom to stop worrying about sin?

Paul:

Interviewer: Paul, suppose a Christian were to say to you: "Aw, come on—sin can't hurt that much. I don't need to be concerned about my sin. Why, that might lead to some kind of unhealthy obsession." How would you convince that person that letting sin go unchecked might have serious consequences?

Paul:

Option

Have students break into groups of four. Allow twenty minutes for them to read Romans 6 and discuss these three questions:

1. Based on Romans 6, why should I live in obedience to God rather than live in sin?

2. Based on Romans 6, how can I live in obedience to God?

3. Based on Romans 6, what takes place in baptism? How should that affect our attitude toward sin?

When time is up, discuss as a class.

Into Life

Have students remain in their small groups to discuss the questions below:

1. How can I keep focused on my death to sin and my new life in Christ? (Colossians 3:1-4; Galatians 2:20).

2. How should I deal with sin in my life when I become aware of it? (1 John 1:9; James 4:7-10).

Allow about twelve minutes for discussion. Then give each student an index card. Have students work individually to write a plan that will help them to live obediently before God each day. Encourage them to jot down ideas that are as specific and practical as possible. Allow a few minutes for this, then close with prayer.

Let's Talk It Over

The questions on this page are designed to encourage review of the lesson Scriptures and to promote discussion of the lesson by the class. The answers provided are only discussion starters. Let your class talk it over from there.

1. This writer has seen a bumper sticker bearing the question, "How much sin can I get away with and still go to Heaven?" What is wrong with this viewpoint?

The bumper sticker reflects the world's popular idea that people can make it to Heaven if their good works outweigh their evil deeds. There is no acknowledgment here of the grace of God or of the need of Jesus Christ as Savior. However, in another way the bumper sticker's message may accurately portray the thinking of even some Christians. Since we are saved by grace, so the reasoning goes, we ought to be able to "get away with" some sin. In Romans 6 Paul combats this type of reasoning. Instead of wanting to get away with sin, we should be so appreciative of God's grace and Jesus Christ's death on our behalf that we will want to be done with sin in all its forms.

2. How can we keep in our minds the fact that we are dead to sin, but alive to God?

An excellent way is by memorizing Scripture. Besides our text, a fitting passage for this purpose is Colossians 3:1-17. If we have difficulty memorizing, we can still gain tremendous benefit by reading such passages and praying that God will help us put into practice the principles they contain. Another help is found in our Christian fellowship. Hebrew 3:13 reminds us to "exhort one another daily, while it is called Today; lest any of you be hardened through the deceitfulness of sin." As we share our views on current events, let us take the opportunity to remind one another that we are dead to sin. Another source of help is the vast array of Christian books available that deal with holiness of life, overcoming temptation, living a victorious life of service for Christ, and the like.

3. It is quite a challenge to "yield . . . your members as instruments of righteousness unto God." What is involved in doing this?

Frances R. Havergal's hymn, "Take My Life, and Let It Be," is something of a commentary on this portion of Scripture. She specifies hands, feet, voice, and lips as instruments to be consecrated to the Lord. It is an excellent exercise to consider our hands and make a list of how many good things they can do for the glory of God. We could list distributing Christian literature in our community, preparing a meal for a family in need, or writing a note of encouragement to someone who is depressed. We could make such a list regarding our feet, our lips, our ears, etc. With such general lists in mind we could begin each day with a specific plan as to how to employ hands, feet, lips, and other physical faculties in service to God and to our fellow beings.

4. What comparisons and contrasts may be drawn between the payment of wages for earthly labor and the payment of the wages of sin?

We frequently speak of "an honest day's work for an honest day's pay." A worker who conscientiously fulfills the responsibilities given him by his employer rightfully expects to be paid for his labor. The Bible states that the wages of sin is death. Should not one expect to receive sin's wages who devotes himself or herself to sin in this life? Also, in the workaday world we occasionally hear of one who declines to accept wages for a job completed, but in the spiritual realm one who keeps on sinning will be unable to refuse the terrible wages sin pays. Further, a laborer may not receive due wages immediately, but must wait for a time. The wages of sin may likewise be long in coming, but such wages will surely at last be paid.

5. How would we go about instituting a program of personal spiritual improvement?

Such a program should begin in prayer, in which we seek God's guidance. We would then naturally turn to God's Word to search out His will for our lives. An inventory of our attitudes and habits would then reveal where improvement is needed. It might be helpful to ask a minister, elder, teacher, or other mature Christian the question that the rich young ruler asked Jesus: "What lack I yet?" (Matthew 19:20). An answer to the same question might be gained through participation in a small Bible study group. Perhaps we would feel it necessary to curtail friendships or change jobs or avoid certain amusements that could hinder our attempts at improvement. Some means of keeping track of our progress would be important also. A personal journal could serve that purpose.

A Glimpse of Glory

DEVOTIONAL READING: Luke 24:1-10.

LESSON SCRIPTURE: Mark 16:1-8; Romans 8:12-27.

PRINTED TEXT: Mark 16:1-8; Romans 8:12-17.

Mark 16:1-8

1 And when the sabbath was past, Mary Magdalene, and Mary the mother of James, and Salome, had bought sweet spices, that they might come and anoint him.

2 And very early in the morning, the first day of the week, they came unto the sepulchre at the rising of the sun.

3 And they said among themselves, Who shall roll us away the stone from the door of the sepulchre?

4 And when they looked, they saw that the stone was rolled away: for it was very great.

5 And entering into the sepulchre, they saw a young man sitting on the right side, clothed in a long white garment; and they were affrighted.

6 And he saith unto them, Be not affrighted: ye seek Jesus of Nazareth, which was crucified: he is risen; he is not here: behold the place where they laid him.

7 But go your way, tell his disciples and Peter that he goeth before you into Galilee: there shall ye see him, as he said unto you.

8 And they went out quickly, and fled from the sepulchre; for they trembled and were amazed: neither said they any thing to any man; for they were afraid.

Romans 8:12-17

12 Therefore, brethren, we are debtors, not to the flesh, to live after the flesh.

13 For if ye live after the flesh, ye shall die: but if ye through the Spirit do mortify the deeds of the body, ye shall live.

14 For as many as are led by the Spirit of God, they are the sons of God.

15 For ye have not received the spirit of bondage again to fear; but ye have received the Spirit of adoption, whereby we cry, Abba, Father.

16 The Spirit itself beareth witness with our spirit, that we are the children of God:

17 And if children, then heirs; heirs of God, and joint-heirs with Christ, if so be that we suffer with him, that we may be also glorified together.

GOLDEN TEXT: We are . . . heirs of God, and joint-heirs with Christ, if so be that we suffer with him, that we may be also glorified together.—Romans 8:16, 17.

Good News for God's People
Romans—Unit 2: Empowered by the
Spirit (Lessons 5-8)

Lesson Aims

After this lesson a student should be able to:
1. Glimpse and briefly describe the glory of Jesus and the glory of His people.
2. Realize that our own glory waits for our own service and our own sacrifice.
3. Make some sacrifice this week.

Lesson Outline

INTRODUCTION
    A. Return to Life
    B. Lesson Background
I. GLIMPSE OF CHRIST'S GLORY (Mark 16:1-8)
    A. Sad Mission (vv. 1-4)
    B. Glad Tidings (vv. 5-8)
    Laughing at Death
II. GLIMPSE OF OUR GLORY (Romans 8:12-17)
    A. Death and Life (vv. 12, 13)
    B. Sons of God (vv. 14-16)
    C. Heirs of God (v. 17)
    Heirs to a Fortune
CONCLUSION
    A. If
    B. Prayer
    C. Thought to Remember

Visual 5 of the visuals packet asks a penetrating question in light of Christ's sacrifice for us. The visual is shown on page 269.

Introduction

In the springtime hearts beat faster as we see new signs of life in field and forest and our own backyards. New leaves and bright flowers give a lift to winter-weary spirits. When our hearts are glad in springtime, it is fitting to be gladdened also by the thought of life beyond the grave—of Jesus' resurrection and ours.

Christ is risen! Of course the thought is with us always. The fact is the cornerstone to faith's foundation. Our day of meeting is the first day of every week, the day Jesus arose.

Still, it is fitting in the springtime to hold a special celebration. This not only is the time when new life is bursting out around us; it is also the time of year when Jesus died and rose. Indeed the Lord is risen, and let us all be glad.

A. Return to Life

Last week our lesson turned our minds to Jesus' resurrection. As He died and rose again, we also die to sin and rise again to life and purity. This week we interrupt our work in Romans to look briefly at the first announcement of our Lord's return to life. To that brief look we add another look at Romans and our own new life.

B. Lesson Background

It was springtime when our Savior rode in triumph to Jerusalem, while multitudes were hailing Him as king (Mark 11:7-10). The rulers had said the man would be arrested (John 11:57), but when He came they dared not touch Him. They were afraid the happy crowd would start a riot if their hero were arrested (Mark 14:2). So Jesus taught among them day by day (Luke 21:37, 38).

But then the rulers bribed a man of His own company to help them find Him when no crowd was present (Mark 14:10, 11). And so our Lord was taken in Gethsemane (Mark 14:43-50). A swift pretense of trial followed (Mark 14:53-65). The governor gave in to pressure and condemned a man unjustly (Mark 15:1-15). So the Lord was crucified and buried (Mark 15:21-47). The funeral was quick because the Preparation Day was ending, and the Sabbath was about to begin (Luke 23:54).

A group of faithful women had followed Jesus from Galilee to Jerusalem. Now they followed His body to the tomb. Then they quickly prepared materials to anoint that body later (Luke 23:55, 56).

Sunset brought the end of Preparation Day and the beginning of the Sabbath. Normally that was a happy day. Now the rulers had succeeded in crucifying Jesus, and perhaps this was the most gleeful Sabbath of their lives. They ignored the no-work rule to go to the governor and get the tomb of Jesus sealed and guarded (Matthew 27:62-66). That done, they could enjoy their triumph on the day of rest.

The followers of Jesus also rested "according to the commandment" (Luke 23:56). To them it certainly was the saddest Sabbath of their lives. Our text takes up the story on the next day.

I. Glimpse of Christ's Glory (Mark 16:1-8)

The Jewish rulers were not unanimous in their condemnation of Jesus. There were at least two dissenters among them, and those two obtained the crucified body of Jesus and placed it in a costly tomb. They wrapped the body in linen with a hundred pounds of myrrh and aloes

How to Say It

GETHSEMANE. Geth-*sem*-uh-nee.
MAGDALENE. *Mag*-duh-leen or Mag-duh-*lee*-nee.
SALOME. Suh-*lo*-me.

(John 19:38-42). That might seem to be spices enough, but the devoted women from Galilee wanted to add their own contribution.

A. Sad Mission (vv. 1-4)

1. And when the sabbath was past, Mary Magdalene, and Mary the mother of James, and Salome, had bought sweet spices, that they might come and anoint him.

These ladies were ready to get an early start, for they had prepared their *spices* in the closing moments of Preparation Day before the Sabbath began (Luke 23:56).

Mark names three of these devoted ladies. There may have been others in the group (Luke 24:10).

2. And very early in the morning, the first day of the week, they came unto the sepulchre at the rising of the sun.

John 20:1 says Mary Magdalene came "while it was yet dark." Probably that was when she started, but the ladies arrived about sunrise. We are not told how far they had to go. Besides, an earthquake may have delayed them on the way (Matthew 28:2) There was great excitement with the earthquake before they arrived. The tomb was opened by an angel so brilliant that no soldier drew a sword against him. Instead, the guardsmen dropped like dead men (Matthew 28:2-4). Probably they recovered strength and courage enough to take to their heels before the women got there.

3. And they said among themselves, Who shall roll us away the stone from the door of the sepulchre?

Apparently the tomb was like some that still are seen in Palestine. There was a large outcrop of limestone in a hillside. The face of the stone was cut straight up and down like a wall, and then a chamber was chiseled into the rock. A big stone was cut in the shape of a wheel. It rolled back and forth in a groove to close and open the doorway.

The women, or some of them, had been there to watch when the body of Jesus was laid away and the door was closed. Then they had hurried away to get their spices before the beginning of the Sabbath. They did not know the stone had been sealed and a guard had been set to be sure

no one would tamper with it (Matthew 27:62-66). Now, as they were coming back to the tomb, they were wondering whom they could find to roll back that heavy stone and open the doorway. They knew nothing of the angel who was there ahead of them.

4. And when they looked, they saw that the stone was rolled away: for it was very great.

The stone was big: they could see it from a distance, and they saw that they would have no problem about getting it moved away from the doorway. It seems that Mary Magdalene was first to look through the open doorway and see that the body of Jesus was gone. Naturally supposing that someone had taken it away, she raced to tell Peter and John. John tells her story without mentioning the other women (John 20:1, 2). When she had gone, the other women went on into the opened tomb.

B. Glad Tidings (vv. 5-8)

5. And entering into the sepulchre, they saw a young man sitting on the right side, clothed in a long white garment; and they were affrighted.

Undoubtedly this young man was an angel from Heaven. No wonder the women were affrighted. Not long before, the angel had appeared like lightning, and even the soldiers on guard had been terrified (Matthew 28:3, 4). Luke records that there were two angels in dazzling robes (Luke 24:4), but Mark mentions only the one who spoke.

LAUGHING AT DEATH

Most people would agree that the "right side" of a tomb is the *outside*.

We sometimes joke about funerals and cemeteries because we are mystified and apprehensive about death. A certain fear grips us when we are confronted by mortality, when we realize that life as we know it must eventually come to an end. Perhaps it is the fear of the unknown.

Friends of Jesus were afraid when they found the tomb occupied not by a corpse, but by an angel. We can only guess what all their fears were, because they were afraid even to speak.

The good news for them and for us is that we don't have to fear death anymore. Think about it—because Jesus lives, we too can live beyond the grave, and forever! Praise the Lord!

—R. W. B.

6. And he saith unto them, Be not affrighted: ye seek Jesus of Nazareth, which was crucified: he is risen; he is not here: behold the place where they laid him.

"Don't be afraid." Isn't that exactly how any kindhearted angel or man would reassure some frightened women? This angel had good news for the ladies. His dazzling appearance was not to scare them; it was to let them know he was no ordinary young man. Realizing that a Heavenly angel was talking, they would not be inclined to doubt what he said.

The angel continued his reassurance. He knew why the women were there, but their coming was in vain. There was no dead body to be covered with spices. Jesus was alive again. There was only an empty *place where they laid him.*

The angel also reminded the ladies that Jesus had foretold that He would die and rise again (Luke 24:6, 7). He had repeated that promise so often that we wonder how His followers could be so shocked when He kept it (Matthew 16:21; 17:22, 23; 20:18, 19). Apparently the disciples thought He was using figurative language that they did not understand. But now the promise was literally fulfilled.

7. But go your way, tell his disciples and Peter that he goeth before you into Galilee: there shall ye see him, as he said unto you.

The women were to be the first human messengers of the resurrection. They were to *tell his disciples* that Jesus was alive and would meet them in *Galilee* as He had promised to do.

Tell his disciples and Peter. Why was Peter singled out for special mention? Perhaps he was overcome with remorse over his denial of Jesus (Matthew 26:69-75), so overcome that he thought Jesus no longer would consider him a disciple. For his reassurance he had the women's message and more. Before that day was over, Jesus came to him in person (Luke 24:34). Peter was still a disciple, and Jesus took care to keep him.

8. And they went out quickly, and fled from the sepulchre; for they trembled and were amazed: neither said they any thing to any man; for they were afraid.

When the Heavenly messenger told them to go, the women lost no time in going. The appearance of the shining angel was intimidating, and the message was awesome. He had told them not to be afraid (v. 6), but fear does not vanish on command. The women were still trembling, amazed, and afraid. They got away from that place as fast as they could. *Neither said they any thing to any man.* That is, they did not stop to talk with anyone along the way, but went straight to "tell his disciples and Peter," as the angel had told them to do (Matthew 28:8)

It seems that the disciples were not all together, so the women had to go from place to place with their message. To some disciples they reported that they had seen angels who said Jesus was alive (Luke 24:22, 23). But before they reached all the disciples, Jesus himself met them and repeated the instructions the angel had given (Matthew 28:9, 10). As they went on to the other disciples, surely they reported that they had seen the Lord himself.

The disciples were skeptical when they heard the message from the women (Luke 24:11), but they were thoroughly convinced when Jesus came to their group on two different occasions (John 20:19-29). Then they went to Galilee as they were told to do. There Jesus came unexpectedly to seven of them by the sea (John 21:1-14), and also met a larger group at an appointed place and gave them their marching orders (Matthew 28:16-20). Later He was with them again in Judea. They saw Him rise from the Mount of Olives and vanish in a cloud (Luke 24:50, 51; Acts 1:6-9). If that glimpse of glory was not enough, bright angels said the Lord was coming back (Acts 1:10, 11). He himself had promised to come "in a cloud with power and great glory" (Luke 21:27, 28).

The apostles waited briefly as Jesus had told them to do (Acts 1:4). Then the Holy Spirit came to guide them as they began the great work of preaching the gospel (Acts 2). Now that work is in our hands as we wait for our Lord to come "in a cloud with power and great glory."

II. Glimpse of Our Glory (Romans 8:12-17)

Refreshed by remembering that Christ rose from the dead, we turn again to our study in Romans. Last week our lesson introduced Christ's resurrection and compared our experience with it. As Jesus died and rose again, we have died to sin and risen to walk in newness of life (Romans 6:1—7:6).

Still sin has not given up. It is eager to capture us again. Sometimes we do wrong, or at least fail to do right, through ignorance or carelessness or our own lust (James 1:14). But the grace of God and the sacrifice of Jesus still cleanse us. "I thank God through Jesus Christ our Lord" (Romans 7:7-25).

Chapter 8 of Romans then begins with a ringing assurance: "There is therefore now no condemnation to them which are in Christ Jesus, who walk not after the flesh, but after the Spirit." There are two factors in our freedom from condemnation. First is the grace of God, who forgives our sins if we confess them (1 John 1:9). The second factor is our determination to be guided by God's Spirit rather than the craving of our physical bodies: to "walk not after the flesh, but after the Spirit." "For to be carnally minded is death; but to be spiritually minded is life and peace" (Romans 8:1-8).

God's Spirit lives in Christians (1 Corinthians 6:19). Without Him, we are not Christians at all (Romans 8:9). Through His Spirit in us God gives life to our mortal bodies (Romans 8:11).

A. Death and Life (vv. 12, 13)

12. Therefore, brethren, we are debtors, not to the flesh, to live after the flesh.

Therefore, because we have our life through God's Spirit (v. 11), we owe nothing to our physical bodies. We have no obligation to cater to their selfish wishes. We cherish them as temples of God's Spirit. We keep them clean and use them as He directs. We keep them under control.

13. For if ye live after the flesh, ye shall die: but if ye through the Spirit do mortify the deeds of the body, ye shall live.

To *live after the flesh* is to let the physical nature take control, to give priority to its desire for indulgence, pleasure, comfort, luxury. It is to surrender the mind to such desires of the body, to take pride in possessions and prestige rather than goodness. If you do that, *ye shall die.* That is the way of uncounted millions, as anyone can see; but it is the way to destruction (Matthew 7:13).

The way to *live* is to be controlled by *the Spirit,* by God's Spirit who lives in you (vv. 9-11). Even from a selfish viewpoint it is better to be led by the Spirit, for it is our own life that is at stake. To *mortify* is to kill. If we let the Spirit lead us, He leads us to kill all the sinful *deeds of the body.* The body then is free to be Spirit-led in deeds that give glory to God and benefit to our fellowmen. If we do not kill those evil deeds of the body, they will kill us.

B. Sons of God (vv. 14-16)

14. For as many as are led by the Spirit of God, they are the sons of God.

This is the practical demonstration by which *sons of God* can be recognized. They are *led by the Spirit of God.* That means they do right instead of wrong. They are unselfish rather than greedy and demanding. They delight in serving others, not in being served, "even as the Son of man came not to be ministered unto, but to minister" (Matthew 20:28). They have received Jesus, the Word who became flesh (John 1:12). They have been born of God (John 1:13); born of water and of the Spirit (John 3:5). They have died to sin and risen to walk in newness of life (Romans 6:1-12). Their mind is like the mind of Christ, a mind to sacrifice for the good of others (Philippians 2:5-8).

15. For ye have not received the spirit of bondage again to fear; but ye have received the Spirit of adoption, whereby we cry, Abba, Father.

Before becoming Christians, we were slaves of sin. We had reason then to be afraid, for "the

visual 5

I GAVE MY LIFE FOR THEE, WHAT HAST THOU GIVEN FOR ME?
—FRANCIS R. HAVERGAL

wages of sin is death" (Romans 6:16, 23). When we became Christians we received the Holy Spirit of God (Acts 2:38; Romans 8:9). We are controlled by Him (v. 14), but we are not frightened slaves as we used to be. The Spirit who controls us is *the Spirit of adoption.* The Greek word for *adoption* is formed by putting together the word for *son* and a verb meaning *put.* We have received the Spirit of son-putting: He was given to us when we were put in the position of sons. Led by Him, we do not cringe in fear; happily *we cry, Abba, Father.* In the language of the Jews, *Abba* is the word for *Father.* Probably that was the word Jesus used as He prayed in Gethsemane; but Mark wrote the record of it in Greek, and therefore added a translation of *Abba* (Mark 14:36). Perhaps Christians came to have a custom of using the two words together in prayer, and the Holy Spirit leads us also to call on God as our Father (Galatians 4:6).

16. The Spirit itself beareth witness with our spirit, that we are the children of God.

Within ourselves, in our own spirits, we feel that we are God's children; and we testify to that when we address God as Father. The Holy Spirit also testifies through the inspired writers who call us *children of God* in this text and elsewhere in the Scriptures.

C. Heirs of God (v. 17)

17. And if children, then heirs; heirs of God, and joint-heirs with Christ, if so be that we suffer with him, that we may be also glorified together.

Children expect to inherit their father's wealth when he dies. Our Father in Heaven will never die, but still we are His *heirs.* We shall share both His boundless riches and His endless life. Jesus is God's Son in a unique way, in a way that we are not. Our version indicates this by calling Him "only begotten" (John 3:16). Very reasonably God has made Him "heir of all things" (Hebrews 1:2). And we are *joint-heirs with Christ!* We too are heirs of all things, *if so be that we suffer with him.* Do we do that?

Paul gives a partial list of his own sufferings in 2 Corinthians 11:24-29. We do not know what suffering the Roman Christians were enduring at the time they received this letter; but it was not many years later that the emperor and his gestapo were driving them into the arena to battle with ferocious wild beasts for the amusement of the pagan population.

Christianity has so leavened the world that you and I are not likely to suffer in such ways. Our suffering is mostly in the form of scorn and ridicule from the pagans around us. But we can at least give up some of our pleasures in order to devote more time and energy to the Lord's work. Isn't your congregation needing a volunteer for some task worth the sacrifice of some soap-opera time? Doesn't it need a lot more money for its local program and its missionary outreach? If we are not making any real sacrifice for our Father in Heaven and our brothers on earth, what does that say about our sonship?

At this point, however, the apostle Paul does not dwell on sufferings. Quickly he goes on to a reason for enduring them: *that we may be also glorified together*. "For I reckon that the sufferings of this present time are not worthy to be compared with the glory which shall be revealed in us." Not only all mankind, but all creation is suffering because of man's sin. And not only mankind, but all creation "shall be delivered from the bondage of corruption into the glorious liberty of the children of God" (Romans 8:18-25). Praise the Lord!

HEIRS TO A FORTUNE

Once in a while I see senior citizens driving fancy motor homes that have a sticker or plate on the back that reads, I'M SPENDING MY CHILDREN'S INHERITANCE. Fact is funnier than fiction. The truth is, not many of us are very concerned about leaving our children wealth in our wills. We simply would like to get through our retirement years with a measure of comfort, and without bankrupting our kids to care for us.

I'm glad, however, that God isn't driving around in a Winnebago, squandering my Heavenly inheritance! His riches are unsearchable and inexhaustible.

In her hymn " A Child of the King," Harriet E. Buell states, "My Father is rich in houses and lands; He holdeth the wealth of the world in His hands."

We are children of the King, and Christ is our brother. If we share His suffering, we shall share His glory also. God's will names every Christian as an heir to eternity; the names are written in "the Lamb's book of life."

In a sense, the children of God begin enjoying eternal life as soon as the "adoption papers" are sealed by the Holy Spirit—God's gift to us when we claim Christ as our Savior   —R. W. B.

Conclusion

Our lesson is titled "A Glimpse of Glory," but really it brings two glimpses. Briefly before us flashes the glory of our risen Lord, who "was received up into heaven, and sat on the right hand of God" (Mark 16:19). Then there is a flash of our own glory, for "we may be also glorified together" as "heirs of God, and joint-heirs with Christ" (Romans 8:17).

A. If

There is a solemn warning in the condition that goes with the glimpse of our own glory: "If so be that we suffer with him" (Romans 8:17). Christ suffered crucifixion for us; can we afford to evade all suffering for Him? (Luke 14:27).

Our service may not be spectacular. It may be unappreciated among men, even unnoticed. Isn't that the way we want it? (Matthew 6:1). Not to be seen by men, but for the benefit of men and the glory of God comes the call to "present your bodies a living sacrifice, holy, acceptable unto God, which is your reasonable service" (Romans 12:1).

B. Prayer

Abba, Father, how good it is to be Your children! May Your Spirit guide us into humble, fruitful service now, and into Your presence forever. In Jesus' name, amen.

C. Thought to Remember

Sacrifice is reasonable service.

Home Daily Bible Readings

Monday, Mar. 28—He Has Risen! (Mark 16:1-8)

Tuesday, Mar. 29—Who Are the Children of God? (Romans 8:12-18)

Wednesday, Mar. 30—All Things Work Together for Good (Romans 9:28-32)

Thursday, Mar. 31—More Than Conquerors (Romans 8:33-39)

Friday, Apr. 1—The Glory of the Lord (Isaiah 6:1-8)

Saturday, Apr. 2—Visions of God (Ezekiel 1:15-28)

Sunday, Apr. 3—Commissioned to Prophesy (Ezekiel 2:1-7)

Learning by Doing

This page contains an alternate lesson plan emphasizing learning activities. Classes desiring such student involvement will find these suggestions helpful.

Learning Goals

During the study of this lesson your students will:

1. Compare and contrast Christ's glorification with their own future glorification in Christ.

2. Consider how their promised glorification in Christ can motivate them to serve Him more consistently.

Into the Lesson

Begin by asking, "What are some ways in which people honor another person?" Your students may suggest such methods as these: by presenting a trophy or plaque, by having a banquet in another's honor, or by placing a crown on the person honored. More ways than these can be mentioned. Discuss briefly some of the reasons why people honor another person.

Lead into the Bible study by saying, "Today we are going to consider how Jesus was honored following His crucifixion. This is sometimes referred to as His glorification. In addition we will look at what Scripture teaches about our future honor—our glorification."

Into the Word

Give a copy of the following questions to each class member.

1. What was involved in Christ's glorification, according to the passages listed below?
Mark 16:1-8, 19
Philippians 2:6-11
Acts 2:22-24, 32-36
Hebrews 2:9
Revelation 5:8-14
2. What is involved in our future glorification, according to the following passages?
Romans 8:12-30
James 1:12
Matthew 5:10-12
Philippians 3:20, 21
1 Corinthians 15:42-44
3. In what ways is our glorification similar to Christ's?
4. In what ways is our glorification different from Christ's?

Have class members form groups of six to discuss the questions. Appoint a discussion leader for each group, and inform the groups that they have twenty-five minutes to explore the passages. When time is up, ask each group to share with the class some of their observations for questions three and four.

Some of the similarities of Christ's glorification and ours are these: Christ experienced resurrection from the dead, and so shall we; since Christ has been raised from the dead, He can never die again (Romans 6:9); likewise when we are raised our bodies shall be imperishable and immortal (1 Corinthians 15:53). We will live together in Heaven.

Some of the differences are these: Jesus will be worshiped by all creation, we will not; Jesus will reign over all, we will not; Jesus is exalted to the right hand of the Father, we are not; Jesus has power over death, but our victory over death is because of His power, not ours.

After sufficient discussion write these words on the chalkboard: *humiliation, resurrection, glorification.* Point out that Jesus experienced humiliation in order to make possible our salvation. Ask the class what was included in His humiliation. (This included His relinquishing Heaven's glory and yielding His privileges as God to come to earth and live among us; rejection by His people; ridicule and suffering associated with His arrest, trial, and crucifixion.)

Jesus' glorification began when He was resurrected, and it continued when He ascended to Heaven and was exalted at the right hand of God. His glorification will culminate when He returns to defeat His enemies and to take His followers to be with Him forever in Heaven. State that as followers of Jesus, we may experience ridicule and rejection. But that will be accounted as nothing when we have experienced our resurrection, and in our new, glorified bodies dwell forever with the Lord.

Into Life

Read 1 Corinthians 15:50-58, which speaks of our future glorification. Point out that our hope of this blessed, eternal future should have a tremendous impact on how we live right now. Verse 58 deals with this truth. Provide each class member with a sheet of paper and a pen. Ask the students to rewrite this verse in their own words to make the meaning as clear as possible. After three or four minutes, ask volunteers to share their paraphrases with the class.

Let's Talk It Over

The questions on this page are designed to encourage review of the lesson Scriptures and to promote discussion of the lesson by the class. The answers provided are only discussion starters. Let your class talk it over from there.

1. "Ye seek Jesus of Nazareth, which was crucified: he is risen; he is not here" (Mark 16:6). This announcement by the angel at the tomb is a dramatic high point of Mark's Gospel. What makes it so dramatic?

When we begin reading the final chapter of Mark, we already know what is going to happen. And yet we tend to fall in step with the women as they make their sad journey to the tomb. We hear them discuss the very practical problem of how to get the heavy stone rolled away from the tomb's entrance. We share their perplexity also as they approach the tomb and see it open. It is thrilling to try to identify with their soaring emotions as they hear the angel's pronouncement and as they rush from the tomb to share the exciting, though still somewhat frightening, news. Such a reading of the resurrection accounts is good for us, since it reminds us that we also have exciting news to tell.

2. How can we tell if we are being led by the Spirit of God?

It is a principle of the New Testament that the Holy Spirit draws the believer's attention to Jesus and glorifies Him (see John 15:26; 16:12-15). One's attitudes regarding Jesus will reveal if one is being led by the Spirit. The Spirit will lead us to Jesus, to follow Him, to fellowship with Him, and to desire to introduce Him to others. The fruit of the Spirit (Galatians 5:22, 23) is a list of Christlike characteristics that will grow in us if the Spirit is leading us. A desire for Heaven and the intimate fellowship with God and Christ that we will experience there is another evidence that God's Spirit is dwelling in us and leading us (see Colossians 3:1-4)

3. God's revelation of himself as Father to those who are in Christ is one of the New Testament's most comforting and encouraging teachings. How can we gain the maximum benefit from this teaching?

It is unfortunate that too many human beings have grown up with a negative impression of the word *father*. The man they called father was either indifferent and uncaring or cruel and abusive. He may have been a slave to alcohol, a stern disciplinarian, or a man who was too busy to take time for his family. If persons with such fathers are to appreciate the wisdom, understanding, goodness, and love of God, our Heavenly Father, they must see within the church some shining examples of human fathers who are sincerely patterning themselves after Him. We all need to contemplate what is best in human examples of fatherhood and then remind ourselves that these examples provide us with only the smallest hint of the grandeur of God's Fatherhood.

4. Why should it stir us to excitement to discover that we are heirs of God?

We certainly would be excited if we were to learn that we had inherited millions of dollars. Our minds would leap from one item to another as we anticipated what we might purchase with that money. But if we thought about it further, we would be sobered by the realization that everything that money could buy would ultimately fade and crumble. However, as heirs of God we come to possess "treasures in heaven, where neither moth nor rust doth corrupt, and where thieves do not break through nor steal" (Matthew 6:20). God grants us an inheritance that features eternal life with Him, eternal fellowship with Jesus Christ, and eternal citizenship in Heaven with our fellow saints. We should think about this inheritance frequently and let the excitement of it vibrate within us.

5. How can we combat the temptation to do Christian service for the applause of men?

It is sad but true that there are church members similar to the chief rulers of Jesus' time who "loved the praise of men more than the praise of God" (John 12:43). And even those who serve humbly and quietly may occasionally be troubled because they receive no public acknowledgment for their work. We must grow in our ability to see our service being rendered directly to God for His glory and His approval. To hear God say one day, "Well done, good and faithful servant" (Matthew 25:23) should be our heart's greatest desire. Or perhaps it will be easier for us to picture ourselves serving in a direct relationship to Jesus Christ. Then we can aim at a consistent fulfillment of Colossians 3:23: "And whatsoever ye do, do it heartily, as to the Lord, and not unto men."

The Lord is the Center of my Joy

Life in the Spirit

April 10
Lesson 6

Apr
10

DEVOTIONAL READING: Romans 8:26-28, 35-39.

LESSON SCRIPTURE: Romans 8:1-11.

PRINTED TEXT: Romans 8:1-11.

Romans 8:1-11

1 There is therefore now no condemnation to them which are in Christ Jesus, who walk not after the flesh, but after the Spirit.

2 For the law of the Spirit of life in Christ Jesus hath made me free from the law of sin and death.

3 For what the law could not do, in that it was weak through the flesh, God sending his own Son in the likeness of sinful flesh, and for sin, condemned sin in the flesh:

4 That the righteousness of the law might be fulfilled in us, who walk not after the flesh, but after the Spirit.

5 For they that are after the flesh do mind the things of the flesh; but they that are after the Spirit, the things of the Spirit.

6 For to be carnally minded is death; but to be spiritually minded is life and peace.

7 Because the carnal mind is enmity against God: for it is not subject to the law of God, neither indeed can be.

8 So then they that are in the flesh cannot please God.

9 But ye are not in the flesh, but in the Spirit, if so be that the Spirit of God dwell in you. Now if any man have not the Spirit of Christ, he is none of his.

10 And if Christ be in you, the body is dead because of sin; but the Spirit is life because of righteousness.

11 But if the Spirit of him that raised up Jesus from the dead dwell in you, he that raised up Christ from the dead shall also quicken your mortal bodies by his Spirit that dwelleth in you.

GOLDEN TEXT: The law of the Spirit of life in Christ Jesus hath made me free from the law of sin and death.—Romans 8:2.

Good News for God's People
Romans—Unit 2: Empowered by the Spirit (Lessons 5-8)

Lesson Aims

After this lesson a student should be able to:

1. Explain why there is now no condemnation to Christians.

2. Tell what duty or obligation we have as children of God

3. Find some way of doing his or her duty better this week.

Lesson Outline

INTRODUCTION
  A. What Is Life?
  B. Lesson Background
I. FREE FROM CONDEMNATION (Romans 8:1-4)
  A. The Liberating Law (vv. 1, 2)
  B. The Liberating Method (vv. 3, 4)
II. MINDS IN CONFLICT (Romans 8:5-8)
  A. Flesh and Spirit (v. 5)
  B. Death and Life (v. 6)
    Wrong Side of the Brain
  C. Explanation (vv. 7, 8)
III. THE LIFE-GIVING SPIRIT (Romans 8:9-11)
  A. We in Him and He in Us (v. 9)
    Flesh or Faith
  B. Result (vv. 10, 11)
CONCLUSION
  A. What We Owe
  B. What We Shall Receive
  C. Prayer
  D. Thought to Remember

Display visual 6 of the visuals packet and let it remain before the class. The visual is shown on page 277.

Introduction

A grisly story was on the radio news today. Prodded by older friends, a teen-age boy drank gin till he passed out. It was a great joke, the others thought, till they tried to rouse him. He made no response; they could find no pulse, no breath. Frantically they called 911.

The paramedics came with screaming sirens, but they could only confirm the friends' opinion. The boy was pronounced dead.

On a slab in the morgue, the "dead" boy stirred. Then he sat up and vomited. He had a monstrous hangover, but he was very much alive.

A. What Is Life?

Life is an elusive thing. Who can define it? We are sure we have it when we shout for joy or scream with pain; but no one sees it when it slips away, and sometimes we are not even sure it is gone.

One thing is certain: most of us who have life want to keep it. Jesus said, "Whosoever will save his life shall lose it: and whosoever will lose his life for my sake shall find it" (Matthew 16:25). We who love life will do well to study the Word of God, for God is the giver of life.

B. Lesson Background

Two weeks ago we were thinking thankfully of our transformation. Once we were slaves of sin, utterly unable to escape from bondage; but Christ broke the chains and set us free. The change is as drastic and dramatic as death and resurrection. "Therefore we are buried with him by baptism into death: that like as Christ was raised up from the dead by the glory of the Father, even so we also should walk in newness of life." Now we are "dead indeed unto sin, but alive unto God through Jesus Christ our Lord." That makes a difference in the way we live, of course. "Let not sin therefore reign in your mortal body, that ye should obey it in the lusts thereof. . . . For sin shall not have dominion over you" (Romans 6:1-14).

Last week's resurrection lesson lent power to those thoughts. Our victory over sin should be as complete as Christ's victory over death. But then chapter 7 of Romans calls attention to something we all know from our own experience. Christ has set us free from sin, but sin is not content to leave us free. Sin dogs our steps continually, nipping at our heels, eager to capture us again. By the grace of God it does not have dominion over us, but sometimes it does trip us so that we stumble into wrong. "For the good that I would, I do not: but the evil which I would not, that I do" (Romans 7:15-19).

I. Free From Condemnation (Romans 8:1-4)

Who among us has not felt the same frustration? "I delight in the law of God after the inward man: but I see another law in my members, warring against the law of my mind, and bringing me into captivity to the law of sin which is in my members." In such frustration Paul's voice rises to a wail: "O wretched man that I am! who shall deliver me from the body of this death?" but Paul has the answer: "I thank God through Jesus Christ our Lord"

(Romans 7:22-25). How frequently we all thank God because He still delivers us "through Jesus Christ our Lord"! This grateful thinking is continued in our text.

A. The Liberating Law (vv. 1, 2)

1. There is therefore now no condemnation to them which are in Christ Jesus, who walk not after the flesh, but after the Spirit.

No condemnation? Not even if we do wrong? (7:19). There is condemnation for the wrong (8:3), but we escape because we are *in Christ Jesus.* In Him we *walk not after the flesh, but after the Spirit.* The wrong we do is no part of our customary walk, no part of the life we want to live (7:22). It is an accident, a stumble. It grieves us even as it grieves God. By His grace and our effort we recover quickly and once more walk *after the Spirit:* we live as God's Spirit leads us to live.

At this point some of the most valued ancient manuscripts do not have the clause *who walk not after the flesh, but after the Spirit.* For this reason the clause is left out of some English versions. It appears in verse 4, however, so we know it is a proper description of a Christian's way of living.

2. For the law of the Spirit of life in Christ Jesus hath made me free from the law of sin and death.

The law of sin and death is plain: "The soul that sinneth, it shall die" (Ezekiel 18:4). Adam was warned of that in the beginning (Genesis 2:17), and warnings have been multiplied since that time. I have sinned, and so have you. There's no question about that. Then how can there be "no condemnation" to us? That too is simple. Another law overpowers the law of sin and death. That other law is called *the law of the Spirit of life in Christ Jesus.*

When we hear the word *law,* we may think of something written, like the law of God that Moses wrote in a book, or the law of our nation that fills other books. But the word has a deeper meaning. Basically a written law is an expression of the will of the lawgiver. When we think in terms of will, our case is simplified. Sin wants us dead. The Spirit want us alive. The Spirit prevails, and we live.

Then what happens to the law that prescribes death for sinners? After all, that was God's own decree to Adam and to all the rest of us. Does God's Spirit in us break God's law that has been so often repeated?

No. The law demands death for sin. Christ died for our sins. The law's demand is satisfied, and we live.

Then why doesn't everybody live? Christ died for the sins of the whole world (1 John 2:2). This brings us back to the proposition we have seen before in these studies from Romans. Our fate depends on our faith. Abraham was credited with righteousness because he believed in God (Romans 4:3), and so are we. Thus God can both be just and make us sinners just. He does it because we believe in the Savior He sent (Romans 3:26).

B. The Liberating Method (vv. 3, 4)

3. For what the law could not do, in that it was weak through the flesh, God sending his own Son in the likeness of sinful flesh, and for sin, condemned sin in the flesh.

The law could not make us free from sin. It pointed out our sin and prescribed punishment, but it could not take away either the guilt of sin or the power of sin. God had another method of doing that. He did it by *sending his own Son in the likeness of sinful flesh, and for sin.* Jesus was sent in a human body like our sinful bodies in every way but one: His body was not sinful. Being sinless himself, He was an acceptable sacrifice for sin in us. So *in the flesh,* the sinless body of Jesus, God *condemned sin* in two ways.

First, sin is shown to be utterly wrong and without excuse. Since "all have sinned" (Romans 3:23), some people suppose that all have to sin, that no one can live in the flesh without sinning. But one can. Jesus proved that by doing it. We can resist the devil and drive him away (James 4:7). Temptation does not overwhelm and overpower us (1 Corinthians 10:13). If we give in to temptation, it is because we fail to do our best. So sin is condemned as both bad and unnecessary.

Second, sin so condemned is put down from its ruling position. It no longer has power to dominate and destroy us. Not only do we have the ability to resist the devil and defeat sin; we also have forgiveness for our failures. So "sin shall not have dominion over you" (Romans 6:12-14).

4. That the righteousness of the law might be fulfilled in us, who walk not after the flesh, but after the Spirit.

The righteousness required by *the law* was never attained by those who tried to keep the law. It is not attained by us either, but it is God's gift to us when He redeems us and pardons our sin. "This righteousness from God comes through faith in Jesus Christ to all who believe" (Romans 3:22, *New International Version*).

Being so gifted, we *walk not after the flesh.* We do not gratify every desire of our physical bodies; even their genuine needs do not have first place in our lives. We follow the leading of God's *Spirit* instead. He does lead us to give proper care to our bodies, for they are His temples (1 Corinthians 6:19). That does not mean we pamper them with luxury; rather, we keep them strong and fit for His service. We find the Spirit's leading in the Bible He inspired; His presence within us, coupled with our own best effort, gives us power to follow His leading.

II. Minds in Conflict (Romans 8:5-8)

Every Christian wants to follow the Spirit's leading, but that is easier said than done. Most of us falter and fail sometimes, and Paul understood that. Earlier lessons and this one have referred to his discussion in Romans 7:15-25. We are tempted by the devil and his angels and his people; and to make matters worse, something inside of us seems to be on their side. As the apostle Paul put it, the will of our mind is opposed by a contrary will in the members of our bodies. So "when I would do good, evil is present with me" (Romans 7:21, 23). The next verses of our text speak of conflicting minds trying to control us.

A. Flesh and Spirit (v. 5)

5. For they that are after the flesh do mind the things of the flesh; but they that are after the Spirit, the things of the Spirit.
Flesh is literally the meat of our physical bodies. What it likes is not always best for us. Our muscles like ease and comfort rather than hard work. Our skin likes to feel soft fabrics rather than durable work clothes. Our tongues like too much sugar and salt and cholesterol. Our noses like expensive fragrances rather than the smell of sweat. Given a chance, our bodies quickly become addicted to nicotine, alcohol, cocaine, or heroin. In all these ways and more, *the flesh* craves instant pleasure rather than permanent good. So Paul uses the term *flesh* to include some attitudes of mind such as greed and selfish pride. Among the Corinthians, "envying, and strife, and divisions" indicated that they were "carnal," which means fleshly (1 Corinthians 3:3). Trying to sum up all of this, the *New International Version* translates *flesh* as "sinful nature." While that is not a literal translation, it does present the meaning of our text clearly: "Those who live according to the sinful nature have their minds set on what that nature desires; but those who live in accordance with the Spirit have their minds set on what the Spirit desires." The *flesh* craves what is most pleasant at the moment; the *Spirit* chooses what is best for eternity. We choose to live according to one or the other, and we set our minds according to the choice that we make.

B. Death and Life (v. 6)

6. For to be carnally minded is death; but to be spiritually minded is life and peace.
It is wise to think about results before we set our minds one way or the other. *To be carnally minded* is to "mind the things of the flesh" (v. 5). That is easy, comfortable, pleasant. Therefore it is attractive. But it results in *death,* and we had better take that into account. *To be spiritually minded* is to mind "the things of the Spirit," to set our minds and devote our energies to doing what God's Spirit leads us to do. That is not so easy, but the result is *life and peace.* Isn't that worth whatever effort it takes to follow the Spirit's leading?

WRONG SIDE OF THE BRAIN

Fascinating research suggests that men tend to use the left hemisphere of their brain more, and women use the right side more. Women are said to be "right-brained," more given to creative and abstract thinking, while males are usually "left-brained," more programmed for calculating, logical thought. All available evidence seems to support the theory. God apparently created complementary characteristics for ideal male/female relationships.

Paul wasn't concerned about right-brained and left-brained natures. He was deeply distressed by the human tendency to be *"wrong-brained"*—carnally minded. Those who allow themselves to be directed by fleshly appetites are thinking with only the dark side of their brains.

Christians, indwelt by the Holy Spirit, are enlightened. We can, and should be, *right-minded*—rejecting fleshly appetites and desiring only what the Spirit desires for us. Spiritually speaking, there is no difference between male and female (Galatians 3:28), for we are all heirs to life and peace.   —R. W. B.

C. Explanation (vv. 7, 8)

7. Because the carnal mind is enmity against God: for it is not subject to the law of God, neither indeed can be.
God's mind is set on long-term benefits for mankind and for each person. *The carnal mind* is set on present pleasure for one person regardless of the rest of mankind. It follows that *the carnal mind is enmity against God,* for momentary pleasure often damages long-term welfare, and gratification of one's own wish often damages the welfare of others. *The carnal mind,* pleasure-bent and selfish, is a rebel, *not subject to the law of God.* It cannot be subject to God's rule, because its aims are contrary to God's aims.

8. So then they that are in the flesh cannot please God.

In this verse, being *in the flesh* is not simply living in a physical body. It is walking after the flesh (v. 4), minding the things of the flesh (v. 5), being carnally minded (v. 6). As the phrase is used here, to be *in the flesh* is to be in rebellion against God; so of course *they that are in the flesh cannot please God.*

III. The Life-Giving Spirit (Romans 8:9-11)

The Spirit of God, the Spirit of Christ, the Holy Spirit—these are different ways of describing the same Spirit. This divine Spirit is given to us when we become Christians (Acts 2:38), and thereafter lives in us (1 Corinthians 6:19). In this lesson we have seen that His guidance makes us free from the rule of sin and death (v. 2). Gratefully then we walk after the Spirit (v. 4): we follow His leading. We set our minds on the things He wants for us (v. 5), knowing they will result in life and peace (v. 6). All these thoughts and more are tied together in the closing verses of our text.

A. We in Him and He in Us (v. 9)

9. But ye are not in the flesh, but in the Spirit, if so be that the Spirit of God dwell in you. Now if any man have not the Spirit of Christ, he is none of his.

Being *in the flesh* is not simply living in a physical body (v. 8), and being *in the Spirit* is not being without a physical body. It is walking after the Spirit (v. 4), minding the things of the Spirit (v. 5), being spiritually minded (v. 6). We do all this *if so be that the Spirit of God dwell* in us. And if *the Spirit of Christ* does not dwell in us, we are *none of his*: we are not Christians at all.

The Spirit is not perceived by our physical senses, and our understanding of Him is limited. It seems clear, however, that the same Spirit is both *the Spirit of God* and *the Spirit of Christ*. If that divine Spirit is in us, both God and Christ are in us. Recall that wonderful night when Jesus promised to send to His apostles another Comforter, the Spirit of truth (John 14:16, 17). He said also, "If a man love me, he will keep my words: and my Father will love him, and we [the Father and Jesus] will come unto him, and make our abode with him" (John 14:23). There is nothing lacking of God's presence in us: Father, Son, and Holy Spirit are there. They are in us fully. If our fellowship is less than complete, it is because we are not fully in them: because we do not always follow their leading (v. 4), because we do not always set our minds firmly on their will (v. 5), because we are not entirely spiritually

minded (v. 6). The Spirit in us is powerful but gentle. He leads, but does not drive. He does not chain us and beat us and compel us to do His will; He waits for us to want to serve Him.

FLESH OR FAITH

The wife of a friend died a few years ago. Her passing was not unexpected; the last years of her life had been stolen by a struggle with Parkinson's disease. Her body gradually had been debilitated until she could do nothing for herself. Her husband bravely bore the sadness of seeing her suffer.

Almost everyone has known at least one person who, due to stroke, accidental injury, birth defect, or incurable illness, has been "trapped" in a body that has quit functioning to one degree or another. Some such victims cannot move part or any of their body; some cannot speak; but their minds are alive, alert, and active.

In one sense, all of us are "trapped" in our bodies. Our flesh is weak and mortal, and we must experience the trials and temptations of our carnal existence. If we allow ourselves to be enslaved by the flesh, we "cannot please God." A corollary to that truth is found in Hebrews 11:6: "Without faith it is impossible to please God" (*New International Version*).

The positive implication of these negative teachings is that we can please God and be free from the oppression of the flesh by choosing to live lives of faith. We can throw off the flesh's mastery over us by yielding our spirits to the Spirit of God.

—R. W. B.

B. Result (vv. 10, 11)

10. And if Christ be in you, the body is dead because of sin; but the Spirit is life because of righteousness.

If Christ be in you. We have just seen that He is in us if we are Christians (v. 9). So now we are reading that if we are Christians *the body is dead because of sin.* Obviously this does not mean literally and physically *dead.* Our eyes see; our

visual 6

ears hear. In the literal sense our bodies are alive. Then in what sense are they dead?

Is Paul saying our bodies are still under the sentence of death, that they will die because of sin, even though our sin is forgiven? Forgiven Christians do die physically; we all know that. Possibly Paul is reminding us of it in order to add that these bodies that will die will also be restored to life (v. 11).

Or is Paul reminding us again that we have died to sin (Romans 6:1, 2), that our sinful bodies have been crucified and destroyed so that we are not servants of sin anymore? (Romans 6:6). Both chapter 6 and chapter 8 make it plain that the body is dead as a controlling force in our lives. We "walk not after the flesh, but after the Spirit" (v. 4).

In contrast with the *body* that is *dead, the Spirit is life because of righteousness.* Our version spells *Spirit* with a capital S, meaning the Holy Spirit in us is life. Certainly He is, and He shares His life with us. But some versions here spell *spirit* with a small letter, meaning that our spirits are alive. They do not share the death of the body. That also is true. In Christ we are alive forevermore *because of righteousness:* because our sins are forgiven and we have the righteousness that God gives us because we have faith in Jesus (Romans 3:21, 22).

11. But if the Spirit of him that raised up Jesus from the dead dwell in you, he that raised up Christ from the dead shall also quicken your mortal bodies by his Spirit that dwelleth in you.

God is the one who *raised up Jesus from the dead.* The Holy Spirit is His Spirit and Christ's Spirit (v. 9). This Spirit does dwell in us who are Christians (v. 9). Therefore we are assured that God *shall also quicken* our *mortal bodies.* To *quicken*

is to make alive. Already He has made us alive after we were dead in our sins (Colossians 2:13). When our bodies are literally dead, God will make them alive when Jesus again appears on earth (1 Thessalonians 4:16). This He will do *by his Spirit* who lives in us.

Conclusion

The conclusion of this lesson is seen in the latter part of last week's text (Romans 8:12-17). That section of Scritpure was transferred to that resurrection lesson to add a glimpse of our glory to a glimpse of the glory of our risen Lord. It is a twofold conclusion: it tells first what we owe, and then what we shall receive.

A. What We Owe

In verses 12-15 Paul says we are in debt. We owe full allegiance and faithful following. But we do not owe these to the flesh, the physical body that cares for nothing but its own comfort and pleasure. The flesh is a deadly master. If we choose to serve it above all, we shall die. We owe our loyal service to the Spirit, God's Spirit, who leads us to kill the flesh before it kills us. God's Spirit leads God's children, and He leads them to say, "Abba, Father." This is the way of life.

B. What We Shall Receive

Verses 16 and 17 tell what we shall receive. God's children are God's heirs. They are joint-heirs with Christ, who is heir of all things. All of the boundless universe is ours, and all of the glory of Heaven. Best of all, the companionship of Father, Son, and Holy Spirit is ours, for we are children of God.

How foolish it is, and how sad, to value things that are seen rather than things that are unseen! (2 Corinthians 4:16-18). Amos R. Wells wrote this lament:

Many a soul,
Gifted with realms in all God's universe,
Cramping his soul within a kennel space,
Lives in the moment for the moment's end,
Squanders his hours on instants, days on hours,
And being heir of God's eternity,
Begs of the petty years a crust of bread.

C. Prayer

Abba, Father, how glorious it is to be Your children! You have sent the Savior to redeem us and the Spirit to live within us. By His leading we find our footsteps guided, our spirits lifted, our minds set on things eternal. Thank You, Father.

D. Thought to Remember

Let's remember who we are.

Home Daily Bible Readings

Monday, Apr. 4—"Free! Free! I'm Free at Last!" (Romans 8:1-5)

Tuesday, Apr. 5—Mind on Flesh or Spirit? (Romans 8:6-11)

Wednesday, Apr. 6—The Work of the Spirit (Romans 8:18-27)

Thursday, Apr. 7—A Vision of the Exalted God (Revelation 4)

Friday, Apr. 8—There Shall Be Showers of Blessings! (Ezekiel 36:22-26)

Saturday, Apr. 9—I Will Pour Out My Spirit (Acts 2:14-21)

Sunday, Apr. 10—God Gives a New Spirit (Ezekiel 11:14-21)

Learning by Doing

This page contains an alternate lesson plan emphasizing learning activities. Classes desiring such student involvement will find these suggestions helpful.

Learning Goals

In this lesson you will lead your students to:

1. Contrast life in the Spirit with life in the flesh.

2. Consider how they can live according to the Spirit rather than the flesh.

Into the Lesson

Before class write this statement on the chalkboard: *Living according to the Holy Spirit is natural for Christians.*

Begin class by calling attention to the statement. Then ask students to form two groups, with half of the class gathering on one side of the classroom, and the other half on the other side. Inform the class that you want them to participate in a brief, informal debate. One side is to defend the statement on the chalkboard, the other side is to oppose it.

Have a volunteer from the defense support that position. Then let someone from the opposition counter. Allow discussion to go back and forth, but cut it off after four or five minutes.

Now ask students which position they really agree with. Ask those who agree with the statement to raise their hands. Then ask those who disagree to raise theirs. This will give you a feel for what the class thinks about the difficulty of living in the Spirit.

Lead into the Bible study time by saying, "Our lesson today focuses on the difference between living according to the Holy Spirit and living according to the flesh. The Scriptures indicate that we have a battle going on within us. The battle is between our fleshly nature and the desire within to obey God. In our study we will contrast the two options and pinpoint ways we can live more consistently in submission to the Holy Spirit."

Into the Word

Ask a volunteer to read Romans 8:1-14 aloud. Then state that in Scripture the term *flesh* usually refers to the physical body. But Paul gives the term a moral meaning in Romans 8. He uses the expressions "after the flesh" and "in the flesh" to describe the person who gives himself to the pursuit of that which is carnal, temporal, worldly. It indicates a commitment to please self rather than God. Note that the *New International Version* renders the word for flesh as "sinful nature."

Put the following two column headings on the chalkboard: *Living in the Spirit* and *Living in the Flesh.* To show the difference between the two, have the students examine Romans 8:1-14 to find the characteristics mentioned there for each. Write their suggestions under the appropriate heading.

After discussion, have class members turn to Galatians 5 and ask a volunteer to read verses 13-16. Ask students, "According to this passage, what are differences between living in the Spirit and living in the flesh?" Again, record their observations on the chalkboard.

Next, divide the class into groups of four. Provide each student with a sheet of paper and a pencil. Ask students to write these verse numbers on their papers: 1-4; 5-8; 9-11; 12-14.

In their groups they are to work together and summarize each of these sections of Romans 8. Each summary should be twelve words or less. Appoint a discussion leader for each group, and allot fifteen minutes for this project.

When time has expired, consider the verse sections one by one and let each group give their summary.

Summarize the principal teachings of the text by leading a discussion of the following two questions:

1. Why should we live according to the Spirit?

2. How can we live according to the Spirit?

Into Life

Have students work in their groups of four to consider and make application of two principles from Romans 8. Assign half of the groups to discuss principle one, and half to discuss principle two. Give each group a copy of the appropriate questions below. The principles are as expressed in the *New International Version.*

Principle One—Set your mind on what the Spirit desires (v. 5)

a. What does the Spirit desire?

b. How can we develop the habit of setting our minds on what the Spirit desires? Be practical.

Principle Two—Put to death, by the Spirit, the misdeeds of the body (v. 13)

a. What are the misdeeds of the body?

b. How can we, through the Spirit, put these misdeeds to death? Be practical.

Let the groups share their conclusions.

Let's Talk It Over

The questions on this page are designed to encourage review of the lesson Scriptures and to promote discussion of the lesson by the class. The answers provided are only discussion starters. Let your class talk it over from there.

1. Those who are in Christ have the promise of "no condemnation." How does this bring comfort now?

The memory of past sins is not erased when one becomes a Christian. The apostle Paul late in his life was still mindful of his earlier failings (see 1 Timothy 1:12-16). Some, however, remembering their past sins, continue to feel discomfort over them. It may be said that they condemn themselves, dragging the painful memories of past sins through their conscious mind again and again. So we should thrill to the pronouncement of "no condemnation"; we can joyously appropriate to ourselves Jesus' words to the woman taken in adultery: "Neither do I condemn thee: go, and sin no more" (John 8:11). When old guilt rises up to vex us, we should lay hold on such sources of comfort.

2. We can resist sin; we can overcome temptation. Why do we need to be reminded of this?

It may be said that we live in a "no-fault" society. Some think that the power of our physical appetites is so intense and the pressures of life so unrelenting that people can hardly be blamed for giving in to temptations. If one advocates sexual abstinence for teen-agers, for example, critics scoff and claim that it is unrealistic to expect young people to control their sexual urges. But the Bible indicates that we do have the power to say no. In at least two different places we are exhorted to resist the devil, who is the author of temptation (see James 4:7; 1 Peter 5:8, 9). In connection with the example given earlier, it is noteworthy that Paul urges us to "flee fornication" (1 Corinthians 6:18). Whatever the temptation, we have the power to resist (1 Corinthians 10:13). To help us we have the presence of God's Spirit, the enlightenment of the Scripture, the resource of prayer, and the encouragement of fellow Christians.

3. How can we legitimately care for our bodies without becoming preoccupied with keeping them comfortable and attractive?

Thinking seriously about our bodies as temples of the Holy Spirit (1 Corinthians 6:19) should affect the way we treat them. For example, we will observe a diet that will keep our bodies presentable and useful for the Lord. In regard to rest and relaxation we will refrain from mere idleness or laziness and will aim instead to regain energy for further work to God's glory. Physical exercise will serve not as an end in itself, but it too will be a means of keeping us fit for our God-given duty. We will clothe our bodies in a way that will be in harmony with the fact that God lives in us and that we live to honor Him. Since both men and women are quite conscious of outward appearance today, both may benefit from a look at 1 Peter 3:3, 4.

4. A person with a carnal mind seeks immediate pleasure and gives little thought to its long-range effects. What are some common examples of carnal behavior and their consequences?

Perhaps illicit sexual behavior offers the clearest example of the painful consequences of a few moments of careless pleasure. And yet, in spite of the threat of AIDS, unwanted pregnancies, and conflict within and between families, carnal persons still mishandle sex. Another example is the abuse of alcoholic beverages. Physical illnesses, accidents, and fights frequently result from excessive drinking, but carnal people still let alcohol overtake them. The practices of lying and deception offer one more example. The long-range effects of these are misunderstanding, distrust, and conflict. But those who are carnal still tell their lies and sow the seeds of a bitter harvest in their lives and the lives of those around them.

5. The lesson writer states that "the Spirit in us is powerful but gentle. He leads, but does not drive." What are some ways in which the Spirit administers gentle leadership?

Of course, He speaks to us through the Scriptures. There are some harsh warnings in the Word of God; but if they apply to our life situation, the Spirit of God still leaves it up to us to respond. He speaks to us through the counsel of friends. Paul's exhortation in Galatians 6:1 certainly speaks of gentle guidance. The Spirit speaks to us through our problems and opportunities also. We need to be alert when facing any crisis or opportunity to perceive what God's Spirit wants us to learn through it.

Using Our Gifts in Serving

DEVOTIONAL READING: Philippians 2:1-4, 14-16; 4:8, 9.

LESSON SCRIPTURE: Romans 12.

PRINTED TEXT: Romans 12:1-18.

Romans 12:1-18

1 I beseech you therefore, brethren, by the mercies of God, that ye present your bodies a living sacrifice, holy, acceptable unto God, which is your reasonable service.

2 And be not conformed to this world: but be ye transformed by the renewing of your mind, that ye may prove what is that good, and acceptable, and perfect will of God.

3 For I say, through the grace given unto me, to every man that is among you, not to think of himself more highly than he ought to think; but to think soberly, according as God hath dealt to every man the measure of faith.

4 For as we have many members in one body, and all members have not the same office:

5 So we, being many, are one body in Christ, and every one members one of another.

6 Having then gifts differing according to the grace that is given to us, whether prophecy, let us prophesy according to the proportion of faith;

7 Or ministry, let us wait on our ministering; or he that teacheth, on teaching;

8 Or he that exhorteth, on exhortation: he that giveth, let him do it with simplicity; he that ruleth, with diligence; he that showeth mercy, with cheerfulness.

9 Let love be without dissimulation. Abhor that which is evil; cleave to that which is good.

10 Be kindly affectioned one to another with brotherly love; in honor preferring one another;

11 Not slothful in business; fervent in spirit; serving the Lord;

12 Rejoicing in hope; patient in tribulation; continuing instant in prayer;

13 Distributing to the necessity of saints; given to hospitality.

14 Bless them which persecute you: bless, and curse not.

15 Rejoice with them that do rejoice, and weep with them that weep.

16 Be of the same mind one toward another. Mind not high things, but condescend to men of low estate. Be not wise in your own conceits.

17 Recompense to no man evil for evil. Provide things honest in the sight of all men.

18 If it be possible, as much as lieth in you, live peaceably with all men.

GOLDEN TEXT: I beseech you therefore, brethren, by the mercies of God, that ye present your bodies a living sacrifice, holy, acceptable unto God, which is your reasonable service.—Romans 12:1.

Good News for God's People

Romans—Unit 2: Empowered by the Spirit (Lessons 5-8)

Lesson Aims

After this lesson a student should be able to:

1. Identify some ability that God has given him or her to be used in the service of God and humanity.

2. Use that ability energetically this week.

Lesson Outline

Visual 7 of the visuals packet highlights a truth included in verse 1. The remaining verses of the text expand on it. The visual is shown on page 284.

Introduction

A. What Shall We Do?

In our lessons from Romans we have seen much of what God has done for us. Since God has done so much for us, what shall we do?

B. Lesson Background

Last week we were reading from the eighth chapter of Romans about "Life in the Spirit": about being guided by the Spirit of God rather than the desires of our physical bodies. In the closing verses of chapter 8, Paul acknowledges that living in the Spirit may bring trouble and persecution; but he ends the chapter with this

triumphant assurance: "In all these things we are more than conquerors through him that loved us. For I am persuaded, that neither death, nor life, nor angels, nor principalities, nor powers, nor things present, nor things to come, nor height, nor depth, nor any other creature, shall be able to separate us from the love of God, which is in Christ Jesus our Lord."

Then chapters 9-11 bring us a long discussion of the state of Jews and Gentiles. This discussion is omitted from our present series of lessons, but we need to take notice of the conclusion of it. In the sight of God, all people, Jews and Gentiles, are shut up in unbelief and disobedience so that God may have mercy on all of them (Romans 11:32). His generous mercy is the basis of Paul's plea in our text.

I. A Living Sacrifice (Romans 12:1, 2)

Both Jewish Romans and heathen Romans were well acquainted with the idea of sacrifice. Christians, whether they had been Jews or Gentiles, learned that Christ's sacrifice of His life was the only one that was needed to atone for sin (Hebrews 10:12-14). But that does not mean there are no sacrifices for Christians to make. Our text describes a very important one.

A. Holy and Reasonable (v. 1)

1. I beseech you therefore, brethren, by the mercies of God, that ye present your bodies a living sacrifice, holy, acceptable unto God, which is your reasonable service.

By the mercies of God both Jews and heathen had been rescued from bondage to sin and from certain death. Certainly this provided a sound basis for asking them to do something in return, and Paul asked a very big thing. To the Roman Christians and to us he says, *Present your bodies.* Jews and heathen presented the bodies of animals, but we are asked for something better—our own bodies. Jews and heathen presented bodies killed at the altar, but we are asked for *a living sacrifice,* bodies alive and useful, bodies able and willing to do what God wants them to do. Our sacrifice then is described in two other ways. First, it is *holy.* That means set apart, dedicated, completely turned over to God. Second, it is *acceptable unto God.* Translated more literally, *acceptable* is *well pleasing.* We dedicate our living bodies to do whatever will please God.

Paul says such a sacrifice is *your reasonable service.* Some versions translate *worship* instead of *service.* Instead of choosing between the translations, let's include both of them.

Our complete worship and service to God are *reasonable*. Surely all He has done for us provides reason enough for all we can do for Him. But some versions have *spiritual* instead of *reasonable*. Again we can include both translations instead of choosing one. We present our physical bodies in sacrifice, but this is much more than a physical sacrifice. It involves our minds and spirits, our emotions and wills. It involves all that we are.

The sacrifice we present is our total selves, living and worshiping and serving. And let's not forget that phrase, *acceptable unto God*, or *well pleasing unto God*.

B. Renewed and Transformed (v. 2)

2. And be not conformed to this world: but be ye transformed by the renewing of your mind, that ye may prove what is that good, and acceptable, and perfect will of God.

The non-Christian *world* of Paul's time was much like the non-Christian world of today. People are selfish, greedy for profit and pleasure and prestige. Instead of sacrificing themselves in service to God and mankind, they try to use other people and God for their own advantage. Even if we were trained in Christian ways from infancy, *this world* still tries to capture us and force us into its mold. We are to resist the worldly pressure and be transformed, reshaped, in the likeness of God's Son (Romans 8:29).

This transformation is accomplished *by the renewing of your mind*. We have to reshape and redirect our thinking. We have to tear it away from worldly profit and pleasure and power. We have to fix it on things that are true, honest, just, pure, lovely, and of good report (Philippians 4:8). Then the well-directed mind must direct the body. Transformed by such a mind, we can *prove what is that good, and acceptable, and perfect will of God*. In this context it seems clear that Paul is thinking specifically of God's will for us: that is, of what God wants us to do and what He wants us to be. That is what we can *prove*, and the Greek word for *prove* is a very interesting one. Sometimes it means *discern* or *recognize*, as in Luke 12:56. Sometimes it means *test*, as in 1 Thessalonians 5:21. Sometimes it means *approve*, as in 1 Corinthians 16:3. And sometimes it means *show* or *demonstrate*, as in 1 Corinthians 3:13. Again, let's not choose one meaning, but consider all of them. Transformed by a renewed mind, we can *discern* or *recognize* God's will for us. We can *test* it in our living, and surely we will then approve it. Finally we can *demonstrate* His will for us as we let our light shine so people around us will see our good works and glorify our Heavenly Father (Matthew 5:16)

II. Using Our Gifts
(Romans 12:3-8)

All of us are called to present our bodies in sacrifice, not killed at the altar, but living and serving God; but we do not all serve in the same way. The kind of service we give to God depends on the kind of ability He has given to us.

A. Know Yourself (v. 3)

3. For I say, through the grace given unto me, to every man that is among you, not to think of himself more highly than he ought to think: but to think soberly, according as God hath dealt to every man the measure of faith.

Grace often is defined as favor that is not deserved, the favor by which sinners are saved (Ephesians 2:8). That definition is correct, but it is not complete. God's favor brings salvation, and it brings also different kinds of gifts and abilities. The rest of our text will call attention to some of them. The special *grace* that was given to Paul included the summons and the inspiration to be an apostle, a specially authorized representative for the Lord (Romans 1:5; 15:15; Ephesians 3:7, 8). Through that grace, with special inspiration and authority, he gave the instruction that follows.

Every man means every person; the ladies are not left out. Each one is urged *not to think of himself more highly than he ought to think*. Conceited, arrogant thinking is part of the worldly mold from which we have been transformed (v. 2). Our renewed minds are *to think soberly*. Sober thinking is sound thinking. Each of us is to have a correct and accurate opinion of himself—not too high, but not too low either. We need to look at ourselves objectively and form an opinion that fits the facts.

According as God hath dealt to every man the measure of faith. This does not mean God arbitrarily hands out a lot of faith to one person and only a little faith to another. It seems that the phrase *of faith* is possessive. Faith's measure is the measure of ability that God gives to a person who has faith. That person's faith controls whatever portion or measure of ability the person receives. Verses 6-8 mention some of the different abilities that are given. The amount or *measure* of ability God gives is the proper basis for that person's opinion of himself.

B. Members of One Body (vv. 4, 5)

4, 5. For as we have many members in one body, and all members have not the same office: so we, being many, are one body in Christ, and every one members one of another.

A human body has many parts, and the parts are constructed in different ways to serve different purposes. Each member of the church has his or her own way of helping the others and being helped by them. The help one can give depends on the ability God has given that person.

C. Different Gifts (vv. 6-8)

6. Having then gifts differing according to the grace that is given to us, whether prophecy, let us prophesy according to the proportion of faith.

Whatever abilities we have are *gifts* of God's *grace,* His favor that we neither earn nor deserve. In His grace and goodness He gives us *differing* abilities so we can help one another. Do we sometimes wish others were like us? Or do we wish we could be more like others? No! A body would be worthless if all the parts were just alike.

Some Christians had the gift of *prophecy,* the ability and privilege of receiving information and instruction directly from God and passing His messages on to others. That gift was very helpful to the church in the days before God's messages were recorded in the New Testament to guide all of us. The prophet was a link with Heaven. Perhaps that is why the gift of prophecy is at the top of the list. Anyone who had that gift should prophesy *according to the proportion of faith.* Having faith in God, he received from God a certain portion of information or instruction. He should pass on to his fellow Christians exactly what he received: he should give God's message, not his own.

7. Or ministry, let us wait on our ministering; or he that teacheth, on teaching.

Ministry is service. Many Christians are gifted with the ability to serve in various ways. They visit the sick, they bring comfort to the sorrowing, they spend time with the lonely, they read to people whose eyes are dim, they take hot meals to people whose cook is sick, or perhaps they give some help with the housework. Or they mow the lawn when the homeowner is disabled. They help to clean and maintain the meeting house, they come early to unlock the doors and stay late to lock them again. Almost any Christian has a gift of ministry, an ability to serve in some way. Many Christians serving in many ways provide a broad base to support the leaders.

To *wait on our ministering* is not to delay it. It is to be diligent in our service, to give it time and attention, to look for opportunities to serve, and to serve well, as a good waiter in a fine restaurant is alert and quick to see and meet every need of a customer.

He that teacheth should likewise give time and attention to his *teaching.* He should be well acquainted with the truth he will teach, and he should be well prepared to teach in the best way to make the truth plain and attractive. He too should be alert, watching for opportunities to present the truth.

8. Or he that exhorteth, on exhortation: he that giveth, let him do it with simplicity; he that ruleth, with diligence; he that showeth mercy, with cheerfulness.

One who teaches may also exhort people to do what they are taught to do: but some are specially gifted with ability to stir others to action, to encourage and strengthen and motivate. Anyone with that gift should give time and attention to the encouragement and help he can provide.

He that giveth should do it *with simplicity,* with single-mindedness, thinking only of the need to be met and the good to be accomplished by the gift. Without such simplicity we complicate our giving by thinking of how many ways we could use the money selfishly instead of giving it. Consequently we do not give as much as we really can. In effect, then, giving *with simplicity* is giving generously. In 2 Corinthians 8:2 the same Greek word is translated *liberality* instead of *simplicity.*

He that ruleth refers to those who are in a position of authority or leadership in the church (1 Thessalonians 5:12), the elders (1 Timothy 5:17). Like those with other gifts, they should give time and attention to what they are doing. They should be careful, thorough, zealous in guiding those who are under them.

We show *mercy* when we forgive someone who has done wrong, or when we help someone who is in trouble. The good Samaritan showed mercy to the wounded man he found along the road (Luke 10:37). The good we do is marred when we do it grudgingly. We are robbed of the joy of helping, and the one we help is robbed of the joy of being helped. How much better to show mercy *with cheerfulness!*

IT DOESN'T
TAKE MUCH
OF A MAN
TO SERVE

GOD

BUT
IT TAKES
ALL THERE IS
OF HIM.
—ANONYMOUS

visual 7

III. Advice for All

(Romans 12:9-18)

We have been reading advice for different people: one who prophesies, one who ministers, one who teaches, one who exhorts, one who gives, one who rules, one who shows mercy. Still the advice is much the same for all of them. Whatever ability one has, he should use it well, thoroughly, wholeheartedly, happily. Now we go on with advice, not for specific people with specific gifts, but for all of us.

A. Love and Goodness (vv. 9, 10)

9. Let love be without dissimulation. Abhor that which is evil; cleave to that which is good.

Dissimulation is *deceit*, hypocrisy. We are to "love one another with a pure heart fervently" (1 Peter 1:22). More than that, we are to love our enemies (Matthew 5:44). Love is not always warm, personal affection; it is sincere good will, eagerness for the good of the loved one, readiness to help that person if we can.

To *abhor* is to hate and avoid. This is our attitude toward *that which is evil.* This does not mean we hate and avoid and fear any evil that may be done *to* us. We can accept that with composure, even with joy (James 1:2, 3; 1 Peter 4:12, 13, 16). But if anyone or anything tempts us to *do* evil, that suggestion is to be rejected with contempt and disgust.

To *cleave* is to cling, to be attached. Our attachment to *that which is good* ought to be as firm and resolute as our separation from *that which is evil.*

10. Be kindly affectioned one to another with brotherly love; in honor preferring one another.

The love of brothers at its best is the model for the relation of Christian to Christian. Such love is unselfish: each of us prefers to honor another rather than to be honored.

HATING SIN

The nightly news has become a horror show! One murderer's crimes include cannibalism. Another man is charged with sodomizing his two nephews, ages two and four. A mother disposes of her newborn in a garbage dumpster. An arsonist incinerates his entire family when he burns down their home.

Celebrities acknowledge their homosexual sins when they contract the AIDS virus. Others admit promiscuous sex lives without a hint of remorse over their fornication/adultery.

Rapists pornographers, and prostitutes continue to make the news. Muggings, bank robberies, embezzlements, and tax frauds—all sorts of crimes are reported nightly.

Christians are rightly horrified at such behavior. How much do *you* hate sin? Enough to elect legislators who oppose it? Enough to turn off TV shows that condone and glorify it? Enough to resist the devil who creates it? Enough to avoid even the "appearance of evil"? (1 Thessalonians 5:22).

We must not forget the positive part of Paul's exhortation: "Cleave to that which is good." On the Christian team, our *offense* must be as strong as our *defense.* Then our victory is assured.
—R. W. B.

B. Service and Joy (vv. 11-14)

11. Not slothful in business; fervent in spirit; serving the Lord.

Business here is not buying and selling; it is busy-ness, earnest attention and effort. We are not to be *slothful,* slow or reluctant or lazy, in giving our best to whatever we ought to do. Instead, we are to be *fervent in spirit.* Literally, *fervent* means *boiling.* Our spirits ought to be "all steamed up" and "boiling over" with eagerness in *serving the Lord.*

12. Rejoicing in hope; patient in tribulation; continuing instant in prayer.

Why are we continually happy and energetic in serving the Lord? One reason is the *hope* we have. We are convinced that God rules, that everything will turn to right in the end, and that we shall have a share in God's victory and glory. Such a hope makes us not only happy and enthusiastic (v. 11), but also *patient in tribulation.* The Greek word for *tribulation* has the primary meaning of *pressure.* In today's English, *pressure* is used as that Greek word is, meaning all the troubles and difficulties and opposition and frustrations that try our souls. And in today's English, *patient* has become too weak a word to express the meaning here. We are to be strong and steadfast in enduring all the pressures of our modern life.

To keep up our vigor and enthusiasm, we need to be *continuing instant in prayer.* In the antique English of our version, *instant* means constantly and earnestly. We need God's help in keeping up our strength and enthusiasm under all the pressures that come to us.

13. Distributing to the necessity of saints; given to hospitality.

Saints are Christians. They take care of each other. When some of them are in need of food or clothing or shelter, the others distribute as much of their own goods as it takes to supply the need. This generosity may take the form of *hospitality* to saints from out of town.

14. Bless them which persecute you: bless, and curse not.

Can you bring yourself to keep on doing good to people who keep on doing wrong to you? This may be a difficult part of being patient in tribulation, but it is an important part.

C. Fellowship and Peace (vv. 15-18)

15. Rejoice with them that do rejoice, and weep with them that weep.

Envy makes some people feel bad when others are rejoicing, but Christians have no envy. Each one loves his neighbor as himself, and so each one is sincerely happy with the happiness of another, or sorrowful with another's sorrow.

16. Be of the same mind one toward another. Mind not high things, but condescend to men of low estate. Be not wise in your own conceits.

The first part of this verse does not say we should have no differences of opinion; it says we should be considerate of one another. All of us should think of the good of others as well as our own good. We should wish for others to have just what we would want for ourselves. It is the Golden Rule in the realm of thought.

Mind not high things does not forbid us to think of Heavenly things. We ought to do that (Colossians 3:1, 2). But we are not to set our minds on things that are *high* in the worldly sense: riches and fame, prestige and power. Rather, we should *go along with lowly people.* This is a better translation than *condescend,* for *condescend* suggests that we are lowering ourselves. That suggestion is not in the Greek word. We are not to lower ourselves to share with the lowly; we are to be lowly with them. The last clause of the verse is aptly translated in *The New English Bible*: "Do not keep thinking how wise you are."

17. Recompense to no man evil for evil. Provide things honest in the sight of all men.

Christians do right. If others do wrong, that is no excuse for us to respond in the same way. Instead, we take care not only to do what is *honest*—honorable, right, good—but also to do it so humbly and modestly and cheerfully that *all men* will see it as right.

18. If it be possible, as much as lieth in you, live peaceably with all men.

Sometimes it is not possible to *live peaceably with all men.* Paul knew that very well. He himself was opposed and beaten and jailed. But we do our best to keep the peace. We try to be sure no wrong act or word of ours will give anyone an excuse to oppose us.

COMPATIBILITY

In our 1992-93 Christian preschool, our enrollment for Fall was nearly full by February 1992! The success of our Christian Preschool is just one indicator of the boom in child-care en-

terprises. Day-care, latchkey, and kindergarten programs proliferate.

Some children are enrolled in preschools to give them a "head start" when they go to public school. Most parents want their youngsters to "learn how to get along with others." In other words, the kids are learning *compatibility.*

Paul realized that grownups in the church need to learn and practice getting along with each other, too. In this text, he lists several characteristics of compatibility: modesty (v. 3), geniality (v. 10), generosity (v. 13), empathy (v. 15), humility (v. 16), and honesty (v. 17).

Robert Fulghum was close to the truth when he wrote *All I Really Need to Know I Learned in Kindergarten.* He says wisdom can be found "in the sandpile at Sunday school." He's definitely right about that. God's Word contains the most important truths we can learn.   —R. W. B.

Conclusion

A. This Week

Yes, you have a gift. If it is not one of those mentioned in our text, you can add it to the list. If you neglect it, it will fade away. If you use it, it will grow. So put it to work this week.

B. Prayer

Our Father in Heaven, it is by Your grace that we have the many abilities that make us helpful to one another and to Your church. By Your grace may we have also the willingness to sacrifice our selfish interests and use Your gifts for You and Your people. In Jesus' precious name we pray. Amen.

C. Thought to Remember

You are gifted.

Home Daily Bible Readings

Monday, Apr. 11—Depths of God's Riches, Wisdom, Knowledge (Romans 11:25-36)
Tuesday, Apr. 12—Many Gifts, One Body (Romans 12:1-8)
Wednesday, Apr. 13—Outdo One Another in Showing Honor (Romans 12:9-13)
Thursday, Apr. 14—Live Together in Integrity and Harmony (Romans 12:14-21)
Friday, Apr. 15—"Love Your Neighbor As Yourself" (Romans 13:5-10)
Saturday, Apr. 16—Salvation Is Near to Us (Romans 13:11-14)
Sunday, Apr. 17—To God Be Glory Through Jesus Christ (Romans 16:17-27)

Learning by Doing

This page contains an alternate lesson plan emphasizing learning activities. Classes desiring such student involvement will find these suggestions helpful.

Learning Goals

As a result of this lesson your students will:

1. Review how God has demonstrated His mercy in their lives.

2. Identify specific responses to God's mercy that are commanded in Romans 12.

3. Commit themselves to presenting their lives as sacrifices offered to God.

Into the Lesson

Begin class by asking your class members, "What are some hymns or choruses that tell of God's love and mercy for us?" As students suggest examples, ask them what phrases or ideas in the hymn or chorus emphasize God's love and mercy.

Option

Give each class member a slip of paper and a pencil. Encourage students to reflect on the way God has shown mercy to them. Then ask them to write on the slip the title of a hymn that expresses their thoughts about this. If they prefer, they may create a hymn title of their own. After a few minutes ask volunteers to share their titles.

Lead into today's study by saying, "The book of Romans is drenched in mercy. In the first eleven chapters Paul explains God's mercy; in chapters twelve through sixteen, he exhorts us to respond appropriately to it. Let's explore some ways in which we can show our gratitude to God for His mercy."

Into the Word

Part One: Lead your students to review Paul's teachings of God's love, grace, and mercy that are recorded in chapters 1-11 of Romans. Have different students read aloud these passages: Romans 3:21-26; 5:1-11; 8:15-18; 8:28-39. After the reading of each passage ask, "Based upon this passage, how has God been merciful to us?" Discuss briefly.

Part Two: Read Romans 12:1-18 aloud. Then give each class member a copy of the following questions based on this text.

In response to God's mercy—

1. How should we relate to God?

2. How should we relate to the world?

3. How should we relate to ourselves?

4. How should we relate to other believers?

Have students form groups of six to discuss the questions for about fifteen minutes. Then call the class together again and say, "Perhaps all of Paul's instruction in this passage can be summed up in verse 1. What do you think is involved in offering ourselves to God as living sacrifices?" Allow for discussion.

Option

Complete Part One above. Then divide the class into groups of four students each. Provide each group with several sheets of paper, pens, a felt-tip pen, and masking tape. Appoint a leader in each group to direct the following activity.

Each group is to read Romans 12:1-18. Then they are to create four bumper sticker slogans, one to summarize each of four topics that are related to the text.

The slogans are to express our response to God's mercy as seen in our relationship with—

God (v. 1)

the world (v. 2)

ourselves (v. 3)

other believers (vv. 4-18).

Suggest that the students within each group brainstorm several ideas for each topic. Then they can select the slogan they think best expresses the ideas of the passage. They are then to cut a sheet of paper into four strips about the size of a bumper sticker and write a slogan on each.

Allow about fifteen minutes for this activity. Then have the groups affix their bumper stickers to the wall with the tape. The class should then select the bumper sticker they like the best for each of the four topics.

Into Life

Write the following incomplete statements on the chalkboard:

When I think of offering my life to God as a living sacrifice, I—

The biggest obstacle to offering myself to God as a living sacrifice is—

I will seek to offer myself to God as a living sacrifice this week by—

Give each class member a sheet of paper. Ask the students to complete these statements honestly as they apply to their lives. Let them know that they need not share these with anyone. Ask them to review the statements in the coming week as a reminder of the sacrifice they are to present to God.

Close with prayer in the small groups students worked in earlier.

Let's Talk It Over

The questions on this page are designed to encourage review of the lesson Scriptures and to promote discussion of the lesson by the class. The answers provided are only discussion starters. Let your class talk it over from there.

1. What comparisons can be drawn between the living sacrifice we are to make of our bodies and the animal sacrifices of the Old Testament era?

In Old Testament times, the sacrifice was to be the best the worshiper could offer. God's law specified that deformed and blemished animals were not to be offered. Likewise, we should give God the best of our time and energy and not merely what is left over from all our other activities. The worshiper in Israel was to offer the sacrifice willingly. The New Testament counsels us to present our gifts "not grudgingly, or of necessity: for God loveth a cheerful giver" (2 Corinthians 9:7). Surely this applies to our gifts of time and service as well as our money. The Old Testament sacrifices were to be offered according to God's design. Detailed instructions were included in the law regarding these sacrifices. Although it does not contain detailed regulations, the New Testament makes it clear that we should engage in corporate worship, private worship, Christian fellowship, sharing of our faith, and service.

2. Why is it important that we learn to look objectively at our abilities and strengths and weaknesses?

By overestimating our abilities we may waste our own time and other people's time by attempting tasks we are not capable of doing. In the church we may accept responsibilities that are beyond our capability, and thereby contribute to dissatisfaction and disharmony among the members. On the other hand, by failing to recognize and acknowledge our actual abilities we deprive our church, our family, our employer, and perhaps our society of notable benefits we are capable of producing. How tempting it is, when faced with a new challenge, simply to say, "I can't," before assessing whether or not we can. As we study the Scriptures, we need to pray, "Lord, help me to perceive the talents You have given me, and guide me in putting them to work for Your glory."

3. How can persons who have the gift of motivating others benefit the church?

Perhaps every church committee should have one person like this, who will say, "We can do it! Let's get to work on it! God will surely bless our efforts." Such a motivator would also help to stir up the entire congregation's enthusiasm for the committee's project. The role of the motivator could be especially vital in urging the members of the congregation to take the gospel to the lost in their community, and to support the Lord's work by giving generously. A motivator has the ability to present facts known and accepted by all in such a way as to get people to do what they know they should be doing. Obviously this kind of person can be a tremendous asset in any church.

4. How can we teach Christians to "abhor [or hate] that which is evil"?

One benefit of reading the Bible is that it enables us to look at evil from God's viewpoint. Occasionally the Bible tells us what God hates. A notable example is Proverbs 6:16-19, which lists seven sins that the Lord hates and that "are an abomination unto him." It is clear that we also should hate such sins. Another benefit the Bible provides is its description of sin's fruits. We read of family conflict, national decline, poverty, disease, death, and eternal punishment in Hell as results of wicked behavior. Surely anything that produces such a bitter harvest should be hated. Christians should be urged also to ponder the experiences in their own lives that confirm the Bible's revelation of sin as a horrible, destructive reality.

5. Paul urges Christians to be "fervent in spirit." Why is this significant today?

We regard enthusiasm as natural in connection with sporting events or some other forms of entertainment, but not so in our daily walk with Christ. This is a strange situation, since our worship, fellowship in Christ, and study of the Scriptures are the very activities that should generate the greatest level of enthusiasm. Of course we are wary of becoming emotionalistic or of exhibiting a false enthusiasm. But Paul's phrase, "fervent in *spirit*," points away from the artificial atmosphere of religious zeal. It speaks instead of a zeal that radiates out from the truth, the joy, and the power that God's Spirit ministers to our own spirits. This is a fervor that we should not hesitate to express.

Living for Others

DEVOTIONAL READING: Romans 15:1-17.

LESSON SCRIPTURE: Romans 14.

PRINTED TEXT: Romans 14:7-19.

Romans 14:7-19

7 For none of us liveth to himself, and no man dieth to himself.

8 For whether we live, we live unto the Lord; and whether we die, we die unto the Lord: whether we live therefore, or die, we are the Lord's.

9 For to this end Christ both died, and rose, and revived, that he might be Lord both of the dead and living.

10 But why dost thou judge thy brother? or why dost thou set at nought thy brother? for we shall all stand before the judgment seat of Christ.

11 For it is written, As I live, saith the Lord, every knee shall bow to me, and every tongue shall confess to God.

12 So then every one of us shall give account of himself to God.

13 Let us not therefore judge one another any more: but judge this rather, that no man put a stumblingblock or an occasion to fall in his brother's way.

14 I know, and am persuaded by the Lord Jesus, that there is nothing unclean of itself: but to him that esteemeth any thing to be unclean, to him it is unclean.

15 But if thy brother be grieved with thy meat, now walkest thou not charitably. Destroy not him with thy meat, for whom Christ died.

16 Let not then your good be evil spoken of:

17 For the kingdom of God is not meat and drink; but righteousness, and peace, and joy in the Holy Ghost.

18 For he that in these things serveth Christ is acceptable to God, and approved of men.

19 Let us therefore follow after the things which make for peace, and things wherewith one may edify another.

Apr
24

GOLDEN TEXT: Let us therefore follow after the things which make for peace, and things wherewith one may edify another.—Romans 14:19.

Lesson Aims

After this lesson a student should be able to:

1. Recall at least one of two problems that Paul saw in the church at Rome.

2. Recall at least one way Paul suggested to deal with the problems.

3. "Follow after the things which make for peace."

Lesson Outline

INTRODUCTION

    A. War and Peace

    B. Lesson Background

  I. THE LORD UNITES US (Romans 14:7-9)

    A. The Lord's People (vv. 7, 8)

    B. The Lord's Purpose (v. 9)

  II. THE LORD JUDGES US (Romans 14:10-15)

    A. Christ Judges All (vv. 10-12)

       Class-Action Suit

    B. We Help One Another (vv. 13-15)

 III. THE KINGDOM AND US (Romans 14:16-19)

    A. The Kingdom (vv. 16-18)

       First Sermon

    B. Our Part (v. 19)

CONCLUSION

    A. Harmony Among Brethren

    B. Harmony With Heaven

    C. Think and Pray

    D. Prayer

    E. Thought to Remember

Visual 8 of the visuals packet highlights some thoughts in the Lesson Background section. The visual is shown on page 293.

Introduction

A. War and Peace

Our battle song written by Sabine Baring-Gould, has a stirring sound: "Onward, Christian soldiers, marching as to war." And we are in a war. We are called to "put on the whole armor of God" (Ephesians 6:11) and "fight the good fight of faith" (1 Timothy 6:12). On the other hand, Jesus said, "Blessed are the peacemakers" (Matthew 5:9), and the apostle Paul calls us to "follow after the things which make for peace" (Romans 14:19).

How can we be both warriors and peacemakers? First, we need to recognize our Leader and never turn aside from following Him. We march "with the cross of Jesus going on before." Then we need to know the enemy and not be shooting down our fellow soldiers. "We wrestle not against flesh and blood, but against principalities, against powers, against the rulers of the darkness of this world, against spiritual wickedness in high places" (Ephesians 6:12). And we need to choose our weapons carefully. They are "not carnal, but mighty through God to the pulling down of strongholds" (2 Corinthians 10:4).

Yes, we have a warfare, but this lesson is directed rather to peace in our own camp. "We are not divided; all one body we."

B. Lesson Background

In the background of this lesson lie two questions that might possibly threaten the peace of the church in Rome. One is a question about food; the other is a question about special days.

A question about food. Heathen Romans sometimes offered animals in sacrifice to their imaginary gods. Usually only a small part of the carcass was burned on the altar. Another part was given to the priest who conducted the ceremony of sacrifice, and the rest of the meat belonged to the worshiper who brought the sacrifice. He might have a feast with friends, or he might sell the meat. Probably some of the priests' portions also found their way to the market. Some students suppose that most or all of the meat in Roman markets was from such sacrifices.

Some Christians would not use such meat. To eat it, they thought, would be to take part in the heathen worship in which it had been offered. But other Christians thought there was not necessarily any connection between the eating and the worship. Perhaps some of them even thought they could go to a banquet in a heathen temple and join in the eating without joining in the worship (1 Corinthians 8:10).

Paul discusses this question at length in 1 Corinthians 8—10. In the first part of Romans 14, however, he merely says a Christian should not condemn or despise a fellow Christian who disagrees with him on this matter (vv. 1-4).

We are not faced with the same problem today, but perhaps the same answer can be given to some questions on which we differ. Shall we avoid all movies because most of them are dirty? Shall we boycott a restaurant that offers intoxicating drinks? Shall we stay away from a community fund raiser because it has gambling along with other amusements? Shall we denounce dancing because it is sensual? Is

"Christian rock" worshipful or intolerable? Can we apply Paul's principle to such questions, refusing to condemn or despise one who does not agree with us?

A question about special days. Jewish Christians in Rome kept the Sabbath, and perhaps observed the monthly New Moon Day and the annual festivals as well. Most of the Gentile Christians observed none of these. Nowadays some Christians meet for worship on the Sabbath, Saturday; but most do not. Most Christians celebrate Christmas and Easter, but some object to these celebrations because no such annual observances are recorded in the New Testament.

Paul says each Christian should make up his own mind. He need not try to force his opinion on others, however; for people on both sides of the question are equally devoted to the Lord (Romans 14:5, 6). That leads directly to the first verse of our text.

I. The Lord Unites Us
(Romans 14:7-9)

In an extreme case, it may become necessary to get rid of some sinner who has made his way into the fellowship of the church without giving up his sin (1 Corinthians 5:9-13). But most of us in the church are sincerely devoted to Christ and His will. We therefore can tolerate many differences of opinion among ourselves, even some big differences.

A. The Lord's People (vv. 7, 8)

7. For none of us liveth to himself, and no man dieth to himself.

"Living for Others" is the title of our lesson. When we have that in mind, verse 7 naturally makes us think of our relationship with the people around us; but that is not Paul's thought at this point. It is true, of course, that we have an influence on others and they have an influence on us. We ought to think about others and order our lives for their good as well as our own. That thinking will appear later in our text; but in this opening verse the theme is not our relationship with fellow Christians, but our relationship with the Lord. See how this is brought out in verses 6 and 8.

8. For whether we live, we live unto the Lord; and whether we die, we die unto the Lord: whether we live therefore, or die, we are the Lord's.

Our relationship with the Lord not only continues as long as we live, but also involves our whole life: all that we do is devoted to Him. Furthermore, we are not separated from the Lord even when *we die.* Our relationship is eternal.

Both before and after death *we are the Lord's.* This is the nature of our relationship: He owns us. We owe Him the full service of happy slaves.

B. The Lord's Purpose (v. 9)

9. For to this end Christ both died, and rose, and revived, that he might be Lord both of the dead and living.

Our eternal relationship with the Lord is the *end,* the purpose, of His death and resurrection. He "was delivered for our offenses, and was raised again for our justification" (Romans 4:25). He died to redeem us (Titus 2:14); He "ever liveth to make intercession" for us (Hebrews 7:25).

II. The Lord Judges Us
(Romans 14:10-15)

In the background of our lesson we see that one Christian is so strong, so confident in his freedom from idolatry, that he does not hesitate to eat the meat from an idolatrous sacrifice. Another does not share that confidence, and he will not eat the meat. Neither of these two should criticize the other; for both are servants of the same Master, and the Master's judgment is what counts (Romans 14:1-4). Now Paul returns to that thought.

A. Christ Judges All (vv. 10-12)

10. But why dost thou judge thy brother? or why dost thou set at nought thy brother? for we shall all stand before the judgment seat of Christ.

One man thinks it is a sin to eat the meat of an idolatrous sacrifice. Then he should not eat it, but neither should he condemn another who has a different opinion. That other is confident that there is no sin in his eating, but he should not look down on the brother who lacks that confidence. Christ is the Master of both; His judgment is the only one that matters.

11. For it is written, As I live, saith the Lord, every knee shall bow to me, and every tongue shall confess to God.

The judgment of Christ (v. 10) is also God's judgment, for Christ "was ordained of God to be the Judge of quick and dead" (Acts 10:42). Paul now quotes from Isaiah 45:23 to remind us that everybody, believer or unbeliever, will finally accept that judgment.

12. So then every one of us shall give account of himself to God.

Like the rest of mankind, all of us Christians will submit to God's judgment; and any unjustified condemnation of our brethren will be among the things we shall have to answer for.

CLASS-ACTION SUIT

News in our neighborhood periodically focuses on the ongoing dispute involving owner/operators of a uranium processing plant. The residents of the community immediately surrounding the plant site, and workers too, filed charges of pollution and life-endangerment against the industry. High levels of radiation in the plant and toxic waste from its disposal system alledgedly have threatened the lives of people both inside and outside.

The Environmental Protection Agency investigated and ordered a major clean-up and overhaul to satisfy federal regulations. Now the plaintiffs have brought a class-action suit against both the plant and the EPA for not issuing proper warnings and for taking so long to accomplish the required modifications.

Paul describes a "class action" when he writes, "We shall all stand before the judgment seat of Christ." In that action, however, all humans as a class will be defendants, not plaintiffs, before the righteous Judge. "All have sinned" (Romans 3:23), and "there is none righteous" (Romans 3:10).

We who are in Christ must not consider ourselves better than others. Sin condemns us all, so we cannot, *we must not*, judge our brothers and sisters. Judgment is reserved for Christ.

—R. W. B.

B. We Help One Another (vv. 13-15)

13. Let us not therefore judge one another any more: but judge this rather, that no man put a stumblingblock or an occasion to fall in his brother's way.

Instead of criticizing others, each Christian ought to take a critical look at himself. He should examine what he does and what he says; he should make sure no deed or word of his will be an obstacle to someone else. To fall into sin is a serious thing, a tragic thing; and to cause someone else to fall into sin is tragic too.

14. I know, and am persuaded by the Lord Jesus, that there is nothing unclean of itself: but to him that esteemeth any thing to be unclean, to him it is unclean.

There is nothing unclean of itself. Of course this does not refer to such things as murder, mayhem, adultery, theft, malice, lust, and envy. Paul is returning to the background thought of meat from heathen sacrifices. That is not *unclean of itself.* Roast beef from an ox killed at the altar is exactly like it would be if the ox were killed somewhere else. The apostle Paul, living in communion with *the Lord Jesus* and enlightened by His Spirit, had been brought to this conviction.

But there is more to be said. Sin lies in the heart, not just in the action. If one thinks an act is wrong and does it anyway, he is a sinner at heart even if the act is harmless. He thinks he is doing wrong; he means to do wrong. That intention is wrong whether the act in itself is wrong or not.

15. But if thy brother be grieved with thy meat, now walkest thou not charitably. Destroy not him with thy meat, for whom Christ died.

You understand, as Paul does, that the meat from a sacrificed ox is not unclean. You eat it without offending either God or your conscience. But *thy brother* does not know what you and Paul know. He thinks anyone who eats that meat is taking part in heathen worship. Because you are his brother in Christ, he is *grieved*, pained, distressed, when you do such a thing. When you cause such distress to a brother, you are not acting *charitably.* In the *King James Version*, the word *charity* means the unselfish kind of love that moves you to help others even if helping them is costly. Such a love would lead you to pass up the beef and be content with a vegetable plate to avoid distressing your brother.

Though your brother is deeply grieved by your eating, his grief would not be expected to *destroy* him. But there is an added possibility that Paul describes in 1 Corinthians 8:9-13. Your brother does not want to offend or embarrass you by denouncing what he sees as your sin. To avoid any embarrassment, he takes a helping of beef along with you. But he thinks that beef is unclean, so to him it is unclean. In his own mind he is renouncing Christ and worshiping an idol just to keep from embarrassing you, and that can destroy him for eternity. Are you willing to do that for the sake of a piece of roast beef? Paul would rather be a vegetarian for the rest of his life (1 Corinthians 8:13).

III. The Kingdom and Us (Romans 14:16-19)

Would you insist on enjoying your roast beef regardless of the distress it caused your brother? Paul says that would be not only a wound to the brother, but also a sin against Christ (1 Corinthians 8:12). That is to be avoided at all costs. Above all things we want to be ruled by God: we want to do His will (Matthew 6:33).

A. The Kingdom (vv. 16-18)

16. Let not then your good be evil spoken of.

The thought is not that we should rebuke and denounce and shut up anyone who may speak evil of the good we do. Rather, we try to do good in such a way that no one will think of speaking evil of it. In this context it means that we turn down the roast beef, no matter how good it is, rather than let a misinformed brother say we are joining in idol worship—or rather than let an outsider say Christians are always quarreling among themselves.

17. For the kingdom of God is not meat and drink; but righteousness, and peace, and joy in the Holy Ghost.

Doing God's will and being ruled by Him is not a matter of what we eat and drink, but our wish to do God's will controls our eating and drinking along with everything else we do. The kingdom of God, His rule, His dominion, involves many things, reaching into every nook and cranny of our living. Here we see three of the things that are involved.

Righteousness consists of two things: doing right and being forgiven when we fail to do right. Seeking God's kingdom and His righteousness includes seeing both of these.

Peace includes harmony with our Father in Heaven and harmony with our brothers and sisters on earth. Seeking God's kingdom includes seeking both of these.

Joy in the Holy Ghost, or *in the Holy Spirit*, is the natural result of following the Spirit's leading. We find His leading in these verses we are reading, and elsewhere in the Bible. He leads us to seek first "the kingdom of God, and his righteousness" (Matthew 6:33). When we are eagerly seeking these, joy comes unsought. Joy is with us even in our troubles, for we know these troubles will do us good (James 1:2-4).

18. For he that in these things serveth Christ is acceptable to God, and approved of men.

The instructions in this chapter help us to find righteousness, peace, and joy in God's kingdom, so we can be sure all these instructions help us to win the approval of God and men.

FIRST SERMON

I was just eighteen when I preached from my father's pulpit for the first time. Like most first-year Bible college students, I told that captive congregation everything I knew—and the sermon lasted at least ten minutes! My text was Luke 2:52, and naturally the outline had four points: Jesus grew in *wisdom*, in *stature*, in *favor with God*, and in *favor with man*. The last two points I elaborated as Christ's example of growth spiritually and socially.

Paul underlines the importance and possibility of spiritual and social maturity for Christians. He as much as promises that those who serve Christ in "righteousness, and peace, and joy in the Holy Ghost" will enjoy acceptance from God and approval from man.

visual 8

What might it be instead of meat?

Every human heart craves acceptance and affirmation. When we believe in God, we want to be "right" with Him. When we become socially aware, we want to be approved by those in our social circle. Our spirits want to relate to others in friendship.

Jesus makes it possible for us to be friends with (reconciled to) God. And in Him we experience sweet fellowship with those of "like precious faith" (2 Peter 1:1). Though non-believers may not affirm us, they can do nothing to break these precious bonds of Christian fellowship.

—R. W. B.

B. Our Part (v. 19)

19. Let us therefore follow after the things which make for peace, and things wherewith one may edify another.

One of *the things which make for peace* is to be considerate of others, not to grieve them by doing what they think is wrong (v. 15). We can easily think of other things that *make for peace* rather than strife. We are to *follow after* those things, to pursue them and capture them and make them a part of our way of living. We will not do wrong for the sake of peace, of course; but we may leave undone some things that are not wrong but may have harmful results.

We are also to pursue *things wherewith one may edify another.* Literally, *edify* means "build up." How do we build up anyone in Christian faith and conduct? Obviously we do not do it by destroying him for the sake of a dinner of roast beef (v. 15). We do it by teaching and encouraging, by praising those who do well and being patient with those who falter, by thanking those who are strong and giving a hand to those who are weak. We do it by setting an example of vigorous Christian living and unfailing helpfulness. "Therefore, strengthen your feeble arms and weak knees. 'Make level paths for your feet,' so that the lame may not be disabled, but rather healed" (Hebrews 12:12, 13, *New International Version*).

Conclusion

The twentieth century is near its end, and in this entire century perhaps no Christian has been destroyed or even grieved because a brother was eating the meat of a heathen sacrifice. But is it possible that some Christians have been grieved, or even destroyed, because of something no more important than that?

A. Harmony Among Brethren

Think of a dispute in your congregation, now or in the past. Does it involve something that is surely wrong, something that the Bible clearly says is wrong? Or is it like the roast-beef question in Rome, a question on which brethren can have different opinions and still work together in harmony, neither condemning nor despising those who differ?

Think of the last quarrel you personally had. Was the issue so important that you *had* to take a firm stand? Or could you have given in as easily and gracefully as a Roman beef-eater could have become a vegetarian to avoid offending a brother?

B. Harmony With Heaven

Above all things, of course, we want to live in harmony with our Father in Heaven and our Savior who gave His life for us. We will be true to them, even if it means offending someone on earth, and even if that someone is a brother dearly beloved. But we need to remember the penetrating declaration of 1 Corinthians 8:12: "When ye sin so against the brethren, and wound their weak conscience, ye sin against Christ." Harmony with Heaven comes first; but if harmony with brethren is marred carelessly or needlessly, harmony with Heaven is marred as well.

C. Think and Pray

This matter of harmony may be far from simple. It may be well to give up our own way to avoid conflict, but it is not well to let a noisy minority rule the congregation. It may be well to give up our own way and go along with the majority, but not if the majority is certainly wrong. It may be well to give up some rights to avoid offending a brother, but it is bad to let the Lord's work go undone because a few brethren are easily hurt.

There is a time when we ought to take a firm stand for God's truth, and oppose those who deny or twist it. When the apostles were commanded to stop doing what the Lord sent them to do, their reply was uncompromising: "We ought to obey God rather than men" (Acts 5:29). But a stand for God's truth may be different from a stand for our own judgment or our own way.

There is a time when we ought to work harmoniously with others who disagree with us. Paul said, "Let not him that eateth despise him that eateth not; and let not him which eateth not judge him that eateth" (Romans 14:3). Let them ignore their difference and get on with the Lord's work. But we cannot join in doing wrong in order to have harmony.

There is a time when we ought to give up our rights and go along with a brother in order to avoid conflict. "If thy brother be grieved with thy meat, now walkest thou not charitably" (Romans 14:15). But giving up one's rights is not the same as giving up God's truth.

When a difference of opinion is seen, how can we know what to do? We need to think about it, and pray about it. We need to listen to James: "Let every man be swift to hear, slow to speak, slow to wrath" (James 1:19). We need to study God's Word and follow it. We need to give up our pride, abandon our stubbornness, and make every effort to be "acceptable to God, and approved of men" (Romans 14:18). After all our thinking and praying, we need to face the possibility that we are mistaken. It is not possible for God's Word to be wrong, but it is possible for us to misunderstand it. Let's keep on thinking and praying.

D. Prayer

Our Father in Heaven, may we have the courage to stand firm for You and Your way when a firm stand is needed, and may we have grace to give up our own way when that is the right thing to do, and may we have wisdom to know what is best. In Jesus' name we ask, amen.

E. Thought to Remember

"Every one of us shall give account of himself to God" (Romans 14:12)

Home Daily Bible Readings

Monday, Apr. 18—The Strong and the Weak (Romans 14:1-4)

Tuesday, Apr. 19—Honor God at All Times (Romans 14:5-10)

Wednesday, Apr. 20—The Weak and the Strong (Romans 14:13-23)

Thursday, Apr. 21—Be Like-Minded to Glorify God (Romans 15:1-6)

Friday, Apr. 22—"Praise the Lord, All Gentiles!" (Romans 15:7-13)

Saturday, Apr. 23—Paul's Ministry to the Gentiles (Romans 15:14-21)

Sunday, Apr. 24—Paul Seeks the Romans' Prayers (Romans 15:22-33)

Learning by Doing

This page contains an alternate lesson plan emphasizing learning activities. Classes desiring such student involvement will find these suggestions helpful.

Learning Goals

In this lesson your students will:

1. Formulate principles for dealing with conflicts over matters of opinion.

2. Apply these principles to specific issues.

Into the Lesson

Write these words on the chalkboard:

In matters of faith, unity

In matters of opinion, liberty

In all things, love.

Read this statement and tell the class that it is a paraphrase of a popular slogan from a few centuries ago. Lead your students in a discussion by asking, "What does this slogan mean?"

Your students should conclude that there are some issues that are essential to the Christian faith, and that concerning these issues Christians must be in agreement.

The slogan recognizes also that there are issues in life about which Christians may hold differing opinions. In these matters, regarding which the Scriptures do not give specific direction, we have freedom to differ. But regardless of whether the issue is a matter of faith (essential) or of opinion (nonessential), we must always extend love toward our fellow Christians.

At this point ask your students, "What are some issues that are matters of faith?" Record their ideas on the chalkboard. Then ask, "What are some issues that are matters of opinion?" Again, jot their suggestions on the chalkboard.

Then state, "From the beginning of the church until today, Christians have had disagreements. Sometimes these were regarding nonessential issues. As Christ's people, it is important that we learn to deal with such issues as Christ desires. That is what we will explore today."

Into the Word

Part One. Ask a volunteer to read Romans 14:1-6. Then present a two-minute lecture on the two issues presented: eating meat and observing special days. Be sure to communicate information from the Lesson Background section.

Lead your students in a discussion of these three questions:

1. According to this passage, who was right, those who ate meat or those who didn't? Why?

2. Who was right, those who observed special days or those who didn't? Why?

3. Why didn't Paul (the writer) take sides on these issues?

Part Two. Ask a volunteer to read Romans 14:7-21. Have students form groups of four to six to complete this assignment. They are to discuss this question, based upon the passage: *What principles are suggested for dealing with conflict over matters of opinion?*

Provide each group with paper and pencils. Appoint a discussion leader for each group and allow ten minutes for them to complete the assignment.

Part Three. After ten minutes ask the groups to report their principles. List them on the chalkboard and let them remain there for the remainder of the lesson. Then ask, "How can we learn to love in a genuine way those with whom we have conflict?" Allow for discussion.

Into Life

Before class write each of these issues on a small strip of paper and put them in a bowl:

Singing primarily hymns in worship services versus singing primarily worship choruses

Owning a church building versus renting a facility

Raising hands in worship versus not raising hands

Using the *King James Version* versus using a modern translation

Allowing women to baptize in a worship service versus not allowing women to baptize

Having refreshments in Bible school versus not having refreshments

Continue with the small groups. Ask each group leader to pick one of the strips of paper from the bowl. Each group is to discuss three questions regarding that issue:

1. What does the Bible say about this issue?

2. How can principles from Romans 14 be applied to this issue?

3. What other factors need to be considered when dealing with this issue?

Distribute a copy of these questions for each group leader. After ten minutes ask the groups to report their conclusions.

Finally, ask the class, "Which principle from Romans 14 do you personally need to focus on most?" Ask students to discuss the question in their groups.

Close the class session with prayer.

Let's Talk It Over

The questions on this page are designed to encourage review of the lesson Scriptures and to promote discussion of the lesson by the class. The answers provided are only discussion starters. Let your class talk it over from there.

1. Eating meat offered to idols could lead a first-century Christian into idol worship. Is the dabbling of Christians in occult practices a parallel situation today? If so, how do we deal with such a circumstance?

There are Christians who give some attention to astrology or read books about clairvoyance. They may regard all this as harmless diversion, and they may scoff at anyone who speaks of these as dangerous practices. Such persons may feel they can have contact with the occult and not suffer harm. However, the principle Paul discusses in Romans 14 is applicable here. We may know of Christians young in the faith or persons contemplating becoming Christians who have been deeply and dangerously involved with the occult. If they are struggling to leave such a life behind them, it can be a terrible temptation for them to see a veteran believer dabbling in these things.

2. There are various opinions as to what Christians should and should not do on Sunday. How may we achieve harmony in this matter?

Most will agree that the early Christians met on the first day of the week for worship, and that it is most fitting for us to do so. But are activities of a different nature fitting? Should Christians do lawn work or repairs on Sunday? Should they go shopping? How about attending football or baseball games? These are some activities that may be a focus of disagreement among believers. The New Testament does not give specific regulations regarding what activities are appropriate on the first day of the week, so it is left for believers to exercise their own judgment. In deciding this question, each believer should consider what will please the Lord, what will avoid offending other Christians, and what will constitute the best witness to non-Christians.

3. Why is it important for us to examine our words and actions from the standpoint of other persons?

Perhaps it had not occurred to some believers in Paul's time that by eating meat sacrificed to idols they could offend Christians who were weak in faith. But such offers could be given. So today, it may not always be obvious to us how our words or deeds may affect other persons. We do well, therefore, to review objectively our speech and conduct so as to keep from turning anyone away from Christ. Also, those who are more spiritually mature and who understand the liberty that is theirs in the Christian walk are tempted to be a bit impatient with those who do not share their understanding. They may look down on the less mature and be inclined to dismiss their scruples. But that is not the way of love or compassion. The strong in faith will be willing to "bend over backward" at times, relinquishing some of their liberty, so as not to cause "the weak brother [to] perish, for whom Christ died" (1 Corinthians 8:11).

4. We must recognize that Paul's challenge to "follow after the things which make for peace" (v.19) has some limitations. What are these?

We can never preserve peace at the cost of compromising Biblical teaching. There is a great deal of false doctrine being propagated today, and we are not serving the cause of Christ well if we allow it to be taught in the church, and we refrain from objecting in the name of peace. Another kind of peace that is foreign to Paul's way of thinking is the kind that involves "sweeping under the rug" some problem that has arisen in the church. Problems that are handled in this way tend to grow even worse, affecting more and more persons, until leaders are forced to deal with them.

5. Paul urges Christians to edify, that is, build up, one another. Why is his exhortation pertinent today?

Paul repeatedly refers to this principle in his discussion of spiritual gifts (1 Corinthians 14:3, 5, 12, 17, 26). This is an important principle: anything we do in the church should be for the building up of the church and our fellow members. How much service in the church is performed for personal satisfaction or pride or merely because one is obligated to do it? How common is it for church members to assess any program in the church on the basis of "What's in it for me?" If we could get across this concept of a mutual ministry of upbuilding, there would be greater benefits in the church for everyone.

Delivered From Bondage

DEVOTIONAL READING: 1 Timothy 1:12-17.

LESSON SCRIPTURE: Galatians 1, 2.

PRINTED TEXT: Galatians 1:6, 7; 2:11-21.

Galatians 1:6, 7

6 I marvel that ye are so soon removed from him that called you into the grace of Christ unto another gospel:

7 Which is not another; but there be some that trouble you, and would pervert the gospel of Christ.

Galatians 2:11-21

11 But when Peter was come to Antioch, I withstood him to the face, because he was to be blamed.

12 For before that certain came from James, he did eat with the Gentiles: but when they were come, he withdrew and separated himself, fearing them which were of the circumcision.

13 And the other Jews dissembled likewise with him; insomuch that Barnabas also was carried away with their dissimulation.

14 But when I saw that they walked not uprightly according to the truth of the gospel, I said unto Peter before them all, If thou, being a Jew, livest after the manner of Gentiles, and not as do the Jews, why compellest thou the Gentiles to live as do the Jews?

15 We who are Jews by nature, and not sinners of the Gentiles,

16 Knowing that a man is not justified by the works of the law, but by the faith of Jesus Christ, even we have believed in Jesus Christ, that we might be justified by the faith of Christ, and not by the works of the law: for by the works of the law shall no flesh be justified.

17 But if, while we seek to be justified by Christ, we ourselves also are found sinners, is therefore Christ the minister of sin? God forbid.

18 For if I build again the things which I destroyed, I make myself a transgressor.

19 For I through the law am dead to the law, that I might live unto God.

20 I am crucified with Christ: nevertheless I live; yet not I, but Christ liveth in me: and the life which I now live in the flesh I live by the faith of the Son of God, who loved me, and gave himself for me.

21 I do not frustrate the grace of God: for if righteousness come by the law, then Christ is dead in vain.

GOLDEN TEXT: I am crucified with Christ: nevertheless I live; yet not I, but Christ liveth in me: and the life which I now live in the flesh I live by the faith of the Son of God, who loved me, and gave himself for me.—Galatians 2:20.

Lesson Aims

After this lesson a student should be able to:
1. Tell when and how Paul "withstood" Peter.
2. Explain why Peter's action was wrong.
3. Examine his own living to see how well it agrees with his belief.

Lesson Outline

INTRODUCTION
  A. Breaking the Barrier
  B. Lesson Background
 I. TRAGIC CHANGE (Galatians 1:6, 7)
  A. Being Removed (v. 6)
  B. Twisting the Good News (v. 7)
II. MISTAKE CHALLENGED (Galatians 2:11-14)
  A. Mistake (vv. 11-13)
    Pretense
  B. Challenge (v. 14)
III. EXPLANATION (Galatians 2:15-21)
  A. Wrong Rebuilding (vv. 15-18)
  B. Cooperating With God's Grace (vv. 19-21)
    Figuratively Speaking
CONCLUSION
  A. Our Doing
  B. Prayer
  C. Thought to Remember

Display the map (visual 9 of the visuals packet) and locate the places mentioned in the lesson background. The map is shown on page 301.

Introduction

We today can hardly realize how fanatically the first-century Jews held themselves apart from Gentiles. To go into a Gentile's house was out of order; to eat with him was unthinkable (Acts 10:28; 11:2, 3). The first Christians were Jews, and it seems that they thought no one but Jews would ever be Christians.

A. Breaking the Barrier

Acts 10:1—11:18 records the unusual methods God used to break down the barrier between Jews and Gentiles. Simon Peter and some others were first convinced, and members of a Roman household became Christians. Peter was sharply criticized when he went back to Jerusalem, but his explanation convinced the Jewish Christians that the Lord meant His salvation for Gentiles also—and the Jewish Christians had grace enough to be glad.

Then some of the Jewish Christians took another tack. It was well and good for Gentiles to become Christians, they said; but Gentile Christians must become Jews as well. Otherwise they could not be saved.

That position was challenged, and the debate was vigorous. As we see in the fifteenth chapter of Acts, the Holy Spirit led apostles and elders and church to a firm decision. Jews and Gentiles alike are saved through faith in Christ. Jewish law was a yoke that even the Jews could not bear; Gentile Christians were free of it (Acts 15:6-11, 28, 29).

Unfortunately some of the Christian Jews were not convinced. They kept on teaching their false doctrine, and some of the results are seen in our lesson.

B. Lesson Background

The Roman province called Galatia was a strip of land about a hundred miles wide that ran crookedly across the middle of Asia Minor from north to south. Its north end was near the Black Sea and its south end near the Mediterranean, though it did not touch either sea.

Acts 13:14—14:23 records that Paul and Barnabas started several churches in the southern part of Roman Galatia. Later Paul visited those churches again, bringing the good news that Gentile Christians did not need to become Jews (Acts 16:1-5). Still later Paul came to Galatia a third time as he began his third missionary journey (Acts 18:23). Going on to the west, he spent about three years in Ephesus and then visited Macedonia and Greece before starting to Jerusalem (Acts 19:1—20:6).

Scholars disagree about when the apostle Paul wrote his letter to the Galatians, but it seems probable that he sent it to those churches in southern Galatia near the end of his third missionary journey, about three years after visiting them for the third time. During those three years some Jewish Christians in Galatia had been arguing that all Christians must be Jews as well. It seems that some of the Galatians were giving up their freedom in Christ and accepting the yoke of the law, and Paul felt that he must warn them (Galatians 5:1).

How to Say It

HYPOKRISIS (Greek).   Who-*pah*-krih-sis.

I. Tragic Change

(Galatians 1:6, 7)

We are not told how Paul knew what was happening in Galatia. Many people were traveling in those days, however, either on business or on pleasure. Christian travelers often looked up Christians in towns they visited. Probably someone from Galatia brought the news to Paul.

A. Being Removed (v. 6)

6. I marvel that ye are so soon removed from him that called you into the grace of Christ unto another gospel.

Details of this verse offer some difficulties, but the general meaning is clear. *Him that called you* has been taken to mean God, or Christ, or Paul. As a matter of fact, all of these did call the Galatians from sin and death to forgiveness and life, and all of them sounded the call through the gospel that Paul preached. But now the Galatians were hearing a different message. They were being told that Christ could not save them unless they would become Jews and keep the laws of Moses. Some of the Galatians were beginning to believe the new message. *Removed* is better translated *being moved* or *moving yourselves*. The move to a different message was not completed, but it was under way. Paul wrote this letter to stop it.

B. Twisting the Good News (v. 7)

7. Which is not another; but there be some that trouble you, and would pervert the gospel of Christ.

As the *New International Version* puts it, that different gospel (v. 6) *is really no gospel at all*. The word *gospel* means good news. The good news is that Jesus' death on the cross atoned for our sins, and we who believe in Jesus are saved by God's grace and our faith (Ephesians 2:8). The Galatians were being told that that way of salvation would not work. They were being told that they must keep the law of Moses in order to be saved. In truth, the law was a way of salvation that would not work, and centuries of history had proved that it would not work. Probably those who were turning toward that message did not realize that it actually contradicted the true gospel, but it did. The gospel proclaims that Christ is all we need. "Ye are complete in him" (Colossians 2:10). To deny that is to deny Him. Those who look for salvation through the law have fallen from grace, and Christ will do them no good (Galatians 5:4).

The gospel Paul preached is dependable and right. That is elaborated in the rest of chapter 1 and all of chapter 2. Paul got his message directly from the Lord, not from men. The earlier apostles confirmed it. It was the same message they preached. The falsehood now troubling the Galatians had been investigated and proved to be false (Acts 15). Don't be fooled by falsehood!

II. Mistake Challenged

(Galatians 2:11-14)

Some students of the Bible make much of Paul's "quarrel" with Peter at Antioch. Some suppose the two were antagonists as long as they lived, but the Scriptures do not support this.

Actually, no quarrel is recorded, much less a lifelong grudge. Paul caught Peter in a mistake, and promptly told him about it. Thus he gave us a fine example of courageous confrontation. Peter gave us an example that is harder to follow. He accepted the rebuke in good spirit and profited by it. That is not recorded in so many words, but it can be inferred from Peter's attitude afterward. To him Paul was "our beloved brother" (2 Peter 3:15).

This lesson teaches that we are saved through Christ, not through the law of Moses or through any good we do. There is no distinction between Jews and Gentiles, or between people of different nations or races. All are saved through Christ, or not at all.

The Lord chose Peter to lead the church to that truth (Acts 15:7). Peter defended the truth as ardently as Paul did. There never was any conflict between the teaching of these great leaders. Peter once failed to live up to what they taught, as we see in the following text. Paul pointed out his mistake, and the two went forward in unbroken fellowship.

A. Mistake (vv. 11-13)

11. But when Peter was come to Antioch, I withstood him to the face, because he was to be blamed.

Probably the first great church among the Gentiles was at Antioch, about three hundred miles north of Jerusalem. Antioch became the home base for Paul's three famous missionary journeys, the first of which is recorded in Acts 13 and 14. At Antioch arose a great debate on this question: Must Gentile Christians become Jews as well? At Jerusalem that question was answered with a firm no, as we see in the fifteenth chapter of Acts. Paul was in complete agreement with Peter and other leaders in Jerusalem (Galatians 2:9). Subsequently, however, *when Peter was come to Antioch*, Paul felt compelled to take a firm stand against him. Peter was wrong, not in what he taught, but in what he did.

12. For before that certain came from James, he did eat with the Gentiles: but when they were come, he withdrew and separated himself, fearing them which were of the circumcision.

At Antioch Peter *did eat with the Gentiles* in the church, indicating full and complete Christian fellowship with them. Probably he did not now insist on kosher food, as he had done earlier (Acts 10:14). But Peter made a change when *certain came from James*. Does this mean that James personally sent these people on some special mission to Antioch? Or does it mean simply that they came from Jerusalem, where James was an outstanding leader in the church? We cannot be sure. However, the men from Jerusalem must have known about the decision reached there, that Gentiles might become Christians without accepting Jewish laws and customs. Therefore we suppose these Jews from Jerusalem were happy to see many Gentiles becoming Christians. But at the same time the Jews were not ready to give up their lifelong habit of separation or to eat any food that was not kosher. When the church at Antioch had a fellowship dinner these newcomers brought kosher food and grouped together in a part of the area where the meeting was held.

These people from Jerusalem were Peter's old friends, and now they were newcomers where Peter had been staying for some time. It would seem ungracious for him to turn his back on them to eat with Gentile brethren as he had been doing. Peter is famous for acting or speaking impetuously, without thinking things through. Now impulsively he turned away from the Gentile brethren to eat with his old friends. Probably the implications that were plain to Paul did not enter Peter's mind at all. Luke notes that Peter was *fearing* the Jews. He had been sharply criticized for eating with Gentiles (Acts 11:2, 3), and might be criticized again. But *fearing* does not necessarily mean he was afraid of that. *Fear* often means a proper respect. In Ephesians 5:33, for example, the same Greek word is used to urge a wife to "reverence" her husband. Peter ought to respect his old friends, but not to respect them more than the truth.

13. And the other Jews dissembled likewise with him; insomuch that Barnabas also was carried away with their dissimulation.

Dissimulation represents the Greek word *hypokrisis*, from which we have our word *hypocrisy*. Primarily it means playacting. Peter was hypocritically playing a part: he was acting as if he thought it was wrong to eat with Gentiles, but really that was not his thought at all. To make matters worse, the other Jewish Christians in Antioch followed his lead—even bighearted Barnabas, who had been quick to rejoice at the conversion of the Gentiles (Acts 11:22, 23). The great church at Antioch was being split into two sections, Jewish and Gentile.

PRETENSE

"Let's pla'ke we're firemen; you drive the truck, and I'll hold the hose."

"Let's pla'ke we're models in a fashion show; you wear this dress, and I'll put on this hat."

Kids can have a good time pretending, playing like people they would like to be. Such pretenses in children are typically healthy expressions of creative thinking.

Problems arise, however, when adults seriously pretend to be someone or something they are not. Jesus labeled such behavior of the religious leaders of His day as "hypocrisy," and He strongly condemned the play-actors (see Matthew 23). When Peter and the other Jewish Christians at Antioch acted in a manner not consistent with their convictions, their action was labeled hypocrisy. They separated themselves from the Gentile Christians so as not to offend the Jewish Christians who had come from Jerusalem. In so doing, they gave the appearance that they approved such discrimination. This dissimulation was contrary to the gospel and threatened the unity of the church.

Walking "uprightly according to the truth of the gospel" requires integrity. At all times let's be careful that our words and actions truly reflect the convictions of our hearts.   —R. W. B.

B. Challenge (v. 14)

14. But when I saw that they walked not uprightly according to the truth of the gospel, I said unto Peter before them all, If thou, being a Jew, livest after the manner of Gentiles, and not as do the Jews, why compellest thou the Gentiles to live as do the Jews?

The truth of the gospel includes the truth that Christian Jews and Christian Gentiles are one in the sight of God. Peter and the other Jews were not acting according to that truth. Peter was leading the way, so Paul challenged him personally; but he did it openly *before them all* because all of them were making the same mistake.

Peter was *a Jew*; but before those other Jews came from Jerusalem, he had been living *after the manner of Gentiles*. He had been associating freely with Gentile brethren, eating with them, probably accepting their food. That was right. It was in accord with Peter's true belief, in accord with the truth of the gospel, in accord with God's will that had been made plain in the revelations and decisions recorded in Acts 10:1— 11:18 and Acts 15.

Then if Peter the Jew was acting as a Gentile, why in the world did he want to make the Gentiles act like Jews? Until Paul pointed it out, probably Peter had not realized that he was doing that. Not by words, but by actions, he was taking the side of those false teachers who said Gentiles must become Jews (Acts 15:1). He separated himself from Gentile brethren to be with Jewish brethren; and that action said clearly to the Gentiles, "If you want to be fully accepted in our brotherhood, you must do as we Jews are doing." Thus he would bind on the Gentiles the yoke of bondage that he himself had said they should not bear (Acts 15:10).

III. Explanation
(Galatians 2:15-21)

To clarify his challenge, Paul argued that Jewish laws and customs had never been enough to save the Jews. That was why Jesus' sacrifice and the gospel were necessary. Peter could hardly dispute that. He had used the same argument forcefully in the earlier meeting in Jerusalem (Acts 15:7-11).

A. Wrong Rebuilding (vv. 15-18)

15. We who are Jews by nature, and not sinners of the Gentiles.

Being *Jews,* both Paul and Peter had been guided by God's law and had not fallen into the depths of depravity that were common among the *Gentiles* (Romans 1:22-32).

16. Knowing that a man is not justified by the works of the law, but by the faith of Jesus Christ, even we have believed in Jesus Christ, that we might be justified by the faith of Christ, and not by the works of the law: for by the works of the law shall no flesh be justified.

With all their effort to keep the law, both Paul and Peter knew they had fallen short. Neither they nor anyone else could be justified by the law. The only way to become just is to be forgiven. Since Jesus died to atone for human sin, forgiveness is offered to those who believe in Him. Knowing this, both Paul and Peter had put their trust in Jesus, depending on Him for forgiveness and justification.

17. But if, while we seek to be justified by Christ, we ourselves also are found sinners, is therefore Christ the minister of sin? God forbid.

Both Paul and Peter were seeking *to be justified by Christ,* as Peter had stated in Jerusalem (Acts 15:11). But now Peter was acting as if they were not justified, as if they were still sinners who must be justified by keeping the Jewish law and separating themselves from Gentiles. They were followers of Christ; if then they were sinners not

visual 9

justified by their following of Him, then it would seem that Christ was a *minister of sin,* not of justification. That thought was so abhorrent that Paul renounced it instantly and vigorously: *God forbid!*

18. For if I build again the things which I destroyed, I make myself a transgressor.

Paul used the word *I* to make a general statement: "If I, or anyone else, rebuilds what he has destroyed, he shows that he is *a transgressor.* If it was right to tear it down, then it is wrong to build it up again." Actually, of course, it was Peter, not Paul, who was doing this. Peter had been first to take the gospel to Gentiles, and he had successfully defended that action before his fellow Jews in the church (Acts 10:1—11:18). Thus he had taken the lead in tearing down the barrier between Jews and Gentiles. He knew that was right, for God was leading him every step of the way. But now he was separating himself from the Gentiles. Thus he was taking the lead in building again the barrier that he had torn down. That had to be wrong!

B. Cooperating With God's Grace
(vv. 19-21)

19. For I through the law am dead to the law, that I might live unto God.

The law could not justify anyone; it could only condemn (v. 16). Jews and Gentiles alike are condemned as sinners; but Jesus died to atone for sin (1 John 2:2), and "there is therefore now no condemnation to them which are in Christ Jesus" (Romans 8:1). Being baptized into Christ, we are baptized into His death (Romans 6:3). Thus we are "dead indeed unto sin" (Romans 6:11) and also *dead to the law.* Neither sin nor law dominates us any longer, but we *live unto God.*

20. I am crucified with Christ: nevertheless I live; yet not I, but Christ liveth in me: and the life which I now live in the flesh I live by the faith of the Son of God, who loved me, and gave himself for me.

"If any man be in Christ, he is a new creature" (2 Corinthians 5:17). I used to be a sinner, but that sinner has been crucified (Galatians 5:24). *Nevertheless I live.* I have new life because I have faith in *the Son of God,* whose loving sacrifice redeemed me. Now I live in Christ, and *Christ liveth in me* to control everything I think or say or do. A new creature in Christ is free from sin, from death, from condemnation, and from the law.

FIGURATIVELY SPEAKING

Figures of speech can be effective devices of communication. A familiar simile is found in Psalm 1:3, which states that a godly person is "like a tree planted by the rivers of water." Had the psalmist chosen to use a metaphor instead, the psalm would read; "A godly person *is* a tree planted by rivers of water." The difference in meaning is slight but the force of the metaphor is stronger.

"Our God is a consuming fire" (Hebrews 12:29) is far more arresting than, "Our God is like a consuming fire."

Paul uses a memorable metaphor when he states, "I am crucified with Christ." We understand his meaning to be figurative, for we know that Paul had not literally hung upon a cross. He is telling us that his spiritual surrender to Jesus was so complete, it was *as if* he had died to the law and was born again to faith in Christ. His transformation was so dramatic, it was *like* a crucifixion and subsequent resurrection.

The circumstances of Christian conversion vary, but death to old, corrupting loyalties, and birth to new loyalties are basic. *Death* and *birth* are metaphors here, but they help us to understand the serious implications of repentance and regeneration. —R. W. B.

21. I do not frustrate the grace of God: for if righteousness come by the law, then Christ is dead in vain.

Home Daily Bible Readings

Monday, Apr. 25—Paul Accuses Any Who Dispute the Gospel (Galatians 1:6-9)
Tuesday, Apr. 26—Paul's Gospel Based on Revelation From Jesus Christ (Galatians 1:10-17)
Wednesday, Apr. 27—The Church Rejoices With Paul (Galatians 1:18-24)
Thursday, Apr. 28—Paul's Ministry to the Gentiles (Galatians 2:1-10)
Friday, Apr. 29—The Law Cannot Justify (Galatians 2:11-16)
Saturday, Apr. 30—Only Christ Justifies (Galatians 2:17-21)
Sunday, May 1—Rejoice in the Lord, Always (Philippians 4:4-10).

The grace of God is offered to us freely; and it is able to save us from our sins, to make us new creatures, to bring us to life and joy forever. But God's grace is frustrated and powerless unless we trust it freely and completely. If we think it is not enough, if we think we must also become Jews and adhere to their ancient law, then we have fallen from grace and will have no benefit from Christ (Galatians 5:4). If we become righteous by keeping the law, then Christ's death is *in vain,* useless. But we know our efforts to make ourselves righteous are all in vain without God's grace and Christ's death.

Conclusion

"By grace are ye saved through faith; and that not of yourselves: it is the gift of God" (Ephesians 2:8). What we earn is death, but God gives us life (Romans 6:23). Life beyond death depends on God's grace, not on our doing. That is the truth.

Nevertheless, our doing is important too. Let's conclude with a glance at that side of the truth.

A. Our Doing

Jesus said the Holy Spirit would guide Peter and others "into all truth" (John 16:13). Acts 2 records some of the truth Peter taught with the power of the Spirit. From that time on, as far as we know, there was never any error in what Peter said. But at one point, what he did was not in agreement with what he said; and what he did threatened to nullify his faith and frustrate God's grace. Then was his doing important?

Sometime everybody will agree that "Jesus Christ is Lord" (Philippians 2:11). We Christians believe that now. But if what we do denies what we say we believe, we show that our belief is a sham and we rob God's grace of its power. "Ye see then how that by works a man is justified, and not by faith only" (James 2:24). This too is the truth.

> Trust and obey.
> For there's no other way
> To be happy in Jesus,
> But to trust and obey.

B. Prayer

How gracious You are, our Father, to give us what our doing could never earn, a place in Your eternal kingdom! Father, we do believe that Jesus Christ is Lord, and we plead for Your help as we try to live by that belief. In Jesus' name, amen.

C. Thought to Remember

Trust and obey—both.

Learning by Doing

This page contains an alternate lesson plan emphasizing learning activities. Classes desiring such student involvement will find these suggestions helpful.

Learning Goals

After completing this session the students should be able to:

1. Understand the futility of seeking to be saved by works.

2. Contrast the life-style of one who receives salvation by faith with the life-style of one who seeks salvation by works.

Into the Lesson

Read the following case study to your class. (It is included in the student book.) Then lead students in a discussion of the questions that follow it:

Jason was distressed. He had been attending First Church for months and loved it. The church was alive, the people warm, the worship dynamic, and the minister was clearly a man of God.

Recently, however, Jason heard some conversations in his Bible class that concerned him. A number of the members of his class talked as if they knew for certain that they would go to Heaven when they died. That seemed cocky to Jason. He wondered how anyone could ever know if he was good enough to get to Heaven. He felt that that was for God to decide, not for Christians to claim.

Lead the class in discussing:

1. What would you say to Jason if he expressed these concerns to you?

2. Which of these motives do you think might be the strongest in causing Jason to obey God: love, gratitude, fear, guilt, pride? Why?

Lead into the Bible study by saying, "In our study today we begin exploring Paul's letter to the Galatians. The Galatian Christians were like Jason in the case study, in that they thought they had to measure up to God's standards to be saved. Let's observe how Paul deals with the problem."

Into the Word

Before class prepare copies of the six questions that follow (or use the student book). Be sure to make enough copies so there will be one for each person in class.

1. Read Galatians 1:6, 7. Why is Paul distressed with the Galatian Christians?

2. The gospel was being perverted in Galatia by those who taught that a person is saved by good works, not by faith in Christ. According to these passages in Galatians, how serious was this problem among the Galatian Christians? Why?

3:1-3, 10, 11
4:8-11
5:2-6
6:12-15

3. Read Galatians 2:11-21. What was the real problem with Peter's behavior? What did it imply about salvation?

4. In your own words, summarize Paul's reply to Peter's behavior.

5. According to this passage (see especially verse 16) what effect does a person's good works have on his being justified (made righteous and worthy of salvation)?

6. Read Ephesians 2:8-10. What is the relationship between one's doing good works and receiving salvation? What is the relationship between one's receiving salvation and doing good works? (v. 10).

Divide the class members into groups of six and give a copy of the questions to each member. Appoint a discussion leader for each group and allow twenty-five minutes for the groups to discuss the questions.

When time expires, bring the groups together and ask, "What did your group conclude about the seriousness of believing we are saved by our works?" Allow for discussion. You will want your class to understand that we can never be saved by our works. We are saved completely by Christ's work on the cross. Once we are saved, however, we express our gratitude and obedience by doing the good works God wants us to do (Ephesians 2:10; Galatians 2:20).

Into Life

Have the class members work in groups once again. Instruct half of the groups to write a page in the journal of an imaginary person who seeks to be saved by works. Instruct the other half of the groups to write a page in the journal of an imaginary person who seeks to be saved by faith. Encourage all the groups to highlight the person's activities, thoughts, attitudes, and motives.

Allow twelve minutes. Then allow the groups to share their journal entries. Close with prayer, thanking God for His gracious gift of salvation.

Let's Talk It Over

The questions on this page are designed to encourage review of the lesson Scriptures and to promote discussion of the lesson by the class. The answers provided are only discussion starters. Let your class talk it over from there.

1. Paul was distressed that the Galatians were turning to "another gospel." What are some examples of "another gospel" that are being proclaimed in our time?

Since the gospel involves the literal death, burial, and resurrection of Christ (1 Corinthians 15:1-4), we can classify as "another gospel" that widespread teaching of today that denies those historical realities. We are aware that in many pulpits, classrooms, and books these fundamental facts of the gospel are treated as myth or exaggeration. Paul's emphasis in Galatians demonstrates that any teaching that negates the significance of Christ's death and resurrection must be labeled as "another gospel." It is an error held in common by the major cults that they distort the Biblical teaching about the significance of these events. They, therefore, are guilty of propagating "another gospel."

2. Paul's confronting of Peter in regard to his inconsistent behavior indicates that there are times when even people of authority and prominence within the church must be called to account for their errors. How may this apply to the church today?

Perhaps we know of ministers, elders, or other church leaders whose Biblical knowledge, personal piety, and forceful character would make one extremely hesitant to question their judgment or offer them constructive criticism. But like Peter, even the most capable leaders can fall prey to unconscious prejudice or poor judgment. We dare not allow ourselves to be intimidated into remaining silent when we see such a leader making a mistake that will harm the body of Christ. While we are obligated to submit to those in authority, we must resist if by word or example they would influence us into doing what is contrary to the truth of the gospel.

3. Leaders and workers in the church frequently allow fear of disapproval or criticism to hinder their work. How can such fear be overcome?

One concept that each Christian must fix in mind is this: all of us are still imperfect; we all have learning and growing to do. The criticism we receive from others may be God's way of helping us to grow. This is a positive way of viewing criticism. On the other hand, it is clear that some criticism results from ignorance, prejudice, and the critic's wounded pride. Much of the murmuring and complaining directed at Jesus was of this kind. Jesus rose above such petty sniping at His ministry, and so must Christian workers today. It is essential that we pray for discernment, so that we may profit from the legitimate criticism and ignore the other.

4. In the event recorded in our text, the conduct of Peter and Barnabas was inconsistent with their beliefs; hence, they were being hypocritical. What does that fact indicate about hypocrisy in the church?

We are familiar with the common excuse some people have for staying away from the church: "There are too many hypocrites in the church!" Perhaps that may be said of any congregation. If Peter and Barnabas could be guilty of hypocrisy, then anyone in any church is vulnerable to it. With only a few moments' reflection most of us could recall occasions when we put on a "false front," when we pretended to be happier, holier, or more sympathetic than we really were. Of course, those who complain about hypocrites in the church would have to admit that they are not always honest in the way they project themselves. Nevertheless, we should be growing more honest, and more sincere as Christians, striving to avoid hypocrisy.

5. How can we make sure that our conduct as Christians is consistent with our profession?

We need to take inventory of the faith we profess. Perhaps it would be helpful for us to write down the principles of faith that we hold dear. With these spelled out before us, we will be in a good position to ask ourselves how well we live up to each principle. If we claim that we believe the gospel is meant for all mankind, then what are we doing to support missionary work? If we affirm that the people within our own community need salvation, then how about our involvement in evangelism? If we regard it as essential that Christians meet regularly for worship, how does our own church attendance tie in with that? If we believe all Christians should engage in personal Bible study and prayer, what is the status of our own devotional life?

Adopted as God's Children

DEVOTIONAL READING: Romans 11:11-33.

LESSON SCRIPTURE: Galatians 3:1—4:7.

PRINTED TEXT: Galatians 3:1-5, 23—4:7.

Galatians 3:1-5, 23-29

1 O foolish Galatians, who hath bewitched you, that ye should not obey the truth, before whose eyes Jesus Christ hath been evidently set forth, crucified among you?

2 This only would I learn of you, Received ye the Spirit by the works of the law, or by the hearing of faith?

3 Are ye so foolish? having begun in the Spirit, are ye now made perfect by the flesh?

4 Have ye suffered so many things in vain? if it be yet in vain.

5 He therefore that ministereth to you the Spirit, and worketh miracles among you, doeth he it by the works of the law, or by the hearing of faith?

. . . .

23 But before faith came, we were kept under the law, shut up unto the faith which should afterward be revealed.

24 Wherefore the law was our schoolmaster to bring us unto Christ, that we might be justified by faith.

25 But after that faith is come, we are no longer under a schoolmaster.

26 For ye are all the children of God by faith in Christ Jesus.

27 For as many of you as have been baptized into Christ have put on Christ.

28 There is neither Jew nor Greek, there is neither bond nor free, there is neither male nor female: for ye are all one in Christ Jesus.

29 And if ye be Christ's, then are ye Abraham's seed, and heirs according to the promise.

Galatians 4:1-7

1 Now I say, That the heir, as long as he is a child, differeth nothing from a servant, though he be lord of all;

2 But is under tutors and governors until the time appointed of the father.

3 Even so we, when we were children, were in bondage under the elements of the world:

4 But when the fulness of the time was come, God sent forth his Son, made of a woman, made under the law,

5 To redeem them that were under the law, that we might receive the adoption of sons.

6 And because ye are sons, God hath sent forth the Spirit of his Son into your hearts, crying, Abba, Father.

7 Wherefore thou art no more a servant, but a son; and if a son, then an heir of God through Christ.

GOLDEN TEXT: God sent forth his Son . . . to redeem them that were under the law, that we might receive the adoption of sons.—Galatians 4:4, 5.

Set Free by God's Grace
Galatians
(Lessons 9-13)

Lesson Aims

After studying this lesson a student should be able to:

1. Recall several different meanings of the terms *children of God* and *sons of God.*

2. Tell how Jesus is different from any other son of God.

3. Tell how people become children of God.

4. Discover some way in which he or she can grow to be more like Jesus.

Lesson Outline

INTRODUCTION
    A. Slavery Bad and Good
    B. Lesson Background
  I. BE REASONABLE (Galatians 3:1-5)
    A. Basic Truth (v. 1)
    B. Sharp Questions (vv. 2-5)
 II. GOD'S CHILDREN (Galatians 3:23-29)
    A. The Law's Work (vv. 23-25)
      School's Out!
    B. Children by Faith (vv. 26-28)
    C. Abraham's Children (v. 29)
III. HEIRS (Galatians 4:1-7)
    A. Young Children (vv. 1-3)
    B. Grown-up Children (vv. 4-7)
      Kin
CONCLUSION
    A. God's Various Children
    B. God's Only Begotten Son
    C. God's Christian Children
    D. Prayer
    E. Thought to Remember

Visual 10 of the visuals packet emphasizes a truth found in Galatians 3:23-29. The visual is shown on page 309.

Introduction

A. Slavery Bad and Good

Slavery has existed among mankind in many times and in many places, and its evils are well known. Who among us, having experienced freedom, would willingly submit to a life of bondage and place himself or herself under the total rule of another person? The thought is appalling, for we are aware of the severe and de-meaning treatment that those in such a position too often have received.

There is a Master, however, whose purposes are only good, not evil. His resources, which are available to His servants, are unlimited, and His love for those who yield to Him knows no bounds. We speak, of course, of God. Paul willingly chose to submit to this Master. Consequently, he describes himself as the slave of Christ or of God (Romans 1:1; Philippians 1:1; Titus 1:1). Such is the situation of all who give themselves to Jesus. They renounce evil masters and joyfully serve a good one. Being set free from sin, they become slaves of righteousness (Romans 6:18).

Last week's lesson was titled "Delivered From Bondage," for Jesus' slaves are truly free (John 8:31, 32). This week's lesson takes that truth a step farther. Jesus' slaves are "Adopted as God's Children."

B. Lesson Background

This week's text follows that of last week. We have seen that Jews under the law were burdened with an unbearable yoke (Acts 15:10) and Gentiles without the law were destined to perish (Romans 2:12). But in God's grace, Jews and Gentiles alike were set free from their burdens and bondage by faith in Christ (Galatians 2:16). Then some of the Gentiles free from their bondage were being led to take upon themselves the bondage from which the Jews had been set free. What nonsense!

I. Be Reasonable (Galatians 3:1-5)

Quickly the Galatians were turning to a different way (Galatians 1:6). Paul urged them to be reasonable, to stop and think about what they were doing. First he reminded them of a basic truth; then he asked a series of sharp questions to help them see how absurd it was to change as they were changing.

A. Basic Truth (v. 1)

1. O foolish Galatians, who hath bewitched you, that ye should not obey the truth, before whose eyes Jesus Christ hath been evidently set forth, crucified among you?

When Paul was in Galatia, he very *evidently,* plainly, clearly, set forth the truth about *Jesus Christ,* especially the fact that He was *crucified.* This was basic in Paul's teaching everywhere. "Christ died for our sins according to the Scriptures" (1 Corinthians 15:3). See also 1 Corinthians 1:23; 2:2. Jesus offered His life in sacrifice, and that sacrifice is enough to make atonement for all the sins of the world (1 John 2:2).To be forgiven and cleansed, we need only to put our trust in Jesus and obey Him. That is the truth, and the Galatians did not *obey the truth* when they began to look for salvation by keeping the Jewish law. To do that was to fall from grace (Galatians 5:4). How could they do it? They must be *bewitched!*

B. Sharp Questions (vv. 2-5)

2. This only would I learn of you, Received ye the Spirit by the works of the law, or by the hearing of faith?

All Christians receive the gift of the Holy Spirit (Acts 2:38), and He gives different abilities to different ones (1 Corinthians 12:4-11, 28-30). Some Christians are gifted teachers or helpers or administrators; in apostolic times some were gifted with the power to do miracles such as healing, prophesying, or speaking in tongues. Some of the Galatians did such miracles, and this showed plainly that the Spirit was there among them. Did He come because they obeyed the Jewish law? Certainly not! He came while Paul was preaching among them, before other teachers began trying to bring them under the law. They received the Holy Spirit *by the hearing of faith*: that is, by hearing the gospel and believing it. Wasn't that proof that they received salvation without keeping the Jewish law?

3. Are ye so foolish? having begun in the Spirit, are ye now made perfect by the flesh?

Each Christian in Galatia, like each Christian anywhere, began his new life by being born of water and the Spirit, the Holy Spirit (John 3:5). Though the body was born of water, the new creature born of the Spirit was spirit (John 3:6). Each Christian then was a spiritual being, and the Spirit who fathered him became his companion to give guidance and power. Could any Christian then expect to be *made perfect* or mature by a mass of regulations about physical things like kosher food, ceremonial washing, and pilgrimages to Jerusalem for special feasts? How *foolish!* God's design was just the opposite. He meant the regulations about physical things to bring people to Christ. In Christ they are justified by faith, not by the old regulations (v. 24).

4. Have ye suffered so many things in vain? if it be yet in vain.

In Galatia Paul had warned the Christians "that we must through much tribulation enter into the kingdom of God" (Acts 14:22). Unbelieving Jews had persecuted Paul himself (Acts 13:45, 50; 14:2, 19). No doubt the Christians had to endure similar persecution after Paul left. Was it all for nothing? It was if they now were going to become Jews and try to be saved by the law.

That would be to forsake Christ (Galatians 5:4) and end the persecution. But Paul added, *if it be yet in vain.* He was not convinced that the Galatians would be foolish enough to desert Christ and become Jews.

5. He therefore that ministereth to you the Spirit, and worketh miracles among you, doeth he it by the works of the law, or by the hearing of faith?

The question of verse 2 is repeated in a different way. God had given the Holy Spirit to Galatian Christians and had done miracles among them. He had done this before false teachers began urging the Christians to live by Jewish laws. Therefore it was plain that God had done it because they heard His gospel and believed, not because they lived by the law.

II. God's Children (Galatians 3:23-29)

Verses 6-22 remind us of God's promise to Abraham. Long before the law was given, He promised a blessing for the whole world. The law did not make the promise invalid, but neither did it bring the blessing to the world. What it did was to show that Jews as well as Gentiles were sinners, so Jews and Gentiles both needed the promise of salvation by faith in Christ.

A. The Law's Work (vv. 23-25)

23. But before faith came, we were kept under the law, shut up unto the faith which should afterward be revealed.

Christians are saved by faith in Christ, but that was not revealed till Christ came. In the meantime, the law was given to the Jews to govern and control them. *We,* Paul and the other Jews, were like prisoners held under guard to wait for the time when Christ would come and the way of salvation by faith would be revealed.

24. Wherefore the law was our schoolmaster to bring us unto Christ, that we might be justified by faith.

The Greek word for *schoolmaster* is literally *child-leader.* This was not a teacher in school, but a servant who took the child to school and made sure the child did not get into mischief on the way. Likewise the law was designed to lead the Jews *unto Christ* and supervise their conduct on the way.

25. But after that faith is come, we are no longer under a schoolmaster.

The child-leader's work was done when he arrived at school and turned the boy over to the teacher. So the law's work is done when one under the law becomes a Christian. The Christian is no longer under the law.

SCHOOL'S OUT!

In a few weeks, youngsters all over the nation will be jumping for joy when schools close their doors for the summer. For three months they will be free from the structure and restrictions imposed in the classroom.

School regulations and requirements, of course, are for a good purpose—educational discipline. In school, students are guided through the learning process that can help them find success in life.

Secondary education is not nearly so structured or restrictive. Students are given more and more personal responsibility. Definite requirements must be met, but students are free from close, rigid supervision.

Thus Paul contrasts living under law and living by faith. It is like the difference between kindergarten and the university. In the Christian age, disciples enjoy freedom, and bear personal responsibility for their destiny. It is phase two of God's plan of redemption. Phase one was preparatory, not permanent. God never intended for His people to stay in "kindergarten" forever. School's out!   —R. W. B.

B. Children by Faith (vv. 26-28)

26. For ye are all the children of God by faith in Christ Jesus.

In verses 23-25, *we* means Paul and the other Jewish Christians. They were under the law till they came to faith in Christ, and then they were no longer under the law. Now in verse 26, *ye* means the Gentile Christians in Galatia. They had never been under the law; it had not led them to Christ. Nevertheless they had come to Christ when they had heard the gospel. Without any help from the law, they were *children of God by faith in Christ Jesus.*

27. For as many of you as have been baptized into Christ have put on Christ.

When one is *baptized into Christ* one emerges from the water to begin a new life, but he or she does not emerge from Christ. That person has *put on Christ* permanently. No doubt the Galatian Christians sometimes failed to live up to their commitment, as we do; but their commitment and ours is to be like Jesus.

28. There is neither Jew nor Greek, there is neither bond nor free, there is neither male nor female: for ye are all one in Christ Jesus.

The difference between *male* and *female* does not cease to exist, of course. A Christian is still a man or a woman, still an employer or an employee, still red or yellow, black or white. But none of these has any effect on the Christians' standing as a child of God. A Gentile Christian

in Galatia became a child of God "by faith in Christ Jesus" (v. 26). That person's relationship with God was exactly the same as that of a Jewish Christian who had been led to Christ by the law. The Jew also became a child of God "by faith in Christ Jesus." To us Christians today, this means that no Christian should feel either above or below another Christian because of his or her gender or job or race.

C. Abraham's Children (v. 29)

29. And if ye be Christ's, then are ye Abraham's seed, and heirs according to the promise.

This is another way of saying all faithful Christians, regardless of differences, have the same standing before God. The crown of God's covenant with Abraham was the promise of blessing for "all families of the earth" (Genesis 12:3). That promise looked far into the future. The worldwide blessing would not come through Abraham personally, but through his "seed," his progeny. That was made plain to Abraham's grandson (Genesis 28:14). Paul points out that "seed" refers especially to Christ (Galatians 3:16). He is the one who offers the blessing of salvation and eternal life to "all families of the earth." Since Christ is Abraham's seed, all who are in Christ are *Abraham's seed, and heirs according to the promise.*

III. Heirs
(Galatians 4:1-7)

Being God's children is an honor and a privilege to be cherished, but there is more. It means God has made us fit to have a share of "the inheritance of the saints in light" (Colossians 1:12). What a treasure! It is "an inheritance incorruptible, and undefiled, and that fadeth not away, reserved in heaven for you" (1 Peter 1:4). Furthermore, if we are steadfast in the faith, God's power will keep us safe through all the uncertainties of earth till our inheritance is revealed with our completed salvation "in the last time" (1 Peter 1:5).

A. Young Children (vv. 1-3)

1, 2. Now I say, That the heir, as long as he is a child, differeth nothing from a servant, though he be lord of all; but is under tutors and governors until the time appointed of the father.

A rich man's son may be the heir to a billion-dollar estate; but when he is five or ten or fifteen years old, his position is like that of a household slave. He has to do whatever he is told. He has to obey not only his parents, but also whatever baby-sitters, nannies, and teachers his parents choose.

3. Even so we, when we were children, were in bondage under the elements of the world.

Before Christ came, the Jews were like young children, and therefore like slaves. Their baby-sitters were the laws of the Old Testament. These are called *the elements of the world.* They were elementary regulations about things in the world, childish rules about special days and times (v. 10), also about diet and drink and cere-monial cleansing (Hebrews 9:10). Grown-up people should be able to follow Jesus without all those minute regulations.

B. Grown-up Children (vv. 4-7)

4, 5. But when the fulness of the time was come, God sent forth his Son, made of a woman, made under the law, to redeem them that were under the law, that we might receive the adoption of sons.

For many centuries the Jews lived as young children, or as slaves in bondage to the law (v. 3). Then came the time appointed by the Father (v. 2), the time for their liberation. Then *God sent forth his Son,* Jesus. *Made of a woman* is better trans-lated *born of a woman.* Thus God's Son became a human being "like unto his brethren" (Hebrews 2:17), like other human beings. He was also *made* (or *born*) *under the law,* as were the Jews who had been so long in bondage to that law. Being one of them, He was in a position *to redeem them that were under the law,* to set them free from bondage to that law. Thus *we,* Paul and the other Jews under the law, *might receive the adoption of sons.* Here the word *adoption* does not mean strangers were received into the family. It means those who had been living as young children now were re-garded as grown-up sons, capable of understand-ing the Father's will and doing it without a multitude of rules to govern their every move.

6. And because ye are sons, God hath sent forth the Spirit of his Son into your hearts, cry-ing, Abba, Father.

Jesus was born under the law to redeem those who were under the law (vv. 4, 5), and He was born of a woman (v. 4) to redeem all who are born of women. In verses 3-5, *we* refers to Paul and other Jews born under the law. Now in verse 6, *ye* refers to Gentile Christians in Galatia. They had never been under the law, but they had been in bondage to sin (John 8:34). Jesus had redeemed them from that bondage, and they were sons of God just as were the redeemed Jews. Therefore God sent to them *the Spirit of his Son,* the Holy Spirit. Moved by the Spirit of Jesus, those Chris-tians cried *Abba, Father* just as Jesus had done (Mark 14:36. *Abba* is *Father* in the language of the Jews. The Gentile Christians were children of God exactly as the Jewish Christians were.

visual 10

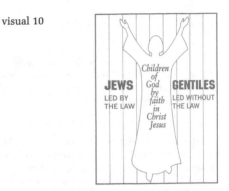

7. Wherefore thou art no more a servant, but a son; and if a son, then an heir of God through Christ.

Both here and in verse 1, *servant* represents the Greek word for slave. The Jews had been slaves of the law and the Gentiles had been slaves of sin, but Jesus had redeemed both Jews and Gentiles. Every Christian was no longer a slave, *but a son.* He was a son of God, and there-fore *an heir of God through Christ.* Can you imag-ine what it means to be an heir to all the infinite wealth of the Almighty? Yet some teachers were urging those Gentile Christians to volunteer for the slavery from which the Jewish Christians had been liberated. How silly!

KIN

When I was a very small child, I was "adopted" by a kind, Christian man who was such a special friend that he became like another grandfather or uncle to me. His name was Quinn, but when I tried to pronounce it, it came out "Kin." Soon my whole family called him by that nickname, and really, Kin was as close to us as kin.

Kin was a selfless servant of God. His positive influence upon my life and upon the lives of my parents and siblings cannot be measured. Kin even invited our family to live with him in his house, which seemed to me a mansion—three stories with spacious rooms. Ultimately we be-came heirs in his will, but the far greater inheri-tance was the impact of his generous love and gracious spirit.

The apostle Paul states that we have been adopted by God. Redeemed from slavery to sin, we are now God's sons; and as sons of God, we are His heirs. When Jesus gave His life on the cross, God's new will became effective; thus we are recipients of an abundant inheritance, now and forever.

One day all of God's children will dwell in the Father's mansions prepared for them and will share in the indescribable joy of His presence.

—R. W. B.

Conclusion

In the Bible, the phrases *children of God* and *sons of God* are used with various meanings. We may become confused if we suppose they always mean the same.

A. God's Various Children

Adam was God's son (Luke 3:38). That means God created him. The Lord formed Adam's body from the materials of earth, and breathed life into it (Genesis 2:7). No one else is God's son in exactly the same way. But since Adam was God's son, all of Adam's children are children of God in a way.

We have no record of how God created the angels, but probably they are called *sons of God* in Job 1:6. Who else was present to shout for joy when the foundations of the earth were laid? (Job 38:4-7). Only rarely are angels called God's sons, but the name is appropriate both because God created them and because they are obedient to Him.

In Genesis 6:2 it seems that *sons of God* means good men. Unfortunately they were not as wise as they were good. They married bad girls because the girls were pretty. So the human race became rapidly worse (v. 5). In Psalm 82:6 judges of Israel, even unjust judges, are called *children of the Most High*. Even more surprising, they are called *gods*. This reminds us that the word *gods* also has different meanings. Basically it means powerful ones, and *children of the Most High* means that God gave them the power of government (Romans 13:1).

B. God's Only Begotten Son

In all the history of mankind, only once has a virgin become pregnant. The Holy Spirit worked this miracle without any physical contact at all, and so the virgin's Son is literally the Son of God (Luke 1:30-35). The *King James Version* calls Him God's only begotten Son (John 3:16), for God has never begotten anyone else in the same way. Jesus is both divine and human, both God and man. He is Immanuel, which means God with us (Isaiah 7:14). Whatever other sons God has, He has no other Son like Jesus. God gave this unique Son "that whosoever believeth in him should not perish, but have everlasting life" (John 3:16). For lost mankind there is no other Savior (Acts 4:12).

C. God's Christian Children

God's only begotten Son came into the world to save the world (John 3:17). Sad to say, many people in the world did not welcome Him. Some did welcome Him, however. To them He gave the power and right to be God's children. They too were born of God (John 1:11-13), not as Jesus was, but in a spiritual sense. God begot them by means of the word of truth, His message of salvation (James 1:18). They were born again; they were newborn spirits (John 3:5, 6). They were children of God, and so are those who are born in the same way in our time.

Children should honor their parents (Exodus 20:12; Ephesians 6:1-3). We recognize God as our Father, as Galatians 4:6 indicates. We have a keen appetite for His Word, the food by which we grow (1 Peter 2:2). We are not content to be infant children. We read the Scriptures and listen to Christian teaching in order to grow more and more like Jesus (Ephesians 4:13-16).

There was a special doorway in the farmhouse where I lived as a child. There I stood on my birthday while Dad used a carpenter's square and a pencil to mark my precise height on the door jamb. He and I would have been unhappy if I had not been taller every year. The Bible is not only the food that makes us grow; it is also the yardstick to measure our growth as children of God. (See Galatians 5:19-26; Ephesians 4:25-32; Romans 12:3-21.) Are you growing in all the right ways?

D. Prayer

Abba, Father, it is a precious privilege to be Your children. Thank You for giving us a new birth, and thank You for providing in Your word the nourishment by which we grow. As we feed on it day by day, may we truly be more and more like Your only begotten Son. Amen.

E. Thought to Remember

Children ought to grow.

Home Daily Bible Readings

Monday, May 2—Miracles by Way of Law or Faith (Galatians 3:1-5)

Tuesday, May 3—People of Faith: Children of Abraham (Galatians 3:6-10)

Wednesday, May 4—The Spirit Comes Through Faith (Galatians 3:11-15)

Thursday, May 5—The Righteous Live by Faith (Galatians 3:16-22; Habakkuk 2:1-4)

Friday, May 6—Christians Are All Children of God (Galatians 3:23-27)

Saturday, May 7—No Longer Slaves, but Adopted Children (Galatians 3:28—4:7)

Sunday, May 8—Let Your Faith Rest in God (1 Corinthians 2:1-5)

Learning by Doing

This page contains an alternate lesson plan emphasizing learning activities. Classes desiring such student involvement will find these suggestions helpful.

Learning Goals

After this session students will be able to:

1. Trace Paul's line of reasoning in Galatians 3 and 4 that shows we are saved through faith in Christ, not by works that we do.

2. Identify thinking that is consistent with the teaching of salvation by faith.

Into the Lesson

Begin class by saying, "God's Word clearly teaches that we are saved by God's grace through our faith. We cannot be saved by works. Yet many faithful churchgoers still think they must do a certain amount of good works to get to Heaven. They may talk about being saved by God's grace, but their thinking still focuses on how good they must be."

Lead your class in a discussion of this question: "What causes churchgoing people to think they must earn their salvation rather than receive it as a free gift from God?"

Allow discussion for no more than three minutes. Then lead into the Bible study by saying, "The apostle Paul was greatly concerned about the Galatian Christians. Though they had been taught that salvation comes through faith in Christ, not by works, they had strayed away from that thinking. Today we will explore Paul's line of reasoning to convince the church at Galatia that they must reject the teaching that says we are saved by our works, and they must embrace the truth that salvation comes through faith in Christ. Then we will analyze some statements and determine if they reflect thinking that is consistent with salvation by faith."

Into the Word

Divide Galatians 3:1—4:7 into several sections, and have a like number of volunteers read this text aloud to the class. Then divide your class members into groups of four to six. Give half of the groups Assignment One below and the other half Assignment Two,

Assignment One: Based upon Galatians 3:1-14, why should the Galatians trust Christ for salvation and reject law-keeping as a means of salvation? List the reasons given. Then create a television advertisement designed to persuade the viewer that we receive salvation through faith in Christ, and not because of any amount of good works we do.

Assignment Two: Based upon Galatians 3:19—4:7, why should the Galatians trust Christ for salvation and reject law-keeping as a means of salvation? List the reasons given. Then create a newspaper advertisement designed to persuade the reader that we receive salvation through faith in Christ, and not because of any amount of good works we do.

Allow the groups thirty minutes to complete their assignments. Then reassemble the class and allow each group to present its ad to the rest of the class.

Into Life

Make enough photocopies of the following activity so each student may have one.

FAITH or WORKS

Which of the following statements are consistent with trusting Christ for our salvation? Which are consistent with seeking salvation by good works? Put a check mark in the appropriate space for each statement.

Faith   Works

_____ _____   1. Since I have accepted Christ as Savior, I know that God has accepted me.

_____ _____   2. Because I believe Jesus took God's wrath for me, I can approach God boldly.

_____ _____   3. I have to try to do more good works to make sure I will go to Heaven.

_____ _____   4. Of course I'm going to Heaven; I've been a pretty good person.

_____ _____   5. I deserve God's wrath for my sins, but I know I'm forgiven. That's because Jesus took my punishment and gives me His righteous standing with God.

Allow three minutes for this activity. Then take a tally of each statement. Reveal that statements 1, 2, and 5 are consistent with trusting Christ for our salvation.

Conclude by having the class sing the hymn, "Rock of Ages."

Let's Talk It Over

The questions on this page are designed to encourage review of the lesson Scriptures and to promote discussion of the lesson by the class. The answers provided are only discussion starters. Let your class talk it over from there.

1. In some places we still hear of the tendency to define a Christian as a person who refrains from certain practices, such as smoking, drinking, and gambling. What shall we say of this emphasis?

It resembles the Galatians' tendency to insist that Christians must abide by the Jewish regulations and restrictions regarding diet, ceremonial cleansing, feast days, etc. While there are excellent Scriptural reasons that may be given for avoiding smoking, drinking, gambling, and similar vices, we dare not make prohibitions of these into a new law code for Christians. Instead, we must emphasize our salvation by grace, and the divine principles of behavior that grow out of it. Because we are saved, we will want to care for the body God has given us and not destroy it with harmful substances. Because we are saved, we will want to practice good stewardship of the material wealth God gives us and not waste it foolishly.

2. We who have been baptized into Christ have put on Christ. How is this a helpful way of viewing the Christian life?

The clothing we put on our bodies tells a lot about us. Those who wear uniforms or working clothes reveal something about their occupations. Whether our clothes are clean and neat or dirty and unkempt will say quite a bit about our personal habits. If we take seriously the matter of putting on Christ, we will show by our words, actions, and attitudes that we belong to Him. People who watch us will be able to witness Christ's own holiness, compassion, and love reflected in us. Paul uses the same figure in Romans 13:14: "Put ye on the Lord Jesus Christ, and make not provision for the flesh, to fulfil the lusts thereof."

3. How does the Holy Spirit help us to recognize and appreciate God as our Father?

The Holy Spirit has given us many precious passages in the Scriptures that reveal God as a caring Father. Jesus spoke of the Father's love for us (John 16:27). In Matthew 7:11 and James 1:17 we read of the Father's willingness to give gifts to His children. In Matthew 6:25-34 we learn of the Father's awareness of our needs and readiness to supply them. Many other Scriptures speak of our response to the Father. We are to worship the Father (John 4:23), pray to the Father (Matthew 6:9-13), call upon the Father (1 Peter 1:17), and praise the Father (1 Peter 1:3). Surely it is the indwelling Spirit who causes us to recognize the good things our Father has already given us and who urges us to thank Him as appreciative children should.

4. All people are children of God by virtue of being descendants of Adam. Why should we mention that fact in connection with our evangelistic efforts?

People need to be assured that they are not merely highly evolved members of the animal kingdom, nor just insignificant specks on a tiny planet of the universe. As people come to understand that we exist because of the action of a loving Creator, they can be led to see that God had an ultimate purpose in creating us. This is a vital prelude to the presentation of the plan of salvation. We need to show the unsaved that while it is wonderful to know that we are all God's children because He has made us His unique creation, it is far more sublime to discover that He offers us a means to an eternal, spiritual sonship through the death and resurrection of His Son, Jesus Christ.

5. One way Christians grow as God's children is by feeding upon His Word. What comparisons can we draw between the feeding of natural children and Christians' feeding on the Scripture?

Children are fed regularly so they may grow and have healthy bodies. Likewise, Christians need regular nourishment from God's Word. Without it, spiritual malnutrition will set in, as will stunted spiritual growth. Children are fed a balanced diet, so their bodies may acquire a variety of nutrients. Christians need a balanced spiritual diet. Rather then concentrate on favorite passages or on a single, appealing topic, we need to digest doctrinal truths, commands, promises, warnings, practical counsel, and expressions of praise. Children are taught to eat slowly and chew their food well. Many passages of Scripture cannot be assimilated quickly; we must "chew" on them in thoughtful study to gain the maximum benefit from them.

Given the Birthright of Freedom

DEVOTIONAL READING: Titus 2:11-13; 3:1-8.

LESSON SCRIPTURE: Galatians 4:8-31.

PRINTED TEXT: Galatians 4:8-20.

Galatians 4:8-20

8 Howbeit then, when ye knew not God, ye did service unto them which by nature are no gods.

9 But now, after that ye have known God, or rather are known of God, how turn ye again to the weak and beggarly elements, whereunto ye desire again to be in bondage?

10 Ye observe days, and months, and times, and years.

11 I am afraid of you, lest I have bestowed upon you labor in vain.

12 Brethren, I beseech you, be as I am; for I am as ye are: ye have not injured me at all.

13 Ye know how through infirmity of the flesh I preached the gospel unto you at the first.

14 And my temptation which was in my flesh ye despised not, nor rejected; but received me as an angel of God, even as Christ Jesus.

15 Where is then the blessedness ye spake of? for I bear you record, that, if it had been possible, ye would have plucked out your own eyes, and have given them to me.

16 Am I therefore become your enemy, because I tell you the truth?

17 They zealously affect you, but not well; yea, they would exclude you, that ye might affect them.

18 But it is good to be zealously affected always in a good thing, and not only when I am present with you.

19 My little children, of whom I travail in birth again until Christ be formed in you,

20 I desire to be present with you now, and to change my voice; for I stand in doubt of you.

GOLDEN TEXT: But now, after that ye have known God, or rather are known of God, how turn ye again to the weak and beggarly elements, whereunto ye desire again to be in bondage.—Galatians 4:9.

Set Free by God's Grace

Galatians

(Lessons 9-13)

Lesson Aims

After this lesson students should be able to:
1. Treasure the freedom that Christ gives.
2. Resist efforts to enslave them.
3. Trust God's Word and follow it better.

Lesson Outline

INTRODUCTION
 A. Captivity and Freedom
 B. Lesson Background
 I. DON'T CHOOSE A CAGE (Galatians 4:8-11)
 A. The Former Cage (v. 8)
 B. Another Cage (vv. 9, 10)
  Comfortable Prison
 C. Frightening! (v. 11)
 II. TRUE TEACHER (Galatians 4:12-16)
 A. Choose Freedom (v. 12a)
 B. Joyous Welcome (vv. 12b-14)
 C. Why Change? (vv. 15, 16)
 III. FALSE TEACHERS (Galatians 4:17-20)
 A. Selfish Affection (v. 17)
 B. Better Affection (v. 18)
 C. True Teacher's Agony (vv. 19, 20)
  Labor Pains
CONCLUSION
 A. They Zealously Affect You
 B. They Would Exclude You
 C. Don't Go Backward
 D. Be a Skeptic
 E. Prayer
 F. Thought to Remember

Display visual 11 of the visuals packet and refer to it when appropriate. The visual is shown on page 316.

Introduction

An intriguing book by Joy Adamson is titled *Born Free*. It tells of Elsa, a lion cub born free in the wilds of Kenya, but reared in affectionate captivity after losing her mother. As a mature lioness, however, Elsa was returned to the wild and to the life of freedom to which she was born.

A human cub also is born free; but all too soon he or she is taken captive, for everyone who sins is a slave of sin (John 8:34). Sin does not willingly release a captive. The only way to escape his clutches is to be born again (John 3:5).

A. Captivity and Freedom

On Paul's first missionary journey he brought the gospel to Galatians held captive by sin. Some of them believed the message and were born again, born to be free from sin's control. But when Paul was gone, other teachers tried to persuade those free Galatians to enter another cage, to become captives of the Jewish law that was powerless to make men free. Paul was unhappy about that.

B. Lesson Background

For centuries the Jews had been captives of the law and the Gentiles had been captives of sin, but through Christ both of them escaped to freedom. As we read in last week's text, they became children of God and therefore God's heirs (Galatians 4:1-7). In this lesson we are to read Paul's call for them to cherish and keep their freedom.

I. Don't Choose a Cage (Galatians 4:8-11)

Who would choose a cage rather than freedom? As a matter of fact, that is what all sinners do. They are fooled by "the deceitfulness of sin" (Hebrews 3:13). Sin baits his cage with something that looks good, and the unwary victim does not see the bars till he or she is entrapped. But when one has been rescued from a cage, shouldn't that person be too wise to walk into another?

A. The Former Cage (v. 8)

8. Howbeit then, when ye knew not God, ye did service unto them which by nature are no gods.

The Jews knew God through the writings of the Old Testament, but the Gentiles in Galatia did not have that advantage. Before Paul came with the gospel, they *knew not God.* At that time they were enslaved and did service to various imaginary deities *which by nature are no gods.* (See Acts 14:8-18).

B. Another Cage (vv. 9, 10)

9. But now, after that ye have known God, or rather are known of God, how turn ye again to the weak and beggarly elements, whereunto ye desire again to be in bondage?

Some of the Galatians had *known God* through Paul's preaching. More than that, they had become *known of God*: they had believed Paul's message and had become Christians; they had been born again; God had recognized them as His children. No longer were they captives of imaginary gods; they were sons of the almighty Creator and heirs of all His wealth (Galatians 4:7).

Sons of the true and living God, liberated from the cage of imaginary deities, how could the Galatians think of walking into another cage? Misled by false teachers, some of them were beginning to *desire again to be in bondage.* They were willing to be captives of the laws that had held the Jews in bondage for centuries (Galatians 4:3). Those laws were elementary rules designed to bring people to Christ, not to bind people who already had come to Him (Colossians 3:24, 25). Those *elements,* those laws, were *weak,* powerless, "for the law made nothing perfect" (Hebrews 7:19). They were *beggarly,* poverty-stricken: they had no wealth to compare with the inheritance of God's children. Only false teaching could make those outmoded laws seem attractive; only lies could lure God's children into such a cage.

10. Ye observe days, and months, and times, and years.

Happy holidays and festival weeks were attractive features of the Jewish system: the weekly Sabbath, the monthly new moon feast, the three annual festivals prescribed by law, and others added by tradition. Probably the false teachers were clever enough to lead into these first. Then other regulations could be added in connection with them: rules of diet and ceremonial cleansing, the mournful Day of Atonement, the long pilgrimages to Jerusalem.

COMFORTABLE PRISON

Some prisoners experience culture shock when they are released from prison to reenter society. Perhaps the biggest adjustment involves their independence. Now they must make their own decisions, manage their own time, and provide their own food and shelter. They are free, but they must fend for themselves. Some, unable to do this, decide that they are more comfortable *inside* then *outside* the prison.

Galatian Christians, having been freed from their heathen religions, were being misled into accepting the Jewish law with all its rules and regulations. Perhaps they felt that observing the law's prescribed statutes and ceremonies would relieve them of the necessity of making thoughtful decisions.

A Christian's freedom in Christ carries with it certain responsibilities that require mature thinking and behavior. But why would the Galatians want it any other way? Why would we? Why go back to prison?   —R. W. B.

C. Frightening! (v. 11)

11. I am afraid of you, lest I have bestowed upon you labor in vain.

What was wrong with a happy feast on the first day of the month? It could be harmless in itself, but the false teachers that were in Galatia were using it to start the process of bringing Christians into the captivity of the whole Jewish law. Their proposition was that Christians could not be saved unless they became Jews and kept the whole law (Acts 15:1, 5). To say that was to deny that Christ alone was capable of saving His people. To depend on the law for salvation was to fall from grace and lose the benefit that Christ alone can give (Galatians 5:1-4). If the Galatian Christians would follow the false teachers, all of Paul's work with them would be wasted. The thought was frightening.

II. True Teacher
(Galatians 4:12-16)

Now Paul reminded the Galatians of his ministry among them. Gladly they had received him and the truth he brought. Could they not still find gladness in that same truth?

A. Choose Freedom (v. 12a)

12a. Brethren, I beseech you, be as I am; for I am as ye are.

The apostle Paul, once called Saul, had been a captive of the law (Galatians 4:3). He was such a devoted and vigorous slave of the law that he wanted to destroy the church of Christ (Acts 8:3). But he had learned that the church was right and the claims of Christ were true (Acts 9:1-19). Thereupon he had become a Christian like the Galatian Christians, free from the law and depending on Christ alone. Now the Galatians were thinking of becoming as Paul had been before, captives of the law. He strongly urged them to be as he was now, free from the law and relying on Christ.

B. Joyous Welcome (vv. 12b-14)

12b. Ye have not injured me at all.

Paul had been seriously wronged and injured in Galatia. He had been driven out of town, he had been stoned and left for dead (Acts 13:50; 14:5, 6, 19). But the Jews and heathen had done this; the Christians had not wronged him in any way.

13. Ye know how through infirmity of the flesh I preached the gospel unto you at the first.

Paul first preached the gospel in Galatia because of some *infirmity* or sickness. The Galatians knew all about that, so it was not necessary for Paul to describe the sickness to them. Therefore we are left without any further information regarding it.

14. And my temptation which was in my flesh ye despised not, nor rejected; but received me as an angel of God, even as Christ Jesus.

Some of the most trusted Bible manuscripts read *your temptation* instead of *my temptation*. With that reading the verse says Paul's sickness tempted the Galatians to despise and reject him. Who would expect almighty God to send His message by a feeble sick man? If we prefer the reading of the *King James Version*, then *temptation* can be taken to mean a trial or tribulation or trouble. The Greek word sometimes has that meaning. Paul's sickness certainly was a trial to him as well as a temptation to the Galatians. With either reading, the main thought of the verse is clear. The Galatians did not despise or reject Paul because he was sickly. They welcomed him as gladly as if he had been *an angel of God*, or even if he had been *Christ Jesus*. Of course this was not true of all Galatians, but it was true of those who became Christians.

C. Why Change? (vv. 15, 16)

15. Where is then the blessedness ye spake of? for I bear you record, that, if it had been possible, ye would have plucked out your own eyes, and have given them to me.

The Galatians had considered themselves blessed by Paul and his message, and indeed they had been blessed. They had been delighted with the presence of the Holy Spirit and the miracles He had done among them (Galatians 3:5). So what had become of that *blessedness* they had enjoyed? What had happened to make them turn from the message that had blessed them? Why were they accepting a different message, one that really was not a gospel at all? (Galatians 1:6, 7). It was utterly unreasonable to make such a change, for they had been so happy with Paul's message and so grateful to him that they gladly would have given him their eyes. This statement leads many students to think that Paul's infirmity (v. 13) had damaged his eyesight.

16. Am I therefore become your enemy, because I tell you the truth?

Paul had been a very good friend to the Galatians, bringing them the truth that had blessed

them. They had recognized this; they had been willing to reward him with anything they had, even their eyes. But now he was critical of them because they were looking with favor at a different message. His criticism was true, but would it anger them? Would they now consider him an *enemy* because he told them *the truth*?

III. False Teachers
(Galatians 4:17-20)

Having spoken of himself and recalled his own relationship with the Galatians, Paul now turns to tell about the false teachers who were upsetting those Galatians by perverting the gospel of Christ (Galatians 1:7).

A. Selfish Affection (v. 17)

17. They zealously affect you, but not well; yea, they would exclude you, that ye might affect them.

Affect here means to show affection for. The false teachers were lavishing special attention on the Galatian Christians, courting them with flattery and pretended friendship—*but not well*, not with any good purpose. What those teachers wanted to do was to *exclude* the Galatian Christians, to cut them off from the affection and fellowship of Paul. They hoped the Galatians then would bestow their affection on the false teachers instead of Paul, and would believe their falsehood instead of Paul's truth. Paul's complaint was not that the Galatians were turning away from him, but that they were turning away from the truth. He did not at any time ask loyalty to himself, but only loyalty to Christ. He wanted the Galatians to remember that Christ had saved them when they had heard and believed the gospel, not because they had faithfully kept the law (Galatians 3:2).

B. Better Affection (v. 18)

18. But it is good to be zealously affected always in a good thing, and not only when I am present with you.

The zealous attention and affection given by false teachers to the Galatian Christian was bad because its purpose was bad. The apostle Paul himself had given similar attention and affection in a *good* cause, and that was good. The Galatian Christians and all Christians ought to accept such attention in a good cause *always*, not just when Paul is present with them. The message that Paul preached is the truth by which other messages are tested. If anyone comes with a message that contradicts it, Christians should reject both the message and the messenger (Galatians 1:9).

visual 11

C. True Teacher's Agony (vv. 19, 20)

19. My little children, of whom I travail in birth again until Christ be formed in you.

In a striking figure Paul pictures himself as the mother who gave birth to the Christians in Galatia. In pain and affliction (v. 13) he brought them to be born as children of God (John 1:12; 3:5). But now they were turning from truth to falsehood in a way unworthy of God's children. Paul was in agony like the pangs of childbirth, and would be in agony till Christ's mind, Christ's purpose, and Christ's will would be formed in those Galatian Christians so fully and firmly that they would not be led away by any false teaching.

LABOR PAINS

Our children were born B. L.—before lamaze. My wife wasn't eager to endure the pain of childbirth without medication, and I certainly wasn't keen on witnessing it. These days, it seems that many prospective parents choose the French technique. Dr. Heathcliff Huxtable delivered scores of babies each TV season, and I never heard him speak of any method other than "natural childbirth."

Labor pains are no joke, though. God declared to Eve, "In pain you shall bring forth children" (Genesis 3:16, *New American Standard Bible*).

Paul used the childbirth metaphor to illustrate his spiritual and emotional pain as he assisted in the birth of converts to Christianity. He agonized over their struggle with the Spirit as Christ was formed in them. And when they backslid, as did the Galatians, Paul's anguish was intensified.

Those who share the gospel with the lost still "travail" as they assist in the "delivery" of newborn babes in Christ. But just as a mother soon

Home Daily Bible Readings

Monday, May 9—Christ the Power/Wisdom of God (1 Corinthians 1:17-25)

Tuesday, May 10—Let Those Who Boast, Boast in God (1 Corinthians 1:26-31)

Wednesday, May 11—Paul's Demonstrations of the Spirit (1 Corinthians 2:1-5)

Thursday, May 12—No One Comprehends God's Thoughts (1 Corinthians 2:6-13)

Friday, May 13—Paul Reproves Galatians for Immaturity (Galatians 4:8-11)

Saturday, May 14—Paul's Eye Problems Blessed Galatians (Galatians 4:12-20)

Sunday, May 15—Allegory of Two Covenants: Hagar, Sarah (Galatians 4:21-31)

forgets the pains of childbirth when she holds her newborn in her arms, these dedicated Christians disregard the spiritual travail of evangelism when they experience the rewards and satisfaction of fulfilling Christ's commission.

—R. W. B.

20. I desire to be present with you now, and to change my voice; for I stand in doubt of you.

To *stand in doubt* is to be perplexed, puzzled. Paul had taught the Galatians truly. How could they be so bewitched by falsehood? (Galatians 3:1). What could he say? How could he stop them in their mistaken course and get them to obey the truth? He longed to see them, to talk face to face, to hear and answer their reasoning, to see them renounce falsehood and cling to the truth, to change his voice from harsh criticism to hearty praise.

Conclusion

Not many of us today are troubled by persons insisting that Christians cannot be saved unless they become Jews also (Acts 15:1, 5). But that does not mean there are no false teachers.

A. They Zealously Affect You

"They zealously affect you, but not well" (Galatians 4:17). We are besieged by advertisers who seek our favor with pretended friendship and flattery. You "deserve" this or that, they say. "You're worth it." But we know their real interest is in their profit, not our welfare. We look carefully before we buy.

The religious world has its share of those who seek our favor with flattery and pretended friendship. How many devoted Christians have given generously to some popular preacher on TV, only to learn that he squandered their gifts on extravagant living, or even on rank immorality?

There are many faithful people who devote their lives to the honest teaching of God's Word. It is good to support them generously, for "the laborer is worthy of his reward" (1 Timothy 5:17, 18; see also 1 Corinthians 9:14). But there are some pretenders who pervert the Word for their own selfish purposes (Galatians 1:7). To support them in their wrong is to be a partner in it (2 John 10, 11). We need to look carefully before we give, but not to stop giving to those who do well.

B. They Would Exclude You

False teachers wanted the Galatians to be severed from Paul and to give their affection to the false teachers. (See Galatians 4:17). Be wary of anyone who wants to be the one and only teacher, who tells you not to listen to anyone but him, who says he alone has the truth. Many of us remember a time years ago when an ardent religious group made headlines by mass suicide. In a radio interview, a former member of the group revealed that its leader had forbidden the members to have any unnecessary contact with people outside the group. He wanted his people to hear no voice but his. The young lady giving the interview said she herself had twice been whipped for associating with outsiders. She felt no resentment: she had been whipped for her own good, she said. But she was glad she had separated from the group before its revered leader led it to commit suicide. We need to be careful about what we hear, but also to be careful about refusing to hear.

C. Don't Go Backward

"The law was our schoolmaster to bring us unto Christ" (Galatians 3:24). It is a backward movement that turns from Christ to the "weak and beggarly elements" of law (4:9). Still there are many people who like to make rules and regulations that are not in the Bible. There are church-made creeds. There are rules of social life and diet, "forbidding to marry, and commanding to abstain from meats" (1 Timothy 4:3). There are earnest Christians who quote, "Touch not; taste not; handle not" as if it were a commandment of the Lord. Actually, Colossians 2:20-22 is a warning against such rules.

There are rules that are Biblical and necessary. "Be not deceived: neither fornicators, nor idolaters, nor adulterers, nor effeminate, nor abusers of themselves with mankind, nor thieves, nor covetous, nor drunkards, nor revilers, nor extortioners, shall inherit the kingdom of God" (1 Corinthians 6:9, 10). Christians also obey the laws of the land, unless those laws command them to disobey God; and they obey those laws as a part of their duty to God (1 Peter 2:13-15).

When someone says we must obey this rule or that regulation, it is pertinent to ask, "Who says so?" Is it the Word of God? Is it someone "ordained of God"? (Romans 13:1, 2). Or is it some unauthorized person or group trying to bring us under its own authority? "Stand fast therefore in the liberty wherewith Christ hath made us free, and be not entangled again with the yoke of bondage" (Galatians 5:1).

D. Be a Skeptic

Looking into an old blacksmith shop, the poet saw discarded on the floor the many hammers that had been worn out by beating on the anvil; but the original anvil was still in use, and good as new.

And so, thought I, the anvil of God's Word
For ages skeptic blows have beat upon;
Yet though the noise of falling blows was heard,
The anvil is unharmed—the hammers gone.

It is no longer wise to be skeptical about the Bible. It has stood the test of time, the attacks of enemies, and the desertion of friends. Modern skeptics can only recycle the worn-out arguments of ancient ones. But once in a while someone claims to have a new revelation from God. It is well to be skeptical about that. If that "revelation" contradicts the Bible, it is false. If it agrees with the Bible, what's new? And once in a while there is someone who claims to have found a new way of interpreting the Bible, some magic key by which all the mysteries of Scripture are made plain. Again we may well be skeptical about such a claim. Wise and devoted people have been studying God's Word minutely for centuries. Not very often does a scholar of our time find in it a profound truth that no one has ever discovered before. Remember these lines from poet John Greenleaf Whittier:

We search the world for truth; we cull
The good, the pure, the beautiful,
From graven stone and written scroll,
From all old flower-fields of the soul;
And, weary seekers of the best,
We come back laden from our quest,
To find that all the sages said
Is in the Book our mothers read.

Paul counsels us clearly and well: "Though we, or an angel from heaven, preach any other gospel unto you than that which we have preached unto you, let him be accursed. As we said before, so say I now again, If any man preach any other gospel unto you, than that ye have received, let him be accursed" (Galatians 1:8, 9).

Our Lord Jesus Christ also addressed the subject clearly and well: "If ye continue in my word, then are ye my disciples indeed; and ye shall know the truth, and the truth shall make you free" (John 8:31, 32).

E. Prayer

How graciously You have made us free, our heavenly Father! At what great cost our Savior redeemed us, when He gave His life on the cross at Calvary! Guided by Your faultless Word, may we never again allow ourselves to be entangled with any yoke of bondage. As we meet the trials and temptations of our daily lives, may we ever stand fast in the freedom Christ has given. In Jesus' precious name we pray. Amen.

F. Thought to Remember

"The truth shall make you free."

Learning by Doing

This page contains an alternate lesson plan emphasizing learning activities. Classes
desiring such student involvement will find these suggestions helpful.

Learning Goals

By the end of this session each student should be able to:

1. Explain the spiritual bondage to which the Christians in Galatia were turning.

2. Identify various kinds of spiritual bondage in which some Christians today allow themselves to become ensnared.

3. Determine how Christians can protect their freedom in Christ.

Into the Lesson

Begin the lesson by giving a brief synopsis of the book *Born Free*. The synopsis is found in the Introduction to the lesson on page 314.

Point out that people are born free also, but that in committing sin we become enslaved to sin (John 8:34). In Christ, however, we are set free. Explore this thought briefly by asking, "In what ways are Christians free?" Allow a few minutes for discussion.

Tell the class, "The Galatian Christians had been made free in Christ. They were free from sin, free from fear of the imaginary gods they worshiped before they learned of the one true and living God. But some religious teachers had come among them and were persuading many to accept another kind of spiritual bondage. As we examine the situation of the Galatian Christians recorded in today's lesson text, let's look for principles to help us keep from losing the freedom that is ours in Christ Jesus.

Into the Word

Read Galatians 4:8-20 aloud to the class. Then have the students form groups of six and discuss the following questions in their groups. Give each group several photocopies of the commentary section of this lesson for their study.

1. How were the Galatian Christians becoming enslaved again?

2. How would you describe the relationship between Paul and the Galatians when he first came to them with the gospel?

3. How would you describe the relationship between Paul and the Galatians at the time Paul wrote this letter to them?

4. What caused the change in their relationship?

5. What was Paul's greatest concern for the Galatians?

6. Describe the spiritual condition of the Galatians at each of these stages: before they came to Christ; right after they came to Christ; when this letter was written.

Allow twenty minutes for the groups to work. After reassembling the class, consider each of the questions and let the groups share their conclusions.

Option

Ask a volunteer to read Galatians 4:8-20 aloud to the class. If there are eighteen or fewer persons in your class, have them form three groups. Divide the Scripture text into three portions and give a different portion to each of the three groups. (If you have more than eighteen persons in class, form groups of five and give some of the groups the same portion of the text. Divide the text as follows: verses 8-11, 12-16, and 17-20.)

Each group is to study its passage and write a paraphrase of it in language an eight-year-old can understand. Appoint a leader for each group. Provide the groups with paper, pens, and photocopies of the appropriate portions of the commentary section of this lesson for their reference. Allow twenty minutes for this activity.

When the time has expired, ask the group leaders to read the paraphrases to the entire class. Add any information you feel is necessary for further clarification.

Then use question six from the study option above to analyze the Galatians. Put the three headings on the chalkboard and list the students' observations as they give them.

Into Life

Christ had set the Galatians free from the bondage of sin, and yet they were being persuaded to look to law-keeping to save them. Paul described such foolish action as a return to bondage. Ask "In what ways have some Christians today adopted the Galatians' attitude?" (Some answers are, by yielding to man-made rules and regulations that are not in the Bible, such as rules of social life and diet; by submitting to a strong leader who says he alone has the truth.)

Read Galatians 5:1 aloud to the class. Urge the students to read that verse regularly and to pray that God will help them to cherish and protect their freedom in Christ.

Let's Talk It Over

The questions on this page are designed to encourage review of the lesson Scriptures and to promote discussion of the lesson by the class. The answers provided are only discussion starters. Let your class talk it over from there.

1. Many human beings seem to possess an unfortunate inclination toward attitudes and habits that lead to their eventual enslavement. What can be done to overcome this tendency?

We see this tendency in the physical realm as people bind themselves to drugs and alcohol. We witness it in the realm of politics, when citizens allow a dictator to dominate them. We view it in the context of religion, also, as adherents of certain cults or followers of a strong, charismatic leader cease to think for themselves and thus allow themselves to be mentally enslaved. The simple answer to this is to point people to the only legitimate slavery: being a slave of Jesus Christ. "For he who was a slave when he was called by the Lord is the Lord's freedman; similarly, he who was a free man when he was called is Christ's slave" (1 Corinthians 7:22, *New International Version*). Ironically, the more completely one binds oneself to Christ, the greater is that person's true freedom.

2. Like the false teachers in Galatia, members of cults today often present a strong display of friendship to outsiders. How should that fact affect us?

If we are ever tempted to join one of these cults because of the apparent warmth of their friendship, let us remember that such warmth and cordiality can be used to lure us into spiritual enslavement. We might see how well the facade of friendship holds up if we persist in asking probing questions about the group's beliefs and practices, and the basis for them. Another aspect of this matter is our own church's level of friendship. Is it genuine? Is it deep? Let us determine to be unsurpassed in the warmth of the welcome we extend and the depth of friendship we offer to our own members and to those people who visit our services.

3. Like Paul, those today who share the life-giving gospel with the lost can truly say they have assisted in the birth when those persons are born as children of God. What is the church's responsibility following their birth?

In the natural realm a mother nourishes and nurtures the child to whom she has given birth. Christians should have that same concern for the spiritual babes in their midst. Too often, however, we allow newborn Christians to struggle along on their own. As a result, many of them drift away from the household of faith, and some who stay never reach maturity in Christ. Those who are young in faith require a balanced diet of the Word of God, which will include a healthy measure of doctrine, calls to praise and worship, and promises of Heavenly triumph and rest, among other benefits. We also need to nurture them by offering them encouragement, comfort, and guidance in avoiding moral and spiritual pitfalls.

4. How can we get into the habit of testing all things by the Word of God?

Paul urges us, "Test everything. Hold on to the good" (1 Thessalonians 5:21, *New International Version*). In order to accomplish such testing we need to have a thorough grasp of Biblical doctrines and principles. Then, if we hear a religious leader espouse an unscriptural doctrine or advocate a moral principle contrary to the Word, we will recognize it. It is vital that Christians discuss together the kinds of teachings, philosophies, and moral principles that receive prominence in our society today. Such discussions will give us exercise in drawing out the Biblical passages that speak to human error, and it will aid us in being alert to anti-Scriptural principles when we encounter them in our work, recreation, and social contact.

5. Why is it important for each person to know the Bible and not to depend solely on the interpretations of other human beings?

Even the most sincere teachers of the Bible may overstress some doctrines to the exclusion of others. And of course there are teachers and preachers who espouse false doctrine and make a show of supporting it with Biblical passages. To know the Bible accurately, in its entirety, we must study it for ourselves. We will need to make use of the sermons, lessons, commentaries, and other learning tools provided by men, but we must learn to distinguish between Biblical truth and human opinion. Since we are capable of being experts in such areas as automobiles, sports, sewing, cooking, and the like, should we not be able to develop expertise in handling Biblical truth also?

Bear Fruit of the Spirit

DEVOTIONAL READING: 1 Timothy 6:6-12.

LESSON SCRIPTURE: Galatians 5.

PRINTED TEXT: Galatians 5:1, 13-26.

Galatians 5:1, 13-26

1 Stand fast therefore in the liberty wherewith Christ hath made us free, and be not entangled again with the yoke of bondage.

. . . .

13 For, brethren, ye have been called unto liberty; only use not liberty for an occasion to the flesh, but by love serve one another.

14 For all the law is fulfilled in one word, even in this; Thou shalt love thy neighbor as thyself.

15 But if ye bite and devour one another, take heed that ye be not consumed one of another.

16 This I say then, Walk in the Spirit, and ye shall not fulfil the lust of the flesh.

17 For the flesh lusteth against the Spirit, and the Spirit against the flesh: and these are contrary the one to the other; so that ye cannot do the things that ye would.

18 But if ye be led of the Spirit, ye are not under the law.

19 Now the works of the flesh are manifest, which are these, adultery, fornication, uncleanness, lasciviousness,

20 Idolatry, witchcraft, hatred, variance, emulations, wrath, strife, seditions, heresies,

21 Envyings, murders, drunkenness, revelings, and such like: of the which I tell you before, as I have also told you in time past, that they which do such things shall not inherit the kingdom of God.

22 But the fruit of the Spirit is love, joy, peace, long-suffering, gentleness, goodness, faith,

23 Meekness, temperance: against such there is no law.

24 And they that are Christ's have crucified the flesh with the affections and lusts.

25 If we live in the Spirit, let us also walk in the Spirit.

26 Let us not be desirous of vainglory, provoking one another, envying one another.

GOLDEN TEXT: The fruit of the Spirit is love, joy, peace, long-suffering, gentleness, goodness, faith, meekness, temperance.—Galatians 5:22, 23.

Set Free by God's Grace

Galatians

(Lessons 9-13)

Lesson Aims

After this lesson a student should be able to:

1. Briefly describe works of the flesh and fruit of the Spirit.

2. Search his or her life for a trace of fleshly works to be eliminated.

Lesson Outline

INTRODUCTION
  A. Understanding Freedom
  B. God's Spirit and Ours
  C. Lesson Background
 I. TURNING POINT (Galatians 5:1, 13-18)
  A. Call (v. 1)
  B. Warning (vv. 13-15)
    Christian Liberty
  C. Lust Against Lust (vv. 16-18)
 II. WORKS OF THE FLESH (Galatians 5:19-21)
  A. Bad Works (vv. 19-21a)
  B. Bad Result (v. 21b)
III. FRUIT OF THE SPIRIT (Galatians 5:22-26)
  A. Good Fruit (vv. 22, 23)
  B. Death to the Flesh (v. 24)
  C. Life in the Spirit (vv. 25, 26)
CONCLUSION
  A. Stay Free
  B. How to Stay Free
  C. Prayer
  D. Thought to Remember

Display visual 12 of the visuals packet and refer to it as you consider the main points of the lesson text. The visual is shown on page 325.

Introduction

It is wonderful to be redeemed from captivity and ushered into "the glorious liberty of the children of God" (Romans 8:21). We must cherish that liberty and take care to keep it. So our lesson text begins: "Stand fast therefore in the liberty wherewith Christ hath made us free."

A. Understanding Freedom

Christ has made us free, but that freedom is not a permit to do anything wrong. We are free in Christ, not free to do anything that cannot be done in His name (Colossians 3:17). If we think

Christian liberty makes us free to sin, then we give up our liberty and become slaves of sin again.

We are free Christians. Can we do right without laws to compel us? Can we avoid wrong without laws to restrain us? It is a narrow road that leads to life (Matthew 7:14). How can we find it? Paul gives the answer: "Walk in the Spirit, and ye shall not fulfil the lust of the flesh" (Galatians 5:16).

B. God's Spirit and Ours

In our text the word *Spirit* is printed with a capital S to show that it means God's Spirit, the Holy Spirit. This divine Spirit is in conflict with the human flesh, which often seems bent on doing wrong.

Some good Bible students think the word *spirit* in these verses means the Christian's own human spirit, which also opposes wrong desires of the flesh. We all know the Christian's human nature has a better side in conflict with the flesh. Paul describes that conflict in Romans 7:22-25, but he calls the better side of human nature "the inward man" and "the mind" rather than "the spirit."

The practical teaching of our lesson is the same, whether Paul meant God's Spirit or the Christian's spirit. If he meant the human spirit, he meant the reborn human spirit, the spirit born of God's Spirit (John 3:6). That reborn human spirit and the divine Spirit are together in opposing evil desires of the flesh.

Since God's Spirit and the Christian's spirit are united in the struggle, we may do well to bypass the question of which one the apostle Paul meant. For the purposes of this lesson, we will go along with the majority of translators and suppose the word *Spirit* in our text means the Holy Spirit.

C. Lesson Background

The first four chapters of Galatians are designed to guide our thinking. From facts of history and with powerful logic, Paul shows that Christ is supreme and sufficient. If we believe in Him and follow Him, we are safe for eternity. Galatian Christians would gain nothing by becoming Jews. Today's Christians likewise need no other Savior and no other Master. To look to another for salvation is to forsake Christ.

How to Say It

EROS (Greek). *air*-oce.
AGAPE (Greek). uh-*gah*-pay.

I. Turning Point
(Galatians 5:1, 13-18)

The last two chapters of Galatians turn from thinking to doing. What is involved in following Jesus? This lesson and the next will not tell all the details of our duty, but they will give us some guidelines.

A. Call (v. 1)

1. Stand fast therefore in the liberty wherewith Christ hath made us free, and be not entangled again with the yoke of bondage.

Here is the summary and conclusion of what Paul has said in the first four chapters. Heathen had been slaves of sin before they knew Jesus. Jews had accepted *bondage* to the law to keep them from wrong, but even so they had not escaped the *bondage* of sin. Christ had brought freedom to heathen and Jews alike. Paul calls them to cherish and keep their freedom.

B. Warning (vv. 13-15)

13. For, brethren, ye have been called unto liberty; only use not liberty for an occasion to the flesh, but by love serve one another.

Christian liberty is to be treasured, but not to be misused. It must not be used for *an occasion to the flesh*, a permit for our physical natures to satisfy their selfish desires regardless of other people. Rather, our physical natures are to be controlled by godly minds and used in unselfish service to fellow Christians, whom we love as we love ourselves.

14. For all the law is fulfilled in one word, even in this; Thou shalt love thy neighbor as thyself.

See Romans 13:8-10, where Paul states this more fully.

A sane person does not intentionally injure himself in any way, and a loving Christian does not intentionally injure anyone else. More than that, a sensible person plans and works for his or her own benefit. A loving Christian plans and works also for the benefit of others.

CHRISTIAN LIBERTY

America is the "land of the free." Citizens are free to express opinions, free to assemble for causes, free to worship as they please, and free to vote for leaders of their choice. To guarantee these freedoms for everyone, however, laws must be made and enforced. One persons' exercise of freedom must not infringe upon another person's freedom. To ensure "liberty and justice for all," individual human rights must be protected by lawmakers and peacekeepers.

So, democratic freedom is not absolute. We are not free to speed, murder, deal drugs, or evade income tax. Actually, there are many prohibitions that people who live in a free society must abide by.

Christian liberty is not absolute either. In this era of grace, we are not bound by the statutes of Mosaic law, but we are compelled by love for God and our fellowman and by the conviction of the Holy Spirit to subject ourselves, not only to civil law, but to God's moral law as well.

In Christ we are free, not to indulge every impulse of the flesh, but to please God and to love our neighbors. We are free from the bondage of selfishness, free from the domination of carnal instincts. Let us use our freedom as God intends.
—R. W. B.

15. But if ye bite and devour one another, take heed that ye be not consumed one of another.

People in Galatia were not literally devouring the flesh of others. No country, however, is free of biting insults, sarcasm, scorn, ridicule. One who likes to bite is likely to be bitten in return. In every country there are some who devour the property of others by clever fraud or outright theft. Such cheaters are likely to be cheated. There are some who destroy reputations with slander, and they are likely to be destroyed in the same way. So Paul warns, *Take heed that ye be not consumed one of another.* In a crooked world without love, those who are not consumed by others destroy themselves—their own character, their own goodness and decency, and sometimes their own physical bodies.

C. Lust Against Lust (vv. 16-18)

16, 17. This I say then, Walk in the Spirit, and ye shall not fulfil the lust of the flesh. For the flesh lusteth against the Spirit, and the Spirit against the flesh: and these are contrary the one to the other; so that ye cannot do the things that ye would.

Both in the Bible and in modern English, *lust* usually appears as something evil: "Every man is tempted, when he is drawn away of his own lust, and enticed" (James 1:14). But lust is not always bad. In this verse we see that the Spirit lusts too—the Holy Spirit. He lusts always for what is right and good. To lust is simply to desire. It is good to lust for what is good; it is bad to lust for what is bad.

There is constant conflict between the good and the bad. The Holy Spirit wants only good, but *the flesh lusteth against the Spirit.* This leads us to stop and think about what is meant by that word *flesh.*

Obviously our physical bodies are not all bad. Hands of flesh prepare meals to feed the family, build and maintain the house where it lives, make clothes for warmth and beauty. Hands of flesh care for the sick, set broken bones, earn money for charitable giving. Physical lips and vocal cords teach God's Word. What good thing do we do that is not done by our flesh?

Then why does *flesh* appear so often as something bad, something that *lusteth against the Spirit?* It is because the flesh itself has no moral standards. It desires food and clothing, which is right and proper. But it likes ease and comfort too, so it may want to get food and clothing in the easiest way, by stealing or fraud instead of earning them. The flesh craves sexual satisfaction, but it may want to avoid the responsibility of marriage. The flesh is selfish. It does not feel the discomfort of someone else who is hungry and cold. In order to do good, the flesh needs to be controlled by a mind that is set on doing good. So Paul uses the word *flesh* to mean the selfish side of human nature, the greedy side that impels one to do what is pleasant and profitable to oneself, disregarding the leading of God's Spirit and the needs of other people. Paul writes, therefore, that nothing good lives in his flesh: that is, in that greedy side of his nature (Romans 7:18). Consequently, the Spirit of God and that greedy side of human nature *are contrary the one to the other.* They are in constant conflict *so that ye cannot do the things that ye would.* If you want to satisfy every lust of the flesh and live for your own pleasure alone, the influence of the Spirit makes your conscience uneasy and slows your mad pursuit of pleasure. If you want to follow the Spirit's leading, the lusts of the flesh get in the way. Paul describes this conflict more fully in Romans 7:15-25. What we need in our own minds and hearts is a firm decision to *walk in the Spirit* and *not fulfil the lust of the flesh.*

18. But if ye be led of the Spirit, ye are not under the law.

This is explained in verses 22 and 23. There is no law against those things to which the Spirit leads us. To be free from law, we need only to follow the Spirit's leading.

II. Works of the Flesh (Galatians 5:19-21)

Now it is time to be specific. Do we have any doubt about what happens when people "fulfil the lust of the flesh" (v. 16), when they let the selfish part of their nature have its way? In the following verses the apostle Paul is going to give some plain examples.

A. Bad Works (vv. 19-21a)

19. Now the works of the flesh are manifest, which are these, adultery, fornication, uncleanness, lasciviousness.

Works are things that are done. The more the selfish and sensual side of human nature is loosed, the more the following things will be done. *Manifest* means apparent, easily and plainly seen. *Works of the flesh* that were plainly seen in the first century are seen even more plainly now because we have newspapers, magazines, and television to advertise them.

Sexual sins are at the top of the list, perhaps because they were as popular among ancient pagans as they are among modern pagans. *Fornication* is any sexual union between a man and woman not married to each other. Fornication is *adultery* when either fornicator is married.

Uncleanness and *lasciviousness* include a wide range of things that encourage fornication: impure thoughts, foul language, dirty jokes, lewd movies, indecent stage plays, the whole field of pornography. Such things are produced and purchased because of "the lust of the flesh" (v. 16), or "the desires of the sinful nature," as the *New International Version* has it.

20. Idolatry, witchcraft, hatred, variance, emulations, wrath, strife, seditions, heresies.

Perhaps the Galatians in Lystra offered sacrifices to a statue of Jupiter (Acts 14:13). We are not tempted by that kind of *idolatry*, but Paul warns that covetousness is idolatry too (Colossians 3:5). If we crave something we do not have, and that craving has more influence in our lives than God has, then we are idolaters. Money and comfort and pleasure and prestige—these are some of the modern idols. It is the flesh, the selfish part of human nature, that cares more for these than for truth and goodness.

Witchcraft is *sorcery* in some versions, *magic* in others. There were and there are people who claim to have magical ways of knowing what is going to happen in the future. Some claim to have magical ways of managing the future events. Such magic often is used for selfish gain or advantage: it is a work of the flesh.

The rest of verse 20 lists some very common things in which people are set against people. They arise from the selfish side of human nature: they are works of the flesh. The *New International Version* makes them plainer to our modern minds: "hatred, discord, jealousy, fits of rage, selfish ambition, dissensions, factions."

21a. Envyings, murders, drunkenness, revelings, and such like.

Envyings and *murders* may be added to the list that ends verse 20. They are things in which one

person is selfishly set against another. Some of
the oldest manuscripts do not have *murders* here,
and so it is left out of some modern versions. It
is notable also that Paul does not mention such
obvious sins as lying, stealing, and defrauding.
Everybody knows these are bad. Even heathen
who do them try to keep them hidden. Paul lists
things that ancient and modern heathen do with
no pangs of conscience. The same things can en-
trap Christians too, so Paul gives this warning.

Also among works of the flesh are *drunkenness,
revelings, and such like.* These are popular with
heathen bent on pleasure; and if a Christian is
bent on pleasure, he had better beware.

B. Bad Result (v. 21b)

**21b. Of the which I tell you before, as I have
also told you in time past, that they which do
such things shall not inherit the kingdom of
God.**

I tell you before means *I am warning you in advance.* Before the time came for those Galatians
to go from this life to the eternal inheritance of
God's children, Paul was warning them *that they
which do such things shall not inherit the kingdom of
God.* Paul had told them the same thing *in time
past,* probably when he was teaching among
them in person. But hearing it again was good
for them, and it is good for us. The liberty of
God's children (v. 1) does not mean they are free
to live like children of the devil. Being recognized as a church member will not get one to
Heaven if he ignores the leading of the Spirit
and lives according to the lust of the flesh.

III. Fruit of the Spirit
(Galatians 5:22-26)

The Spirit opposes all the bad works listed
above, and so guides us away from the bad result seen in verse 21. The Spirit has works too,
good works with good results. They include
such things as sharing with the needy, helping
the weak, encouraging the strong; and they result in the glorious inheritance that is lost if we
choose to let the flesh have its way (Matthew
25:31-40). But in our text Paul speaks rather of
fruit of the Spirit. Works are deeds that are done;
fruit consists of feelings, attitudes, and traits of
character that grow and ripen when we follow
the Spirit's leading.

A. Good Fruit (vv. 22, 23)

**22. But the fruit of the Spirit is love, joy,
peace, long-suffering, gentleness, goodness,
faith.**

Love in the New Testament is not *eros,* the sexual desire that is called love in modern songs

visual 12

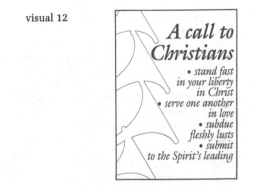

A call to Christians
• stand fast in your liberty in Christ
• serve one another in love
• subdue fleshly lusts
• submit to the Spirit's leading

and literature. Paul writes of *agape,* the earnest
affection that longs to do good to the loved one
even if it is costly to the one who loves.

Joy is gladness compatible with love and truth
(1 Corinthians 13:6), joy that comes from knowing the truth (1 John 1:3, 4), even if it is accompanied by "much affliction" (1 Thessalonians 1:6).
Joy persists through great troubles (1 Peter 1:3-7),
even because of troubles (James 1:2-4). It is such
happiness that it impels Christians to give generously even when they are poor (2 Corinthians
8:1-4). It is pleasure in the progress of others (3
John 4). Being fruit of the Spirit, *joy* is delight in
things that delight the Spirit, especially "the salvation of your souls" (1 Peter 1:8, 9).

Peace is the sense of well-being and content-
ment that comes when one is in tune with God.
"Thou wilt keep him in perfect peace, whose
mind is stayed on thee: because he trusteth in
thee" (Isaiah 26:3). As joy does not depend on
pleasure, peace does not depend on comfort.
Jesus was facing the cross when He said, "My
peace I give unto you" (John 14:27). With Calvary just ahead, how could He have any peace to
give? He was at peace because He was accepting
the Father's will, He was doing right, He was giving His life for others. He trusted God, and God
kept Him in perfect peace while the nails were
driven. Such peace is the Spirit's fruit in us
when we are in tune with Him.

Long-suffering is translated *patience* in some versions. It means putting up with a lot. This is the
characteristic of one who is slow to anger, and
such a one is better than the mighty (Proverbs
16:32). The flesh, the selfish side of our nature, is
inclined to demand our rights, to stand up for
ourselves, to be aggressive, to get even with anyone who harms us. But revenge belongs to God
(Hebrews 10:30), and God's Spirit does not lead
us to steal it. God's Spirit is fruitless in us if we
choose to let the flesh have its way.

Gentleness is *kindness* in other versions. While
long-suffering means putting up with some un-
pleasantness, *kindness* goes a step farther. It

means reaching out actively to help others, to be useful to them.

Goodness is of many kinds, and all of them are fruit of the Spirit. Here goodness appears as the climax of three things we can express in our relationships with others. *Long-suffering* means putting up with the imperfections of others; *gentleness* or *kindness* means reaching out to help others; *goodness* means doing good to others.

Faith here may mean faithfulness, perseverance, dependability. As this grows and ripens in us, people come to know they can count on us to be standing firmly for the right.

23. Meekness, temperance: against such there is no law.

Meekness is not weakness. As many sermons have pointed out, Greeks used the word *meek* to describe a horse trained and harnessed and put to work. With that in mind, we can see *long-suffering* as the patience to accept wrong without doing wrong in return, and *meekness* as the humility to accept good direction. The direction given by God's Spirit is always good, and often we can profit by accepting good direction from others.

Temperance appears as *self-control* in other versions. When this fruit is ripened, the flesh is so well managed that it does none of the evil works listed in verses 19-21. Laws are needed to keep those works of the flesh from being disastrous, but *there is no law* against the fruit of the Spirit. When such fruit is abundant in us, we naturally do nothing against the law. Therefore we are gloriously free from the law.

B. Death to the Flesh (v. 24)

24. And they that are Christ's have crucified the flesh with the affections and lusts.

When we belong to Christ we kill the selfish side of our nature, the side that "lusteth against the Spirit" (v. 17). Crucifixion is not a quick and easy death. The flesh and its lusts and its works do not vanish in an instant when we become Christians. Getting rid of them is painful as well as slow. But they do die as the fruit of the Spirit grows and ripens.

C. Life in the Spirit (vv. 25, 26)

25. If we live in the Spirit, let us also walk in the Spirit.

We do *live in the Spirit*. He causes our new birth as Christians (John 3:5). "It is the Spirit that quickeneth; the flesh profiteth nothing" (John 6:63). Then *let us also walk in the Spirit:* that is, let Him be in control of everything we say and do.

26. Let us not be desirous of vainglory, provoking one another, envying one another.

Vainglory is empty honor. It is the flesh that lusts for the praise of men instead of the praise of God (John 5:44; 12:42, 43). The desire for men's honor leads to *provoking one another*, challenging one another, competing, trying to get ahead of our brethren. The same lust for men's honor leads to *envying one another*, feeling bitter and hostile because someone else has the honor and recognition we crave. Do you ever feel a nagging wish to put someone down so you can be above him or her? Do you ever feel a surge of bitterness because someone's wealth, or accomplishment, or honor is greater than your own? If you do, the flesh you crucified is not quite dead yet. Don't let him escape from the cross!

Conclusion

To bring this lesson to a close, let's quickly look again at its two main thoughts.

A. Stay Free

"Stand fast therefore in the liberty wherewith Christ hath made us free, and be not entangled again with the yoke of bondage" (Galatians 5:1).

B. How to Stay Free

"Walk in the Spirit, and ye shall not fulfil the lust of the flesh" (Galatians 5:16).

C. Prayer

Gracious Heavenly Father, how good it is to have before us the Bible inspired by Your Spirit and to have within us the presence of Your Spirit himself! Today we promise again that where He leads us we will follow. In Jesus' name we pray. Amen.

D. Thought to Remember

Walk in the Spirit.

Home Daily Bible Readings

Monday, May 16—Wait for Righteousness by Faith (Galatians 5:1-5)

Tuesday, May 17—Basic Value: Faith Working Through Love (Galatians 5:6-12)

Wednesday, May 18—You Were Called to Freedom (Galatians 5:13-15)

Thursday, May 19—Name the Works of the Flesh (Galatians 5:16-23)

Friday, May 20—Avoid the Fruits of Darkness (Galatians 5:24-26; Ephesians 5:18-20)

Saturday, May 21—Obtaining the Grace of God (Hebrews 12:12-17)

Sunday, May 22—Bear Fruit in Every Good Work (Colossians 1:3-13)

Learning by Doing

This page contains an alternate lesson plan emphasizing learning activities. Classes desiring such student involvement will find these suggestions helpful.

Learning Goals

Choose two of these goals for this session. In this session the students will:

1. Illustrate Paul's teaching about Christian liberty by means of a simple diagram.

2. Contrast life controlled by the Holy Spirit with life that is dominated by the desires of the flesh.

3. Examine their own lives for indications of the leading of the Holy Spirit or the dominance of fleshly desires.

4. Determine to allow the Spirit to be in control in their lives.

Into the Lesson

Before class begins, put the following diagram on the chalkboard:

Law---------------Liberty----------------License
Galatians 5:1   Galatians 5:13

When you are ready to begin the session, draw your class members' attention to the diagram on the chalkboard and say, "Our lesson text from Galatians 5 can be summed up with this simple diagram. By His death on the cross Christ set us free from the bondage of sin and the bondage of the law given through Moses. Some were trying to influence the Galatians to turn back to the rules and regulations of the Jewish law (point to the word *law*), and Paul warned against that, as we have seen in our lessons from Galatians in the past three weeks. But a danger lay in the other direction, in that some might think Christian liberty was a synonym for license (point to *license* on the diagram). As we shall see, today's lesson touches on both of these extreme views. Then we shall consider some specific attitudes and behaviors that are in no way associated with Christian liberty, as well as those that are."

Into the Word

Divide your class into groups of four students each. Give each group a copy of the commentary section of this lesson, a copy of the questions below, and pencil and paper. Appoint a leader for each group to guide the group's research and discussion of the questions. Allow twenty-five minutes for this activity.

1. Chapters 1-4 of Galatians contain Paul's response to the Galatians' desire to turn to the law of the Jews for salvation. Galatians 5:1 is a summary of his teaching about it. Paraphrase this verse.

2. Galatians 5:13 contains Paul's instruction to those who might regard their liberty in Christ as freedom to do anything they please. Paraphrase this verse.

3. Galatians 5:13-26 contrasts a life that is led by God's Spirit with a life that is lived governed by the desires of the flesh. Write a brief summary statement for each.

4. We are saved by faith, not works. Yet Paul lists specific works that will keep a person out of God's kingdom (vv. 19-21). How do you harmonize these truths?

When the time is up, ask the groups to share their paraphrases of Galatians 5:1 and 13. Make certain that the students understand the nature of our liberty in Christ and the importance of standing firm in it. Then summarize their study by leading a discussion of the following two questions:

What does it mean to walk in the Spirit?

What is the key to walking in the Spirit?

Into Life

Give each student paper and pencil. Ask each to write a letter to an imaginary new Christian, encouraging the new Christian to walk in the Spirit. The letter should provide basic principles or practical suggestions for doing so. Students are to work individually. Allow seven minutes for completion. Then ask for several volunteers to read their letters to the rest of the class.

Option

Give each student a pencil and a copy of the following incomplete statements. Allow space after each one for writing.

1. Evidence of the Spirit's leading in my life:

2. Evidence that I allow the desires of the flesh dominance in my life:

3. My strategy for living consistently by the Holy Spirit:

Have students work alone. Let them know that they will not be asked to share their answers.

After four minutes, close the session by having the students bow their heads while you read aloud all stanzas of J. Edwin Orr's hymn, "Cleanse Me."

Let's Talk It Over

The questions on this page are designed to encourage review of the lesson Scriptures and to promote discussion of the lesson by the class. The answers provided are only discussion starters. Let your class talk it over from there.

1. "By love serve one another" (Galatians 5:13). What does this simple exhortation say about the basic duty of Christians?

It reminds us that our duty is more than merely saying we love one another. Many Christians have been disillusioned and crushed when they were neglected by their fellow Christians who claimed to love them. We need to practice the serving love that provides genuine comfort to a bereaved brother or sister in Christ, that supplies food and clothing in a time of financial crisis, that offers a listening ear when frustration must be expressed, etc. Paul's exhortation also reminds us that while on occasion we may need to be served by other Christians, our primary aim should be to serve rather than to be served. Too many church members are willing to sit back and let the minister, the elders and deacons, the teachers, and the musicians serve them. Not only are they neglecting the duty of serving, but also they are missing the joy that serving brings.

2. Paul's listing of the works of the flesh begins with sexual sins. These sins appear to be as much of a snare for human beings today as they were in New Testament times. Why is this a remarkable fact?

After two thousand additional years of human history it seems that people would be significantly more aware of the destructive effects of illicit sexual behavior. And yet human beings today are ruining marriages, destroying homes, soiling reputations, and damaging their health pursuing the same kind of immoral activities that people in Paul's day pursued. People today are better educated, more aware of the psychological factors that influence their behavior, and better informed as to matters of disease and health, but they are still afflicted by the weakness of the flesh and prone to misuse God's gift of sex.

3. Why should we carefully define the joy that is the fruit of the Spirit?

Certainly some of the joy we experience as Christians differs little from the world's kind of joy. It is joyous, for example, to partake of a fellowship dinner or play games at a Sunday-school class party or cheer the church's softball team to victory. There is nothing wrong with ex-

periencing the joy of "good times," but the Holy Spirit leads us to joy of another kind. Some joyous experiences that are unique to Christians are the sense of relief we gain when we prayerfully yield a burden to God, the exhilaration we feel when our devotional Bible reading uncovers a verse that speaks to a pressing need in our lives, and the satisfaction we receive in serving another person in Jesus' name. These are surely occasions of joy that the Spirit produces.

4. The lesson writer speaks of meekness as "the humility to accept good direction." Why do we need this fruit of the Spirit?

Early in life we develop the spirit of independence that says, "I want to make up my own mind, and I want to do things my way." Basically this is a healthy development, since we cannot go through life allowing others to make all our decisions for us. Too often, however, we carry the spirit of independence to extremes and refuse to heed the worthwhile counsel others offer. Apparently the indwelling Spirit tames this independent spirit, so that we become more sensitive to God's leading and more willing to listen to sensible advice from our fellow human beings. This definition of meekness ties in well with Jesus' teaching about dealing with our enemies (Matthew 5:38-48). His advice runs counter to our natural instincts; but when we follow it, we discover that it produces the best results.

5. It almost seems a contradiction to say that self-control is a fruit of the Spirit. How do we balance this effort of the self with the Spirit's working?

Paul described this cooperation of the human with the divine when he exhorted the Philippians to "work out your own salvation with fear and trembling: for it is God which worketh in you both to will and to do of his good pleasure" (Philippians 2:12, 13). We are responsible to work at exercising control over our appetites and desires, but God's power at work within us helps us succeed in our effort. It is wrong for us to assume that we can achieve mastery over all temptation through our own power. It is equally wrong, however, for us to throw up our hands and say, "There is nothing I can do to control myself—I will just leave it up to God."

Express Christ's Love in All Relationships

DEVOTIONAL READING: 1 Corinthians 13:1-7.

LESSON SCRIPTURE: Galatians 6.

PRINTED TEXT: Galatians 6:1-10, 14-18.

Galatians 6:1-10, 14-18

1 Brethren, if a man be overtaken in a fault, ye which are spiritual, restore such a one in the spirit of meekness; considering thyself, lest thou also be tempted.

2 Bear ye one another's burdens, and so fulfil the law of Christ.

3 For if a man think himself to be something, when he is nothing, he deceiveth himself.

4 But let every man prove his own work, and then shall he have rejoicing in himself alone, and not in another.

5 For every man shall bear his own burden.

6 Let him that is taught in the word communicate unto him that teacheth in all good things.

7 Be not deceived; God is not mocked: for whatsoever a man soweth, that shall he also reap.

8 For he that soweth to his flesh shall of the flesh reap corruption; but he that soweth to the Spirit shall of the Spirit reap life everlasting.

9 And let us not be weary in well doing: for in due season we shall reap, if we faint not.

10 As we have therefore opportunity, let us do good unto all men, especially unto them who are of the household of faith.

. . . .

14 But God forbid that I should glory, save in the cross of our Lord Jesus Christ, by whom the world is crucified unto me, and I unto the world.

15 For in Christ Jesus neither circumcision availeth any thing, nor uncircumcision, but a new creature.

16 And as many as walk according to this rule, peace be on them, and mercy, and upon the Israel of God.

17 From henceforth let no man trouble me: for I bear in my body the marks of the Lord Jesus.

18 Brethren, the grace of our Lord Jesus Christ be with your spirit. Amen.

GOLDEN TEXT: Let us do good unto all . . . , especially unto them who are of the household of faith.—Galatians 6:10.

A. Then and Now

Set Free by God's Grace
Galatians
(Lessons 9-13)

In Romans and Galatians we have seen two problems that troubled the early churches: (1) May a Christian use meat from an animal sacrificed in heathen worship? (2) Must all Christians be Jews as well? Neither of these problems troubles us now. Isn't it amazing that Paul's answers to them are so helpful with the problems that do trouble us?

B. Lesson Background

Lesson Aims

When this lesson has been completed, a student should be able to:

1. Briefly outline a Christian's responsibility to others.

2. Tell what responsibility a Christian has for himself or herself.

3. Find a way to meet his or her responsibility better this week.

Lesson Outline

Display visual 13 of the visuals packet and refer to it as you consider verses 1 and 2 of the text. The visual is shown on page 333.

Introduction

We come now to the last lesson of our three-month study of Romans and Galatians. If you want to begin with a quick review of the series, "Preview" on page 227 may be used as a guide. Or you may prefer to use this lesson first and then have the review at the end of your class period.

Last week's lesson portrayed "works of the flesh" in stark contrast with "fruit of the Spirit" (Galatians 5:16-26). The last verse of that text called us to turn away from selfish competition, strife, and envy. Now this new lesson calls us to turn to brotherhood, cordial cooperation, sharing. As the lesson title puts it, "Express Christ's Love in All Relationships."

I. Sharing Responsibility (Galatians 6:1-5)

When one becomes a Christian, "he is a new creature" (2 Corinthians 5:17). He is "born of water and of the Spirit." This is a spiritual rebirth, for "that which is born of the Spirit is spirit" (John 3:5, 6). But the newborn spirit lives in the same old physical body. "The flesh" has the same old desires and demands. Each Christian has the responsibility of keeping his or her body under control and following the leading of the Holy Spirit. But that is not all. Each Christian also shares the responsibility of helping other Christians continue in the Spirit's way. This week's text begins with responsibility for others and goes on to responsibility for oneself.

A. Responsibility for Others (vv. 1, 2)

1. Brethren, if a man be overtaken in a fault, ye which are spiritual, restore such a one in the spirit of meekness; considering thyself, lest thou also be tempted.

We and our *brethren* intend to subdue "the flesh" and follow the leading of the Spirit, but most of us confess that we sometimes fail. We ought to be eager both to help others when they falter and to accept help when we need it. So what do we do when we see that a brother is caught in something wrong? If we are *spiritual*, led by the Holy Spirit, we do not abandon the brother.

First, we *restore such a one*. We help that person back to the Spirit's way.

Second, we do it *in the spirit of meekness*.

Third, we watch ourselves lest we be tempted too. If the erring brother is doing something profitable or pleasant, we may be tempted to join him instead of restoring him. If his error is revolting, we may be tempted to take a "holier-than-thou" attitude that will alienate him instead of help him. If the effort to restore him leads us into a fault as bad as his, matters will be worse instead of better.

2. Bear ye one another's burdens, and so fulfil the law of Christ.

The idea is not to whip our erring brother back into line; it is to help him with his load. In some way he has stumbled under the weight of temptation. He needs a helping hand rather than a kick. Provide the help he needs. This is the way to *fulfil the law of Christ.* Christ's law is the one that fulfills all the law: "Thou shalt love thy neighbor as thyself" (Galatians 5:14). That law is not fulfilled by talking about love, but by bearing *one another's burdens.*

B. Responsibility for Self (vv. 3-5)

3. For if a man think himself to be something, when he is nothing, he deceiveth himself.

How easy it is to fool myself! How readily I get the idea that I am better than those around me! (Luke 18:11). How blindly I ignore my faults while condemning yours! (Luke 6:41, 42). How glibly I make excuses for my failures; how foolishly I imagine my motives are always pure and noble! Am I the only one who is sometimes self-deceived, or do you fool yourself too?

4. But let every man prove his own work, and then shall he have rejoicing in himself alone, and not in another.

Prove means test. I need to examine what I am doing, examine with a critical eye, checking it by the teaching of God's Word. I need to examine not only what I do, but also why I do it. Are my motives really as unselfish as I like to think they are? This critical examination, if I do it honestly and objectively, will keep me from thinking I am something when I am nothing.

Honest self-examination may stop me from thinking of myself more highly than I ought to think (Romans 12:3), but it will not reveal that I am nothing at all. Paul says *every man* will *have rejoicing in himself.* Even If I find shortcomings in myself, I am God's son and heir (Galatians 3:26; 4:7). That alone is reason enough for rejoicing. But examination will show also that I am gifted with abilities and possessions that can be used for the Lord. Honest examination will not show that any devoted Christian is worthless; it will not give one any excuse to be idle.

Too often a Christian neglects his own duty and development and is content to find his rejoicing *in another.* "I'm as good as the others in the church," one says complacently. But as "good as others" is not good enough unless it is as good as I can be. Or one may be proud of his accomplishment, when really it is due to brethren who have helped him with his load. Examination will help him evaluate himself correctly and give proper credit to others. Or one may be content to do little or nothing, but find his rejoicing in another who does much. He takes pride in belonging to the party of Paul or Apollos or Cephas—or of some modern leader (1 Corinthians 1:12). Much as I admire the great work of Paul, self-examination turns the spotlight on what *I* am doing. That is where *I* can make some improvements with the help of the Lord, and perhaps with the help of brethren.

5. For every man shall bear his own burden.

Does this contradict the direction in verse 2, "Bear ye one another's burdens"? Not at all. It completes the thought of verse 2. I ought to help you with your burden. That is a part of my responsibility, my load. But you are responsible for your load whether I help you or not. Likewise you ought to help me with my burden, but I am responsible for my burden whether you help me or not. That is why I should examine my own work and you should examine yours. For eternity we shall be judged by what we do (2 Corinthians 5:10), and here and now we can improve what we do.

II. Responsible Sharing (Galatians 6:6-10)

Our word *common* belongs to a large family. Members of that family are *community, commonwealth, communion, communicate,* and others. Such words indicate that people have something in common, something shared. Each one of us has something to share with others, and each one is responsible for his own unselfish sharing.

A. Pupil and Teacher (v. 6)

6. Let him that is taught in the word communicate unto him that teacheth in all good things.

Communicate unto can as well be translated *share with.* Pupil and teacher share the word that is taught, God's precious message. But that is not all. They share *all good things,* and these include material things such as food, clothing, and shelter. The teacher brings the word and shares it with the pupil; the pupil brings material things and shares them with the teacher, for the Lord ordained that preachers of the gospel should have their living from that work (1 Corinthians 9:14). Such sharing may be within a local congregation where an able preacher receives a regular salary, or it may reach across many miles and many years. The apostle Paul himself sacrificed and suffered to share the word in Philippi (Acts 16:11-34). Years later, when he was far away in Rome, the Philippians still shared their material things with him (Philippians 4:14-18). Likewise Christians in many lands today are sharing their living with missionaries who teach the word thousands of miles away. This thought provides an opportunity to review and promote the missionary program of your own congregation.

B. Sowing and Reaping (vv. 7, 8)

7. Be not deceived; God is not mocked: for whatsoever a man soweth, that shall he also reap.

Anyone is greatly *deceived* if he thinks he is going to laugh in God's face and produce a crop of wheat from a planting of weed seed. Like seeds, thoughts and words and deeds have consequences; and the consequences are of the same kind as the thoughts and words and deeds from which they spring.

8. For he that soweth to his flesh shall of the flesh reap corruption; but he that soweth to the Spirit shall of the Spirit reap life everlasting.

He that soweth to his flesh scatters the kind of seed that appeals to his flesh, the selfish and sensual side of his nature. No one would be foolish enough to plant cockleburs and expect a harvest of wheat, but a man may be so deceived that he expects to reap some benefit from a planting of impure thoughts, false and angry and arrogant words, and acts that are greedy and heartless. Indeed, such a planting may produce a sort of pleasure; or it may produce riches and the respect of those who respect riches. But these benefits are only temporary, like the luxuriant leaves of growing cockleburs. The ripened harvest is *corruption*—decay and destruction.

He that soweth to the Spirit plants such seed as the *Spirit* likes: thoughts that are pure and noble, words that soothe and instruct and encourage, and acts that are kind and helpful. The first growth from such planting may be worldly loss instead of gain, but the ripened harvest is *life everlasting.*

Past lessons from Romans and Galatians have taught us that we are not saved by what we do. Is that teaching now being denied? Certainly not. It is true that we are justified by faith, not by works. But faith cannot live alone. Without works it is dead (James 2:17, 20, 26), and dead faith is fruitless and worthless.

It is true also that we are saved by grace, not by works. But even God's grace will not save those who scorn the Spirit's leading and prefer the works of the flesh that loomed so horribly in last week's lesson. In faith we plant good seed.

In faith we weed and water it day by day as it grows. But when we have done all we can, God's grace is the sunlight that brings the harvest of life everlasting.

AXIOM OF AGRICULTURE

In *Wise Words From a Wise Guy,* Vern McLellan has paraphrased proverbs with wit and humor, while retaining the underlying truths. For example: "He who sows wild oats should not expect a crop failure."

You don't have to be a PhD in agriculture to understand this one. It is axiomatic: given the proper environment, and barring contingencies, corn planted will result in a harvest of corn.

Paul uses this self-evident truth to illustrate an equally absolute principle of human behavior: under ordinary circumstances, carnal behavior will produce a crop of corruption. A promiscuous sexual life-style will result in ruined relationships, guilt for sin, divine condemnation— not to mention the real risk of unwanted pregnancies, abortions, venereal disease, and AIDS. Alcoholism and drug abuse produce family breakups, highway accidents, all kinds of crime, ruined careers, debilitated health, and premature death.

Paul's admonition is clear: put the Spirit in charge of your crop rotation, and keep on doing good. The harvest will be abundant and everlasting.

—R. W. B.

C. Don't Stop Now (vv. 9, 10)

9. And let us not be weary in well doing: for in due season we shall reap, if we faint not.

Sowing to the Spirit is not something we do in a day and then no more. It is something we continue day after day for sixty or seventy or eighty years before we reap the full benefit of life everlasting. But the harvest is assured if we keep on keeping on. To *faint* is to loosen our grip, to relax our effort, to drop out, to give up. If we do that, no harvest is promised, no life everlasting.

10. As we have therefore opportunity, let us do good unto all men, especially unto them who are of the household of faith.

Do good unto all men. This is a large part of what is meant by sowing to the Spirit (v. 8). *As we have therefore opportunity,* whenever we have a chance, we are to do good in any way we can to as many people as we can—but *especially unto them who are of the household of faith.* We hear of uncounted millions of hungry people far away, and certainly there is boundless opportunity to do good; but we see that our own families have enough before we make a contribution to a relief fund. Likewise we give preference to the family of God, our Christian brothers and sisters. If we give help to the hungry and sick far away, we like to channel it through people and organizations that carry the gospel of Christ along with food and medicine. Here we may take some time to consider the benevolent work of our own congregation.

III. End of the Letter
(Galatians 6:14-18)

In verses 11-13, Paul writes again of those false teachers who were saying the Galatian Christians could not be saved unless they would become Jews. He reveals their selfish purposes: to escape persecution, and to boast about making converts to the Jewish religion. In verse 14 Paul points out a better reason for pride.

A. Glory in the Cross (v. 14)

14. But God forbid that I should glory, save in the cross of our Lord Jesus Christ, by whom the world is crucified unto me, and I unto the world.

To *glory* is to be proud, to boast. Paul could understand the false teachers' pride in their Jewishness. He once had held an enviable position among the Jews, and no doubt he had been proud of it (Philippians 3:4-6). But now he was proud of one thing only: *the cross of our Lord Jesus Christ.* By the cross, that is, by Jesus' sacrifice, Paul had been redeemed, set free from bondage to sin and bondage to the law, transformed into a child of God, and destined for an eternal inheritance (1 Peter 1:4). Paul took no pride in anything he had done, but only in what Jesus had done. In redeeming Paul, Christ had also separated him from the world as if by death. His allegiance now was to a kingdom not of this world (John 18:36). Now he could write, "Our citizenship is in heaven" (Philippians 3:20, *American Standard Version*).

BOASTING

Have you noticed how many award programs are shown on TV? Oscars, Emmys, Tonys, and Grammys are handed out by the dozens. Then come the People's Choice Awards, the Country Music Awards, and several others. Throw in the beauty pageants, the World Series, the Super Bowl, and celebrity roasts—it's easy to conclude that Americans are preoccupied with recognition and honor. We seem obsessed with selecting "the best" of everything.

The typical acceptance speech of winners and honorees is one of humble appreciation for all the "little people" who contributed to the success of the recipients. Very often it includes "thanks to God."

Modesty is a personality characteristic that most of us respect, and even expect. Paul, despite his many skills and achievements, was modest and humble. His only boast, he said, was in the cross of Jesus.

So we today boast not in perfect attendance, tithing, or even going to the "mission field." We, like Paul, glory only in the cross of the Christ and the Christ of the cross.   —R. W. B.

B. A Rule to Live By (vv. 15, 16)

15. For in Christ Jesus neither circumcision availeth any thing, nor uncircumcision, but a new creature.

Circumcision was the mark of a Jew. When one is *in Christ Jesus,* it makes no difference whether he is a Jew or not. What makes a difference is to be *a new creature,* to be born again (John 3:5). Such a new creature finds glory and pride, in the cross, for Christ's death on the cross atoned for human sin and made it possible for sinners to be forgiven and born again.

16. And as many as walk according to this rule, peace be on them, and mercy, and upon the Israel of God.

Salvation depends on being born again, being new creatures in Christ. To *walk according to this rule* is to live by it, to become Christians, to trust Christ completely and follow Him faithfully. Paul prays for *peace* and *mercy* for all who do that. They are the real *Israel of God.*

C. An End of Trouble (v. 17)

17. From henceforth let no man trouble me: for I bear in my body the marks of the Lord Jesus.

False teachers had insisted that only Jews could be included in the Israel of God. They had troubled the Galatians with that perversion of the gospel (Galatians 1:7). That had troubled Paul too, and no doubt they had troubled him also by saying that he was no true teacher of Christ's way. Such troubling ought to stop. Paul was really Christ's man, and he had *marks* on his

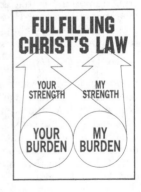

visual 13

body to prove it—the marks of whips and stones that had scarred him because he had preached Christ's message (2 Corinthians 11:23-25). This letter should end the false teaching and put a stop to the trouble.

D. Benediction (v. 18)

18. Brethren, the grace of our Lord Jesus Christ be with your spirit. Amen.

Last week's lesson called us to walk in the Spirit and avoid the works of the flesh. This week's lesson repeated that message in a different way, calling us to sow to the Spirit and reap life everlasting (v. 8). But all our walking and all our sowing are not enough to produce that harvest. Life everlasting is not our pay; it is a gift from God to us (Romans 6:23). Of course it is not given to those who prefer the works of the flesh; it is for those who try earnestly to follow the Spirit's way. But it is still a gift, not a payment for services. It comes to us through *the grace of our Lord Jesus Christ,* through His favor that we do not earn nor deserve, His favor given because we believe in Him (Ephesians 2:8). The Galatians were called into that grace (Galatians 1:6); they fell away from it if they thought Christ was not enough to save them (Galatians 5:4). So in closing Paul wished for Christ's grace to be with them still, not only to forgive any new sins, but also to provide gifts to be used in serving the Lord and His people (Romans 12:6-8). All of us need our Lord's forgiving favor as we try to subdue the flesh and follow the leading of the Spirit. May the grace we need be with us now and always.

Conclusion

We cherish the beautiful thirteenth chapter of 1 Corinthians; unanimously we applaud its last line: "The greatest of these is love" (*American Standard Version*). But our lesson title speaks of expressing love, and that is not so easy as praising it. The text says nothing about saying, "I love you." Important as that is, there are other ways of expressing love. How are we doing with those? Shall we conclude the lesson by asking some questions of ourselves?

A. Bearing One Another's Burdens

More or less generously we give money to support a Christian family whose breadwinner is out of a job. With a little urging we even contribute time and energy to cooking and child care when a mother is disabled. But our text begins with a burden that is harder to bear. Questions:

1. If I see a brother in a fault, will I dare undertake to restore him?

2. If a brother sees me in a fault and undertakes to restore me, will I accept his effort gratefully and profit by it?

B. Sowing to the Spirit

Most of us appreciate the teachers who instruct us in God's Word. Most of us willingly share our incomes to pay the preacher's salary. Most of us sow to the Spirit by joining in the worship and work of the church, by honesty in business, by good Christian living, clean talk, pure thoughts. Some of us even help with evangelistic calling. Questions:

1. Do I do all I can to discourage pornography in print and licentiousness in entertainment, or do I privately enjoy TV shows in which fornication is flaunted and crookedness is considered clever?

2. Am I as enthusiastic as I ever was about Christian fellowship and work and worship, or have I grown a bit weary in well doing?

C. Living by the Rule

Most of us are modest enough to realize that we do not deserve to be saved, but must rely on our Savior's grace and forgiveness. Questions:

1. Do I pause often to consider my daily living and ask forgiveness if I have acted selfishly, or wounded someone with an unkind word, or soiled my mind with a sordid thought?

2. How will my daily living be better this week than it was last week?

D. Prayer

Our Father who art in Heaven, forgive us our debts as we forgive our debtors.

E. Thought to Remember

Jesus saves.

Home Daily Bible Readings

Monday, May 23—Bear One Another's Burdens (Galatians 6:1-5)

Tuesday, May 24—Let Us Do Good to All People (Galatians 6:6-10)

Wednesday, May 25—In the Cross of Christ I Glory (Galatians 6:11-18)

Thursday, May 26—God Desires All Persons to Be Saved (1 Timothy 2:1-7)

Friday, May 27—"Fight the Good Fight" (1 Timothy 6:11-16)

Saturday, May 28—Fulfil Your Ministry (1 Timothy 4:1-5)

Sunday, May 29—"I Have Kept the Faith" (2 Timothy 4:6-18)

Learning by Doing

This page contains an alternate lesson plan emphasizing learning activities. Classes desiring such student involvement will find these suggestions helpful.

Learning Goals

In this session you will lead your class members to do the following:

1. Recognize that every Christian is accountable to God for his or her own life.

2. Distinguish between one's responsibility for helping other believers to live faithfully for Christ and each person's own responsibility to be faithful.

Into the Lesson

Prepare copies of the following Agree/Disagree activity for your students. Be sure to make enough copies for each student to have one:

SA MA MD SD

— — — — 1. We are responsible for helping other Christians live in the way of Christ.

— — — — 2. Ultimately, no one is responsible for my life except me.

— — — — 3. Our choices shape our character, and our character shapes our destiny.

— — — — 4. We cannot solve other people's problems. Our role is to help them take responsibility for their own problems.

At the beginning of class, distribute copies of the Agree/Disagree statements. Ask the students to read the statements and determine their response to each. They should put a check mark in the column that most nearly represents their thinking. The key is as follows:

SA=means Strongly Agree
MA=means Mildly Agree
MD=means Mildly Disagree
SD=means Strongly Disagree

Allow two or three minutes for the students to complete the activity. Then take a tally of each statement. Allow brief discussion to explain why they responded as they did.

Lead into the Bible study by saying, "As we complete our study of Galatians, we will continue to explore how we are to express our freedom in Christ. In last week's lesson, we saw that we are not to use our liberty to satisfy fleshly lusts; instead, we are to live in the Spirit and produce the fruit He desires. Living in the Spirit involves being sensitive to others' needs, and is given expression in such ways as serving others in love and bearing the burdens of fellow Christians who have carelessly departed from the way the Spirit leads. But we may wonder, What is the extent of our responsibility in these areas, and what is the other person's own responsibility? Today we will consider this issue.

Into the Word

Ask a volunteer to read Galatians 6:1-18 aloud to the class. Then divide the students into groups of four. (If your class is smaller than twelve, have students work in groups of two or three.) Assign one of the situations below to each group.

Situation One

I know that Jim is involved in immorality, and I know he is in serious trouble spiritually as a result. But who am I to condemn him? What he does is none of my business.

Situation Two

Sue surely has it rough, being a single mother with two preschoolers. She really struggles. But I don't see how our class can help her. I mean, everyone is so busy. Who has the time?

Situation Three

Our preacher puts too much emphasis on obedience to God. Oh, sure, he teaches that we are saved by grace, not works. He insists there is nothing we can do to add to Christ's saving work on the cross. But he keeps stressing that sin is serious business. He talks about our accountability to God for our lives. If you ask me, that sounds like an unnecessary guilt trip.

Instruct each group to discuss these questions in relation to the situation they were given: *What principles from Galatians 6 are relevant to this situation?* and, *What specific course of action would you recommend a Christian to take regarding it?* Allow fifteen minutes for discussion. Then bring the groups together to share their conclusions.

Into Life

Lead your class in discussing the following two questions:

1. How do we know when we are responsible to help others, and when our help may lead them to be irresponsible?

2. How can we help others without leading them to believe that we, not they, are responsible for their actions?

Let's Talk It Over

The questions on this page are designed to encourage review of the lesson Scriptures and to promote discussion of the lesson by the class. The answers provided are only discussion starters. Let your class talk it over from there.

1. Why is the concept of responsibility one that needs strong emphasis in the church and in our society generally?

Much is said today in regard to people's *rights*, while the responsibilities that go with them are often neglected. We hear, for example, of a woman's supposed *right* to an abortion, but so little is said about the responsible sexual behavior that would prevent many unwanted pregnancies. Purveyors of pornography insist on their *right* to publish what they please, while they irresponsibly pollute the minds of fellow citizens. In the church we may exercise our *right* to be absent from services or to withhold our offering or to make uncomplimentary remarks about the leaders or other members. But to be a responsible member of the church is to recognize that our attendance, financial support, and positive contribution to the unity of the congregation are matters that we dare not neglect.

2. Why is Paul's exhortation that we bear one another's burdens" a vivid way of describing our responsibility to one another?

We use the word *burden* to apply to various problems that people encounter. For example, we speak of the "burden of grief." When our fellow Christians are weighed down with grief because of a death, that is a burden we can help them bear. We speak also of the "burden of responsibility or of leadership." Leaders or persons in positions of responsibility must in the end make their own decisions and judgments, but we can support them with prayer and encouragement and thereby share their burden. We may speak of the "burden of guilt." While we are taught to cast our burden on the Lord (Psalm 55:22), it is also helpful to confess our guilt to other human beings (see James 5:16) and experience forgiveness and acceptance from them (see James 5:16).

3. It is sometimes difficult for us to think of sharing our material wealth with a missionary thousands of miles away. How can we deal with this difficulty?

We sometimes hear of church members who complain of sending money overseas because there are so many people in our own country who need the gospel. They may feel this way in part because the people in those foreign countries and the missionaries who are trying to reach them are only names devoid of faces and personalities. It is vital for the church to provide opportunities for members to develop a personal knowledge of and involvement with Christian missionaries and the people with whom they are working. How helpful and enriching it would be, for example, if every church family could have the experience of entertaining missionaries as guests.

4. Why is the concept of sowing to the Spirit a helpful way to describe how we can grow in Christ?

Even those of us who are not farmers or backyard gardeners have an appreciation for the basic truth that we reap what we sow. We should be able to appreciate how this principle works in the spiritual realm. It is obvious that sowing pride, jealousy, hatred, etc. into our relationships with other people will result in a bitter harvest of shattered friendships and strife-ridden families. How much better it is when we sow the kinds of attitudes Paul listed in Philippians 4:8! In the church those who sow inconsistent attendance, careless financial support, and indifference toward duties are most likely to be among those who lament, "I'm not getting anything out of church!" Far better is it to sow habits of faithful discipleship and reap a Christian life that is exciting and rewarding.

5. Paul promises that "we will reap a harvest if we do not give up" (Galatians 6:9, *New International Version*). How can Christian workers keep from giving up?

Christian workers should occasionally inventory what they have already reaped. The minister who is discouraged by a lack of recent responses to the gospel invitation can usually find encouragement in noting the growth of those he has led to Christ in the past. The teacher who is struggling with an unresponsive class may recall previous students who have since become leaders in the church. Any worker in the church can look back to previous successes as a way of getting through times of discouragement. Most important, however, is the certainty of God's eternal blessing promised to all those who remain faithful in serving Him.

Summer Quarter, 1994

Theme: God Redeems a People
(Exodus—Deuteronomy)

Special Features

Lessons

Unit 1. Deliverance From Oppression

Unit 2. Provision for Present and Future

Unit 3. Instructions for Life

About these lessons

The study for the Summer Quarter is based on the books of Exodus, Leviticus, Numbers, and Deuteronomy. God's redemption of Israel from Egyptian bondage, His provision for them in their wilderness journey and beyond, and His basic instructions for the continuance of Israel's favored relationship with Him are the focus of these lessons.

Jun 5
Jun 12
Jun 19
Jun 26
Jul 3
Jul 10
Jul 17
Jul 24
Jul 31
Aug 7
Aug 14
Aug 21
Aug 28

Quarterly Quiz

The questions on this page may be used in several ways: as a pretest at the beginning of the quarter; as a review at the end of the quarter; or as a review after each lesson. The questions are based on the Scripture text of each lesson (King James Version). **The answers are on page 344.**

Lesson 1

1. For how long after Moses' birth did his mother hide him from the Egyptians? *Exodus 2:2*
2. Where was the baby Moses when Pharaoh's daughter found him? *Exodus 2:5, 6*
3. Pharaoh's daughter recognized the baby Moses as being one of whom? *Exodus 2:6*

Lesson 2

1. Who was Moses to say had sent him to the children of Israel? *Exodus 3:14*
2. What did God tell Moses to do with his shepherd's rod? *Exodus 4:3*
3. What happened to Moses' rod when he did what God told him to do with it? *Exodus 4:3*

Lesson 3

1. At what hour did the Lord bring death upon all the firstborn of Egypt? *Exodus 12:29*
2. The first thing in the morning, after the death of Egypt's firstborn, Pharaoh summoned Moses and Aaron and commanded them to take their people and leave. T/F *Exodus 12:31*

Lesson 4

1. What did the Lord use to cause the Red Sea to divide so the Israelites could cross on dry land? *Exodus 14:21*
2. How many of the Egyptians who followed Israel into the Red Sea escaped? *Exodus 14:28*

Lesson 5

1. When Israel complained in the wilderness because of their hunger, what did God tell Moses He would rain from heaven for them? *Exodus 16:4*
2. On that occasion, what did God provide for the Israelites in the evening? *Exodus 16:13*

Lesson 6

1. Who observed Moses sitting from morning till evening by himself judging the people of Israel? *Exodus 18:14*
2. What did this person say would happen to both Moses and the people if he continued to do this? *Exodus 18:18*

Lesson 7

1. In describing the way He rescued Israel from the Egyptians, God said He bore them on ____ wings. *Exodus 19:4*

2. If Israel would keep God's covenant, they would be His peculiar ____, and unto Him a kingdom of ____, and a holy ____. *Exodus 19:5, 6*

Lesson 8

1. Who was coming down Mount Sinai with Moses when the noise of singing could be heard coming from the camp of Israel? *Exodus 32:17*
2. Moses offered himself for Israel's sin. God refused, however, saying He would do what to one who sinned against Him? *Exodus 32:33*

Lesson 9

1. At Sinai the Israelites were asked to give a freewill offering to support the priesthood of Aaron and his sons. T/F *Exodus 25:2, 8*
2. What two manifestations of God's presence were given when the construction of the tabernacle was completed? *Exodus 40:34*

Lesson 10

1. How often was Israel to celebrate the year of jubilee? *Leviticus 25:10*
2. A man who had sold his ancestral land would do what in the jubilee year? *Leviticus 25:28*
3. An Israelite was not to force a fellow Israelite to serve in what way? *Leviticus 25:39*

Lesson 11

1. How many of the twelve men whom Moses sent to spy out Canaan said Israel would be unable to defeat the people who lived there? *Numbers 14:6-9, 36-38*
2. Name the spies who believed that God would help Israel take Canaan. *Numbers 14:6-9*

Lesson 12

1. If the Israelites kept all of God's commandments when they lived in the promised land, their days would be ____. *Deuteronomy 6:2*
2. Moses warned Israel not to ____ the Lord after they entered the promised land. *Deuteronomy 6:12*

Lesson 13

1. What word did Moses use to describe how Israel would be treated by God if they obeyed His laws? *Deuteronomy 28:2-6*
2. How would Israel be treated by God if they disobeyed Him? *Deuteronomy 28:15-19*

From Slavery to a Nation

by John W. Wade

THE LESSONS FOR THIS QUARTER deal with a relatively brief but a very important segment of Israelite history—the forty-year period beginning with the exodus from Egypt and continuing through the wilderness wanderings to the border of the promised land. During this period, recorded in Exodus, Leviticus, Numbers, and Deuteronomy, the Israelites were transformed from a hapless group of slaves in Egypt to a nation poised to enter the land that God had promised to their forefathers.

This was not an easy time for the Israelites. As slaves, they had been under the control of the Egyptians, thus having little opportunity to learn self-discipline. Their lack of self-discipline, and their stubborn determination to do their own thing, almost led to their destruction in the wilderness. Through God's intervention, through the law given on Mount Sinai, through the tabernacle that gave them a common center of worship, and through Moses' patient leadership they managed to survive this forty-year ordeal. By the time they reached the promised land, they had learned to obey God's chosen leaders and had acquired enough discipline that they were ready to embark on the military conquest of Canaan.

Deliverance From Oppression

Unit I in this quarter's lesson studies deals with material that will be familiar to many Bible students.

Lesson 1 opens with the Israelites in Egypt, where they found prosperity. But that prosperity was not to last, for there arose over Egypt a new king, who "knew not Joseph." This new king, probably representing a new dynasty, felt no gratitude for what Joseph had done to help Egypt, and so he began to impose restrictions on the people, reducing them to slavery. Even in slavery, however, the people continued to grow in strength, causing the Egyptians to impose even more stringent restrictions on them. Finally, the order went out that all boy babies born to the Israelites were to be killed. Into this situation Moses was born. For a time his parents were able to evade the king's edict, but eventually they had to place him in a basket and put him in the river. Most of your students know the story of his rescue by Pharaoh's daughter. Use this lesson as an opportunity to show that this rescue was an act of God's providence, not just an accident.

Lesson 2 picks up the story of Moses' life years later. He is an exile from Egypt, tending his father-in-law's sheep in a remote area near Mount Horeb. Here God confronts him through the burning bush, challenging him to return to Egypt and liberate the people of Israel. Moses makes one excuse after another to avoid this call, but finally agrees to go. This lesson will give you an opportunity to challenge your students to accept the Lord's call to serve, avoiding the excuses that people often make.

Lesson 3 tells of the ten plagues that God sent upon Egypt because Pharaoh stubbornly refused to free the Israelites. You will want to read Exodus 6-12 to refresh your memory about the plagues. If you have access to a video of the movie, *The Ten Commandments*, you may want to view it. The details may not always be accurate, but it will give you a feeling for the situation.

Lesson 4, the final lesson in this unit, recounts the crossing of the Red Sea. God usually works in quiet, undramatic ways to carry out His will, but occasionally He reveals himself in a mighty act such as this. You may want to use this lesson to help your students understand how God has worked in the past and may still work. Again, viewing *The Ten Commandments* may enhance your ability to present this exciting event to your students.

Provision for Present and Future

Unit II in this study emphasizes five ways God provided for His people during this time period.

Lesson 5 finds the Israelites something less than happy campers. The supplies they had brought with them were running low, so they began to complain. God knew their need and supplied them with manna and quail. The people were given specific instructions about gathering and using the manna, but some displeased God by refusing to heed these instructions. Use this lesson to help students understand that while God provides for our needs, He expects us to obey His commandments.

Lesson 6 shows how God helped Moses to provide leadership for the people. Moses was wearing himself out trying to meet the people's needs. He had to learn how to delegate responsibility. Probably every congregation would be strengthened if it did a better job of training people for work in the church and then delegating jobs to them.

Lesson 7 features one of the great texts of the Bible—the Ten Commandments as found in Exodus 20. Even though this text is familiar to many of your students, it is a text that needs to be re-examined regularly by all of us. These few verses provide a solid foundation for proper relations between man and God, and also among men. Any group of people that attempts to build a society without such a foundation is doomed to failure. Our nation is in serious trouble today because it has ignored this foundation, and if we are to survive, we must restore that foundation.

Lesson 8 also has its setting at Mount Sinai. Even as Moses remained on the mountain to receive the law, the people fell into grievous sin. Coming down from the mountain to the camp, Moses found the people reveling before the golden calf they had made during his absence. In his anger Moses threw down and shattered the stone tablets upon which were inscribed the Ten Commandments. Yet Moses loved the people, and in spite of his anger and disappointment in them, he made intercession before God on their behalf. Because of Moses' prayer, God spared them. Two emphases can be made in this lesson. This first is to show how readily people can turn away from God, even when He has blessed them greatly. The second is to help your students understand the power of intercessory prayer.

Lesson 9 tells of God's instruction for the people to make an offering for the building of the sanctuary, so that He might dwell among them. The pillar of fire and the pillar of cloud hovering over the tabernacle were visible manifestations of God's presence. A stewardship emphasis may be given to this lesson by pointing out that the Israelites gave a generous offering to build the tabernacle and its furniture. God's people today may be assured of His presence in His Spirit.

Instructions for Life

The third and final unit of the quarter's lessons gives some practical applications of the law to real-life situations.

Lesson 10 is taken from the book of Leviticus, where the rules establishing the year of jubilee are set forth. These rules would go into effect when the Israelites entered the promised land. According to these rules, all land would revert to the original owner or his heirs in the year of jubilee. The intention was that the rich would be prevented from exploiting the poor. This lesson also may be given a stewardship emphasis, for it teaches that all possessions belong to God.

Lesson 11 tells of the exciting adventure of the twelve men who were sent to spy out the promised land. They all brought back glowing reports of the wealth of the land, but ten of them were pessimistic about their chances of taking the land from its occupants. The had forgotten how God had guided and protected them thus far on their journey. Two of the spies, however, assured the people that with God's help the land could be taken. Lacking in faith, the people chose to believe the ten, and as a result they had to spend forty years wandering in the wilderness. You will want to remind your students that modern doubters often miss God's blessings because of their lack of faith.

Lesson 12, based upon Deuteronomy 6:1-13, allows us to study the teaching that is at the very heart of the faith of Israel. God is one Lord! There is not a plurality of gods, such as was supposed by the heathen, whose diverse and often conflicting activities led only to moral confusion. Because God is one, everything He does is in keeping with His one purpose. The belief in one God is not just a theological tenet that we hold remote from reality. It touches our lives, and, indeed, every aspect of the whole universe.

Obviously, there are implications when one holds such a belief. First, it is a belief that cannot be held lightly. To hold it casually is to deny it. Further, such a belief requires that it be shared with others, especially with one's own family. You won't want to miss this opportunity to encourage your students to be involved in home Bible study and in the various educational programs of the church. Encourage them to share their faith with others both in word and action.

Lesson 13, a look at Moses' farewell address, emphasizes obedience. He lays before the people two clear, but quite different, options. The people may choose to obey God and enjoy the promise of His blessings, or they may disobey Him and suffer the dire consequences. Since we are studying this as history, we know what happened. The Israelites too often made the wrong choices with tragic results. We need to do everything we can to avoid their mistakes.

Since most of us are not as well versed in this part of the Old Testament as we are in other parts of the Bible, you may need to spend some extra time studying the background for these lessons. You will need to share this information with your students to give them an understanding of the historical setting for the lessons. You will want to use maps to show the travels of the Israelites from Egypt to the borders of Canaan. A plan of the tabernacle will give the students a better understanding of lesson 9. These can be among the most interesting lessons during the whole year, and they are quite relevant, touching on the everyday needs of all of us.

Seeking God's Ways

by Douglas Redford

ALL OF US know people who have attempted to study the Bible but have come away frustrated. "I just can't understand it," they say. These folk may feel confused or disappointed, but they need never feel alone. The people who lived during the time of the events recorded in Scripture were often just as frustrated in discerning the will of God as we who are privileged to read about them. If someone were to compose a record of our spiritual progress, our experiences might be surprisingly similar to those individuals of Scripture whom we often consider champions and stalwarts of faith.

A Perplexed People

The children of Israel often must have wondered about God's purpose for them and whether He had abandoned them to perish under the cruel bondage of the Egyptians. With some of them, perhaps wondering had given way to bitter resignation. More than four hundred years passed since Jacob and his family had found in Egypt a respite from famine in Canaan. God in His gracious providence had raised up Joseph to be His people's deliverer. Those days, however, were a distant memory; new rulers had arisen who "knew not Joseph." For the Israelites, the larger question had become, "Does God know us? Does He even care?"

The impression that God is distant and uncaring or that He has somehow forgotten our circumstances can gnaw at the soul of any of us, despite what we may claim to have believed for years. Certain situations that we thought were indicative of God's blessing seem to turn sour, leaving us in bondage to feelings and questions from which we find it difficult to escape.

Often these feelings and questions arise because we are not fully acquainted with the ways of God as they apply to a given situation. We limit God to a particular course that *we* have charted and become disenchanted when He does not cooperate. Yet God, in His time and by His methods, provided an "exodus" (literally a "way out") for the Israelites, and He will likewise be faithful in doing so for us.

Miscalculating the Time

One of the most frustrated Israelites was Moses. He chafed under the tyranny of the Egyptians and longed to see his people break free. Perhaps he felt a certain degree of guilt because of the years he had spent as part of the Egyptian government. He may have been eager to even the score. One day he saw what he perceived to be his opportunity, and he seized it with vigor. He killed an Egyptian whom he saw abusing one of his fellow Israelites.

The New Testament provides a significant insight into Moses' thinking at this point. It is recorded in Acts 7:25 that "Moses thought that his own people would realize that God was using him to rescue them, but they did not."* Certainly the day came when God *did* use Moses to rescue His people, but Moses' enthusiasm caused him to move much too quickly. He was operating within a "time zone" that was different from that of Heaven.

The tension between the sovereignty of God and the free will of man is often viewed as a deep theological question. In reality it has extremely practical implications. It is not at all easy to draw the line between "making things happen" and "letting the Lord lead." Moses' slaying of the Egyptian was clearly an act of impulse, performed with absolutely no consideration of the divine perspective on his actions. It is noteworthy that while Moses glanced "this way and that" before carrying out his deed, he failed to glance upward (Exodus 2:12).

It is best for us today, in seeking to be used of God, to give time to any impulse that we deem to be "spiritual"—and to spend that time in prayer and in consultation with others. It is far better first to confer with others about our intentions than to act first and later be forced to undo any harm caused by our hasty action. What Moses saw as a courageous, uniting act only widened the gap between him and his fellow Israelites (Exodus 2:13, 14).

Misusing the Method

"There is a way that seems right to a man, but in the end it leads to death" (Proverbs 16:25). Frequently this verse is applied to unbelievers who have chosen to live by a standard other than God's. Yet Christians can be just as guilty of following after what seems or feels the right thing to do, without regard to the ways of God.

Although Moses' desire for his countrymen was sincere, his method was terribly mistaken. He could never become Israel's deliverer by borrowing from Egypt's techniques. Had Moses remembered Joseph's patience and quiet trust while imprisoned in Egypt, perhaps Moses would have reevaluated his tactics.

If our efforts to follow what we understand as God's will involve us in something wrong, or for that matter even questionable, we ought to withdraw immediately from that course of action and look for another. Moses' impetuous act drove a wedge between him and the Israelites and made the Egyptian authorities even more hostile. When we behave in an offensive manner toward others because we believe ourselves to be on God's side, we alienate those persons from ourselves—and from Him. We become guilty of trying to fight Satan by using his methods, a path of certain failure.

Paul's words in 2 Corinthians 8:21 provide a standard worthy of emulation in our conduct before the unbelieving world: "For we are taking pains to do what is right, not only in the eyes of the Lord but also in the eyes of men." We should note that even Moses, after employing God's methods for delivering His people, eventually earned the respect of the officials in Egypt as well as the general populace in that nation (Exodus 11:3)

By the time of the crossing of the Red Sea, Moses possessed a far better understanding of God's methods. While the Israelites were casting verbal stones at him for leading them into what they thought was certain doom, Moses simply responded, "Do not be afraid. . . . The Lord will fight for you; you need only to be still" (Exodus 14:13, 14). If we are not confident that our timing or our methods are in tune with God's, the best advice is to "be still" and to follow perhaps the most difficult command of the Scriptures—"wait."

Misinterpreting the Event

In baseball, players have a particular set of signs that are used to communicate what a batter or runner should do in a given situation. The coach "flashes" a sign, and the players attempt to carry out their assignments. Occasionally, however, a batter or a runner will "miss" a sign. The ensuing confusion can result in a missed opportunity to score.

Moses, as we have observed from Acts 7:25, believed that his countrymen would recognize that God was the real power behind his slaying of the Egyptian. He was convinced that he was reading God's "signals" correctly and assumed that everyone else would understand that and fall in step.

Later, when Moses found himself tending sheep in the desert of Midian, he likely was convinced that God no longer needed his services. Yet, in that barren wilderness, God was working in a way Moses never could have imagined. The Potter was molding His servant for His work in His time.

How dangerous if we become obsessed with the notion that God has stamped His seal of approval upon our plans! How impatient we then become with people who just can't see things "His way!" How easily we may view them as obstacles blocking the path of progress in the kingdom of God!

Even if we are fairly certain that the steps we are taking are God's, it can be risky to use such language in the present day. In recent years we have been exposed to numerous examples of religious leaders who boldly proclaimed themselves as "chosen instruments" of God, while simultaneously engaging in blatantly sinful conduct. All anyone has to do to guarantee rejection of his message is to begin with the words, "God has spoken," or, "The Lord has led me."

The news is not all bad, however. We still possess the most important means for communicating God to a needy world, and it is just as effective as ever. Jesus said, "By this all men will know that you are my disciples, if you love one another" (John 13:35). Jesus has assured us that His voice will be heard when His people show by their actions that they sincerely love one another. In fact, if we have first established ourselves as a caring, committed people of unshakable integrity, others will be far more apt to listen to us when we speak of God's guidance.

Loved Always

Someone has wisely stated, "God is too kind to do anything cruel . . . too wise to make a mistake . . . too deep to explain himself." Like most "wise statements," this one is cleverly put, easily remembered, but learned only with immeasurable patience and not without some mistakes. We should not be surprised when what God is seeking to accomplish seems too intricate for us to grasp. Finite man is incapable of fully understanding the Infinite One. This is why faith is necessary (Hebrews 11:6), and it is also why errors are committed by human beings who presume to know what God is doing.

Yet God loved Moses even during his mistakes—even when he had struck the fatal blow upon the Egyptian. As Christians today we are not primarily God's servants, workers, ambassadors, or ministers. We are first and foremost His children. In spite of our misgivings, misunderstandings, and mistakes, as we sincerely strive to honor Him, we are never misplaced.

Our Father loves us, too.

---

*Scripture quotations in this article are taken from the *New International Version.*

God Redeems a People

by J. Lee Magness

THE EVENTS FOR OUR STUDY in this series of lessons are as dramatic as any that may be found in the pages of the Bible. They occurred during that crucial period of Israel's history recorded in the books of Exodus through Deuteronomy. Among them were a miraculous sea crossing, a dangerous wilderness journey, desert battles, and rebellions. These lessons are filled with importance for us, because of the parallels that may be noted between Israel's experience and ours in the Christian life.

The events of Israel's exodus from Egypt to their entrance into the land of Canaan weave a grand tapestry adorned with the wondrous, redemptive deeds of God. This lesson series, which highlights some of these events, is not entitled, "Israel Escapes From Egypt" nor, "Israel Endures the Desert"; it is entitled, "God Redeems a People." The series has been given this title because the dominant figure in the tapestry is not mighty Pharaoh, nor faithful Moses, nor even the people of God, but God himself.

The impetus for the exodus came from God, who saw the Israelites, the instruments of His eternal plan, slipping into faithlessness and uselessness. God called Moses to lead His people out of bondage, not at a time when Moses was eager for the responsibility of leadership, but when he would evade it. Every move of the people was spurred on by the word of God and the power of God and the guidance of God. When the wandering people wondered where the next step would lead, God guided them on. And God continued to lead them, finally bringing them to the promised land.

At the end of their journey, as Israel camped east of the Jordan River, Moses reviewed all that had happened to them since they left Egypt. He reminded the people that it was the Lord who had redeemed them from bondage to Pharaoh and had given them life and hope (Deuteronomy 7:7, 8).

God Redeemed His People

The tapestry held up to our view is dominated by the loving acts of God. He redeemed His chosen people from bondage, but this redemption was much more than rescue from the bondage of hard labor and cruel taskmasters and heartless midwives. Israel's situation was much more critical than the loss of their economic independence.

The people of Israel had lost their geographical identity. But a dim memory, if even that, was the promised land, a land to which they had no desire to return, even if they had had the ability. After more than four hundred years of exposure to Egyptian culture, they were on the verge of losing their national identity. And, most crucially, they were not far from forsaking or forgetting their spiritual identity. When God called him, Moses feared that the people would not remember the God of their fathers and would ask, "What is his name?" (Exodus 3:13). Later at Sinai, in their first crisis of confidence, the people instinctively turned to an Egyptian calf-god.

When God redeemed His people, He gave them the opportunity to escape physical and economic oppression. But He also gave them the opportunity to escape the bondage of lost identity and lost purpose and lost relationship. He gave them the opportunity once again to become a distinctive people, one with a distinctive homeland, a distinctive life-style, a distinctive purpose, and a distinctive commitment to Him, the one true and living God. Truly, God redeemed His people.

The People Redeemed

God occupies the center of the tapestry, and His calling, guiding, redemptive work is its subject. But woven into the fabric are the people of Israel themselves.

First, the Israelites were the chosen people, those whom God had chosen to be the instruments through whom He would restore humanity to himself. However else He could have acted, He chose to act in and through them, not so much in spite of their human frailty, but in the light of it.

Second, although God had chosen them to be the agents of redemption and had redeemed them so they could fulfill that high calling, they had to choose to be chosen. They had to seize God's redemptive moment when it came. They had to choose to leave their homes in Egypt, to enter into a covenant relationship with God at Sinai, and to journey through the wilderness with Him as their guide. They had to say "yes" or "no" to the call to come out, the call to obey, the call to follow.

The completion of God's purpose for His chosen people depended on their choosing to be His people and to walk in His way, and this they did. Only then could God redeem them.

Seizing the Opportunity

God's chosen people eventually made it through the wilderness and entered into the land He had promised them. In time, His purposes for Israel were accomplished. Through this people Christ, the Redeemer, came into the world. Through Him God offers redemption to all who are enslaved to sin, guidance for their journey through life, and victory over even the most formidable foes. As with Israel, however, those whom He calls must choose to be chosen, and they must seize the opportunities presented to them if their spiritual journey is to be successful.

The apostle Paul knew it is crucial for God's people, the church, to seize the opportunity that His redemptive action presents to them. Paul wrote, "Be very careful, then, how you live—not as unwise but as wise, making the most of every opportunity, because the days are evil" (Ephesians 5:15, 16, *New International Version*). The days in which we live are perilous. Wisdom is more a matter of which way we go than of how much we know. And the opportunities are still before us. Will we seize them or not?

Remaining for us is the opportunity for exodus, for escape from the bondages of lost identity, lost purpose, and lost relationship with God. Some Christians have become so enamored of the surrounding Christless culture that they are in danger of losing their distinctive identity as God's "peculiar people." Some Christians have become so habitual in their Christian living that they are in danger of losing their distinctive purpose as God's agents of change in the world. Some Christians are so trapped in the bondage of materialism that they are in danger of losing their spiritual identity. We must seize the opportunity of exodus that God continues to hold out for us.

The opportunity of renewal and realignment with God remains for us, too. Christians often find themselves, as it were, like Israel at the foot of Mount Sinai, facing the renewal of their relationship with God, but fearing the commitment of obedience to Him. Christians sometimes find themselves in a wilderness fraught with spiritual obstacles within and without. The temptation to rebel, to return to our comfortable bondages, is ever present. The perils of spiritual malnutrition and drought constantly beset our journey. But so does the opportunity to choose God at every point along the way.

Remaining for us also is the opportunity for entrance into a new land, with its new challenges, new relationships, and new arenas of service. The temptation to maintain the status quo in our spiritual lives, however stifling it may be,

is very real. We know that entering the land of God's promise does not mean entering a land of complete ease, but one more challenging, more demanding, than the old. When we choose God's way and God's guidance, we choose to face those changes and those challenges.

The lessons that comprise this series hold up to our view the tapestry of God at work in ancient Israel. In spite of their doubt, hesitation, stumbling, grumbling, and at times open rebellion, they eventually seized God's moment of redemption and restoration. The challenge is ours as the people of God's new covenant, the church, to weave ourselves into this work in progress, the fabric of God's intentions. The obstacles are numerous. But God is ever present to lead us safely onward.

When Moses stood before Israel in the plains of Moab, near the end of Israel's epic journey, he reminded the people of God that it was not their doing that had brought them to the borders of the promised land—it was the work of God. Now the hour they had anticipated for so long had arrived. Would they enter the land and confront the enemy in his stronghold? Would their experiences in the wilderness give them confidence that God would not fail them now? Once again they must act, they must seize the opportunity when it came to them.

If we learn but one thing from our study it surely must be that God will never abandon that person who loves and honors Him, and who makes the most of every opportunity to fulfill God's will in his or her life.

Answers to Quarterly Quiz on page 338

Lesson 1—1. three months. 2. in a basket among the flags by the river's edge. 3. the Hebrews' children. **Lesson 2**—1. I AM. 2. cast it on the ground. 3. it became a serpent. **Lesson 3**—1. midnight. 2. false. **Lesson 4**—1. a strong east wind. 2. none. **Lesson 5**—1. bread. 2. quails. **Lesson 6**—1. Moses' father-in-law. 2. they would both wear away. **Lesson 7**—1. eagles'. 2. treasure, priests, nation. **Lesson 8**—1. Joshua. 2. God would blot him out of His book. **Lesson 9**—1. false. 2. a cloud covered the tent, the glory of the Lord filled the tabernacle. **Lesson 10**—1. every fifty years. 2. return unto his possession. 3. as a bondservant. **Lesson 11**—1. ten. 2. Caleb, Joshua. **Lesson 12**—1. prolonged. 2. forget. **Lesson 13**—1. blessed. 2. cursed.

God Remembers

DEVOTIONAL READING: Exodus 2:16-24.

LESSON SCRIPTURE: Exodus 1, 2.

PRINTED TEXT: Exodus 1:8-11a; 2:1-9a, 23-25.

Exodus 1:8-11a

8 Now there arose up a new king over Egypt, which knew not Joseph.

9 And he said unto his people, Behold, the people of the children of Israel are more and mightier than we:

10 Come on, let us deal wisely with them; lest they multiply, and it come to pass, that, when there falleth out any war, they join also unto our enemies, and fight against us, and so get them up out of the land.

11a Therefore they did set over them taskmasters to afflict them with their burdens.

Exodus 2:1-9a, 23-25

1 And there went a man of the house of Levi, and took to wife a daughter of Levi.

2 And the woman conceived, and bare a son: and when she saw him that he was a goodly child, she hid him three months.

3 And when she could not longer hide him, she took for him an ark of bulrushes, and daubed it with slime and with pitch, and put the child therein; and she laid it in the flags by the river's brink.

4 And his sister stood afar off, to wit what would be done to him.

5 And the daughter of Pharaoh came down to wash herself at the river; and her maidens walked along by the river's side: and when she saw the ark among the flags, she sent her maid to fetch it.

6 And when she had opened it, she saw the child: and, behold, the babe wept. And she had compassion on him, and said, This is one of the Hebrews' children.

7 Then said his sister to Pharaoh's daughter, Shall I go and call to thee a nurse of the Hebrew women, that she may nurse the child for thee?

8 And Pharaoh's daughter said to her, Go. And the maid went and called the child's mother.

9a And Pharaoh's daughter said unto her, Take this child away, and nurse it for me, and I will give thee thy wages.

. . . .

23 And it came to pass in process of time, that the king of Egypt died: and the children of Israel sighed by reason of the bondage, and they cried, and their cry came up unto God by reason of the bondage.

24 And God heard their groaning, and God remembered his covenant with Abraham, with Isaac, and with Jacob.

25 And God looked upon the children of Israel, and God had respect unto them.

GOLDEN TEXT: God heard their groaning, and God remembered his covenant with Abraham, with Isaac, and with Jacob.—Exodus 2:24.

God Redeems a People

Unit 1: Deliverance From Oppression

(Lessons 1-4)

Lesson Aims

After this lesson, each student should:

1. Have a better understanding of the historical setting of the Israelites' bondage in Egypt.

2. Realize more fully that God watches over the destinies of men and nations.

3. Feel a stronger sympathy for those who suffer oppression.

4. Make a stronger commitment to bring the message of freedom to those who are in bondage to sin.

Lesson Outline

INTRODUCTION
    A. "Give Me Liberty!"
    B. Lesson Background
I. GOD'S PEOPLE ENSLAVED (Exodus 1:8-11a)
    A. A New King Arises (vv. 8, 9)
    B. Egyptian Fear of the Hebrews (v. 10)
    C. The Egyptian Answer (v. 11a)
        Undeserved Affliction
II. GOD'S PLAN BEGUN (Exodus 2:1-9a)
    A. The Birth of Moses (vv. 1, 2)
    B. Act of Desperation (vv. 3, 4)
    C. Discovery by Pharaoh's Daughter (vv. 5, 6)
    D. Provision by Pharaoh's Daughter (vv. 7-9a)
III. GOD'S COVENANT REMEMBERED (Exodus 2:23-25)
    A. The Death of Pharaoh (v. 23)
    B. God Sees the People's Plight (vv. 24, 25)
        Remembering
CONCLUSION
    A. God Hears, but Waits
    B. All Kinds of Bondage
    C. Let Us Pray
    D. Thought to Remember

Display visual 1 of the visuals packet and let it remain before the class. The visual is shown on page 349. The map, visual 14, may be displayed for reference throughout this quarter of study.

Introduction

A. "Give Me Liberty!"

"Give me liberty or give me death!" cried Patrick Henry, whose challenge became a rallying cry for the American Revolution. But no such champion arose to provide leadership for the downtrodden children of Israel, who had been caught up in a much more dreadful bondage in Egypt. For one thing, it was far easier for Henry to make his statement in the relative safety of the Virginia House of Burgesses than it would have been for an Israelite toiling beneath the lash and bludgeon of an Egyptian taskmaster. Henry's act may have been courageous, but the Hebrew slave's act would have been foolhardy or even fatal.

But more was involved. God in His infinite wisdom was using this long bondage as a training ground to prepare for himself a people who would be called upon to undergo even more severe challenges and sufferings in the centuries to come. We who take the short view of history have trouble understanding this. We want our problems solved now and our wishes gratified at once. In this lesson, we learn that God takes the long view, because that is the only view that works in the long run.

B. Lesson Background

How many times small sins lead to far greater ones! Out of hatred and jealousy the brothers of Joseph had sold him into slavery in Egypt. By God's providence, however, Joseph rose to a position of great power and leadership in the land. Later, during a time of famine, his brothers joined him there. Because of the great service that Joseph had rendered Pharaoh, Joseph's father and all of Joseph's brothers and their families were made welcome in the land. They lived in the northeastern corner of the Nile Delta called Goshen, and over the years they multiplied and became great in number. That fact caused a later Pharaoh great alarm and led him to take action against the Israelites. So, hundreds of years after the sin of Joseph's brothers, the whole Hebrew nation suffered the consequences of it.

Scholars do not agree about the dating for the exodus. Some place it in the Eighteenth Egyptian Dynasty, about 1450 B.C. Others argue for a Nineteenth Dynasty date, sometime after 1300 B.C. There are factors, however, that argue for the earlier date. For example, a Pharaoh's daughter, Hatshepsut, did emerge as a strong figure in the Eighteenth Dynasty and later became ruler of Egypt. A temple that was built in her honor still stands as an impressive monument to her power. Just such a woman would have been strong enough to adopt a Hebrew baby and rear him as her own.

The lessons we will be studying this quarter begin at the time of the political change in Egypt that had such a profound effect on the people of Israel.

I. God's People Enslaved (Exodus 1:8-11a)

A. A New King Arises (vv. 8, 9)

8, 9. Now there arose up a new king over Egypt, which knew not Joseph. And he said unto his people, Behold, the people of the children of Israel are more and mightier than we.

Joseph had rendered a great service to Egypt and her rulers, and he had been appropriately rewarded. By this time, however, he had been dead for many years, and political memories are notoriously short. The new ruler may not have known of the work of Joseph, or he may have chosen to ignore it in order to build up his own reputation. Perhaps he had ambitious plans, and this prosperous minority, alien Hebrews, posed a threat to these plans. Our own times afford countless examples of how minorities can be exploited by greedy oppressors.

Being a minority, the children of Israel posed no real threat to Egypt. But the king of Egypt needed to arouse his own people against them, and so he did not hesitate to use the big lie, a technique still used by exploiters. If he could make his people fearful and jealous of the Hebrews, then his people would be more likely to support him in a crusade against them.

B. Egyptian Fear of the Hebrews (v. 10)

10. Come on, let us deal wisely with them; lest they multiply, and it come to pass, that, when there falleth out any war, they join also unto our enemies, and fight against us, and so get them up out of the land.

Egypt was well protected from invasion on all sides. The most likely invasion route would have been across the northeastern part of the Nile Delta, the land of Goshen, where the Israelites lived. Had the Egyptians treated the Israelites fairly, they would have had good reason to fight alongside the Egyptians in helping to repel any invaders. Clearly, however, more was involved. The Egyptians wanted the Israelites' possessions and their labor, and so they conjured up this excuse to hide their real motives. The Hitlers, the Stalins, the Husseins may well have learned their tactics from this ancient king.

It seems certain that another factor was involved in the Egyptians' changed feelings toward the Israelites. The Egyptians feared and hated the Israelites for no other reason than that they were different. We don't have to look to ancient history to find examples of the same problem. The Soviet Union, one of the largest empires in all history, is breaking up because the many ethnic groups within it cannot get along. Yugoslavia, a similar ethnic and religious conglomerate, is disintegrating. The only hope for any such situations is Jesus Christ "who hath made both one, and hath broken down the middle wall of partition between us" (Ephesians 2:14).

C. The Egyptian Answer (v. 11a)

11a. Therefore they did set over them taskmasters to afflict them with their burdens.

Though the Israelites were numerous, they were not organized to defend themselves against the Egyptians. They were forced to build "treasure cities" of Pithom and Raamses (v. 11b). Strategically located in the Nile Delta, these were probably cities where provisions and weapons were stored for use by the military in the event of an invasion. The Egyptians considered their own safety more important than the rights of the Hebrews, who were considered outsiders.

Undeserved Affliction

In the mid-eighteenth century there were established traditions of self-government among the American colonies, among which was the practice of taxation through representative provincial assemblies. Through a series of acts passed by Parliament, however, the British imposed taxation directly on the colonists. Among them were the Sugar Act of 1764, the Stamp Act of 1765, the Townshend Acts of 1767, and the Tea Act of 1773. These were denounced by colonial leaders, and soon the cry went up against taxation without representation. The Boston Tea Party on December 16, 1773, was a dramatic protest by American colonists against such unfair taxation.

Two and one-half years later, the separated colonies were united in their resistance to British rule. When emerging leadership forged the Declaration of Independence, the course that would produce freedom for the colonies was set in motion.

Like Israel of old, who cried out to God in their bondage and undeserved affliction, our forefathers called on God to bless their desire to be free.

Much of the unrest and revolution taking place in our time is the protest against undeserved affliction. People want to be free.   —W. P.

How to Say It

Jochebed.   *Jock*-ih-bed.
Pithom.   *Py*-thum.
Raamses.   Ray-*am*-ses.

II. God's Plan Begun

(Exodus 2:1-9a)

The king of Egypt soon found that hard bondage did not hinder the continued growth of the Israelites. So he decided upon an even more horrible scheme: he ordered the Hebrew midwives to kill all male babies born to Hebrew women. The midwives, however, refused to cooperate with this scheme. The king next issued an order that all male Hebrew babies were to be thrown into the river. He was certain that this would soon weaken the Hebrews. But he failed to make allowance for God, who had other plans.

A. The Birth of Moses (vv. 1, 2)

1, 2. And there went a man of the house of Levi, and took to wife a daughter of Levi. And the woman conceived, and bare a son: and when she saw him that he was a goodly child, she hid him three months.

God often begins great plans with small, relatively insignificant events. A Levite man married a Levite woman, an event that probably occurred almost daily. We later learn that the man's name was Amram and his wife's name was Jochebed (Exodus 6:20). They were married several years before Moses was born to them, for they had a daughter, Miriam, and a son, Aaron, who were older than Moses. The baby was a *goodly child*, that is, strong and healthy. For *three months* Jochebed was able to hide him, but concealing an active baby soon became impossible. He was certain to be discovered and killed.

B. Act of Desperation (vv. 3, 4)

3. And when she could not longer hide him, she took for him an ark of bulrushes, and daubed it with slime and with pitch, and put the child therein; and she laid it in the flags by the river's brink.

The horrible dilemma finally had to be faced. As agonizing as it must have been, Jochebed had to choose between the baby and the rest of the family. Only a mother could know the pain that rent her heart as she made the fateful decision. Yet she was not willing to abandon hope completely and throw the baby into the river as the king had directed. Hoping against hope, she prepared a container of papyrus, the reeds that grew so bountifully along the banks and in the backwaters of the Nile River. Carefully she *daubed it with slime and with pitch*. The *New International Version* says that she "coated it with tar and pitch." These substances made the little ark waterproof. The Egyptians made reed boats in a similar fashion that were remarkably durable.

Still, her plan seemed farfetched. Even if the little ark with its precious cargo stayed afloat several days or even weeks, worldly wisdom would say that she was only postponing the death of her loved one. We can only imagine her thoughts as she carefully lowered the ark into the water among the *flags*, the reeds and other water plants that would keep it from drifting away. But hope is hope because it can foresee the impossible. We are told that "by faith" Moses' parents hid him three months after he was born (Hebrews 11:23). Surely that same faith sustained Jochebed when she placed her baby in the river. She was determined to do everything she could to save her son and then trust God.

4. And his sister stood afar off, to wit what would be done to him.

Miriam, Moses' older sister, was strategically placed where she could watch the ark. There is little she could have done to protect the baby if a heartless Egyptian had happened upon him at the river's edge. From her position *afar off*, Miriam waited to see what might happen so she could report it to her parents.

C. Discovery by Pharaoh's Daughter (vv. 5, 6)

5. And the daughter of Pharaoh came down to wash herself at the river; and her maidens walked along by the river's side: and when she saw the ark among the flags, she sent her maid to fetch it.

There is no suggestion that the baby was deliberately placed where he might be found by Pharaoh's daughter. In fact, discovery by Egyptians could very well seal his doom. We have to see in this the working of God's divine providence. In situations where our best efforts fall short, He can intervene to bring about His will. Once Pharaoh's daughter saw the floating ark, her curiosity was aroused, and *she sent her maid*, probably her personal attendant, to bring the basket to her.

6. And when she had opened it, she saw the child: and, behold, the babe wept. And she had compassion on him, and said, This is one of the Hebrews' children.

VISUALS FOR THESE LESSONS

The *Adult Visuals/Learning Resources* packet contains classroom-size visuals designed for use with the lessons in the Summer Quarter. The packet is available from your supplier. Order no. 492.

The princess herself opened the ark, not knowing exactly what she would find. To her surprise it was a baby, and the baby wept. She immediately recognized that it was a Hebrew baby, but that did not destroy her compassion. Racial hatred and politics may lead people to do many terrible things. Yet there is something about an innocent baby that can melt away even this kind of bitterness. Even Pharaoh's daughter could not resist this innocence.

D. Provision by Pharaoh's Daughter
(vv. 7-9a)

7-9a. Then said his sister to Pharaoh's daughter, Shall I go and call to thee a nurse of the Hebrew women, that she may nurse the child for thee? And Pharaoh's daughter said to her, Go. And the maid went and called the child's mother. And Pharaoh's daughter said unto her, Take this child away, and nurse it for me, and I will give thee thy wages.

Miriam, who had been watching all of this, must have been close enough to understand what was happening. We don't know how old she was at the time, but she probably displayed a keen wit beyond her years. Even as the princess pondered what to do with the child, Miriam spoke up at just the right time to appeal to her compassion. If she kept the baby, she would need a nurse, and that was what Miriam offered. Little did the princess realize that the woman Miriam brought was the baby's own mother. Surely prayers of thanksgiving filled Jochebed's heart as she hurried to the princess and to her own son.

The arrangement that Pharaoh's daughter worked out with Jochebed was common practice among mothers of noble rank. Wet nurses were employed to care for their children until they were weaned, which often occurred at age three or four. If this was true in Moses' case, then there was ample time for the mother and child to become firmly bonded together.

III. God's Covenant Remembered
(Exodus 2:23-25)

The intervening verses tell of Moses' coming to maturity as the son of Pharaoh's daughter. On one occasion, as he went out among the Hebrews to observe their hard labor, he saw an Egyptian mistreating one of them. In his anger he killed the Egyptian and hid his body, thinking that his act had gone unnoticed. The next day, however, when he attempted to settle a dispute between two Hebrews, he learned that his act had not gone undetected. Realizing that his own life was now in danger, Moses fled to the

visual 1

land of Midian, a desert area that probably included Sinai and areas east of it. Here he was to remain in exile for forty years.

A. The Death of Pharaoh (v. 23)

23. And it came to pass in process of time, that the king of Egypt died: and the children of Israel sighed by reason of the bondage, and they cried, and their cry came up unto God by reason of the bondage.

Eventually the Pharaoh who sought Moses' life died. The Israelites may have hoped that their burdens would now be lightened, but such was not the case. The Egyptians had found that it was profitable to keep the Hebrews as slaves and so they were not inclined to change the arrangement. The Hebrews' heavy burdens continued, and, presumably, their sons were still under a death threat. Apparently enough male babies escaped the king's decree that the labor pool was maintained. Disappointed that their burdens were not lessened under the new Pharaoh, the Israelites groaned and cried out in anguish to God.

The Israelites' knowledge and understanding about God may have been limited at this time. Their later experiences in the desert suggest that their long years of bondage had left them in ignorance about Jehovah. Although some individuals may have remembered the God of their fathers, there is nothing to indicate that they worshiped Him in any regular or organized way. Yet their cries went up to Him, because they had no one else to whom they could appeal. Like many people today, they appealed to God when everything else failed.

B. God Sees the People's Plight
(vv. 24, 25)

24, 25. And God heard their groaning, and God remembered his covenant with Abraham, with Isaac, and with Jacob. And God looked upon the children of Israel, and God had respect unto them.

Of course, God hears all prayers; but the Scriptures often say He "hears" those prayers that He grants and is "deaf" to those He rejects. God had not forgotten the covenant that he had made with Abraham, Isaac, and Jacob. He had already fulfilled part of that covenant by greatly increasing the descendants of Abraham as He had promised (Genesis 12:2; 22:17). Other promises included in the covenant remained to be fulfilled. Now God was preparing to fulfill some of them.

REMEMBERING

Patti Sharp was a passenger in a small plane piloted by her father when he was suddenly stricken with a heart attack and died.

Patti had never piloted a plane. Often, however, she had flown with her father, who was an experienced pilot, and had heard him tell her the procedures required for landing. Now, as she reached over his body, his words came clearly to her mind. She said she could hear her father telling her how to fly the plane. At 4:30 P.M. of that early fall day, Patti successfully landed the Super Cub on an Eastern Oregon airstrip. She had prayed to stay calm. Her confidence in her father's guidance helped her through. Her words were, "I know my dad would never let anything happen to me!"

In tough situations we need someone on whom we can confidently rely.

Israel, under the pressure of bondage in Egypt, cried out to God for help. Because of His covenant with Abraham, Isaac, and Jacob, God heard, and soon the deliverer whom He was preparing was sent to rescue them.

Through His Son, God has made known His desire to rescue all from the bondage of sin. Don't delay coming to Him, who alone can save. —W. P.

Home Daily Bible Readings

Monday, May 30—A New Harsh King Ruled Egypt (Exodus 1:5-10)

Tuesday, May 31—More Oppressed, More Hebrews! (Exodus 1:11-16)

Wednesday, June 1—Midwives Feared the Lord, Not Pharaoh (Exodus 1:17-21)

Thursday, June 2—Mother Made a Basket; Sister Watched (Exodus 1:22—2:4)

Friday, June 3—Princess Called for Nurse for Moses (Exodus 2:5-9)

Saturday, June 4—Moses Killed an Egyptian (Exodus 2:10-14)

Sunday, June 5—Moses Fled to Midian; Marries in Midian (Exodus 2:15-23)

Conclusion

A. God Hears, but Waits

For centuries people have wrestled with the problem of why God permits suffering. For one who believes in an all-powerful, all-loving God, the issue will not go away. Of course, much suffering can be attributed to human sinfulness. Yet this does not begin to account for all of the suffering in the world. In the end we must confess that we do not have all the answers. We must admit our ignorance and submit to the infinite wisdom of God.

We have no basis on which to argue that the Israelites were worse sinners than the Egyptians and thus deserved the harsh treatment they received. The sin of the Egyptians, on the other hand, is very apparent. Fear, prejudice, and desire for material gain were among the obvious motives for their mistreatment of the Israelites. Whatever else may be said, the Israelites' long and painful bondage in Egypt bonded them together as a people with a common cause. And it prepared them to receive Moses when God sent him back to lead them out of that bondage.

B. All Kinds of Bondage

The kind of bondage that the Israelites suffered in Egypt supposedly no longer exists in our modern world. But there are many oppressive political regimes that allow people little freedom and force them to live under extremely adverse conditions.

If the whole world enjoyed the blessings of prosperity and democracy, we would not be free of bondage. None is more prevalent nor more devastating than bondage to sin. In the final analysis, every other form of bondage stems from it. Fortunately, we know the way to break out of this bondage. Paradoxically, the way to escape is another form of bondage—total submission to Jesus Christ. Only as we yield ourselves to Him, and make His will our will, do we know true freedom (John 8:36).

C. Let Us Pray

Dear God, we pray for those who are suffering. Give us strength and wisdom to help those we can. May we see in the suffering of the Hebrews how You work in history, sometimes slowly but always certainly, to bring about Your will. In Jesus' name we pray. Amen.

D. Thought to Remember

Remember the Lord's promise, "If the Son therefore shall make you free, ye shall be free indeed" (John 8:36).

Learning by Doing

This page contains an alternate lesson plan emphasizing learning activities. Classes desiring such student involvement will find these suggestions helpful.

Learning Goals

As students participate in today's class session, they should:

1. Survey Exodus 1 and 2 and list what these chapters teach about God's faithfulness, providential care, and forgiveness.

2. Thank God for His faithfulness, providence, and forgiveness demonstrated in their own lives.

Into the Lesson

Before class write the following statements on sheets of posterboard or shelf paper and display them in your classroom. Use a bright-colored felt-tip marker so that the statements catch the attention of the students as they enter the classroom:

"God's greatness is seen in man's weakness."

"Waiting on God is always worth it."

"When the hour seems the darkest, God's light shines the brightest."

Use these statements in one of the following ways to introduce today's lesson:

Stand beneath them. For this activity, mount the statements in different corners of the classroom. Students are to choose the statement with which they most identify. At your signal, they are to go and stand by that statement.

Ask volunteers in each of the groups to share why they chose that statement.

Tell a neighbor. Divide your students into pairs. Students are to choose the statement they most relate to and tell their partners which statement they chose, and why.

After either activity, explain to the class that today's lesson illustrates the ideas expressed in the statements.

Into the Word

If you have time, ask for three or four volunteers to share in a reading of more than today's printed text. Have them read aloud to the class Exodus 1:6—2:23. As the students listen, they should decide how this story illustrates each of the sentences written on the posters.

Discuss the students' responses to the text, and then choose one of the following activities:

Sixty-second monologues. Divide the students into groups of about three, and from the following list choose a different Bible character for each group:

"I am Moses—"

"I am Pharaoh—"

"I am Pharaoh's daughter—"

"I am the sister of Moses—"

"I am Zipporah—"

The students within each group are to study Exodus 1 and 2 and work together to prepare a sixty-second speech that expresses the point of view of their assigned character. Then one member of each group is to deliver the speech to the whole class. Allow ten minutes for the groups to prepare before you call for the speeches.

Reflection questions. Have the students discuss these Bible-study questions in groups or pairs:

1. How did God see to it that the baby Moses was protected? Why do you suppose He did this? How do you suppose Moses' mother reacted to what happened?

2. Suppose you had never heard this story before, and the person reading it to you stopped immediately after Exodus 2:15. Would you suspect that Moses would become a great leader for God? Why, or why not?

3. How do you think the events of Exodus 2:1-25 prepared Moses for future service?

What does this lesson teach? Divide students into small groups and give each group a copy of the following statements:

• God uses unlikely people to accomplish His purposes.

• From failure God sometimes fashions a person He can use.

• God always keeps His promises—but not always in the way we expect.

• Despite what they may suffer, those who love God will not be forgotten by Him.

The groups are to examine Exodus 1 and 2 and decide which verses teach these truths. Lead the groups in sharing their conclusions.

Into Life

If you used the statements in "What does this lesson teach?" they will lead into a challenging conclusion for this session. If you did not use them, read them aloud and ask how this week's text teaches each truth.

Then ask, "Have any of these truths been demonstrated in the lives of Christians you know? If so, how?"

Close with prayers of thanks for God's faithfulness, providential care, and forgiveness.

Let's Talk It Over

The questions on this page are designed to encourage review of the lesson Scriptures and to promote discussion of the lesson by the class. The answers provided are only discussion starters. Let your class talk it over from there.

1. Pharaoh's tyranny caused some of the Hebrews to resist his injustice (Exodus 1:17; 2:2; 2:11, 12). Quite often, what is needed to awaken one's sense of justice to wrongs that exist in society? What are some specific wrongs that we may encounter in our families, on our jobs, or in our communities?

Often an injustice must touch our lives personally before our sense of justice is aroused. Nevertheless, all defenseless persons are the objects of God's special concern, and He would have His people be sensitive to the defenseless simply because they are made in His image and loved by Him. Insensitivity, favoritism, and prejudice are just a few of the injustices that are prevalent in our society.

2. Human history is replete with examples of the devaluation of human life and dignity, and of man's inhumanity against man. Throughout time, however, there have been courageous individuals who have dared to stand against the callous mistreatment of other humans. How can we oppose oppression and injustice in our modern world?

God values every human life and calls upon each Christian to take a stand of tenderness and compassion in the face of tyranny and prejudice. In our personal world, we can strive to treat our co-workers, neighbors, and fellow citizens with dignity and worth, even if we are mocked or ridiculed for our position. Our voice should be a voice for the weak, the helpless, the hurting, and the victimized. Each of us should be willing to take a stand and speak out for the value of each human life.

3. Human injustice and oppression exists in many forms. How can we recognize situations where human distress is present? In what ways can we respond to the needs of others when we recognize their pain?

Overbearing bosses, domineering family members, and demanding friends and neighbors often produce unjust and difficult environments in which persons must live. Greed, pride, selfishness, and lust for power frequently are at the root of suffocating circumstances, and these ungodly attitudes are outwardly manifested in deceit, abuse, and repression. Concerned

Christians can help by intervening with aid or counsel, by comforting the downtrodden, by working for change, and by praying for the alleviation of the distress.

4. At the time of Pharaoh's edict of infanticide, Hebrew parents faced a horrible dilemma over which they had no control. Even today, life often brings trying times and spiritual crises over which we have little or no control. In tough circumstances, why is faith so important? How can our faith be strengthened when we face such situations?

Faith is an essential ingredient for surviving the perplexing difficulties of life, because it maintains the hope that God will work out His good for His people (Romans 8:28), and because it encourages a trust in the goodness and power of God (Psalm 100:5). So often we attempt to control and manipulate the circumstances of our lives, thinking that merely by our actions or force of will we will accomplish our desires. Too often we forget that God is ultimately in control of all things. Faith drives us into the arms of God with humility and dependence, and it has confidence that God will help at just the right time and in just the right way (1 Peter 5:5, 6). As unpleasant as conditions beyond our control can be, they bring opportunities to deepen our reliance upon God and to intensify our relationship with Him.

5. As powerful as world leaders may be, even they cannot thwart the will of God. What comfort and encouragement do we receive when we understand that nothing can come between God and His plan for those who are His people?

The knowledge of God's sovereignty in His universe provides enormous consolation to us who are His children, especially during those times when we may be tempted to give up or to wonder whether anybody cares about us. Such a realization reminds us that God is active in the world and in our lives, that He is aware of our needs, that He is concerned for our welfare, that He has the power to accomplish His will, and that He will keep His promises to bring eternal blessing to those who place and keep their trust in Him.

God Calls and Moses Responds

DEVOTIONAL READING: Exodus 3:16-20.

LESSON SCRIPTURE: Exodus 3:1—4:17.

PRINTED TEXT: Exodus 3:10-15a; 4:1-5, 10-12.

Exodus 3:10-15a

10 Come now therefore, and I will send thee unto Pharaoh, that thou mayest bring forth my people the children of Israel out of Egypt.

11 And Moses said unto God, Who am I, that I should go unto Pharaoh, and that I should bring forth the children of Israel out of Egypt?

12 And he said, Certainly I will be with thee; and this shall be a token unto thee, that I have sent thee: When thou hast brought forth the people out of Egypt, ye shall serve God upon this mountain.

13 And Moses said unto God, Behold, when I come unto the children of Israel, and shall say unto them, The God of your fathers hath sent me unto you; and they shall say to me, What is his name? what shall I say unto them?

14 And God said unto Moses, I AM THAT I AM: and he said, Thus shalt thou say unto the children of Israel, I AM hath sent me unto you.

15a And God said moreover unto Moses, Thus shalt thou say unto the children of Israel, The LORD God of your fathers, the God of Abraham, the God of Isaac, and the God of Jacob, hath sent me unto you.

Exodus 4:1-5, 10-12

1 And Moses answered and said, But, behold, they will not believe me, nor hearken unto my voice: for they will say, The LORD hath not appeared unto thee.

2 And the LORD said unto him, What is that in thine hand? And he said, A rod.

3 And he said, Cast it on the ground. And he cast it on the ground, and it became a serpent; and Moses fled from before it.

4 And the LORD said unto Moses, Put forth thine hand, and take it by the tail. And he put forth his hand, and caught it, and it became a rod in his hand:

5 That they may believe that the LORD God of their fathers, the God of Abraham, the God of Isaac, and the God of Jacob, hath appeared unto thee.

. . . .

10 And Moses said unto the LORD, O my Lord, I am not eloquent, neither heretofore, nor since thou hast spoken unto thy servant; but I am slow of speech, and of a slow tongue.

11 And the LORD said unto him, Who hath made man's mouth? or who maketh the dumb, or deaf, or the seeing, or the blind? have not I the LORD?

12 Now therefore go, and I will be with thy mouth, and teach thee what thou shalt say.

GOLDEN TEXT: Come now therefore, and I will send thee unto Pharaoh, that thou mayest bring forth my people the children of Israel out of Egypt.—Exodus 3:10.

God Redeems a People

Unit 1: Deliverance From Oppression

(Lessons 1-4)

Lesson Aims

As a result of studying this lesson, each student should:

1. Have a better understanding of God's call to Moses to lead the children of Israel from their bondage in Egypt.

2. Be able to name some of the excuses Moses gave to avoid God's assignment.

3. Be ready to say "yes" when asked to take an active role in the work of the church.

Lesson Outline

INTRODUCTION
  A. Excuses
  B. Lesson Background
I. GOD CALLS MOSES (Exodus 3:10-15a)
  A. God's Commission (v. 10)
  B. Moses' Excuse (v. 11)
  C. God's Reassurance (v. 12)
  D. Moses' Next Excuse (v. 13)
  E. God's Special Name (vv. 14, 15a)
II. GOD GIVES A SIGN (Exodus 4:1-5)
  A. Moses' Further Complaint (v. 1)
  B. Moses' Rod Becomes a Sign (vv. 2-5)
III. STILL ANOTHER EXCUSE (Exodus 4:10-12)
  A. Moses' Slowness of Speech (v. 10)
    I Am Not Eloquent!
  B. God Made Man's Tongue (vv. 11, 12)
    A Deliverer
CONCLUSION
  A. A Leader Shortage
  B. Instant Gratification
  C. Let Us Pray
  D. Thought to Remember

Display visual 2 of the visuals packet and let it remain before the class throughout this session. The visual is shown on page 358.

Introduction

A. Excuses

Excuses come in all shapes and forms. Every church worker has heard his or her share of them, some reasonable and some ridiculous. I once heard of a lady who had a prize parrot. She couldn't attend church or Sunday school, she said, because she had to baby-sit her bird. We

have to struggle to smother a laugh at such a feeble excuse.

We wonder if God didn't feel the same way at some of the excuses Moses offered to escape the call to relieve the suffering of his people in Egypt. Moses obviously did not think himself qualified for such a great task, and in that frame of mind it probably never occurred to him how feeble some of these excuses must have seemed to God.

B. Lesson Background

Last week's lesson ended with Moses fleeing Egypt for his life, and the Israelites ground ever deeper into bondage. For forty years Moses remained in the wilderness, hundreds of miles east of Egypt. He had married the daughter of Jethro, the priest of Midian, and had become a dutiful son-in-law, caring for Jethro's flock. Had Moses become so busy that he had forgotten his people in Egypt? They had rejected his efforts to help them forty years ago (see Acts 7:23-29). Had he been so chastened by that rejection that he put them out of his mind? Or did he remember them, and remember with a sense of guilt?

Moses had become more and more identified with the nomadic life of the Midianites. He was now eighty years old, and his physical powers would not have been the same as when he fled Egypt. Life for him had become comfortable, and he was not seeking to change it.

Leading Jethro's flock to pasture, Moses came to the region of Mount Sinai. There God intervened in a miraculous manner, calling to Moses from a bush that burned but was not consumed. And Moses' life was forever changed.

I. God Calls Moses (Exodus 3:10-15a)

The bush that burned but was not consumed caught Moses' attention. Then from the bush came a voice calling Moses by name and warning him to remove his shoes, because he stood on holy ground. Following this, God identified himself as the God of Abraham, Isaac, and Jacob, informing Moses that He had not forgotten His people. Moses now knew that he was standing in the presence of almighty God!

A. God's Commission (v. 10)

10. Come now therefore, and I will send thee unto Pharaoh, that thou mayest bring forth my people the children of Israel out of Egypt.

God was prepared to deliver His people from the oppression of the Egyptians, and Moses was to be His chosen instrument to accomplish this task. Moses must have been overwhelmed by this thought. Only a few moments before, he had been but a shepherd minding Jethro's flock in the quiet of the desert. Suddenly, without any warning, he was challenged to confront the monarch of a mighty nation, and to demand that the Hebrew people be freed.

B. Moses' Excuse (v. 11)

11. And Moses said unto God, Who am I, that I should go unto Pharaoh, and that I should bring forth the children of Israel out of Egypt?

Moses certainly must have had mixed emotions as the implications of God's call began to sink in. Moses was a humble man, and his lack of experience as a leader must have left him feeling totally inadequate for such a task. Doubtless, most of us would feel the same way in such a situation. Humility is an attitude that every leader should have, and so in demonstrating humility, Moses showed that he had one of the qualifications needed.

Yet, in showing humility, Moses also revealed more. Apparently he thought he was going to have to free the Israelites on his own, a thought that would humble anyone. He should have realized, however, that since God was calling him to this task, God would be with him to strengthen him so he could do it. In thinking of his own weaknesses first, he revealed that his trust in God was less than complete.

C. God's Reassurance (v. 12)

12. And he said, Certainly I will be with thee; and this shall be a token unto thee, that I have sent thee: When thou hast brought forth the people out of Egypt, ye shall serve God upon this mountain.

When he was challenged to serve, Moses' first thought was of himself and his weaknesses. In this respect most of us are like him. Unless we possess an overweening ego, we see our weaknesses when we are called to serve God. But God turned Moses' thoughts away from himself. "Look to me," said God, "for I will be with you." We too can find strength in the assurance that God will be with us when we labor in His service.

God had already given Moses a visible sign in the burning bush, but this had not been enough to stimulate his faith. Instead, God gave him a pledge that had to be taken completely on faith. God promised Moses that after he had brought the Israelites out of Egypt, they would return to this very location and would *serve God.* (Some versions translate this "worship God," which is, of course, one form of service.) If Moses would believe that, he would have full assurance that all the obstacles that stood in the way of Israel's departing Egypt would be removed.

D. Moses' Next Excuse (v. 13)

13. And Moses said unto God, Behold, when I come unto the children of Israel, and shall say unto them, The God of your fathers hath sent me unto you; and they shall say to me, What is his name? what shall I say unto them?

Moses' next problem dealt with the matter of authority. He anticipated that the Israelites would demand to know by what right he came claiming to be a leader over them. In any encounter with the heavily armed Egyptians, the Israelites would be at a severe disadvantage. They had every right to check on the credentials of anyone who came claiming to be their emancipator.

The appropriate answer to their question would have been, *The God of your fathers hath sent me unto you.* That answer was adequate for Moses, but he feared that it would not do for the Israelites. They had been surrounded for so long by the idolatry of the Egyptians that for most the knowledge of the God of Abraham, Isaac, and Jacob had grown vague. No doubt they were familiar with the names of the numerous Egyptian gods, and Moses was quite sure that they would want to know the special name of the God he represented.

At first glance this may not strike us so much as an excuse as a request for information Moses would need on his mission. Yet, underneath, it reveals his lack of faith that God would provide whatever was needed to accomplish that mission. When God has given us a promise of victory, we ought not be too particular about the details of how it will be carried out.

E. God's Special Name (vv. 14, 15a)

14, 15a. And God said unto Moses, I AM THAT I AM and he said, Thus shalt thou say unto the children of Israel, I AM hath sent me unto you. And God said moreover unto Moses, Thus shalt thou say unto the children of Israel, The LORD God of your fathers, the God of Abraham, the God of Isaac, and the God of Jacob, hath sent me unto you.

In these verses, God's special name is given to Moses to give him assurance as he returned to Egypt to free his people. Scholars have written much on the meaning and implication of this special name. In Hebrew the word has four letters—YHWH—and it means "I am" or "I am the existing one." The Hebrews came to consider this name so sacred that they would not even

---

How to Say It

YAHWEH.   *Yah*-weh.

pronounce it, substituting some other word for God when they were reading the text aloud. Since ancient Hebrew did not have vowels, people eventually forgot how to pronounce the name. Some suggest that the word should be pronounced "Yahweh." *The American Standard Version* has it "Jehovah" (Psalm 23:1, for example). In many editions of the *King James* and *Revised Standard Version* it is printed as "LORD" in large and small capitals.

The point to stress here is that Yahweh or Jehovah is the God who alone exists; He has always been, and He will always be. This is the God who would guide Moses in his mission, not some imaginary god such as those the Egyptians worshiped. This should have been enough to convince Moses of the success of the mission on which he was being sent, but it wasn't.

II. God Gives a Sign
(Exodus 4:1-5)

The intervening verses record God's instructions to Moses. He was to return to Egypt, gather the elders of Israel together, and inform them that the God of their fathers had heard their cry and was ready to deliver them from bondage. Together they were to go to Pharaoh and ask to be released so they could worship God. Furthermore, God told Moses what the result would be. Pharaoh would refuse their call for emancipation, and finally God would stretch out His hand and smite Egypt with many wonders. After that, Pharaoh would let them go.

A. Moses' Further Complaint (v. 1)

1. And Moses answered and said, But, behold, they will not believe me, nor hearken unto my voice: for they will say, the LORD hath not appeared unto thee.

Moses still had his doubts. He knew that when he presented himself to the leaders, they would have to take his statements on faith. Moses knew these people well enough to know that they would not accept his word without some additional proof.

B. Moses' Rod Becomes a Sign (vv. 2-5)

2, 3. And the LORD said unto him, What is that in thine hand? And he said, A rod. And he said, Cast it on the ground. And he cast it on the ground, and it became a serpent; and Moses fled from before it.

The *rod* was the shepherd's staff, the ordinary working tool of every shepherd. It served as a walking stick for the shepherd, a weapon to fend off wild animals, and its crook was useful in retrieving sheep that had fallen into dangerous

places. God told Moses to throw it to the ground, and when he did, it immediately became a snake. We are not told what kind of snake it was, but apparently it was poisonous, for Moses, whose long experience in the desert trained him to know snakes, wisely fled from it.

4, 5. And the LORD said unto Moses, Put forth thine hand, and take it by the tail. And he put forth his hand, and caught it, and it became a rod in his hand: that they may believe that the LORD God of their fathers, the God of Abraham, the God of Isaac, and the God of Jacob, hath appeared unto thee.

Moses faced still another test of faith, one that most of us might have trouble passing. God asked him to pick up the snake by its *tail*. An experienced snake handler might pick up a snake by its head, but not by its tail, which would leave it free to inflict its deadly wounds. But Moses passed the test. Without hesitation he reached down and picked up the serpent, just as God had ordered. Immediately it became *a rod* once again. Apparently the sign of the rod was one of the signs to convince the Israelite leaders that Moses indeed had been sent from God (Exodus 4:28-31).

III. Still Another Excuse
(Exodus 4:10-12)

Verses 6-9 record two additional signs by which Moses would bring the Israelites to belief. In one of these, God caused Moses' hand immediately to become leprous. Then instantaneously He made it healthy again. The second sign was one that Moses would use when he returned to Egypt. There he would take water from the Nile River and pour it upon the dry land where it would instantly become blood.

A. Moses' Slowness of Speech (v. 10)

10. And Moses said unto the LORD, O my Lord, I am not eloquent, neither heretofore, nor since thou hast spoken unto thy servant; but I am slow of speech, and of a slow tongue.

Moses still had excuses to offer in order to escape his mission. He was not an eloquent man, he protested, and never had been. He would never be able to deliver God's message effectively, either to the Israelites or to Pharaoh. Even his confrontation with God in the previous few minutes had not given him the gift of ready speech.

Perhaps there was some truth in what Moses said. His long and lonely years as a shepherd had not given him much opportunity to sharpen his speaking skills. Like most beginning speakers when they face their first audience, he may have feared that he would be tongue-tied. Living among the Midianites for so long, he had had little opportunity to use the languages of the Egyptians and the Hebrews. He may have felt that he could no longer express himself fluently in those languages. Some have even suggested that he suffered from a speech impediment, but there is nothing in the text to indicate this.

I AM NOT ELOQUENT!

No one seemed less qualified to communicate the Word of God to a different culture than Mr. Hyde. Every mission board he approached turned him down because of his severe stuttering. Believing still that he was called to share the gospel in India, he signed on as a seaman on a freighter until he reached that land.

Hyde's stutter remained, and he struggled to learn the dialect of the Indian state now called Kerala. Then he made a discovery. Although he could not preach without stuttering, he had no speech difficulties when he prayed. Staying in the homes of the people, he simply prayed for them. Soon he was renamed "Praying Hyde." His ministry grew, and young men who had found Christ through Hyde's prayers began to reach thousands for the Lord.

At large conventions the believers, after hearing fine preaching, still wanted to hear Praying Hyde. They would chant, "Praying Hyde." Now an old man, Mr. Hyde would come to the platform and pray for God's people and for those who did not know Jesus as Savior and Lord.

Mr. Hyde died in a native hut. Found in the morning he was on his knees.

Will we allow anything to impede our service for Christ? Can we offer a valid excuse for not serving?   —W. P.

B. God Made Man's Tongue (vv. 11, 12)

11, 12. And the LORD said unto him, Who hath made man's mouth? or who maketh the dumb, or deaf, or the seeing, or the blind? have not I the LORD? Now therefore go, and I will be with thy mouth, and teach thee what thou shalt say.

Even if Moses had some basis for his excuse, he revealed a lack of faith in God. Since God was sending him on this mission, Moses should have trusted God to provide the means to accomplish it. God reminded him that he had made man's mouth and ears and eyes. The Creator certainly could control what He had made. Once again God assured Moses that He would be with him, and then He promised to *teach* him what to say. Centuries later Jesus would make a similar promise to his twelve disciples when sending them out to announce the nearness of the kingdom of Heaven. When they were brought before governors and kings, they would not have to worry about what to say. The Spirit would give them the words to speak (Matthew 10:18-20).

One more attempt by Moses to refuse the divine commission kindled God's anger against him. It was clear that at the moment Moses did not have sufficient faith in God to provide for his proclaimed deficiencies, so God told him that He would provide Aaron, Moses' brother, to be his spokesman (Exodus 4:13-16). That announcement, it seems, gave Moses the encouragement to do as God had bidden him.

A DELIVERER

A hero may come in a strange package! Alvin Cullum York was a man who was reluctant to go to war. When he was convinced that it was duty, however, he volunteered for service in World War I and was soon on the front lines in France.

In the great Argonne-Meuse offensive of 1918, this quiet man silenced an entire enemy machine gun emplacement. He killed more than twenty enemy soldiers and single-handedly took 132 prisoners. It was the most outstanding achievement by any individual in battle in the entire war. In recognition of his heroic achievement, this man who was famed as Sergeant York was awarded the Congressional Medal of Honor, the highest recognition his nation could offer.

Moses was a "strange package" for God to call to be the deliverer of His people, Israel. A shepherd, eighty years old, slow of speech, and unsure of his leadership ability, Moses seemed an unlikely candidate to become the instrument of God to create a new nation, but Moses was God's choice.

When we are willing to do what the Lord asks of us, He will supply all we need to do His work. Don't be fearful that you are not strong enough to be all He wants you to become.   —W. P.

Home Daily Bible Readings

Monday, June 6—God Speaks to Moses (Exodus 3:1-6)

Tuesday, June 7—God Came to Deliver Israel (Exodus 3:7-10)

Wednesday, June 8—But, Who Are You? God? (Exodus 3:11-15)

Thursday, June 9—God of Abraham, Isaac, and Jacob (Exodus 3:16-22)

Friday, June 10—Take Your Rod—Cast It Away (Exodus 4:1-5)

Saturday, June 11—If Rod and Leprosy Fail, Pour Water (Exodus 4:6-17)

Sunday, June 12—Moses and Aaron Go to Israel's Elders (Exodus 4:18-31)

Let's Talk It Over

The questions on this page are designed to encourage review of the lesson Scriptures and to promote discussion of the lesson by the class. The answers provided are only discussion starters. Let your class talk it over from there.

1. Moses was reluctant to accept God's call to service, and he offered some feeble excuses to try to get out of doing what God wanted him to do. Many Christians today aren't much different. How can we combat the tendency of offering excuses to avoid doing the Lord's work?

When asked to accept a responsibility in the church, many Christians have a natural tendency to procrastinate, to protest, and to resist. Our busy schedules, our limited abilities, our lack of training, our health, our age, and our fear of failure are just some of the excuses we offer to avoid the tasks we are asked to do. We can fight the inclination to reject God's call by developing a healthy view of the resources He has given us for ministry (Romans 12:3-8), by cultivating an attitude of willingness (Hebrews 10:7), and by learning to depend on God's strength and power for the task (Philippians 4:13; 2 Corinthians 12:9, 10).

2. Years earlier, Moses' attempt to provide leadership for the Israelites had ended in failure (Exodus 2:11-15). Perhaps he was reluctant to leave the security of his life as a shepherd because he didn't want to risk failure again. What does the fear of failure do to a person? How can we overcome this fear? What benefits accrue to those who are willing to leave familiar and secure surroundings to undertake an unfamiliar task for the Lord?

Fear of failure immobilizes a person, causing one to take no risks, to avoid new opportunities for growth, and to miss many of life's joys. Victory over such fear is possible as we develop confidence in God who holds the future (Jeremiah 29:11), as we find our sufficiency for every task in Christ Jesus (Ephesians 3:20, 21), and as we build trust in God's goodness and grace (Psalm 34:8, 15, 19). Daring to step out into the unknown will deepen our faith and encourage a more childlike trust in the Lord. As we do so, our abilities will be sharpened, the Lord's kingdom will be strengthened, and we will experience a satisfaction the timid can never know.

3. Many persons prefer to function in situations where they feel experienced and qualified. How can a church be sensitive to this natural desire as it seeks to find willing workers to fill positions of service? At the same time, how may we be benefited if we stretch ourselves beyond the comfortable and known to discover new avenues of ministry in the church?

A church that matches the tasks that need to be done with those members who possess the talents, gifts, and abilities to do those tasks will generally have more satisfied and productive workers (Romans 12:6-8; 1 Peter 4:10, 11). Having members fill out talent survey sheets is one way to accomplish this. Everyone's God-given contribution to the church's ministry should be held in esteem and acknowledged as vital to the work of the kingdom (1 Corinthians 12:4-6, 14-17). Nevertheless, all of us should be willing to try new jobs, to experiment with undeveloped talents, and to undertake challenging opportunities. In doing so, we may discover talents that we didn't know we had. Furthermore, being involved in new tasks and responsibilities may bring reinvigoration to our spirits and renewed joy in our Christian walk.

4. Like Moses, we may sometimes lack the faith that God will provide what we need in order to fulfill the task He sets before us. How can we develop a greater faith in God? What can be the effects of such a faith?

Our faith in God is cultivated as we come to know Him and His character more intimately, as we remind ourselves of the almighty works of God in our lives and in the lives of other saints. As such confidence in God grows, we will experience greater peace, deeper conviction, stronger assurance, intensified boldness, and increased victories.

5. When God called Moses to lead the Israelites to freedom, God promised to be with him (Exodus 3:12). Likewise, Jesus' commission to us includes the promise of His divine presence (Matthew 28:20). How does this promise of Christ help us face difficult tasks?

The promise of the Lord's constant presence helps us to focus on His strength instead of our weaknesses. Knowing that the Lord is very near brings assurance of His care for us, of His guidance when the way is unclear, of His encouragement when times are tough, and of His comfort when we face the anxieties of life.

Although Moses had given Pharaoh advance notice of the tenth plague, most of the people would not have known of its coming. Some may have observed the Israelites as they marked their doorposts with blood, but they would not have understood what this meant.

At midnight the terrible blow struck with swiftness and certainty. Death knew no exceptions. From the palace of Pharaoh, to the miserable dungeons, to the lowly maidservant (11:5), the firstborn of every household fell victim. Even the animals of the Egyptians did not escape the hand of death.

B. Mournful Cry (v. 30)

30. And Pharaoh rose up in the night, he, and all his servants, and all the Egyptians; and there was a great cry in Egypt: for there was not a house where there was not one dead.

Apparently death struck instantaneously and without any prior warning. Grandparents, fathers, mothers, children, uncles, aunts, cousins—in some way every Egyptian household was touched. In the middle of the night someone noticed that the body of a loved one was cold and still, and a cry of anguish went up. That cry was heard by others who made the same gruesome discovery. Soon the whole Egyptian community echoed with wails of mourning. Just as Moses had predicted, "There shall be a great cry throughout all the land of Egypt, such as there was none like it, nor shall be like it any more" (11:6), the terrible prediction came true.

Although the royal palace was isolated from most of the people, the multiplied cries reached even the ears of Pharaoh. Remembering with chilling accuracy the pronouncement of Moses, the king must have made a quick inventory of the palace. He may have discovered the lifeless body of his firstborn, as well as those of his advisors and servants. We can only imagine the panic that seized his heart when he realized the magnitude of the disaster. Many times he had hardened his heart against the will of the Lord, but now that heart was shattered by the disaster that had beset him and his kingdom.

C. Complete Surrender (vv. 31, 32)

31, 32. And he called for Moses and Aaron by night, and said, Rise up, and get you forth from among my people, both ye and the children of Israel; and go, serve the LORD as ye have said. Also take your flocks and your herds, as ye have said, and be gone; and bless me also.

Only a short time before, the king had chased Moses and Aaron from his presence, threatening to kill them if he saw them again. Now his arrogant threats had changed to pleas for mercy.

The earlier plagues had brought suffering and inconvenience and in some cases even the fear of death. But this final plague brought death itself—cold, stark death that left no household untouched. Pharaoh's stubbornness had brought great suffering to his people. If he had been isolated from any of the earlier plagues, he had to suffer this one along with his people. Many a modern dictator has followed a similar career, seeking power no matter what it has cost his people. For that matter, is there any area involving human relationships that has not felt the destructive force of someone's pursuit of selfish power?

Pharaoh granted each of Moses' requests. Moses and his people were allowed to leave Egypt, they were allowed to go and serve the Lord as they had asked, they were allowed to take their flocks and herds.

In his desperation and weakness, he made one last request. He asked Moses to bless him. Just what he expected this blessing to be, we have no idea. We have known many persons in similar desperate situations to ask Christians to intercede with God for them. Whether these are but empty words or a serious cry for help, we may never know. Yet we have an obligation to offer what comfort and ministrations we can, leaving the rest up to God.

D. A Terrified People (v. 33)

33. And the Egyptians were urgent upon the people, that they might send them out of the land in haste; for they said, We be all dead men.

Even in the face of the earlier plagues, perhaps the Egyptian populace, as well as Pharaoh, had been loath to let the Hebrews leave the land because of the loss it would mean to them. But now they were terrified, and understandably so. In this night, all had lost their firstborn. They were certain that further delay in granting the Hebrews' release would bring the loss of more life. So they rose up everywhere and urged the Hebrews to leave. Willingly, nay eagerly, they gave them the gold and silver they requested to hasten their departure.

A DECISION MADE TOO LATE

"Will, it's time you got a good hasp and padlock on the well house. One of these days some of our small animals will get in that door when the wind blows it open, and they'll fall into the well and drown." Will's wife had told him that several times, and Will's answer was always the same. "You're right, June. I bought the new hasp and lock last December. As soon as there is a little free time I'll do it."

Spring and summer passed, and the farm work never slowed down. Finally the bountiful harvest was reaped. The joy of that season was enriched with the coming of children and grandchildren for a visit.

Early the next morning Tim rushed into the kitchen. "Grandpa, Susan's in the well! She followed the banty rooster into the well house. I can't get her out." Will and Susan's father rushed to the building. Susan could swim, but she couldn't catch the bottom rung of the ladder to get out. After several heart-stopping moments, loving arms were able to reach Susan and pull her and the banty rooster to safety. In an hour the new hasp and padlock were in place, and the well house door was locked shut!

We are all a little like Will. We know what we should do, but, for reasons known only to ourselves, we put it off.

Pharaoh waited too long to prevent disaster. His right decision came too late to bring life back to Egypt's firstborn.   —W. P.

Conclusion

A. Hardened Hearts

As we study this passage about the ten plagues, we read that the Lord hardened Pharaoh's heart, causing him to reject Moses' request that the Israelites be permitted to leave (Exodus 7:13; 9:12; 10:1, 20, 27; and 11:10). This would lead us to suppose that Pharaoh lacked any freedom of will to make a choice in the matter, that he was simply a helpless pawn in the hands of almighty God. We might think that if we based our conclusion on these verses alone.

Yet other verses suggest a different conclusion. Exodus 8:15, 32 and 9:34 indicate that Pharaoh hardened his own heart. In the face of obvious miracles, the king chose deliberately to reject them.

Still other verses (8:19; 9:7, 35) simply state that his heart was hardened, leaving the conclusion ambiguous as to whether God hardened the king's heart or he did it of his own free will. Is there a logical solution to this apparent contradiction?

To begin, we must recognize that Pharaoh, like every one of us, possessed the freedom to make moral decisions. Whether he made right decisions or wrong decisions depended upon his understanding of the situation and the condition of his heart. Pharaoh knew very well the nature and results of the decisions that he was called upon to make. He knew that if he obeyed God's order to let the Israelites go, he would be losing a vast pool of free labor for the projects he wanted to build. He was unwilling to make this kind of sacrifice, and so he willfully rejected God's order.

We ourselves sometimes go through the same process. We know that certain habits are bad for our health. Yet we persist in them, convincing ourselves that the pleasures we derive from them outweigh the eventual consequences.

In what sense, though, can it be said that God hardened Pharaoh's heart? God did not act directly upon the king's heart and force him to make the wrong choice. Rather, God allowed the occasion that gave the evil inclination of Pharaoh's heart opportunity to be expressed in action. The action taken was the responsibility of Pharaoh, not God. We may express it another way. The rays of the sun that melt the wax harden the clay. The rays of the sun are exactly the same. The different responses are caused by the different natures of the substances upon which the rays fall. God by His nature does not deliberately tempt any of us. Yet the nature of the world in which we live is such that on occasion He must allow temptations to come our way. We make the decisions about how we handle them.

One of the tragic aspects of sin is that the innocent must suffer its consequences as well as the guilty. We may protest that this isn't fair, and, it isn't. That's what makes sin so evil!

B. Let Us Pray

Dear God and Father, we thank You that You watch over Your people from age to age. Through our Lord Jesus Christ, You have brought us out of our bondage to sin. May we walk in Your ways always, looking to the Scriptures as our infallible guide. In Jesus' name we pray. Amen.

C. Thought to Remember

"Let my people go, that they may serve me" (Exodus 8:1).

Home Daily Bible Readings

Monday, June 13—I Will Redeem You With Great Acts (Exodus 6:2-9)

Tuesday, June 14—Hebrews Asks Egyptians for Gold/Silver (Exodus 6:10-13; 11:1-3)

Wednesday, June 15—Preparations for Passover Meal (Exodus 12:1-6)

Thursday, June 16—The Lord Will Pass Over Israel's Homes (Exodus 12:7-13)

Friday, June 17—The "Passover" Is a Memorial Day (Exodus 12:14-20)

Saturday, June 18—Hebrews Saved; Egyptians Slain (Exodus 12:21-32)

Sunday, June 19—The Hebrews Despoiled the Egyptians (Exodus 12:33-39)

Learning by Doing

This page contains an alternate lesson plan emphasizing learning activities. Classes desiring such student involvement will find these suggestions helpful.

Learning Goals

In today's class session, the students should:

1. Review the story of Moses, Pharaoh, and the plagues God sent on Egypt to convince Pharaoh to release the Israelites.

2. Discuss implications of this story for believers today.

Into the Lesson

Begin today's class session by asking your students "What do you know about the story of Moses and Pharaoh?" Challenge each to write down on a slip of paper one fact that he or she knows about this story.

Collect the slips of paper, and then redistribute them to the class. Each member should read the statement he or she received and mark it either "True" or "False."

Collect the statements one more time and read them to the whole class. Help the group to see whether each of the statements is true or false.

Discuss with the class, "What can we learn from the story of Pharaoh and Moses?"

Into the Word

In the spirit of questions and quizzes with which you began today's session, conduct a brief "Ten Plagues Quiz" with the class. List each of the plagues on a different flash card and give each card to a different class member. Those ten class members are to come to the front of the class, hold the cards so the class can read them, and then arrange themselves so that the plagues are listed chronologically from the first through the tenth. If you wish, the whole class can help the ten card holders.

You may want to accomplish the same goal in the following manner: List the plagues in random order on your chalkboard and ask each class member to list them in the correct order on his own slip of paper. Then discuss the correct order of the plagues.

Read today's Scripture text aloud. Then conduct the following "Comments and Questions" discussion with the class. The following quotations are from the comments in the first lesson plan. Read the quotations (or ask a member to do so). Then discuss the questions after each one. (Both the quotations and the questions are in the student book, if you would like to make this a small-group activity.)

• "Moses had done God's bidding once and had failed. It would have been completely human for Moses to have been reluctant to try again what had already failed. Most of us have had experiences like this. On occasion we have done what we thought God wanted us to do, only to have our efforts collapse in our face. 'Once burned is twice wise,' we say. We'll not try that again."

What gives us resolve to keep on serving God, even when our efforts haven't seemed successful?

• "Pharaoh's stubbornness had brought great suffering to his people. If he had been isolated from any of the earlier plagues, he had to suffer this one along with his people. Many a modern dictator has followed a similar career, seeking power no matter what it has cost his people. For that matter, is there any area involving human relationships that has not felt the destructive force of someone's pursuit of selfish power?"

Share examples of ways that the lust for power can corrupt family life, work situations, or the work of a local church.

• "[Pharaoh] somehow convinced himself that the price he would have to pay would not be as great as the price of losing the slaves. We ourselves sometimes go through the same process. We know that certain habits are bad for our health. Yet we persist in them, convincing ourselves that the pleasures we derive from them outweigh the eventual consequences."

Why is this tendency so strong in us? Is it any different for Christians than non-Christians? How would you use the story of Pharaoh and Moses to convince a chronic sinner to reconsider his ways?

Into Life

Divide the class into groups of three and ask each member of each group to complete one or both of these sentences:

"One time when I saw God's answer to prayer after a very long wait—"

"One time when I saw the truth of God exposed publicly—"

In their small groups, some students may wish to share a request that they've been praying about for a very long time. Or they may be able to think of a way that God's truth needs to be exposed for all the world to see. Let them share either or both of these ideas and then pray together in their groups of three.

Let's Talk It Over

The questions on this page are designed to encourage review of the lesson Scriptures and to promote discussion of the lesson by the class. The answers provided are only discussion starters. Let your class talk it over from there.

1. Remembering His covenant with Abraham, Isaac, and Jacob, God acted with loving care and concern for their descendants, the children of Israel. How does recognizing God's faithfulness and compassion help us who are His people today face difficult situations?

One of the most precious promises given to Christians is that of God's presence and abiding love, even in the times of great difficulty and apparent defeat in this life (see Matthew 28:20; John 14:23; Romans 8:35-39). Our awareness that God cares for us restores hope in the face of calamity, supplies strength in the midst of troubles, preserves joy amid affliction, and strengthens trust in God's ultimate goodness. Consequently, our attitude can be one of optimism and hope, rather than discouragement and defeat.

2. Like Pharaoh, many persons resist the warning signs that personal disaster is about to strike, and they persist in failing to address a spiritual problem in their lives. What can be the consequences of such willful avoidance and procrastination? What changes should such a person make in his or her life to avoid those consequences?

If a person stubbornly refuses to address a problem in his or her life, that refusal may result in harm to himself and those he loves, broken relationships, and irretrievable loss. While there is yet time, such a person must be willing to admit wrong, seek and heed wise counsel, and read God's Word, allowing it to correct error in his or her life (Proverbs 15:31, 32; 2 Corinthians 7:9-11; 2 Timothy 3:16, 17).

3. Only complete obedience to God's instructions protected the Israelites when He brought death to the firstborn in Egypt. What can keep us from giving unreserved obedience to God? How can we as Christians develop hearts of resolute devotion to the will of God?

Peer pressure, greed, pride, selfish ambition, laziness, and physical desires are just a few of the things that become obstacles to our wholehearted obedience to God. All of these can have a powerful pull in our lives because they appeal to our sinful nature and its weaknesses. We must come to the realization that that which is physical and material in nature is temporary

and gives only momentary satisfaction. Only our relationship with God the Father through His Son Jesus Christ has lasting importance. By opening our hearts to God's Word and surrounding ourselves with those persons who are committed to Him we will be equipped to resist our sinful desires and fears, which impede our obedience to God.

4. God has granted to us, as He did Pharaoh, the freedom to make moral choices. What are some benefits that come to us when we choose to do what is right in God's sight? What measures can we take to enlarge our understanding of God's will and to increase our willingness to do it?

Pharaoh chose to disobey the commands of God, and as a result he and his people suffered destruction and death. Ultimately, disobedience to God can produce no other results. It is a different story, however, for the one who chooses to do what God has commanded. Such a person knows the peace and calm of a clear conscience in his daily life, the satisfaction of growth in character and maturity, the delight of pleasing God, and the strengthening of his relationship with God and often with others as well. And finally, that person will escape the eternal wrath of God that is reserved for those who persist in their disobedience. As we emphasize the disciplines of Bible reading and study, prayer, and meditation on spiritual matters, we will more readily discern God's will. As we down-play the role of possessions, power, and prestige in our lives, we will experience a greater desire and willingness to do His will.

5. The blood of the Passover lamb protected the Israelites from the judgment of death that God brought on Egypt. What is the meaning of Paul's statement that Christ is our passover sacrificed for us? (1 Corinthians 5:7). How should we respond to this fact?

The apostle Paul's statement proclaims that the blood of Christ, which was shed on the cross at Calvary, enables us who are sinners to escape eternal death, which our sins deserve. Such miraculous and undeserved salvation should cause us to love God with all of our being and to do all that He asks of us.

God Brings Victory

DEVOTIONAL READING: Exodus 15:22-27.

LESSON SCRIPTURE: Exodus 13:17—14:31.

PRINTED TEXT: Exodus 14:21-31.

Exodus 14:21-31

21 And Moses stretched out his hand over the sea; and the LORD caused the sea to go back by a strong east wind all that night, and made the sea dry land, and the waters were divided.

22 And the children of Israel went into the midst of the sea upon the dry ground: and the waters were a wall unto them on their right hand, and on their left.

23 And the Egyptians pursued, and went in after them to the midst of the sea, even all Pharaoh's horses, his chariots, and his horsemen.

24 And it came to pass, that in the morning watch the LORD looked unto the host of the Egyptians through the pillar of fire and of the cloud, and troubled the host of the Egyptians,

25 And took off their chariot wheels, that they drave them heavily: so that the Egyptians said, Let us flee from the face of Israel; for the LORD fighteth for them against the Egyptians.

26 And the LORD said unto Moses, Stretch out thine hand over the sea, that the waters may come again upon the Egyptians, upon their chariots, and upon their horsemen.

27 And Moses stretched forth his hand over the sea, and the sea returned to his strength when the morning appeared; and the Egyptians fled against it; and the LORD overthrew the Egyptians in the midst of the sea.

28 And the waters returned, and covered the chariots, and the horsemen, and all the host of Pharaoh that came into the sea after them; there remained not so much as one of them.

29 But the children of Israel walked upon dry land in the midst of the sea; and the waters were a wall unto them on their right hand, and on their left.

30 Thus the LORD saved Israel that day out of the hand of the Egyptians; and Israel saw the Egyptians dead upon the seashore.

31 And Israel saw that great work which the LORD did upon the Egyptians: and the people feared the LORD, and believed the LORD, and his servant Moses.

GOLDEN TEXT: The LORD saved Israel that day out of the hand of the Egyptians. . . . And Israel saw that great work which the LORD did upon the Egyptians: and the people feared the LORD, and believed the LORD, and his servant Moses.
—Exodus 14:30, 31.

God Redeems a People

Unit 1: Deliverance From Oppression

(Lessons 1-4)

Lesson Aims

As a result of studying this lesson, each student should:

1. Understand that God saved the Israelites from the Egyptians by a great miracle.

2. Realize that while God sometimes acts through mighty deeds, He does not always work in this way.

3. See in God's miraculous rescue of the Israelites His involvement in this world and His concern for His people.

4. Develop a deeper faith in God.

Lesson Outline

INTRODUCTION
    A. Love and Judgment
    B. Lesson Background
  I. PROVISION BY GOD (Exodus 14:21, 22)
    A. Divine Passageway (v. 21)
    B. Dry Land (v. 22)
      "Sail On!"
  II. PURSUIT BY THE EGYPTIANS (EXODUS 14:23-25)
    A. Headlong Rush Into the Sea (v. 23)
    B. Trouble (v. 24)
    C. Panic (v. 25)
III. PUNISHMENT OF THE ENEMY (Exodus 14:26-28)
    A. Divine Directive (v. 26)
    B. Destruction (vv. 27, 28)
      Escape Versus Entrapment
IV. EPILOGUE (Exodus 14:29-31)
    A. Salvation for Israel (vv. 29, 30)
    B. Faith Strengthened (v. 31)
CONCLUSION
    A. God Specializes in the Impossible
    B. Let Us Pray
    C. Thought to Remember

Display visual 4 of the visuals packet throughout this session. This visual is shown on page 372.

Introduction

A. Love and Judgment

A Christian family decided to spend an evening watching a video of the classic movie *The Ten Commandments*. Because of the nature of the movie, even the preschool daughter was allowed to stay up and watch. While she didn't understand much of the plot, she understood what was happening when Pharaoh's army had the Israelites trapped against the Red Sea ready to annihilate them. "Doesn't God love the Israelites? Can't He save them?" she cried out. Then the problem was solved as the waters were parted and the Israelites were able to cross over on dry land. The little girl clapped for joy when she realized what had happened. Then the sea closed in upon the Egyptians, and they were dramatically destroyed. Now the girl had another problem. "Doesn't God love the Egyptians?" she asked.

Innocent children have a way of asking profound questions. If we reply, "Yes, God loved the Egyptians," the next question will be, "Then why did He destroy them?" There are no simple answers that will satisfy either a five-year-old or a learned philosopher. Some things we just have to accept on faith. We believe that God watches over the destiny of nations, showering blessings upon them. We believe also that He holds every nation accountable before the bar of justice. A nation may conduct itself in such a way that it fills its cup of wrath. When that time comes, judgment is poured out upon it. For generations the Egyptians had brutally mistreated the Israelites. Now the time of judgment had come. The Egyptian army was destroyed, not because God hated the people, but because justice demanded punishment.

On the other side of the sea was another scene, a scene of victory. The Israelites could rejoice, not just because their enemies were destroyed, but more important because they had been spared a dreadful fate. Their feeble faith had been stirred, and they would begin to believe God's messengers. Many times in the future they would doubt and their faith would waver, but they never forgot this experience at the Red Sea.

B. Lesson Background

When Pharaoh realized the magnitude of the loss of life suffered by the Egyptians as a result of the tenth plague pronounced by Moses, he was gripped by fear and thrust Israel from the land. The Israelites were dressed for travel, having observed Moses' command for the eating of the Passover meal (Exodus 12:11). Thus, when the word came there was no delay—the children of Israel left the land of Egypt in haste.

The most direct route from Goshen to Palestine was across the corridor of land that bordered the Mediterranean Sea, a distance of no more than one hundred and fifty miles. But there was a problem in taking this route. The Philistines had entered southern Palestine and had made some settlements in the area where Israel would have had to go. The Philistines, though not nearly as numerous as the Israelites, were a powerful and warlike people. Rather than bring Israel into direct confrontation with the Philistines, God directed them southward along the Red Sea (Exodus 13:21).

Scholars debate the exact route they took. Over the centuries the topography of the shifting desert sands have so changed that there is no way that we today can trace the route with certainty. The route took them by the sea and placed them in a precarious position when Pharaoh changed his mind and set out with his army to bring them back. When the Israelites saw the pursuing Egyptians, they went into a panic. They immediately blamed Moses, feeling quite certain they would perish there.

Moses tried to reassure them that God would fight for them, but calming a terrified, undisciplined multitude was not an easy task. God then instructed Moses to speak to the people "that they go forward." This may be good advice for us in time of crisis: act, don't argue.

I. Provision by God
(Exodus 14:21, 22)

As we have explained, God did not choose the shortest and most obvious route for the Israelites to take to the promised land. Instead, He led them southward into difficult terrain where they could readily be trapped if Pharaoh chose to pursue them. It may have been that God made the Israelites appear to be leaderless and in total disarray. Perhaps their actions caused Pharaoh to think that they could readily be rounded up and herded back to Goshen. The king couldn't resist the temptation. God used the situation to harden Pharaoh's heart (14:8), and so he set after them in full pursuit with his foot soldiers and six hundred chariots leading the way. With such a formidable force coming after them, the Israelites had good reason to fear.

God did not leave the Israelites completely helpless, however. The "angel of God," which had gone ahead of them, moved between them and the Egyptians, and the pillar of cloud that had guided them moved behind them, separating them from the advancing army. The pillar gave light to the Israelites but darkness to the Egyptians who had to halt their charge (14:19, 20).

A. Divine Passageway (v. 21)

21. And Moses stretched out his hand over the sea; and the LORD caused the sea to go back by a strong east wind all that night, and made the sea dry land, and the waters were divided.

> **How to Say It**
>
> PHILISTINES.   Fi-*liss*-teens or *Fil*-iss-teens.

With the approach of the Egyptian troops, Moses had been given instructions about how to handle the situation (14:16). Now the time had come for him to carry out the instructions. *Moses stretched out his hand over the sea*, and immediately God caused *a strong east wind* to move the water aside and dry the bottom of the sea.

The reference to the east wind causes various commentators to note that the purpose of God was accomplished by use of a natural phenomenon. Indeed, it must be acknowledged that God has used natural forces to accomplish His purposes. Yet obviously in this case His use of the wind was beyond the ordinary. What occurred was miraculous. A further indication of this was the timing involved. It was only after Moses *stretched out his hand over the sea*, in response to God's command, that the wind began to blow. Therefore, we do not need to ask ourselves how it was possible for the wind to divide the waters. In the words of the psalmist who sang about this event, "The waters saw thee, O God, the waters saw thee; they were afraid" (Psalm 77:16).

B. Dry Land (v. 22)

22. And the children of Israel went into the midst of the sea upon the dry ground: and the waters were a wall unto them on their right hand, and on their left.

The blowing of the wind not only separated the waters, but it also dried the bottom of the sea, which made it possible for the Israelites to walk across the seabed. We can only guess how wide the passageway through the sea was or how wide the sea was at this point. Under normal marching conditions, a trained army can cover about three miles an hour. If the sea had been about five miles wide at this point, a trained army would cross in about an hour and a half. But the Israelites were not a trained army, so they probably wouldn't have moved that quickly. Estimates as to their number range from two to three million. Among them were old people and small children who would have slowed the pace. The cattle would have been further cause for a somewhat slow pace. The safe channel through the sea must have been hundreds of feet wide or wider to accommodate such a group. So several hours in the early part of the night would have been required for the entire throng to cross over the sea.

"SAIL ON!"

There is a place in the Hudson River where, as you sail, you seem to be entirely hemmed in with hills. The boat drives on toward a rocky wall, and it seems as if it must either turn back or be dashed to pieces. But if you have the courage to sail on you will find that, just as you come within the shadow of the great rocky cliff, an opening suddenly appears, and the boat can pass into one of the grandest bays on the river.

Imagine the scene as the Israelites were caught between the Egyptians and the sea. There appeared to be no way forward. They feared that they would have to turn back and submit. But Moses urged them on. Suddenly an opening appeared—the waters parted. More than two million men, women, and children, and flocks and herds of animals, plunged into the passageway, with walls of frothing water on each side of them; a howling wind; the glow of the pillar of fire; the threat of Pharaoh's horses and chariots behind them. The epistle to the Hebrews says, "By faith they passed through the Red sea as by dry land" (11:29). Truly it must have taken great faith.

Our faith, too, is often challenged to venture on perilous paths. The picture of Israel's crossing the sea carries eternal truth for us all. The way of safety may not open till we are hemmed in and Pharaoh's chariots are almost upon us. Faith often leads into the very thick of what we think at first are perils.

II. Pursuit by the Egyptians (Exodus 14:23-25)

A. Headlong Rush Into the Sea (v. 23)

23. And the Egyptians pursued, and went in after them to the midst of the sea, even all Pharaoh's horses, his chariots, and his horsemen.

The pillar of cloud that separated the Israelites from the Egyptians during the night provided light for Israel's safe passage while enshrouding Pharaoh's army in unnatural darkness. Seemingly, when the last of the Israelites had entered the channel and left its western end vacant, the cloud withdrew with them. It seems that this permitted enough pre-dawn light to reveal to the Egyptians what had happened, and they immediately plunged into the midst of the sea after the Israelites. An intelligent tactic would have been to wait and send out scouts to investigate this strange phenomenon. Pharaoh's heart was hardened, however, and he was determined to recapture the Israelites. And since he gave the orders, the troops had little choice but to obey.

visual 4

B. Trouble (v. 24)

24. And it came to pass, that in the morning watch the LORD looked unto the host of the Egyptians through the pillar of fire and of the cloud, and troubled the host of the Egyptians.

In the morning watch. The morning watch extended from 2:00 A.M. until sunrise, which occurred at about 6:00 A.M. Apparently it was near the end of this period, immediately before sunrise, that God *looked unto* Pharaoh's army and *troubled the host of the Egyptians.* This may suggest that strange phenomena associated with the moving pillar created panic among the Egyptians and threw them into confusion. The six hundred chariots, all attempting to advance at once, may have gotten in each other's way and become entangled.

C. Panic (v. 25)

25. And took off their chariot wheels, that they drave them heavily: so that the Egyptians said, Let us flee from the face of Israel; for the LORD fighteth for them against the Egyptians.

Soon Pharaoh's charioteers had worse problems. God caused the wheels to come off their chariots, making it almost impossible for the horses to pull them. The *Revised Standard Version* has "clogging their chariot wheels." Perhaps the wheels sank in the sandy sea bottom and became clogged and were broken off. Faced by these unexpected circumstances, it did not take the Egyptian soldiers long to understand the real problem: God was fighting against the Egyptians. They wanted nothing to do with a fight against a divine enemy and they made a very logical decision: "Let's get out of here!" The problem was that by the time their decision was made it was too late.

III. Punishment of the Enemy (Exodus 14:26-28)

A. Divine Directive (v. 26)

26. And the LORD said unto Moses, Stretch out thine hand over the sea, that the waters may come again upon the Egyptians, upon their chariots, and upon their horsemen.

The Egyptian host had pursued the Israelites far into the sea. Then the wheels of their chariots had come off, broken, or become mired in the sandy sea bottom. At this point, God was ready to bring His judgment upon them. By now the Israelites were safely on the eastern shore, so God told Moses to stretch out his hand over the sea so it would resume its natural state.

B. Destruction (vv. 27, 28)

27, 28. And Moses stretched forth his hand over the sea, and the sea returned to his strength when the morning appeared; and the Egyptians fled against it; and the LORD overthrew the Egyptians in the midst of the sea. And the waters returned, and covered the chariots, and the horsemen, and all the host of Pharaoh that came into the sea after them; there remained not so much as one of them.

Morning appeared, and this particular morning brought with it the close of a long, dark period of Israel's bondage in Egypt and the dawn of a new day of freedom and nationhood under the leadership of God. At God's command, Moses stretched out his hand over the sea, and as he did so, the waters began to flow back over the channel that had been opened up. The chariots of the Egyptians could not carry them to safety, and the onrushing waters swept them into the sea, and they all drowned. Their arrogance had doomed them.

Had the opening of the sea been a natural phenomenon, the waters would have returned more slowly, giving some of the Egyptians a chance to escape. But this was the work of God's mighty hand, and it happened so swiftly that none was able to escape.

From time to time archaeologists and others have attempted to find remains of this catastrophe, but after more than three thousand years we would hardly expect to find any recognizable evidence of this great defeat. But even though there is no physical evidence for this great event, it remained indelibly burned into the memories of the Israelites. Throughout the rest of their history they never forgot it, and it is mentioned again and again in their later writings.

ESCAPE VERSUS ENTRAPMENT

In 1952 the "Black Storm," a hurricane packing winds of over two hundred miles per hour, raked all the south shore of the island of Jamaica in the West Indies. Twenty-two inches of rain fell on the island in a period of twenty-four hours.

Every stream became a torrent. The Rio Cobre, usually a placid stream, became a raging instrument of death. It funneled fifty-two feet of water through its narrow canyon, tearing away homes, bridges, and anything else in its path. In the hours before midnight, preceding the full fury of the storm, the canyon was an escape route for people fleeing to higher ground. Within two and one-half hours after the torrential rain began, what had been a road to safety became a death-dealing monster. No one knows how many persons were swept away and drowned when the high wall of water made its unrelenting rush toward the sea.

Israel, under the command of God, walked through the Red Sea on dry land. When Egypt's army followed, Israel's divine way of escape and life suddenly became an engulfing flood. If we walk with the Lord in our journey through this life, we can have assurance that He will bring us through death to life eternal. Those, however, who make the same journey without Him are in grave peril. Are you walking life's ways alone or with Him?   —W. P.

IV. Epilogue
(Exodus 14:29-31)

A. Salvation for Israel (vv. 29, 30)

29. But the children of Israel walked upon dry land in the midst of the sea; and the waters were a wall unto them on their right hand, and on their left.

This summary statement is given to show the sharp distinction between the fate of the Israelites and the Egyptian host. What was a way of escape for the Israelites became a fatal trap for the Egyptians. The *dry land* on which the Israelites walked to freedom became a snare for the heavier chariots of Pharaoh. The *waters* that *were a wall* on either side of the Israelites and that created a channel for their safe crossing of the sea became the instrument for the annihilation of their enemy.

30. Thus the LORD saved Israel that day out of the hand of the Egyptians; and Israel saw the Egyptians dead upon the seashore.

None among the Israelites could doubt that the protecting hand of God was upon them. Their previous fears and distrust of Moses should have been laid aside for good. The bodies of the dead Egyptians washed upon the shore provided further evidence of this great miracle by which they gained their freedom.

B. Faith Strengthened (v. 31)

31. And Israel saw that great work which the LORD did upon the Egyptians: and the people feared the LORD, and believed the LORD, and his servant Moses.

Seeing is believing, and Israel certainly had plenty of evidence to convince them that God had worked a great miracle that day. Not only did they believe God, they believed Moses—for a time. Within weeks, however, they were rebelling against God and rejecting Moses' leadership. For the most part, the faith of the Israelites was strong only when the physical evidence to support it was abundant. When such evidence was not present, their faith began to waver and soon turned to open rebellion.

Conclusion

A. God Specializes in the Impossible

"Got any rivers you think are uncrossable? Got any mountains you can't tunnel through?" These words from a chorus that we used to sing conclude with the thought that God specializes in the impossible. The Israelites, who had witnessed the ten plagues and then the destruction of Pharaoh's army in the Red Sea, would have no trouble believing the words of this song. In the months that followed they would have further opportunity to see evidences of God's power at work in their lives.

In this demonstration of God's power, Israel could see His judgment against the Egyptians for all the atrocities they had committed against them. They could also see God as a deliverer, a God who was concerned for them in their time of troubles. This understanding of God gave them the faith and courage to face the many trials that lay ahead of them. No matter how difficult a situation might seem, they could believe that God would intervene in a dramatic way to rescue them.

There are dangers, however, in such a position. Persons or nations who expect God to rescue them every time they get into a difficult situation may be tempted to take unnecessary moral and physical risks. Later on, the Israelites fell into this trap. Their sinfulness led them to stray from God and His teachings. Then they expected God to step in at the last minute and rescue them. Sometimes He did, in spite of the fact that they had brought their problems upon themselves. But there were times that He didn't, leaving them to suffer the fate that they so properly deserved.

The Israelites had to learn that God does not always work in obvious and dramatic ways. Sometimes He works slowly and quietly through the minds of people to achieve His purposes. At other times He may marshal the forces of providence to gain His ends. When God works in this fashion, the persons involved are usually not even aware that He is at work. Only as they look back after months or even years can they see the hand of God in what has happened.

We who live today are not likely to experience anything as dramatic as a miraculous crossing of the Red Sea. But because it did happen to the Israelites, we can know that God is a God of power, that He is involved in our world and is concerned about His people. On many other occasions God intervened in the history of the Hebrew people to protect and guide them, as He prepared them to receive the Messiah who would bless the whole world.

God's miraculous dealings with mankind have been relatively rare. Far more often He has worked through the Scriptures to reveal knowledge of His will and to sensitize the consciences of people to do His will. Through other modes of revelation He has made known His will, and He has inspired His spokesmen to pronounce that will to others.

It is good to know that God has performed great and mighty acts in the past and that He can still do so if He chooses. It is reassuring to know that God is all-powerful. But it is also comforting to know that He can and does work in our lives every day without vast displays of power.

B. Let Us Pray

Almighty God, we recognize that You are the Creator and Controller of the universe. We praise You because of Your great power. We thank You that Your power is available to guide and protect us. May we learn to trust You to provide all that we need for our journey through this life and our safe arrival on the Heavenly shores. In the name of our Master we pray. Amen.

C. Thought to Remember

Faith is kept strong by walking daily with God, not by observing miraculous deeds.

Home Daily Bible Readings

Monday, June 20—Passover: "Night of Watching" (Exodus 12:40-51)
Tuesday, June 21—Consecration of Israel's Firstborn: Man/Beast (Exodus 13:1-10)
Wednesday, June 22—Ask: "What Does This Mean?" (Exodus 13:11-16)
Thursday, June 23—God Led Israel by Cloud and Fire (Exodus 13:17-22)
Friday, June 24—Fear Not, Stand Firm, See Salvation (Exodus 14:10-20)
Saturday, June 25—Israel Walked on Dry Land (Exodus 14:21-31)
Sunday, June 26—Moses and Miriam Sing and Dance in Praise to God (Exodus 15:1-21)

Learning by Doing

This page contains an alternate lesson plan emphasizing learning activities. Classes desiring such student involvement will find these suggestions helpful.

Learning Goals

Today's session will help students to:

1. Review the account of Israel's crossing of the Red Sea to escape from the Egyptians.

2. Reflect on the "Red Sea experiences" in their lives and their personal trust in God in those trials.

Into the Lesson

Begin today's session with a discussion about traveling. Many people travel in the summer, so this is an appropriate time to remember the good things and the bad things about going on a trip. Here are a few questions you could use:

1. Of all the things you must do to get ready for a trip, which do you dislike the most?

2. What is the one thing you're most likely to forget or overlook?

3. Think of a trip you anticipated more than any other. Share the circumstances with the class and tell why the trip was so special.

4. Have you ever dreaded a trip? Why?

Tell class members that today's lesson involves the most important trip that one generation of Israelites would ever take. It was a trip that they probably anticipated and dreaded.

Into the Word

Continue the idea of anticipation and dread as you share the background for this lesson. Why would the Israelites look forward to leaving Egypt? In what sense might they dread it?

The event in today's text is one of the most dramatic in all of Scripture. You may want to choose a special and dramatic way to retell it. For example, you could play a videotape of the classic movie *The Ten Commandments*. Instead of reading today's Scripture text, show a brief portion of the movie, including the portrayal of the dividing of the sea and the escape on dry ground. You might give most of your class period to showing a portion of the video.

If you can obtain an audio tape of this portion of the Bible, play Exodus 14:5-31. Before you play the tape, instruct class members to listen for:

"Something I discovered for the first time about this event,"

"Something about this event that surprises me,"

"Something about this event that inspires me,"

"Something in this account that teaches a lesson for life today."

After students have heard the text read, give them the following scrambled list of elements of the account. (Omit the numbers in parentheses, which indicate the correct order of these sentences.) Have students work in pairs to put the elements in the correct order.

(6) "Tell the Israelites to go forward."

(3) The Egyptian army overtook the Israelites as they camped near the sea.

(4) "Why did you bring us out of Egypt? We'll die in the desert!"

(2) Pharaoh ordered all the chariots of Egypt to pursue the Israelites.

(14) Seeing the Egyptians lying dead on the shore, the Israelites put their trust in the Lord.

(1) Pharaoh changed his mind about letting the Israelites go.

(8) With a nightlong east wind God divided the waters.

(12) At daybreak Moses stretched his hand back over the sea.

(5) "Stand firm and you'll see the deliverance of the Lord."

(10) God caused a problem for the wheels of the Egyptian chariots.

(13) The entire army of Pharaoh was swallowed in the sea.

(9) The Israelites went through the sea on dry ground.

(7) The pillar of cloud stood between the Israelites and the Egyptians.

(11) "The Lord is fighting for the Israelites against Egypt."

Into Life

Use the following discussion questions to help students discover implications of this event for their lives.

1. What do you make of the plea of the people in verses 11 and 12? Why should they have displayed more faith than this? (Consider the ten plagues.) How did Moses respond to them? How did God respond?

Have you ever been frightened by some enemy? How may this account prepare you to face such fears in the future?

2. What would you label as a "Red Sea experience" in your life? How did God help you get through the trial "on dry land"? What did you learn about trusting God? What did you learn about coping with fear?

Let's Talk It Over

The questions on this page are designed to encourage review of the lesson Scriptures and to promote discussion of the lesson by the class. The answers provided are only discussion starters. Let your class talk it over from there.

1. Why was the plight of Israel at the Red Sea a great trial for their faith?

From a human standpoint Israel's situation seemed hopeless. They were hemmed in by the Red Sea in front of them and the army of Egypt behind them. They had to choose between meekly surrendering to Pharaoh or placing themselves in God's care, not knowing exactly how He would save them.

2. After the waters of the Red Sea parted, creating a passageway through which Israel could walk, did it require faith for Israel to step out onto the dry seabed? Explain.

Yes. When they started they did not know (a) how long it would be before the waters returned, perhaps trapping them, and (b) whether the waters would return in time to protect them from the Egyptians. They had to trust.

3. Often we are seized by panic and fear when faced with an impossible situation, just as the Israelites were when sandwiched between the approaching Egyptian army and the Red Sea. In such circumstances how can we move from fear to faith? What can be the advantages of having confidence in God to work things out?

Faith can overcome fear when we fix our eyes on the Lord, seek His help, and remember His unchanging nature and faithfulness. Recalling the Biblical accounts of the triumphs of God's people, and remembering the testimony of other Christians who have faced similar predicaments, will give us encouragement to trust in God's care for us (Psalm 34:15; Hebrews 12:1-3). As we nurture our trust and confidence in God, we will maintain purpose for the present and hope for the future.

4. Although the Egyptians were powerful, they were not victorious over Israel. What does this remind us about human resources? What effect should this awareness have on our approach to personal skills, goals, and attitudes at home and on the job?

Human resources are frail and fragile, and human strength can quickly slip away. If we depend solely upon our own strength, abilities, and ingenuity, we can falter and fail. This realization should cause us to place our trust in God, not in ourselves, and to avoid excessive pride in our accomplishments. Such an attitude of humility will keep us from being overbearing or oppressive toward family, friends, and co-workers, and will lead us to honor God in what we do.

5. Although God already had demonstrated His power in the ten plagues and had proved His resolve to deliver His people, Pharaoh persisted in hardening his heart and in fighting God. Pharaoh's obstinacy led to his humiliation and destruction. How may we harden our hearts toward God and others? What can be the effects of resisting God in our lives?

A person may harden his or her heart by persisting in ungodly attitudes and actions. Some of these are selfishness, pride, a refusal to forgive, a failure to listen, a compulsion to control, and the clinging to unrighteous habits. The consequences of such behavior can be hurt, disgrace, dishonor, brokenness, loneliness, and even physical and spiritual death.

6. The Hebrews should have realized after the Red Sea crossing that their departure from Egypt was an irreversible decision. Why do Christians need to give more thought to making irreversible decisions in serving Christ?

So many of the spiritual commitments that church members make prove to be rather half-hearted and conditional. We may decide to accept a teaching position, but when we discover how much preparation time it requires, we want to back out. We promise to do some evangelistic calling, but when we have a door or two close in our faces, we want to quit. We accept a membership on a committee, but we find that some of the committee's decisions stir up criticism, and we are not willing to endure such "heat." The church's endeavors are thereby crippled by positions left unoccupied and tasks left undone. One recalls the description of our Lord in Luke 9:51: "As the time approached for him to be taken up to heaven, Jesus resolutely set out for Jerusalem" (*New International Version*). The church is in dire need of workers who will follow their Master's example in irreversibly committing themselves to the completion of their God-given mission.

Bread From Heaven

DEVOTIONAL READING: Exodus 17:1-13.

LESSON SCRIPTURE: Exodus 16.

PRINTED TEXT: Exodus 16:2-7, 13-18.

Exodus 16:2-7, 13-18

2 And the whole congregation of the children of Israel murmured against Moses and Aaron in the wilderness:

3 And the children of Israel said unto them, Would to God we had died by the hand of the LORD in the land of Egypt, when we sat by the fleshpots, and when we did eat bread to the full; for ye have brought us forth into this wilderness, to kill this whole assembly with hunger.

4 Then said the LORD unto Moses, Behold, I will rain bread from heaven for you; and the people shall go out and gather a certain rate every day, that I may prove them, whether they will walk in my law, or no.

5 And it shall come to pass, that on the sixth day they shall prepare that which they bring in; and it shall be twice as much as they gather daily.

6 And Moses and Aaron said unto all the children of Israel, At even, then ye shall know that the LORD hath brought you out from the land of Egypt:

7 And in the morning, then ye shall see the glory of the LORD; for that he heareth your murmurings against the LORD: and what are we, that ye murmur against us?

. . . .

13 And it came to pass, that at even the quails came up, and covered the camp: and in the morning the dew lay round about the host.

14 And when the dew that lay was gone up, behold, upon the face of the wilderness there lay a small round thing, as small as the hoar frost on the ground.

15 And when the children of Israel saw it, they said one to another, It is manna: for they wist not what it was. And Moses said unto them, This is the bread which the LORD hath given you to eat.

16 This is the thing which the LORD hath commanded, Gather of it every man according to his eating, an omer for every man, according to the number of your persons; take ye every man for them which are in his tents.

17 And the children of Israel did so, and gathered, some more, some less.

18 And when they did mete it with an omer, he that gathered much had nothing over, and he that gathered little had no lack; they gathered every man according to his eating.

GOLDEN TEXT: I will rain bread from heaven for you; and the people shall go out and gather a certain rate every day, that I may prove them, whether they will walk in my law, or no.—Exodus 16:4.

God Redeems People

Unit 2: Provision for Present

and Future (Lessons 5-9)

Lesson Aims

As a result of studying this lesson, students should:

1. Understand how God provided food for the Israelites in the wilderness.

2. Be less inclined to complain about adverse conditions in which they find themselves.

3. Be less tempted to amass more material possessions than they need or can use.

4. Be convinced to trust God for the necessities of life.

Lesson Outline

INTRODUCTION

    A. Ever Been Hungry?

    B. Lesson Background

  I. ISRAEL COMPLAINS (Exodus 16:2, 3)

 II. GOD PROMISES BREAD (Exodus 16:4-7)

    A. Test of Obedience (v. 4)

       Daily Bread

    B. Double Portion (v. 5)

    C. Double Manifestation (vv. 6, 7)

III. GOD PROVIDES FOR HIS PEOPLE (Exodus 16:13-18)

    A. Quail in the Evening (v. 13)

    B. Bread in the Morning (vv. 14, 15)

    C. Gathering the Bread (vv. 16-18)

       Enough

CONCLUSION

    A. Learning to Trust

    B. Learning to Obey

    C. Let Us Pray

    D. Thought to Remember

Display visual 5 of the visuals packet throughout this session. The visual is shown on page 379.

Introduction

A. Ever Been Hungry?

Have you ever been hungry, really hungry, when no food was available, and there were no prospects that any food would be available? While there are places in the world where this is a continuing problem, probably most of us in our nation have never faced this kind of a bleak situation. Since this is true, we are not likely to feel greatly sympathetic with the Israelites in the

wilderness as they came face to face with this reality. We notice only their complaining.

When the events we are studying in this lesson took place, the Israelites had been in the wilderness about a month. That was long enough for the poorest among them to exhaust the food they had brought with them from Egypt. To the rest it was clear by now that in the barren wilderness upon which they had entered they must eventually succumb to starvation when all their cattle had been eaten up or had died from lack of nourishment. So they were facing reality, and they began to murmur. The fact that God heard their complaining and provided food is proof enough that their problem was real. Their offense was not that they were complaining about a minor problem or one that they simply imagined. Rather, it lay in their lack of faith in God. They did not trust Him to provide a solution to the problem. This lesson should remind us that we at times are like those Israelites in this regard. We don't trust God enough to believe that He will provide answers to our problems—or we don't trust Him enough to believe that He will answer them His way, not ours.

B. Lesson Background

A month had passed since Israel had left Egypt (see Exodus 16:1; Numbers 33:3). Their campsites along the way are listed in Numbers 33:5-11. Numerous attempts have been made to identify these sites, but there is no general agreement as to their exact location. The Bible does not give a detailed description of them.

We are told of only a few of the events that occurred after the Israelites left the eastern shore of the Red Sea. They moved into the wilderness of Shur and went three days without finding water. They found water at Marah, but they could not drink the water because it was bitter, and so they began to murmur. God instructed Moses to cut down a certain tree and throw it into the water. When he followed the instructions, the water was miraculously sweetened (Exodus 15:22-25). Later they came to Elim, where there were twelve wells, or springs, and seventy palm trees, a pleasant site for camping indeed. From Elim the Israelites moved into the wilderness of Sin, where today's lesson begins.

I. Israel Complains
(Exodus 16:2, 3)

2, 3. And the whole congregation of the children of Israel murmured against Moses and Aaron in the wilderness: and the children of Israel said unto them, Would to God we had died by the hand of the LORD in the land of Egypt,

when we sat by the fleshpots, and when we did eat bread to the full; for ye have brought us forth into this wilderness, to kill this whole assembly with hunger.

The Israelites had brought some food with them from Egypt, and they had milk and meat from their flocks and herds. They had also brought gold and jewelry with them, but as yet they had not established relations with any desert tribe so that they could buy food from them. As we have already indicated, some had not brought as much as others, and they were probably beginning to experience want. They would be the first to complain, but others, anticipating that they would soon be in the same situation, no doubt joined in the choruses of complaint.

The Israelites blamed Moses and Aaron, rather than God, for their predicament. Their two leaders were visible and available, while God's presence was not so immediately obvious. Anyone who would be a leader in the church must, like Moses, learn to accept complaints from the people.

The people emphasized their complaint by indicating that they wished they had died in Egypt rather than having gone through all the hardships of leaving Egypt only to starve in the wilderness. Whether or not they really felt this way is impossible for us to know. By making the statement, however, they got Moses' attention. In Egypt, they insisted, they had plenty of meat and were able to eat bread until they were stuffed. They exaggerated how good their situation had been in Egypt. If they had been so happy there, why had their complaints gone up continually to God? (Exodus 3:7). How unreasonable was their complaint! Do not people behave in a similar way today when they are dissatisfied with the present situation? How typical it is to magnify the bad points of the present circumstances and to remember the good of the past, while forgetting its drawbacks.

II. God Promises Bread
(Exodus 16:4-7)
A. Test of Obedience (v. 4)

4. Then said the LORD unto Moses, Behold, I will rain bread from heaven for you; and the people shall go out and gather a certain rate every day, that I may prove them, whether they will walk in my law, or no.

At the critical moment God intervened and revealed to Moses that the problem the people were facing would be resolved. God would send *bread from heaven*. The word *bread* sometimes refers to any kind of food. Here it refers specifically to the small pieces of food that God was going to pro-

visual 5

vide for the people's sustenance during their stay in the wilderness. The Israelites came to call it "manna" (v. 15). It came *from heaven*, first in the sense that it came from the surrounding atmosphere, and second because it came miraculously from God, who resides in Heaven.

The people were to gather *a certain rate* of the manna each day. The *Revised Standard Version* renders this "gather a day's portion"; the *New International Version* has, "gather enough for that day." They were not to be greedy and gather too much, nor were they to be lazy and not gather enough. Every day they were to gather enough for that day only. The rules God attached to this gift would *prove* the Israelites, that is, be a test of their obedience day by day. He desired to create in the people habits of obedience, for soon He would give them the law at Mount Sinai. Their obedience or disobedience to that law would determine their future course as a nation.

DAILY BREAD

A young married couple attending Bible college in the 1940s provided this testimony: "We were at the end of our money, food, and in one more week, housing. Jobs were hard to find, and Bill got the flu and missed a week of work. We ate our last oatmeal with coffee because we had no milk. On the shelf in our one and one-half room apartment was exactly three cents.

"We thanked the Lord for our oatmeal and coffee and asked Him to somehow multiply our three cents. That afternoon Bill's boss said there was work for him beginning the next week. That was good news! In the early evening we were visited by a friend who owed us five dollars for a radio we had sold him on the promise that he would pay later. He gave Bill the five dollars, and that provided food for a week. Back at work the following week, Bill earned enough for our rent. God did multiply our three cents!

"Never again were we that close to having nothing. We learned that 'daily bread' was enough, and we have never forgotten that lesson."

Israel was hungry, and God gave them manna—not a week or a month's supply, just daily bread! Do we trust Him enough to be satisfied day by day with His provision for our needs? Bread from Heaven given in daily portions challenges us to believe that God can supply. Trust Him. His promises are reliable. —W. P.

B. Double Portion (v. 5)

5. And it shall come to pass, that on the sixth day they shall prepare that which they bring in; and it shall be twice as much as they gather daily.

The Israelites were instructed to gather enough of the manna for each person each day. *On the sixth day* they were to bring in *twice as much* so that they would not have to gather any on the seventh day. The Israelites had not yet reached Mount Sinai, so the law with its Sabbath-keeping regulations had not yet been given. The practice of gathering the manna only on six days was established in order to prepare them for the Sabbath when the law was given.

C. Double Manifestation (vv. 6, 7)

6, 7. And Moses and Aaron said unto all the children of Israel, At even, then ye shall know that the LORD hath brought you out from the land of Egypt: and in the morning, then ye shall see the glory of the LORD; for that he heareth your murmurings against the LORD: and what are we, that ye murmur against us?

Once Moses had received word from God, he and Aaron addressed the complaining people. In the evening they would see evidence that God had brought them out of Egypt. As we learn in verses that follow, this evidence was the flight of quail that descended upon their camp, providing them meat.

In the morning they would see God's glory. Some Bible students believe that this is a reference to the visible appearance described in verse 10. We are not told exactly what this manifestation of God was, but perhaps it was a brilliant cloud that appeared in an otherwise clear sky. This particular evidence of the Lord's presence is not to be confused with the pillar of cloud and the pillar of fire that guided the Israelites on their journey.

Other Bible students, however, believe that God's glory *in the morning* is a reference to the fall of the manna. They call attention to the balance of the two clauses in verses 6 and 7, and feel that two similar manifestations of God's presence and power are implied thereby. The first of these manifestations (the quail) would occur at evening, followed by the one in the morning (the manna). The manifestation mentioned in verse 10, they point out, preceded the coming of the quails; it did not follow it.

Finally Moses chided the people for blaming him and Aaron for their hunger and made it clear that they were really murmuring against God when they blamed God's representatives for their plight.

> ### How to Say It
>
> BDELLIUM. *del*-e-um.
> ELIM. *Ee*-lim.
> EPHAH. *ee*-fah.
> MARAH. *May*-rah.
> SINAI. *Sye*-nay-eye or *Sye*-nye.

III. God Provides for His People (Exodus 16:13-18)

A. Quail in the Evening (v. 13)

13. And it came to pass, that at even the quails came up, and covered the camp: and in the morning the dew lay round about the host.

The Israelites had longed for the fleshpots of Egypt. Now God answered that longing with a huge flock of *quails* that settled on the camp. This bird was a native of the Mediterranean area, and is not to be confused with the North American bobwhite. In the spring it migrated from the interior of Africa across the Sinai Peninsula and along the eastern Mediterranean coast into southern Europe. This route would take the quails over the route traveled by the Israelites. Some, seeking a naturalistic explanation of this event, suggest that the quails were exhausted by their flight over the Gulf of Suez and settled for rest in the Israelite camp, where they could be easily captured. Even if this is an adequate explanation of their arrival, the time of their arrival, coinciding precisely with Moses' announcement, shows God's controlling hand in this event.

B. Bread in the Morning (vv. 14, 15)

14. And when the dew that lay was gone up, behold, upon the face of the wilderness there lay a small round thing, as small as the hoar frost on the ground.

When the dew evaporated in the morning, the substance that had been promised by God was lying on the ground. The Bible does not provide us an exact description of it, so we can only guess as to what it actually looked like. It was small and delicate, perhaps round in shape and flaky in texture, since it resembled the frost on the ground. Exodus 16:31 informs us that it was like coriander seed and white, and that it tasted like wafers made with honey. Numbers 11:7-9 also suggests that it looked like a coriander seed, and describes its color as that of bdellium, which was an amber-colored resin that exuded from certain trees. Apparently manna was white, tinged with amber. Its comparison to the coriander seed suggests that it was small, no more than an eighth of an inch in diameter. We are told that the people "ground it in mills, or beat it in a mortar, and baked it in pans, and made cakes of it: and the taste of it was as the taste of fresh oil" (Numbers 11:8). Altogether, it was suited to be a substitute for bread and thus to be the main source of nourishment for the people.

Some who seek a naturalistic explanation for the manna suggest that it was the secretion of the tamarisk tree or of certain insects that fed on the sap of the tamarisk. This theory will not stand, for this secretion appeared only in certain seasons of the year and in certain areas, whereas the Israelites were supplied with this food the year around for the forty years they spent in the wilderness. The only adequate explanation for this bread or manna is that it was a miraculous provision of God for His people.

15. And when the children of Israel saw it, they said one to another, It is manna: for they wist not what it was. And Moses said unto them, This is the bread which the LORD hath given you to eat.

The people could not identify the small round things lying on the ground. In most modern translations, *It is manna* is translated as a question, "What is it?" Apparently they had never seen anything like it. The word *manna* used in this question was later applied to this substance, and it has been called by that name ever since.

Moses explained that the substance they could not identify was the bread the Lord had promised to give them. It didn't look like bread, and it may not have tasted like bread, but it was to be their "staff of life" for the next forty years.

C. Gathering the Bread (vv. 16-18)

16. This is the thing which the LORD hath commanded, Gather of it every man according to his eating, an omer for every man, according to the number of your persons; take ye every man for them which are in his tents.

The people were to gather enough for each person, an amount said to be an *omer*. This measure is mentioned only in this chapter. We are told that an omer was a tenth of an ephah (v. 36). Scholars differ as to how much this was, but it was probably less than two quarts dry measure. This may seem a lot for each person to eat, especially small children, but the manna

was light, rather like corn or bran flakes, and the omer of manna served for all the meals in the day. Probably everyone went to work gathering it. Since it was on the ground, even small children could help.

17, 18. And the children of Israel did so, and gathered, some more, some less. And when they did mete it with an omer, he that gathered much had nothing over, and he that gathered little had no lack; they gathered every man according to his eating.

Heeding Moses' orders, the people began to gather what they thought would be about an omer. Some, however, gathered somewhat more, others somewhat less. Yet amazingly, when they measured it in their tents, each had enough for his family's needs. Whether by means of a miracle or the working of His providence, God made adequate provision for each person's requirement for food.

In the verses that follow the printed text, we learn that the people were not to save any of one day's provision of manna against the next day's need. When some tried to do that, it became infested with worms and rotted. There was one exception to this command, however. They were instructed to gather two omers on the sixth day so that they would not be required to gather any on the seventh day, which was to be observed as the Sabbath (v. 26). Those who went out to gather on the seventh day found nothing.

ENOUGH

"He who dies with the most toys wins." This bumper sticker is seen in some affluent areas of the western states. Perhaps you have seen it where you live. It is probably intended as a humorous statement about the acquisition of gimmicks and gadgets, which fill our lives, our garages, and occupy so much of our thought. In truth, however, the statement reflects an underlying philosophy that governs the lives of many persons in our society. It is a blatant materialism that is both unsatisfying and frightening; unsatisfying because anyone who lives by it can never have enough things, and frightening because it throws one into conflict with the life and teaching of Jesus Christ, who taught us to share with those who are in need.

The manna was a gift from God to feed Israel in the wilderness. They were to gather only enough for each day's need. Any excess, kept in fear that there would be no supply for tomorrow, would become unfit for human consumption. When those in a family shared what they had gathered, they discovered that "he that gathered much had nothing over, and he that gathered little had no lack."

When we manage our material blessings God's way, by using what we need and sharing with others, we will find that we will have enough. Can we live out that principle in our present world order?   —W. P.

Conclusion

A. Learning to Trust

The Israelites murmured against Moses and Aaron because they were facing a food shortage. This was a situation that would cause serious concern, of course. Their failing was that they did not trust God enough. They had seen His mighty acts in the ten plagues in Egypt. They had participated in the miraculous crossing of the Red Sea and had witnessed the destruction of Pharaoh's army. They had seen the miracle that converted the bitter water of Marah into sweet water. Yet they did not have enough faith in God to believe that He would provide food for their daily needs.

Are we any different? We see God's wonderful power in nature. He uses the rain, the sunshine, and fertile soil to produce the food we require. In a thousand other ways He provides for our needs. We need not expect Him to shower manna upon us or to make provision for us by some other miraculous means. Instead, he has endowed us with strength and has allowed us to develop skills that enable us to produce not only the necessities of life, but things that in any other age would have been considered luxuries. Yet some complain because they don't have more. Is not such complaining an expression of a person's doubt that God will provide what he or she needs?

If God took note of the complaining of the Israelites, who had just come out of slavery and had received little instruction about Him, will our complaints escape His notice? What must He think of us, who have known Him most of our lives and have received so much from Him, if we entertain doubts about His care for us?

B. Learning to Obey

Our relationship with God begins with our knowledge about Him. In time that knowledge develops into faith or trust. In time this faith leads us beyond our knowledge about Him, and we learn to trust Him even though we don't know everything about Him. As we trust Him, we come to love Him. Our relationship to God does not end with knowledge, faith, and love, however. It must also involve obedience.

The Israelites got into trouble at this point. They knew a little about God, and they no doubt trusted Him a little—not enough to believe He could supply them food, to be sure—but a little. However, they still had to learn to obey Him. Their first big test had come while they were yet in Egypt. They had been instructed to sprinkle the blood of the lamb on the doorposts and lintels of their houses. If any did not obey, they paid a terrible price—the loss of their firstborn.

Now with God's provision of the manna, the people were given some new tests. They were told to eat each day the manna they had collected and not to try to keep any until the next day. Those who didn't obey found that this extra manna had become worm-infested and spoiled. They were told to gather extra manna on the sixth day so they would not need to gather any on the seventh. Some disobeyed, however, and tried to collect food on the seventh day, but there was none to be found.

These may seem like minor infractions of God's orders, but in the small things we often reveal the true nature of our hearts. Jesus said that if we love Him, we will keep His commandments. He did not distinguish between big commandments and little ones, allowing us to disobey or ignore the ones that we don't think are important. An unchecked spirit of disobedience will ultimately lead to consequences that are disastrous—and eternal!

C. Let Us Pray

Dear God and Father, we pause now to give You thanks for all the wonderful blessings You have given us. Forgive us when we complain. Teach us to be even more appreciative of Your blessings. In Jesus' name, amen.

D. Thought to Remember

"Those who complain most are most to be complained of."   —Matthew Henry

Home Daily Bible Readings

Monday, June 27—God Will Be Our Health (Exodus 15:22-27)
Tuesday, June 28—God Will Rain Bread From Heaven (Exodus 16:1-5)
Wednesday, June 29—Each Morning Look for God's Glory (Exodus 16:6-10)
Thursday, June 30—In Evenings, Eat Flesh; Mornings, Bread (Exodus 16:11-15)
Friday, July 1—The People Gathered According to Needs (Exodus 16:16-21)
Saturday, July 2—A Double Supply the Sixth Day (Exodus 16:22-30)
Sunday, July 3—Keep a Jar Full of Manna (Exodus 16:31-36)

Learning by Doing

This page contains an alternate lesson plan emphasizing learning activities. Classes
desiring such student involvement will find these suggestions helpful.

Learning Goals

As students participate in today's class session, they should:

1. Review the main topics of the five lessons in the unit that begins with this week's lesson.

2. Understand how God provided food for the Israelites and what He was trying to teach them with His provision.

3. Acknowledge the gifts God gives them.

Into the Lesson

This lesson is the first of five lessons based on the theme of God's provisions. Introduce this idea in one of the following ways:

If you teach young adults, pair them off and ask each pair to discuss this question: "What is the most significant gift you ever received from your parents?"

If you teach middle adults, ask them to discuss, "What is the most important gift you can give your children?"

If you teach senior adults, ask them to discuss, "What is the most valuable gift you ever received?"

Tell the class that today's lesson begins a unit entitled "Provision for Present and Future." It describes several ways God provided for the Israelites after they left Egypt. The lessons will prompt us to consider how God provides for similar needs that we experience.

Into the Word

Give students an overview of this five-lesson unit. Before class, write the following words in large letters on sheets of paper or posterboard, one word per sheet: *Food, Advice, Covenant, Restoration,* and *Presence.*

On the back of the sheet labeled "Food," write or type this sentence: "God provided for the physical needs of the Israelites after their provisions ran out in the wilderness."

On the back of the paper labeled "Advice," write this: "Through the advice of Jethro, God helped Moses learn how to govern his people."

On the back of the "Covenant" paper write, "God provided a covenant for the nation of Israel, showing them how to be God's own special people."

On the back of the "Restoration" paper write, "God restored the people, even after they disobeyed Him terribly."

On the back of the "Presence" paper write, "Through the tabernacle, God provided a way to be present continually with the people."

Before class ask five volunteers to read these sentences aloud to the class. Each reader should display his word, like a flashcard, while reading his sentence.

Before the readings tell the class that each of these sentences summarizes one of the lessons in this unit and tells of a different provision that God made for the Israelites. As they listen to the sentences, students should decide which provision they feel is most important.

Discuss this briefly before looking specifically at today's text.

Briefly explain the background to today's text. Then ask a volunteer to read Exodus 16 aloud to the class. (Perhaps four volunteers could do this: one could read all the narration, another the words spoken by the people of Israel, another the words of Moses, and another the words of the Lord.)

Jot the following questions on your chalkboard or distribute a handout. Students should listen for answers to these questions as the Scripture is being read.

1. How would you describe the attitude of the Israelites at this time? What was God trying to teach them with these events?

2. What are the evidences that God's provision of food for Israel in the wilderness was miraculous?

Into Life

Discuss some or all of the following questions to summarize today's session:

1. Have you ever been totally dependent on someone else for your basic needs? How did it make you feel? How do you suppose the Israelites felt as their provisions ran out and they didn't know where food would come from? Were their reactions justifiable? If so, in what ways? In what ways were they wrong?

2. How have you already learned what God was trying to teach the Israelites? How does our culture make it difficult for us to truly depend on God?

3. Think of five or six specific gifts that have come to you from God alone. Which of these are physical? Which are spiritual? Which are you most grateful for? Why?

Let's Talk It Over

The questions on this page are designed to encourage review of the lesson Scriptures and to promote discussion of the lesson by the class. The answers provided are only discussion starters. Let your class talk it over from there.

1. How can we develop the hunger and thirst Jesus described (Matthew 5:6) rather than complain about what we lack?

It cannot be denied that we all have physical needs. Yet, in truth, most of us aren't experiencing life-threatening hunger. The first concern of each of us, therefore, should be to seek God and His righteousness (Matthew 6:33). When we give priority to physical wants and needs, we invariably find ourselves complaining and lamenting what we lack. As we give our energies to knowing God in daily life and seeking His will first, we become more aware of how blessed we are and how many material things He has already given us. Our awareness of our blessings, especially those that are ours in Jesus, will lead us to seek to know God even better and to help others find both physical and spiritual food.

2. How much do we feel that following God means life should always be easy with never an inconvenience or hardship?

Even as the Israelites misunderstood and thought that leaving Egypt would be an easy task, some Christians distort the call of discipleship to Jesus and give in to the feeling that all of life will now be comfortable and pleasant. If we develop that feeling and then encounter illness, grief, or broken dreams, we almost invariably question why God has "let us down." Remembering what Jesus' disciples went through as His witnesses will help us realize that He never promised ease. Most people who have lived through several decades can testify that the really worthwhile things of life seldom come easily. Hardship accompanies most of the best parts of life (marriage, childrearing, church work, etc.), and believers can testify that God continues faithful even in the most difficult of times.

3. In their complaint to Moses, Israel extolled the good times of their life in Egypt. Do we engage in a similar memory fantasy today? What is the danger in this?

For Israel to imply that their condition had been better in Egypt than it was in the wilderness is amazing! They engaged in "selective memory" to come to that conclusion. On occasion our recollections of former times may be just as selective. It is true that we derive great spiritual benefit in recalling how God has led us in times past. When times are tough, however, it can be spiritually crippling for us to long for a former time rather than face the challenge of trusting God to provide for present needs. It has been said that each stage of life gets harder and harder, but in Christ each also gets better and better. Childhood has more challenges than infancy; adolescence is yet more difficult. Young adulthood, adulthood, maturity, and older age bring with them demanding challenges, but also greater blessings and more evidence of God's working, until finally we see Him fully.

4. God's provision of manna for Israel was miraculous. In what other ways has God provided for the needs of His people?

We sometimes fail to appreciate God's power and provision in our behalf by taking life's blessings for granted and failing to see His hand in the giving of our "daily bread." Could it be that some of our complaining and lack of faith come from this failure to appreciate how God has built marvelous benefits into the universe and how He is at work among us moment by moment? Not only can we not adequately describe manna, we have no reason to expect that we will ever personally experience anything like it. However, some thought and reflection may help us realize that God has been directly involved in providing what we have needed when we have most needed it, and often in ways we never would have expected.

5. What is the danger in trying God's patience? How can we keep from doing that?

Israel's murmurings against God soon turned to open rebellion against Him, and God considered destroying them completely. Does our view of God allow for Him to consider "giving up" on people? Paul used those very terms in telling the Roman Christians that persons who engage in a godless way of life will be given up to the results of such (Romans 1:18-32). And he warned the Corinthian Christians to learn from Israel's mistakes and not to ignore a vital relationship with God (1 Corinthians 10:1-13). The Bible clearly teaches that faithful obedience, accompanied by sincere gratitude (even in hard times), is the only way to develop and maintain a good relationship with God in Christ Jesus.

Leadership for Meeting Needs

DEVOTIONAL READING: Exodus 18:1-12.

LESSON SCRIPTURE: Exodus 18.

PRINTED TEXT: Exodus 18:13-25.

Exodus 18:13-25

13 And it came to pass on the morrow, that Moses sat to judge the people: and the people stood by Moses from the morning unto the evening.

14 And when Moses' father-in-law saw all that he did to the people, he said, What is this thing that thou doest to the people? Why sittest thou thyself alone, and all the people stand by thee from morning unto even?

15 And Moses said unto his father-in-law, Because the people come unto me to inquire of God:

16 When they have a matter, they come unto me; and I judge between one and another, and I do make them know the statutes of God, and his laws.

17 And Moses' father-in-law said unto him, The thing that thou doest is not good.

18 Thou wilt surely wear away, both thou, and this people that is with thee: for this thing is too heavy for thee; thou art not able to perform it thyself alone.

19 Hearken now unto my voice, I will give thee counsel, and God shall be with thee: Be thou for the people to Godward, that thou mayest bring the causes unto God:

20 And thou shalt teach them ordinances and laws, and shalt show them the way wherein they must walk, and the work that they must do.

21 Moreover thou shalt provide out of all the people able men, such as fear God, men of truth, hating covetousness; and place such over them, to be rulers of thousands, and rulers of hundreds, rulers of fifties, and rulers of tens:

22 And let them judge the people at all seasons: and it shall be, that every great matter they shall bring unto thee, but every small matter they shall judge: so shall it be easier for thyself, and they shall bear the burden with thee.

23 If thou shalt do this thing, and God command thee so, then thou shalt be able to endure, and all this people shall also go to their place in peace.

24 So Moses hearkened to the voice of his father-in-law, and did all that he had said.

25 And Moses chose able men out of all Israel, and made them heads over the people, rulers of thousands, rulers of hundreds, rulers of fifties, and rulers of tens.

GOLDEN TEXT: Thou shalt provide out of all the people able men, such as fear God, men of truth, hating covetousness; and place such over them, to be rulers of thousands, and rulers of hundreds, rulers of fifties, and rulers of tens.—Exodus 18:21.

God Redeems a People

Unit 2: Provision for Present

and Future (Lessons 5-9)

Lesson Aims

As a result of studying this lesson, the students should:

1. Understand that work in the Lord's kingdom can be done more efficiently when it is divided among many people.

2. Appreciate the fact that effective leaders delegate work to others.

3. Evaluate the work of the congregation of which they are a part to find more efficient ways to do the work of the Lord.

Lesson Outline

INTRODUCTION
  A. Many Hands
  B. Lesson Background
  I. MOSES JUDGES HIS PEOPLE (Exodus 18:13-16)
    A. Full-Time Job (v. 13)
    B. Tactful Questions (v. 14)
    C. Explanation (vv. 15, 16)
    It's My Job!
 II. JETHRO GIVES COUNSEL (Exodus 18:17-23)
    A. Jethro's Concern (vv. 17, 18)
    B. Moses' Task (vv. 19, 20)
    C. Shared Responsibility (vv. 21-23)
III. MOSES HEEDS THE COUNSEL (Exodus 18:24, 25)
    A. Humility Demonstrated (v. 24)
    B. Leaders Chosen (v. 25)
    Qualified Assistants
CONCLUSION
  A. A Matter of Leadership
  B. Let Us Pray
  C. Thought to Remember

Display visual 6 of the visuals packet. It contains a truth relative to the work in God's kingdom today. The visual is shown on page 387.

Introduction

A. Many Hands

Where there is a picnic, there will be ants, and our picnic that day was no exception. When I looked under the table, I saw a number of ants scurrying about as if aroused by our arrival. As we started our meal, I tossed a small piece of bread on the ground three or four feet from them to see what they would do. It wasn't long before

one of the scouts found it. I watched him to see what he would do. He carefully examined the crumb and may even have taken a bite or two of it. Then he tried to move the crumb, but it was just too much for him. I watched him struggle with it a while longer, then I turned to my meal. After a few minutes, I glanced back at the piece of bread, and to my surprise it was gone. Then I saw it a few feet away, so I got up and went over and examined it closely. When I did, I saw that the crumb was surrounded by ants, who, by combining their efforts, were able to pull it along. The scout ant had gone back and gotten help to move the crumb back to the nest. As my grandmother used to say, "Many hands make light work."

King Solomon had some good advice about watching the ants and learning from them. We would be wise to follow that advice (see Proverbs 6:6-8; 30:25). Ants have survived for centuries because they do many things right. Among other things, they share burdens that are too large for any one or two ants to carry.

Most churches face the problem of having a few leaders and a handful of people do most of the work necessary to keep a congregation thriving. The more people who can become involved in a church program, the more successful it is likely to be. As leaders are freed up from some of the tasks they are now doing, they will have more time to plan and organize others for more effective service. We would do well to learn some things from the ants and from Jethro, Moses' father-in-law.

B. Lesson Background

After leaving the wilderness of Sin, the setting for last week's lesson, the Israelites moved on to Rephidim, where they camped. *(Refer to the map of the Sinai peninsula, visual 14 of the visuals packet.)* The location of Rephidim is not known for certain today, but it was somewhere between the wilderness of Sin and Mount Sinai. Immediately the people had a problem—there was no water. Once more a murmuring went up from the camp, and once more the people blamed Moses for their problem. Answering Moses' plea for help, God instructed him to take some of the elders of Israel and go on before the people to a certain rock. He was to strike the rock with his shepherd's rod in the sight of the elders. Moses did as he was instructed, and water came forth from the rock to assuage the people's thirst. Thus the people were quieted for a little while.

Israel's troubles were not over, however. Their travels brought them into contact with the Amalekites, a nomadic group that roamed from Canaan to the area of Mount Sinai. As the

Israelites entered this territory, the Amalekites insidiously attacked them from the rear and cut off those who, because they were weary and exhausted, were lagging behind (see Deuteronomy 25:17, 18). The Amalekites then attacked the main army of Israel at Rephidim. Moses, Aaron, and Hur climbed a hill to watch the battle. When Moses held up his hand with the rod of God in it, the Israelites prevailed, but when he became tired and let it down, the Amalekites prevailed. Finally, Aaron and Hur had Moses sit on a stone and they stood on either side of him, holding up his hands till the setting of the sun. Thus the Israelites administered a resounding defeat to their enemy.

I. Moses Judges His People
(Exodus 18:13-16)

While the Israelites were camped at Rephidim, Jethro, Moses' father-in-law, came bringing Moses' wife, Zipporah, and his two sons. Moses recounted to Jethro all the things that had happened since he had returned to Egypt to free the Israelites. Jethro rejoiced in this good news, and offered a burnt offering and a sacrifice to God in thanksgiving (Exodus 18:1-12).

A. Full-Time Job (v. 13)

13. And it came to pass on the morrow, that Moses sat to judge the people: and the people stood by Moses from the morning unto the evening.

The next day *Moses sat to judge the people*, which apparently had become a customary practice. We don't know where he conducted his court, but it was probably in front of his tent. We are not told when this practice began, but in all likelihood people began to bring their grievances to Moses almost as soon as they started on their exodus from Egypt. What had started as a few cases had now grown into a full-time job, and then some. Probably most of the disputes the people brought to Moses were minor in nature, but Moses, wanting to keep peace among the people, was willing to hear them all. It is surprising that Moses did not quickly see what a burden he had taken upon himself. But he was like many good people in the church today who take on one job after another and soon find themselves so burdened that their effectiveness is diminished.

B. Tactful Questions (v. 14)

14. And when Moses' father-in-law saw all that he did to the people, he said, What is this thing that thou doest to the people? Why sittest thou thyself alone, and all the people stand by thee from morning unto even?

visual 6

Jethro spent the whole day watching the people come before Moses. As an outsider and one who observed from the sidelines, Jethro was in an excellent position to make an objective evaluation of the process. The first thing he noted was that the people were being inconvenienced by having to wait such long hours to get justice. It is interesting that Jethro observed that this system was inconveniencing the people before he spoke about its effect on Moses himself. He may have recognized that this contributed to the people's ill temper and discontent, which made them more inclined to murmur about other things. Good morale can be destroyed by relatively minor issues as well as by matters of greater importance. Church leaders need to keep this in mind.

C. Explanation (vv. 15, 16)

15, 16. And Moses said unto his father-in-law, Because the people come unto me to inquire of God: when they have a matter, they come unto me; and I judge between one and another, and I do make them know the statutes of God, and his laws.

Moses responded to Jethro's questions by indicating that he had not really planned this method of dispensing justice. It had started when the people began coming to him to settle their disputes. Before he realized it, the people were coming in increasingly greater numbers. They came to Moses to *inquire of God,* for they recognized that Moses enjoyed a special relationship with Him.

At the time of this event, God had not yet given His law to the people. That law, which would soon be given at Mount Sinai, would include detailed regulations governing civil as well as religious matters. Apparently, until the law was given, the people depended on Moses to make known God's will. As they traveled across the wilderness, their day-by-day experiences gave rise to many disputes. Those that they could not solve among themselves they brought to Moses. When they came, Moses made them *know the statutes of God, and his laws.* In addition to dispensing justice, Moses also began to teach them God's laws in the process.

IT'S MY JOB!

The office was a busy place, but it was obvious that the workload was not equal. Several secretaries were busily typing, producing letters that would be in the mail later that day. In another, more central, area of the office things were not going as well. A group of workers were standing around one desk, waiting for their turn to have the office manager answer their questions as to what they should do next or how they should handle various phases of the day's work. The manager was careful and meticulous in giving directions to each one and then checking to be certain each understood what he had said should be done.

The system was working, but at the end of the day just as many workers were standing around his desk as there had been at the beginning of the workday. An efficient work schedule was not in evidence, and too much time was wasted in the eight-hour period the office was in operation.

To the office manager's amazement, he was dismissed after being in this new position for only three months. He was hurt and angry. His comment was, "It was my job to give directions and make decisions, and I made them correctly." Apparently the efficient use of time and available resources was not important in his mind.

Are we ever guilty of doing more than we need to do because we don't want to share responsibility? After all, "It's my job."   —W. P.

II. Jethro Gives Counsel (Exodus 18:17-23)

A. Jethro's Concern (vv. 17, 18)

17, 18. And Moses' father-in-law said unto him, The thing that thou doest is not good. Thou wilt surely wear away, both thou, and this people that is with thee: for this thing is too heavy for thee; thou art not able to perform it thyself alone.

Moses had lived closely with his father-in-law for the past forty years, and so Jethro's relationship with his son-in-law was good enough that he did not hesitate to speak frankly to him. Earlier Jethro had implied that the judicial process Moses had in place was not good for the people (v. 14). Now he pointed out clearly that it would be harmful both to Moses and them. Although sitting and listening to people's problems all day might not be physically tiring, it would be emotionally draining. The strain of this would eventually take its toll on Moses' strength and lead to the sacrifice of his health and usefulness. The people too would suffer from the long delays they were forced to endure. Moses was so involved in the process that he did not realize what it was doing to him and his people. Clearly he was trying to do more than one person alone could do. It took an outsider to see the situation and provide a solution to the problem.

B. Moses' Task (vv. 19, 20)

19. Hearken now unto my voice, I will give thee counsel, and God shall be with thee: Be thou for the people to Godward, that thou mayest bring the causes unto God.

In his remarks Jethro emphasized Moses' role as the intermediary between God and the people. One element in this function would involve Moses' bringing the people's *causes unto God* when they involved new matters requiring special instructions from Him.

20. And thou shalt teach them ordinances and laws, and shalt show them the way wherein they must walk, and the work that they must do.

The second part of Moses' role as the one who stood between God and the people was that he was to teach the people the *ordinances and laws* that God revealed to him. Only in this way would they learn how they were to conduct themselves and what duties they were to perform in everyday life.

Moses' situation was not greatly different from that of Christian leaders today. Many people today do not know God's commandments for their lives. They need to be taught these, but they also need to be taught how to apply these teachings to their lives. The Israelites had at least some excuse for their ignorance, for God had not yet revealed His law to them. But the same cannot be said of us. The Bible is readily available to us, and Christian teachers are available for every age group. We are without excuse if we are unaware of the Christian principles that are to motivate and guide our daily lives.

C. Shared Responsibility (vv. 21-23)

21. Moreover thou shalt provide out of all the people able men, such as fear God, men of truth, hating covetousness; and place such over them, to be rulers of thousands, and rulers of hundreds, rulers of fifties, and rulers of tens.

Jethro next suggested that Moses select men to help him provide guidance for the people. These were to be *able men.* They were to be competent men, possessing good judgment and leadership qualities. They were to *fear God,* recognizing their accountability to Him.

Although the Israelites had received very little formal teaching about God, some had grown in faith to the point that they could serve as leaders and examples for the others. They were to be *men of truth*. No quality is more important for a judge than the commitment to seek and uphold the truth. The final quality Jethro mentioned was that the leader/judge must also hate covetousness. Men who were not covetous would not be tempted to take bribes.

The leaders were to be set over thousands, hundreds, fifties, and tens, indicating different levels of authority. We are not told here, but it seems safe to assume that this was a system of lower courts, appeals courts, and higher courts, with Moses serving as the supreme court in hard cases.

22. And let them judge the people at all seasons: and it shall be, that every great matter they shall bring unto thee, but every small matter they shall judge: so shall it be easier for thyself, and they shall bear the burden with thee.

These courts presided over by the leaders were to be convened *at all seasons,* whenever needed. They were not just a temporary expediency, but were to be permanent. The courts were to be in session whenever and wherever Israel would encamp. It seems likely that most of the people's disputes would have been resolved on the lowest level. It can be easily seen, therefore, how much this sharing of the judicial burden would make Moses' task *easier*. Since the people would have the right of appeal, they knew that in matters of major importance Moses would still be in control.

23. If thou shalt do this thing, and God command thee so, then thou shalt be able to endure, and all this people shall also go to their place in peace.

If . . . God command thee. Jethro did not presume to think that Moses should act on this advice without first consulting God. We are not told how Moses could refer a matter to God to obtain a decision on it, but apparently there was an established means for him to do so. The benefits of this system were twofold. Moses would be relieved of the great burden he had taken upon himself and he would be *able to endure*. The second benefit would be that the people

would be better satisfied. Usually the closer to home justice is, the happier people are.

Their place. This seems to be a reference to Canaan. Jethro was certain that the people would make the journey to the promised land contentedly if his proposal were acted upon.

III. Moses Heeds the Counsel (Exodus 18:24, 25)

A. Humility Demonstrated (v. 24)

24. So Moses hearkened to the voice of his father-in-law, and did all that he had said.

Moses accepted the wise advice of his father-in-law. This speaks well of Moses' humility. A less humble man might have resented the advice and refused to follow it. How often our pride keeps us from accepting advice from others! We especially seem to resent advice from those who are closest to us. In rejecting wise counsel we may protect our precious egos, but as a result we miss many wonderful blessings.

We are not told how soon Moses implemented Jethro's plan. Deuteronomy 1:6-18 seems to indicate that he did not implement it until after the law was received on Mount Sinai. If this is the case, it would make good sense, for with the coming of the law the judges would have a written basis for their decisions.

B. Leaders Chosen (v. 25)

25. And Moses chose able men out of all Israel, and made them heads over the people, rulers of thousands, rulers of hundreds, rulers of fifties, and rulers of tens.

Deuteronomy 1:13 indicates that the people were involved in the selection of these men. This seems reasonable since Moses could not have known the whole nation well enough to know who would make the best leaders. Some scholars have suggested that the division by thousands, hundreds, fifties, and tens represented natural groupings within the nation. If that was the case, the number under each leader may not have been precisely a thousand or a hundred. Further, the number in each group would change as some died and some were born.

It is also worth noting that these leaders were called *rulers*, indicating that they did more than administer justice in disputes. They were heads over their respective groups, having authority over them as they journeyed in the wilderness.

QUALIFIED ASSISTANTS

The efficient operation of all the coalition forces against Iraq during the Gulf War was outstanding. The coordination of this multinational effort began with the commander in chief and his

---

How to Say It

AMALEKITES. *Am*-uh-leck-ites.

REPHIDIM. *Ref*-ih-dim.

SINAI. *Sye*-nay-eye or *Sye*-nye.

ZIPPORAH. Zi-*po*-ruh.

military advisors and was carried out through the entire chain of command. Officers of every branch of service and on every level, enlisted personnel in combat positions and in support positions—all worked in harmony and all were important in the victory. They were a magnificent team!

Israel needed an efficient "chain of command." Moses was bearing an impossible administrative, legislative, and judicial load. When he accepted the advice of his father-in-law and saw to it that able assistants were selected, Moses' crushing burden was lifted and all Israel was blessed.

Do we apply this principle in our churches? "Like a mighty army moves the church of God." Each person needs to fulfill his or her role and also help equip others in the body to share the work of ministry and evangelism. —W. P.

Conclusion

A. A Matter of Leadership

When Jethro came to visit Moses, he found him overwhelmed in trying to serve his people. After observing the situation, Jethro recommended that Moses appoint leaders to serve under him in administering justice to the people. Moses wisely took the advice of his father-in-law and sought out others to assist him. This problem sounds very modern. During the course of a year, we have an opportunity to visit many different congregations. When we ask about problems a congregation may have, almost invariably we hear, "Our biggest problem is the lack of leadership."

What steps can a church take to overcome this problem? Here are a few suggestions:

1. *The congregation should seek out able people from their midst.* One of the qualifications for those who would serve under Moses was that they be "able." Today we would consider an able person one who is intelligent, reasonably well educated, and who possesses those qualities of personality that cause others to recognize him as a leader. Perhaps somewhere there is a congregation so unfortunate that it has no member who possesses any of these qualifications. But in most congregations there are some. In remote areas in New Guinea, we have seen villages where no one has had any formal education, and everyone is illiterate, and yet they have leaders.

2. *The people need to be challenged.* It is easy for members of a church to get into a rut with the same people doing the same things in the same old way. The danger in this is that the rut becomes comfortable and most people don't want change. It takes a challenge to stir people out of their accustomed ways. When they are chal-

lenged it is often discovered that many have hidden talents they can use for the Lord. Our task is to find ways to challenge them.

3. *The people must be trained.* Many would be willing to serve if they knew what to do. One may be born with certain qualities that are necessary for leadership, but many of the necessary skills must be acquired through education and training. A congregation ought to have regular educational programs that not only teach the Bible but also prepare its members to be teachers, youth leaders, deacons, elders, and other types of leaders needed by every church.

4. *Care must be taken not to overwork the leaders.* We hear much these days about burnout. There are many reasons for burnout, but one of the most common ones in a church is that a few are overworked while most people do little. Moses was headed for burnout when Jethro gave him sound advice about how to avoid it.

5. *Current methods and programs should be analyzed.* When Jethro came to visit Moses, he watched what Moses was doing. By standing on the sidelines and observing, he quickly was able to analyze the problem and offer solutions for it. It may help to have a person from the outside take a look at the programs we have in our local church. An outsider may see things that those involved miss. But we must have the humility to listen and the willingness to change.

B. Let Us Pray

Dear Lord, we pray that we will take what we have learned in this lesson and apply it to our lives and the work of the church. In Jesus' name we pray. Amen.

C. Thought to Remember

Many hands make light work.

Home Daily Bible Readings

Monday, July 4—Water From the Rock (Exodus 17:1-7)

Tuesday, July 5—War With Amalek (Exodus 17:8-16)

Wednesday, July 6—Moses' Family Reunited (Exodus 18:1-5)

Thursday, July 7—Jethro Rejoiced for Moses' Good News (Exodus 18:6-9)

Friday, July 8—Jethro Offered Sacrifices to God (Exodus 18:10-12)

Saturday, July 9—Jethro Suggested a Better Way (Exodus 18:13-27)

Sunday, July 10—"Oh That I Were Made Judge" (2 Samuel 15:1-6)

Learning by Doing

This page contains an alternate lesson plan emphasizing learning activities. Classes desiring such student involvement will find these suggestions helpful.

Learning Goals

As students participate in today's class session, they should:

1. Describe the effect Jethro's advice had on Moses' success as a leader.

2. Decide how they can either (1) give advice to someone who needs it to succeed as a Christian leader, or (2) ask for advice to succeed as Christians themselves.

Into the Lesson

Write, "Who needs advice?" in big letters on your chalkboard. To begin today's session, divide your class into thirds. Have each third do one of the following assignments:

1. Turn to your neighbor and discuss, "The best advice I ever received."

2. Turn to your neighbor and discuss, "If I could give one piece of advice to someone famous, here's what it would be."

3. Look through a stack of newspapers (provided by the teacher) and find a story or advertisement that depicts someone who really needs advice. Share your "finding" with the person next to you, and be ready to share it with the class.

Give students between five and ten minutes for this assignment. Then let volunteers from each group share with the whole class. Discuss, "What role does receiving advice usually play in a person's overall success in life? What happens to the person who refuses to receive advice? What role does advice play in the success of a leader, especially in the church?"

Tell class members that this week's lesson continues our study of Moses and his leadership. We'll see how good advice made a difference in his ability to lead Israel.

Into the Word

Briefly connect this lesson to last week's by summarizing the events of Exodus 17 (see "Lesson Background" on page 386). Ask your students to number themselves off by fives, so that everyone has a number from one to five. As you read aloud today's printed text to the class, students should listen for the answer to the question below that corresponds to their assigned number.

1. What does this passage demonstrate about the relationship between Jethro and Moses?

2. What does this passage demonstrate about the attitude of the people toward Moses?

3. What does this passage demonstrate about the attitude of Moses toward the people?

4. What does this passage teach about the qualities of successful leaders?

5. What does this passage teach about the responsibilities leaders have for each other?

After the text is read, ask each student to find someone else in the room who has the same number as he or she. Once the pairs or groups have assembled, they should discuss their assigned question for about five minutes. Then lead a class discussion of all five questions.

Into Life

Of all the important lessons suggested by the event in today's text, most fall into one or the other of these two categories: "The Need for Mentors," and "The Need for Qualified Leaders." Discuss one or both of these needs with your class.

The Need for Mentors. A mentor is a person who advises and helps another person, usually someone who is younger, to reach his or her full potential. Ask class members if they can think of any examples from history in which a person's success was largely due to the advice, support, and encouragement of a mentor. Who was the mentor in their own lives?

If your class members are older, ask them to think of younger members of your congregation who have potential for leadership. Can your class members help these persons so they can reach their leadership potential?

If your class members are younger, ask them to identify leaders in your congregation who might be able to help them reach their potential for God. Mentoring can take place in every arena of life—parenting, business, and marriage, as well as leading in the church.

Your class members may want to jot down the names of potential mentors. Suggest that beside each name they write ways to establish a relationship with this person (if they haven't already). In what context will they be able to receive the influence they want?

The Need for Leaders. Ask, "Why doesn't the church have more and better leaders?" Discuss briefly, then consider the five suggestions for improving the church's leadership that are mentioned in the "Conclusion" section on page 390. Discuss how your class members can help solve your church's need for leaders.

Let's Talk It Over

The questions on this page are designed to encourage review of the lesson Scriptures and to promote discussion of the lesson by the class. The answers provided are only discussion starters. Let your class talk it over from there.

1. In what ways may our church have customs or practices that really do not serve people's needs (or, how do we know "the way we've always done it" is best)?

By nature churches tend to be conservative, and that obviously is best in matters involving doctrine and faith. However, that tendency can cause us to close our minds to needs or problems that may be diminishing our service to the Lord. Moses was a strong leader and yet, remarkably, he was receptive to positive suggestions from other people, including his own father-in-law! As the lesson points out, Jethro drew attention to both the people's needs and Moses' method, which was causing him to overextend himself. Churches today need to look at the same issues (people's needs and leaders' energy) and then reconsider whether or not to hold on to long-standing methods, if to do so keeps the church from being as effective as it can be in advancing the Lord's cause today. By changing his procedures, Moses did not diminish or alter the effect of communicating God's word. Rather, he helped it.

2. How can our church help more people get involved in meaningful ways of serving and participating in the body of Christ?

Most congregations suffer from what is called the "80/20 syndrome." This simply means that eighty percent of the giving, working, etc. is done by twenty percent of the members. In some churches the ratio is even worse, possibly 90/10. When that condition exists, that church finds itself in a situation similar to that of Moses. It is not healthy either for the few who may "burn out" or for the church as a whole. Some churches use a talent/service survey to let the members express what service they would like to perform or what they have done in the past. Others offer a "Gifts Inventory" of some kind to help people sense what spiritual gifts they may possess and thus encourage them to use those for the Lord's service. And quite a few have visionary leaders, who encourage younger members to be understudies in service roles so they eventually will be equipped to assume full responsibility for a given task. The methods available are numerous, and they certainly provide healthy alternatives to keep us from using guilt as a means of motivation to service.

3. How can our church help people become effective leaders?

Rather than assume that anyone chosen as an elder or deacon automatically receives divine guidance, could the church have classes to study the Scriptural roles of leaders? A church could invite a guest speaker in for a weekend or a retreat to teach these leaders, or several smaller churches could go together to have a seminar on church leadership. Ongoing Scripture study in the first few minutes of regularly scheduled meetings of the leaders could help improve the service of leadership in a church. Likewise, classes in evangelism or witnessing (whether traditional visitation or "life-style"), or for any position of service in the church, could aid in the development of leaders. Always, however, one of the best methods for teaching leadership is "on-the-job" training.

4. How can our church best determine who are qualified to be placed over "tens" and who over "thousands"?

In relating the parable of the pounds (Luke 19:11-27), Jesus taught that the person who is faithful in small matters pertaining to God's kingdom will be rewarded with a greater measure of authority when Jesus returns. The application of this principle is seen often in this life, and it certainly is fitting in the life of every congregation of Christians. As people are faithful in performing less important tasks, leaders may discern their readiness to be given greater responsibility. Those who regularly study churches point out that the newest members are usually eager to have opportunities to serve. Of course, babes in Christ should not be put in positions of high authority in the church. But there are many tasks they may be given. Some churches, however, wait too long to give new Christians any opportunity whatsoever to serve. The longer a church waits to utilize the talents of new Christians, the harder it will become to get them involved. Likewise, most teenagers in churches would be honored to be asked by the leaders to have a responsibility that is important in the church. One's showing that he or she can be faithful in a little depends on that person's being given a chance to serve. How is your congregation doing at that?

A Covenant to Keep

DEVOTIONAL READING: Deuteronomy 5:2-21.

LESSON SCRIPTURE: Exodus 19:1—20:17.

PRINTED TEXT: Exodus 19:4-6a; 20:2-4, 7-17.

Exodus 19:4-6a

4 Ye have seen what I did unto the Egyptians, and how I bare you on eagles' wings, and brought you unto myself.

5 Now therefore, if ye will obey my voice indeed, and keep my covenant, then ye shall be a peculiar treasure unto me above all people: for all the earth is mine:

6a And ye shall be unto me a kingdom of priests, and a holy nation.

Exodus 20:2-4, 7-17

2 I am the LORD thy God, which have brought thee out of the land of Egypt, out of the house of bondage.

3 Thou shalt have no other gods before me.

4 Thou shalt not make unto thee any graven image, or any likeness of any thing that is in heaven above, or that is in the earth beneath, or that is in the water under the earth.

· · · · · · · · · · · · ·

7 Thou shalt not take the name of the LORD thy God in vain: for the LORD will not hold him guiltless that taketh his name in vain.

8 Remember the sabbath day, to keep it holy.

9 Six days shalt thou labor, and do all thy work:

10 But the seventh day is the sabbath of the LORD thy God: in it thou shalt not do any work, thou, nor thy son, nor thy daughter, thy manservant, nor thy maidservant, nor thy cattle, nor thy stranger that is within thy gates:

11 For in six days the LORD made heaven and earth, the sea, and all that in them is, and rested the seventh day: wherefore the LORD blessed the sabbath day, and hallowed it.

12 Honor thy father and thy mother: that thy days may be long upon the land which the LORD thy God giveth thee.

13 Thou shalt not kill.

14 Thou shalt not commit adultery.

15 Thou shalt not steal.

16 Thou shalt not bear false witness against thy neighbor.

17 Thou shalt not covet thy neighbor's house, thou shalt not covet thy neighbor's wife, nor his manservant, nor his maidservant, nor his ox, nor his ass, nor any thing that is thy neighbor's.

GOLDEN TEXT: If ye will obey my voice indeed, and keep my covenant, then ye shall be a peculiar treasure unto me above all people.—Exodus 19:5.

Lesson Aims

As a result of studying this lesson, the students should:

1. Understand that the children of Israel were chosen by God as His covenant people.

2. Recognize the unchanging nature of the moral principles of the law given through Moses.

3. Appreciate the impact God's law has had on the world's civilizations.

4. Be challenged to honor God and respect their fellowmen in thought, word, and deed.

Lesson Outline

INTRODUCTION
   A. Roots of Our Civilization
   B. Lesson Background
 I. A CHOSEN PEOPLE (Exodus 19:4-6a)
   A. Careful Protection (v. 4)
   B. Conditional Promise (vv. 5, 6a)
      A Big "If"
 II. THE TEN COMMANDMENTS (Exodus 20:2-4, 7-17)
   A. A Right Relationship With God (vv. 2-4, 7-11)
      No Substitutes
   B. A Right Relationship With One Another (vv. 12-17)
CONCLUSION
   A. Rules for Living
   B. Let Us Pray
   C. Thought to Remember

Display visual 7 of the visuals packet throughout this session. The visual is shown on page 397.

Introduction

A. Roots of Our Civilization

Colleges traditionally have required students to take a course in Western civilization. Now a debate is raging throughout the academic community regarding this requirement. Some insist that it is too narrow because it suggests that only European ideas are really important. The critics assert that Africa and Asia have made many contributions to modern civilizations and that these contributions ought to be recognized.

While much of Western civilization is certainly based on the civilizations of Greece and Rome and Western Europe, we must recognize that others have made contributions that influence how we think, what we eat, and what we wear.

In all the debate, however, one important source seems to have been overlooked, a source that many believe is more important than any of the others. We speak, of course, of the Israelites and Christianity, which has its roots in ancient Israel. Whether one is talking about art, or literature, or the basic elements that hold society together, it would be difficult to overestimate the influence that the Israelites and their spiritual descendants have had on modern civilization. Ancient Israel never occupied more than a small area at the eastern end of the Mediterranean. Even under Solomon, when Israel reached its peak, these people could not rival in power or size the great empires of the ancient world.

Yet we are in debt for what has come down to us through this people. This lesson focuses on one of those benefits—that of law. The Ten Commandments, and the supporting laws that come with them, have been the basis for much of our modern law. To deny this is to deny the obvious. Let us then not look upon today's lesson dealing with the Ten Commandments as the study of some ancient law code that has no relevancy to modern civilization. Rather, these Commandments have provided the very backbone of our culture, and most of the problems that plague our world would be solved if people would adhere to their basic truths.

B. Lesson Background

Last week's lesson found the people of Israel camped at Rephidim, where Jethro, Moses' father-in-law, came to visit him. After Jethro departed to go to his own land, the Israelites moved from Rephidim and came to the desert of Sinai, where they camped before Mount Sinai. They arrived at Mount Sinai in the third month after their exodus from Egypt, seemingly on the first day of the third month (Exodus 18:27—19:2).

After the Israelites had set up their camp at the base of the mount, Moses began to ascend the mountain, expecting to receive revelations from God. God called to him, however, and sent him back to the people with the message contained in the first portion of our lesson text. God was prepared to enter into further direct relations with the people of Israel, but first He desired a positive commitment from them.

Moses did as he was instructed. Gathering the elders of the people together, he delivered the following words of God to them.

I. A Chosen People
(Exodus 19:4-6a)

A. Careful Protection (v. 4)

4. Ye have seen what I did unto the Egyptians, and how I bare you on eagles' wings, and brought you unto myself.

God had first established His covenant with Abraham, and He had reaffirmed it with Isaac and Jacob (Genesis 17:1-8, 19; 26:24; 35:10-12). Now He was ready to reaffirm that covenant with their descendants, the Israelites. God began by reminding the people how He had dealt with the Egyptians, who had enslaved them and stubbornly refused to let them leave Egypt. The power that God had unleashed against the Egyptians would assure the Israelites that He had the power to enforce any covenant He made with them. Then He reminded them that He had brought them out of Egypt *on eagles' wings*, providing them direction and food and water.

B. Conditional Promise (vv. 5, 6a)

5, 6a. Now therefore, if ye will obey my voice indeed, and keep my covenant, then ye shall be a peculiar treasure unto me above all people: for all the earth is mine: and ye shall be unto me a kingdom of priests, and a holy nation.

God's offer to Israel was conditional—*if ye will obey my voice*. This is the way God has always dealt with people. The promises He makes are conditioned upon people's obedience.

Once God made clear to the Israelites the need for their obedience to Him, He began to spell out the blessings that they would enjoy if they obeyed Him. The first blessing was that they would be *a peculiar treasure*. The *Revised Standard Version* has "my own possession," while the *New International Version* renders this, "my treasured possession." As God's "own possession" or His "treasured possession," Israel would enjoy His special protection and care. This was a unique blessing, one they would enjoy *above all people*. If any should doubt that God could provide them with these blessings, He reminded them that all the earth was His. This reminder was necessary for a people who had just come out of Egypt, whose inhabitants worshiped so-called gods that were regarded as having only limited power.

God then revealed some of the details of this special relationship. They were to be *a kingdom of priests*. This speaks of Israel's role as mediator. Through this people God's revelation of himself, and His provision of redemption for the world through Jesus Christ, would be made. Thus, through them other people of the world would be brought to God. They were also to be *a holy nation*. They were to be set apart or dedicated to God. This dedication was to be demonstrated in lives that were morally pure and that glorified Him. It is worth noting that under the New Covenant, Christians constitute a royal priesthood and a holy nation, whose task is to declare God's praise for bringing us out of sin's darkness into the light of salvation in Jesus Christ.

The elders of Israel took this message to the people and brought back their response to Moses: "All that the Lord hath spoken we will do" (v. 8). Moses then returned to the Lord with the people's promise of obedience.

God then informed Moses that He was prepared to make a special revelation to the people. In preparation for this the people were to wash their clothing. Further, they were warned at the risk of death not to ascend the mountain, nor even to touch the foot of it.

On the third day there were thunderings and lightnings and a thick cloud on the mountain. Trumpets sounded, the Lord descended in fire, smoke billowed up, and the mountain shook. God then spoke to Moses, ordering him to climb to the top of the mountain. As Moses went up, God halted him and sent him back down the mountain to warn the people not to go beyond the boundary or barrier that was at the foot of the mountain. Moses came down and delivered this message and then went back up the mountain, where he received the Ten Commandments.

A BIG "IF"

In recent years an increasing number of colleges and universities have been under investigation by the National Collegiate Athletic Association for violation of the rules that govern the athletic programs of member institutions. These rules pertain to recruiting, academic requirements, scholarship benefits, and any other type of aid offered to athletes being "courted" to enroll in a member school. Their purpose is to ensure that all who receive athletic scholarships will acquire a good education in a valid degree program, while promoting fairness in competition among the participating schools. All schools in the NCAA know the rules and agree to abide by them.

Violation, if discovered, will bring penalties to the offending institution. The number of

---

How to Say It

REPHIDIM. *Ref*-ih-dim.
SINAI. *Sye*-nay-eye or *Sye*-nye.

athletic scholarships the school can offer may be reduced. The team can be disallowed to compete in post-season tournaments, and appearances on TV can be forbidden. Unfortunately, an entire school program will suffer for the violations of a few.

Life is like that. Many suffer for the wrongdoing of those who will not abide by laws enacted to protect and benefit all. The blessings of any covenant can remain ours only if we meet its requirements. The "if" clause is a big one many ignore to their shame and the injury of others.

—W. P.

II. The Ten Commandments (Exodus 20:2-4, 7-17)

This scene at Mount Sinai is one of the high points in the history of the human race. These Ten Commandments, or "Ten Words" as they are sometimes called, form the foundation for a person's relations with God and one's relations with other human beings. These laws are profound in their simplicity. They have been the basis of legal systems that have governed nations. It is impossible to calculate the impact these laws have had in shaping Western civilization.

A. A Right Relationship With God (vv. 2-4, 7-11)

2, 3. I am the LORD thy God, which have brought thee out of the land of Egypt, out of the house of bondage. Thou shalt have no other gods before me.

God begins His presentation of the laws by stating that He is Jehovah, the covenant God, who brought the Israelites out of Egypt. He does not present himself as the Creator, the God of power and authority, but as the Deliverer, the God of mercy and protection. In the Commandments that follow, He shows what the people must be and do if they are to continue to enjoy His protection.

The first Commandment is foundational to everything that follows. If Jehovah God is not the one and only God, then the other nine Commandments lose much of their force. *Thou* is singular, indicating that even though the covenant is with all the people, yet each individual is responsible for obeying the laws. The mention of *other gods* is not to be understood in the sense that there actually were other gods and that Jehovah was only the most important of these. Rather, it is a concession to the fact that the Israelites lived for many years in Egypt, amidst a people who worshiped what they thought were gods. Perhaps some Israelites still harbored some notions about these.

Monotheism, the teaching that there is but one God, is reiterated time and again in the Old Testament. For example, Deuteronomy 6:4 states, "Hear, O Israel: The Lord our God is one Lord." Some scholars argue that the Israelites borrowed the idea of monotheism from the Egyptians or some of their other neighbors. But there is nothing to suggest that any of their neighbors came even close to the concept of one God. Instead, their neighbors were always tempting the children of Israel to pursue many other gods. Jehovah is the one and only God. To proclaim another god is to lie; to accept one is to be deluded.

4. Thou shalt not make unto thee any graven image, or any likeness of any thing that is in heaven above, or that is in the earth beneath, or that is in the water under the earth.

The first Commandment teaches God's uniqueness and thus rejects polytheism. The second teaches His spiritual nature and thus rejects idolatry. A *graven image* is one that has been carved from wood or stone. However, the same word is used of an image cast from melted metal (Isaiah 40:19; 44:10; Jeremiah 10:14), so it may be regarded as a general term for an image. Included in this prohibition were images of anything in the whole material creation—in the sky, on the earth, or in the sea.

This verse and verse 5 are to be taken together. It seems clear that it is not the mere making of images that is forbidden. Soon after giving this Commandment, God gave directions for the making of the cherubim of gold for the mercy seat of the ark of the covenant, the design of pomegranates in the high priest's robe, and the figures of fruits and flowers on the candlestick in the tabernacle. So we cannot suppose that He intended to prohibit the arts of sculpture and painting. What is forbidden is the making and worshiping of any physical object, whether as a figure for a false god or as one that in any way symbolizes Jehovah.

NO SUBSTITUTES

The bottles looked alike. Both were dark brown, but each had its own label firmly attached making known its contents. The problem was that it was dark, and Grandpa O'Kelly didn't want to read. He was in a hurry to get relief from his overindulgence in eating at the church picnic. Reaching for the bottle he was sure would bring relief, he took a big gulp to quiet his aching stomach. It didn't taste quite right. Now he turned on the light. To his dismay the label read, "Castor Oil." He would get relief, but not at that moment nor of the kind he wanted.

Disturbed by his moans and the light, his wife, Helen, entered the room. She took one good look, picked up the bottle, and remarked,

"Well, Colin, it serves you right. I always knew you would do something like this. You could have killed yourself. The directions on anything in that cabinet are to be read and followed."

Grandpa O'Kelly wasn't going to get any sympathy from Helen for what must have been a habit of doing things without paying any attention to instructions and warnings.

God's Word is even more important than the label on a bottle. A person who puts anyone or anything in place of God in his or her life makes a substitution that will produce terrible, and lasting, consequences.   —W. P.

7. Thou shalt not take the name of the LORD thy God in vain: for the LORD will not hold him guiltless that taketh his name in vain.

The *name of the Lord* stands as a symbol of God's majesty, power, and holiness. To take lightly His name is to take lightly God himself. The Hebrew term translated *in vain* (or "for vanity") can mean "for evil," "for falsehood," or "for nothing." To call on God to damn anyone or anything that displeases one is to use His name for evil. To invoke God's name for the purpose of leading others to believe a lie is to use His name for falsehood. To use the divine name in a thoughtless or frivolous way is to use it for nothing, with no understanding of its proper meaning. Although the punishment is not mentioned, God *will not hold* anyone *guiltless* who dishonors His name in any of these ways.

8. Remember the sabbath day, to keep it holy.

A few weeks before this time God had prohibited the Israelites from gathering manna on the seventh day, declaring that it was "a sabbath unto the Lord" (Exodus 16:25). Now He commanded them to remember that day and *keep it holy*, that is, set it apart.

9, 10. Six days shalt thou labor, and do all thy work: but the seventh day is the sabbath of the LORD thy God: in it thou shalt not do any work, thou, nor thy son, nor thy daughter, thy manservant, nor thy maidservant, nor thy cattle, nor thy stranger that is within thy gates.

From the beginning man was designed to be a worker (Genesis 2:15). Having created us, God also knows what is best for us. He knows that a person should not work continuously. So He decreed that the Israelites should labor six out of every seven days and rest from work on the seventh. This law applied to the whole family, to servants, to beasts of burden, even to foreigners in Israel's midst.

11. For in six days the LORD made heaven and earth, the sea, and all that in them is, and rested the seventh day: wherefore the LORD blessed the sabbath day, and hallowed it.

visual 7

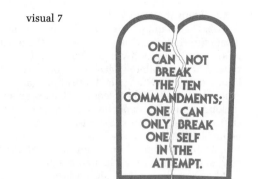

ONE CANNOT BREAK THE TEN COMMANDMENTS; ONE CAN ONLY BREAK ONESELF IN THE ATTEMPT.

Two reasons are given for the distinctiveness of the seventh day. The first and principal reason is given here, namely the fact that God's work of creation was accomplished in six days, and that He rested on the seventh. Thus the resemblance of God's nature and man's nature is shown. Second, the Sabbath was to be a sign between God and Israel (Exodus 31:13) and a memorial of God's redemption of them from bondage in Egypt.

The words of Jesus emphasize God's beneficence in instituting the Sabbath: "The sabbath was made for man" (Mark 2:27). It is for our good that we have a day each week in which to rest from our routine of work.

B. A Right Relationship With One Another (vv. 12-17)

12. Honor thy father and thy mother: that thy days may be long upon the land which the LORD thy God giveth thee.

As we consider our relationship with other human beings, we can see that the relationship between parents and children is foundational to all the rest. It is in the home where love for God and man, respect for each other, obedience to authority, honesty, indeed all godly virtues, are to be transmitted to the younger generation. When parents give these to their children, they fulfill the task assigned to them by God and thus prove themselves worthy of being honored by their children.

Sadly, however, in many homes children learn disrespect for God and their fellowmen, disobedience, and dishonesty. If children learn the selfish way rather than God's way, they behave selfishly even toward the parents who taught them. Honoring neither father nor mother, church nor country, God nor man, they race madly after money or pleasure or power. Children who learn the selfish way become leaders in crooked government or crooked business, or become supporters of those who do. Crookedness can bring any nation to ruin.

13. Thou shalt not kill.

This Commandment invests life with sanctity, a sanctity that found little respect in the ancient world. Yet that sanctity is not absolute, for while murder was prohibited, legal executions were not (Exodus 21:12). The ancient world was a violent place, but the twentieth century has seen more violence and less respect for life than any century that preceded it. We speak of crime, wars, and genocide. But we also speak of abortion, in which human life is snuffed out even before the innocent unborn child draws its first breath.

14. Thou shalt not commit adultery.

Adultery, according to the Old Testament law, was sexual relations between two persons, one or both of whom were married to another person. When marriage was first instituted, it was declared that the husband and wife became "one flesh" (Genesis 2:24). Adultery profanes this divinely recognized union between a husband and wife. The seriousness of the sin of adultery is indicated by the severe penalty it drew—both persons were to be put to death (Leviticus 20:10). The fate of adulterers, described in the New Testament, is no less frightening (1 Corinthians 6:9, 10; Galatians 5:19-21).

15. Thou shalt not steal.

Stealing is the taking of anything that belongs to someone else. It may be done secretly, as in shoplifting, or it may involve taking by force. Fraud is stealing that is done by deceit. Implied in this Commandment is the right of private ownership of property. Stealing is more than just a crime against property; it is a crime against the sanctity of personhood. To take a person's property is to take a part of that person's life.

16. Thou shalt not bear false witness against thy neighbor.

In its strictest sense this refers to the legal process, lying under oath in a trial. But lying under any conditions is a violation of this Commandment. Lying is anything told or withheld for the purpose of deceiving. Lying began in the Garden of Eden with Satan's deceit of Eve and continues right up to the present time.

17. Thou shalt not covet thy neighbor's house, thou shalt not covet thy neighbor's wife, nor his manservant, nor his maidservant, nor his ox, nor his ass, nor any thing that is thy neighbor's.

To *covet* is to have an improper desire for anything that belongs to another. Some specific examples are given, but the last item mentioned, *any thing,* is all-inclusive. This tenth Commandment indicates that God is concerned with more than a person's outward deeds. It teaches that He sees the heart and is concerned with the thoughts and motives from which those acts proceed.

Conclusion

A. Rules for Living

At Mount Sinai God entered into a covenant relationship with the people of Israel, promising them that above all other nations they would occupy a favored position with Him. As such they would receive His special protection and care. Their part of the covenant was to obey Him. God made sure that there would be no misunderstanding about what He expected of them. In the Ten Commandments and the numerous laws that were given through Moses, God gave detailed regulations that were to govern the lives of the people. By keeping them, Israel would remain in a proper covenant relationship with Him.

Some persons, viewing the negative nature of these Commandments, have concluded that this code of laws is restrictive, designed to inhibit the enjoyment of life. Nothing could be farther from the truth. (See Deuteronomy 6:24). God's laws of human conduct are designed to keep people orderly, happy, and prosperous. Anyone who has lived by the moral and ethical standards established by Him can testify to the happiness and harmony of life that result.

B. Let Us Pray

Dear God and Father in Heaven, we thank You that through the experience of the people of Israel we can learn what You expect of those who live under the divine covenant. Help us to accept Your will for our lives as we live under the new covenant in Jesus Christ. In His name we pray. Amen.

C. Thought to Remember

"The Lord our God made a covenant with us in Horeb" (Deuteronomy 5:2).

Home Daily Bible Readings

Monday, July 11—Yahweh Offers a Covenant With Israel (Exodus 19:1-6)
Tuesday, July 12—Kingdom of Priests and Holy Nation (Exodus 19:7-15)
Wednesday, July 13—Moses Brings People to Meet God (Exodus 19:16-20)
Thursday, July 14—Moses Takes Aaron to God (Exodus 19:21-25)
Friday, July 15—Commandments for Man and God (Exodus 20:1-11)
Saturday, July 16—Commandments for Human Relationships (Exodus 20:12-17)
Sunday, July 17—The People's Fear (Exodus 20:18-26)

Learning by Doing

This page contains an alternate lesson plan emphasizing learning activities. Classes desiring such student involvement will find these suggestions helpful.

Learning Goals

Before we begin, let us note that the Ten Commandments were the foundation of the law that was given specifically to Israel. As Christians we are not under the Old Testament law, for Christ fulfilled it (Matthew 5:17, 18), and in fulfilling it He "took it out of the way, nailing it to his cross" (Colossians 2:14). Yet the prohibitions and requirements stated in these commands apply to Christians today. This is so, not because we are under the law, but because we are followers of Jesus, and Jesus and His apostles included them in their teaching. With this in mind, students participating in today's class session should:

1. Survey these commands to notice what a person gives and what a person receives by obeying them.

2. Thank God for the good life He provides us as we walk in His ways.

Into the Lesson

Before class prepare sheets of paper containing the questions and directions shown in italics here:

What is the last promise you made? To whom did you make it? On this paper, write—

1. Your name.

2. The last promise you made.

3. The person to whom you made the promise.

After completing the paper, give it to another class member to do the same.

If your class sits at tables, put one of these papers on each table. If your class sits in chairs, put one paper at the end of each row.

As class members arrive, encourage them to find and complete the sheet. They should have fun as they notice what other class members have written.

To begin today's session, allow a few volunteers to share what they have written. Allot just a few minutes for this.

Tell the class that today's lesson is about promise-keeping. Lead a brief discussion about the idea of covenants and covenant-keeping, the subject of today's lesson.

Ask class members to mention some covenants of which they are a part. Examples include real estate agreements, other kinds of purchase agreements, and marriage vows. Pick one example and ask these questions: What does each party agree to *give* in this covenant? What does each expect to *receive*?

To make the transition to the Bible-study portion of this lesson, mention that at Mount Sinai God was prepared to enter into a covenant with Israel. We will consider what both parties to this covenant were to give and to receive.

Into the Word

This lesson comes in the middle of a unit of lessons that focus on what God provided for His people. Ask class members to think of the last two lessons and recall God's provision that was the subject of each. Then refer to the "Lesson Background" section to establish the historical setting for this lesson. Explain that all was in readiness for God to establish His covenant with His people.

Before a volunteer reads Exodus 19:4-6a aloud, ask class members to listen for the answer to four questions:

1. What did *God give* to this agreement?

2. What did *God receive* from this agreement?

3. What would the *Israelites give* to this agreement?

4. What would the *Israelites receive* from this agreement?

You may want to write across the top of your chalkboard the eight italicized words above. After the verses are read, ask for answers to the four questions. Write them under the appropriate headings and discuss briefly.

Then turn to Exodus 20, which is the core of today's study. Students are to look at each of the commands with the idea in mind of giving and receiving.

Ask them to complete a Bible-study chart with these three headings: Commandment, What a Person *Gives*, What a Person *Receives*.

Let the students work in groups of five for ten minutes. Then lead the class in a discussion of each Commandment and its implication for Israel, and also for us today.

Into Life

Close with the following prayer activity:

Write a prayer. Have class members work in pairs to write a prayer in which they (1) thank God for what we receive by obeying His Commandments, and (2) ask God for help to obey where we have failed.

Let's Talk It Over

The questions on this page are designed to encourage review of the lesson Scriptures and to promote discussion of the lesson by the class. The answers provided are only discussion starters. Let your class talk it over from there.

1. God has commanded that we have no other gods before Him (Exodus 20:3). What are some of the gods that claim people's allegiance today?

Some people yet today worship the creation rather than the Creator. Others worship the works of their own hands. Another worships the product of his mind, such as the theory of evolution or other theories and philosophies. Hero worship is another prevalent form of idolatry, whether the hero be rock star or famous preacher. Perverse people even worship Satan and demons directly. Perhaps the most prevalent "other god" that people worship today is self. Worship of self is expressed in such slogans as, "Do your own thing," or, "If it feels good, do it."

2. What is the connection between those Commandments that deal with our relationship with God and those that speak of our relationship with other people?

Although our increasingly secular society would try to separate the first four Commandments (pertaining to our relationship with God) from the last six, neither these Commandments nor our lives can be segmented that easily. God spoke these words to Moses as a unit for the benefit of Israel; even so, all ten of these Commandments speak to the very basis of our lives. In a sense, the rest of the Old Testament and all of the New Testament show the bearing that our relationship with God has on our relations with other people. In general, one who believes that God is the supreme being to whom he shall one day give account of his life will more likely respect and treat well all others whom God has created. One who does not hold that belief will more likely act in a contrary manner.

3. Can a "day of rest" every week be forced upon people? What are the benefits of observing such a day on a regular basis?

Down through the years of church history various attempts have been made to mandate that Christians observe the Sabbath and avoid specific activities on that day. However, there have been those who resisted these attempts, stating that such a requirement is an example of what the apostle Paul and other leaders in the early church had in mind when they insisted that in Christ we are no longer bound by the law. At the same time, most people recognize that there are numerous rhythms built into our bodies as well as the universe. Taking a day in seven to rest makes sense for our health. It also reminds us of God's ownership of all of life, and of His loving concern for our welfare. Our busy schedules wrongly convince some persons that such resting is mere luxury. Many of us might be surprised to discover that taking one day a week for rest and spiritual reflection not only preserves our health but heightens our productivity in the other six days of the week. Just as many who tithe their income have discovered that the remainder goes farther when God's part is taken out first, so we may discover a similar benefit in our use of time.

4. The fifth Commandment states that parents are to be honored. To whom was this Commandment given—minor children only, or persons of all ages?

We generally think of the fifth Commandment as applying to young children. The context, however, does not permit such a limitation; all the rest of the Commandments point toward adult hearers, and adults certainly are included in this one also. Thus, more than just learning obedience in childhood and adolescence is intended by the Commandment; it speaks of caring for one's parents in their old age, when they are declining in health both in body and in mind. Every society has had to face the painful truth that a person's worth can be called into question when he or she is not "productive"— whether that be a fetus, a person with disabilities, or an older person. God has always spoken out for those who are left out by the rest of society (as witness the prophets of Israel and Jesus himself). This Commandment teaches that we are never relieved of our debt of honor to our parents while they are living.

5. Why are the Ten Commandments more than just arbitrary rules? What was their purpose?

The Commandments are expressions of eternal and unchangeable values of right and wrong. Their purpose was to lead the Israelites to the fullest, happiest, and best life.

Restoration After Wrongdoing

DEVOTIONAL READING: Numbers 12:1-16.

LESSON SCRIPTURE: Exodus 32; 34:1-10.

PRINTED TEXT: Exodus 32:15-19, 30-34; 34:4-6.

Exodus 32:15-19, 30-34

15 And Moses turned, and went down from the mount, and the two tables of the testimony were in his hand: the tables were written on both their sides; on the one side and on the other were they written.

16 And the tables were the work of God, and the writing was the writing of God, graven upon the tables.

17 And when Joshua heard the noise of the people as they shouted, he said unto Moses, There is a noise of war in the camp.

18 And he said, It is not the voice of them that shout for mastery, neither is it the voice of them that cry for being overcome; but the noise of them that sing do I hear.

19 And it came to pass, as soon as he came nigh unto the camp, that he saw the calf, and the dancing: and Moses' anger waxed hot, and he cast the tables out of his hands, and brake them beneath the mount.

. . . .

30 And it came to pass on the morrow, that Moses said unto the people, Ye have sinned a great sin: and now I will go up unto the LORD; peradventure I shall make an atonement for your sin.

31 And Moses returned unto the LORD, and said, Oh, this people have sinned a great sin, and have made them gods of gold.

32 Yet now, if thou wilt forgive their sin—; and if not, blot me, I pray thee, out of thy book which thou hast written.

33 And the LORD said unto Moses, Whosoever hath sinned against me, him will I blot out of my book.

34 Therefore now go, lead the people unto the place of which I have spoken unto thee: behold, mine angel shall go before thee: nevertheless, in the day when I visit, I will visit their sin upon them.

Exodus 34:4-6

4 And he hewed two tables of stone like unto the first; and Moses rose up early in the morning, and went up unto mount Sinai, as the LORD had commanded him, and took in his hand the two tables of stone.

5 And the LORD descended in the cloud, and stood with him there, and proclaimed the name of the LORD.

6 And the LORD passed by before him, and proclaimed, The LORD, The LORD God, merciful and gracious, long-suffering, and abundant in goodness and truth.

GOLDEN TEXT: The LORD passed by before him, and proclaimed, The LORD, The LORD God, merciful and gracious, long-suffering, and abundant in goodness and truth.
—Exodus 34:6.

Lesson Aims

Because of this lesson the students should:

1. Be alert to influences that seek to diminish their devotion to God.

2. Have a better understanding of God's mercy.

3. Appreciate Moses' love and concern for his people.

4. Commit themselves to worship and serve God only.

Lesson Outline

INTRODUCTION

  A. A Violent Temper

  B. Lesson Background

  I. MOSES' UNEXPECTED RETURN (Exodus 32:15-19)

    A. The Stone Tablets (vv. 15, 16)

    B. Noise From the Camp (vv. 17, 18)

    C. Vented Anger (v. 19)

      Celebrating Sin

  II. MOSES' UNUSUAL RESPONSE (Exodus 32:30-34)

    A. Intention Revealed (v. 30)

    B. Intercessory Request (vv. 31, 32)

    C. Individual Responsibility (vv. 33, 34)

  III. MOSES' UNEQUALED PRIVILEGE (Exodus 34:4-6)

    A. Preliminary Requirement (v. 4)

    B. Divine Revelation (vv. 5, 6)

      The Nature of God

CONCLUSION

  A. Restoring What Was Messed Up

  B. A Loving Intercessor

  C. Let Us Pray

  D. Thought to Remember

Display visual 8 of the visuals packet and refer to the points emphasized on it as you develop the lesson. The visual is shown on page 405.

Introduction

A. A Violent Temper

In the early years of the church there lived in Egypt a very pious man, who was loved and respected by all who knew him. He had one fault, however—a terrible temper. After one bad display of his temper, he decided to withdraw from the society that irritated him and live in a monastery. There, he thought, among other pious men he would have no problems. He was wrong, though, for even without intending to they sometimes irritated him, and then his temper would show itself.

Finally he decided to leave the monastery and live out in the desert by himself. When he left the monastery, he took with him only the ragged clothes on his back and a pot to get water from a spring near the cave where he planned to live. One day as he carried the pot of water up the hill from the spring to his cave, he stumbled and fell, spilling the water. He returned to the spring and refilled his pot, but halfway up the hill he stumbled again and once more spilled the water. Picking up the pot, he angrily hurled it to the ground, where it struck a rock and shattered into a dozen pieces. Looking down at the broken vessel he said to himself, "What a fool I am! Now I have nothing with which to carry water. First I was angry with people. Now I vent my rage against an earthen pot."

When Moses returned from the mountain and found the people reveling before the golden calf, he had good reason to be angry. But after he had smashed the two tablets that God had provided, he must have felt as foolish as the Egyptian monk. Because Moses had broken the original tablets, God required that he cut out two stone tablets to replace them. No doubt Moses learned a lesson from this experience, and hopefully so can we.

B. Lesson Background

The Ten Commandments were spoken by the Lord from Mount Sinai in the hearing of all the assembly of Israel (Deuteronomy 5:4, 22). At the people's request, God did not speak again directly to them, but communicated the remainder of His commandments and statutes to Moses alone (vv. 23-31). The children of Israel remained camped at the foot of Mount Sinai while Moses went up on the mountain to receive the law. He stayed there forty days (Exodus 24:18). It wasn't long before the people became restless, and fearing that Moses would not return, asked Aaron to "make us gods, which shall go before us" (Exodus 32:1). Aaron asked the people to donate their golden earrings, and from these he fashioned a golden calf. When the calf was finished, Aaron proclaimed the next day a feast day. After the people brought their offerings, they "sat down to eat and to drink, and rose up to play" (vv. 2-6).

While Moses was still on the mountain, God informed him about what the people were doing. God's wrath was kindled against the people to the point that He was ready to destroy them and raise up a people from Moses. But Moses pleaded with God on behalf of the people, and God was so moved by his plea that He spared them (vv. 7-14). Today's lesson begins as Moses and Joshua make their way down the mountain to confront the people.

I. Moses' Unexpected Return (Exodus 32:15-19)

A. The Stone Tablets (vv. 15, 16)

15, 16. And Moses turned, and went down from the mount, and the two tables of the testimony were in his hand: the tables were written on both their sides; on the one side and on the other were they written. And the tables were the work of God, and the writing was the writing of God, graven upon the tables.

Moses had spent forty days on the mountain. During that time God had revealed to him the detailed aspects of the law. Now it was time for Moses to reveal these laws to the people, and so he started down toward the camp at the base of the mountain.

He carried with him the two stone tablets upon which were engraved the Ten Commandments. We are not told their size or shape. They were small enough that Moses could carry them and later they could be deposited in the ark of the covenant. Interestingly, the tablets were inscribed on both sides, which is not the way they are usually depicted by artists. God himself had prepared the first two tablets and had inscribed the words upon them (Exodus 31:18).

B. Noise From the Camp (vv. 17, 18)

17, 18. And when Joshua heard the noise of the people as they shouted, he said unto Moses, There is a noise of war in the camp. And he said, It is not the voice of them that shout for mastery, neither is it the voice of them that cry for being overcome; but the noise of them that sing do I hear.

Joshua is first mentioned as the leader of the Israelites when they fended off the attack of the Amalekites (Exodus 17:8-16). He was the son of Nun from the tribe of Ephraim, but we know nothing else of his background. We don't know why Moses selected him as the military leader, since he was a young man (Exodus 33:11), but it

---

How to Say It

AMALEKITES. *Am*-uh-leck-ites.
SINAI. *Sye*-nay-eye or *Sye*-nye.
YAHWEH. *Yah*-weh.

---

was a good choice. When Moses started up the mountain, Joshua, acting as Moses' aide, accompanied him part of the way (24:12-14). Then when Moses came back down, he met Joshua and together they went down the mountain until they came within earshot of the camp.

When Joshua heard the sounds that were coming from the camp, his first thought was that it was military action he heard. His experience in fighting the Amalekites may have conditioned him to anticipate other attacks. But Moses knew better, for he had already been informed by God of the people's sin of idolatry (32:7, 8). Apparently, however, he was not yet ready to share all of this information with Joshua, and so he said that what he heard sounded more like singing.

C. Vented Anger (v. 19)

19. And it came to pass, as soon as he came nigh unto the camp, that he saw the calf, and the dancing: and Moses' anger waxed hot, and he cast the tables out of his hands, and brake them beneath the mount.

Moses' reaction here contrasts sharply with his response at the top of the mountain not long before when God first told him of the sin of the people. At that time God informed Moses of His intention to blot the people out, and Moses pleaded their case before God. But when Moses actually saw what they were doing, he reacted angrily and violently. The golden calf the people made must have reminded him of the idols he had seen in Egypt. And the dancing must have been terribly licentious. The worship of many of the ancient gods involved dancing, which usually degenerated into sex orgies. This leads us to believe that their sin was greater than Moses had at first supposed.

In his anger, which *waxed hot*, he hurled the tablets to the ground, breaking them. This was no childish temper tantrum. It was righteous indignation, engendered by his bitter disappointment at the behavior of the people.

CELEBRATING SIN

Peter was an eager student, a quick learner, and an active church member, who talked of dedicating his life to the Christian ministry. He had a flaw, but church friends felt he would outgrow it: he resented regulations and did not accept leadership when he could not be in charge.

The rock music craze hit the west coast, and Peter's church warned their young people against its subtle lyrics celebrating drugs, immorality, and rebellion against established social order. Peter thought his church leaders were too conservative and not open to new ideas in music. He saw them as tied to Bible standards, which were out of touch with the "new morality" and situation ethics.

Soon Peter was an advocate of Gay Rights, repeal of drug laws, and completely antiestablishment. He no longer attended church but marched in any protest that celebrated sin or civil disobedience. Ridiculing righteousness, he was determined to try everything that would give him momentary pleasure. This was his downfall. Peter died a youthful victim of AIDS.

When Peter chose to overturn the Word of God in favor of the idol of self-indulgence, he started on the road to destruction. Israel made the same choice in Moses' day. Don't let yourself be led from life back to death.   —W. P.

II. Moses' Unusual Response (Exodus 32:30-34)

Moses wasted no time in taking steps to punish the people for their idolatrous behavior. The intervening verses tell how he ground up the golden calf to powder, mixed it with water, and made the Israelites drink the water. Then he turned to Aaron and demanded an explanation. We would laugh at Aaron's excuse if the situation had not been so serious. All he had done, he said, was throw the gold jewelry into the fire, and, lo and behold, out came the calf!

Moses' return to the camp and his destruction of the idol did not at once bring an end to all of the revelry (v. 25). Although for the most part it seems to have ceased, yet, there were groups who persisted in licentious behavior. They had to be stopped, lest they provoke God's anger and He come and destroy the entire nation. Therefore Moses stood in the main gate of the camp and issued a call for all who were on the Lord's side to come and stand by him. The Levites responded, and Moses, with God's sanction (v. 27), sent them among the people to execute those who were still rebellious or had been leaders in the great sin. About three thousand were killed before the orgy was stopped.

A. Intention Revealed (v. 30)

30. And it came to pass on the morrow, that Moses said unto the people, Ye have sinned a great sin: and now I will go up unto the LORD; peradventure I shall make an atonement for your sin.

The next day Moses spoke to the people again, reminding them of their *great sin.* So soon after hearing the Ten Commandments, they had at the very least broken the first two of them, if not more. Then he promised to go before the Lord on their behalf; it might be that he could make *atonement* for their sins.

B. Intercessory Request (vv. 31, 32)

31, 32. And Moses returned unto the LORD, and said, Oh, this people have sinned a great sin, and have made them gods of gold. Yet now, if thou wilt forgive their sin—; and if not, blot me, I pray thee, out of thy book which thou hast written.

Once again Moses ascended the mount to come into God's presence. Moses began his petition to God by frankly and fully admitting the people's guilt, which is the way that every prayer for forgiveness must begin. There can be no forgiveness unless there is complete admission of guilt. Then, as Moses began to ask God for forgiveness of the people's sin, he did not finish the sentence. Did he wonder if God could not, or would not, forgive such a heinous act, whose very essence showed such disregard for the divine Being? To complete the sentence, we might add something like "well and good" or "so be it."

If God would not forgive the people, Moses offered himself as a sacrifice for them. *Blot me . . . out of thy book.* Some interpret this to mean that Moses was willing to die for them. But more than this seems to be involved. Moses apparently was willing even to surrender eternal life for the people. We are reminded of the apostle Paul's expression of his willingness to become accursed if it would save his kinsmen after the flesh (Romans 9:3).

C. Individual Responsibility (vv. 33, 34)

33. And the LORD said unto Moses, Whosoever hath sinned against me, him will I blot out of my book.

Even though Moses offered himself up for his people, God could not accept this offer. A sinner cannot be an atonement for another sinner. Only one who was perfect man and God, Jesus Christ, could atone for the iniquities of sinners. God made plain the responsibility that each individual has for his or her own sin. He emphasized this truth centuries later through the prophet Ezekiel. (See Ezekiel 18:20.)

34. Therefore now go, lead the people unto the place of which I have spoken unto thee: behold, mine angel shall go before thee: nevertheless, in the day when I visit, I will visit their sin upon them.

The matter was closed as far as God was concerned, and He would not accept any more pleas from Moses. Moses' job was to carry out the commission to lead the people to the promised land. To insure that Moses would accomplish this mission, God would send His *angel* before him to guide him.

Even though God had spared the lives of the people for the present (Exodus 32:14), yet He would *visit their sin upon them*, that is, punishment would certainly come. Verse 35 tells us that "the Lord plagued the people, because they made the calf." Some scholars believe that this refers to some kind of epidemic disease that God visited upon the people immediately. Other scholars hold that it refers to God's judgment that none of the adults who left Egypt (except a few of the faithful) would see the promised land but would perish in the wilderness (Numbers 14:32-35).

III. Moses' Unequaled Privilege (Exodus 34:4-6)

Moses returned to the camp, and chapter 33 records the ensuing discussion that took place between him and God. Having won God's assurance that He would continue to be with the people, Moses then asked to see God's glory. In response, God told Moses that there was a special place in the mount where he could stand and catch but a glimpse of His glory.

A. Preliminary Requirement (v. 4)

4. And he hewed two tables of stone like unto the first; and Moses rose up early in the morning, and went up unto mount Sinai, as the LORD had commanded him, and took in his hand the two tables of stone.

God promised to continue to be with the people. In order for the covenant to be fully restored, however, the two tables that Moses had shattered had to be replaced. God required Moses to hew out the *two tables* upon which the laws would be inscribed. Since Moses had destroyed the original tables, it seems appropriate that he should be required to hew out a new set.

After the blank stones were prepared, Moses once more ascended Mount Sinai to come into the presence of God. He went alone, and the people and their flocks were to be kept off the mountain.

B. Divine Revelation (vv. 5, 6)

5, 6. And the LORD descended in the cloud, and stood with him there, and proclaimed the name of the LORD. And the LORD passed by before him, and proclaimed, The LORD, The LORD God, merciful and gracious, long-suffering, and abundant in goodness and truth.

The Lord had previously shown His presence through a pillar of cloud as He had talked to Moses at the door of the tent of meeting (Exodus 33:9, 10). Once more He used this method to indicate His presence. He then *proclaimed* His

visual 8

name—*the Lord* (Yahweh or Jehovah, God's special name for His covenant people).

Before God appeared, He had placed Moses in a cleft of the rock and covered him with His hand, for no man could look upon God and live (33:20-23). Then God permitted him just a glimpse of His back parts. This experience prepared Moses for the Lord's revelation. Twice God proclaimed His special name, Jehovah, and listed some of His attributes, a list that continues through verse 7. It is significant that His mercifulness is the first attribute named, for this above all was what the Israelites needed in the face of their idolatry with the golden calf.

THE NATURE OF GOD

Two little neighbor girls, Marci and Jill, were playing house with their dolls. Marci kept punishing the dolls for various acts of disobedience, such as not doing the dishes, forgetting to clean up their rooms, and taking another doll's clothes. One of Marci's favorite rebukes was, "You know I have told you a thousand times not to do that!"

Jill never protested the dolls' punishment. After a few minutes she would pick up the offender, hold the doll lovingly in her arms, and say, "You were bad to do that. You must not do it again. I love you and forgive you. Don't make Marci angry by doing what she tells you not to do or you will be punished again." Each little girl was playing out her own perception of how a home was to be managed in order to gain the obedient cooperation of all family members.

God is our Heavenly Father, and in His dealing with us we see two aspects of His nature: His righteousness and His mercy. His righteousness demands that our sin be punished, but His mercy causes Him to yearn to forgive us. The dilemma is resolved in Jesus. By giving His life on the cross He took the punishment for our sins, thus allowing the Father to forgive us completely. If we come to Him with open hearts, He will receive us with open arms.   —W. P.

Conclusion

A. Restoring What Was Messed Up

We camped along an isolated stretch of beach, and when my two sons and I walked down to the beach, we found that we had it all to ourselves. There were no footprints in the smooth, white sand, and there was nothing to indicate that anyone else had been there all day. The boys thoroughly enjoyed themselves playing in the surf and in the beautiful white sand. They built sand castles, dug for clams, and disturbed the sand in other ways. As we started to leave, one of them looked around and said, "We sure made a mess of the sand. We ought to smooth it off so it doesn't look so bad." I assured them that that wouldn't be necessary. We came back the next morning to find the sand as smooth as we had found it the day before. When the boys asked what happened, I explained that during the night the tide had come in and restored the sand to its original smoothness.

In a way this resembles God's dealings with the Israelites. In worshiping the golden calf, they had committed a terrible sin; and by their own efforts there was no way they could ever restore the covenant relationship with God that they had destroyed. God had threatened to blot them out, and that is exactly what they deserved. Moses had intervened, however, even expressing his willingness to die in their stead.

God is a holy God, who demands righteousness and obedience of those who would be His followers. But He is also a merciful God, who can and does forgive. In spite of Israel's terrible rejection of God, He was willing to forgive them and restore them to the blessings of the covenant. God has not changed. He is still a holy God, who requires His followers to be faithful and righteous. But His mercy is abundant to all who come to Him in Christ Jesus (Ephesians 2:4-7).

B. A Loving Intercessor

Measured by any of several standards, Moses was a great man. He was great because of his humility, his wisdom, and his patience. In no attribute, however, was he greater than in his love and concern for his people, a concern that led him to intervene with God on their behalf. When he pleaded their case before God, he began by acknowledging their great sin. He made no excuses for them. If people seek reconciliation with God, they must begin by honestly acknowledging that they have sinned.

Once this was settled, Moses offered himself for his people. But God did not accept Moses' offer, for ultimately every person must bear the responsibility for his or her sins. It is not certain if God immediately brought judgment upon the people, but punishment did come to this generation of Israelites over the forty years they spent wandering in the wilderness.

How fortunate the Israelites were to have an intercessor such as Moses! Yet we are far more fortunate, for we have the perfect intercessor, Jesus Christ, God's own Son. Moses pleaded for his people as a sinner pleading for sinners, but Christ, the sinless one, pleads for us. Even though Moses offered to sacrifice himself, such a sacrifice could not ultimately atone for the people's sins, for Moses himself was a sinner. Christ is not only our great high priest, He is also the perfect sacrifice for our sins (2 Corinthians 5:21).

Even though we have an Advocate who pleads our case before the Heavenly Father, we cannot expect to escape all of the consequences of our sins. We may be freed of punishment for our sins in the final judgment, but like the Israelites in the wilderness, we must expect some consequences in this life. A murderer, an adulterer, a liar, or a thief whose sins have been forgiven may not have to bear the consequences of those sins at judgment, but that person cannot avoid all of the consequences of those sins in this life.

C. Let Us Pray

Dear God and Father, we thank You for the life of Moses, who was not only a wise leader but one who was willing to offer himself for his people. Grant that we might have such a spirit of self-sacrifice. In Jesus' name, amen.

D. Thought to Remember

The Lord God is merciful.

Home Daily Bible Readings

Monday, July 18—What Happened to Aaron's Faith? (Exodus 32:1-6)

Tuesday, July 19—Is the Molten Calf Your Savior? (Exodus 32:7-14)

Wednesday, July 20—Moses Destroys the Golden Calf (Exodus 32:15-20)

Thursday, July 21—"Out Came This [Golden] Calf" (Exodus 32:21-24)

Friday, July 22—Who Is on the Lord's Side? (Exodus 32:25-35)

Saturday, July 23—God Makes a Distinct People (Exodus 33:12-23)

Sunday, July 24—God Abounds in Love and Faithfulness (Exodus 34:1-10)

Learning by Doing

This page contains an alternate lesson plan emphasizing learning activities. Classes desiring such student involvement will find these suggestions helpful.

Learning Goals

As students participate in today's class session, they should:

1. Review Exodus 32 and 34 to understand why Israel needed to be restored to God.

2. Decide how they need a second chance, or how they should extend a second chance to someone they know well.

Into the Lesson

Write the words, *A Second Chance*, on a large piece of poster board to mount before the class as members arrive.

To begin today's discussion, ask if anyone can remember when someone gave him or her a second chance. Ask volunteers to share their stories. After they have done this, discuss some or all of these questions with the whole class:

1. How important can a second chance be?

2. How does a second chance motivate the person who receives it?

3. What fears may make a person hesitate to offer someone a second chance?

4. What fears may make a person hesitate to *accept* a second chance?

5. How many second chances do you suppose the average person receives in a lifetime?

Explain to the class that today's lesson deals with a time in Israel's history when God's people desperately needed a second chance with Him. There are times when we too recognize such a need in our lives. Today's Scripture indicates how God may feel about offering it.

Into the Word

Before students turn to their Bibles, ask them to remember the different provisions of God that you have studied in the last three weeks. Then use the material in the "Lesson Background" section on page 402 to remind them of the setting of this week's lesson.

Exodus 32 and 34:1-10 form the text for our study in this lesson. Have the students examine this text according to the following divisions: 32:1-10; 11-14; 15-18; 19-24; 25-35; 34:1-10. Choose one of the following activities to accomplish this.

• *Bible-study chart.* In groups of about five, students should answer the following questions for each of the above paragraphs: What does this passage teach about God? What does this passage teach about the people of Israel? What does this passage teach about Moses?

If you wish, a different third of the class could answer only one of the questions about all of the paragraphs. After several minutes of study in groups, students should share as a whole class. Summarize by deciding what the whole passage teaches regarding each of the questions.

• *One-word summaries.* Working in pairs or groups as large as five, students should write one word to summarize each of the paragraphs of the text.

After students have worked for several minutes, ask for volunteers to share their words. Look at one paragraph at a time, comparing the summaries and asking students to explain why they chose as they did.

• *Picture the paragraph.* Students work with partners or in small groups to draw simple stick pictures to illustrate each of the paragraphs. When they have finished, have them mount the pictures around the room and review the chronology of the account.

• *Personalized perspectives.* In groups, students should assume the perspective of one of the main characters or groups in this account: Moses, God, the Israelites, or Aaron. For each paragraph, they are to write a few words or a sentence to explain how their character is reacting to the events recorded there.

After students have written their perspectives, look at the Scripture paragraph by paragraph and let the groups share their perspectives about how each character is involved and what each character is thinking.

Into Life

Ask students to decide how they identify with Aaron, the Israelites, and Moses in the text. Then distribute note cards and ask students to write down a situation in their lives in which they would like to receive a second chance. This may be something large (a habit to break, a career change, the restoration of a damaged relationship) or something relatively small. (Tell them that their notes will be kept private.) Then have them write down the name of a person who deserves a second chance from them.

Close with a guided prayer, asking students to silently pray about the people and situations they have noted.

Let's Talk It Over

The questions on this page are designed to encourage review of the lesson Scriptures and to promote discussion of the lesson by the class. The answers provided are only discussion starters. Let your class talk it over from there.

1. What kinds of things can be broken in a flash of anger that cannot be remade later?

Moses reacted to Israel's idolatry by angrily breaking the stone tablets God had given him. Yet God inscribed His laws on a second set of tablets, this time provided by Moses. Sometimes our tempers may break a relationship with another person in such a way that it may never be restored. That is true, in part, because no person has the capability of God to forgive and restore. It is true also because people are fragile. Each person is unique and each relationship equally so, and no "special glue" can guarantee to restore either if broken. This should give us pause before we let our tempers flare: people and relationships are worth holding tight. Since this kind of self-calming is beyond the ability of most persons, God has offered us His Spirit in Christ Jesus, and He works to develop long-suffering (or patience) in us.

2. Moses was willing to offer himself for the sins of Israel. How can a person today offer himself or herself on behalf of another?

As the lesson writer stated, no fallible human can make atonement for the sins of other fallible persons, so Moses' offer was refused. And yet it is not uncommon to hear the sentiment expressed. Even Paul stated his willingness to sacrifice himself for his countrymen (Romans 9:1-5) in order to get them to respond to the gospel. Many a parent has prayed the same kind of prayer for an errant child, and the feeling is not unknown to quite a few caring and loving Christians. Even though we are not capable of providing a substitutionary sacrifice for other people, yet we can offer ourselves as living sacrifices in the sense of modeling Christian faith, seeking every opportunity to tell others of Jesus, and giving sacrificially in order to support the outreach of the church (Romans 12:1). It is never enough in one sense, but it may be used greatly by God anyway.

3. Why may one suffer for one's misdeeds or sins even after he or she has received forgiveness for them?

Generally we assume that a wrongdoer is either forgiven or is punished; the thought that both could come to a person seems contradictory. However, we must clarify that there may be more than one level of guilt/responsibility involved in the same act of sin/error. God offers us forgiveness eternally in Christ Jesus, and that is unconditional in the sense that God's grace provides what we could never achieve on our own. At the same time there may be human guilt from the violation of civil or criminal laws. It often happens that persons may be forgiven through acceptance of Christ and still have to serve time in prison, pay a fine, or suffer social ostracism for crimes committed. God's mercy is such that we know He has granted us full and complete pardon; but while we live in society, we may still suffer the effects of our sins and bad choices.

4. How is it that we sometimes experience the best of blessings in the worst of times?

It frequently happens that we discover greater measures of God's goodness when we seem at our lowest points. In what must have been a terribly low point of Moses' life (when his people sinned so grievously and he destroyed the very tablets God had given him), he had the amazing privilege of receiving a special vision of God's glory. The apostle Paul related that in his time of greatest weakness and frustration God's strength sustained him more than ever before (2 Corinthians 12:7-10). Could it be that not only is God increasingly helpful when we are at our weakest and lowest, but also that in those times we may be much more attentive to Him and cleansed of any thoughts of our self-sufficiency?

5. How should every Christian view the suffering of Christ on the cross? Why?

Often we think about the cross of Christ in an abstract and general way. We tend to think only in terms of the sins of humanity as the reason for His atoning death. However, when we are confronted with the reality of our own sins each of us must admit to himself or herself, "Jesus died because *I* rebelled against God and distorted His will for my life." To think that each of us has caused great pain and sorrow to God himself is not pleasant, but it is necessary if we would fully appreciate the meaning of His grace in a personal way. Then each can say, "The amazing reality that God loves and forgives *me* overwhelms me with gratitude and a desire to give Him my life."

God Is With Us

DEVOTIONAL READING: Exodus 33:12-16.

LESSON SCRIPTURE: Exodus 25:1-9; 29:38-46; 40:16-38.

PRINTED TEXT: Exodus 25:1-8; 29:42-46; 40:33b-38.

Exodus 25:1-8

1 And the LORD spake unto Moses, saying,

2 Speak unto the children of Israel, that they bring me an offering: of every man that giveth it willingly with his heart ye shall take my offering.

3 And this is the offering which ye shall take of them; gold, and silver, and brass,

4 And blue, and purple, and scarlet, and fine linen, and goats' hair,

5 And rams' skins dyed red, and badgers' skins, and shittim wood,

6 Oil for the light, spices for anointing oil, and for sweet incense,

7 Onyx stones, and stones to be set in the ephod, and in the breastplate.

8 And let them make me a sanctuary; that I may dwell among them.

Exodus 29:42-46

42 This shall be a continual burnt offering throughout your generations at the door of the tabernacle of the congregation before the LORD, where I will meet you, to speak there unto thee.

43 And there I will meet with the children of Israel, and the tabernacle shall be sanctified by my glory.

44 And I will sanctify the tabernacle of the congregation, and the altar: I will sanctify also both Aaron and his sons, to minister to me in the priest's office.

45 And I will dwell among the children of Israel, and will be their God.

46 And they shall know that I am the LORD their God, that brought them forth out of the land of Egypt, that I may dwell among them: I am the LORD their God.

Exodus 40:33b-38

33b So Moses finished the work.

34 Then a cloud covered the tent of the congregation, and the glory of the LORD filled the tabernacle.

35 And Moses was not able to enter into the tent of the congregation, because the cloud abode thereon, and the glory of the LORD filled the tabernacle.

36 And when the cloud was taken up from over the tabernacle, the children of Israel went onward in all their journeys:

37 But if the cloud were not taken up, then they journeyed not till the day that it was taken up.

38 For the cloud of the LORD was upon the tabernacle by day, and fire was on it by night, in the sight of all the house of Israel, throughout all their journeys.

GOLDEN TEXT: I will dwell among the children of Israel, and will be their God.
—Exodus 29:45.

God Redeems a People

Unit 2: Provision for Present and Future (Lessons 5-9)

Lesson Aims

As a result of studying this lesson, each student should:

1. Have a better understanding of the tabernacle, its purpose, and its place in Israel's worship.

2. Appreciate the sacrifices the Israelites made in order to build the tabernacle.

3. Recognize the importance of having a designated place of worship.

4. Have a greater sense of reverence for God who dwells among us.

Lesson Outline

INTRODUCTION
   A. From the Foundation to the Steeple
   B. Lesson Background
 I. AN OFFERING FOR GOD (Exodus 25:1-8)
   A. Attitude (vv. 1, 2)
   B. Building Materials (vv. 3-5)
   C. Supplies (vv. 6, 7)
   D. Purpose (v. 8)
      Make Me a House
 II. A SANCTUARY FOR GOD (Exodus 29:42-46)
   A. A Place of Meeting (vv. 42, 43)
   B. A Place of Ministry (v. 44)
   C. A Place of God's Presence (vv. 45, 46)
III. THE TABERNACLE COMPLETED (Exodus 40:33b-38)
   A. God's Presence Indicated (vv. 33b-35)
   B. God's Guidance (vv. 36-38)
CONCLUSION
   A. God's Presence
   B. Meeting Needs
   C. A Lost Reverence
   D. Let Us Pray
   E. Thought to Remember

Display visual 9 of the visuals packet and let it remain before the class. The visual is shown on page 413.

Introduction

A. From the Foundation to the Steeple

A church in a remote village in New England had no church building and only occasional preaching. After many years, and by much sacrifice and hard work, they were able to build a meetinghouse. When it came time to dedicate the building, they had to invite a minister from a neighboring town to lead in the service because they had no minister.

The visiting minister, who was accustomed to participating in dedication services in which several ministers shared, asked, "What part do you want me to take in the dedication?"

One of the members, thinking that the question referred to the part of the building that was to be included in the dedication, replied, "Oh, the whole thing. We want everything from the foundation to the top of the steeple to be dedicated to the Lord."

Even so, when the Lord gave Israel instructions for the building of the tabernacle, He intended that every piece of it and every act of worship performed in it be dedicated to Him.

B. Lesson Background

While the Israelites were encamped at Mount Sinai, God called Moses to the top of the mount several times to communicate His laws to the Israelites' leader. Apparently the first of these ascents involved God's giving the instructions that are recorded in Exodus 20:22—23:33. After Moses delivered these to the people and received their commitment to obey them, he ratified their covenant with God through the offering of sacrifices and the sprinkling of blood on the representatives of the twelve tribes (Exodus 24:3-8).

Moses then took Aaron, two of Aaron's sons, Joshua, and seventy of the elders of Israel and returned to the mount. Leaving the others behind at various stages on the mount, Moses alone proceeded to the top in order to commune with God. In all, Moses was in the mount for forty days. During this time he received the directions for the building of the tabernacle and its furniture, for the making of the priest's garments, for the consecration of the priests, and for the services that were to be conducted in the tabernacle, as well as other instructions (Exodus 24:9—31:17). The first two portions of the printed text for this lesson contain some of the instructions that God gave Moses during this forty-day period.

We should note also that while Moses was meeting with God on this occasion, God gave him the original stone tablets of testimony. The event we studied in last week's lesson occurred when this meeting with God had ended.

How to Say It

EPHOD.   *ee*-fod.

I. An Offering for God
(Exodus 25:1-8)

A. Attitude (vv. 1, 2)

1, 2. And the LORD spake unto Moses, saying, Speak unto the children of Israel, that they bring me an offering: of every man that giveth it willingly with his heart ye shall take my offering.

God was about to reveal to Moses the specifications for the tabernacle and its furniture. The tabernacle was to be a physical structure, so physical materials would be needed for its construction. God instructed Moses, therefore, to ask the people to offer the needed materials. Since the people would be the primary beneficiaries of God's presence among them, it was altogether fitting that they provide the materials for the tabernacle's construction.

Literally, the phrase *of every man that giveth it willingly with his heart* may be translated "of every man whose heart drives him." God seeks only those gifts that are freely given, from persons whose hearts prompt them to give. "God loveth a cheerful giver" (2 Corinthians 9:7). God rejects gifts that are given grudgingly or of necessity. The Israelites had little experience in bringing gifts to God, and so it would have been no surprise if they had responded to this appeal in a stingy fashion. Amazingly, however, when Moses later requested this offering of the people, they gave generously, to such an extent that Moses finally had to tell them to bring no more (Exodus 36:4-7).

B. Building Materials (vv. 3-5)

3-5. And this is the offering which ye shall take of them; gold, and silver, and brass, and blue, and purple, and scarlet, and fine linen, and goats' hair, and rams' skins dyed red, and badgers' skins, and shittim wood.

The materials here requested were the most expensive available. Nothing about the tabernacle was to be cheap. The metals requested—*gold, and silver, and brass*—are listed in the descending order of their value. The ark of the covenant, made of wood, was to be overlaid with gold, inside and out. The mercy seat, the lid for the ark, was to be of pure gold with a gold cherub on each end of the seat. The table of showbread was to be overlaid with pure gold, and the seven-branched candlestick and the utensils used with it were to be of pure gold. The sockets to hold the boards of the tabernacle were to be silver, as were the bands for the posts and the hooks for the curtains. *Brass*, or more correctly, bronze, was used as a covering for the altar and for some of the vessels used at the altar and for other items used in the construction of the tabernacle.

Blue, and purple, and scarlet. These referred to cloth dyed these different colors. The cloth was probably wool from the Israelites' flocks. The *blue* was dyed by indigo, which was widely used in Egypt. The *purple* dye came from a shellfish found in the eastern Mediterranean, and since each one produced only a tiny drop, purple cloth was very expensive. The *scarlet* dye, called cochineal, came from an insect that fed on the holm oak. The *fine linen* was a product of Egypt and usually was not dyed. The *goats' hair* was a fabric made from the soft inner wool of certain goats. This fabric was frequently used for tents.

The Egyptians had developed considerable skill in tanning and dyeing animal skins, and so it is likely that the *rams' skins dyed red* had been brought from Egypt when the Israelites left. Many Bible students question the translation *badgers' skins*, since this animal is not found in Egypt and rarely in the wilderness. Some think that the word used here is a general term for dolphins, seals, or sea cows, which are found in the Red Sea. The *shittim wood* is usually translated "acacia wood" in modern versions. The acacia is a small tree that usually grows in arid places. Its wood is hard, heavy, and fine grained, making it very suitable for use in making furniture.

C. Supplies (vv. 6, 7)

6, 7. Oil for the light, spices for anointing oil, and for sweet incense, onyx stones, and stones to be set in the ephod, and in the breastplate.

The *oil* was olive oil for the lamps in the candlestick, to be located in the Holy Place (Exodus 27:20). The *spices* were to be mixed with oil to make a holy ointment, which would be used to consecrate the tabernacle, all the items in it and the vessels associated with them, and also to consecrate Aaron and his sons to the priesthood (30:22-31). Spices would be used also in making *sweet incense* for use in the tabernacle (30:34-36). The *onyx stones* were mounted in gold settings and placed on the shoulders of the *ephod*, a garment worn by the high priest. A dozen precious stones were needed for the *breastplate* worn by him (Exodus 28:9-21).

D. Purpose (v. 8)

8. And let them make me a sanctuary; that I may dwell among them.

After specifying the items the people were to give, God revealed the purpose for them. *A sanctuary*, that is, a hallowed place. This comprehensive term included the tabernacle with its furniture, its tent, and its court. This sanctuary would be hallowed as God's dwelling place among the Israelites.

MAKE ME A HOUSE

Grandfather Carson was a master carpenter. When he brought his family to the Willamette Valley in the new state of Oregon, his skills in carpentry provided a living for them. His excellent work and honesty kept him in constant demand in the city where he had settled.

One day his wife, Alameda, said, "George, its time for you to build a house for our growing family. I know just how it must be to meet our needs." Over a period of weeks Alameda told George her dream for their home, and he planned how he would proceed. He bought the best material available, and he didn't hurry in building the house. In a few months he had constructed his wife's dream. It was a house that would stand as the center for family life until it was destroyed by fire two generations later. It was a house for fun, hard work, hospitality, and love.

George Carson lived out his years in that house. There is no need to describe the structure—its purpose is what is important. Here family could come and find comfort, rest, and renewal. Here children were born, and they and grandchildren were taught the moral and spiritual truths that guided the family. Here guests were welcomed and made to feel at home.

To Moses God said, "Make me a house." It was God's desire to dwell among the people. The house would be a place where Israel could come and worship and learn God's laws. It would be the center of the nation's spiritual life.

God still wants to dwell among His people today, not so much in a house, however, as in their hearts. Is He welcome in your life? —W. P.

II. A Sanctuary for God (Exodus 29:42-46)

A. A Place of Meeting (vv. 42, 43)

42, 43. This shall be a continual burnt offering throughout your generations at the door of the tabernacle of the congregation before the LORD, where I will meet you, to speak there unto thee. And there I will meet with the children of Israel, and the tabernacle shall be sanctified by my glory.

The altar of burnt offering stood in the court that surrounded the tabernacle. The *burnt offering,* consisting of two lambs, was placed upon this altar. One lamb was offered in the morning and one in the evening (Exodus 29:38-41). This offering was to be made every day *throughout your generations,* that is, for generation after generation. Here God promised to meet His people and communicate with them. Every spot in God's creation is holy because He made the

physical world and because He inhabits it. But some places enjoy greater sanctity because of their function, in this case the place where God revealed His will to His people.

B. A Place of Ministry (v. 44)

44. And I will sanctify the tabernacle of the congregation, and the altar: I will sanctify also both Aaron and his sons, to minister to me in the priest's office.

This verse summarizes chapter 29, which deals with the consecration of the priests.

God promised that when the materials for the tabernacle were assembled and it was erected, then He would *sanctify* it. He would also sanctify *the altar.* Leviticus 9:24 tells us that the first time a sacrifice was offered upon the altar, fire from the Lord came out and consumed the sacrifice. The people who witnessed that scene shouted and fell on their faces.

God also promised to sanctify *both Aaron and his sons* in the priesthood. This would mark the beginning of the Aaronic priesthood. Only descendants of Aaron would serve as priests in the tabernacle and later in the temple. The reference here undoubtedly includes the public service in which Aaron and his sons were formally set apart for their offices. The deeper sanctification, however, was that performed by God as He accepted the offerings and sacrifices of the people and set His approval upon them.

The priests in ancient Israel had certain specific duties. They were to burn incense on the altar in the Holy Place, put the showbread on the table each Sabbath, and trim the lamps of the candlestick daily so the light would burn continually. They were also required to attend the altar and offer various sacrifices there. Further, they were responsible for instructing the people in the law. Thus it was no light service into which Aaron and his sons were called.

C. A Place of God's Presence (vv. 45, 46)

45, 46. And I will dwell among the children of Israel, and will be their God. And they shall know that I am the LORD their God, that brought them forth out of the land of Egypt, that I may dwell among them: I am the LORD their God.

God's most precious promise was that He would *dwell among the children of Israel, and . . . be their God.* In fact, He had brought them out of Egypt for this very purpose. We read later of God's presence in the tabernacle, indicated by the manifestation of His glory (Numbers 14:10; 16:19, 42; 20:6). God's glory would dwell specifically in the Holy of Holies, resting between the cherubim above the mercy seat (Leviticus 16:2). God's presence with His people would be made known in other ways as well, as He led, sustained, and defended them in the future, just as He had done in bringing them *out of the land of Egypt*.

Christians enjoy a similar blessing in the indwelling of the Holy Spirit. The gift of the Holy Spirit marks the beginning of the Christian life (Acts 2:38). One cannot belong to Christ unless he has the Spirit of Christ (Romans 8:9). One's life shows the presence of the Spirit by definite fruit (Galatians 5:22-25). And the Spirit provides guidance and comfort.

III. The Tabernacle Completed (Exodus 40:33b-38)

After his final descent from Mount Sinai (Exodus 34:29), Moses gathered the people together and told them of God's instructions for the building of the tabernacle. The people responded generously to the call for an offering of the needed materials. Two men, whom God had endowed with wisdom and understanding in all manner of workmanship, led in the construction of the tabernacle, its furnishings, its court, and in the making of the priests' garments. This is recorded in Exodus 35:4—39:43.

Exodus 40:1-33a records God's command and Moses' fulfillment of the command to set up the tabernacle, to place all the furniture in it, and to set up the court round about. Following this, Moses consecrated the entire sanctuary to God, and anointed Aaron and his sons to minister to God in the priest's office.

A. God's Presence Indicated (vv. 33b-35)

33b-35. So Moses finished the work. Then a cloud covered the tent of the congregation, and the glory of the LORD filled the tabernacle. And Moses was not able to enter into the tent of the congregation, because the cloud abode thereon, and the glory of the LORD filled the tabernacle.

So Moses finished the work. God ordered the sanctuary to be set up on the first day of the first month (of the second year) after Israel's departure

visual 9

from Egypt (40:2), and Moses did as instructed (v. 17). We are not told how long this job took, but since all of the parts of the tabernacle and its surrounding court were already finished, the whole task may have been completed in one day.

As soon as this work was finished, the *cloud* that had guided them through the wilderness covered the tabernacle. At the same time *the glory of the Lord*, appearing as a brilliant light, filled the interior of it. Both manifestations signified God's approval of the work that was done in constructing the tabernacle, and His willingness to dwell among the people of Israel. Moses, it seems, would have reentered the tabernacle, but he could not because of the brilliance of God's glory.

B. God's Guidance (vv. 36-38)

36-38. And when the cloud was taken up from over the tabernacle, the children of Israel went onward in all their journeys: but if the cloud were not taken up, then they journeyed not till the day that it was taken up. For the cloud of the LORD was upon the tabernacle by day, and fire was on it by night, in the sight of all the house of Israel, throughout all their journeys.

These three verses, which conclude the book of Exodus, tell how God guided the Israelites as they traveled through the wilderness. The *cloud* showed them not only where to go but when to go. It was above the tabernacle during the daytime, and at night *fire* replaced the cloud. Jehovah's presence was indicated by both of these manifestations. They were visible to all who were in the camp, giving assurance to everyone that God was in their midst.

Conclusion

A. God's Presence

The Israelites had considerable evidence that God was watching over them and guiding them. They had seen the mighty miracles that occurred just before and during their escape from Egypt. In the wilderness God provided food and water. He led them with the pillar of cloud by day and the pillar of fire by night, and He would continue to do this in their wilderness journey. Because the Israelites had received very little teaching about Jehovah, they needed some obvious signs to assure them that He was really in their midst. And God provided the physical signs the people needed.

We today may be better educated and more sophisticated than were these Israelites just freed from slavery, yet we also need to be reassured of the presence of God in our lives. Some believe that God ought to reveal himself to us in some physical, dramatic way so that the people of our generation would believe in Him. But that's not the way it worked out for the Israelites. Even with the evidence of God's presence before them day and night, they murmured against Him and His appointed leaders. On occasion they even engaged in open rebellion (Numbers 16:1-35).

We have one very important advantage that the Israelites didn't have. We have God's revelation through the written Word, and thus we don't really need the dramatic revelation that He provided for them. For the Israelites to become believers they needed to see the pillars of cloud or fire or witness some of the miracles associated with the exodus from Egypt. In a similar way, we need to experience God's Word firsthand before it can move us to faith. For that reason we need to be involved in regular, systematic Bible study. We need to study the history of God's chosen nation just as we are doing in this series of lessons to appreciate His long and patient relationship with them, a relationship that culminated in the coming of His Son, Jesus Christ.

B. Meeting Needs

The building of the tabernacle met two of man's needs: his need for a specific place in which to worship and his need to make a tangible expression of his love for God.

Certainly God can be worshiped in any place, but we worship more easily and are inclined to worship more regularly if we have surroundings appointed for worship. The spiritual life of Israel was richer because of the tabernacle.

Opportunity for the Israelites to make a tangible expression of their love for God was provided in the bringing of offerings to build the tabernacle. Thus we see that worship involves both subjective and objective elements. It is good for one to contemplate God in one's own heart. It is also good for a person to go to a place of worship. It is good for a person to praise and adore God in prayer, but that person also needs to make a material offering to God. If one's religion is to be meaningful, one's entire being must participate in it. That is why a religion apart from offerings of tangible things to God is virtually meaningless.

God needed neither the sanctuary nor the offerings of the people. Israel was not building a place to which God needed to come, but a place to which they needed to come. God did not need their offerings, for "the earth is the Lord's." He did not need their gifts—they needed to bring their gifts. Here, as in all things, God showed His love by meeting the needs of man.

C. A Lost Reverence

Ours is an irreverent age. We have lost our respect for even the holiest things. Several factors may account for this. First, science has pushed the boundaries of our knowledge into areas that were once thought almost beyond belief. Second, familiarity breeds contempt. When we deal day after day with things that once amazed us, we soon come to take them for granted. This can happen even in our relationship with God. The prayer time that we once approached with such reverence becomes a habit we casually accept. The awe we once had as we approached the Communion table gradually erodes.

Perhaps the greatest threat to our sense of reverence has come because we have lifted ourselves into the place that properly belongs to God. Our Western culture emphasizes the individual, insisting that each person is sovereign. People's desire to "do their own thing" leads them to turn aside from the things God would have them do. A God who is casually or ignorantly neglected is a God who soon is rejected. The unsophisticated Israelites came into God's presence with awe because they had seen His power. Should not we who have known His power many times over show similar reverence?

D. Let Us Pray

Almighty God, high, holy, and lifted up, let us never forget that You are God and we are but mortal humans. Keep us humble in the knowledge that You are ever present both to protect us and to judge us. In Jesus' name we pray. Amen.

E. Thought to Remember

"I will dwell among the children of Israel, and will be their God" (Exodus 29:45).

Home Daily Bible Readings

Monday, July 25—Israel to Bring an Offering (Exodus 25:1-9)

Tuesday, July 26—Make a Beautiful Sanctuary (Exodus 25:10-22)

Wednesday, July 27—Priests to Wear Beautiful Robes (Exodus 28:1-5)

Thursday, July 28—Service for Consecrating Priests (Exodus 29:1-37)

Friday, July 29—Daily Offerings (Exodus 29:38-46)

Saturday, July 30—The Erection of the Tabernacle (Exodus 40:16-33)

Sunday, July 31—The Glory of the Lord (Exodus 40:34-38)

Learning by Doing

This page contains an alternate lesson plan emphasizing learning activities. Classes desiring such student involvement will find these suggestions helpful.

Learning Goals

As students participate in today's class session, they should:

1. Review how the tabernacle became the means for Israel to experience God's presence among them.

2. Decide how Christians today can be aware of God's presence in their lives.

3. Choose one specific way to build their own sense of God's presence in their lives.

Into the Lesson

Write the following open-ended sentence on the chalkboard for class members to see as they arrive: "I feel closest to God when—"

Distribute slips of paper and ask class members to jot on them their completions of the sentence. Class members should *not* write their names on their papers. Collect the papers and read them back to the class.

Discuss some or all of these questions with the class:

1. Do you think it is easy or difficult to experience the presence of God? Why?

2. What are the biggest factors affecting whether or not you feel close to God?

3. What part of the church's worship services helps you feel close to God? Is there any part of the worship services that hinders your closeness to Him? If so, what is it?

4. Do you have some other special place that helps you focus on God? Describe it to the class.

Today's lesson discusses God's gift of His presence to the Israelites. Tell class members that while they are studying that gift, they can also reflect on how He has provided His presence for every Christian today.

Into the Word

Use the "Lesson Background" section on page 410 to prepare a two-minute lecture that connects this week's study with last week's.

As a volunteer reads Exodus 25:1-8 aloud to the class, your students should listen and decide, "How did God provide materials for the tabernacle?"

Ask for brief answers to the question, and then explain the significance of the various materials listed in this passage. (See the explanations under the appropriate verses of the Scripture text.) Discuss, "How do you think the Israelites'

gifts for the tabernacle affected the quality of their worship there? Why did God prescribe such expensive materials for the tabernacle?"

As another volunteer reads Exodus 29:42-46 to the class, class members should listen and decide, "How were the people to be represented before God?"

Hear answers, and then explain the Aaronic priesthood (once again using information from the comments of explanation of these verses).

Ask a third volunteer to read Exodus 40:33b-38 while class members listen and decide, "How did God indicate to the Israelites His presence with them?"

Once again hear answers, and then share insights given under these verses of the text.

Into Life

Discuss, "Would it be easier for us today to realize God's presence if we had a physical manifestation of it among us? Why do you suppose God does not appear to us today in a cloud or a pillar of fire or a lightning bolt?"

Read two passages that speak of God's presence among Christians in the church: Matthew 18:20 and 28:20.

Write this line on your chalkboard: "Everywhere I go I see you." Contemporary Christian musical artist Rich Mullins repeats that line again and again at the end of his song, "I See You." (You may want to play it for your class members. It's on the album, "The World as Best as I Remember It, Volume 1," *Reunion Records.*)

Ask class members what Christians can do to foster this attitude in their everyday lives. How can we be aware of God's presence day by day and hour by hour? Is there something special we can do at particular times to stay aware of His presence all the time?

As class members suggest ideas, write them on the chalkboard. (Possibilities to get you started: Commit a regular time to Bible study and prayer; attend church worship services every week; listen regularly to Christian music—perhaps in the car on the way to work; join a small group for Bible study or prayer; find a prayer partner and meet with him or her at least once a month. Once a week is better!)

Ask class members to survey the list of ideas on the board and choose one that they can implement this week.

Let's Talk It Over

The questions on this page are designed to encourage review of the lesson Scriptures and to promote discussion of the lesson by the class. The answers provided are only discussion starters. Let your class talk it over from there.

1. How costly should be the furnishings of our place of worship?

Some plead a concern for stewardship to justify their furnishing the church building with old, used items instead of spending for new things. If a church actually gives to missions or benevolence the money that is saved, that may indeed be good stewardship. Too many churches, however, actually don't give the money at all, and end up just being cheap with God. The Israelites surely had many benevolent needs among them in their wilderness experience, but God called for jewels, rare cloth, and precious metals anyway. We need a point of balance: by being too frugal we may give outsiders the impression that our worship is unimportant and not worth much; yet anyone can be turned off when buildings get too lavish. It takes much thought and prayer, but people who want to glorify God will find the right way.

2. Is the church building more holy than other places? How much respect or special treatment should it be given?

When Jesus spoke with the Samaritan woman at the well, the discussion turned to the subject of where a person ought to worship in order to be pleasing to God. Jesus revealed that the important consideration was not *where* one worshiped, but *how*. He indicated that worship is valid only when it is done in spirit and in truth (John 4:21-24). Christians, therefore, have rightly concluded that there is no special place on earth where God dwells to the exclusion of all others. Nevertheless, the dedicating of a place for the purpose of worship should draw at least an attitude of respect from people. What that means will vary with individual interpretations, but such respect does provide a guideline. Having one place that has that specific purpose does not negate the awareness of the presence of God in all times and places. Rather, it can enhance it, much as celebrating a special day or occasion makes us more aware every day of the blessings we emphasize on that particular day.

3. The tabernacle became the center of the worship of the nation of Israel. List several reasons why the assembling of Christians for corporate worship is still valid and necessary.

Hebrews 10:24, 25 give three reasons for corporate worship. One is the Scriptural command to be faithful in assembling. Thus, assembling for worship is not optional but is a matter of obedience. A second reason is that Christians may stimulate one another to love and good deeds. The implication is that without this stimulation love and good deeds would be lacking. The third reason stated is that Christians encourage one another as they meet together for worship. That this encouragement is necessary may be seen from the fact that very few people who purposely neglect corporate worship remain faithful to the Lord for very long.

4. What should we bring to worship in order to please God?

Just as the Israelites were called to bring their offerings to make the tabernacle a reality, we too are to bring our gifts to Him. Our offering should be brought as a token that all we have belongs to God and as a thanksgiving for what He has given us. Most important, we should come with a reverent and humble heart, willing to be confronted by God in the awesome experience of worship.

5. If we were to receive some visible evidence of God's presence and blessing (such as Israel was given in the pillar of cloud and fire), what effect do you think that would have on our faithfulness to God?

While it is sometimes tempting to think that our trust in God would be stronger if we had all the physical evidence of God's presence that Israel had, an honest appraisal might not support such a conclusion. Although there were times when the Israelites seemed to walk the narrow road of faith, there were other times when they gave way to doubt and disobedience. Even Jesus' disciples fell away from Him in fear, and this while He yet lived among them. The conclusion we must draw, then, is that physical objects and signs do not guarantee one's faithfulness to God or a closer relationship with Him. The key to faithfulness is our willingness to allow God's Spirit to dwell within us and to lead our steps in the ways of righteousness (see John 16:7-11). As we read with open hearts the Word the Spirit inspired and seek divine help through prayer, our trust and obedience will increase.

Celebrate God's Ownership

DEVOTIONAL READING: Deuteronomy 4:5-9.

LESSON SCRIPTURE: Leviticus 25.

PRINTED TEXT: Leviticus 25:8-10, 23-28, 39-42.

Leviticus 25:8-10, 23-28, 39-42

8 And thou shalt number seven sabbaths of years unto thee, seven times seven years; and the space of the seven sabbaths of years shall be unto thee forty and nine years.

9 Then shalt thou cause the trumpet of the jubilee to sound on the tenth day of the seventh month, in the day of atonement shall ye make the trumpet sound throughout all your land.

10 And ye shall hallow the fiftieth year, and proclaim liberty throughout all the land unto all the inhabitants thereof: it shall be a jubilee unto you; and ye shall return every man unto his possession, and ye shall return every man unto his family.

. . . .

23 The land shall not be sold for ever: for the land is mine; for ye are strangers and sojourners with me.

24 And in all the land of your possession ye shall grant a redemption for the land.

25 If thy brother be waxen poor, and hath sold away some of his possession, and if any of his kin come to redeem it, then shall he redeem that which his brother sold.

26 And if the man have none to redeem it, and himself be able to redeem it;

27 Then let him count the years of the sale thereof, and restore the overplus unto the man to whom he sold it; that he may return unto his possession.

28 But if he be not able to restore it to him, then that which is sold shall remain in the hand of him that hath bought it until the year of jubilee: and in the jubilee it shall go out, and he shall return unto his possession.

. . . .

39 And if thy brother that dwelleth by thee be waxen poor, and be sold unto thee; thou shalt not compel him to serve as a bondservant:

40 But as a hired servant, and as a sojourner, he shall be with thee, and shall serve thee unto the year of jubilee:

41 And then shall he depart from thee, both he and his children with him, and shall return unto his own family, and unto the possession of his fathers shall he return.

42 For they are my servants, which I brought forth out of the land of Egypt: they shall not be sold as bondmen.

GOLDEN TEXT: The land shall not be sold for ever: for the land is mine; for ye are strangers and sojourners with me.—Leviticus 25:23.

Lesson Aims

As a result of studying this lesson, the students should:

1. Have a growing appreciation for God's concern for social justice, as revealed in the provisions of the law of Moses.

2. Understand that they are stewards, not owners, of whatever God has placed in their hands.

3. Select one way in which they will be better stewards for God.

Lesson Outline

INTRODUCTION

    A. A Faithful Steward

    B. Lesson Background

  I. THE JUBILEE YEAR (Leviticus 25:8-10)

    A. Establishment (v. 8)

    B. Proclamation (v. 9)

    C. Results (v. 10)

 II. LAWS REGARDING THE LAND (Leviticus 25:23-28)

    A. Recognition of God's Ownership (vv. 23, 24)

    B. Redemption by Kin (v. 25)

    C. Redemption by Owner (vv. 26, 27)

    D. Return in the Jubilee Year (v. 28)

      Redeemed!

III. PROVISIONS FOR THE POOR (Leviticus 25:39-42)

    A. Slavery Forbidden (v. 39)

    B. Servants Until the Jubilee Year (vv. 40-42)

      No Slaves!

CONCLUSION

    A. Neither Communism nor Capitalism

    B. Let Us Pray

    C. Thought to Remember

Display visual 10 of the visuals packet throughout this session. The visual is shown on page 421.

Introduction

A. A Faithful Steward

As a young man Garfield Todd went as a missionary from his native New Zealand to Southern Rhodesia, the nation now known as Zimbabwe. In addition to his work as a missionary, he became involved in farming and ranch-ing. His ranching activities became quite prosperous, and he continued to enlarge his land holdings. He was encouraged to enter politics, and eventually he was elected prime minister. However, his concern for the rights of the nationals and his efforts to seek justice for them alienated the white minority, and he was soon voted out of office. Under the regime that followed he was looked upon as subversive and often was subjected to house arrest.

Eventually nationals were able to gain control of the government, and Todd regained some of his freedoms. Then he began to give away portions of his land to responsible nationals, who became farmers and ranchers. On one occasion he was asked why he was giving away his land. "Oh," he responded, "I'm not giving away *my* land. I only held it as a steward for the Lord. In turning it over to nationals, I'm just exercising that stewardship in a different way."

The Israelites were to be God's stewards of the promised land when they took possession of it. After the Canaanites were driven out, each family among the Israelites would be allotted a portion of the land. A person might sell his family allotment, but in the jubilee year it was to revert to him or to his heirs. In this way the Israelites would be reminded that the land really belonged to God and that they were but exercising stewardship over it.

B. Lesson Background

At first reading, the book of Leviticus may seem to contain little of interest or value to a Christian. The book describes in detail the requirements pertaining to the various types of sacrifices the Israelites were to make. Many of the duties of the priests are given here as well. The book contains various laws that governed Jewish society, and it gives instruction about how to apply the Ten Commandments in everyday life. All of these laws were revealed to Moses by God. One of the recurring clauses scattered throughout the book is, "the Lord spake unto Moses."

The book of Exodus closes with the construction and dedication of the tabernacle. Leviticus, with its detailed description of the ceremonies and activities of the priests who ministered in the tabernacle, logically follows. In and of themselves these activities have no meaning to the Christian, and yet many of them do look forward to the coming of the Savior and His sacrificial death. For instance, the great day of atonement with its sacrifices certainly prefigures the taking away of our sins by Christ (Leviticus 16).

The practical application of some of the laws found in Leviticus would be made when the Israelites were enjoying a settled life in the promised land rather than while they were journeying in the wilderness. At the time these laws were given, however, the people anticipated being in the promised land within a short time. Unfortunately, when the spies were sent out and then returned with their report (Numbers 13, 14), the people began to murmur and complain that they would be unable to take the land from the inhabitants. As a result, God sentenced them to forty years of wandering in the wilderness. Because the people's entrance into the promised land was delayed, so too was the application of some of these regulations.

The book of Leviticus contains very little narrative material. Perhaps the most dramatic event in the book was the death of Nadab and Abihu, sons of Aaron. They ignored the commands of the Lord and offered strange fire before Him. For their presumption and arrogance they were consumed by fire that came out from the presence of the Lord.

Today's lesson deals with the year of jubilee and some of the ways it impacted the lives of the people.

I. The Jubilee Year
(Leviticus 25:8-10)
A. Establishment (v. 8)

8. And thou shalt number seven sabbaths of years unto thee, seven times seven years; and the space of the seven sabbaths of years shall be unto thee forty and nine years.

The first seven verses of this chapter contain God's requirements for observing the sabbatical year. Verse 8 begins instructions for observing the jubilee year. The jubilee year was to be observed every fiftieth year, that is, after the passage of seven sabbatical years. Since it came every fifty years, most people would have an opportunity to observe it only once in a lifetime, and thus it was a very special occasion.

B. Proclamation (v. 9)

9. Then shalt thou cause the trumpet of the jubilee to sound on the tenth day of the seventh month, in the day of atonement shall ye make the trumpet sound throughout all your land.

The beginning of the jubilee year was announced by the sounding of the ram's horn, or *shophar*. The word *jubilee* comes from the Hebrew word that originally meant "a blast of a trumpet." In time it came to mean the year of the trumpet blast, the happy occasion for those who were set free or returned to their lost fields. The trumpet blast announcing this joyous year was to occur *on the tenth day* of Tishri, *the seventh month* in the sacred calendar. This was also *the*

How to Say It

ABIHU.   Uh-*bye*-hew.
NADAB.   *Nay*-dab.
SHOPHAR (Hebrew).   *show*-far.
TISHRI.   *Tish*-ree.

---

day of atonement, one of the most sacred days of the Jewish year. This ordinarily falls during our September or October. By this time in Palestine the harvest of both grain and fruit would have been completed, and men would begin to prepare the soil for planting next year's crop. In the year of jubilee, however, planting was not done, since the fields were to lie fallow (v. 11).

C. Results (v. 10)

10. And ye shall hallow the fiftieth year, and proclaim liberty throughout all the land unto all the inhabitants thereof: it shall be a jubilee unto you; and ye shall return every man unto his possession, and ye shall return every man unto his family.

The people were to *hallow the fiftieth year*. To *hallow* a year is to set it apart, make it a special year. One way they were to hallow this year was by not planting the fields or tending the vineyards. While the people were allowed to gather for immediate use that which grew voluntarily without planting, they were not to systematically plant, cultivate, or harvest any crop during the year of jubilee. The time they normally would spend in agricultural activities could be spent in prayer and meditation, thus making the year more sacred.

The jubilee year was a time of liberation. It freed the land that had been sold so that it could revert back to the original owners or their heirs. It also freed those persons who had sold themselves into bondage to get out of debt. It is worth noting that a portion of this verse is found on the Liberty Bell: *Proclaim liberty throughout all the land unto all the inhabitants thereof.* Those who insist that the Old Testament is not relevant to our times need to be reminded of this passage.

II. Laws Regarding the Land
(Leviticus 25:23-28)
A. Recognition of God's Ownership
(vv. 23, 24)

23, 24. The land shall not be sold for ever: for the land is mine; for ye are strangers and sojourners with me. And in all the land of your possession ye shall grant a redemption for the land.

When the Israelites came into the land that God would give them, they were to understand that that land could not be sold; it could, in effect, only be leased. This regulation was not based on economics or political theories. Rather, it was based on the fact that the land belonged to God. The people who lived on it and used it were but tenants, or stewards. This idea is emphasized in the expression *strangers and sojourners*. Israel was to remember that the land in which they were to dwell was not really theirs; it belonged to God.

Christian stewardship is based on the same principle. Everything that we claim to possess really belongs to God. It is not ours to use simply to indulge ourselves; rather, it is a trust that we are required to exercise under God. He will hold us responsible for how we administer that trust. If Christians understood this principle, most of the hassles associated with church finances and budgets would evaporate.

Verse 24 indicates that those who took possession of the property of others were to *grant a redemption for the land*. This is explained in verses 25-28.

B. Redemption by Kin (v. 25)

25. If thy brother be waxen poor, and hath sold away some of his possession, and if any of his kin come to redeem it, then shall he redeem that which his brother sold.

Because of poor crops, or bad health, or any of many reasons, a person might fall into debt and have to sell his land to pay the debt. The sale of land was never final, however. This verse and the following verses reveal three ways by which the land could be redeemed. The first of these is that a relative might buy the land so it would return to the family of the original owner. Apparently a relative did not have a legal obligation to redeem his kinsman's land, but in a society such as that in ancient Israel, the moral obligation to do so must have been very strong.

C. Redemption by Owner (vv. 26, 27)

26, 27. And if the man have none to redeem it, and himself be able to redeem it; then let him count the years of the sale thereof, and restore the overplus unto the man to whom he sold it; that he may return unto his possession.

The second way that land could be redeemed was for the original owner to redeem it himself. Since this land was agricultural land, its value was based on the crops it would produce each year. The price that a buyer would pay for land would be determined by how many years he would be able to farm it until the next jubilee year, when he would be required to give the land back to its original owner. If the original owner redeemed his land before the year of jubilee, he was to determine how much value the buyer had gotten from the land since the sale, and then refund the balance of the sale price to him. After doing this, the original owner could return to his property. While the price of different parcels of land might have varied because of fertility and location, that variation in price would not have been nearly so great as in our society where development has greatly increased the price of land.

D. Return in the Jubilee Year (v. 28)

28. But if he be not able to restore it to him, then that which is sold shall remain in the hand of him that hath bought it until the year of jubilee: and in the jubilee it shall go out, and he shall return unto his possession.

In cases where neither the original owner nor his relatives could redeem the land, the land would remain in the possession of the buyer until the jubilee year, at which time it reverted back to the original owner or his heirs. In this case the owner or his heirs did not pay anything to redeem the land; it came back to them automatically. But the buyer was not cheated out of the money he had paid for the land. He really had only leased the land, and he had enjoyed its fruits during the years before the jubilee.

REDEEMED!

There it was! In a moment of madness he had sold it. The money gained was wasted months ago, but he couldn't even remember how he had spent it. Was it spent on something to forget the fear of rejection and failure that had dominated his life?

It didn't matter now. There, right before his eyes, was the engagement ring he had purchased to give to Joan but hadn't offered to her. Somehow the moment was never right, or his own insecurity that questioned how she could really love him was always in the way. In a moment of despair he had sold the ring, pocketed the money, and left town.

Now he was back. He was a new man, a redeemed man with faith in the Lord, a job, and a future. Quickly he walked into the shop and repurchased the ring. Without hesitation he headed for Joan's house. Did she still love him? Was she married? A few moments after his knock Joan opened the door, and a smile brightened her face. "Come in, John. I've been waiting; I knew you would return," she said. Without a word John held out the ring and gently placed it on Joan's finger. Redeemed! Not just the ring impulsively sold. John himself was redeemed from his lost, unsure, fearful past and was now the recipient of Joan's undeserved love.

God specializes in redemption. It was a law for personal failures in Israel, and it is now a work of grace by Jesus' love at Calvary for all who will accept Him as their Redeemer. —W. P.

visual 10

III. Provisions for the Poor (Leviticus 25:39-42)

A. Slavery Forbidden (v. 39)

39. And if thy brother that dwelleth by thee be waxen poor, and be sold unto thee; thou shalt not compel him to serve as a bondservant.

Sometimes a person found himself in such dire financial straits that he had to sell not only his land, but he had to sell himself into servitude as well. A fellow Israelite might buy him, but must not treat him as a slave, who was forced to cater to every whim of his master.

B. Servants Until the Jubilee Year (vv. 40-42)

40. But as a hired servant, and as a sojourner, he shall be with thee, and shall serve thee unto the year of jubilee.

Anyone who bought a fellow Israelite must treat him as fairly and kindly as he would treat a hired servant who was free to leave at any time. Exodus 21:2 tells us that one who sold himself into servitude was to be freed after serving for six years. However, the servant was to be freed earlier if the jubilee year came before the six years of service were completed.

41. And then shall he depart from thee, both he and his children with him, and shall return unto his own family, and unto the possession of his fathers shall he return.

The year of jubilee liberation was not limited only to the servant, but it included his family as well. They were all to be freed and allowed to return to their own clan. (If, however, the master had provided a wife for the man while he was in servitude, and the wife bore him children, a different law prevailed—see Exodus 21:4.) The expression *unto the possession of his fathers* refers to the family land. This provision covers a situation where a person had fallen into debt and had been forced to sell his land to cover the debt. Additional debt had forced him to sell himself into bondage. In the year of jubilee not only would he be freed from servitude, but also he would be permitted to return to the land of his forefathers. Thus he would be given a fresh start on the family farm. Such an arrangement would help prevent a family from falling into poverty that became deeper with each succeeding generation.

42. For they are my servants, which I brought forth out of the land of Egypt: they shall not be sold as bondmen.

In this verse we are given the reason for regulating the treatment of Israelites who entered servanthood through debt. Just as the land actually belonged to God, and the people worked it as stewards of God, so all of the Israelites belonged to God because He had redeemed them from bondage in Egypt. For this reason, no Israelite was to be treated as the property of men, bought and sold as slaves. All, master and servant alike, belonged to God. The master had to remember that he was but a steward of what was God's, and he was responsible for how he rendered that stewardship.

The mention of Egypt served to remind the Israelites of their terrible suffering there. The Egyptians had made the Israelites to serve "with rigor," which means that the people had been treated ruthlessly (see Exodus 1:13, 14). Masters were warned not to treat their fellow Israelites in such a cruel manner (Leviticus 25:43).

No Slaves!

Man has a terrifying ability to enslave himself, and once enslaved to show little hesitation or remorse in drawing others into his bondage. A tragedy of our time is that, because of the sins of parents, many children are enslaved at birth. When parents become shackled by drugs, alcohol, or unbridled passion, they enslave their children with injured minds and bodies through birth defects, infant drug addiction, and, increasingly, through the HIV virus, which produces AIDS. There is no freedom for these innocent victims.

This modern slavery exists because our society is one that has promoted the "now" generation. Sadly, the number of persons who feel any responsibility for the well-being of future generations seems to be diminishing.

It is the right of all persons to be free. This freedom demands a discipline that forbids self-indulgence and sees that "my rights" must be limited by "your rights." Only this way can we enjoy the freedom God designed for us. —W. P.

Conclusion

A. Neither Communism nor Capitalism

Not only in America but around the world, a small handful of people have become exceedingly wealthy. On the other hand, large numbers of persons remain in grinding, relentless poverty. Explanations accounting for the wealth of some persons and the poverty of others are numerous and perhaps complex, and it is not our purpose here to consider these. We desire not to enter a discussion about economics and sociology, but to show how God provided ancient Israel with laws that prevented such a wide difference in people's wealth.

According to the laws we have studied in today's lesson, a person in ancient Israel could not sell the land that belonged to him and his fathers before him. He could only lease it until the jubilee year, when the lease expired and the land reverted to the owner or his heirs. Such a law prevented a person from accumulating vast tracts of land that enhanced personal wealth at the expense of landless peasants. This is a problem today, especially among Third World countries, where a few have huge land holdings that are used to keep farm workers as virtual serfs.

We must acknowledge that the jubilee laws applied only to agricultural land. Developments within walled cities were covered by another law, which allowed a person to redeem mortgaged property within a year. If, however, the original owner did not redeem the property within the space of a year, it became the permanent possession of the buyer and his descendants (Leviticus 25:29, 30). Obviously, such a law allowed a person to acquire sizable holdings in buildings and businesses not possible under the jubilee laws.

For forty years after World War II we lived through the Cold War, a life-and-death struggle between Marxian communism and free enterprise capitalism. In recent years we have witnessed the complete collapse of communism as an economic system. Communists insisted that property and the means of production and distribution of goods belonged to the government. Such a philosophy led to the denial of freedoms for individuals, and fostered indolence on the part of workers. Capitalism, however, has not been free of faults. Its emphasis on acquisition and consumption has led to a widening of the gap between the rich and the poor. Worse, it has engendered unbridled greed on the part of both.

Obviously, applying the Mosaic laws to our country would not solve the problems of capitalism, such as we have mentioned. The regulations dealing with the jubilee year were designed for a simple agricultural economy, not for the tremendously more complicated international economy that exists today. And yet, the principles on which the year of jubilee was based are as relevant today as when God's law was first given. They condemn greed and acquisitiveness, which characterize our society, and they require a concern for the poor, regardless of how they got in that condition.

Behind all of the jubilee regulations is the basic principle of stewardship. Israelites were not to hold their fellow Israelites as slaves, nor were they to treat them ruthlessly. The reason was that all Israelites belonged to God, because He had released them from bondage in Egypt. Land was not to be held in perpetuity by purchasers but was to revert to the original owners in the jubilee year. The reason was that all the land really belonged to God. Those who occupied a piece of land at any given time did so as stewards of God, not as owners. If our country, even if just all Christians, could grasp this concept, what a difference it would make in our society. Each one of us, however, can apply it to his or her own life, which is where every revolution must start.

B. Let Us Pray

Dear God and Father, Creator of the whole world and everything that is in it, we come to You recognizing our stewardship of those things You have placed in our trust. May the laws of the ancient Hebrews remind us of that trust. In Jesus' name we pray. Amen.

C. Thought to Remember

"It is required in stewards, that a man be found faithful" (1 Corinthians 4:2).

Home Daily Bible Readings

Monday, Aug. 1—The Land Shall Keep Sabbatical Year (Leviticus 25:1-7)

Tuesday, Aug. 2—Hallow the Fiftieth Year (Leviticus 25:8-12)

Wednesday, Aug. 3—Land Cannot Be Sold in Perpetuity (Leviticus 25:13-24)

Thursday, Aug. 4—Property Is the Lord's Land (Leviticus 25:25-28)

Friday, Aug. 5—Levites May Redeem Property Anytime (Leviticus 25:29-34)

Saturday, Aug. 6—Jubilee Sets Slaves Free (Leviticus 25:35-43)

Sunday, Aug. 7—Israel Is God's Servant—Not Slave (Leviticus 25:44-55)

Learning by Doing

This page contains an alternate lesson plan emphasizing learning activities. Classes desiring such student involvement will find these suggestions helpful.

Learning Goals

As students participate in today's class session, they should:

1. Review God's laws regarding the year of jubilee.

2. Compare this practice with the way we tend to view our possessions today.

3. State a Biblical principle for Christians today that explains the implications of God's ownership of everything.

Into the Lesson

Read the following Agree/Disagree statements to your class members (or have them read them from the student book) and ask for their response to each. Then discuss with them their responses and why they responded as they did.

1. Since God owns everything, I'm responsible only to Him for how I use what I have.

2. God holds me responsible only to return one-tenth of my income to Him.

3. God holds me responsible to use for Him everything I have.

4. God may claim any and all of my possessions for His use.

5. God's claim on my possessions extends to how I use them in the lives of others.

6. I should view my possessions as "on loan" to me from God.

7. Because God owns my possessions, someone else may make a claim on them.

Into the Word

Begin today's class with a brief lecture to establish the background for today's study. Use material from the "Introduction" section of the first lesson plan.

You will need to spend much of this week's Bible-study time explaining the year of jubilee to your students. To orient them to this concept, ask them to spend about ten minutes, in groups of about five, doing one of the following Bible-study activities (you may want to let students choose from among these activities, with each group doing a different activity).

Marked-Bible plan. If class members have the student book, ask them to use today's printed text included there for a marked-Bible exercise. If not, photocopy today's Scripture text and give each student a copy. Students should mark their texts in this way:

1. Circle each phrase that shows something about God's ownership of everything.

2. Put an arrow beside each verse that teaches something about social justice.

3. Put an exclamation point beside each verse that surprises you.

4. Put a question mark beside each verse that you're not sure you understand.

Sentence summaries. For each of the sections of Leviticus 25 in today's text (vv. 8-10, 23-28, and 39-42), class members should write a sentence to summarize what it says about God's ownership of everything.

Background study. Provide several Bible reference books: a Bible dictionary, a Bible encyclopedia, and a commentary on the book of Leviticus. Ask a few students to prepare a brief report on the year of jubilee.

After the groups have completed their activities, let them share and discuss their results with the class. Then go through today's text, enhancing what has already been said about the year of jubilee by using the comments of explanation in this manual.

Into Life

Discuss the following questions with your class:

1. What seems most surprising to you about this passage? What would seem most unusual to most people in our society?

2. What feature of this ancient law is most appealing to you? Why?

3. How would our country change, and how would our community change, if some of these principles were put into practice today?

Read the following Scriptures aloud to the class: Psalm 24:1; 50:10; Matthew 6:33; 1 Corinthians 4:2.

Discuss: How does an awareness that God owns everything affect our outlook on life? How does this perspective liberate us? What kinds of attitudes and conduct will a person have who recognizes God's ownership of all things?

Write this open-ended sentence on the chalkboard, or display it on a poster that you have prepared before class: "Because God owns everything, I—" Ask class members to decide how they should answer the question. Each person should think of an answer before you close the class session with a time of prayer.

Let's Talk It Over

The questions on this page are designed to encourage review of the lesson Scriptures and to promote discussion of the lesson by the class. The answers provided are only discussion starters. Let your class talk it over from there.

1. To what areas of a Christian's life does the concept of "stewardship" apply?

Usually Christians think only of money when the word *stewardship* is mentioned. Preachers and teachers expand the concept with the traditional alliterative treatment of "time, talent, and treasure." Both concepts are defective. God's claim applies to all of life, including, for example, one's body (which is not included in "time, talent, and treasure"). A Christian's body belongs not to himself or herself, but to the Lord. We are to exercise faithful stewardship (care) over our bodies, including our dietary patterns, exercise, and sexual conduct. In 1 Corinthians 6:12-20 Paul asserts God's ownership and the Christian's stewardship of the body, concluding with the reminder, "You are not your own; you were bought at a price. Therefore honor God with your body" (*New International Version*).

2. What are some of the principles that permeate the Biblical concept of "stewardship"?

The basic principle affirms God's ownership of everything, including His people. The land (as indicated in today's lesson), crops and animals (as symbolized by the tithe, the first and the best), and people all belong to Jehovah. The second, and corollary, principle is that we are caretakers, or stewards, of what we possess; we are not owners. All that we call "ours" are really God's gifts to us, entrusted to us. He is the great and good Giver; we are the beneficiaries of His goodness. The third principle is that God requires faithfulness of all His stewards: "It is required in stewards, that a man be found faithful" (1 Corinthians 4:2). How revolutionary it would be if all Christians implemented these principles in their lives!

3. What is the Christian perspective regarding the accumulation of wealth?

First of all, wealth itself is *not* evil. It is the *love* of money that is the root of all kinds of evil (1 Timothy 6:10). Jesus warned of the dangers of wealth because it *can* become your master. Accumulating wealth must be understood in terms of the "how" and the "why." Accumulation must be done by ethical and legal means. If it is accomplished by dishonest methods or through the exploitation of people, it stands condemned.

Motivation also is a key factor. If accumulation is fueled by greed or pride, it stands outside *all* Christian perspective. We are to be motivated by the desire to share, to use accumulated wealth for the benefit of others (see Ephesians 4:28). No single life-style is mandated in Scripture for Christians. Sterling examples are offered of both the life-style of denial (with little or no accumulation) and of wealth (with faithful stewardship and the ensuing benefit to God's people).

4. How should Christians today regard indebtedness?

Debt marks the American way of life. "Go now and pay later" appeals to most of us. For many persons, *consuming* dominates their decisions and behavior. To get more usually means a person must incur more and more debt. Most of us must incur indebtedness in purchasing a house and some "big ticket" items, such as a car. But it's the *abuse* of consumer credit that causes many persons financial problems. They overextend themselves financially and cannot pay the balance due on their credit cards each month. Debt demands that a portion of a person's resources be used in paying his or her creditors for the privilege of using their money, and that interest payment is often a staggering amount. Is that good stewardship? The less debt we carry, the more financial resources we will have to use to support the Lord's work. Christians, as wise and faithful stewards, should work toward eliminating personal debt.

5. Why do people exploit others?

Many reasons may be given. Among them are the following: (1) Greed. Look out for number one, get all you can however you can. (2) Power. A person can feel powerful who bests another in economic struggles. (3) Hostility. Many people, who have been abused and exploited, experience deep-seated hostility and want to "get even." (4) Low self-esteem. Persons who don't feel good about themselves may seek to feel superior to others by taking advantage of them. (5) Sin. Ultimately, sin is the root of all exploitation of others. God created us to love people and use things, but too many love things and use people. In revealing His will and His law to His people, God forbade exploitation.

Accept God's Guidance

DEVOTIONAL READING: Numbers 23:18-23.

LESSON SCRIPTURE: Numbers 13, 14.

PRINTED TEXT: Numbers 13:25-28, 30, 31; 14:6-10a, 28-30.

Numbers 13:25-28, 30, 31

25 And they returned from searching of the land after forty days.

26 And they went and came to Moses, and to Aaron, and to all the congregation of the children of Israel, unto the wilderness of Paran, to Kadesh; and brought back word unto them, and unto all the congregation, and showed them the fruit of the land.

27 And they told him, and said, We came unto the land whither thou sentest us, and surely it floweth with milk and honey; and this is the fruit of it.

28 Nevertheless the people be strong that dwell in the land, and the cities are walled, and very great: and moreover we saw the children of Anak there.

. . . .

30 And Caleb stilled the people before Moses, and said, Let us go up at once, and possess it; for we are well able to overcome it.

31 But the men that went up with him said, We be not able to go up against the people; for they are stronger than we.

Numbers 14:6-10a, 28-30

6 And Joshua the son of Nun, and Caleb the son of Jephunneh, which were of them that searched the land, rent their clothes:

7 And they spake unto all the company of the children of Israel, saying, The land, which we passed through to search it, is an exceeding good land.

8 If the LORD delight in us, then he will bring us into this land, and give it us; a land which floweth with milk and honey.

9 Only rebel not ye against the LORD, neither fear ye the people of the land; for they are bread for us: their defense is departed from them, and the LORD is with us: fear them not.

10a But all the congregation bade stone them with stones.

. . . .

28 Say unto them, As truly as I live, saith the LORD, as ye have spoken in mine ears, so will I do to you:

29 Your carcasses shall fall in this wilderness, and all that were numbered of you, according to your whole number, from twenty years old and upward, which have murmured against me,

30 Doubtless ye shall not come into the land, concerning which I sware to make you dwell therein, save Caleb the son of Jephunneh, and Joshua the son of Nun.

Aug
14

GOLDEN TEXT: If the LORD delight in us, then he will bring us into this land, and give it us; a land which floweth with milk and honey. Only rebel not ye against the LORD.
—Numbers 14:8, 9.

Lesson Aims

As a result of studying this lesson, each student should:

1. See in the example of Caleb and Joshua men who were steadfast in their loyalty to God in spite of the pressure of the crowd.

2. Be encouraged to stand for what he or she believes to be right, even though the majority may disagree.

Lesson Outline

INTRODUCTION
  A. "Once to Every Man and Nation"
  B. Lesson Background
 I. MISSION ACCOMPLISHED (Numbers 13:25-28, 30, 31)
  A. Show and Tell (vv. 25, 26)
  B. Good News and Bad News (vv. 27, 28)
  C. Conflicting Viewpoints (vv. 30, 31)
 II. MOMENT OF OPPORTUNITY (Numbers 14:6-10a)
  A. Agonized Appeal (vv. 6-9)
  B. Threat of Violence (v. 10a)
   Doing What's Right
III. MURMURERS' PUNISHMENT (Numbers 14:28-30)
  A. Request Granted (vv. 28, 29)
  B. Exceptions (v. 30)
   Rejected
CONCLUSION
  A. "One on God's Side"
  B. Let Us Pray
  C. Thought to Remember

Display visual 11 and let it remain before the class. The visual is shown on page 428.

Introduction

A. "Once to Every Man and Nation"

The actions of Joshua and Caleb that are recorded in today's lesson text call to mind the words of the stirring hymn penned by James Russell Lowell:

> Once to every man and nation
>   Comes the moment to decide,
> In the strife of truth with falsehood,
>   For the good or evil side;

These two men had a decision to make. They could take the side of the people, which was the popular and apparently safe side. Or they could stand with Moses and Aaron and face the anger of the people. These two faithful men did not hesitate in making their decision. They stood with Moses and Aaron, willing to accept whatever consequences that decision would bring.

Once more the words of Lowell seem appropriate to the occasion:

> Though the cause of evil prosper,
>   Yet the truth alone is strong;
> Though her portion be the scaffold,
>   And upon the throne be wrong,
> Yet that scaffold sways the future,
>   And, behind the dim unknown,
> Standeth God within the shadow
>   Keeping watch above His own.

B. Lesson Background

The opening chapters of the book of Numbers find the children of Israel still camped at the base of Mount Sinai. While they were there, God ordered them to take a census of the people by tribes. The count revealed that the Israelites "twenty years old and upward, all that were able to go forth to war" numbered slightly more than six hundred thousand (Numbers 1:45, 46).

The tenth chapter begins the account of their journey from Mount Sinai to the promised land, which, apparently, they were to enter from the south. Their journey was not without problems, however. Chapter eleven records that at one point some of the people began to murmur because all they had to eat was manna. They lusted for meat and some of the foods they remembered from Egypt. God answered their murmuring by miraculously supplying an enormous amount of quail. The complaining people greedily gathered large amounts of the birds, in defiance and contempt of God's warning that their greed would lead to loathing of the flesh they craved. While they were in the act of eating, the camp was smitten with a great plague and those that had craved other food died.

After burying the dead, the people journeyed onward. Then Aaron and Miriam attempted to undermine the influence of Moses. God quickly intervened in this effort to usurp Moses' leadership, and Miriam was stricken with leprosy. Aaron acknowledged his foolish sin, and Moses asked God to heal Miriam. At God's direction, Miriam was shut out of the camp for seven days before she was restored (chapter 12).

The Israelites then continued on toward Canaan, stopping when they reached Kadesh-barnea (Deuteronomy 1:19). From this campsite Moses sent twelve men to spy out the land. Their return from this reconnaissance mission marks the beginning of today's lesson text.

I. Mission Accomplished
(Numbers 13:25-28, 30, 31)

A. Show and Tell (vv. 25, 26)

25, 26. And they returned from searching of the land after forty days. And they went and came to Moses, and to Aaron, and to all the congregation of the children of Israel, unto the wilderness of Paran, to Kadesh; and brought back word unto them, and unto all the congregation, and showed them the fruit of the land.

When Moses sent the spies out, they proceeded northward through the wilderness of Zin and the semi-arid region south of Hebron. They went as far north as Rehob, which was in the northern part of Canaan near the headwaters of the Jordan, before turning back south again. The round trip must have covered more than four hundred miles. Since it took them forty days to complete the trip, this would not have been difficult for men who were accustomed to walking and who were traveling light.

The scouts brought back grapes, pomegranates, and figs. The grapes came from the "brook" (or valley) of Eshcol, an area near Hebron that still produces grapes. Since this was the time of the early grape harvest (v. 20), the time of the spies' return must have been in August.

The spies probably made their report first to Moses and Aaron and then to the congregation. It may be that the report was made to the tribal leaders, who in turn reported this information to their tribes.

B. Good News and Bad News (vv. 27, 28)

27. And they told him, and said, We came unto the land whither thou sentest us, and surely it floweth with milk and honey; and this is the fruit of it.

The first part of the spies' report was positive. It is worth noting, however, that they described the land they had spied out as *the land whither thou sentest us* rather than the land that the Lord had given them. God himself had described that land as one flowing *with milk and honey* (Exodus 3:8, 17), and with that description the twelve spies wholeheartedly agreed. This expression refers to the fruitfulness of the land, especially in comparison with the barren desert where they were then camped. As testimony to the land's richness, the spies displayed the fruit they had gathered. A modern visitor to Palestine might wonder about the literal accuracy of the expression, since much of the land seems an arid desert. We must recognize, however, that centuries of overgrazing and the cutting of the trees for firewood have stripped the land of most

of its vegetation, leaving it barren. The Israelis have planted millions of trees in an effort to restore the land's fertility, and in some areas the program has been very successful.

28. Nevertheless the people be strong that dwell in the land, and the cities are walled, and very great: and moreover we saw the children of Anak there.

Now for the bad news—*nevertheless*. What follows are some of the reasons why the majority of the spies believed that the Israelites would not be able to enter the promised land. These men had carried out Moses' orders to find out about the land and its inhabitants (vv. 18-20). The information they brought back was accurate; their problem was the application of that information. The first problem they saw was that the people were strong. Not only were they numerous, but they were well able to defend themselves against any intruders. Further, their cities were walled. This would be a new experience for the Israelites, because few cities in Egypt were walled. In addition, the walled cities were usually located on high ground and were supplied with water from cisterns or springs. Without special weapons and special training, any attackers would have a difficult time against such fortifications.

To clinch their argument, the spies reported that *the children of Anak* were there. We know little about these people, but they had a reputation of being giants. The spies reiterated this, insisting that in the presence of the sons of Anak, they felt like grasshoppers (v. 33).

Verse 29 mentions other tribes the spies had observed. The Amalekites, with whom the children of Israel had already fought a battle (Exodus 17:8-13), occupied the area south of Canaan. The Hittites, a powerful nation centered in Asia Minor, were present, as were the Jebusites, who held Jerusalem. The Amorites lived in the mountainous regions, and the Canaanites lived along the seacoast and in the Jordan Valley.

How to Say It

AMALEKITES. *Am*-uh-lek-ites.
ANAK. *A*-nak.
ESHCOL. *Esh*-col.
JEBUSITES. *Jeb*-yuh-sites.
JEPHUNNEH. Jih-*fun*-eh.
KADESH-BARNEA. *Kay*-desh-*bar*-nee-uh (strong accent on *bar*).
PARAN. *Pay*-ran.
REHOB. *Ree*-hob.
SINAI. *Sye*-nay-eye or *Sye*-nye.

C. Conflicting Viewpoints (vv. 30, 31)

30. And Caleb stilled the people before Moses, and said, Let us go up at once, and possess it; for we are well able to overcome it.

Elsewhere in the Scriptures Caleb is depicted as a man of stalwart courage (see Joshua 14:6-15; 15:13, 14). In this situation he demonstrated his courage by speaking out against the ten spies who brought the discouraging report. Joshua agreed with Caleb, but did not speak up at this point. Joshua, a close confidant of Moses, may have remained silent because he felt the people would have considered his testimony somewhat biased. Caleb's testimony would have been considered more objective by the people.

Caleb began by quieting the people. Probably he gave some of the details of his survey of the land, and what we have here is but the conclusion of his speech. That conclusion was to the point: "Let us go *now*, for we are able to take the land." Caleb's conviction that the people could take the land was based on his faith that they would not be alone; God would be with them.

31. But the men that went up with him said, We be not able to go up against the people; for they are stronger than we.

As soon as Caleb concluded his speech, the other spies joined in rebuttal. In their original report they had given an honest account of the fruitfulness of the land. Now they were distorting facts to support their fears. While the Israelites may have lacked the weapons and skills necessary to capture walled cities, they were not weak. For one thing, they outnumbered any of the enemies they would have to face when they entered the land. Further, they made no allowance for the power of God, who would intervene on their behalf.

Verse 32 records another argument they advanced to justify their fears. The land, they said, "eateth up the inhabitants." We are not sure exactly what they meant, although political arguments do not have to be clear to be effective in swaying people. Surely they did not mean that the land was harsh, for they had already reported that it was fruitful, flowing with milk and honey. They may have meant that because of the geographical location of the land, it was subject to continuous attacks from one side and another, and whoever lived there would have to be forever on the lookout for an invasion.

II. Moment of Opportunity (Numbers 14:6-10a)

Verses 1-5 of chapter fourteen tell of the people's response to the dismal report of the ten spies. They wept through the night. As the evil report spread through the tents of each tribe, the people grumbled because they were certain that God had brought them here so they would be killed by the sword (Deuteronomy 1:27). In the morning their grumblings were directed against Moses and Aaron, culminating in a proposed revolt against Moses' leadership and in the suggestion that they select a new leader to guide them back to Egypt. Faced with such strong opposition, Moses and Aaron fell on their faces in solemn prayer before the congregation (compare Numbers 16:22).

A. Agonized Appeal (vv. 6-9)

6, 7. And Joshua the son of Nun, and Caleb the son of Jephunneh, which were of them that searched the land, rent their clothes: and they spake unto all the company of the children of Israel, saying, The land, which we passed through to search it, is an exceeding good land.

To show their support for Moses and Aaron, Joshua and Caleb stood before the assembly and pled for the people to turn from their proposed rebellion. They *rent*, that is, "tore" *their clothes* in a dramatic expression of their horror at the thought that the people would consider such disobedience. Then, hoping to calm the people's fears and quiet their mutinous spirit, they began to tell them once more how good the land was.

8. If the LORD delight in us, then he will bring us into this land, and give it us; a land which floweth with milk and honey.

The two faithful spies continued their praise of the land as rich and fruitful, and they assured the assembly that God would give them the land. But there was one condition: they had to be pleasing to God. Their present rebellious attitude was anything but pleasing to Him. Not only were they revealing a lack of faith in God to fulfill His promises to them, but they were rejecting the leaders He had appointed.

9. Only rebel not ye against the LORD, neither fear ye the people of the land; for they are

bread for us: their defense is departed from them, and the LORD is with us: fear them not.

Joshua and Caleb recognized that the people's rebellious attitude arose out of *fear*. Their fear is understandable in view of the ten spies' report of the formidable obstacles the Israelites would face in taking the land. The two faithful spies cautioned the people not to rebel against God, but they did not bitterly condemn them. Instead, they spoke words of reassurance. The nations who lived in Canaan would be *bread* for them, that is, Israel would devour them. This is a figurative way of saying that their conquest could readily be accomplished.

One reason that the Israelites could expect to conquer the promised land was that the pagan nations' *defense* had *departed from them*. The expression literally means "a shadow," such as a cloud produces in protecting one from the burning rays of the sun. Now God was about to remove that protection.

The assurance that Joshua and Caleb displayed was not based on their confidence in Israel's strength and ability alone. They had a firmer foundation than that—their faith in God. By reminding their fellow Israelites that God was with them, they tried to convince them that they need not fear the inhabitants of the promised land. Nothing casts out fear better than a solid faith in God, the conviction that He loves us and that He watches over our lives.

B. Threat of Violence (v. 10a)

10a. But all the congregation bade stone them with stones.

The people refused to accept the courageous testimony of Joshua and Caleb. Whether they were whipped into a frenzy by some of their leaders or they spontaneously reacted against the two spies, we do not know. Soon, however, the fear-filled congregation was urging that these two be stoned to death. They likely would have carried out their wicked scheme, if God had not intervened. The glory of the Lord appeared in the tabernacle in the sight of everyone, and He revealed to Moses His judgment upon the people. Only Moses' supplication prevented God from sending a pestilence upon them that would have completely wiped them out (vv. 10-20).

DOING WHAT'S RIGHT

Consensus fidelium is a Latin phrase, which, loosely translated, means, "the common mind." It refers to the way most persons regard a matter. Appeal to "the common mind" in the area of politics is a safeguard against rule by only a few. In a democracy "the common mind" of the people is discovered by means of the ballot box.

There is value in knowing "the common mind." If, however, the majority are self-serving and have regard neither for truth nor the best interests of all the people, disaster will ultimately be the result.

Israel believed the report of ten of the twelve spies that were sent to explore the promised land. In this classic case the majority position stood for rebellion against God, and the results were tragic for Israel.

So, today, moral behavior is not determined by a consensus of people's opinions. It is based on the teachings of God's Word. Regarding any moral issue a Christian will take his or her stand on the Word of God, even if doing so means facing the opposition and threats of the majority.   —W. P.

III. Murmurers' Punishment (Numbers 14:28-30)

The intervening verses record God's words to Moses, in which He revealed to His servant that divine judgment would come upon the people for their mutiny. Moses' intercession on their behalf had spared their lives for the time being, but God's punishment would surely come.

A. Request Granted (vv. 28, 29)

28, 29. Say unto them, As truly as I live, saith the LORD, as ye have spoken in mine ears, so will I do to you: your carcasses shall fall in this wilderness, and all that were numbered of you, according to your whole number, from twenty years old and upward, which have murmured against me.

In these verses Moses revealed to the people what their punishment would be. Their own words came back to haunt them. In their anger against Moses, they asserted that they wished they had died in the wilderness (Numbers 14:2). Now they would have that rash wish carried out. God didn't mince words with them: *your carcasses shall fall in this wilderness*. All those twenty years old and older who had murmured against God would not see the promised land. Instead, they would die in the wilderness.

B. Exceptions (v. 30)

30. Doubtless ye shall not come into the land, concerning which I sware to make you dwell therein, save Caleb the son of Jephunneh, and Joshua the son of Nun.

The death penalty was pronounced upon all the adults who had rebelled against God, but that penalty would not be carried out immediately. Had all of them been struck dead, no one would have been left to care for the children. Instead, the Israelites' trail in the wilderness for the next thirty-eight plus years would be marked by their graves as they fell one by one. The only exceptions were the two faithful spies, Joshua and Caleb. Of all the adults who left Egypt, only these two would live to see the promised land.

REJECTED

One of the stories that impressed school children for several generations was "The Man Without a Country," written by Edward Everett Hale. It is the story of a young army officer, who, during his trial by court-martial, exclaimed that he wished he would never hear of the United States again.

The young man's wish was granted. He was sentenced to spend the rest of his life on a ship, with instructions that no one was ever to give him any news of his homeland. When in port he could never go ashore; when at sea he lived in a solitary cabin and worked as a deckhand. News of his homeland came by chance conversation with new seamen and sometimes by hearing the sailors talk when they returned from shore leave. He had rejected his citizenship, and his country had rejected him.

As the years passed, the nation's westward expansion filled his mind. He created a map to show those changes on a wall of his cabin. When he lay dying he asked the ship's doctor to fill in the map so he could see all he had forfeited. He died wanting above all else to be part of what had been his by citizenship but was lost forever by his wrong decision.

One generation of Israel lost their right to enter the promised land because they rejected God. Let us remain faithful to Him so we may "enter into that rest," which God has prepared for His people (Hebrews 4:11).   —W. P.

Home Daily Bible Readings

Monday, Aug. 8—Miriam and Aaron Rebuked by God (Numbers 12:1-15)

Tuesday, Aug. 9—Moses Sends Spies to Canaan (Numbers 13:1, 2, 17-24)

Wednesday, Aug. 10—Two Spies Vote to Enter Canaan (Numbers 13:25-30)

Thursday, Aug. 11—Fear Dominated the Majority (Numbers 13:31—14:3)

Friday, Aug. 12—Only Caleb and Joshua Confident (Numbers 14:4-19)

Saturday, Aug. 13—Ten Spies Die of Plagues (Numbers 14:20-38)

Sunday, Aug. 14—Doubters: The Lord Is Not Among You (Numbers 14:39-45)

Conclusion

A. "One on God's Side"

Wendell Phillips once observed that "one on God's side is a majority." While Moses did not stand completely alone (Aaron, Joshua, and Caleb, stood with him), yet this little handful of the faithful had to face the wrath of the people who numbered in the hundreds of thousands. In the face of such overwhelming odds they may have been tempted to abandon their convictions and take the side of the crowd. They were unwavering in their faith, however, even though it might have cost them their lives.

At crucial times in the history of the Israelite people, heroes appeared to save the nation from disaster or to lead them in the right direction. We think of David, armed with only a slingshot and his faith in God, going out to meet Goliath. Or the lovely Queen Esther, who was willing to sacrifice herself to save her people.

Yet not all of God's heroes are called to serve under such dramatic circumstances. Some heroes never face bodily harm, even though they stand for the right against the majority. They do face the scorn of the crowd, however, and even social rejection. Others are quiet, even unknown, heroes. They are heroes nevertheless, because in their often monotonous and humdrum lives day by day they stand for what is right. These heroes will never make the evening TV news, yet their faith and their lives are duly recorded in the Lamb's book of life.

We need to recognize also that heroes do not usually stand alone. Behind them are the unsung heroes quietly doing their duties before God. Elijah thought that he alone in all of Israel was faithful to God. God had to remind him that there were still "seven thousand in Israel" who had not "bowed unto Baal" (1 Kings 19:18). Beyond all of this we ought to recognize that wherever God calls us into service, He is there to watch over us and guide us. He may not intervene to spare us as He did Joshua and Caleb, but He is there nevertheless.

B. Let Us Pray

Almighty God, as we study the history of the Israelite people help us to more fully understand that You do watch over the destinies of men and nations. Give us the faith and courage to stand for You, even when that means standing alone. In Jesus' name we pray. Amen.

C. Thought to Remember

No matter what the odds may be, one person and God is a majority.

Learning by Doing

This page contains an alternate lesson plan emphasizing learning activities. Classes desiring such student involvement will find these suggestions helpful.

Learning Goals

As students participate in today's class session, they should:

1. Examine Numbers 13 and 14 to find the lessons these chapters hold for Christians regarding the necessity of taking risk, standing alone against the crowd, and accomplishing one's best for God.

2. Choose at least one of these principles and decide how to put it into practice in their own lives.

Into the Lesson

Use as many of the following open-ended questions as necessary to set the stage for today's Bible study.

1. If the group I'm with wants to do something I don't really prefer, I usually—

2. The last time I stood up for my opinion against a crowd was —

3. When confronted with a challenge greater than I have ever faced before, I usually—

4. If I could live my life again, one thing I would do differently is—

5. My usual approach to really big problems is to —

You may decide to:

Read the statements to the whole class. Have them jot their completions on blank paper you have given them. Then ask volunteers to read their completions as you go through the statements again, one by one.

Distribute the whole set of questions. Ask students to pair off and to choose one or two of the sentences to complete with their partners.

Distribute the statements on slips of paper. Write the statements on slips of paper, one statement per slip. Give the slips to class members as they arrive. To begin today's session, instruct students to find another person in the class who has the same open-ended sentence. Once each has found a partner, they can stand for ninety seconds and share with each other how they complete it.

Into the Word

Summarize your introductory activity by stating that it introduces some of the issues that are at the heart of today's lesson: Willingness to take *courageous action*; how to respond to *peer pressure*; and seizing the opportunity to *accomplish something big in life*. Write each of these italicized words or phrases on the chalkboard as you speak. Point to them now and ask, "How are these issues especially important to Christians? How might Christians look at these issues differently from non-Christians?" Discuss these briefly.

Tell the class that you want them to watch and see how these issues play out in the Bible story to be studied today.

Prepare a brief background lecture based on the material in the "Introduction" section of this lesson, and deliver it at this point. Then ask a volunteer or several volunteers to read the Scripture text aloud.

You may decide to use more than today's printed text. Consider reading all of Numbers 13 and 14 except for Numbers 13:4-15.

You could plan for a *dialogical reading* of the Scripture. In the week before class, recruit class members to read the words spoken by (1) God, (2) Moses, (3) the group of spies (Numbers 13:27-29), (4) Caleb, (5) the Israelites, (6) Joshua, and (7) the narrator. If you choose to do this, make seven copies of the text before class and mark the appropriate sections for each reader.

As the Scripture is read, students should look at the words you have written on the board and think about how each of those issues is present in this account. When the Scripture reading is finished, have class members form groups of five to answer that question together. Allow about six minutes for group discussion, and then lead a class discussion about it.

Into Life

Ask class members to decide individually which of the three issues on the chalkboard is the biggest challenge for them. If you have time, ask them first to share their choice in their small study groups. Then ask for volunteers to share with the whole class. Ask them how the example of Joshua and Caleb motivates them to deal with their challenge.

Close with three prayers:

One person asks God to help class members be courageous in serving Him.

The second asks God to give class members the strength they need to choose His way, regardless of the pressures of society.

The third asks God to lead class members in accomplishing something significant for Him.

Let's Talk It Over

The questions on this page are designed to encourage review of the lesson Scriptures and to promote discussion of the lesson by the class. The answers provided are only discussion starters. Let your class talk it over from there.

1. What was the essential difference in the perspective of Caleb and Joshua and that of the other ten spies?

All of the spies viewed the same picture of Canaan, as it were. The elements in the picture were identical: the land was fertile, the inhabitants were powerful, the cities were well fortified, and some of the inhabitants were very tall. They agreed about the various peoples who lived there. Caleb and Joshua, however, saw the picture within the framework of strong faith. They said, "We can—the Lord is with us!" The other spies said, "We can't!" Notice the frame for the latters' picture: "We seemed like grasshoppers in our own eyes" (Numbers 13:33, *New International Version*). Herein lies a significant lesson for life. The picture (what we experience) is similar or identical for most of us—the frame makes the difference. In counseling, the main task of the therapist is to help the counselee "reframe" experience. The experience *doesn't* change, but one's perspective of it does, and that makes all the difference in the world!

2. Why are some people afraid to take an unpopular stand?

At least four significant reasons usually surface. (1) They fear they will lose popularity. What "others" think dominates their decision-making. They fear relationships will be affected—they may lose friends. Others may reject them. (2) They fear the unpopular stand may cost them financially. One who is in business may lose customers. Alienating people could be costly. (3) They wish to minimize pain. Normal persons don't want to suffer! If one is in the minority (and a very small minority, at that) he or she may end up being a martyr. (4) They fear that the demands may be greater than they feel they can handle. The greater the discrepancy between the demands made upon a person and that person's *perceived* ability to respond, the greater the level of stress and consequent fear.

3. What is the antidote for fear?

The antidote for fear is faith, particularly with the emphasis on the dynamic of faith—*trust*. Fear can eat at a person, if God's assurance is forgotten or rejected. Throughout the Bible we find this word of God's assurance: "Do not be afraid, for I am with you." The ten spies feared to enter the promised land to possess it because they lacked *trust* in God to fulfill His promise to give them victory over their enemies. Their focus was on their fear, not on faith that God, who powerfully delivered them from Egypt, would give them the land He had promised them. Fear will be replaced by peace and confidence when trust persists. "Thou wilt keep him in perfect peace, whose mind is stayed on thee: because he trusteth in thee" (Isaiah 26:3).

4. List some of the characteristics of a "hero."

Not all heroes are alike, particularly those we designate "unsung heroes." But heroes tend to have similar traits. They are as follows: (1) Courage. When we think of heroes, bravery is one of the first traits that comes to mind. The hero often is one who risks greatly (even life) to help, to rescue, to achieve. All heroes possess courage, whether moral or physical. (2) Vision. Particularly, national heroes envision what can be accomplished and then set out to achieve it. They often have the ability to communicate that vision to others, too. (3) Confidence. Even when all others apparently disagree or doubt, the hero is a "believer." The hero's confidence energizes his or her actions. (4) Perseverance. Throughout history, heroes have been those who persisted, come what may. Heroes remain steady when all else seems to be wavering. Caleb and Joshua fit the pattern perfectly—they qualify on all counts as legitimate heroes.

5. In America, what principles are followed in determining what is "right"?

Right is often determined by what the majority deems to be "right." This is the era of polls and surveys. Find out what the majority thinks and accept it. Others subscribe to the principle that "might makes right." Whoever has the power (or the money that buys and wields the power) determines what is right. However, there will always be those who determine what is right on the basis of God's revelation. Sexual promiscuity, abortion, homosexual practice, and greed will never be right, no matter what polls show or power blocs dictate. Choosing the right according to God's revelation puts one in the company of Caleb and Joshua.

Love the Lord Your God

DEVOTIONAL READING: Deuteronomy 7:6-9, 12.

LESSON SCRIPTURE: Deuteronomy 6.

PRINTED TEXT: Deuteronomy 6:1-13.

Deuteronomy 6:1-13

1 Now these are the commandments, the statutes, and the judgments, which the LORD your God commanded to teach you, that ye might do them in the land whither ye go to possess it:

2 That thou mightest fear the LORD thy God, to keep all his statutes and his commandments, which I command thee, thou, and thy son, and thy son's son, all the days of thy life; and that thy days may be prolonged.

3 Hear therefore, O Israel, and observe to do it; that it may be well with thee, and that ye may increase mightily, as the LORD God of thy fathers hath promised thee, in the land that floweth with milk and honey.

4 Hear, O Israel: The LORD our God is one LORD:

5 And thou shalt love the LORD thy God with all thine heart, and with all thy soul, and with all thy might.

6 And these words, which I command thee this day, shall be in thine heart:

7 And thou shalt teach them diligently unto thy children, and shalt talk of them when thou sittest in thine house, and when thou walkest by the way, and when thou liest down, and when thou risest up.

8 And thou shalt bind them for a sign upon thine hand, and they shall be as frontlets between thine eyes.

9 And thou shalt write them upon the posts of thy house, and on thy gates.

10 And it shall be, when the LORD thy God shall have brought thee into the land which he sware unto thy fathers, to Abraham, to Isaac, and to Jacob, to give thee great and goodly cities, which thou buildedst not,

11 And houses full of all good things, which thou filledst not, and wells digged, which thou diggedst not, vineyards and olive trees, which thou plantedst not; when thou shalt have eaten and be full;

12 Then beware lest thou forget the LORD, which brought thee forth out of the land of Egypt, from the house of bondage.

13 Thou shalt fear the LORD thy God, and serve him, and shalt swear by his name.

GOLDEN TEXT: Hear, O Israel: The LORD our God is one LORD: and thou shalt love the LORD thy God with all thine heart, and with all thy soul, and with all thy might.
—Deuteronomy 6:4, 5.

Aug
21

God Redeems a People

Unit 3: Instructions for Life

(Lessons 10-13)

Lesson Aims

As a result of studying this lesson, the students should:

1. Understand the importance of a firm faith in the one true God.

2. Commit themselves to sharing their faith with others.

3. Be able to repeat the key verses of today's lesson (Deuteronomy 6:4, 5).

Lesson Outline

INTRODUCTION

  A. Home Schooling

  B. Lesson Background

 I. COMMANDS AND PROMISES (Deuteronomy 6:1-3)

  A. Reminder of Obedience (v. 1)

  B. Rewards of Obedience (vv. 2, 3)

    Hear and Obey

 II. THE GREATEST COMMANDMENT (Deuteronomy 6:4, 5)

  A. God Is One (v. 4)

  B. Undivided Love (v. 5)

III. TEACHING GOD'S COMMANDMENTS (Deuteronomy 6:6-9)

  A. Within the Family (vv. 6, 7)

  B. In Public (vv. 8, 9)

IV. A WORD OF CAUTION (Deuteronomy 6:10-13)

  A. Blessings Not Earned (vv. 10, 11)

  B. Warning Against Forgetfulness (vv. 12, 13)

    A New Land

CONCLUSION

  A. Jehovah Is One

  B. Let Us Pray

  C. Thought to Remember

Refer to visual 12 of the visuals packet to review the principal elements involved in loving God. The visual is shown on page 437.

Introduction

A. Home Schooling

Growing dissatisfaction with public schools in America has led many parents to turn to alternative ways to educate their children. Some have turned to private schools or Christian schools; a few have used another approach, home school-

ing. This method, which allows the parents or other persons to teach the children at home, is now recognized and accepted in several states.

It is interesting to note that some are hailing this as a new and effective approach to education. Effective it may very well be, but new it is not—unless, of course, one is willing to accept a method more than three thousand years old as new. The agricultural and pastoral life of ancient Israel made a formal school system as we understand it an impossibility. A child's education, therefore, had to be accomplished in a different manner. In Israel it was to be done in the home. There, skills were learned that equipped one to be a productive and contributing member of society. And, more important, there the principles of truth and godliness, woven throughout every daily activity, were to be imparted by parents to their children.

B. Lesson Background

Last week's lesson ended with Moses' pronouncement of God's punishment upon Israel for heeding the report of the ten spies and refusing to trust Him to lead them in conquering Canaan. That unfaithful generation would never enter the promised land; they would die in the wilderness.

When the people realized that the wilderness indeed would be their lot, they had a change of heart. "We will go up and fight, according to all that the Lord our God commanded us," they said (Deuteronomy 1:41). Their willingness came too late, however. Moses warned them that such a course was not the will of God. They went up anyway, armed against the people of the land, and were immediately put to flight. Thirty-eight years went by, years spent in wandering in the wilderness, until the sentence that had been pronounced upon them was executed (2:14).

Israel's journeyings had brought them finally to the plains of Moab, east of the Jordan River. There the exhortations and warnings found in today's lesson were given to Israel by Moses.

The text for today's lesson is taken from the book of Deuteronomy. The name *Deuteronomy* means "second law." This title does not mean to suggest that the book contains a second law, one different from the law that God had already given. Nor is it a repetition of the law in all of its details. The book does repeat and reiterate much of the law as given to Moses at Mount Sinai, but it concentrates on the civil and social, rather than the ceremonial, aspects of it. The book features three addresses of Moses, in which he reminds the people of their responsibilities under the covenant and urges them to remain faithful to those commitments once they enter the promised land.

I. Commands and Promises
(Deuteronomy 6:1-3)

A. Reminder of Obedience (v. 1)

1. Now these are the commandments, the statutes, and the judgments, which the LORD your God commanded to teach you, that ye might do them in the land whither ye go to possess it.

The previous chapter restates the Ten Commandments as found in Exodus 20. This verse may refer back to them, or it may introduce what follows. In the original, the expression *these are the commandments* is singular: "this is the commandment." It is equivalent to the "law" in Deuteronomy 4:44. By this term Moses seems to have in mind the entire body of legislation that God had given. The terms *statutes* and *judgments* explain it, emphasizing the permanence and rightness of God's decrees.

Moses was ordered by God to teach the people these laws, no easy task given the Israelites, long tenure as slaves in Egypt. But this teaching was not just an intellectual exercise. Its purpose was to change the people's conduct—that they *might do them,* live by them, in the land that they soon were to possess.

B. Rewards of Obedience (vv. 2, 3)

2. That thou mightest fear the LORD thy God, to keep all his statutes and his commandments, which I command thee, thou, and thy son, and thy son's son, all the days of thy life; and that thy days may be prolonged.

To *fear the Lord* does not mean to cringe before Him, expecting to be struck down by Him at any moment. It means, rather, to reverence Him in the heart, to exalt Him in the highest because of who He is. All of Israel's experiences could be expected to have led them to such reverence for God. And reverence for God naturally would lead to obedience to *his statutes and his commandments.*

Not only were the people to fear God and obey Him, but it was imperative that they teach their children to do the same, and their children in turn were to teach their children, and so on. If each generation obeyed God *all the days* of their lives, they would enjoy God's special blessing: they would continue long in life.

These words of Moses were directed specifically to Israel, living under the covenant God had established with them. We cannot say, therefore, that every person today who believes and obeys God will live a long and prosperous life. Indeed, one may suffer greatly because he is a believer. Yet, it stands to reason that, generally speaking, those who follow God's instructions for life are more likely to live longer and happier lives than those who disregard them.

3. Hear therefore, O Israel, and observe to do it; that it may be well with thee, and that ye may increase mightily, as the LORD God of thy fathers hath promised thee, in the land that floweth with milk and honey.

Beginning with Abraham, God had promised the *fathers* of Israel a land in which to dwell (see Genesis 12:1; 15:7). At the same time He promised to make of Abraham's descendants a great nation (12:2; 17:6; 18:18). These promises were in process of fulfillment. The richness of the land they would soon inherit is indicated by the familiar expression, *the land that floweth with milk and honey.* Israel's prosperity and increase would occur in that land, but all was conditioned on their obedience to God's law.

HEAR AND OBEY

On the fiftieth anniversary of the Japanese attack on Pearl Harbor, America remembered the pain and shock of that event. Brave men died, not for lack of training, skills, equipment, or personal courage. The American troops were caught unawares because information indicating the movement of ships and aircraft toward Hawaii was handled improperly. Had the warning been heeded and the rules of preparedness obeyed, the outcome could have been different.

As Israel prepared to enter the land God was giving them, Moses reminded them that their obedience to God's laws would ensure their long life there. God's laws for the people's happiness and safety in the land were plain, and each generation was expected to learn them and live by them. Failure to do either would lead to tragedy and loss.

Peter speaks of an adversary who would devour each one of us (1 Peter 5:8). Do you take the warning seriously? Are you prepared for his advances? Will you hear and obey?   —W. P.

II. The Greatest Commandment
(Deuteronomy 6:4, 5)

A. God Is One (v. 4)

4. Hear, O Israel: The LORD our God is one LORD.

Jewish people refer to verses 4-9 as the "Shema," since that is the Hebrew word translated *hear,* with which verse 4 begins. These few verses summarize the very heart of the Jewish faith. This verse stresses either Jehovah God's unity or His uniqueness. Either way, He stood in stark contrast to the pagan gods of the neighbors of the Israelites. Jehovah God was not merely first among many gods, as Amon-Re was in the Egyptian pantheon or Baal in the Canaanite pantheon. Jehovah God was and is the only God. The pagan deities were imagined as often quarreling and fighting among themselves, but Jehovah God faces no such conflicts.

Because Jehovah is holy, He requires man also to be holy. In a pantheon of many gods and goddesses, each deity had his or her own standards of conduct. These standards often were anything but holy, and when human beings attempted to follow one or more of these deities, their lives also were anything but holy.

B. Undivided Love (v. 5)

5. And thou shalt love the LORD thy God with all thine heart, and with all thy soul, and with all thy might.

This verse logically follows the previous verse. If God really is one and unique, then He deserved the total loyalty of the Israelites, and love for God was to be the motivation for it. Faithfulness and duty might be required of the worshipers of pagan deities, but rarely was love made the basis of this devotion. The ancient Hebrews viewed the *heart* not only as the seat of emotions, but they also believed that it was the center of mental activity. They viewed the *soul* as the essence of life or the animating principle that came from God. Thus man is to love God with his mind, his emotions, with all the faculties at his command. Nor was this love to be casual; it was to be with all his might!

It is important to note that Jesus referred to this commandment as the first and greatest commandment, one that took precedent over all others (Matthew 22:37, 38; Mark 12:29, 30). Jesus indicated that people were to love God not only with all their heart and soul and strength, but also with all their mind. Jesus was not adding another element to this, the greatest of commandments, but apparently was recognizing the distinction that people in His time made between heart and mind.

III. Teaching God's Commandments (Deuteronomy 6:6-9)

A. Within the Family (vv. 6, 7)

6, 7. And these words, which I command thee this day, shall be in thine heart: and thou shalt teach them diligently unto thy children, and shalt talk of them when thou sittest in thine house, and when thou walkest by the way, and when thou liest down, and when thou risest up.

The Ten Commandments were inscribed on tablets of stone so that the people would not forget them, but keeping these tablets as a memo-

rial was not enough. The words of God's law were to be carried in the people's hearts so that they would apply them to their lives day by day. Memorials were useful, as was memorizing the law, but none of these mattered at all if the people did not live by the law daily. The same applies today. Studying the Scriptures is very important, as is memorizing Scripture verses. These activities are shown to have accomplished their purpose only as we live according to God's will each day.

Each Israelite had an obligation to take the words of God into his or her heart, but that obligation was more than personal. Every Israelite, especially every father, was required to share those words with his children. This sharing involved more than just repeating the words in the presence of the children now and then. Parents were required to live the words every day, throughout the day—when they were at home and when they were away from home, when they went to bed at night and when they got up in the morning.

B. In Public (vv. 8, 9)

8, 9. And thou shalt bind them for a sign upon thine hand, and they shall be as frontlets between thine eyes. And thou shalt write them upon the posts of thy house, and on thy gates.

God may have intended for these verses to be taken figuratively, but later Jews understood them literally. They made small leather containers and placed in them pieces of parchment on which were written important passages of Scripture, including Deuteronomy 6:4-9. With leather straps one box was fastened to the left arm and another was fastened to the center of the forehead. They were ordinarily worn during certain times of prayer. These boxes were the phylacteries that are mentioned in the New Testament (Matthew 23:5).

Israelites also took literally the commandment to write these verses upon the doorposts of their houses and on their gates. The container for these passages was known as a "mezuzah," a word derived from the Hebrew word for "doorpost." The devout Jew would touch the mezuzah when passing in or out of the house and would repeat Psalm 121:8: "The Lord shall preserve thy going out and thy coming in from this time forth, and even for evermore." Whether God intended these verses to be taken literally or figuratively,

---

How to Say It

SHEMA (Hebrew).   She-*mah*.

the intent is certain. God wanted His words to be integrated into the daily life of the people of Israel. Wherever they were and whatever they were doing, they were to be governed by His commandments. This should serve as a reminder to all of us that Christianity is not just a one-day-a-week religion.

IV. A Word of Caution (Deuteronomy 6:10-13)

A. Blessings Not Earned (vv. 10, 11)

10, 11. And it shall be, when the LORD thy God shall have brought thee into the land which he sware unto thy fathers, to Abraham, to Isaac, and to Jacob, to give thee great and goodly cities, which thou buildedst not, and houses full of all good things, which thou filledst not, and wells digged, which thou diggedst not, vineyards and olive trees, which thou plantedst not; when thou shalt have eaten and be full.

Camped on the plains of Moab, the Israelites were poised to move into the land that had been promised centuries earlier to Abraham, Isaac, and Jacob. As they entered the promised land and possessed it, they would enjoy many blessings, so Moses spoke briefly about them.

The Canaanites and other tribes, who had lived in the land for many generations, had built many strong and comfortable cities. Some of these would be destroyed as the Israelites took the land, but others would be taken over by them. For a people who had been wandering in the wilderness for forty years, these towns and cities with their fully furnished houses would seem luxurious indeed. Canaan had few flowing streams and is a rather dry country, but the Israelites would benefit immediately from the wells and cisterns the occupants had prepared. The vineyards and olive trees were already planted. Had the Israelites been moving into an unoccupied land, they would have been faced with the arduous task of providing all of these things for themselves. It would have taken them years to accomplish this. But all these things were there just for the taking.

B. Warning Against Forgetfulness (vv. 12, 13)

12, 13. Then beware lest thou forget the LORD, which brought thee forth out of the land of Egypt, from the house of bondage. Thou shalt fear the LORD thy God, and serve him, and shalt swear by his name.

Moses concluded his review of the blessings that awaited the people in the promised land with a solemn warning—*beware*. Poverty has its temptations, but so does prosperity, especially when it follows poverty. Often we have seen the tragic results when movie stars or professional athletes are suddenly showered with wealth. Their wealth leads to their undoing. This was exactly the danger that faced the Israelites, and God, through Moses, warned the people of it in advance. To be forewarned is to be forearmed. The people would be equipped to face and overcome this temptation if they took to heart the words Moses spoke to them. If they would fear the Lord, and obey Him, and guide their children in doing so, they would know the continuing blessing of God.

A NEW LAND

Grandfather Phillips loved the new land. When he first stood on the homestead site he had claimed in the Grand Ronde Valley of Northeastern Oregon, the natural prairie grass was almost shoulder high. The beauty of the valley with its fertile soil, the surrounding majestic mountains, lush forests, and free-flowing streams seemed like a rediscovered Eden to him. He bowed his head and thanked God for safe arrival after the long trek across half of the American continent.

Grandfather Phillips always knew that he did not really deserve that land. It was his to develop, use, and preserve for those who would come after him. He felt that God had led him to that place, and his faithful commitment to the Lord and to the church was a witness to his thankfulness for all the blessings he had received in the valley. He never forgot that that beautiful place where he was able to live out his life was a gift from God.

Like Israel entering the promised land, our forefathers occupied territory that their ancestors had never owned. In this land they found new freedom, new life, and new hope. Many were like Grandfather and honored God for the opportunity they were given. Do we now take our blessings for granted? Will we neglect to worship and honor Him?   —W. P.

TO LOVE GOD IS TO:
TRUST HIM WITH CONFIDENCE • OBEY HIM WITH EAGERNESS • REVERENCE HIM IN HUMILITY • OFFER HIM SINCERE WORSHIP

visual 12

Conclusion

A. Jehovah Is One

Monotheism, the belief in one God, set the people of Israel apart from all other peoples. Moses emphasized the oneness and the uniqueness of Jehovah as the Israelites prepared to enter Canaan. He knew that this new venture would bring many challenges to their faith in the one true God, and that they would be faced with many temptations to compromise it.

Our times are not greatly different. In the past three or four decades, the Christian faith has faced many new threats, or old threats in new and camouflaged form. The best defense against these threats is a renewal of our commitment to the one true God.

There are really just three basic views about deity. Polytheists believe in many gods; monotheists believe in one God; and atheists don't believe in any god. Polytheism was prevalent in the period in which today's lesson is set. Egypt, Canaan, and Mesopotamia each had its own pantheon of deities. The attributes and powers ascribed to these gods varied from culture to culture. This was especially true among the Canaanites, where the attributes of their gods might vary even from community to community.

Some may argue that polytheism no longer exists among us. After all, where is one likely to find people bowing before physical images of wood, or stone, or precious metal? Yet we are surrounded by polytheism, in more sophisticated forms, to be sure, but polytheism nevertheless. Among the Canaanites the worship of Baal and other gods and goddesses involved wild sexual orgies. Can any deny that millions in our society fall in worship before the idol of sex? The Canaanites practiced human sacrifice. In America one and one-half million unborn babies are sacrificed every year to the god of personal convenience. The Canaanites offered sacrifices to obtain power and wealth. Have not many in our nation sacrificed decency, mercy, and integrity to gain power and wealth?

Atheism, virtually unknown in the ancient world, is a relatively modern philosophy. Science has given man many tools by which he can control nature, and this power has led him to believe that he can live without God. Marxian Communists are, of course, atheists, but relatively few people in America actually claim to be atheists. Yet, many millions are practical atheists; that is, they live their lives as if there is no God. They plan their lives without taking God into account, and their moral standards reflect an almost complete lack of divine direction. These people wield an influence far beyond their numbers, as evidenced by the deterioration of Christian standards in every aspect of our culture.

The Bible declares that there is but one God—Jehovah. Certain implications, therefore, flow from that fact. The first and most obvious one, pointed out by Moses in verse 5, is that we owe Him our love. No person, no thing, no power has such a claim on our loyalty and our affections. One other very important implication, mentioned by Jesus, comes from the fact that God is one and is the Creator of all that exists. If we love God, we must also love our fellow human beings, whom He created. The Pharisees, who were frequently critical of Jesus, professed great love for God and attempted to demonstrate it by their meticulous attention to the minutia of the law. But they had little desire to care for their fellowmen or minister to their needs. On occasion Jesus characterized them as hypocrites because they professed a faith they were unwilling to put into practice. True love for God will lead us to obey Him wholeheartedly, and that obedience will be demonstrated in our loving concern for others.

B. Let Us Pray

Dear God, we come to You because You are the only God. There is no other power in creation that can claim the love that we owe You. Teach us to give You our undivided love, rejecting the temptations of the materialistic idols we see on every hand. Teach us also to love our neighbors as ourselves. In Jesus' name, amen.

C. Thought to Remember

You can love your neighbor without loving God, but you cannot love God without loving your neighbor.

Home Daily Bible Readings

Monday, Aug. 15—Heads of Tribes Hear God's Word (Deuteronomy 5:22-27)
Tuesday, Aug. 16—The Lord Hears Israel's Words (Deuteronomy 5:28—6:3)
Wednesday, Aug. 17—The Great Commandment (Deuteronomy 6:4-9)
Thursday, Aug. 18—"You Shall Fear, Love, Serve God" (Deuteronomy 6:10-17)
Friday, Aug. 19—Do What Is Right and Good (Deuteronomy 6:18-25)
Saturday, Aug. 20—The Covenanted People (Deuteronomy 7:6-16)
Sunday, Aug. 21—Remember Ways God Has Led You (Deuteronomy 8:1-7)

Learning by Doing

This page contains an alternate lesson plan emphasizing learning activities. Classes desiring such student involvement will find these suggestions helpful.

Learning Goals

As students participate in today's class session, they should:

1. Creatively summarize each of the paragraphs in Deuteronomy 6:1-13 to see how they help us remember the right priorities.

2. State how they can reestablish love for God and His Word as a priority in their lives.

Into the Lesson

Write this question on the chalkboard: "How do you tell a person's priorities?" To begin, have the students pair off and discuss the question. The students in each pair should agree on an answer. As the pairs give their answers, write them on the chalkboard. Then tell the class that today's lesson deals with the issue of priorities and how God's children can remember theirs.

Into the Word

Establish the setting for this week's lesson and give an overview of the book of Deuteronomy. Ample material for this two-minute lecture is in "Lesson Background" on page 434.

Write the following headings on the chalkboard:

Verses 1-3
Verses 4, 5
Verses 6-9
Verses 10-13

Provide half sheets of colored paper and put them where class members can easily get to them. Next to the paper put pencils, felt-tip markers, or even crayons. Tell students that you want them to summarize the meaning of each of the sections of Scripture you have indicated on the chalkboard.

Each student should take four pieces of paper (one for each section) and summarize the meaning of each of these paragraphs on a different sheet. They may do this by drawing a picture or by writing a brief summary. Class members should work on this individually. When they have finished they should find two others and show what they have "created" and discuss the meaning, or share their written summaries.

Option

If you prefer, give the following inductive Bible-study questions to class members to answer in pairs or in groups.

1. Survey today's text to discover the purposes behind God's commands to Israel. What would happen to them if they obeyed God?

2. Read verse 5 from several Bible translations. Paraphrase the verse to explain its meaning.

3. How were the Israelites to regard God's commands? (vv. 6-9). Why did God go into such detail here?

4. God's instruction in verses 10-13 warned against what error?

5. Suppose you were preparing a devotion based on this text. What do you think is the main point that should be communicated from these verses?

Into Life

Discuss these questions with the whole class:

1. Choosing priorities is a common problem for people in our society, both Christians and nonbelievers. How does an understanding of this text help you with the issue of priorities?

2. Most Christian parents today are concerned about whether their faith will be adopted by their children. What help does verse 7 provide in this regard?

3. Which holds the greater threat to a person's remaining faithful to Christ—persecution and trials or blessing and success? What warning did Moses give the Israelites regarding their entrance into the promised land?

4. When have you experienced more spiritual growth—when things have gone well for you, or when you have faced some overwhelming problem? What can we do to grow spiritually in the good times as well as the bad?

Option

In addition to or instead of the above activity, distribute copies of the following self-inventory and ask the students to complete them.

1. The top two priorities in my life are—

2. One way I can reestablish love for God as my top priority is—

3. One way I can demonstrate God's truth to others is—

4. One way I can keep God's Word in my heart every day is—

5. One way I can remember that God is the source of my success is—

Ask the students to think about their answers as you offer prayer about each of these points.

Let's Talk It Over

The questions on this page are designed to encourage review of the lesson Scriptures and to promote discussion of the lesson by the class. The answers provided are only discussion starters. Let your class talk it over from there.

1. How close to extinction is the Christian faith?

The Christian faith is always one generation away from extinction. If one generation does not teach it to the next generation, the faith will die. Moses knew the urgency of passing on faith in God to succeeding generations. Thus, in his "farewell address" he began by telling the people that the commands, decrees, and laws God had revealed were for them, and their children, and their children's children. They were to teach them and observe them. This principle, which Moses stated concerning the law, applies to the Christian faith as well.

2. Who bears the fundamental responsibility for the spiritual education of children?

Three views prevail. They are as follows: (1) *The school.* Education belongs in the classroom. Some feel that schools are to teach more than "reading, writing, and arithmetic"; they are to teach values and morals also. Most American parents, though, are unwilling to regard the schools as the principal agent for teaching morals and values. (2) *The church.* After all, the church is *supposed* to teach the children. The church should teach children in Sunday school, hire a youth minister to get the job done, annually feature vacation Bible school, and support summer youth camps. It appears that the majority of parents have chosen this option. (3) *Parents.* Although relatively few parents accept the primary responsibility for the spiritual education of their children, God has mandated it. If the church fulfills its ministry, it will emphasize *training* and *equipping* parents so that they will fulfill their God-assigned role. Moses revealed God's intent: parents bear the primary responsibility for the spiritual training of their children, and they are to accomplish this by their instruction and example.

3. What practical suggestions that are applicable today did Moses give for teaching the faith?

Regarding God's statutes and decrees, Moses commanded, "Thou shalt teach them diligently unto thy children [suggesting structured teaching], and shalt talk of them" (referring to spontaneous instruction). Thus the faith is communicated at two levels: by formal, planned instruction and in casual conversation. This communication is to pervade family life. This does not mean that it is all one talks about, but talking about God is to be as natural as talking about sports, weather, work, or school. Moses gets very specific: Talk about the faith when you sit in your home (for us, at the table, in the family room); talk about it when you walk together (or ride together in the car); talk about it when you lie down and get up (bedtime provides excellent opportunities for praying with our children, reading the Bible, and talking about the faith). In effect, we should begin and end the day with God, and throughout the day sharing our faith should be as natural as breathing, eating, and sleeping.

4. When is a person most likely to forget God?

The Israelites lived under difficult circumstances as they wandered in the wilderness for forty years. During that time they had to trust God to provide for their daily sustenance. They were soon to be given a land with flourishing cities, well-stocked houses, wells, and plentiful vineyards and groves. They naturally would enjoy these good things, but Moses warned that in their enjoyment was the danger that they might forget God, who provided it all. While we are struggling to get ahead in life, we find it easy to call on God for His help. But once we "make it" and are enjoying prosperity, plenty, and ease, our need for God no longer seems so apparent. Precisely at this time, when we should be most grateful to God for all His blessings, we stand in the greatest danger of forgetting Him.

5. How can we "love God"?

First, we must understand that love isn't something we *feel*, but something that we *do*. So what do we *do* that appropriately says, "I love You, Lord"? We give our whole being, heart and soul, to Him in reverence and praise and obedience and service. And we do it with *all* our might. Our heart (the inner core of our being) thinks God's thoughts and wills what He wills. Then that love is expressed in loving others. See Jesus' statement regarding this in Matthew 25:40.

Choose to Obey

DEVOTIONAL READING: Deuteronomy 29:10-18a.

LESSON SCRIPTURE: Deuteronomy 28.

PRINTED TEXT: Deuteronomy 28:1-6, 15-19, 64-66.

Deuteronomy 28:1-6, 15-19, 64-66

1 And it shall come to pass, if thou shalt hearken diligently unto the voice of the LORD thy God, to observe and to do all his commandments which I command thee this day, that the LORD thy God will set thee on high above all nations of the earth:

2 And all these blessings shall come on thee, and overtake thee, if thou shalt hearken unto the voice of the LORD thy God.

3 Blessed shalt thou be in the city, and blessed shalt thou be in the field.

4 Blessed shall be the fruit of thy body, and the fruit of thy ground, and the fruit of thy cattle, the increase of thy kine, and the flocks of thy sheep.

5 Blessed shall be thy basket and thy store.

6 Blessed shalt thou be when thou comest in, and blessed shalt thou be when thou goest out.

. . . .

15 But it shall come to pass, if thou wilt not hearken unto the voice of the LORD thy God, to observe to do all his commandments and his statutes which I command thee this day; that all these curses shall come upon thee, and overtake thee:

16 Cursed shalt thou be in the city, and cursed shalt thou be in the field.

17 Cursed shall be thy basket and thy store.

18 Cursed shall be the fruit of thy body, and the fruit of thy land, the increase of thy kine, and the flocks of thy sheep.

19 Cursed shalt thou be when thou comest in, and cursed shalt thou be when thou goest out.

. . . .

64 And the LORD shall scatter thee among all people, from the one end of the earth even unto the other; and there thou shalt serve other gods, which neither thou nor thy fathers have known, even wood and stone.

65 And among these nations shalt thou find no ease, neither shall the sole of thy foot have rest: but the LORD shall give thee there a trembling heart, and failing of eyes, and sorrow of mind:

66 And thy life shall hang in doubt before thee; and thou shalt fear day and night, and shalt have none assurance of thy life.

GOLDEN TEXT: All these blessings shall come on thee, and overtake thee, if thou shalt hearken unto the voice of the LORD thy God.—Deuteronomy 28:2.

God Redeems a People

Unit 3: Instructions for Life

(Lessons 10-13)

Lesson Aims

After this lesson, each student should:

1. Come to grips with the Biblical truth that choices bring consequences, both at the personal level and at the national level.

2. Make life choices that are compatible with God's will.

Lesson Outline

INTRODUCTION

    A. "For Want of a Nail"

    B. Lesson Background

I. GOD'S BLESSINGS PROMISED (Deuteronomy 28:1-6)

    A. Obedience Necessary (vv. 1, 2)

    B. Blessings Listed (vv. 3-6)

II. GOD'S JUDGMENT THREATENED (Deuteronomy 28:15-19)

    A. Penalty for Disobedience (v. 15)

    B. Curses Listed (vv. 16-19)

    A Matter of Choice

III. EXILE AND ITS MISERIES (Deuteronomy 28:64-66)

    A. Dispersion (v. 64)

    B. Distress (v. 65)

    C. Despair (v. 66)

CONCLUSION

    A. God's Moral Law

    B. God and the Nations

    C. Let Us Pray

    D. Thought to Remember

Display visual 13 of the visuals packet and let it remain before the class throughout this session. The visual is shown on page 445.

Introduction

A. "For Want of a Nail"

In one of his maxims prefixed to *Poor Richard's Almanac*, Benjamin Franklin once wrote, "For want of a nail, the shoe was lost; for want of a shoe, the horse was lost; for want of a horse, the rider was lost; for want of a rider, the battle was lost; for the loss of the battle, a crown was lost." In other words, actions, sometimes even apparently minor actions, have consequences, and those consequences may be far-reaching. Wrong actions often lead to undesirable results, but sometimes the lack of proper actions also leads to disasters.

This was the message that Moses attempted to convey to the children of Israel as they prepared to enter the promised land. As the result of bad decisions, all the adults who had left Egypt (except Moses, Joshua, and Caleb) perished in the wilderness. Even those who were twenty years of age or younger when they left Egypt suffered because of these bad decisions, for they had had to endure forty years of wanderings in the wilderness.

Those who survived had seen both God's justice and His mercy during their wanderings. Thus they should have been receptive to Moses' message. Perhaps they were attentive, but this message applied not only to them but to all future generations. It is no easy task to convey God's commandments to the next generation, but it must be done. If any generation fails to do it, the process is set in motion that leads to almost certain disobedience and moral and spiritual failure. Today's lesson closes with ominous warnings that applied to Israel's future generations. As it turned out, succeeding generations began to pay less and less heed to those warnings, until finally tragedy befell the nation.

B. Lesson Background

The children of Israel were camped in the plains of Moab, just east of the Jordan River. Their years of wandering in the wilderness were almost finished. Across the river lay their objective, the land God had promised them. Moses, now 120 years old, was nearing the end of his life, so the words he spoke to the people here were his final address to them. The Scripture text for this lesson is taken from near the end of that address. Moses laid before the Israelites a choice: "I have set before thee this day life and good, and death and evil" (Deuteronomy 30:15). He spoke of God's blessings that would attend their way if they were obedient to Him. He also set forth dire warnings of the evil that would befall them if they chose to disobey God.

In his farewell message Moses emphasized God's dealings with the people as a nation. In the final analysis, however, the actions of a nation come down to the actions of its individual citizens. The course a nation takes is but the cumulative result of the decisions that its citizens have made. Imperiled is the nation whose citizens have come to believe that their personal decisions have no effect on the life of that nation. The children of Israel needed both the encouragement that Moses gave and the warnings he extended. And so does modern America!

I. God's Blessings Promised (Deuteronomy 28:1-6)

A. Obedience Necessary (vv. 1. 2)

1. And it shall come to pass, if thou shalt hearken diligently unto the voice of the LORD thy God, to observe and to do all his commandments which I command thee this day, that the LORD thy God will set thee on high above all nations of the earth.

Previously Moses reminded the people that they had entered into a covenant with God. After crossing the Jordan and entering the land of promise, they were to renew this covenant. All the words of God's law were to be recorded there, and the people were to commit themselves to keeping them (Deuteronomy 27:1-8).

The blessings that God extended were both personal and national, even international. God promised to set Israel *on high above all nations of the earth.* This is especially interesting in view of the fact that at that time the Israelites did not even have a land of their own. This reaffirmed the covenant God had made with Abraham centuries before, namely that He would make a great nation of Abraham and that He would make his name great (Genesis 12:2).

2. And all these blessings shall come on thee, and overtake thee, if thou shalt hearken unto the voice of the LORD thy God.

This verse introduces the blessings that God had in store for Israel. These promised blessings were conditional; they would come if the Israelites remained faithful to God. It might appear to some that the Israelites would earn these blessings by their good conduct. We need to understand, however, that God's covenant with Israel was the result of His grace, and His grace alone. They had done nothing to deserve to enter into a covenant relationship with God, and by their actions they could do nothing to deserve keeping the covenant in force. They could, however, lose the blessings of the covenant through their misconduct.

B. Blessings Listed (vv. 3-6)

3. Blessed shalt thou be in the city, and blessed shalt thou be in the field.

The blessings are set forth in poetic form. While these verses do not have rhyme as does much English poetry, they do have a definite rhythmic pattern.

The people would be blessed *in the city* and *in the field.* When they entered the promised land, some would live in villages and towns, while others would live in the rural countryside. Wherever they lived, these blessings would be showered upon them. In the towns and cities their businesses and trades would prosper; in the country their fields would bring forth bountiful harvests.

4. Blessed shall be the fruit of thy body, and the fruit of thy ground, and the fruit of thy cattle, the increase of thy kine, and the flocks of thy sheep.

The fruit of thy body refers to their children. In ancient Israel, children were considered a rich blessing. Those couples who were childless, on the other hand, were greatly pitied. In an agricultural society, children provided needed labor; and when the parents became old, children provided support, the ancient equivalent of Social Security.

The rich soil God would give them in Canaan, along with adequate rainfall properly timed, would insure abundant crops. Their flocks would multiply and find ample pasture on the fertile hillsides.

5. Blessed shall be thy basket and thy store.

The *basket* was used to gather fruit such as figs, grapes, and olives. Here it represents the store in which the fruits of the people's harvests would be kept. The *store* is more accurately translated "kneading trough" in modern versions. It was a vessel in which dough was mixed and allowed to rise from the action of the leaven. It was made of clay or wood or sometimes of a stone hollowed out as a bowl. The kneading trough stands for the people's use of all that God would provide. In sum, this verse says that the people's daily needs for sustaining life would be richly supplied.

6. Blessed shalt thou be when thou comest in, and blessed shalt thou be when thou goest out.

The expression "to come in and to go out" was sometimes used in the Old Testament to indicate a person's ability to be significantly involved in the daily activities of life (see Deuteronomy 31:2; 1 Kings 3:7). God's blessings would extend to the whole range of activities people would engage in. These blessings are just about as important as having ample food and shelter. Even persons of great wealth are likely to be miserable if their daily activities and interactions with the world around them are unpleasant. Verse 7, which is not included in the text, promises God's protection against any

---

How to Say It

BABYLONIANS. Bab-uh-*low*-nee-unz.
MOAB. *Mo*-ab.
HABAKKUK. Huh-*bak*-kuk.

enemies that might rise up against them. God thus promised the people prosperity, personal tranquillity, and a hedge to keep them from external enemies. It is hard to imagine what else they might need.

II. God's Judgment Threatened (Deuteronomy 28:15-19)

A. Penalty for Disobedience (v. 15)

15. But it shall come to pass, if thou wilt not hearken unto the voice of the LORD thy God, to observe to do all his commandments and his statutes which I command thee this day; that all these curses shall come upon thee, and overtake thee.

This verse begins a long list of curses that would befall the Israelite people if they disobeyed God. It is significant that nearly four times as many verses describe the curses as those that describe the blessings. Perhaps this indicates that fallen man needs more warnings than he does promises of blessings. It may, on the other hand, be an example of the Hebrew manner of speaking, in which Moses built to a climax by piling one curse upon another. In either case, Moses painted a very somber picture of what would happen to those who would rebel against God.

We, who are able to view Hebrew history in retrospect, can only marvel at how often these curses fell upon the Israelites almost precisely as Moses pronounced them. His pronouncements seem to take on the character of prophecies that inevitably would be fulfilled. Yet, in every case, a curse came because the people chose of their own free will to disobey God.

B. Curses Listed (vv. 16-19)

16-19. Cursed shalt thou be in the city, and cursed shalt thou be in the field. Cursed shall be thy basket and thy store. Cursed shall be the fruit of thy body, and the fruit of thy land, the increase of thy kine, and the flocks of thy sheep. Cursed shalt thou be when thou comest in, and cursed shalt thou be when thou goest out.

Although the order is not exactly the same, the curses in verses 16-19 parallel the blessings found in verses 3-6. The remainder of chapter 28 is given over to a description of the types of curses that would fall on disobedient Israel. They include destruction and wasting of their crops through disease and drought, physical debilitation as a result of loathsome diseases, subjection and oppression by their enemies, and finally their being given up to the power of the heathen, to be subjected to the utmost indignities and sufferings.

A MATTER OF CHOICE

"Boys, Mom will be gone for the entire day, and we'll eat in town at noon. I have some things that I need to do there." Their dad's decision to eat out sounded good to Joe and Tom, but he had more to say. "I cut two cords of oak wood this week, and it needs stacking. I'll show you where I want you to put it. If you have it all stacked by the time I get back, you can go with me. If not, you'll have to stay here and finish the job. I'll see you later."

Joe and Tom walked to the woodpile. They had just finished a good breakfast and had planned to go fishing that Saturday. School and chores had not given them time during the week.

Joe spoke. "I'm going to the creek. It won't take long to stack the wood. I'll do it later."

Tom was more cautious. "I'll stack wood first," he said. "I'll enjoy fishing more when the job's done."

About noon, Tom was done with his work, but Joe was nowhere to be seen. Just then their father drove up.

"Come on; let's go to town," he called to Tom.

"Dad, Joe's not here. He wanted to fish before stacking wood."

"Too bad," was his dad's reply. "Get in. Joe just missed dinner."

Tom and his Dad drove toward town. Joe saw them leave as he trudged in from the creek with no fish.

"Mean father," you say? "No, disobedient son," is a better answer. Likewise, God never rewards disobedience. He continues to love all persons and is willing to forgive the penitent; but He cannot overlook our willful disregard of His commands.   —W. P.

III. Exile and Its Miseries (Deuteronomy 28: 64-66)

A. Dispersion (v. 64)

64. And the LORD shall scatter thee among all people, from the one end of the earth even unto the other; and there thou shalt serve other gods, which neither thou nor thy fathers have known, even wood and stone.

Among the blessings that God promised to His people if they obeyed Him was protection from their enemies. As mentioned previously, however, those same enemies would become God's instruments of punishment if Israel would depart from His ways. If Israel would refuse to serve God, He would see to it that they would serve their enemies. The neighboring nations would invade their land, steal their crops, take their animals, their sons and daughters, and generally harass and oppress the people until they knew only vexation and anguish of spirit.

If that punishment did not bring the people to their senses, God would eventually allow an even greater misfortune to befall them—they would be scattered among the people of other nations. It would seem as if they had been driven to the ends of the earth. There they would be completely cut off from the worship of God, whom they disdained, and would be obliged to *serve other gods*. Then would they know the depths of degradation to which man, devoid of the knowledge of God, can sink.

B. Distress (v. 65)

65. And among these nations shalt thou find no ease, neither shall the sole of thy foot have rest: but the LORD shall give thee there a trembling heart, and failing of eyes, and sorrow of mind.

The people who would be scattered abroad as a result of their disobedience would have extreme difficulties wherever they went. Children would be taken away from their parents, husbands would be separated from their wives, and all would be forced to serve their captors as slaves or menial servants. In captivity they would find *no ease*, no peace, no calm. So rigorous and wretched would be their servitude that their feet would find no rest. Not only physical exhaustion but inner turmoil would be their lot. In new and different ways they would experience the insecurity and anxiety that their forefathers had known. Given these circumstances, it is little wonder that the people would suffer from *a trembling heart* and *sorrow of mind*.

C. Despair (v. 66)

66. And thy life shall hang in doubt before thee; and thou shalt fear day and night, and shalt have none assurance of thy life.

In their captivity and bondage, the people's very lives would *hang* as suspended by a delicate thread. They would never know when some slight disturbance over which they had no control would cause that thread to snap and jeopardize their lives. The anxiety generated by such conditions would sap their strength, undermine their morale, and leave them almost totally helpless.

As Moses proceeded through his message, his warning of curses became a prediction, clearly foretelling the nation's apostasy. The Biblical record verifies that those predictions were fulfilled. The curses warned against fell on Israel because later generations chose not to obey the word of the Lord spoken by His servant.

Conclusion

A. God's Moral Law

All of us live under a variety of rules and regulations. To disobey these rules can lead to problems, and even disaster. In our homes and families we have understandings (usually not written down and perhaps scarcely even mentioned) about who is to wash the dishes, do the laundry, carry out the garbage, or make the beds. When these simple understandings are regularly ignored or even deliberately flouted, the harmony of the home is disrupted and can even be destroyed.

Our state legislatures and national Congress have passed thousands of laws, many of which we don't know about and probably couldn't understand if we did know about them. We are concerned, however, about those laws that protect our persons and our property from violence. We have many such laws on our statute books, but often the perpetrators of violence and fraud are not caught. If they are caught, sometimes they are not appropriately punished. Because we live in an imperfect society, our legal system falls considerably short of being a perfect instrument of achieving justice.

The laws of nature are different. One does not break the laws of nature; he or she demonstrates them. I may suffer from the delusion that I can defy the law of gravity by jumping from the fortieth floor of a tall building. My broken and lifeless body on the pavement below will give undeniable proof that I didn't break the law of gravity; I only demonstrated it. I may drink a glass of lemonade that is heavily laced with cyanide. The autopsy will reveal that I didn't break a law of nature; I only demonstrated that it was still binding.

Quite early in life we begin to learn the facts about the laws of nature—fire burns, sharp things cut, and falls can be bruising. If we don't learn them early, we are not likely to live to maturity. Violating the laws of nature brings

GODLINESS
HAS
VALUE
for all things, holding promise
FOR
both the present life and the
LIFE
to come.

visual 13

punishment that is certain and swift, with no plea bargaining or time off for good behavior.

God's moral laws are different from household regulations, from legislative statutes, and from the laws of nature. On the one hand, the violation of moral laws brings certain punishment. On the other hand, that punishment may be long delayed and may fall rather lightly upon the guilty. The tragedy of sin, which is another term for the violation of God's moral laws, is that the innocent often have to suffer, sometimes for generations to come.

Early in Israel's history, just as they were about to enter the promised land, Moses set before them the promise of wonderful blessings if they obeyed God, or terrible curses if they disobeyed Him. Sometimes the people obeyed and enjoyed these blessings. More often, however, they fell into disobedience and suffered the curses. Frequently, when Israel became disobedient, God did not administer punishment immediately. Instead, He waited, giving them the opportunity to repent and return to Him. But the people misread God's patience and continued to sin, thinking they could do so with impunity. Israel never did quite learn how moral law works. They never did understand that punishment postponed was not punishment avoided. Eventually God's judgment fell on the nation. Are we any wiser?

B. God and the Nations

God used many different means to punish the wayward Israelites. Sometimes He sent droughts that stunted their crops. On other occasions He sent clouds of locusts to devour the produce of the land. He frequently used marauding neighbors to steal their flocks and even carry some of the people into slavery. Finally God called nations from afar to conquer His people and carry them into captivity: first the Assyrians, then the Babylonians.

The fact that God could use a brutal, pagan nation such as the Babylonians to punish His own chosen people completely overwhelmed the prophet Habakkuk. Although God did not explain His actions, He did assure the prophet that He would deal appropriately with the Babylonians for their cruelty. They were God's instrument to punish Judah, yet they were so terribly brutal that they far exceeded anything that God required. As a result, they, too, were punished and soon passed into oblivion, never to appear again as a distinct nation. A clear teaching of the Scriptures is that by divine providence, God oversees the affairs of men and nations.

America has been blessed as few nations in the world have ever been. Our founding fathers established this nation on their belief in God and on the principles found in His Word. Succeeding generations upheld those principles and nurtured that faith, and, not surprisingly, the nation flourished in many ways. In recent years, however, have seen a growing disregard in many quarters for Christian principles. It should come as no surprise that at the same time there has been an increase in all kinds of sinful and criminal behavior. It appears that the moral and spiritual fabric of our society is disintegrating before our very eyes. Do we think that God is any less concerned about a nation's spiritual and moral health today than He was in Old Testament times? If He punished those peoples then, who disregarded Him and the teachings of His law, what might He do to that nation today, which, having known the greater blessings of His grace in Christ, still chooses to disobey Him? God said to Israel, "Obey and be blessed; disobey and be cursed." That principle is eternally true.

C. Let Us Pray

For Your Word, O Lord, that gives direction to life, we are grateful. We thank You that it is not hidden from our understanding, neither is it far off, beyond our grasp. Nor is it a Word impossible to obey when we are clothed by the nature of Christ. We do desire that life to which You call us, a life to be lived as Your children. We have accepted Christ as our Savior, and now we recommit ourselves to obedience to Him in all things as they are set forth in Your Word. In His name we pray. Amen.

D. Thought to Remember

"Those who cannot remember the past are condemned to repeat it."   —George Santayana

---

Home Daily Bible Readings

Monday, Aug. 22—Blessings of Obedience (Deuteronomy 28:1-9)

Tuesday, Aug. 23—Obedience to God Brings Prosperity (Deuteronomy 28:10-14)

Wednesday, Aug. 24—Curses Come If Disobedient (Deuteronomy 28:15-24)

Thursday, Aug. 25—No One Will Offer to Help (Deuteronomy 28:25-35)

Friday, Aug. 26—Curses Come Through Disobedience (Deuteronomy 28:36-46)

Saturday, Aug. 27—Practice Obedience (Deuteronomy 28:47, 58, 62-65)

Sunday, Aug. 28—The Lord Covenants With Israel (Deuteronomy 29:1-13)

Learning by Doing

*This page contains an alternate lesson plan emphasizing learning activities. Classes
desiring such student involvement will find these suggestions helpful.*

Learning Goals

As students participate in today's class session, they should:

1. Survey the relationship between God's blessings and curses and His people's obedience and disobedience, especially as outlined by Moses in Deuteronomy 28.

2. Examine their own lives to thank God for His blessings and to isolate areas of disobedience that may be bringing them difficulty.

Into the Lesson

Use one of these ideas to introduce today's discussion:

Informal debate. Divide students into groups of two to five and ask them to consider the relationship between obedience to God and blessings from God. One half of the groups should take the position, "The only way to have great blessings is to demonstrate great obedience." The other half should take the position, "Great blessings can come regardless of whether a person obeys God."

Give the groups about six minutes to prepare their positions. Then conduct a discussion with the whole class, allowing those on both sides to propose their ideas.

Newspaper search. Write the question, "Does obedience make a difference?" on the chalkboard. Distribute copies of recent newspapers to groups or pairs of students. Ask them to find news stories that show either problems that arise from disobedience to God or blessings that come from obeying Him. After several minutes, let class members share their articles and their conclusions about them.

"I remember." Have class members pair off and tell their partners what happened to them as children when they disobeyed their parents. After two minutes ask them to share responses with the whole class.

Tell the class that today's lesson deals with the theme of obedience and disobedience and the consequences of each.

Into the Word

Use the introduction to the first lesson plan to prepare a brief lecture that establishes the setting for this text. Then divide the class members into groups of four and have them complete the following Bible-study activities.

Blessings/curses comparison. Students should examine today's text and list the blessings Israel was promised if they would obey God and the curses that would come to them for disobedience. Students should find in the text a curse for disobedience to match each blessing for obedience. They should write them out or paraphrase them side by side on a sheet of paper.

Bible survey. Ask students to use a concordance, topical Bible, or chain-reference Bible to find other Scriptures that describe some of the results of obedience and disobedience to God. If those resources aren't available, here is a list of Scripture references to get them started:

Exodus 19:5	Deuteronomy 5:29
Deuteronomy 11:28	1 Samuel 12:15
1 Kings 3:14	Ephesians 5:6
2 Thessalonians 1:8	Hebrews 2:2, 3
James 1:25	Revelation 22:14

Let the groups share their findings with the class. If you have time, ask students to summarize what they have learned by writing one sentence that explains the relationship between obedience to God and blessings from God.

Into Life

Ask class members to share times when they experienced great blessings from God after they made a difficult decision to obey Him. Were the blessings always physical, or were they sometimes unseen—spiritual or emotional?

Explain that the Bible does not teach that every evil that befalls one of God's children is a direct result of that person's disobedience. Nor does the affluence or fame that comes to some non-Christians say anything about their relationship with God.

Ask the class to name some of the "unseen blessings" that make the Christian life the most worthwhile life to live. Write these on the chalkboard. Then distribute notecards and have each student write down one of these blessings that is lacking in his or her life. Then have each write down one of the blessings he or she is experiencing.

Close with sentence prayers. Class members should pray one of these two prayers: "Dear God, please help (me) (us) to receive the blessing of . . ." or, "Dear God, thank You for letting (me) (us) experience the blessing of. . . ."

Let's Talk It Over

The questions on this page are designed to encourage review of the lesson Scriptures and to promote discussion of the lesson by the class. The answers provided are only discussion starters. Let your class talk it over from there.

1. What is the *ultimate* choice a person can make, as it was expressed by Moses to the people of Israel?

One will literally make millions of choices in one's lifetime. Some are inconsequential, but others are of lasting consequence. Moses presents the ultimate choice in Deuteronomy 30:15 and 19: "See, I have set before thee this day life and good, and death and evil." That's it—no other choice comes even close in ultimate significance. Choose life or death, with the consequent good or evil. These two alternatives are diametrically opposed. In making our choice between the two, we choose our consequences: life brings blessing, death brings the curse. But God does not simply set the two alternatives before us; He declares His desire, His bias: "Choose life, that you may live." The choice and its consequences *ever* remain the same.

2. What punishment eventually fell on the nation of Israel because of their disobedience to Jehovah?

All the blessings were withdrawn and were replaced by curses. Instead of enjoying uninterrupted prosperity, the people experienced diverse and dramatic losses, both "in the city, and . . . in the field" (Deuteronomy 28:15). The curse brought impoverishment instead of plenty, and the withdrawal of protection from ravaging enemies. Most significantly, the people were cursed by being scattered "from the one end of the earth even unto the other" (v. 64), principally by the Assyrian and Babylonian captivities. While in captivity the Israelites were required to serve pagan gods and to endure the rigorous existence of slaves. In their captivity they were condemned to lives of anxiety and hopelessness. All of the curses Moses warned Israel of (see Deuteronomy 28:15-68) eventually fell on them because the succeeding generations made the wrong choice.

3. Cite some major obstacles to our trusting God's promises.

(1) God does not always operate within our time frame. Our patience is tested, our willingness to "wait upon the Lord" is tried. People may give up hope if God doesn't fulfill His promises when they think He should. (2) God calls us to belief and trust that often exceed the limits of human reason. The incredible can become the impossible, in our thinking. The mind may balk at that which it deems irrational. (3) Continuing to trust when the promises remain anchored in the dim future may be very costly. The persistent threat or experience of trouble, danger, and loss may erode our determination to continue to trust. (4) Other people may attempt to sabotage our faith, to cast doubt on God's reliability, to tempt us to distrust. The psalmist experienced the taunt of those who scoffed, "Where is thy God?" (Psalm 42:3, 10). Tragically, sometimes those who become our adversaries to the life of trust may be those closest to us—family and friends. Moses assured the Israelites that God would do as He had promised, both with blessing and punishment. The tragic record stands that Israel neither believed nor trusted God, and they paid the price.

4. The Bible is a big book, yet the basic choice it calls for is clear to see, and the directions are easy to understand. What is the basic message of the New Testament?

The basic message of Christ and the apostles is that Jesus, the Son of God, died for the sins of man, was raised from the dead, and is now exalted to the right hand of God. Men will perish or be saved according to their response to Him and His saving work. The simple instructions to those who believe this are to turn from sin, be baptized, and remain faithful to Christ.

5. What assessment may be made of the contemporary "gospel" that promises "health and wealth"?

It is manipulative, appealing to self-aggrandizement. It will attract some followers of base motives. It will *use* people to gather a following. Ultimately, this is a *false* gospel. Jesus warned of the *cost* of following Him: "Foxes have holes and birds of the air have nests, but the Son of Man has no place to lay his head" (Matthew 8:20, *New International Version*). The example of the apostle Paul may be cited as well. From his description of his experiences as a servant of Christ (see 2 Corinthians 11:23-28), one would hardly conclude that Christians are promised all good things in this life!